Negotiation

Readings, Exercises and Cases

Sixth Edition

Roy J. Lewicki
The Ohio State University

David M. Saunders
Queen's University

Bruce Barry
Vanderbilt University

McGraw-Hill
Irwin

McGraw-Hill
Irwin

NEGOTIATION: READINGS, EXERCISES AND CASES, SIXTH EDITION

Published by McGraw-Hill, a business unit of The McGraw-Hill Companies, Inc., 1221 Avenue of the Americas, New York, NY 10020. Copyright © 2010 by The McGraw-Hill Companies, Inc. All rights reserved. Previous editions © 2007, 2003, and 1999. No part of this publication may be reproduced or distributed in any form or by any means, or stored in a database or retrieval system, without the prior written consent of The McGraw-Hill Companies, Inc., including, but not limited to, in any network or other electronic storage or transmission, or broadcast for distance learning.

Some ancillaries, including electronic and print components, may not be available to customers outside the United States.

This book is printed on acid-free paper.

3 4 5 6 7 8 9 0 DOC/DOC 1 4 3 2 1

ISBN 978-0-07-353031-4
MHID 0-07-353031-X

Vice President & Editor-in-Chief: *Brent Gordon*
VP EDP / Central Publishing Services: *Kimberly Meriwether David*
Publisher: *Paul Ducham*
Managing Developmental Editor: *Laura Hurst Spell*
Editorial Coordinator: *Jane Beck*
Associate Marketing Manager: *Jaime Halteman*
Project Manager: *Robin A. Reed*
Design Coordinator: *Brenda A. Rolwes*
Cover Designer: *Studio Montage, St. Louis, Missouri*
Cover Image Credit: *© Artville (Photodisk)/PunchStock*
Production Supervisor: *Sue Culbertson*
Media Project Manager: *Suresh Babu*
Composition: *S4Carlisle Publishing Services*
Typeface: *10/12 Times Roman*
Printer: *R.R. Donnelley*

All credits appearing on page or at the end of the book are considered to be an extension of the copyright page.

Library of Congress Cataloging-in-Publication Data

Negotiation: readings, exercises, and cases / [edited by] Roy J. Lewicki, David M. Saunders, Bruce Barry.—6th ed.
   p. cm.
   ISBN-13: 978-0-07-353031-4 (alk. paper)
   ISBN-10: 0-07-243255-1
   1. Negotiation in business. 2. Negotiation. 3. Negotiation—Case studies. I. Lewicki, Roy J.
II. Saunders, David M. III. Barry, Bruce, 1958–
HD58.6.N45   2009
658.4′052—dc22   2009039281

The Internet addresses listed in the text were accurate at the time of publication. The inclusion of a Web site does not indicate an endorsement by the authors or McGraw-Hill, and McGraw-Hill does not guarantee the accuracy of the information presented at these sites.

www.mhhe.com

We dedicate this book to all negotiation, mediation, and dispute resolution professionals who try to make the world a more peaceful and prosperous place.

About the Authors

Roy J. Lewicki is the Abramowitz Professor of Business Ethics, and Professor of Management and Human Resources at the Max. M. Fisher College of Business, The Ohio State University. He has authored or edited 32 books, as well as numerous research articles. Professor Lewicki has served as the President of the International Association of Conflict Management, was the founding editor of the Academy of Management Learning and Education, and received the Academy of Management's Distinguished Educator Award for his contributions to the field of teaching in negotiation and dispute resolution.

David M. Saunders is dean of Queen's School of Business. Since joining Queen's in 2003, he has led the internationalization of the school, launched two unique MBA programs and a suite of pre-experience Masters programs, and strengthened Queen's international network with the addition of top business school partners in Europe, Asia, and South America.

Outside of Queen's, David is the co-author of several articles on negotiation, conflict resolution, employee voice, and organizational justice. He sits on the board of the China Europe International Business School (CEIBS) and the European Foundation for Management Development, an international business school association.

Bruce Barry is Professor of Management and Sociology at Vanderbilt University. His research on negotiation, influence, power, and justice has appeared in numerous scholarly journals and volumes. Professor Barry is a past President of the International Association for Conflict Management (2002–2003), and a past chair of the Academy of Management Conflict Management Division.

People negotiate every day. During an average day, they may negotiate with

- the boss, regarding an unexpected work assignment;
- subordinates, regarding unexpected overtime;
- a supplier, about a problem with raw materials inventory management;
- a banker, over the terms of a business loan;
- a government official, regarding the compliance with environmental regulations;
- a real estate agent, over the lease on a new warehouse;
- his/her spouse, over who will walk the dog;
- his/her child, over who will walk the dog (still an issue after losing the previous negotiation);
- and the dog, once out, as to whether any "business" gets done.

In short, negotiation is a common, everyday activity that most people use to influence others and to achieve personal objectives. In fact, negotiation is not only common, but also essential to living an effective and satisfying life. We all need things—resources, information, cooperation, and support from others. Others have those needs as well, sometimes compatible with ours, sometimes not. Negotiation is a process by which we attempt to influence others to help us achieve our needs while at the same time taking their needs into account. It is a fundamental skill, not only for successful management but also for successful living.

In 1985, Roy Lewicki and Joseph Litterer published the first edition of this book. As they were preparing that volume, it was clear that the basic processes of negotiation had received only selective attention in both the academic and practitioner literature. Scholars of negotiation had generally restricted examination of these processes to basic theory development and laboratory research in social psychology, to a few books written for managers, and to an examination of negotiation in complex settings such as diplomacy and labor–management relations. Efforts to draw from the broader study of techniques for influence and persuasion, to integrate this work into a broader understanding of negotiation, or to apply this work to a broad spectrum of conflict and negotiation settings were only beginning to occur.

In the past twenty-five years, this world has changed significantly. There are several new practitioner organizations, such as the Society for Professionals in Dispute Resolution and the Association for Conflict Resolution, and academic professional associations such as the Conflict Management Division of the Academy of Management and the International Association for Conflict Management that have devoted themselves exclusively to facilitating research and teaching in the fields of negotiation and conflict management. There are several new journals (*Negotiation Journal, Negotiation and Conflict Management Research, International Journal of Conflict Management, International Negotiation*) that focus exclusively on research in these fields. Finally, through the generosity of the Hewlett Foundation, there are a number of university centers that have devoted themselves to enhancing the quality of teaching, research, and service in the negotiation and conflict management fields. Many schools now have several courses in negotiation and conflict management—in schools of business, law, public policy, psychology, social work, education, and natural resources. Development has occurred in the practitioner side as well. Books, seminars, and training courses on negotiation and conflict management abound. And, finally, mediation has become an extremely popular process as an alternative to litigation for handling divorce, community disputes, and land-use conflicts. In pragmatic terms, all of this development means that as we assembled this sixth edition, we have had a much richer and more diverse pool of resources from which to sample. The net result for the student and instructor is a highly improved book of readings and exercises that contains many new articles, cases, and exercises, which represent the very best and most recent work on negotiation and the related topics of power, influence, and conflict management.

A brief overview of this book is in order. The Readings portion of the book is ordered into seven sections: (1) Negotiation Fundamentals, (2) Negotiation Subprocesses, (3) Negotiation Contexts, (4) Individual Differences, (5) Negotiation across Cultures, (6) Resolving Differences, and (7) Summary. The next section of the book presents a collection of role-play exercises, cases, and self-assessment questionnaires that can be used to teach about negotiation processes and subprocesses. Complete information about the use or adaptation of these materials for several classroom formats is provided in our accompanying web-based Instructor's Manual, which faculty members may obtain access by contacting their local McGraw-Hill/Irwin representative, by calling (800) 634-3963 or by visiting the McGraw-Hill Web site at www.mhhe.com/lewickinegotiation

For those readers familiar with the previous edition of this book, the most visible changes in this edition are to the book's content and organization, as follows:

- The content of this edition is substantially new. About half of the readings are new to this edition, and there are approximately ten new exercises and cases. Almost all exercises and cases have been revised and updated.

- These 7 sections parallel the 7 sections and 20 chapters of the completely revised textbook, *Negotiation*, 6th edition, by Lewicki, Barry and Saunders, also published by McGraw-Hill/Irwin. The text and reader can be used together, or separately. A shorter version of the text, *Essentials of Negotiation*, 5th edition, by Lewicki, Saunders and Barry, can also be used in conjunction with these readings book (to be published in 2010). We encourage instructors to contact their local McGraw-Hill/Irwin representative for an examination copy (call 800-634-3963, or visit the Web site at www.mhhe.com/lewickinegotiation).

This book could not have been completed without the assistance of numerous people. We especially thank

- The many authors and publishers who granted us permission to use or adapt their work for this book and whom we have recognized in conjunction with specific exercises, cases, or articles.

- The many negotiation instructors and trainers who inspired several of the exercises in this book and who have given us excellent feedback on the previous editions of this book.

- The staff of McGraw-Hill/Irwin, especially our current editor, Laura Spell, and our previous editors, John Weimeister, Ryan Blankenship, John Biernat, Kurt Strand and Karen Johnson; Jane Beck, Allison Cleland and Trina Hauger, editorial assistants who can solve almost any problem; Project Manager Robin Reed; and Lori Bradshaw, tireless developmental editor who turns our confusing instructions and tedious prose into eminently readable and usable volumes!

- Our families, who continue to provide us with the time, inspiration, opportunities for continued learning about effective negotiation, and the personal support required to finish this project.

Roy J. Lewicki
David M. Saunders
Bruce Barry

Contents

Section 6

Resolving Differences

Section 7

Summary

Exercises

Cases

Questionnaires

Appendix

Negotiation Fundamentals

Reading 1.1

Three Approaches to Resolving Disputes: Interests, Rights, and Power

William L. Ury
Jeanne M. Brett
Stephen B. Goldberg

It started with a pair of stolen boots. Miners usually leave their work clothes in baskets that they hoist to the ceiling of the bathhouse between work shifts. One night a miner discovered that his boots were gone.[1] He couldn't work without boots. Angry, he went to the shift boss and complained, "Goddammit, someone stole my boots! It ain't fair! Why should I lose a shift's pay and the price of a pair of boots because the company can't protect the property?"

"Hard luck!" the shift boss responded. "The company isn't responsible for personal property left on company premises. Read the mine regulations!"

The miner grumbled to himself, "I'll show them! If I can't work this shift, neither will anyone else!" He convinced a few buddies to walk out with him and, in union solidarity, all the others followed.

The superintendent of the mine told us later that he had replaced stolen boots for miners and that the shift boss should have done the same. "If the shift boss had said to the miner, 'I'll buy you a new pair and loan you some meanwhile,' we wouldn't have had a strike." The superintendent believed that his way of resolving the dispute was better than the shift boss's or the miner's. Was he right and, if so, why? In what ways are some dispute resolution procedures better than others?

In this reading, we discuss three ways to resolve a dispute: reconciling the interests of the parties, determining who is right, and determining who is more powerful. We analyze the costs of disputing in terms of transaction costs, satisfaction with outcomes, effect on the relationship, and recurrence of disputes. We argue that, in general, reconciling interests costs less and yields more satisfactory results than determining who is right, which in turn costs less and satisfies more than determining who is more powerful. The goal of dispute systems design, therefore, is a system in which most disputes are resolved by reconciling interests.

Source: "Three Approaches to Resolving Disputes: Interests, Rights, and Power," from *Getting Disputes Resolved,* by William L. Ury, Jeanne M. Brett, and Stephen B. Goldberg, 1988, pp. 3–19. New York: Jossey-Bass, Inc., a subsidiary of John Wiley & Sons, Inc. Used with permission.

Three Ways to Resolve Disputes

The Boots Dispute Dissected

A dispute begins when one person (or organization) makes a claim or demand on another who rejects it.[2] The claim may arise from a perceived injury or from a need or aspiration.[3] When the miner complained to the shift boss about the stolen boots, he was making a claim that the company should take responsibility and remedy his perceived injury. The shift boss's rejection of the claim turned it into a dispute. To resolve a dispute means to turn opposed positions—the claim and its rejection—into a single outcome.[4] The resolution of the boots dispute might have been a negotiated agreement, an arbitrator's ruling, or a decision by the miner to drop his claim or by the company to grant it.

In a dispute, people have certain interests at stake. Moreover, certain relevant standards or rights exist as guideposts toward a fair outcome. In addition, a certain balance of power exists between the parties. Interests, rights, and power then are three basic elements of any dispute. In resolving a dispute, the parties may choose to focus their attention on one or more of these basic factors. They may seek to (1) reconcile their underlying interests, (2) determine who is right, and/or (3) determine who is more powerful.

When he pressed his claim that the company should do something about his stolen boots, the miner focused on rights—"Why should I lose a shift's pay and the price of a pair of boots because the company can't protect the property?" When the shift boss responded by referring to mine regulations, he followed the miner's lead and continued to focus on who was right. The miner, frustrated in his attempt to win what he saw as justice, provoked a walkout—changing the focus to power. "I'll show them!" In other words, he would show the company how much power he and his fellow coal miners had—how dependent the company was on them for the production of coal.

The mine superintendent thought the focus should have been on interests. The miner had an interest in boots and a shift's pay, and the company had an interest in the miner working his assigned shift. Although rights were involved (there was a question of fairness) and power was involved (the miner had the power to cause a strike), the superintendent's emphasis was on each side's interests. He would have approached the stolen boots situation as a joint problem that the company could help solve.

Reconciling Interests

Interests are needs, desires, concerns, fears—the things one cares about or wants. They underlie people's positions—the tangible items they *say* they want. A husband and wife quarrel about whether to spend money for a new car. The husband's underlying interest may not be the money or the car but the desire to impress his friends; the wife's interest may be transportation. The director of sales for an electronics company gets into a dispute with the director of manufacturing over the number of TV models to produce. The director of sales wants to produce more models. Her interest is in selling TV sets; more models mean more choice for consumers and hence increased sales. The director of manufacturing wants to produce fewer models. His interest is in decreasing manufacturing costs; more models mean higher costs.

Reconciling such interests is not easy. It involves probing for deep-seated concerns, devising creative solutions, and making trade-offs and concessions where interests are opposed.[5] The most common procedure for doing this is *negotiation,* the act of back-and-forth communication intended to reach agreement. (A *procedure* is a pattern of interactive behavior directed toward resolving a dispute.) Another interests-based procedure is *mediation,* in which a third party assists the disputants in reaching agreement.

By no means do all negotiations (or mediations) focus on reconciling interests. Some negotiations focus on determining who is right, such as when two lawyers argue about whose case has the greater merit. Other negotiations focus on determining who is more powerful, such as when quarreling neighbors or nations exchange threats and counterthreats. Often negotiations involve a mix of all three—some attempts to satisfy interests, some discussion of rights, and some references to relative power. Negotiations that focus primarily on interests we call "interests-based," in contrast to "rights-based" and "power-based" negotiations. Another term for interests-based negotiation is *problem-solving negotiation,* so called because it involves treating a dispute as a mutual problem to be solved by the parties.

Before disputants can effectively begin the process of reconciling interests, they may need to vent their emotions. Rarely are emotions absent from disputes. Emotions often generate disputes, and disputes, in turn, often generate emotions. Frustration underlay the miner's initial outburst to the shift boss; anger at the shift boss's response spurred him to provoke the strike.

Expressing underlying emotions can be instrumental in negotiating a resolution. Particularly in interpersonal disputes, hostility may diminish significantly if the aggrieved party vents her anger, resentment, and frustration in front of the blamed party, and the blamed party acknowledges the validity of such emotions or, going one step further, offers an apology.[6] With hostility reduced, resolving the dispute on the basis of interests becomes easier. Expressions of emotion have a special place in certain kinds of interests-based negotiation and mediation.

Determining Who Is Right

Another way to resolve disputes is to rely on some independent standard with perceived legitimacy or fairness to determine who is right. As a shorthand for such independent standards, we use the term *rights.* Some rights are formalized in law or contract. Other rights are socially accepted standards of behavior, such as reciprocity, precedent, equality, and seniority.[7] In the boots dispute, for example, while the miner had no contractual right to new boots, he felt that standards of fairness called for the company to replace personal property stolen from its premises.

Rights are rarely clear. There are often different—and sometimes contradictory—standards that apply. Reaching agreement on rights, where the outcome will determine who gets what, can often be exceedingly difficult, frequently leading the parties to turn to a third party to determine who is right. The prototypical rights procedure is adjudication, in which disputants present evidence and arguments to a neutral third party who has the power to hand down a binding decision. (In mediation, by contrast, the third party does not have the power to decide the dispute.) Public adjudication is provided by courts and administrative agencies. Private adjudication is provided by arbitrators.[8]

Determining Who Is More Powerful

A third way to resolve a dispute is on the basis of power. We define power, somewhat narrowly, as the ability to coerce someone to do something he would not otherwise do. Exercising power typically means imposing costs on the other side or threatening to do so. In striking, the miners exercised power by imposing economic costs on the company. The exercise of power takes two common forms: acts of aggression, such as sabotage or physical attack, and withholding the benefits that derive from a relationship, as when employees withhold their labor in a strike.

In relationships of mutual dependence, such as between labor and management or within an organization or a family, the questions of who is more powerful turns on who is less dependent on the other.[9] If a company needs the employees' work more than employees need the company's pay, the company is more dependent and hence less powerful. How dependent one is turns on how satisfactory the alternatives are for satisfying one's interests. The better the alternative, the less dependent one is. If it is easier for the company to replace striking employees than it is for striking employees to find new jobs, the company is less dependent and thereby more powerful. In addition to strikes, power procedures include behaviors that range from insults and ridicule to beatings and warfare. All have in common the intent to coerce the other side to settle on terms more satisfactory to the wielder of power. Power procedures are of two types: power-based negotiation, typified by an exchange of threats, and power contests, in which the parties take actions to determine who will prevail.

Determining who is the more powerful party without a decisive and potentially destructive power contest is difficult because power is ultimately a matter of perceptions. Despite objective indicators of power, such as financial resources, parties' perceptions of their own and each other's power often do not coincide. Moreover, each side's perception of the other's power may fail to take into account the possibility that the other will invest greater resources in the contest than expected out of fear that a change in the perceived distribution of power will affect the outcomes of future disputes.

Interrelationship among Interests, Rights, and Power

The relationship among interests, rights, and power can be pictured as a circle within a circle within a circle (as in Figure 1). The innermost circle represents interests; the middle, rights; and the outer, power. The reconciliation of interests takes place within the context of the parties' rights and power. The likely outcome of a dispute if taken to court or to a strike, for instance, helps define the bargaining range within which a resolution can be found. Similarly, the determination of rights takes place within the context of power. One party, for instance, may win a judgment in court, but unless the judgment can be enforced, the dispute will continue. Thus, in the process of resolving a dispute, the focus may shift from interests to rights to power and back again.

FIGURE 1 | Interrelationships among Interests, Rights, and Power

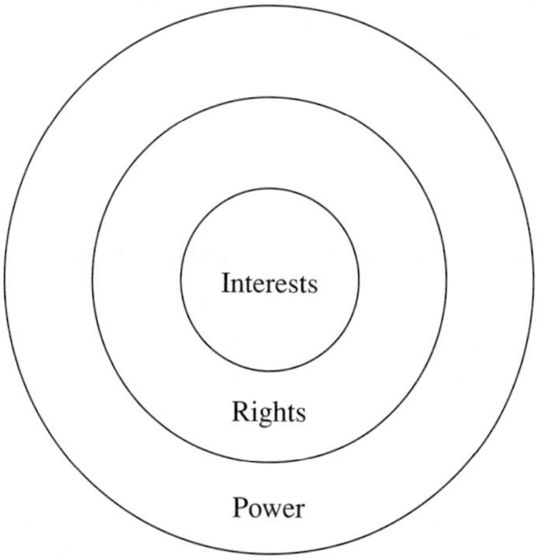

Interests

Rights

Power

Lumping It and Avoidance

Not all disputes end with a resolution. Often one or more parties simply decide to withdraw from the dispute. Withdrawal takes two forms. One party may decide to "lump it," dropping her claim or giving in to the other's claim because she believes pursuing the dispute is not in her interest, or because she concludes she does not have the power to resolve it to her satisfaction. The miner would have been lumping his claim if he had said to himself, "I strongly disagree with management's decision not to reimburse me for my boots, but I'm not going to do anything about it." A second form of withdrawal is avoidance. One party (or both) may decide to withdraw from the relationship, or at least to curtail it significantly.[10] Examples of avoidance include quitting the organization, divorce, leaving the neighborhood, and staying out of the other person's way.

Both avoidance and lumping it may occur in conjunction with particular dispute resolution procedures. Many power contests involve threatening avoidance—such as threatening divorce—or actually engaging in it temporarily to impose costs on the other side—such as in a strike or breaking off of diplomatic relations. Many power contests end with the loser lumping her claim or her objection to the other's claim. Others end with the loser engaging in avoidance: leaving or keeping her distance from the winner. Similarly, much negotiation ends with one side deciding to lump it instead of pursuing the claim. Or, rather than take a dispute to court or engage in coercive actions, one party (or both) may decide to break off the relationship altogether. This is common in social contexts where the disputant perceives satisfactory alternatives to the relationship.

Lumping it and avoidance may also occur before a claim has been made, thus forestalling a dispute. Faced with the problem of stolen boots, the miner might have decided to lump it and not make a claim for the boots. More drastically, in a fit of exasperation, he might have walked off the job and never returned.

Which Approach Is "Best"?

When the miner superintendent described the boots dispute to us, he expressed a preference for how to resolve disputes. In our language, he was saying that on the whole it was better to try to reconcile interests than to focus on who was right or who was more powerful. But what does "better" mean? And in what sense, if any, was he correct in believing that focusing attention on interests is better?

What "Better" Means: Four Possible Criteria

The different approaches to the resolution of disputes—interests, rights, and power—generate different costs and benefits. We focus on four criteria in comparing them: transaction costs, satisfaction with outcomes, effect on the relationship, and recurrence of disputes.[11]

Transaction Costs   For the mine superintendent, "better" meant resolving disputes without strikes. More generally, he wanted to minimize the costs of disputing—what may be called the *transaction costs*. The most obvious costs of striking were economic. The management payroll and the overhead costs had to be met while the mine stood idle. Sometimes strikes led to violence and the destruction of company property. The miners, too, incurred costs—lost wages. Then there were the lost opportunities for the company: a series of strikes could lead to the loss of a valuable sales contract. In a family argument, the costs would include the frustrating hours spent disputing, the frayed nerves and tension headaches, and the missed opportunities to do more enjoyable or useful tasks. All dispute resolution procedures carry transaction costs: the time, money, and emotional energy expended in disputing; the resources consumed and destroyed; and the opportunities lost.[12]

Satisfaction with Outcomes   Another way to evaluate different approaches to dispute resolution is by the parties' mutual satisfaction with the result. The outcome of the strike could not have been wholly satisfactory to the miner—he did not receive new boots—but he did succeed in venting his frustration and taking his revenge. A disputant's satisfaction depends largely on how much the resolution fulfills the interests that led her to make or reject the claim in the first place. Satisfaction may also depend on whether the disputant believes that the resolution is fair. Even if an agreement does not wholly fulfill her interests, a disputant may draw some satisfaction from the resolution's fairness.

Satisfaction depends not only on the perceived fairness of the resolution, but also on the perceived fairness of the dispute resolution procedure. Judgments about fairness turn on several factors: how much opportunity a disputant had to express himself; whether he had control over accepting or rejecting the settlement; how much he was able to participate in shaping the settlement; and whether he believes that the third party, if there was one, acted fairly.[13]

Effect on the Relationship   A third criterion is the long-term effect on the parties' relationship. The approach taken to resolve a dispute may affect the parties' ability to work together on a day-to-day basis. Constant quarrels with threats of divorce may seriously weaken a marriage. In contrast, marital counseling in which the disputing partners learn to focus on interests in order to resolve disputes may strengthen a marriage.

Recurrence   The final criterion is whether a particular approach produces durable resolutions. The simplest form of recurrence is when a resolution fails to stick. For example, a dispute between father and teenage son over curfew appears resolved but breaks out again and again. A subtler form of recurrence takes place when a resolution is reached in a particular dispute, but the resolution fails to prevent the same dispute from arising between one of the disputants and someone else, or conceivably between two different parties in the same community. For instance, a man guilty of sexually harassing an employee reaches an agreement with his victim that is satisfactory to her, but he continues to harass other women employees. Or he stops, but other men continue to harass women employees in the same organization.

The Relationship among the Four Criteria   These four different criteria are interrelated. Dissatisfaction with outcomes may produce strain on the relationship, which contributes to the recurrence of disputes, which in turn increases transaction costs. Because the different costs typically increase and decrease together, it is convenient to refer to all four together as the *costs of disputing.* When we refer to a particular approach as *high-cost* or *low-cost,* we mean not just transaction costs but also dissatisfaction with outcomes, strain on the relationship, and recurrence of disputes.

Sometimes one cost can be reduced only by increasing another, particularly in the short term. If father and son sit down to discuss their conflicting interests concerning curfew, the short-term transaction costs in terms of time and energy may be high. Still, these costs may be more than offset by the benefits of a successful negotiation—an improved relationship and the cessation of curfew violations.

Which Approach Is Least Costly?

Now that we have defined "better" in terms of the four types of costs, the question remains whether the mine superintendent was right in supposing that focusing on interests is better. A second question is also important: when an interests-based approach fails, is it less costly to focus on rights or on power?

Interests versus Rights or Power   A focus on interests can resolve the problem underlying the dispute more effectively than can a focus on rights or power. An example is a grievance filed against a mine foreman for doing work that contractually only a miner is authorized to do. Often the real problem is something else—a miner who feels unfairly assigned to an unpleasant task may file a grievance only to strike back at his foreman. Clearly, focusing on what the contract says about foremen working will not deal with this underlying problem. Nor will striking to protest foremen working. But if the foreman and miner can negotiate about the miner's future work tasks, the dispute may be resolved to the satisfaction of both.

Just as an interests-based approach can help uncover hidden problems, it can help the parties identify which issues are of greater concern to one than to the other. By trading off issues of lesser concern for those of greater concern, both parties can gain from the resolution of the dispute.[14] Consider, for example, a union and employer negotiating over two issues: additional vacation time and flexibility of work assignments. Although the union does not like the idea of assignment flexibility, its clear priority is additional vacation. Although the employer does not like the idea of additional vacation, he cares more about gaining flexibility in assigning work. An agreement that gives the union the vacation days it seeks and the employer the flexibility in making work assignments would likely be satisfactory to both. Such joint gain is more likely to be realized if the parties focus on each side's interests. Focusing on who is right, as in litigation, or on who is more powerful, as in a strike, usually leaves at least one party perceiving itself as the loser.

Reconciling interests thus tends to generate a higher level of mutual satisfaction with outcomes than determining rights or power.[15] If the parties are more satisfied, their relationship benefits and the dispute is less likely to recur. Determining who is right or who is more powerful, with the emphasis on winning and losing, typically makes the relationship more adversarial and strained. Moreover, the loser frequently does not give up, but appeals to a higher court or plots revenge. To be sure, reconciling interests can sometimes take a long time, especially when there are many parties to the dispute. Generally, however, these costs pale in comparison with the transaction costs of rights and power contests such as trials, hostile corporate takeovers, or wars.

In sum, focusing on interests, compared to focusing on rights or power, tends to produce higher satisfaction with outcomes, better working relationships, and less recurrence, and may also incur lower transaction costs. As a rough generalization, then, an interests approach is less costly than a rights or power approach.

Rights versus Power   Although determining who is right or who is more powerful can strain the relationship, deferring to a fair standard usually takes less of a toll than giving in to a threat. In a dispute between a father and teenager over curfew, a discussion of independent standards such as the curfews of other teenagers is likely to strain the relationship less than an exchange of threats.

Determining rights or power frequently becomes a contest—a competition among the parties to determine who will prevail. They may compete with words to persuade a third-party decision maker of the merits of their case, as in adjudication; or they may compete with actions intended to show the other who is more powerful, as in a proxy fight. Rights contests differ from power contests chiefly in their transaction costs. A power contest typically costs more in resources consumed and opportunities lost. Strikes cost more than arbitration. Violence costs more than litigation. The high transaction costs stem not only from the efforts invested in the fight but also from the destruction of each side's resources. Destroying the opposition may be the very object of a power contest. Moreover, power contests often create new injuries and new disputes along with anger, distrust, and a desire for revenge. Power contests, then, typically damage the relationship more and lead to greater recurrence of disputes than do rights contests. In general, a rights approach is less costly than a power approach.

Proposition

To sum up, we argue that, in general, reconciling interests is less costly than determining who is right, which in turn is less costly than determining who is more powerful. This proposition does not mean that focusing on interests is invariably better than focusing on rights and power, but simply means that it tends to result in lower transaction costs, greater satisfaction with outcomes, less strain on the relationship, and less recurrence of disputes.

Focusing on Interests Is Not Enough

Despite these general advantages, resolving *all* disputes by reconciling interests alone is neither possible nor desirable. It is useful to consider why.

When Determining Rights or Power Is Necessary

In some instances, interests-based negotiation cannot occur unless rights or power procedures are first employed to bring a recalcitrant party to the negotiating table. An environmental group, for example, may file a lawsuit against a developer to bring about a negotiation. A community group may organize a demonstration on the steps of the town hall to get the mayor to discuss its interests in improving garbage collection service.

In other disputes, the parties cannot reach agreement on the basis of interests because their perceptions of who is right or who is more powerful are so different that they cannot establish a range in which to negotiate. A rights procedure may be needed to clarify the rights boundary within which a negotiated resolution can be sought. If a discharged employee and her employer (as well as their lawyers) have very different estimations about whether a court would award damages to the employee, it will be difficult for them to negotiate a settlement. Nonbinding arbitration may clarify the parties' rights and allow them to negotiate a resolution.

Just as uncertainty about the rights of the parties will sometimes make negotiation difficult, so too will uncertainty about their relative power. When one party in an ongoing relationship wants to demonstrate that the balance of power has shifted in its favor, it may find that only a power contest will adequately make the point. It is a truism among labor relations practitioners that a conflict-ridden union–management relationship often settles down after a lengthy strike. The strike reduces uncertainty about the relative power of the parties that had made each party unwilling to concede. Such long-term benefits sometimes justify the high transaction costs of a power contest.

In some disputes, the interests are so opposed that agreement is not possible. Focusing on interests cannot resolve a dispute between a right-to-life group and an abortion clinic over whether the clinic will continue to exist. Resolution will likely be possible only through a rights contest, such as a trial, or a power contest, such as a demonstration or a legislative battle.

When Are Rights or Power Procedures Desirable?

Although reconciling interests is generally less costly than determining rights, only adjudication can authoritatively resolve questions of public importance. If the 1954 Supreme Court case, *Brown v. Board of Education* (347 U.S. 483), outlawing racial segregation in public schools, had been resolved by negotiation rather than by adjudication, the immediate result might have been the same—the black plaintiff would have attended an all-white Topeka, Kansas, public school. The societal impact, however, would have been far less significant. As it was, *Brown* laid the groundwork for the elimination of racial segregation in all of American public life. In at least some cases, then, rights-based court procedures are preferable, from a societal perspective, to resolution through interests-based negotiation.[16]

Some people assert that a powerful party is ill-advised to focus on interests when dealing regularly with a weaker party. But even if one party is more powerful, the costs of imposing one's will can be high. Threats must be backed up with actions from time to time. The weaker party may fail to fully comply with a resolution based on power, thus requiring the more powerful party to engage in expensive policing. The weaker party may also take revenge—in small ways, perhaps, but nonetheless a nuisance. And revenge may be quite costly to the more powerful if the power balance ever shifts, as it can quite unexpectedly, or if the weaker party's cooperation is ever needed in another domain. Thus, for a more powerful party, a focus on interests, within the bounds set by power, may be more desirable than would appear at first glance.

Low-Cost Ways to Determine Rights and Power

Because focusing on rights and power plays an important role in effective dispute resolution, differentiating rights and power procedures on the basis of costs is useful. We distinguish three types of rights and power procedures: negotiation, low-cost contests, and high-cost contests. Rights-based negotiation is typically less costly than a rights contest such as court or arbitration. Similarly, power-based negotiation, marked by threats, typically costs less than a power contest in which those threats are carried out.

Different kinds of contests incur different costs. If arbitration dispenses with procedures typical of a court trial (extensive discovery, procedural motions, and lengthy briefs), it can be much cheaper than going to court. In a fight, shouting is less costly than physical assault. A strike in which workers refuse only overtime work is less costly than a full strike.

The Goal: An Interests-Oriented Dispute Resolution System

Not all disputes can be—or should be—resolved by reconciling interests. Rights and power procedures can sometimes accomplish what interests-based procedures cannot. The problem is that rights and power procedures are often used where they are not necessary. A procedure that should be the last resort too often becomes the first resort. The goal, then, is a dispute resolution system that looks like the pyramid on the right in Figure 2: most disputes are resolved through reconciling interests, some through determining who is right, and the fewest through determining who is more powerful. By contrast, a distressed dispute resolution system would look like the inverted pyramid on the left in Figure 2. Comparatively few disputes are resolved through reconciling interests, while many are resolved through determining rights and power. The challenge for the systems designer is to turn the pyramid right side up by designing a system that promotes the reconciling of interests but also provides low-cost ways to determine rights or power for those disputes that cannot or should not be resolved by focusing on interests alone.

FIGURE 2 | Moving from a Distressed to an Effective Dispute Resolution System

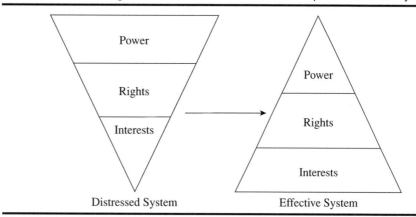

Endnotes

1. In order to steer between the Scylla of sexist language and the Charybdis of awkward writing, we have chosen to alternate the use of masculine and feminine pronouns.

2. This definition is taken from W. L. F. Felstiner, R. L. Abel, and A. Sarat, "The Emergence and Transformation of Disputes: Naming, Blaming, Claiming." *Law and Society Review* 15 (1980–81), pp. 631–54. The article contains an interesting discussion of disputes and how they emerge.

3. See W. L. F. Felstiner, R. L. Abel, and A. Sarat, "The Emergence and Transformation of Disputes: Naming, Blaming, Claiming."

4. In speaking of resolving disputes, rather than processing, managing, or handling disputes, we do not suggest that resolution will necessarily bring an end to the fundamental conflict underlying the dispute. Nor do we mean that a dispute once resolved will stay resolved. Indeed, one of our criteria for contrasting approaches to dispute resolution is the frequency with which disputes recur after they appear to have been resolved. See S. E. Merry, "Disputing Without Culture," *Harvard Law Review* 100 (1987), pp. 2057–73; A. Sarat, "The 'New Formalism' in Disputing and Dispute Processing," *Law and Society Review* 21 (1988), pp. 695–715.

5. For an extensive discussion of interests-based negotiation, see R. Fisher and W. L. Ury, *Getting to Yes* (Boston: Houghton Mifflin, 1981). See also D. A. Lax and J. K. Sebenius, *The Manager as a Negotiator* (New York: Free Press, 1986).

6. S. B. Goldberg and F. E. A. Sander, "Saying You're Sorry," *Negotiation Journal* 3 (1987), pp. 221–24.

7. We recognize that in defining rights to include both legal entitlements and generally accepted standards of fairness, we are stretching that term beyond its commonly understood meaning. Our reason for doing so is that a procedure that uses either legal entitlements or generally accepted standards of fairness as a basis for dispute resolution will focus on the disputants' entitlements under normative standards, rather than on their underlying interests. This is true of adjudication, which deals with legal rights; it is equally true of rights-based negotiation, which may deal with either legal rights or generally accepted standards. Since, as we shall show, procedures that focus on normative standards are more costly than those that focus on interests, and since our central concern is with cutting costs as well as realizing benefits, we find it useful to cluster together legal rights and other normative standards, as well as procedures based on either.

8. A court procedure may determine not only who is right but also who is more powerful, since behind a court decision lies the coercive power of the state. Legal rights have power behind them. Still, we consider adjudication a rights procedure, since its overt focus is determining who is right, not who is more powerful. Even though rights, particularly legal rights, do provide power, a procedure that focuses on rights as a means of dispute resolution is less costly than a procedure that focuses on power. A rights-based contest, such as adjudication, which focuses on which disputant ought to prevail under normative standards, will be less costly than a power-based strike, boycott, or war, which focuses on which disputant can hurt the other more. Similarly, a negotiation that focuses on normative criteria for dispute resolution will be less costly than a negotiation that focuses on the disputants' relative capacity to injure each other. Hence, from our cost perspective, it is appropriate to distinguish procedures that focus on rights from those that focus on power.

9. R. M. Emerson, "Power-Dependence Relations," *American Sociological Review* 27 (1962), pp. 31–41.

10. A. O. Hirschman, *Exit, Voice, and Loyalty: Responses to Declines in Firms, Organizations, and States* (Cambridge, MA: Harvard University Press, 1970). Exit corresponds with avoidance, loyalty with lumping it. Voice, as we shall discuss later, is most likely to be realized in interests-based procedures such as problem-solving negotiation and mediation.

11. A fifth evaluative criterion is procedural justice, which is perceived satisfaction with the fairness of a dispute resolution procedure. Research has shown that disputants prefer third-party procedures that provide opportunities for outcome control and voice. See E. A. Lind and T. R. Tyler, *The Social Psychology of Procedural Justice* (New York: Plenum, 1988); and J. M. Brett, "Commentary on Procedural Justice Papers," in R. J. Lewicki, B. H. Sheppard, and M. H. Bazerman (eds.), *Research on Negotiations in Organizations* (Greenwich, CT: JAI Press, 1986), pp. 81–90.

We do not include procedural justice as a separate evaluation criterion for two reasons. First, unlike transaction costs, satisfaction with outcome, effect on the relationship, and recurrence, procedural justice is meaningful only at the level of a single procedure for a single dispute. It neither generalizes across the multiple procedures that may be used in the resolution of a single dispute nor generalizes across disputes to construct a systems-level cost. The other costs will do both. For example, it is possible to measure the disputants' satisfaction with the outcome of a dispute, regardless of how many different procedures were used to resolve that dispute. Likewise, it is possible to measure satisfaction with outcomes in a system that handles many disputes by asking many disputants about their feelings. Second, while procedural justice and distributive justice (satisfaction with fairness of outcomes) are distinct concepts, they are typically highly correlated. See E. A. Lind and T. R. Tyler, *The Social Psychology of Procedural Justice* (New York: Plenum, 1988).

12. O. E. Williamson, "Transaction Cost Economics: The Governance of Contractual Relations," *Journal of Law and Economics* 22 (1979), pp. 233–61; and J. M. Brett and J. K. Rognes, "Intergroup Relations in Organizations," in P. S. Goodman and Associates, *Designing Effective Work Groups* (San Francisco: Jossey-Bass, 1986), pp. 202–36.

13. For a summary of the evidence of a relationship between procedural and distributive justice—that is, satisfaction with process and with outcome—see E. A. Lind and T. R. Tyler, *The Social Psychology of Procedural Justice* (New York: Plenum, 1988). Lind and Tyler also summarize the evidence showing a relationship between voice and satisfaction with the process. For evidence of the effect of participation in shaping the ultimate resolution beyond simply being able to accept or reject a third party's advice, see J. M. Brett and D. L. Shapiro, "Procedural Justice: A Test of Competing Theories and Implications for Managerial Decision Making," unpublished manuscript.

14. D. A. Lax and J. K. Sebenius, *The Manager as Negotiator.*

15. The empirical research supporting this statement compares mediation to arbitration or adjudication. Claimants prefer mediation to arbitration in a variety of settings: labor-management (J. M. Brett and S. B. Goldberg, "Grievance Mediation in the Coal Industry: A Field Experiment," *Industrial and Labor Relations Review* 37 (1983), pp. 49–69), small claims disputes (C. A. McEwen and R. J. Maiman, "Small Claims Mediation in Maine: An Empirical Assessment," *Maine Law Review* 33 (1981), pp. 237–68), and divorce (J. Pearson, "An Evaluation of Alternatives to Court Adjudication," *Justice System Journal* 7 (1982), pp. 420–44).

16. Some commentators argue that court procedures are always preferable to a negotiated settlement when issues of public importance are involved in a dispute (see, for example, O. M. Fiss, "Against Settlement," *Yale Law Journal* 93 (1984), pp. 1073–90), and all agree that disputants should not be pressured into the settlement of such disputes. The extent to which parties should be encouraged to resolve disputes affecting a public interest is, however, not at all clear. See H. T. Edwards, "Alternative Dispute Resolution: Panacea or Anathema?" *Harvard Law Review* 99 (1986), pp. 668–84.

Selecting a Strategy
Roy J. Lewicki
Alexander Hiam
Karen W. Olander

After you have analyzed your own position and that of the other party and have looked at the contextual issues of the negotiation, you are ready to select a strategy to use in negotiating with the other party. This lengthy preparation allows you to negotiate strategically, adopting a style and plan that are best suited to the situation. As we have noted before, most people skip this preparation; as a result, they negotiate blind. The right strategy greatly improves your odds of a successful outcome.

In this chapter, we will look at five basic strategies that can be used for negotiation. Each strategy applies to a particular set of circumstances and has its own advantages and disadvantages. If you have done your homework, you will be well prepared for selecting the appropriate strategy or combination of strategies for a particular negotiation situation. Note that we say *combination* of strategies. Most negotiations involve a mixture of issues, and each may be best handled with a different strategy. There is usually no single "best" strategy. Variations in the positions of the parties and the context of the negotiation will affect each negotiation differently. And as negotiations continue over time, each side will make adjustments that may call for shifts or changes of strategy by the other side.

Key Factors That Determine the Types of Strategies

The five basic types of negotiating strategies depend on your combination of preferences for two basic concerns: the *relationship with the other negotiator* and the *outcome of the negotiation itself.* The strength or importance of each of these two concerns, and their relative priority, should direct the selection of the optimal negotiation strategy. The other party may select a strategy in a similar manner. If they do not, you will want to give serious consideration as to whether you should share this strategic negotiating model with them. Your chances of a good outcome are often better if both parties agree to play by the same rules. The interaction of the two parties' choices will further influence the negotiation process that actually occurs, and this will have dramatic impact on the outcomes. We will now describe each of these concerns.

Relationship Concerns

First, how important is your past and future *relationship* with the other party? How have the two of you gotten along in the past, and how important is it for the two of you to get along, work together, and like each other in the future? Perhaps it is very important. Perhaps it does not matter at all. Perhaps it is somewhere between these extremes. If maintaining a good relationship with the other party is important to you, then you should

Source: "Selecting a Strategy," from *Think Before You Speak,* by Roy J. Lewicki, Alexander Hiam, and Karen W. Olander, 1996, pp. 54–75. New York: John Wiley & Sons, Inc. Used with permission.

negotiate differently than if the relationship is unimportant, or if it is unlikely that you can repair the relationship.

The importance of the relationship between the two parties will be affected by a number of factors: (1) whether there is a relationship at all; (2) whether that relationship is generally positive or negative (whether the two of you have gotten along well or poorly in the past); (3) whether a future relationship is desirable; (4) the length of the relationship and its history, if one exists; (5) the level of and commitment to the relationship; (6) the degree of interdependence in the relationship; and (7) the amount and extent of free, open communication between the parties.

For example, if you are negotiating the purchase of a new car, you may never have met the salesperson before and may not expect to have a continuing relationship. Therefore, your relationship concerns are low. However, if your business uses a fleet of cars and you expect to work with this person on deals in the future, your relationship concerns are high, and this will affect negotiations. Or if you are buying the car from your neighbor, and want to continue to have a good relationship with that person, you may negotiate differently than if you are buying it from a stranger.

In the case of a party with whom you have an ongoing relationship, it may be congenial, or it may be antagonistic if earlier negotiations have been hostile. If it is a congenial relationship, you may wish to keep it that way, and avoid escalating emotions. If the relationship has a history of hostility, you may prefer not to negotiate, or you may want to lower the emotional level in the negotiations. This is important if you expect the relationship to continue in the future.

Outcome Concerns

The second factor affecting negotiating strategy is the importance of the *outcome* of the negotiation. How important is it for you to achieve a good outcome in this negotiation? Do you need to win on all points to gain the advantage? Or is the outcome of only moderate importance? Or does the outcome not really matter in this negotiation? For example, let us return to the car-buying example. If you are buying a car from a dealer, price may be the most important factor, and you may have absolutely no interest at all in the relationship. If you are buying the car from your neighbor, and you want to keep a good relationship with your neighbor, then you might not press as hard to get a good price. Finally, if you are buying the car from your mother simply so that she doesn't have to worry about it any more, you probably are most concerned about the relationship and care very little about the outcome.

Most of the planning and preparation described in the earlier chapters have focused on the outcome. Hence we will not say much more about outcome concerns here. The important message in this chapter, however, is that the priority of each of the two negotiating concerns, relationship and outcome, will direct the strategy you choose to use for a particular negotiation. The relationship may be your top priority, especially if there is a relationship history and you want to maintain the relationship. In contrast, in many other negotiations, the outcome is the most important factor, as in the example of buying a car. Or relationship and outcome may *both* be important. This will require working together with the other party in some fashion to effect a result. If the relationship concerns have a strong influence on the

FIGURE 1 | Negotiation Strategies

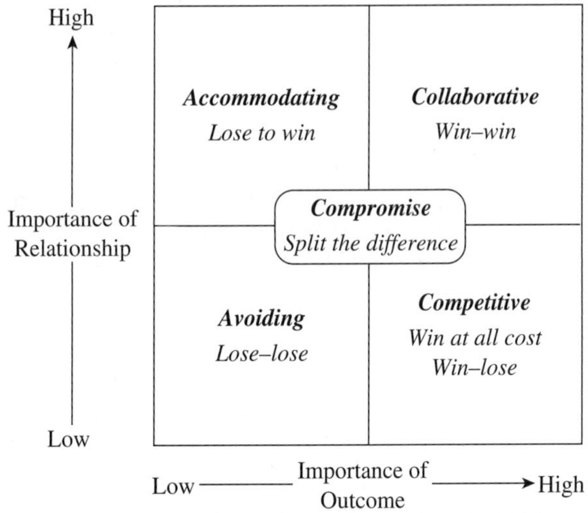

matter at hand, and you decide to emphasize them over the outcome, then you will select a different strategy than you would select where the outcome is more important.

If we show the relationship and outcome concerns on a graph, with high and low priorities for each represented, it looks like Figure 1. The vertical axis represents your degree of concern for the relationship, and the horizontal axis represents your degree of concern for the outcome. When we look at the various quadrants created by different levels of concern for relationship and outcome, five distinctly different strategies emerge:

1. *Avoiding (lose–lose):* This strategy is shown in the lower left of the diagram. In this strategy, the priorities for both the relationship and the outcome are low. Neither aspect of the negotiation is important enough for you to pursue the conflict further. You implement this strategy by withdrawing from active negotiation, or by avoiding negotiation entirely.

2. *Accommodating (lose to win):* This strategy is represented in the upper left of the diagram, where the importance of the relationship is high and the importance of the outcome is low. In this situation, you "back off" your concern for the outcome to preserve the relationship; you intentionally "lose" on the outcome dimension in order to "win" on the relationship dimension.

3. *Competitive (win–lose):* The lower right of the diagram represents high concern for the outcome and low concern for the relationship. You use this strategy if you want to win at all cost, and have no concern about the future state of the relationship.

4. *Collaborative (win–win):*[1] The upper right part of the diagram defines a strategy where there is a high priority for both the relationship and the outcome. In this strategy, the parties attempt to maximize their outcomes while preserving or

enhancing the relationship. This result is most likely when both parties can find a resolution that meets the needs of each.

5. *Compromising (split the difference):* In the middle is an area we will call a compromising, or "satisficing," strategy. It represents a combination approach that is used in a variety of situations. For example, it is often used when the parties cannot achieve good collaboration, but still want to achieve some outcomes and/or preserve the relationship. Thus, for example, if the parties cannot achieve good collaboration but do not want to pursue the outcome and abandon the concern for the relationship (or vice versa), then a compromising strategy can be effective. It is also often used when the parties are under time pressure and need to come to a resolution quickly. Each party will give in somewhat to find a common ground.

These brief descriptions are ideal or "pure" negotiating situations where there may be only one issue at stake. In contrast, most real-life negotiation situations are frequently complex, and thus are often best addressed by using a mix of strategies. Remember, too, that the other party will be formulating a negotiating strategy. You will find your analysis of the other party helpful when you are selecting the appropriate strategy for a particular situation, because you may want to adjust your strategy choice based on what you expect the other to do. If the parties are able to agree on one strategy, negotiations will be easier. In real-life situations, however, each party may start with a different strategy.

We now look at the five basic negotiating strategies in detail. Although you may be inclined to use one particular strategy, it is a good idea to study the components of each strategy carefully. In this way, you can be prepared for the other party's moves, if they use a different strategy than you anticipated.

Avoiding Strategy (Lose–Lose)

The avoiding strategy is used infrequently, but has merit in certain situations. Our nickname of this strategy is actually a misnomer, since an active choice of an avoiding strategy is not necessarily a "loss" on either the relationship or the outcome. However, since we tend to refer to the more active pursuits of relationship and outcomes as "winning," we will call the avoiding strategy a "loss" in terms of the outcome and the relationship.

Why would one choose an avoiding strategy? Because negotiations can be costly (in time, money, and relationships) and there are many cases where negotiators would have been better off to drop the matter entirely! The person employing an avoiding strategy basically sees negotiation as a waste of time—or not worth pursuing. This person may feel that his or her needs can be met without negotiating. In addition, this person may decide that the outcome has very low value and that the relationship is not important enough to develop through the negotiation. As a result, the party reasons that neither the relationship nor the outcome is sufficiently important (at least compared with the costs) and so takes no action or simply refuses to negotiate.

If the "avoider" refuses to negotiate when the other party wants to, this may have a negative effect on the relationship. Even when the outcome is unimportant, many people will prefer to avoid angering the other party. A more moderate method of avoidance may be to not raise any objections to the proceedings, or simply to not show up. If the other party insists on negotiations, and it is important to preserve the relationship, then you might switch to an accommodating strategy.

The avoiding strategy also is a possibility when a party can pursue a very strong alternative outcome. If a strong alternative is available, the person may choose not to negotiate. For example, if you are looking at two different houses to buy, and both meet your needs, you may choose not to negotiate with one seller because you feel the price is too high and the person is inflexible. So you simply select your alternative and pursue an avoiding strategy in the first negotiation.

Alternatives can provide you with bargaining power in other situations, as we will see. If you have no alternatives, or only weak ones, you may also choose not to negotiate. We will discuss alternatives in more depth later in this chapter.

Accommodating Strategy (Lose to Win)

An accommodating strategy is used when the relationship is more important than the outcome of the negotiation. The person using this strategy may prefer to primarily concentrate on building or strengthening a relationship. Since other people are usually happy when we give them what they want, we may simply choose to avoid focusing on the outcome and give it to the other side, thus making them happy. A second reason is that we may want something else in the future. Since many social relationships are built on rather informal expectations and rules of exchange,[2] giving something away now may create the expectation that they need to give us what we want later on. So we give them their preferences now to obtain a better future outcome. A short-term loss is exchanged for a long-term gain.

For example, in a manager–employee relationship, the employee may want to establish a good relationship with the boss now to have a good evaluation, a raise, or a better position in the future. The employee may choose an accommodating strategy and not push for a salary increase now, at her three-month review, if it is expected that this will put her in a better position for a raise at the six-month review.

The accommodating strategy may be used to encourage a more interdependent relationship, to increase support and assistance from the other, or even to cool off hostile feelings if there is tension in the relationship. If the relationship is ongoing, then it may be particularly appropriate to "back down" now, to keep communication lines open and not pressure the opponent to give in on something that they do not want to discuss. In most cases, this strategy is *short term*—it is expected that accommodation now will create a better opportunity to achieve outcome goals in the future. For example, a manager might not urge an employee to take on an extra task right now if the employee is overloaded with projects and the manager can find another person to complete the task, especially if the manager knows that a big project is coming next week, and everyone is going to have to put in overtime.

In a long-term negotiation or over a series of negotiations, it may happen that one side constantly gives in. This precedent may be noted by the other side and seen as accommodating behavior (which it is). It should not be construed as an invitation to the other party to be competitive. But sometimes it is. If this happens to you, the other party will begin to compete and take advantage of your guard being down. You will need to learn how to use damage control and reconnection strategies to overcome these problems.

The accommodating strategy is not usually considered a formal strategy in negotiation. Many negotiation books do not even mention accommodation as a viable strategy; however, most of these books also are based on "high outcome concern" strategies (competing or collaborating) and spend less time on specific strategies to improve or strengthen the relationship. There are two important times to consider an accommodating strategy: first, if the outcome is not very important to you, or pursuing the outcome is likely to create too much tension and animosity, and second, if your primary objective is to improve the relationship. In addition, you might decide to switch to an accommodating strategy during negotiations, particularly when they reach a point where you no longer wish to press for a resolution.

Competitive Strategy (Win to Lose)

When many people think of negotiation and bargaining, this is the strategy they think of. The competitive strategy is used frequently, so it is important to understand how it works, even if you do not plan to use it yourself.

In a competitive strategy, the outcome of the negotiation is more important than the relationship. Because the outcomes (resources, gains, profits, etc.) are seen as finite and limited in amount or size, the person engaging in a competitive strategy wants to get as much of those outcomes as possible. (We will use the term *competition* to denote the person using the competitive strategy.) We call this strategy *win to lose* because it is likely that while competitors may gain on the outcome, they strain and endanger the relationship between the parties. The thinking and goals in this strategy are short term: to maximize the magnitude of the outcome right now, and to not care about either the long-term consequences of this strategy or the relationship. The relationship with the other party does not matter, for one of several reasons: (1) this may be a one-time negotiation with no future relationship, (2) the future relationship may not be important, (3) the relationship exists, but was poor to begin with, or (4) the other party may have a reputation for hard bargaining or dishonesty, and this strategy is adopted for defensive reasons. At any rate, this strategy is undertaken with the assumption that the future relationship with the other party is unimportant, but the specific outcome *is* important.

The competitive strategy tends to emphasize the differences between the parties, promoting a "we/they" attitude. Thus the relationship during negotiation in a competitive situation will be characterized by lack of trust and even by conflict. This contrasts with the collaborative strategy in which differences are minimized and similarities emphasized.

The goal in the competitive strategy is to get the other party to give in, and thus to satisfy the competitor's needs now. It is based on the "I win, you lose" concept. The competitor will do anything to accomplish the objectives and obtain as much of the pie as possible. This can include a variety of behaviors, including hardball tactics.

Critical Factors in a Competitive Strategy

A Well-Defined Bargaining Range   In a competitive strategy, each side has a bargaining range, which consists of a *starting point,* a *target,* and an *ending point* or walkaway. Bargaining occurs because the line bargaining range for each party is different. During bargaining, you attempt to bring the two ranges into overlap so that each party is satisfied.

The *starting point* is announced or inferred as the negotiations begin. Starting points will be different for the two parties. In new car negotiations, for example, the buyer will have a lower starting point, the seller, a higher one. Usually the buyer makes gradual concessions upward, while the seller will make gradual concessions downward, with the expectation that the two will be able to meet somewhere in the middle. In labor negotiations, labor is usually expected to ask "high" and management to offer "low," again with the expectation that concessions on each side will result in finding a meeting ground.

Both parties will have a walkaway point, which is the cutoff point, beyond which they will not go. The walkaway point of the other party is usually not known, and is not stated. In fact, they will actively try to keep you from learning their walkaway point, because if you knew it, you would offer them something slightly above it and expect that they would agree! If talks break off because this point has been reached, then you may surmise that the walkaway point of the other party was probably close to, or at, the last offer that the other side made. If this point is not reached, and the parties agree to a resolution, this point may never be known. In future chapters, we will explore ways of discovering competitors' walkaway points and learn how to turn this knowledge into better outcomes.

As long as the bargaining range for one party in some way overlaps with that of the other party, then there is room for bargaining. (By *overlap,* we mean that the most the buyer is willing to offer is above the least the seller is willing to accept.) If the ranges do not overlap (and this may not be known at the beginning of the negotiations), then there may be no successful negotiation. The parties will need to decide whether to adjust their bargaining ranges, or to end negotiations.

A Good Alternative   An alternative or BATNA[3] (best alternative to a negotiated agreement) is an option that can be pursued if the current negotiation fails. It is an outcome outside the scope of the negotiation with this other party, and can be pursued if it appears more attractive than any potential outcome from this negotiation. Alternatives are good to have because they can be weighed against the value of any particular outcome from this negotiation, to decide which is most advantageous. Not only is an alternative an evaluative tool, it is also a power tool that can be introduced into negotiations in the manner of "I have this alternative that is equally good and costs less. Can you improve on what I will get if I pursue my alternative?"

Alternatives interact with walkaway points to influence the choices you make. For example, say you currently make $25,000 in your job and you are job hunting. You decide that you want to find a job making at least $30,000. What do you do if you find a job you like, but it pays only $28,000? Do you take it or not? If there are no other such jobs available (no alternatives) because the economy is sluggish, then you might take the $28,000 job. However, if many alternative jobs are available for the taking, then you may hold out for a higher salary. On the other hand, suppose you lose your $25,000 job and you are offered $24,000 for another similar job. Will you take it? Perhaps under these circumstances, you will be more likely to do so. In any negotiation, it is wise to be well-informed of your alternatives and, wherever possible, to use them to your advantage.

Tactics   The competitive strategy is also characterized by a number of tactics calculated to enhance the competitor's position and place the other party at a disadvantage. These include behavioral tactics such as bluffing, being aggressive, and threatening, which can give the competitor power over the other party. While these tactics work sometimes, they also have the problem that they can potentially backfire on the person using them, so they must be employed carefully.

Results and Drawbacks of Using a Competitive Strategy

The competitive strategy can be successful, in spite of being one-sided. People using this strategy usually come away from a negotiation with the belief that they obtained the best that they could.

Negotiations that rely on a competitive strategy can be costly and time-consuming, especially if each party holds out for all its demands. Much time is spent researching, pressuring, and "psyching out" the other party. Further time is consumed making moves and countermoves, trying to figure out what the other party will do. Competitive strategies are often compared with strategies used in chess, military warfare, and other tactical, competitive battles. The time spent in these activities is very different from alternative uses of that time; for example, in the collaborative model, this same time could be spent on mutual exploration of issues, sharing of information, and an attempt to find mutually acceptable solutions.

Time and goodwill may also be lost if the competitor anticipates that the other party will be competitive and prepares a competitive strategy. If the other party had not intended to be competitive, they may switch strategies when they discover that you have decided to be competitive, thus escalating emotions and increasing conflict. Not only do you lose time, but you may have alienated the other party, hurt the relationship, and toughened them so that they are now willing to give you far less than they might have on the outcome dimension.

A major problem with the competitive strategy is that it is frequently used by inexperienced or untrained negotiators who believe that competition is the only viable strategy. They may be missing opportunities by automatically selecting the competitive strategy. It is important to select a strategy only after thorough investigation of the issues, an understanding of what strategy the other party is likely to pursue, and some clear decisions about the relative importance of the outcomes and the relationship with the other party.

Likewise, it is possible to underestimate the other parties in a competitive situation. Remember that they, too, have adopted the mission to win at all costs. When using a competitive strategy, we tend to underestimate the strength, wisdom, planning, and effectiveness of the other party and assume that even though they are preparing to be competitive too, we can beat them at their game! If you do not pay close attention to their behavioral and verbal clues, you may set yourself up for manipulation by the other party.

Finally, we need to beware of something called the *self-fulfilling prophecy.* A self-fulfilling prophecy is something we believe so strongly that we actually make it come true. It often happens in negotiation when one party expects the other to behave in a particular way, and as a result, actually makes the party behave that way. This tends to come true if the other party is using the competitive strategy because they think you are. Anticipating that the other is going to be competitive, we prepare to be competitive ourselves. The cues we give off in this preparation—our language, tone of voice, gestures, and behaviors—let the other party believe that we intend to be competitive. So they behave competitively, which only assures us that our initial assumptions were right.

The Collaborative Strategy (Win–Win)

A collaborative strategy is one in which both parties consider the relationship and the outcome to be equally important. This strategy is also referred to as cooperative or win–win.[4] In a collaborative strategy, the parties to the negotiation either begin with compatible goals or are willing to search for ways to pursue their goals so that both can gain. This is in sharp contrast to the competitive strategy, in which the parties believe their goals are mutually exclusive, and only one side can win. The relationship between the parties is very likely an ongoing one, with some established history of give-and-take, so that the parties trust each other and know that they can work together. In addition, collaborative strategies are often initiated when the parties know that they want to establish long-term goals for particular outcomes and for the relationship. For example, many local governments are finding that they simply cannot sustain the operating costs of the past, especially in view of the voters' unwillingness to accept higher taxes. Knowing that city budgets have to be cut, departments need to work collaboratively, with *each* department taking a cut, and try to find creative ways to help each other stay in the black or at least minimize the red.

To make this strategy work, *both* parties to the negotiation must be willing to use the collaborative strategy; if only one side employs it, and the other uses a different one, the chances are that both parties cannot achieve both an optimal outcome and preserve or enhance their working relationship. A collaborative strategy is particularly appropriate within an organization, when two parties have common ground, or in situations where two parties have the same customers, same clients, same suppliers, or same service personnel. In any of these cases, the parties have or want to establish a working relationship, and to keep it working smoothly.

For a collaborative strategy to work, there must be a high degree of trust, openness, and cooperation. The parties look for common needs and goals and engage in mutually supportive behavior to obtain them. Both parties realize that they are interdependent and that their cooperative effort can solve the problems and meet the needs of both sides.

In collaboration, communication between parties is open and accurate. This contrasts greatly with the competitive strategy, in which the negotiators have a high level of distrust and guard information carefully to prevent the other side from obtaining the advantage.

The parties in a collaborative endeavor have support from their constituencies. The constituencies trust the parties to find common ground and support them in doing so.

Doing so may mean not achieving absolutely everything the constituency wanted on the substantive issues, and the constituency has to accept this as valid. In contrast, in the competitive strategy, the constituencies usually push the negotiator to get everything he or she can, regardless of the future of the relationship.

Collaborating parties respect deadlines and are willing to renegotiate the time frame if necessary to achieve their goals. Contrast this with the competitive strategy, where time is used as an obstacle or as a power ploy to accomplish one's own ends.

The collaborative strategy is hard work, but the results can be rewarding. It takes extra time and creativity to build trust and to find win–win solutions. But the outcome and relationship results are usually better for both parties.

Keys to Successful Collaboration

The collaborative strategy has traditionally been underutilized, because most people do not understand the fine points of the strategy and because it is less familiar than the competitive strategy. Many negotiations are based on the competitive model, which is the way most people view negotiation—as a competitive situation where one is better off being suspicious of the other, and the fundamental object is to get all the goodies.

Of key importance in a collaborative strategy is commitment. Both parties need to be committed to (1) understanding the *other* party's needs and objectives; (2) providing a free flow of information, both ways; and (3) finding the best solution(s) to meet the needs of both sides.[5]

Understanding the other party's goals and needs is critical to the collaborative strategy. We suggested that this is important in competitive strategy as well, but for very different reasons. In a competitive strategy, you may know or think you know what the other party wants; but your objective in learning this is to facilitate your own strategy development, and also to strategize how to beat the other side by doing better than them or denying them what they want to achieve. In a collaborative strategy, your objective is to understand their goals and needs so that you can work with them to achieve their goals as well as your own. Good collaboration frequently requires not only understanding their stated objectives, but their underlying needs—*why* they want what they want. In the collaborative strategy, both parties must be willing to ask questions and *listen carefully to the answers,* to learn about the other's needs.

Second, to provide a free flow of information, both parties must be willing to *volunteer* information. The information has to be as accurate and as comprehensive as possible. Both sides need to understand the issues, the problems, the priorities, and the goals of the other. They need to fully understand the important context factors in the negotiation. Compare this with the competitive strategy, in which information is closely guarded, or, if shared, often distorted.

Finally, having listened closely to each other, the parties can then work toward *achieving mutual goals* that will satisfy both parties. To do this, the parties will need to minimize their differences and emphasize their similarities. They will need to focus on the issues and work at keeping personalities out of the discussions. Collaborative goals differ from competitive goals. In competition, the goal is obtaining the largest share of the pie, at any cost, without giving away any information or conceding on any issue. In collaboration, each party must be willing to redefine its perspective in light of the collaboration, knowing that the whole can be greater than the sum of the parts. In this light, having a strong knowledge of the problem area is a definite advantage. While a lack of information can be overcome, starting out with the knowledge is definitely an asset.

To achieve success, each party *from the beginning* must send signals to the other that will help build trust between and among those negotiating.

Obstacles to the Collaborative Strategy

Both parties to a negotiation must be willing to collaborate if this strategy is to be successful. It will be difficult, if not impossible, to employ collaborative strategy under the following circumstances:

- One party does not see the situation as having the potential for collaboration.
- One party is motivated only to accomplish its own ends.
- One party has historically been competitive; this behavior may be hard to change.
- One party expects the other to be competitive and prepares for negotiation based on this expectation.
- One party wants to be competitive and rationalizes this behavior.
- One party may be accountable to a constituency that prefers the competitive strategy.
- One party is not willing to take the time to search for collaborative items.
- The negotiation or bargaining mix may include both competitive and collaborative issues. (Sometimes, the two parties can collaborate on collaborative issues and compete on competitive issues. Our experience, however, is that competitive processes tend to drive out collaborative processes, making collaboration harder to achieve.)

Most of the foregoing obstacles reflect a conflict between the parties' preferences for strategy. It may be possible to get the other party to take a different stance if it appears to be desirable in light of the information. Communication is of major importance when you are trying to establish a collaborative relationship.

Compromising Strategy

Ultimately, most negotiating situations are mixed; some bargaining elements are competitive in nature, and others can be approached collaboratively. There are times when the relationship is only somewhat important, and the outcomes are only somewhat important. This is where the fifth strategy comes in.

The compromising strategy may be thought of as an "adequate for most occasions" approach to negotiation. In this strategy, each side will have to modify its priorities for the relationship and for the preferred outcome(s). In both cases, the parties are making a decision that compromising is preferred because, on the one hand, *both* parties gain something (an advantage over accommodation or competition), both parties gain *something* (as opposed to nothing—an advantage over avoiding), and yet compromising does not require all the intentional effort required for collaboration. For example, if a manufacturing facility has a mandate to contain costs, the union and the factory representatives (whose relationship is usually competitive) will want to find an acceptable way to achieve this. The union will want to avoid layoffs. The company may propose a wage freeze. So the two parties may agree on a small wage increase offset by a decrease of the labor pool by attrition rather than layoffs; this is a compromise.

While negotiators usually don't start off planning a compromise (particularly if a competitive or collaborative strategy is possible), compromising is often seen as an acceptable "second choice." There are three major reasons to choose a compromising strategy (particularly as a "default" alternative to other strategies):

1. A true collaborative strategy does not seem to be possible. One or both parties don't believe that true win–win can be achieved because it is simply too complex or too difficult. Or the relationship may already be too strained for the parties to work together in a manner that fosters and supports good collaboration.

2. The parties are short of time or other critical resources necessary to get to collaboration. Compromising is usually quick and efficient. While it may be suboptimal on the quality of the outcomes achieved, the trade-off between achieving a great outcome and the time required to do it may force one to pick time over quality.

3. Both parties gain something (or don't lose anything) on both dimensions. As opposed to pursuing a competitive strategy (and maximizing outcomes at the expense of the relationship) or an accommodating strategy (and sacrificing outcomes for the relationship), compromising assures some gain on *both* the outcome and relationship dimensions.

When to Choose Which Strategy

Now that we have reviewed the five basic strategies, we come to an important part of this chapter: how to decide which strategy you should use for a negotiation. There are two key factors to consider:

1. How important is the outcome to be gained from this negotiation?
2. How important is the past, present, and future relationship with the opponent? The following paragraphs describe ways to decide about these two questions and other factors to consider in answering them.

Situation

Look at the *situation* and try to figure out which strategy might be best in those circumstances. Do I care a lot about the outcomes in this situation? If I do, am I willing to sacrifice my relationship with the other person? Or, conversely, is the relationship so important that I am unwilling to endanger it by pursuing the outcome? Alternatively, consider the conditions under which each strategy is most effective (see Figure 1 on page 16). Which of these conditions apply to the present situation?

Remember that each strategy has both advantages and disadvantages. One strategy is more or less appropriate depending on the type of conflict and the situation.

Preferences

Analyze your personal *preferences* for the various strategies. You will probably be more successful using a strategy that feels comfortable. Research has shown that people in conflict have distinct preferences for employing certain strategies in conflict situations.[6] These preferences lead individuals to develop distinct *styles* with which they approach many situations. Based on past experience and history, some people have strong biases toward being competitive, collaborative, compromising, accommodating, or avoiding in conflict situations. The stronger your preference for a particular conflict management strategy (style), the more often you will choose it, the more "biased" you become in seeing it as an advantageous strategy, and the more likely you will be to see that strategy (style) as appropriate in a variety of situations. Thus, if you normally respond to conflict (and negotiation) situations in a competitive manner, then you are more likely to see the competitive strategy as widely appropriate—even when it may not be. Similarly, the less likely you are to avoid conflict, the more likely it is that you will not choose the avoiding strategy—even when it may be the most appropriate thing to do. Therefore, understanding your preferences and "biases" is critical, because they will affect your tendency to overselect or underselect strategies in particular situations.

Your preferences for a particular strategy are also influenced by subtle issues such as your *values and principles*. These may be harder, in some ways, to define than your goals, priorities, or limits. But how you evaluate the following will have a great impact on your willingness to use (or not use) certain strategies:

• How much do you value truth, integrity, manners, courtesy?

• Is respect an important issue for you?

• How important is fair play? (And, for that matter, how do you define *fair*?)

• How much of your ego is involved in this—your reputation, your image? How concerned are you about how you will see yourself—or others will see you—if you get what you want, or don't get what you want?

Experience

Next, consider your *experience* using the various strategies. The more experience you have, the better you become at using that strategy—and, probably, the more likely you are to use it. Experience is one of the key factors that works to shape your preferences.

Style

Think about your own style as it interacts with the *other party's style,* and consider the possible consequences. What will be the effect of such a combination? For example, two competitive parties might have more conflict in their negotiation than a competitive party negotiating with a party that usually yields. While it would be too complex to explore all the possible interactions between each of your five possible styles and the styles of the other in detail, we have summarized the possible combinations in Table 1. (Some of the cells in the left side are blank because the information is contained in the "matching cell" on the right side.)

TABLE 1 | Likely Interactions between Negotiators of Different Styles

	Avoiding	Accommodating	Competing	Collaborating	Compromising
Avoiding	Both parties avoid pursuing their goals on the issues, and do not take any action to endanger the relationship.	Accommodator shows strong concern for the avoider, particularly the relationship; avoider attempts to minimize interaction.	Competitor will dominate or avoider will escape. Avoider attempts to minimize interaction, while competitor tries to "engage."	Collaborator shows strong concern for both issues and the relationship while avoider tries to escape. Collaborator may give up.	Compromiser shows some concern for both issues and relationship; avoider tries to escape. Compromiser may give up or avoider may engage.
Accommodating		Both parties avoid pursuing their goals on the issues, give in to the others goals, and try to smooth over relationship concerns.	Competitor pursues own goals on the issues, while the accommodator tries to make the competitor happy. Competitor usually wins big.	Collaborator shows strong concern for both issues and relationship; accommodator tries to make the collaborator happy. Relationship should be very strong, but the collaborator may achieve better outcomes.	Compromiser shows some concern for both issues and relationship; accommodator tries to make the compromiser happy. Relationship will improve, compromiser may entice the accommodator to pursue some issue focus.
Competing			Both parties pursue their goals on the issues and ignore any concern for the relationship; create conflict, mistrust, hostility.	Collaborator shows strong concern for both issues and relationship, while competitor only pursues issues. Competitor usually "wins" and both parties become competitive.	Compromiser shows some concern for both issues and relationship, while competitor only pursues issues. Competitor usually "wins" and both parties become competitive.
Collaborating				Both parties pursue their goals on the issues, show strong concern for the others' goals *and* sustaining trust, openness, and a good relationship.	Compromiser shows some concern. Collaborator shows strong concern for both issues and the relationship. Minimally, good compromise or better.
Compromising					Both parties pursue their goals on the issues in a limited way and attempt to "do no harm" to the relationship.

Perceptions and Past Experience

Consider your *perceptions and past experience* with the other party. How you feel about the other party, and what you want to have happen in that relationship in the future, will drive your strategy. How well do you like each other? How much do you communicate? How much do you need to work with the other party in the future because you are dependent on what they can do for you? How much do you trust them? Your level of trust with the other party will be based on your past experience with them, and on the history and results of other negotiations they have conducted with you or with other parties in the past.

Other Factors

Finally, there are other factors that may affect the selection of strategy but that might be less in your control. Nevertheless they should be part of the planning process. These reflect the following situational or context issues:

- Is this negotiation voluntary or imposed? Are both parties going into it willingly, or has it been assigned by a manager or some other constituency whose voice and support are influential?

- Is the situation highly structured? Are there rules, laws, and management mandates that will direct the negotiation?

- Is the agenda already established? (Can it be changed if necessary?)

- Finally, realize that the setting plays an important part in the proceedings and in the results. Consider not only the physical environment but elements of the psychological setting, including the players, both individuals and groups; their cultures and behavior; and established norms, standards, and processes.

Can You Make a "No Strategy" Choice?

Some people whom we have taught in negotiation have argued that it is possible to adopt *no strategy:* You refuse to make an explicit strategic choice, and "let the chips fall" to determine what you will do next. This allows you "maximum flexibility" to adjust your approach based on what your opponent does first, or as the proceedings change.

This approach has some distinct advantages. You get a chance to find out how your opponent wants to negotiate first, which may tell you a lot about your opponent. It also keeps you from making a commitment to a strategy that may not work or get completed—for example, to be accommodative while the other is being competitive? However, a "no strategy" choice is often the lazy negotiator's way of avoiding a key part of the planning and preparation process. We do not think this is a good choice! While a "no strategy" choice may give you some negotiating leeway, it could also put you in a precarious position if you have not planned well. The result will be that the opposition gains an advantage over you before you realize what is going on!

If you know that you care about the relationship, or the outcome, or both (or neither), select a strategy and begin to plan around it. If you are proactive about strategy choice, you are much more likely to get what you want than if you wait for the other to initiate action. As we have pointed out, you can always adapt your strategy later as necessary.

Moving Forward

As with planning a trip, it is wise to know *where* you want to go and *how* to get there. It is important to have a well-developed plan that includes specific moves and counter-moves. Your game plan can be modified as needed. Modifications will be based on what the other party says and does. Plans start with a strategy.

Endnotes

1. G. T. Savage, J. D. Blair, and R. L. Sorenson, "Consider Both Relationships and Substance When Negotiating Strategically," *Academy of Management Executive* 3, no. 1 (1989), pp. 37–48.

2. G. C. Homans, *Social Behavior: Its Elementary Forms* (New York: Harcourt, Brace & World, 1961).

3. R. Fisher and W. Ury, *Getting to Yes* (Boston: Houghton Mifflin, 1981); R. Fisher, W. Ury, and B. Patton, *Getting to Yes: Negotiating Agreement without Giving In,* 2nd ed. (New York: Penguin Books, 1991).

4. R. E. Walton and R. B. McKersie, *A Behavioral Theory of Labor Negotiations: An Analysis of a Social Interaction System* (New York: McGraw-Hill, 1965); A. C. Filley, *Interpersonal Conflict Resolution* (Glenview, IL: Scott Foresman, 1975); R. Fisher, W. Ury, and B. Patton, *Getting to Yes: Negotiating Agreement without Giving In;* D. G. Pruitt, *Negotiation Behavior* (New York: Academic Press, 1981); D. G. Pruitt, "Strategic Choice in Negotiation," *American Behavioral Scientist* 27 (1983), pp. 167–94; P. J. D. Carnevale and D. G. Pruitt, "Negotiation and Mediation," in *Annual Review of Psychology,* M. Rosenberg and I. Porter (eds.), Vol. 43 (Palo Alto, CA: Annual Reviews, Inc., 1992), pp. 531–82; D. G. Pruitt and P. J. D. Carnevale, *Negotiation in Social Conflict* (Pacific Grove, CA: Brooks-Cole, 1993).

5. Fisher and Ury, *Getting to Yes.*

6. K. Thomas and R. Killman, *The Conflict Mode Inventory* (Tuxedo Park, NY: XICOM, 1974).

Reading 1.3

Balancing Act: How to Manage Negotiation Tensions
Susan Hackley

"The more aware you are of the tensions underlying a negotiation, the greater your chances of success."

Judith Lawson dreaded her upcoming meeting with the mayor. As head of the city's environmental department, she had promised her staff that she would confront the mayor with their complaints. Unless her office was given the budget to implement proposals to improve air quality and deal with polluters, several key members of her staff planned to quit. Furthermore, they would have no qualms about airing their grievances publicly.

Lawson knew this would be a tough negotiation, for several reasons. The mayor would be understandably upset that a high-profile department was threatening mutiny. Lawson wanted to represent her staff aggressively, but she also worried that too assertive a stance might incline the mayor to "shoot the messenger"—which her career couldn't afford.

What made Lawson's task so complicated is that it required her to manage three tensions simultaneously.

1. The tension between creating and distributing value.
2. The tension between empathy and assertiveness.
3. The tension between principals and agents.

These three tensions are "inherent in negotiation, whether the goal is to make a deal or settle a dispute," write Robert H. Mnookin, Scott R. Peppet, and Andrew S. Tulumello in *Beyond Winning: Negotiating to Create Value in Deals and Disputes* (Belknap, 2000). Managing them is vital for successful negotiations.

Distributing Value versus Creating It

Some negotiations are purely *distributive*—the task is to divide a fixed amount of value. When haggling over the price of a suit, you can try to affect the distribution of value (who gets how much), but you're unlikely to create new value. Other negotiations are potentially *value creating:* they offer the opportunity to create value by expanding the universe of what is being negotiated. For example, a celebrity might get a suit for free by agreeing to wear it to a well-publicized event. In a trade negotiation, political face-saving tactics may be as important as the tariffs being decided.

Source: "Balancing Act: How to Manage Negotiation Tensions" by Susan Hackley from the *Program on Negotiation* Newsletter at the Harvard Law School (www.pon.harvard.edu), February 2005, pp. 3–5. Used with permission.

Skillful negotiators make sure they get their fair share while exploring ways to "enlarge the pie," to use a popular negotiation metaphor. If you bargain in a job negotiation for a higher salary but miss opportunities to discuss stock options, merit bonuses, or a more generous retirement package, you may end up with a relatively poor deal. At the same time, you need to protect your core distributive interests, being careful not to share too much information (you're desperate for the job) or give away too much value (you'd take half the salary offered).

Judith Lawson knew there would be value-creating opportunities in her meeting with the mayor. If citizens perceived that the city was handling environmental problems more effectively, both the mayor and the environmental department would score a public relations victory. Moreover, it would be in the mayor's interest not to incur the disruption of a protracted dispute with his environmental department.

Lawson also recognized the distributive issues at stake. What additional resources could the mayor give her department? How much time would he be willing to spend on their concerns and projects?

Empathy versus Assertiveness

In many negotiations, you may find it difficult to truly understand the other side's viewpoint. If you're angry with a supplier who sent you shoddy goods, you won't want to hear his sob story about the poor raw materials with which he had to work. Yet a little empathy could inspire you to help him find ways to solve his problem and, in turn, ensure better-quality goods.

Asking open-ended questions, listening closely, and demonstrating an understanding of the other side's position will not only allow you to explain your own perspective but may also give you new and useful information.

On the other hand, you don't want to be overly swayed by another's story. Being assertive means being able to express your own interests with confidence and clarity. Skilled negotiators have learned how to be assertive *and* empathetic. They make it clear what they want and need, and they also are genuinely curious to discover what the other side wants and needs.

Lawson was tired of the mayor's excuses for undercutting her department's initiatives, yet she knew she needed to see the situation from his point of view. Once their meeting got under way, she learned to her surprise that the mayor had greater sympathy for her requests than she'd expected and that he felt frustrated and hamstrung by the city council's budget decisions. He had avoided engaging with her department because he felt helpless. This new knowledge made it easier for Lawson to engage in creative problem solving that answered her needs as well as the mayor's. What about demonstrating to the council how better air quality would elevate the city's reputation as a desirable place to live, which, in turn, would improve real estate values, public health, and economic development?

Being a Principal versus Serving as an Agent

In her negotiations with the mayor, Lawson was acting as an *agent* for the members of her department, who depended on her to represent their grievances fairly and effectively. As a *principal* in the negotiation, Lawson also had personal interests that were not

Ten Hard-Bargaining Tactics

Don't be caught unprepared by hard bargainers, warn Mnookin, Peppet, and Tulumello in *Beyond Winning*. Here is their top 10 list of common tactics to watch out for:

1. **Extreme claims followed by small, slow concessions.** Don't let a strong demand "anchor" your expectations. Be clear going in about your own demands, alternatives, and bottom line—and don't be rattled by an aggressive opponent.

2. **Commitment tactics.** Your opponent may say that his hands are tied or that he has only limited discretion in negotiating. Make sure that these commitment tactics are for real.

3. **Take-it-or-leave-it offers.** This game of chicken can be countered by making another offer. But watch out: if both parties play this game, you may not get a deal.

4. **Inviting unreciprocated offers.** When you make an offer, wait for a counteroffer before reducing your demands. Don't bid against yourself.

5. **Trying to make you flinch.** Your opponent keeps making demands, waiting for you to reach your breaking point. Don't fall for it.

6. **Personal insults and feather ruffling.** These personal attacks can feed on your insecurities and make you vulnerable. Grow a thick skin.

7. **Bluffing, puffing, and lying.** Exaggerating and misrepresenting facts can throw you off-guard. Be polite but skeptical.

8. **Threats and warnings.** Recognizing threats and oblique warnings as the tactics they are can help you stand up to them.

9. **Belittling your alternatives.** Have a firm sense of your best alternative to a negotiated agreement (BATNA), and don't let your opponent shake your resolve.

10. **Good cop, bad cop.** One of your opponents is reasonable; the other is tough. Realize that they are working together, and get your own bad cop if you need one.

perfectly aligned with those of her staff, including concerns for her career and her professional relationship with the mayor.

Lawyers represent clients. Money managers give investment advice. Labor leaders negotiate on behalf of unions, and real estate agents represent sellers and buyers. People "constantly delegate authority to others so they may act in our place" as agents, note Mnookin, Peppet, and Tulumello. Unfortunately the principal-agent relationship is "rife with potential conflicts." Looking for differences in incentives is an important part of preparing for a negotiation. A victim in a car accident suing for damages needs to examine her lawyer's interests. Does he have a financial incentive to either settle the case early or prolong it unnecessarily?

One way to manage the principal-agent tension is to acknowledge it up front and treat it as a "shared problem." Before her meeting with the mayor, Lawson and her staff agreed that she would not have authority to make commitments without their approval. What if the mayor offered her a promotion without addressing her department's needs? Lawson resolved not to be swayed by bribes, while her staff promised to back her up should the mayor make punitive moves. Recognizing that the "use of agents complicates bargaining by creating a web of relationships in which a variety of actors interact" helped Lawson and her team prepare for the negotiation.

Awareness Is Power

Beyond Winning's authors believe you'll be more likely to succeed if you learn to recognize the three tensions that can exist in negotiations. Overlook them, and you may fail to come to agreement, even when an agreement would be better for both sides.

Sometimes the other side is reasonable, and you can still miss opportunities to create value. You might not pursue the necessary in-depth conversation or, if you do, you might not listen well enough to your counterpart. Another pitfall: not working hard enough to establish the strong relationship that would lead to the give-and-take that results in better deals.

When the other side isn't reasonable, it's that much harder to reach agreement. A divorcing couple may find it impossible to listen and empathize with each other, engaging instead in scorched-earth litigation that depletes the very financial resources in dispute. Beware of tough negotiators, who may employ a variety of strategies ranging from the unpleasant to the unethical. (See the sidebar "Ten Hard-Bargaining Tactics.")

"Making the right moves or using good technique will not cause these tensions to disappear," observe Mnookin, Peppet, and Tulumello. "They are present in most negotiations, from beginning to end, and should be consciously and thoughtfully considered." Learn to seek additional sources of value while also ensuring you get your fair share. Empathize with the other side and assert your own interests convincingly. And when you're employing an agent or acting as one yourself, be aware that your interests may not all be shared.

The Negotiation Checklist

Tony Simons
Thomas M. Tripp

Preparation increases your chance of success, whether in combat, sports, or negotiations. The well-prepared negotiator knows the playing field and the players, is seldom surprised, and can promptly capitalize on opportunities. This article offers a tool for use in effectively negotiating important transactions and disputes.

Making deals is a key part of being effective in business. Managers and executives negotiate constantly over issues as varied as hiring decisions and purchases, corporate resource allocations, and labor contracts. One could argue that the American system of government is based on an ongoing process of negotiation, which is sometimes successful and sometimes not.

The "negotiation checklist" that we present in this article is a systematic way to make sure you are well-prepared before you walk into your next negotiation. It is based on proven principles of negotiation that are taught at several of North America's top business schools. The techniques we describe apply whether you are getting ready for a labor negotiation, a negotiation with a supplier, or a negotiation with a customer. This checklist is not a formula for easy success in negotiations. Rather, it is a methodical approach that requires significant work. The amount of time and effort you spend answering the questions should depend on the importance of the negotiation and on the resources you have available. The payoff for your efforts emerges from the confidence and information that you gain from preparation.

The Negotiation Checklist

The negotiation checklist (in the accompanying box) is a guide for thinking about an important, upcoming negotiation. The pages that follow describe and explain the items on the list.

A. About You

1. What Is Your Overall Goal?   Start with the big picture. What basic need will an agreement address? Why are you talking to this person or this company? What do you hope to accomplish? Understanding your main goal helps put all the other aspects of the negotiation into perspective. Most people begin and end their negotiation planning by determining their overall goal. We suggest that it is just the beginning.

Source: "The Negotiation Checklist," by Tony Simons and Thomas M. Tripp, from *Cornell Hotel & Restaurant Administrative Quarterly* 38, no. 1, February 1997. Used with Permission.

Negotiation Checklist: A systematic way to ensure you are well-prepared before your next negotiation

☑ *Item accomplished*

A. About You

❑ 1. What is your overall goal?

❑ 2. What are the issues?

❑ 3. How important is each issue to you?

Develop a scoring system for evaluating offers:

    ❑ (*a*) List all of the issues of importance from step 2.

    ❑ (*b*) Rank-order all of the issues.

    ❑ (*c*) Assign points to all the issues (assign weighted values based on a total of 100 points).

    ❑ (*d*) List the range of possible settlements for each issue. Your assessments of realistic, low, and high expectations should be grounded in industry norms and your best-case expectation.

    ❑ (*e*) Assign points to the possible outcomes that you identified for each issue.

    ❑ (*f*) Double-check the accuracy of your scoring system.

    ❑ (*g*) Use the scoring system to evaluate any offer that is on the table.

❑ 4. What is your "best alternative to a negotiated agreement" (BATNA)?

❑ 5. What is your resistance point (i.e., the worst agreement you are willing to accept before ending negotiations)? If your BATNA is vague, consider identifying the minimum terms you can possibly accept and beyond which you must recess to gather more information.

B. About the Other Side

❑ 1. How important is each issue to them (plus any new issues they added)?

❑ 2. What is their best alternative to negotiated agreement?

❑ 3. What is their resistance point?

❑ 4. Based on questions B.1, B.2, and B.3, what is your target?

C. The Situation

❑ 1. What deadlines exist? Who is more impatient?

❑ 2. What fairness norms or reference points apply?

❑ 3. What topics or questions do you want to avoid? How will you respond if they ask anyway?

D. The Relationship between the Parties

❑ 1. Will negotiations be repetitive? If so, what are the future consequences of each strategy, tactic, or action you are considering?

❑ 2. ❑ (*a*) Can you trust the other party? What do you know about them?

    ❑ (*b*) Does the other party trust you?

❑ 3. What do you know of the other party's styles and tactics?

❑ 4. What are the limits to the other party's authority?

❑ 5. Consult in advance with the other party about the agenda.

2. What Are the Issues?   What specific issues must be negotiated for the final outcome or agreement to meet your overall goal? For example, if the overall goal is to book a successful convention, what assurances, services, and constraints will be involved? Price may be an obvious component, but it is worthwhile to consider other items, too—items that might make the agreement much more attractive both to yourself and to the other side. Delivery schedules, duration of contract, product or service upgrades, cancellation clauses, contingency plans, transportation services, complimentary room nights, and many other options all have some value to those negotiating a contract. Such side issues may be researched and introduced as part of a food contract, conference booking, or union contract that you are preparing to negotiate.

Consider also whether any of the issues you have considered might be broken down into multiple components or subissues. For the conference-booking negotiation, for example, you might normally consider the room-block guarantee as a single item (i.e., so many rooms reserved until such-and-such a date). In fact, breaking the room reservations down by percentages and multiple deadlines (e.g., 50 percent by one date, 75 percent by another date) might open avenues for mutually beneficial arrangements.

You should anticipate as many issues as possible for the negotiation. By doing so, you will be better informed and thus feel comfortable and confident when negotiating. Also, the more issues you can introduce, the more likely it becomes that creative solutions will arise, as those are often built by packaging or trading off multiple issues. Creative solutions often make it easier to discover an agreement that both parties like.

By adding items to the negotiations agenda, you increase your chance of discovering some issues that you value more than the other party, and discovering other issues that the other party values more than you. Trading off such differently valued issues dramatically increases the value of the agreement to you without costing the other party. Moreover, if you know what issues the other party highly values that you value less, you can use those issues to get concessions on issues that are important to you.

Imagine that you are a food and beverage director of a hotel seeking a dry-goods supplier and that you have written a request for bids from potential vendors. You have considered your storage capacity and specified every-other-week delivery in your request for bids. Now suppose you receive a bid from Alpha Dry Goods, which has another customer in town to whom they deliver once every three weeks. Alpha's quote for biweekly delivery might be mediocre, but it turns out that they could save you substantial money on triweekly delivery. They could save you so much money, in fact, that you consider changing your storage arrangement to accommodate their every-three-weeks delivery schedule. If you had been unwilling to negotiate the delivery schedule, you might never have discovered that opportunity. By adding delivery schedule to the agenda, you were able to discover an issue that improved the business potential for both parties. In this example, you are able to secure a lower overall price in return for a concession on delivery schedule.

In general, the more issues you can put on the table (within reason), the better off you are.[1]

Another reason to consider and discuss many issues in a negotiation is that it minimizes the chance of misunderstandings in the final contract. For any issue that is not discussed, the parties risk the possibility of making different assumptions. For example, the "standard frills" that accompany a banquet may not be known by the person purchasing the banquet.

Once you agree that it's a good idea to discuss many issues, how should you determine how many and which ones? For starters, check with your executive committee or association members. Draw also on outside resources. For example, call some friends and colleagues who have conducted similar negotiations and ask them about what issues they put on the table. Library research and obtaining experts' opinions may be helpful, too. Lawyers can be a marvelous source of ideas about which issues to place on the table, especially for a labor negotiation. Be prepared to include all reasonable and relevant issues that are important to you, even if they are not important to the other party.

You can also call the people with whom you plan to negotiate to ask them what issues they expect to discuss and to share your plans. This kind of conversation will begin the negotiation as a cooperative process and should minimize any delays caused by either negotiator's needing to collect additional information, to get authority, or to figure out the value of issues they had not previously considered. As we discuss later, surprise is usually not conducive to effective negotiations.

3. *How Important Is Each Issue to You?*   Now that you have listed all the different issues that might be negotiated, you need to develop as precise a picture as possible of their relative importance. Which issues are most important to you and which are not particularly important? Knowing the answer to that question will help you answer the next: On which issues should you stand firm and on which issues can you afford to concede? In other words, what issues might you be willing to trade away?

Setting such priorities can be a complex task. To deal with the complexity of rating the importance of individual issues, we suggest you develop a system to keep track of all the issues without losing sight of the big picture. Many different kinds of systems are possible. The key requirement is that you list and prioritize issues so that no issue is left out when you structure and compare potential agreements. The system you use must allow you to readily determine how well each possible agreement addresses every issue. We offer one such scoring system for your use, as described next.[2]

We suggest developing a table that lists every issue in the negotiation. For each issue the table should list the possible range of settlements.[3] You will then assign points to each issue to reflect its relative priority and to every possible settlement of each issue to reflect the relative desirability of resolving the issue in that way. Such a table allows you to assess the value of any proposed agreement by adding up the points it generates. You can then accurately and quickly determine which of several complex agreements you prefer. Moreover, it can help you keep the big picture in mind as you discuss the details of your agreement. We describe additional benefits in the next few pages.

The first part of Exhibit 1 shows an example of a scoring system that a conference organizer might use to negotiate with a hotel representative. In that example, the issues on the negotiation table are the duration of the room-block reservation, the room rate to be charged, the number of complimentary rooms to be provided, and the late-cancellation policy.[4] The maximum number of points possible here is 100. (If the conference organizer gets 100 percent of what she wants, then she gets 100 points; if she gets none of the issues that are important to her, then she gets 0 points.) The organizer has said that

EXHIBIT 1 | Creating a Scoring System

The example shown is a scoring system such as a conference organizer might use.

Issue 1: *Block Reservation*

Maximum value: *40 points*

Rooms reserved until 7 days before conference	40 pts.
Rooms reserved until 10 days before conference	37 pts.
Rooms reserved until 14 days before conference	35 pts.
Rooms reserved until 21 days before conference	15 pts.
Rooms reserved until 30 days before conference	5 pts.
Rooms reserved until 31 days before conference	0 pts.

Issue 2: *Room Rate*

Maximum value: *25 points*

$95 per person single, $70 per person double	25 pts.
$105 per person single, $80 per person double	20 pts.
$115 per person single, $90 per person double	15 pts.
$125 per person single, $100 per person double	10 pts.
$135 per person single, $100 per person double	5 pts.
$145 per person single, $110 per person double	0 pts.

Issue 3: *Number of Complimentary Room Nights*

Maximum value: *20 points*

3 room nights per 100 booked	20 pts.
2 room nights per 100 booked	15 pts.
1 room night per 75 booked	10 pts.
1 room night per 100 booked	5 pts.
1 room night per 150 booked	0 pts.

Exhibit explanation: *Develop a scoring system for evaluating offers.*

To construct your own scoring system, we recommend that you use the following steps:

(a) List all issues of importance for the negotiation, from step 2 in the Negotiation Checklist.

(b) Rank-order all issues according to their value to you. Which is the most important? Next? Last?

(c) Assign points to the issues. The highest-ranked issue gets the most points and the lowest-ranked issue gets the fewest points. The sum of maximum points across all issues should be 100. The purpose of this step is to improve upon the simple rank ordering in step *b* by reflecting the size of the difference between adjacently ranked issues (i.e., how much more important the first issue is than the second, the second issue than the third, and so forth). At 40 points, room-block reservation is worth almost twice as much as the next most important issue, room rate. The number of complimentary rooms and room-cancellation policy are slightly less important than room rate.

(d) List the range of possible settlements for each issue. Identify these ranges using industry or local norms or your best assessments of realistic, high, and low expectations. It may be the case that the longest block-reservation policy in the industry is 30 days. This figure establishes a realistic low boundary. Since a seven-day-out guarantee for block reservation is possible but rare, it establishes a challenging high boundary to which one can aspire.

Issue 4: *Late Cancellations*

Maximum value: 15 points

No penalty up to 14 days before conference	15 pts.
No penalty up to 18 days before conference	9 pts.
No penalty up to 22 days before conference	3 pts.
No penalty up to 26 days before conference	0 pts.

(e) Assign points to the possible outcomes that you identified for each issue. Give the maximum number of points to your preferred settlement for that issue, and assign zero points to any settlement that is least acceptable. Now rank and assign points to the possible settlements in between the best and the worst. Consider that the point values might increase dramatically between certain adjacent pairs of settlements in the range, or might just barely increase. The most important thing to remember about assigning points is that the assignment should reflect what is important to you.

(f) Double-check your scoring system. In completing steps *a* through *e* you undoubtedly will make a few capricious choices based on "gut feeling." For example, you may be so focused on the room-block issue that the points assigned to the other issues could be changed by five points either way without affecting your stance. The point is to make sure your scoring system accurately reflects the important issues and highlights the critical plateaus. To check your numbers, compose three to five completely different hypothetical agreements. Each agreement should emphasize different issues. For example, one agreement might offer a cheap room rate but a short no-penalty cancellation period, while another agreement offers high room rates but a long no-penalty cancellation period. Compare the different agreements on the basis of points and intuitive value. The prospective agreement that has the best "gut feel" should also have the most points. If not, you need to tinker with the values you assigned in steps *a* through *e* or reconsider your priorities.

(g) Use the scoring system to assess any offer that is on the table. You should work toward obtaining the highest-scoring agreement that the other party allows.

keeping the specially priced block of rooms available to last-minute registrants up until the week before the conference is very important. Room rate is somewhat less critical, she says, but is still important. Complimentary rooms and the cancellation policy are also valued by her, but are less weighty than are the first two. Note that it is not critical for all the increments within an issue to be valued equally. The jump from a 21-day-out block reservation to a 14-day-out reservation, for example, is worth 20 points to the conference organizer, while the four-day jump from 14 days to 10 days is worth only two points. Such a difference in value carries an important message. The organizer is saying that it is *very* important to have at least a 14-day-out block reservation, and that any improvement over that would be nice but is not critical.

Constructing a detailed and accurate scoring system can mean considerable work (see the second column of Exhibit 1). However, the task can be worth the effort for several reasons. First, it allows you to compare any package of settlements that may make up an agreement. With large numbers of issues, it quickly becomes difficult to compare different packages without some kind of scoring system.

Second, having a scoring system can keep you analytically focused while keeping your emotions in check. If you force yourself to evaluate each proposal using a predetermined scoring system, you are less likely to lose sight of your original interest during the heat of the actual negotiations. Resist the temptation to revise your scoring system in midnegotiation.[5]

Third, a scoring system is a useful communication tool that gives you a format for soliciting detailed information about the priorities and goals of your boss, your company, or your constituency. Building an accurate scoring system can become the topic of prenegotiation meetings that will improve your chances of pleasing the people you represent.

4. What Is Your BATNA?   Before you begin a negotiation, you need to have a backup plan in case you fail to reach an agreement with the other party. Negotiation scholars refer to this backup plan as the *best alternative to a negotiated agreement,* or BATNA for short. Are you, for instance, negotiating with the only supplier in town, or do you already have several attractive bids in your pocket? Alternatives make all the difference.

Each side's BATNA is a key factor in determining negotiation power. The better your BATNA, the better an offer the other party must make to interest you in reaching an agreement. Your BATNA—what you get if you leave the table without an agreement—determines your willingness to accept an impasse, which in turn tells you how hard you can press for a favorable agreement. You can negotiate hard for a job if you already have a few offers in your pocket. The better your BATNA, the more you can demand.

Having a clear BATNA helps protect you from accepting a deal that you would be better off not taking. Often people get caught up in the negotiation process and accept a contract they should have rejected. Knowing your BATNA can keep you from accepting an agreement that would make you worse off than you were before you started negotiating.

Having identified your BATNA, calculate its value based on the scoring system you developed for step 3. That is, if the other party were to make an offer that was identical to your BATNA, how many points would that offer achieve under your scoring system? Use that score as a reference point to identify those agreements that are worth less to you than your BATNA.

Even if it is difficult to assign a score to your BATNA because it is qualitatively different from the deal under negotiation or because it involves risk or uncertainty, you should nevertheless assign it a rough score for comparison purposes.

5. *What Is Your Resistance Point?*   Your resistance point is the worst agreement you are willing to accept before ending negotiations and resorting to your BATNA. The resistance point is the point at which you decide to walk away from the table for good, and the BATNA is where you're headed when you take that walk.

You should choose your resistance point based primarily on how good your BATNA is. If your BATNA is great, you shouldn't accept anything less than a great offer; if your BATNA is poor, you may have to be willing to accept a meager final offer. Don't forget to factor into your resistance point the switching cost and the risk of the unknown that you would be taking if your BATNA involves changing suppliers.

To illustrate the effect of switching costs, put yourself in the "buying" position of the conference organizer described in Exhibit 1. Suppose the hotel you used last year has already offered to book your conference for $100 a night single occupancy, with a 10-day-out block-reservation clause. If another hotel wants your business, you need to determine your BATNA and decide the margin by which the new hotel must beat the existing agreement—say, five dollars a night—to justify the risk of switching. Conversely, if you are the hotel sales representative in this deal, you have to determine the risks you accept for this new business—namely, that the association might fail to deliver the promised room-nights and the opportunity cost of displacing any existing business. Your BATNA as a hotel sales representative is the probability of your booking the rooms that the conference would otherwise occupy at a given rate, adjusted by the effort (labor and expenses) it will take to book them.

The resistance point is meant to encompass all the issues at the same time rather than each issue independently. If you set a resistance point for each issue under consideration, you sacrifice your strategic flexibility. Your BATNA might include a room rate of, say, $100 a night. If you set a resistance point for room rate, rather than for the agreement as a whole, then you might walk away from what is, in fact, an attractive offer—for example, a $105 per night rate that includes more amenities and a better booking policy than your BATNA. So there should be just one resistance point and not a collection of them. The resistance point should be set just slightly better than your BATNA. Numerically, it will be the sum of the points from your scoring system that represents your minimum requirements for all the issues being negotiated.

Being aware of the resistance point is useful in negotiations. It converts a good BATNA into a powerful negotiating stance. Unless you have previously decided how far you can be pushed, you are vulnerable to being pushed below your BATNA, and thereby may accept an agreement that is worse for you than no agreement at all. The more precise your resistance point, the better.

It may seem awkward to apply a precise resistance point, particularly if your BATNA is vague or not strong. In such circumstances, you might consider setting a "tripwire" or a temporary resistance point. Set it slightly above your actual resistance point; the tripwire then gives you the chance to suspend negotiations for further consultation with your team. For example, imagine that you are booking the conference as discussed earlier. Your members have expressed a slight preference for exploring new places, and so you are negotiating with a new hotel. You are willing to pay more for a new location, but you are not sure exactly how much more your membership will accept. You know that members will balk at an exorbitant room rate. Your BATNA is to stay at the same hotel as last year and face an uncertain amount of members' disappointment. To deal with the uncertainty, you can set a tripwire. If you are comfortable signing a contract that entails a $10-a-night increase, but if you are unable to secure a rate that low or better, the tripwire tells you that you should check with your membership before you make a commitment. You have, in effect, built a "safety zone" around an uncertain BATNA.

B. About the Other Side

Good negotiators seek to understand the other party's needs and limits almost as well as they know their own. Such negotiators might be able to accomplish this understanding before the negotiations begin, or early in the negotiation process. Obviously, the final agreement will reflect not only your own preferences and BATNA, but the other party's as well. Thus it is useful to ask the same questions about the other party as you ask about yourself.

1. How Important Is Each Issue to Them (Plus Any New Issues They Added)? Consider and attempt to estimate the other party's priorities. What trade-offs can you offer that enhance the agreement's value for both sides, or that might be neutral for the other side but a boon for you? If your counterpart had a scoring system like yours, what do you think it would look like? Call people who might have information or insight into the other party's priorities. Build a scoring system like your own that estimates their priorities, and use it to design some potential trade-offs.

As the negotiation proceeds, try to test, correct, and complete your picture of the other party's scoring system. Try to fill out your understanding of what that scoring system might look like if one existed. Gather more information during the negotiations by asking direct questions about priorities, and also by judging the other negotiator's responses to your different offers and proposed trade-offs.

You might also want to probe whether there are any issues about which the other side will completely refuse to negotiate. Such a refusal might simply be a ploy, or it might be a genuine constraint on the way it does business.

2. What Is the Other Side's BATNA? What are your counterpart's alternatives to doing business with you? How much do you think she or he values those alternatives? How badly does this company want to do business with you? Realize that the other party will probably accept an agreement only if it improves on her or his BATNA.

The other side's BATNA contains key information about how far you can push those negotiators before they walk away. If you are selling, the buyers' BATNA should determine the maximum price they would be willing to pay for your services or product. If you are buying, it should determine the lowest price at which they will sell. If you are booking a hotel conference in Hawaii in December, the hotel representative, who has a waiting list of customers, has a much stronger BATNA than the same representative has in July. If you are absolutely certain of the other side's BATNA, and if you propose an agreement that is just a little more attractive than the other side's BATNA, then those negotiators might accept your proposal.

3. What Is the Other Side's Resistance Point, if Any?   Given your assessment of the other party's BATNA, you can estimate the least favorable deal for which the other party might settle. We say "might" because the other party may not have considered his or her resistance point. We have found, though, that it is wise to assume the other party is well prepared. If you know the other party's resistance point, as noted earlier, you can push for an agreement that barely exceeds it. This kind of lowball deal is often better for you than an "equitable" deal, though not always.

If you are the type of negotiator who prefers amiable negotiation tactics over lowballing, then you still may want to know the other side's resistance point for two reasons. First, the other party may try to lowball you. Knowing the party's resistance point will give you the information and confidence to counter a lowball tactic. Second, many negotiators consider a fair deal to be one that falls halfway between the two parties' resistance points. To find the halfway point, you need to know both resistance points. Since experienced negotiators consider their true resistance point to be confidential information, you will most likely have to make a best guess about how far you can push the other party before seriously risking impasse or generating ill will.

Openly asking for the other party's resistance point carries risks. The other party might lie and therefore be forced to take an uncompromising stance to avoid disclosing that misrepresentation. Or if the other party honestly reveals his or her resistance point to you, that negotiator may expect you to reveal your resistance point, too. At this point, you have two choices. One, you reveal your resistance point and open yourself to being lowballed or, at best, to being offered an agreement that reaches no farther than the halfway point between the two resistance points. Two, if you don't reveal your resistance point, you may violate the norm of reciprocity.

4. What Is Your Target?   You set your target based on what you know about the other side. By this point, you should know what is the least favorable agreement that you will accept, and you have estimated the other side's least favorable, acceptable agreement. Now consider the most favorable agreement for you. This is your upper limit—the top of your range. If you focus primarily on your resistance point, which is the bottom of your range, you are unlikely to secure an agreement that is far superior to that resistance point.

To properly set your target, you must consider the bargaining zone, and to do that you have to sum up the other side's situation. The bargaining zone is the range between the two parties' resistance points, comprising the range of mutually acceptable agreements.

C. The Situation

By this point you have drawn up a fairly accurate picture of the issues and the priorities that constitute the negotiations. Here are some additional contextual factors to consider to help you maximize your advantages and minimize your risk of making mistakes.

1. *What Deadlines Exist? Who Is More Impatient?*   The negotiator who feels a greater sense of urgency will often make rapid concessions in an effort to secure a deal quickly. Many Western cultures have a quick-paced approach to negotiations. When paired with negotiators from cultures that negotiate deliberately (e.g., Japan, India), quick negotiators risk getting unfavorable agreements. A good way to slow down your pace is to avoid negotiating under a close deadline. Flexibility with regard to time can be a negotiating strength.

2. *What Fairness Norms or Reference Points Apply?*   Negotiations often involve a discussion of what might constitute a "fair deal." In fact, some experts recommend the approach of always negotiating over the "principle" or standard that you will use to assess fairness before getting down to details and numbers. The abstract discussion may be less threatening or emotionally charged than the details, and may result in a more cooperative tone and outcome for the negotiation.

Recognize, however, that there are many valid ways to determine fairness, and each negotiator will often choose the fairness norm that most favors his or her position. Both parties know that the other is doing this; just the same, each party expects the other to justify an offer as fair by showing how an offer complies with some fairness norm. Because offers that are unaccompanied by a fairness argument will rarely be accepted, you should consider alternative norms of fairness for each negotiation. Ask yourself, which ones justify your demands and which ones defeat them? Which ones best reflect your conscience?

An associate of one of the authors, for example, faced a salary negotiation upon considering a new job. The potential employer stated an intent to pay "market value" and thought it fair to define market value as the salary that other starting local faculty members were paid. The job seeker, on the other hand, judged that as unfair and argued that market value should be defined as the salary paid to starting management faculty members at comparable nationally ranked universities. The candidate thereby successfully redefined "market value" by describing the salaries drawn by other graduates of his program who took management faculty jobs. Since the employer had already agreed to pay market value, the employer found itself making concessions to do the fair thing of acting consistently with its own stated principles.

That example shows how a negotiation often hinges on a discussion of fairness. Prepare for each negotiation by considering alternative norms of fairness.

3. *What Topics or Questions Do You Want to Avoid? How Will You Respond If the Other Side Asks Anyway?*   You might find yourself in a position where there is something that you do not want the other negotiator to know. Your BATNA may be weak, for instance. Good negotiators plan in advance how to respond to questions they do not want to answer. Prepare an answer that is in no way dishonest but does not expose your weaknesses. Preparation means rehearsing your answer until you can deliver it smoothly, just as if you were practicing for a play. If you do not prepare and practice your answers to dreaded questions, then you risk an awkward pause or gesture that will tip off the other negotiator to a potential weakness. Awkward gestures might even cause the other party to believe you are lying when you are not. We suggest preparation so that you avoid looking like a liar when you tell the truth but choose not to reveal confidential information. If there are things you do not want to discuss, prepare your deflections in advance and polish them until they are seamless.

D. The Relationship between the Parties

1. Are the Negotiations Part of a Continuing Series? If So, What Are the Future Consequences of Each Strategy, Tactic, or Action You Are Considering? Consider whether you expect or want to continue a business relationship with the party across the table. If the answer is yes, then you probably want to be careful about using negotiation tactics that the other side might perceive as bullying, insulting, or manipulative. Extracting those last few additional concessions out of the other party is usually not worth the loss of goodwill.

The fact that you plan to do business with the other party in the future offers a few freedoms as well as restrictions. The trust and goodwill that you develop in the current deal may have a payoff for the next time. Also, if you can safely assume that the other party wants a relationship with you, then you can worry less about them negotiating in bad faith. Trust facilitates successful negotiations much more than does paranoia.

2. Can You Trust the Other Party? What Do You Know About Them? Call around to inquire how this company conducts negotiation. How much you trust the other party will influence your negotiation style. To find the trade-offs and creative solutions that ensure that everyone gets a fair deal, you have to share information about your needs and priorities. Unfortunately, though, sharing your information makes you vulnerable to an unscrupulous negotiator across the table. Untrustworthy opponents can ascertain your priorities before you know theirs and use this knowledge to gain maximum concessions from you. They might also lie about their own priorities.

The extent to which you trust the other party should determine your approach to sharing and collecting information. A series of small information "trades" is a good way to build mutual trust without opening either side to exploitation. A second approach to gathering data when you do not trust or know the other party well is to offer multiple proposals and see which ones the other side prefers. Be careful in this approach, however, as you must be willing to live with all the proposals you offer. It is considered a breach of faith if you propose an offer (for any reason) but have no intention of carrying through with the deal even if the other party says OK.

If you already know and trust the other party, your task is much easier. In such cases negotiations can involve an extensive exchange of information about interests and priorities.

3. What Do You Know of the Other Party's Styles and Tactics?   Different negotiators have different personal or cultural preferences. You are likely to secure the best deal and have the most positive interaction if you learn about their style in advance and try to accommodate it.

We have observed three types of negotiators. One type prefers to ease into the issue at hand after some personal contact. Once that negotiator is at ease with you as a person, she or he will be comfortable revealing information afterward.

Another type of negotiator prefers a direct approach and eschews disclosure and creative problem solving. Such a negotiator requires a competitive approach to the interaction.

The third type of negotiator enters the process having carefully computed and decided what is the best deal—and makes that offer up front and announces that it is nonnegotiable. Having already made up his or her mind about what the agreement must be, this negotiator will likely become impatient and annoyed at any attempt at give-and-take. If you know that the person you face prefers to do business this way, recognize that it is probably not a ploy. Simply assess the offer to see if it beats your BATNA. If it does, take it. If it does not, then politely refuse.

Some negotiators use either of two common gambits. One is to return from a break with a request for just one more concession that can seal the deal. This tactic, known as "taking a second bite of the apple," is common among car dealers. The appropriate response is to suggest that if the other party would like to reopen negotiations, you are willing to reopen them, too—but on all the issues, not just one.

"Good cop, bad cop" is a tactic whereby the person with whom you negotiate plays the role of "wanting" to meet all your needs, but "demands" are being made by someone who is higher up and usually absent from the actual negotiation (e.g., the sales manager). One response to this approach is to take a break to reassess the other side's stance compared to your tripwire. Another is to insist on speaking directly with the final decision maker.

4. What Are the Limits to the Other Party's Authority?   Establish early the level of authority held by your counterpart. Most negotiators, unless they are the CEOs of their companies, are authorized to negotiate only certain specified issues and within certain ranges. Determine whether you are negotiating with the right person, or whether far more latitude in generating resolutions might be available if you negotiated with someone else.

5. Consult in Advance with the Other Party about the Agenda.   As we stated earlier, consider calling the other party beforehand to share what issues you plan to discuss and to ask what issues the other party might raise. In general, holding back information is counterproductive, and introducing unexpected issues generally delays the proceedings.

Although good negotiators often get creative in their approach to the issues, this creativity must be well grounded in an understanding of the issues and of both parties' priorities. A well-prepared negotiator has considered these factors in depth, and has also considered the past and future context of the business relationship between the parties. It has been said that no plan survives contact with the enemy—but it remains true that the shrewd general will have memorized the terrain and analyzed the strengths and weaknesses of both sides before an engagement. Fortune favors the prepared mind.

Endnotes

1. There is some risk of overwhelming oneself—and one's negotiation partner—with too many issues. We suggest a combination of moderation in adding issues with an effective system of note taking and organization.

2. Any method that serves as a mnemonic device to track and evaluate multiple issues and deals may work. The one we describe is one that has received much attention in negotiation courses and research. See D. A. Lax and J. K. Sebenius, *The Manager as Negotiator* (New York: Free Press, 1986).

3. Several negotiation sessions may take place before you can identify all the issues and the range of possible resolutions for those issues. However, we recommend that you list in advance as many issues as you know about and then update the table between negotiation sessions to include additional issues and settlements.

4. Note that we have simplified the issues of such a negotiation for expository purposes. Additional issues might include cancellation clauses, airport transportation, continental breakfasts, function space, additional events or amenities, and so on.

5. In the interest of maintaining your original goals, do not adjust your scoring system while in the middle of discussion with the other party. During negotiations you may hear things that suggest your original preferences and priorities may be in error. Such new information might be valid, or it might simply be the other negotiator's effort to mislead you. There are a bad way and a good way to deal with the uncertainty such rhetoric may cause you. The bad way is to lose confidence in the accuracy of your scoring system, throw it out, and continue to negotiate. The good way is to take a break and verify the information as both true and relevant to your preferences. If it is, during that break adjust your scoring system to reflect the new information and restart negotiations with the new scoring system.

Effective Negotiating Techniques: From Selecting Strategies to Side-Stepping Impasses and Assumptions

Gerard I. Nierenberg
Henry H. Calero

"It's not what you do that works; it's how you do it!"

After many years of our combined negotiating experiences, and hundreds of seminars conducted worldwide that were attended by thousands of negotiators, we are thoroughly convinced that the above expression sums up our thoughts concerning whatever strategies or tactics you may choose to use when negotiating. Every high-school football player is told by his coach, many times before the game on Friday night or Saturday afternoon, "No matter how much we have worked on our game plan this week, the most important factor is how well you execute it!" And it is exactly the same for every negotiation you will ever spend time developing techniques for. Whatever success you will achieve is directly related to how well you handled and executed the many things planned.

Once you have your goals set, it is time to select techniques. This chapter discusses some of the most effective techniques out there. It also offers quite a few ways to handle an impasse if those techniques aren't getting you very far. Finally, this chapter covers the dangers of hidden assumptions, because assumptions might be the very reason why generally effective techniques aren't producing progress.

Studying Strategies and Tactics

Now it's time to turn to a number of time-tested negotiating techniques that if chosen wisely, can really work for you and your team. The ones we discuss are extremely varied. We hope you find yourself motivated to try a few new ones, as negotiators who are willing to take risks and tackle the unfamiliar tend to be more creative and more successful.

Forbearance

Sometimes forbearance, referred to as "waiting in haste," requires a great amount of patience in order to work well. And age is a great teacher. Seldom will you see this strategy used by young negotiators who are in a hurry to get things done as quickly as possible. The circumstances and elements involved in the use of this strategy are capable of provoking anger, frustration, and impetuous action. But when used properly, the rewards are great.

Someone who practices forbearance holds his tongue despite temptation to react. Sometimes one party will intentionally provoke the other in order to distract that team

Source: "Effective Negotiating Techniques: From Selecting Strategies to Side-Stepping Impasses and Assumptions," from *The New Art of Negotiating: How to Close Any Deal*, by Gerard I. Nierenberg and Henry H. Calero, 2009, pp. 99–134. Garden City Park, NY: Square One Publishers. Used by permission.

or throw it off kilter. Quite differently, sometimes a party will enthusiastically offer to fulfill 90 percent of the other party's requests in hopes that the opposition will be charmed by the thought of resolution and go for a settlement. Forbearance is a great response in either case, for it involves a patient, self-controlled withholding of reaction until further thought can be given to the situation.

Forbearance is effectively used by the Quakers, a religious organization, during meetings when they are divided in reaching agreement. At such times, they will declare a period of silence before continuing. And afterwards, if the matter is still unsettled and a division still exists, the clerk postpones the question and assigns it to be discussed at another meeting. As you are probably thinking, this process might possibly continue for a longer duration than planned. However, what it does achieve is acknowledgement of direct conflict and disagreement, as well as the hopes for eventual resolution.

Former President Franklin Roosevelt enjoyed telling a story about the Chinese use of forbearance based on 4,000 years of civilization. Two workers were arguing in the middle of a crowd of people. A foreigner expressed surprise that no blows were struck. His Chinese friend explained, "The man who strikes first admits that he no longer has any more ideas!"

Silence

Silence is powerful. During our seminars, we ask attendees to share what strategies and tactics they prefer. Looking back on all the information we have received from them, the most often mentioned response is silence. There's something about silence that demonstrates self-control, confidence, discipline, and calm. And if you can appear to be gifted with those characteristics, you will be considered a gifted negotiator.

An attendee once said, "What has worked very well with us for many years is to say as little as possible and force the other side to convince and sell to us!" Indeed, one of the greatest mistakes often made is talking too much. Most successful negotiators are not only great speakers but also great listeners. They know that in order to persuade others and ultimately sell ideas, concepts, and things, there must be a healthy balance of talk and silence. Whether we're revealing too much or grating against the other party's nerves by being too verbose, words can sometimes become our worst enemies. So successful negotiators know that silence is just as important as talking.

In order for silence to work, the negotiator has to know when to stop talking and when to start talking. He must not undermine his position with too many words, but he also must not undermine it with too much aloofness. This is especially important when he has already achieved his objective and the thought is that he can possibly get "a little bit more." In such cases, the wisdom of Benjamin Disraeli should be considered: "Next to knowing when to seize an advantage, the most important thing in life is to know when to forego an advantage." Negotiators who understand this will seldom lose what they have gained.

Surprise

This strategy involves a sudden shift in whatever course you may have taken. It is swift, drastic, and even emotionally dramatic. However, it doesn't have to involve a loud, high energy shift. The surprise actually can simply be lowering the tone of your voice and speaking much more slowly, with greater word emphasis. The idea is to make yourself less predictable so that the other party doesn't get too confident in their assumptions and demands.

Hank recalls someone he worked for in the aerospace industry who normally spoke loudly and rapidly. When this man was "dressing someone down" and very, very angry, instead of booming even more loudly, he would speak slowly and lower his voice. This would surprise the other party—throw them off. The other side was geared up to fight, yet this man would catch them off guard and calmly pressure them.

So when someone pushes your emotional "hot buttons" in the hopes of making you lose control, why not surprise him? When he attempts to get you angry, react like a judo expert. Don't oppose him, but work with him, using his energy to your advantage. It is possible to disarm even the most hostile individual in a negotiation with a faint smile on your face and a lowering of your voice.

Fait Accompli

In some situations this technique may be risky because it forces you to act and then to wait and see what the response may be. In other words, fait accompli involves offering or declining something—whatever the case may be—in the hopes that the other party will react desirably to your move. It would be wise to first appraise what the consequences might be if it should fail. This technique could also be called "taking a chance."

An interesting illustration of the *unsuccessful* use of the strategy was the attack by England, France, and Israel upon Egypt during the Suez Crisis. They acted without prior consultation with the United States and hoped to present to the world with a "fait accompli," or accomplished fact. To those countries' dismay, the United States intervened and forced them to abandon the attack and withdraw. The example proves that fait accompli is risky, and if the climate isn't right, it could cause much embarrassment. So use this technique prudently.

Apparent Withdrawal

Whenever this strategy is used there is mixture of forbearance, self-discipline, and deception involved. The strategy is an attempt to convince the other person that you have withdrawn, when actually you haven't. The hope is that the other team will scramble to keep you in the negotiations.

Jerry used this approach once in litigation with the Rent commission of the City of New York. The commission determined that a hearing be scheduled, but that hearing would ultimately prove to be detrimental to Jerry's client, a landlord. The commission agreed with Jerry's claim that his client would be disadvantaged. When the issue was taken to the supreme court in the state, the court suggested to the Rent Commission that it should postpone the hearing.

In spite of the request of the court, the Rent Commission went ahead with the hearing. Jerry attended the hearing, but before it began, he had the official stenographer take down a statement for the record in which he warned everyone in attendance that the hearing was being held against the wishes of the supreme court. In addition, Jerry also advised them that he would see to it that the court was informed about the hearing. And then, once he had advised them, he walked out of the room putting "the icing" on his apparent withdrawal strategy.

What the hearing officer of the Rent Commission didn't realize was that an associate of Jerry's remained in the hearing room, seated with a group of witnesses that had been called. Prior to the hearing, Jerry and his associate had decided that the associate would take over in the event that the Rent Commission chose to go ahead with the hearing. His strategy worked perfectly because the individual in charge of the hearing was unsure of how to proceed. After some thought, he called the Rent Commission for advice, and he was told to adjourn the meeting. As a result of this, afterwards the commission was persuaded that landlords are members of the community, and therefore, no one can be victimized without causing harm to everyone.

Reversal

"You can go forward by going backward." When using this strategy, you act in opposition to what may be considered to be the popular trend or goal. Let's look at a financially based example. Bernard Baruch once said that people who make money in the stock market are those who are the first in and the first out. By this he meant that successful investors usually buy when everyone is pessimistic and sell when the prevailing atmosphere is optimistic. Sounds backwards, right? But it works.

The strategy of reversal may sound easy to execute, but in reality it is extremely difficult. Timing has to be perfect. Technically, the power dynamics must shift for reversal to work. The skilled negotiator knows when that's possible and when it's not. Were this approach not so difficult, we would all immediately take advantage of it and become successful at our goals, whether for wealth, prestige, or the like.

Interestingly enough, modern methods of communication have caused a reverse in many traditional negotiating roles. So this technique sometimes happens automatically. For example, Jerry once had occasion to accompany a coffee buyer on a trip to the Amazon jungle. During the trip, Jerry asked the individual if he had a special method of negotiating when purchasing coffee in that part of the world. The man laughed at Jerry and replied, "The most remote tribes in the Amazon that gather coffee beans have shortwave radios. And they get the latest prices from the New York Coffee Exchange. They then add the cost of transportation, allow a small handling charge, and tell the buyer the price he has to pay." One would think the tribes would be concerned with compromising in order to make a sale, but they figured out how to be on top when it came to power dynamics. They performed a reversal of power.

Probing/Testing

Perhaps the most common tactic is one in which a person attempts to acquire additional information. Questions that pose hypotheticals, pry for more details, and seek deeper clarification are the stuff that probing/testing is made of. This strategy can help you to identify the other party's goals, areas of possible compromise, and limits. The trick is not to make yourself sound too unstable, and not to inflame the other party by digging too deeply. This, perhaps, is one of the most important tactics when used properly, because in many instances, it narrows the distance between the negotiators.

There are many expressions that verbally pave the way for the use of probing/testing. Consider several examples: "In order to better understand . . ."; "What if . . ."; "In the event of . . ." All of these phrases seek a response that will give the inquirer a broader vision of what the other party wants, needs, is looking for, is willing to compromise on, plus many other matters. The most important thing to keep in mind when preparing to use any of these expressions is that the words you use don't intimidate, undermine, criticize, offend, or cause the other party any discomfort or anger that, in turn, makes them defensive.

Setting Limits

Setting limits is when someone states he will negotiate only under certain conditions, in a certain location, at a certain time, or in a certain manner. It could also be when a party limits the venue of the negotiation so that they communicate only through their attorney, agent, or some other third party. In history, the French culture has become famous for using time limit in their overall strategy. But it also happens every day in, for example, the food service industry—when someone introduces restrictions on the menu, that's a form of limits!

This technique can really challenge the power dynamics of a negotiation. And it can be done verbally or nonverbally. You might be wondering how the latter works. A nonverbal type of setting limits, known as a "silent barter," is conducted by some tribes in Central Africa. They are engaged in a unique method of negotiating. Whenever a tribe desires to exchange its goods with those of another tribe, the first group leaves the goods on the bank of a river. The other tribe is expected to take the goods and leave their own goods, considered of equal value, in order to end the negotiation. However, if the second party is not satisfied with the goods, then the goods are simply left on the bank. The first tribe must add to their offerings or else the transaction has ended. The fact that the second tribe will walk away if displeased with the final amount of goods left is an example of setting limits.

Feinting

Feinting is best summed up by a simple phrase: "Look to the right, go to the left." The three elements involved in most negotiations are concealment, disclosure, and diversion. Feinting is the diversion part, and it occurs whenever someone attempts to divert the other party's attention toward some other issue or matter. In many circumstances, you would use feinting at a time when the other party is getting close to the main source or something that is very important or sensitive to you.

Yet feinting can also be used to promote a false impression. Perhaps you want to convince another person that you have greater knowledge or more information on a subject than you actually have. You would distract them away from what you don't know and suggest that you are more knowledgeable in certain areas than you are.

In some negotiations, feinting can be accomplished by a *conscious* "slip of the tongue," especially when used by someone who is acting as an agent or third person in the transaction. That agent could use such expressions as, "I'm not at liberty to . . .", or "I wish I could tell you more, but . . ." Then he would go on pretending he's actually getting close to revealing something he shouldn't. Such phrases are excellent hooks that grab immediate attention from those who want to get more information and get to the bottom of matters.

Association

Those who have grown up in large families and are one of the younger members will easily be able to remember how many times their parents negotiated with them using association. This technique is applied effectively when parents present older brothers and sisters as examples of certain types of conduct and behavior. It is a means of getting a younger child to follow in those footsteps. So a parent might say, "Don't you see how well studying has worked out for David? He just got into one of the best colleges in the nation!" Then the younger sibling, wanting to mimic the older one, will work hard to meet those expectations.

In a negotiation, this tactic is used when a party advises you that a group, company, association, or other party whom you know and respect well has previously done business with them. Association is a powerful magnet not only in drawing attention to what is said but also in influencing others. And no other industry understands such power better than the advertising community. They pay millions of dollars to well-known personalities who positively advertise their products. Consumers *associate* the product with the celebrity and believe that if they buy and use the product, they will be as attractive or successful as that celebrity.

Disassociation

Disassociation is the opposite of association. It is not only used in politics but also in business. It's pretty straightforward: one party tries to belittle, discourage, or ruin another party by linking them with someone or something undesirable.

In some negotiations, a company comes under scrutiny simply because other firms who manufacture the same or a similar product are under investigation. That first company needs immediately to distance itself from those organizations. Disassociation will be the first tactic out of the bag when the negotiation begins. The first party must assure the other side that "we are the good guys."

Crossroads

Visualize a crossroads—several paths intersect, entwine, or entangle. When someone uses this tactic, he introduces several matters or issues into the discussion for purposes of getting concessions on one and paving the way or gaining ground on another. Using this method, approaching the other party from several directions, actually forces that other side to see a myriad of issues and concentrate on one of them. In order to feel like they are making progress, that other party will tackle one issue and get the negotiation ball rolling. Then they are more vulnerable and open to others you have placed on the table.

Blanket

When a person uses the blanket technique, he tries to hit the other party with as many issues as possible, believing that some of them will stick and be resolved. The principle theory in blanketing is, if you cover a wide enough area, you're bound to be successful somewhere. It's like using a shotgun and aiming at a large area, instead of using a rifle and aiming at a much smaller target.

Jerry likes to use the example of a young man who would always select a seat at a movie theatre next to a beautiful woman. In the event you are wondering how he did it in a darkened theatre, the man would choose his seat while the lights were on, before the movie started. As soon as it was dark, he would lean towards the woman and ask for a kiss. There were many times when he received a slap on the face, and many other times the lady would simply get up and select another seat. However, there were also those times when he found someone who was in an equally romantic and daring mood. During those rare finds, the guy was successful at getting a kiss from a pretty girl.

Randomizing

Randomizing involves picking a sample and assuming that it represents the whole. This is the negotiating method used by someone who is trying to sell a food product in a supermarket or on the sidewalk. The seller offers something to eat for free to those who are passing by. Then, after tasting it, the prospective buyer may be motivated to buy a bagful. However, the sample might have been a particularly sweet or fresh batch. When the consumer gets home and tastes the bagged product, he might find that it is not as good as the morsel he was given by the seller.

There are some negotiations in which the party who is selling products actually brings merchandise, films, or other material for the purpose of convincing the buyer of the quality and performance of his product. The "random" sampling of merchandise will present well. It is an age-old method of closing a deal in business negotiations by letting the other party use the product free of charge.

Bracketing

The term *bracketing* is actually an old artillery term referring to when a shell is fired in order to register the guns in an artillery battalion. Since Hank was in combat during the Korean War and his responsibility was in "fire direction," he knows a great deal about this technique. It is extremely valuable when negotiating because it not only establishes the upper and lower ranges you are dealing with but also the specific areas at which to "aim your guns."

Bracketing directs you toward where it is best to concentrate. It shows you where the majority of troops and equipment are located, so to speak. In other words, it isolates where your best chances for negotiations are.

Salami

By taking one slice at a time, you can end up with the whole salami. That's the philosophy behind this next approach. The salami technique works exceptionally well in negotiations that involve multiple elements of cost, such as with cases concerning construction. You negotiate not only the overall cost of the project, but such things as design, materials, labor, subcontracts, and more. When Hank was negotiating major weapons contracts with subcontractors in the aerospace industry, this was a major tactic used. Little by little, you gather your information and form a deal.

Quick Close

The quick close is sometimes saved for when a stalemate must be managed. It is applicable to a situation that seems to be going nowhere, when something has to be done quickly. The quick close occurs when compromising measures are necessary, and so a negotiator will say, "Let's split the difference and get this contract signed," or, "We're willing to meet you halfway."

During our seminars, we have asked attendees if this tactic had worked well for them. The overwhelming response from them has been positive. They claim this tactic remains part of their negotiating techniques. Usually, by the time the quick close is used, both parties are ready to resolve issues; neither is threatening to walk away. And there is usually an urgency involved because of time or financial constraints.

The Agent of Limited Authority

We will close this long list of effective negotiating techniques with a tactic that allows you to send someone else into the fray. It's for a situation in which you might wish to use an agent rather than to handle it personally because that agent can play the old "I'm not at liberty to make that concession" approach. Thus, he is called the agent of limited authority. If you are a senior member of the negotiating team, the company, the firm, or whatever applies, you probably cannot claim to have your hands tied in too many knots. But an agent of lesser authority cannot be pinned down to anything much because he is locked into an agent-principal relationship and understandably required to respect that relationship.

During negotiations, the agent will make it clear that he is unable to make a firm or final decision without acceptance by the principal. Meanwhile, you can gather a great amount of information concerning what the other party is looking for. This technique also buys you time to really think about what is being proposed. These benefits will greatly assist you when the time comes to make a final decision or judgment.

We have covered eighteen different techniques that are commonly used in negotiations. Believe it or not, there are numerous others—too many to cover all of them here. The ones discussed above are intended to generate some new possibilities in your negotiation repertoire. But always remember to choose strategies that work well with your particular personality and presentation style. You do not want to use a strategy that will appear awkward or disingenuous.

Overcoming an Impasse

The best way to prepare yourself for an impasse is to have knowledge of more than three or four resolving tactics. Gather as many approaches as you can, so that you won't be at a loss when the "old faithful" don't work. When we originally covered this subject in our seminars, we used to discuss approximately six to nine different methods of breaking an impasse. Then we would open up the program to all the attendees and invite them to share with us any other suggestions. As a result, we enlarged our list of how to deal with an impasse. When you have completed reading them, perhaps you can add a few more to the list.

Take a Break

Take a break or caucus for a few minutes—or longer. If you are part of a team, use the time to discuss matters and brainstorm with the other team members. If you are working alone, get up from the table and walk around the room, look out the window, or simply go to the water fountain or the bathroom down the hall. Such periods of reassessment can often generate new ideas and fresh insights.

We believe it is very important during your recess not to talk about throwing in the towel and walking away. Always save that as the very last resort and action. Such negative thinking has a habit of becoming contagious and can destroy productive and creative thinking.

Recap What Has Occurred

Together, both your party and the other party should review and discuss what has been agreed upon so far, or what exactly is causing disagreement. Also, discuss the agreements-in-principle that were reached over the course of the negotiation thus far, as well as common interests. Sometimes you will discover that the results you have mutually achieved are more significant than perhaps realized. This will spark you on to further resolution. And whenever you talk about something positive, it reflects that the time spent has not been wasted.

Decide What Will Be Lost

Mutually clearly find the answer to the question, "What will be lost if we call it quits at this point?" There are times during an impasse when both sides temporarily forget the negative side of not reaching a settlement. Terminating the negotiation is an outcome that will be detrimental to all concerned. This is a time when it is important to discuss the "minuses" of not resolving the issues.

Hank recalls a negotiation in which he described a possible negative outcome if the two sides were not to reach a settlement. The visualization of failure that he provided actually triggered new resolve in the other party. Someone interrupted him and stated, "Your crystal ball is cloudy. And I'll clear it up for you." And then that person proceeded to speak in a much more positive manner. The tide was turned and negotiations continued. Thus we have discovered that, in some instances, when a person creates a negative image, another individual often tries to make it look less detrimental. Perhaps this occurs because most of us carry around a positive self-image. And whenever it is challenged, we psychologically rise to the occasion to make it less negative. We're not suggesting you harp on the dark side of matters throughout your negotiations, but at certain times, a little talk of the "doom" that might follow if the impasse continues can actually inspire a break in the impasse.

Express How You Feel

When you communicate your feelings, you present yourself as very relatable. Others will acknowledge that you have let your guard down and then possibly do the same. This tactic may uncover and reveal that the other side feels exactly the same way. Even if you haven't reached agreement on any issue, at least you can admit that you have similar emotions.

Once you have honestly expressed how frustrated you feel about the impasse and hopefully heard the return frustration from the other party, take a deep breath and say, "Since it appears that we both feel the same way, let's do something about it!" Make the statement nonverbally convincing by moving your upper body forward and rubbing your palms together in a gesture of expectation. You will appear to be a team player for both sides, amiable and optimistic.

Change the Subject

Although this sounds like you are throwing a red herring into the mix, introduce another issue, view, or approach. Don't belabor the subject that has gotten both of you tied up in knots. Whenever you do this, you're not sweeping the topic under the table; you're simply setting it aside for a while. If the other side refuses to change subjects, explain that moving to other issues does not mean you are forgetting the unresolved ones. Instead, you believe that the "cooling" effect of switching to other matters can be very effective.

Attempt to Secure an Agreement-in-Principle

We define agreements-in-principle as mutual goals to which the parties commit themselves, such as the agreement not to walk away without some sort of resolution, or not to drag the negotiations on beyond two weeks. There are some agreements-in-principle that are rather simple to get because they formulate the fundamental reason why the two sides are negotiating. They may be stated as, "We agree we have to work out some kind of compromise in order to . . .," or "We're both here to negotiate whatever differences exist . . .," and also, "We both are aware we need each other, therefore we have to . . ." Such statements pave the way for getting agreements-in-principle, regardless of how flimsy they may be.

Needs are the cornerstones of why we negotiate. Sometimes parties' needs differ, and sometimes they don't. But usually you can find something in common with the other side. Always rely on those needs that you both have. In the long run, finding common ground won't let you down.

Try Bridge-Issue Agreements

In many negotiations there are innocuous issues that are of little importance and can be easily agreed to. These rather benign issues are also sometimes used in breaking a situation that is deadlocked. No one understands this better than a marriage counselor acting as a third party in negotiating differences in a troubled marriage. Such a counselor would work on establishing common basic agreements from the couple on relatively minor issues in their union. Once he has accomplished that, he will then move on to tacking other, more sensitive issues.

A good example can be found in a labor dispute in which the union demands were as follows: (1) a 17 percent increase in pay; (2) greater retirement benefits; (3) more voice in management decisions that affect workers; (4) changes in the grievance procedures; and (5) changes in the color (black) of the uniforms worn by employees because it was too depressing. In this negotiation, it would be wise for management to use the last demand as the bridge-issue. Once establishing an agreement on it, a more relaxed and less defensive attitude might exist in discussing and negotiating the other issues.

Discuss What Alternatives Remain

The effect of redirecting the discussion from an impasse to what alternatives remain may switch the negotiation from a negative to a positive course. And if the response is that there are no other alternatives, don't let it bother you. Get creative! In a buy-sell situation in which you are the seller, discouragement makes it very easy for the buyer to say goodbye. Developing creative alternatives is what separates the successful negotiator from those with much lower batting averages. We have a colleague who loves telling others in such situations, "There are always other alternatives. We just haven't found them yet!" And he uses emphasis on the word "yet."

Make an Important Disclosure

In most negotiations, each party knows something the other one doesn't know. And some of this knowledge is more important than the rest. Therefore, in some sense, negotiating is a process of, "What do you know that I don't know?" Whenever important disclosures are made, they are usually received with enthusiasm.

In an impasse, disclosing something of importance that will benefit the other party is like a peace offering. It usually breaks through the bottleneck. But a word of caution is necessary: should you disclose something of major importance, always do it incrementally, instead of blurting it out all at once. Make the other party work to get the information, don't merely "spill your guts." The more they work at squeezing all the information out of you, the more they will have a tendency to believe it is the truth, and nothing but the truth. You will also, therefore, have opened up the doors of communication, convincing them that if they keep working at this negotiation, their time and efforts will be worth it.

Ask a Hypothetical Question

Asking a "what if" question may be very effective when used at the appropriate moment in your negotiation. And if you choose to do this, don't allow the words you use to get you into hot water by saying something that may possibly be misinterpreted. During your preparation, give some thought as to how hypothetical questions should be worded in order not to be misunderstood. We have seen instances in which the words were carelessly spoken and the listener heard something that was different. Remember again, the message is always in the receiver's ear, not in the sender's mouth. But an effective hypothetical question can extend the range of vision, helping the negotiators to see the bigger picture and work for resolution.

Ask for or Offer Empathy

When negotiating, we've all heard expressions like, "I know exactly how you feel," "I've been in your shoes," or "I see your position, but . . ." There are times when showing empathy towards others is beneficial. When your hands are tied by individuals or conditions, words of empathy are truly heartening. When others can understand the limits that have been imposed on you, they are more likely to be empathic. So don't be afraid to ask for such understanding. Perhaps you could say, "If I could ask you to step into my shoes for a moment and see things from my position, together we might be able to find another way to handle this situation." Asking for empathy is especially effective in a situation in which you are acting as an agent for a principle and unable to make a total settlement without your principle's concurrence.

It is also important to remember to offer empathy once in a while. It is possible that when you display empathetic responses towards others, some individuals will take it as sign of weakness and attempt to squeeze you in order to get as much as they can. If they try, you should certainly pull back and explain that your intention was to be responsibly open-minded, not taken advantage of. But the other party might also appreciate your willingness to see things their way. Emphasize the fact that you are trying to see the situation from all angles. They might very much respect your fairness and respond to you in a like manner. Don't forget that the negotiating process is giving and getting, getting and giving, hopefully in equal measure!

Try Using a Quick Close

In some negotiations, the impasse has occurred for a very simple reason. One or both sides have been jockeying for position and the negotiation has reached a point at which the players intuitively sense a "quick close" offer may work. This approach has already been defined as a negotiation technique on page 55. However, it is worth mentioning as a possible route to break an impasse as well. When a quick close is timed correctly, a phrase such as, "Will you take $49,000 for it, and that way we can finish today?" or "What do you say we settle this at $25,400 and both get back to work?" can bring closure to a trying negotiation.

As so often occurs in life, three things are likely to happen. First, the other party may readily accept the close and then shake your hand, cementing the deal. Second, they may reject the offer and call it quits. Third, they might counter with another figure. Regardless of what happens, the impasse has been broken.

Diagram Differences

A seminar attendee once told us that she disliked negotiating at locations that didn't have a blackboard or a flipchart in the room. And the main reason for this was because she felt using visual aids for purposes of illustrating differences was extremely important in breaking deadlock and differences. She firmly believed that visualization is a key to opening up closed doors when communicating with others. So she would literally make a list of the points of disagreement, and then work through them.

And we agree with her. When something is illustrated, the narrowness of differences between two parties becomes apparent. As that old expression states, "Seeing is believing!" Whenever narrow differences are seen instead of heard, it seems to have a completely different compromising effect on people.

Give Something to Get Something

A surefire tactic that will overcome an impasse is making a compromise offer. Perhaps one of the most frequently asked questions by workshop attendees is, "When do I make a compromise?" That question may be answered by looking at the many different reasons for making compromises. And the reason we put in last place is that you feel compelled or forced to do it. That brings to mind the words of Winston Churchill when describing an appeaser: "Someone who feeds a crocodile, hoping it will eat him last!"

The word *compromise* culturally seems to convey a more negative than positive image. Perhaps most of us grow up with this negative conception because when we were young, an adult told us, "Never compromise!" Apparently they didn't have the wisdom to realize that life is a long process of negotiating with others, and in order to satisfy our own and others' needs, we must compromise! The *art of negotiating* consists of knowing how, why, where, to whom, and when to make concessions.

Bring Up Future Needs

In most negotiations, present needs are the most important and critical in discussions, despite the fact that the same needs often existed yesterday, and will tomorrow. All of our needs fall into one or all three of those categories. However, during negotiations, present needs always seem to take center stage. Have you ever considered trying the approach of pointing out how you can help the *future* of the other party if they work on a deal with you now?

In some negotiations, individuals are truly unaware of future needs they may have unless you open their eyes and mind to them. Most of us are locked into what needs are pulling at us today, but tomorrow's needs are equally important. Breaking an impasse by bringing up the possibility that you'll be in position to satisfy their future needs, if required, is a great bargaining chip.

Discuss Good Association

An impasse may sometimes be handled by talking about all the favorable and productive dealings the two sides have shared. Bring up all of those "remember when's." Can you retrieve a desperate and difficult time you both faced that was overcome by your mutual cooperative efforts? Every personal or business relationship you have in life is full of such experiences. And turning to that page of the scrapbook, so to speak, can and may be used effectively during times of stress, conflict, or other difficulties. It's the "we've gotten through this before" approach.

Also, it is worthwhile remembering that *trust and goodwill* are not mere words to negotiators. They are the backbone and cornerstone of the negotiating process. Therefore, when facing an impasse, returning to them and reflecting on past periods of trust and goodwill may bridge present differences.

Change Locations

In some instances, simply changing locations might help overcome the impasse and save your negotiation. Getting out of the conference room or office and walking to the manufacturing area, touring the accounting department, or looking at engineering drawings may influence attitudes. Even simply standing up by the coffee machine may do it. Consider the fact that negotiations conducted while standing up don't last as long as those when seated!

Call It Quits

We have saved this alternative for last simply because it should only be employed as the last resort. It doesn't take much creativity to stand up and leave when things aren't going well for you. And if you choose to do it, remember you may have to "eat crow" at a later time. Walking out may require you to come back and later apologize or ask forgiveness. So unless you're sure your departure will jolt the other party and change their attitude concerning making a compromise, it's probably in your best interest not to do it.

There is no other time during a negotiation when you must become more creative than when the process has reached a stalemate—when it's going nowhere, when both sides are deadlocked. That's usually the point when you believe you have two options, which are to "punt the ball" or to "run like hell" for the nearest exit. Yet that's also a time for realizing that you have a great number of creative alternatives for purposes of breaking the impasse and continuing to earnestly negotiate. We hope that our suggestions have inspired you to keep trying and to venture outside of your comfort zone if the old familiar tactics just aren't making headway for you.

Avoiding the Pitfall of Hidden Assumptions

As we near the end of this chapter on effective things to do in the negotiation process, we have to include a discussion of something *not* to do. Most people rely on assumptions when trying to make a decision, resolve an issue, or argue a point. The problem is that the majority of people never examine their assumptions, let alone test them to see if they are worth maintaining. Whoever first wrote or said, "When we assume, we make an 'ass' out of 'u' and 'me,'" was a very wise person. Interestingly, there are very few additional quotations that have been written on the word *assume* and its effect on our lives. Dictionaries hold multiple definitions for the word, but the one that most directly pertains to negotiating involves the idea that when we assume something, we take it for granted that a projected circumstance is true or that a projected outcome will occur.

For a long time, we thought that the words *assume* and *believe* were very similar and should be synonyms. Yet when used in conversation, the word *assume* seems weaker in conviction than the word *believe;* the latter seems to have a much stronger basis than the former. Starting from a very early age, we begin to make assumptions and develop beliefs; it is a process that continues throughout life. In fact, we must accept that assuming and believing are part of human nature. And human nature is definitely present at the negotiating table. Therefore, since we're going to continue making assumptions, there are two things we can do. The first is to become aware that we're making them. And the second thing is to test them, to see if they are true or false. Let's learn just how to do that.

A More Thorough Definition of Assumptions

Some assumptions are relatively simple. For example, we hand a store clerk our money and expect her to give us our merchandise and sometimes also change in return. Whenever we mail a check along with a subscription to a magazine, we expect to subsequently receive that publication. And a traveler who boards an airliner destined for Chicago assumes it will land at O'Hare Airport—or at a more convenient airport in the event of any emergency.

But assumptions brought to negotiations are different. Every assumption made before, during, or after a negotiation may turn out to be a serious mental error that will later keep us awake at night. Furthermore, all of our assumptions are fundamentally based on perception. And to make matters worse, humans don't see everything they look at. "Looking" is two-dimensional, while "seeing" is three-dimensional.

During our seminars on negotiating we used to prove this point very easily by asking the attendees how many of them had ever seen a rainbow. Usually, all or most of them would raise their hands. And then we would ask who, of those who had seen a rainbow before, was absolutely sure of how many colors they perceived (saw). After this question, the number of raised hands considerably lessened. Of those whose hands still remained raised, approximately only one-half answered accurately, stating they saw five colors. Finally, we asked how many knew the exact color sequence of a rainbow, from the inside out. In all the years we asked this question, we never had a single attendee give us the correct color sequence. Then we would drive our point home on the difference between "looking" and "seeing." We would inform them, "You have looked at a rainbow, but you have never actually seen one. If you had, you would have observed that the color sequence is violet, blue, orange, yellow, and red." (By the way, if you want to remember this little bit of trivia, think of the letter "V," followed by the word "boy," and then the letter "R.")

There are times when making an assumption and later finding out that it was false causes no harm because it wasn't serious. However, there are also times in life when the consequences are very grave. In the medical profession, a doctor's worse nightmare is if his "anchor" judgment is wrong. The medical term *anchor* refers to a quick, snap diagnosis the doctor makes the first time he examines you. Based on his initial assumption, he will then pursue testing and/or treat you accordingly.

As negotiators, we are not in life-or-death types of situations like medical doctors are. Yet the false assumptions we make and perpetuate can and do eventually lead to serious consequences. It is true that assumptions are a valid and important part of negotiations. But we must be extra careful not to make them unnecessarily. Unfortunately, there are many who don't realize a large part of our beliefs are based on unconscious, hidden assumptions that are biased.

Hidden assumptions are not subject to rational verification, as other assumptions might be. If we make an open assumption that a certain chair will support our weight and it does, then our assumption was correct. If it doesn't, we take a "pratfall" and land on our behind. In such a case, we get an immediate verification that our assumption was either right or wrong. And if wrong, it is easy to laugh off—no big deal, just select another, stronger chair to sit on. There is absolutely nothing wrong with making the assumption that most chairs will hold your weight. But a problem does arise when we think and behave as if an assumption that judges people is absolutely a proven fact.

In our seminars we deal with assumptions. We hold up a pencil and ask the attendees to describe and write down what they see. Everyone thinks it's a normal pencil they're seeing. However, they are surprised when we bend the pencil and they see it's an artificial rubber pencil bought at a novelty store.

What's the point in discussing hidden assumptions? Well, if we become sensitive to the fact that we all make assumptions and act accordingly, we can be prepared for the unexpected and are less likely to dogmatically defend our positions if we are proven to be wrong.

Evaluations of Assumptions

The assumptions we make are a vital part of our human communication system. We use them continuously in sorting out and trying to make sense of the millions of ambiguous mental stimuli that confront us. We receive a communication, quickly interpret it, and make a first guess—an assumption that we stay with until it is disproved. As the Gestalt school of psychology puts it, to probe a hole we first use a stick to see how far it takes us. We might paraphrase this and say that, to understand the world by probing, we use assumptions until they are disproved. It must be remembered that simple assumptions are easy to refute. However, hidden ones are very difficult to recognize and refute or correct.

Yet during a negotiation there are ways of testing the assumptions you've made. One of them is by asking questions. For example, you've made the assumption that the person with whom you're negotiating has the authority to settle and make a deal with you. All the inductive and deductive information you've received and perceived, verbally and nonverbally, indicates this. But, early in the discussion, you should ask: "In the event you find our terms and conditions acceptable, are you willing to sign the contract today so we can get started on your project?" This question will normally receive one of three responses: "Yes," "No," or "It all depends." Then he will give you additional information that tells you if the assumption is correct or not.

Another method of testing assumptions you've made is by using hypothetical situations. For example, imagine that you are negotiating with a firm that may be protected by some recently legislated environmental laws. In your negotiation, you're dealing with several issues that require knowledge concerning prospective problems—the type of issues your corporate attorneys believe will require escape clauses. You have assumed that any subsequent changes calling for your company's implementation will be separately negotiated. Furthermore, you have assumed that your firm will be reimbursed for any such expenses incurred, which are over and above what you are presently negotiating. You can then test your assumption by creating a hypothetical situation in which a worse case scenario becomes a reality. And then you ask questions relative to who will be responsible for the expenses. In this scenario, you will not only discuss any changes, but also, how soon you will know about them, and how long it will take to implement them.

Sometimes you can also use the old standby, "What if . . ." It is especially useful in negotiating construction contracts that may later be affected by federal, state, or local building codes. In many instances, the firm responsible for the construction *assumes* that any such incurred changes will be borne by the customer or buyer. You need to know how such a situation would be managed. So ask, "What if electrical codes change and the building has to be retrofitted?" During the course of a negotiation, you seldom are privy to seeing the "boiler plate" clauses in a prospective customer's contracts. Even if you have many years of experience, don't assume that you know exactly what the small print on a document covers.

And a final method of testing assumptions is accomplished by listening carefully to what is said, what is implied, and most important, what is not said. This requires full-time attention throughout the negotiation, not simply at the beginning as so many negotiators think. For this reason, we strongly recommend that in a team-type negotiation, one person be assigned the specific task of being the listener. And don't give the assignment to the person who will be the scribe. If you do, you will regret it because an individual cannot take adequate notes and listen carefully at the same time. The scribe records what is said, while the listener hears things between the lines.

Closing Your Business Negotiations
Claude Cellich

Bringing business negotiations to a close requires special skills and techniques. As no two negotiation situations are alike, it is not possible to recommend any one approach. Negotiators must use their own judgment in selecting the most appropriate method.

A wide range of techniques exist from which to select. The choice will depend on the existing relationship between the parties, the objectives of the negotiations, the cultural environment, the negotiating styles of the participants, the state of discussions, and whether the talks concern new business opportunities or the extension of existing contracts. A description of the better known techniques is given below.

Most Common Techniques

The most frequently used methods for closing negotiations can be referred to as the *alternative, assumption, concession, incremental, linkage, prompting, summarizing, splitting the difference, trial,* and the *ultimatum/or else* techniques.

Selected Closing Techniques

Most Commonly Used:

- *Concession*
- *Summarizing*
- *Splitting the difference*

Others:

- *Alternative*
- *Assumption*
- *Incremental*
- *Linkage*
- *Prompting*
- *Ultimatum*

Alternative

Also known as the "either/or close" technique, in this approach one party makes a final offer consisting of a choice for the other side. For example, one party is willing to lower its commission rate if the other agrees to deliver the goods to the warehouse at its own cost.

Source: "Closing Your Business Negotiations," by Claude Cellich, from *International Trade Forum,* no.1, 1997, pp. 14–19. Used with permission.

Assumption

With this method the negotiator assumes that the other side is ready to agree and proceed with detailed discussions of delivery dates, payment schedules, and so forth. This is a technique used frequently by sellers to rush buyers into agreement. It is a useful approach when the initiating party has more than one option to offer to the other side.

Concession

This technique is characterized by the negotiator keeping a few concessions in reserve until the end to encourage the other party to come to an agreement. It is particularly effective in situations in which concessions are expected as a sign of goodwill before final agreement is given. These last-minute concessions should not be overly generous; they should however be significant enough to encourage the other party to finalize the talks.

Incremental

Another approach is for the negotiator to propose agreement on a particular issue and then proceed to settle others until accord is reached on all pending matters. This method is used when the negotiation process follows an orderly sequence of settling one issue after another.

Linkage

Linking a requested concession to another concession in return is still a different approach. Linkage is usually most effective when both sides have already agreed on the outstanding issues and need to settle remaining ones prior to reaching consensus.

Prompting

Prompting is used to reach immediate agreement by making a final offer with special benefits only if accepted immediately. For example, this may consist of overcoming all objections and offering special incentives, e.g., free installation and maintenance, no price increase for next year's deliveries, and free training, if the other party agrees to conclude the transaction on the spot.

Summarizing

This is a technique requiring one negotiator to summarize all the issues being discussed, emphasize the concessions made, and highlight the benefits the other side would gain by agreeing to the proposal. As the discussions near the deadline and consensus is reached on all outstanding issues, one side summarizes the points and asks the other to approve them. The summaries should be short and reflect accurately what has been discussed. This is an approach that can be applied in any cultural environment or business situation.

Splitting the Difference

A useful closing technique is splitting the difference, in which both parties are close to agreement and the remaining difference is minimal. At that point, it may be preferable to split the difference rather than continuing endless discussion on minor issues that may be secondary to the overall objectives and possibly jeopardize the relationship. Splitting the difference supposes that both sides started with realistic offers—otherwise it would give an unfair advantage to the party with an extremely low offer (by the buyer) or a high offer (by the seller). This is a common technique that can expedite closure, but negotiators must ensure that it does not result in an unbalanced agreement.

Trial

Trial is a technique used to test how close the other side is to agreement. In a trial offer, one party makes a proposal, giving the other an opportunity to express reservations. Objections to the trial offer indicate the areas requiring further discussion. By making a trial offer, the initiating party is not committing itself, while the other party is not obligated to accept. Generally, a trial offer results in a constructive discussion on remaining issues while maintaining a fruitful dialogue between the parties until a consensus is reached. This is a useful technique to test the remaining matters to be clarified.

Ultimatum or Else

Another technique is to force the other side to make a decision on the last offer. If the other side fails to respond or accept the offer, the initiating party walks away from the negotiation. The "or else," also known as ultimatum, is generally not recommended for negotiations in which trust and goodwill are required to execute the agreement.

Choosing a Method

The closing technique should be selected during the pre-negotiation phase. Once chosen, it must be carefully prepared to ensure that it is mastered. The technique selected should fit the environment in which the discussions will take place and should match the overall objectives of the negotiations.

With experience, negotiators can shift from one closing technique to another or combine one or more as part of their negotiating tactics.

Overall, experienced negotiators prefer the approaches of concession, of summarizing and of splitting the difference, although the techniques of assumption, prompting, linkage, and trial closing are effective in certain types of negotiations and cultures.

Common mistakes can be avoided in this process provided that negotiators prepare in advance. A selected list of dos and don'ts, as well as key points to remember when closing negotiations, is given in the box above.

When to Close

As nearly every negotiation is different, particularly in international business, the time to bring the discussions to a close varies greatly from one situation to another. Timing is also highly influenced by the cultural background of the negotiators, the complexity of the deal, the existing relationships, and the degree of trust between the parties. For example, when two companies have been doing business for years and are discussing repeat orders, they are likely to arrive at a settlement rather rapidly. Discussions concerning the setting up of a joint venture, however, may take months or years to finalize.

It is important when making the final offer to ensure that the other person has the authority to decide otherwise, additional time may be required to discuss the offer

Closing a Negotiation: Some Dos and Don'ts

Dos:

- Anticipate last-minute demands when planning your negotiating strategy and tactics.
- Agree to an agenda that reflects your objectives and to realistic deadlines.
- Listen to the other party's objections and ask why they are not agreeing.
- Emphasize the benefits to be gained by the other side by accepting your proposal.
- Look for a change in the pattern, size, and frequency of the other party's concessions.
- Overcome objections by giving clear explanations.
- Take notes throughout the discussions, including your concessions and the ones made by the other party.
- Make your "last offer" credible and with conviction.
- Examine the draft agreement and clarify any points that you don't understand, before signing.

Don'ts:

- View closing as a separate step in the negotiations. Be in a hurry to close.
- Make large concessions at the last minute.
- Rush into costly concessions because of deadlines.
- Push your advantage to the point of forcing the other side to leave the negotiations.
- Lose sight of your long-term objectives when getting blocked on minor issues.
- Become too emotional when closing (you need to think as clearly as possible during the close).
- Discuss the deal with the other side once you have agreed (you run the risk of reopening the negotiations).

Remember:

- Flexibility is at the heart of closing a deal.
- Experienced negotiators plan their closing tactics during their preparations for the negotiations.
- Successful negotiators follow their pre-set goals and concentrate their efforts on essential issues.
- Encourage the other party to close, when the time is appropriate, since many negotiators either fear or do not know how and when to close.

(continued)

- The best time to close is when both sides have achieved their expected goals.
- Close only if the deal is good, not only for you but for the other party as well.
- The notion of closing varies in different parts of the world because of cultural factors requiring closing techniques.
- Closing is not done in a hurry.
- Overcoming objections is a part of getting approval of proposals.
- Successful closers seek consensus.
- Buyers often say "no" one more time before saying "yes."
- Nothing is agreed until everything is agreed.
- Not all negotiations lead to closing on a deal—sometimes no deal is better than a bad deal.

within that organization. In some countries, closing is time-consuming, as negotiators need to consult other members of the organization for approval. These additional discussions may result in delays as well as further demands for last-minute concessions. To counter such demands, the initiating party must state clearly when making the final offer that any further changes requested will call for a review of all the issues on which agreement has been reached.

A few clues can help experienced negotiators detect when it is time to close the talks. The most obvious one is when the concessions by one party become less important, less frequent, and are given more reluctantly. Generally, this is a sign that no further compromises are possible. Any concessions beyond that point may lead to a break in the negotiations.

In nearly all negotiations, a time comes when both parties have met most of their objectives and are ready to concede on some lesser issues to reach agreement. Up to that point, both sides exchange views to determine their respective needs, validate their assumptions, and estimate the negotiating range and the type of concessions required. Most concessions are made towards the end of the discussions, particularly as the deadline approaches. It is generally accepted that as much as 80 percent of all the concessions are exchanged in the closing phase of the talks. By this stage the parties have become familiar with each other's interests, tend to take a problem-solving attitude, and usually consider making concessions to reach agreement.

Another clue that it is time to close the discussions is when one party considers it has reached its maximum outcome and decides to make a final offer. This final offer must be made with conviction and followed by a request for a firm commitment from the other party. It is sometimes difficult to determine if the party making the final offer is trustworthy or is rather simply employing a closing tactic to arrive at a settlement in its favor.

Again, a great deal depends on the relationship and trust between the two sides, as well as the cultural environment in which the negotiation is taking place. In some countries, a final offer is considered final, while in others, it conveys willingness to reach agreement. When making a final offer, the party initiating the proposal must be willing to terminate negotiations if the other side refuses to accept. To avoid breaking the negotiation process, however, the party making the final offer can introduce a deadline for the other side to consider the "final" offer. This gives the receiving side more time to reexamine the proposal or to obtain additional facts enabling the continuation of negotiations.

In some countries, negotiators begin the discussions with general principles followed by more specific issues. The party shifting to specific issues is usually expressing its interest in bringing the discussions to a close. In other countries, however, negotiators start to compromise on specific issues one by one until all outstanding matters have been agreed to. These different approaches illustrate the influence of the cultural background on business negotiations and the need to be flexible in concluding international transactions.

It is widely accepted that negotiators, before agreeing to a final offer, ask for last-minute concessions. Such requests are expected and are part of the negotiating process. To be prepared to respond to last-minute requests, negotiators should keep a few concessions in reserve to maintain the momentum and to encourage the other party to close. These concessions should preferably be valued and appreciated by the requesting party, yet not be too costly to provide. For this reason, negotiators should identify the real needs of the other party and the likely concessions to be made just before closing and build them into the overall package.

Before applying any of the closing techniques mentioned above, the negotiators should ask themselves the following questions:

- Does the agreement meet our goals?
- Will we be able to fulfill the agreement?
- Do we intend to commit the resources to implement the agreement?
- Do we consider the other side capable of meeting its commitment to the agreement?

Only when each question is answered with a yes can both parties be ready to bring the discussions to a close.

Deadlines

The most obvious sign that it is time to close discussions is when the deadline approaches. It is important that the deadline be agreed to in advance by both sides, at the initial stage of the negotiations or when setting the agenda. A deadline arbitrarily set by one party in the course of the talks can lead to undue pressure on the other to close.

Deadlines should however be flexible. They can be renegotiated to allow the discussions to proceed until agreement is reached. In particular, when negotiators enter into complex talks in different cultural environments, the possibility of allowing extra time should be built into the planning.

Final Points

When a deal is about to be concluded negotiators need to ask themselves certain questions to avoid unpleasant experiences in the implementation phase. In most cases agreements that run into problems do not suddenly become difficult to implement. Instead it is generally minor issues that are unattended to or left to degenerate over time that lead to major crises. To ensure smooth implementation, negotiators should ask themselves the following questions:

- Have all the essential issues been discussed?
- Is the agreed proposal workable by both parties?
- Does the agreement clearly specify what is to be done by both sides, including payment terms, delivery schedules, product specifications, and so on?
- Have the major barriers to implementing the deal been identified and the means to overcome them agreed to?
- In case of potential disputes during implementation, what mechanisms have been instituted to resolve them?
- If either of the parties needs to renegotiate the terms, what procedures should be followed?

It would be advisable for the persons engaged in the talks to remain involved in the implementation phase. Each side should monitor the execution of the contract through the agreed procedures, and by periodic visits and ongoing communications. By maintaining regular contact and paying attention to minor details, the parties can help to ensure smooth business relations.

Conclusion

Many negotiators do not know how to bring their business talks to a successful close. They should be thoroughly prepared including knowing when and how to apply appropriate techniques and to respond to the other party's use of closing tactics. By mastering closing techniques, negotiators can achieve agreements that both sides can implement smoothly throughout the life of the agreed transaction. In closing a deal, it should be remembered that negotiations based on trust and fair play may lead to repeat business and referrals. As it is expensive and time consuming to find new business partners, it is advisable to retain existing ones by agreeing to terms and conditions with which both sides feel comfortable.

Defusing the Exploding Offer: The Farpoint Gambit
Robert J. Robinson

Situations in which offers are made with an expiration date attached are common in negotiation. In a way, all offers are inherently limited by time: One cannot, for example, leave a car dealership, return several years later, and attempt to accept the last offer made by a dealer who may or may not be employed there any longer. Obviously, the validity of an offer is affected by the passage of time. "Exploding offers," in contrast, are deliberate, calculated strategies. They are typically offered together with an extremely short, artificially imposed time limit. Consider, for instance, the following common manifestations of this phenomenon:

- Mary is looking for an apartment in a new city, and finally finds one that suits all her needs. When she asks about the rent, the landlord says, "The rent is $900 per month, but I tell you what—give me a check for the security deposit today, and I'll make it $850. Otherwise it's $900."

- John needs to buy a car. He haggles for several hours with a dealer, getting the price lower and lower. Finally an impasse is reached: John is still not happy with the price, but the dealer is unable to offer a more attractive deal. As John gets up to leave, the dealer says, "Look, it's the end of the month. If we can do this today, I'll make my quota, and that's worth another $500 off the price to me. But if you come back on Monday, we start all over again."

- Pat is an MBA student looking for a summer job between the first and second years of the program. The school has a recognized recruitment "season" when various companies come on campus, interview students, and, in many instances, offer summer employment. On the first day of the interviews, Pat interviews with Company X. After about 30 minutes, the Company X spokesperson says, "Well, we'd like to offer you the job," (and names a very generous salary) "but you must say yes or no right now."

Each of these examples illustrates what has become known as an *exploding offer.* However, each case probably evokes a different affective response in the reader, and has different implications for the protagonists in the vignettes. Mary has the choice of saving $50 per month on rent but can still have the apartment if she delays until the following day; John probably will not purchase the car unless he takes advantage of the temporary $500 concession; and Pat has the chance to get an attractive summer job—which disappears if Pat's next response is anything but acceptance of the offer. In this brief article my goal is to further refine the notion of exploding offers (the problem faced by Mary, John, and Pat) and suggest some ideas on how to deal with them, including a tactic that I call the "Farpoint Gambit."

Source: "Defusing the Exploding Offer: The Farpoint Gambit," by Robert J. Robinson, from *Negotiation Journal,* July 1995, Vol II, Issue 3, pp. 277–285. Used by permission.

Characteristics of Exploding Offers

Many negotiation scholars use the notion of an exploding offer in informal discussion, and the concept is directly related to analyses of the role of threats and time in negotiating. [S]pecifically, what makes an offer "exploding"? In my opinion, five characteristics separate exploding offers from offers that have naturally decaying life spans.

Power Asymmetry   Exploding offers generally only exist in situations where there is a considerable asymmetry of power between the offeror and the person receiving the offer. Thus in the cases of Mary and John, one might consider the offers as tactics being used between consenting adults in relatively equal power positions, which might not arouse any sense of discomfort. In Pat's case, the situation is more ambiguous. Faced with a large company offering a choice between a job or possible unemployment for the summer, a student burdened with loans might feel great pressure to accept as a result of the exploding offer. An even more extreme example is provided by the academic job market, which is filled with newly minted PhD recipients who are looking for faculty positions. Colleges routinely make exploding offers, which are the equivalent of offering a person dying of thirst a glass of water—if the person accepts right away. This leads to the second condition of concern.

A Pressure-Inducing "Test of Faith"   The exploding offer often places great pressure on the person receiving the offer. This is not in itself unusual or necessarily reprehensible. However, the situation becomes more complex when the pressure is excessive and is built on power imbalances. Thus in the case of the faculty candidate, I have personally witnessed situations where the person receiving the offer is placed under excessive pressure by the argument that "if you're one of us you'll accept now." This not only applies "normal" negotiation pressure but also raises the threat that accepting later risks making the organization angry with you for "holding out." This makes the act of attempting to negotiate further somehow vaguely (or explicitly, depending on the degree of coercion being applied) treasonable, and leaves the person receiving the offer with no options but to accept or withdraw completely. In another situation I witnessed, excessive pressure was applied by means of an interesting variation, which consisted of offering the job to the individual and telling them that they were the person that the company wanted above all others—followed by informing the individual that if they were unable to accept the job *that day,* the offer would be withdrawn, at least until "further candidates have been considered and interviewed for the position."

Restricting Choice   Another characteristic of the exploding offer is its use as a tool that deliberately restricts the choice of the individual. While there is an element of this factor in the case of Mary (the landlord does not want her looking at other apartments) and John (the salesperson does not want him looking at other cars), it is somewhat peripheral in both of these negotiations, which are aimed at closing a deal. In Pat's case, however, the exploding offer as a means to restrict comparative shopping *is the primary tactic,* and rests on not letting Pat get any other offers or even see representatives of other companies. In fact, it might even emerge that Company X is interviewing particularly early in order to prevent the candidates from seeing anyone else.

Lack of Consideration and Respect   Exploding offers involve arbitrary deadlines that are unnecessarily rigid. They can create enormous hardship for the individual involved, who may be called from family duties, may be forced to break leases, or may suffer other financial hardships in order to accept the offer. Appeals for flexibility and consideration are routinely ignored by the offeror, displaying an utter lack of regard for the other negotiator.

Lack of Good Faith   Exploding offers are sometimes made because a negotiator is ambivalent about the person or proposal in question, or is using this strategy as a means of resolving internal strife within the negotiator's organization. This is a somewhat cynical viewpoint, and it is not uncommon for one side to make an exceptionally self-advantageous exploding offer. If the offer is accepted, then a fine bargain has been achieved; and if the offer is rejected, the offeror can move on to other options. The problem is that the offer, as made, was not a serious, good faith attempt to reach a settlement. Thus while Pat might be told that he or she is the candidate that Company X wants, the reality is more likely that Company X wants a warm body with Pat's qualifications, and if Pat won't accept, then an interchangeable individual will be substituted.

Why Are Exploding Offers Made?

It is not difficult to understand the thinking behind the use of exploding offers, in terms of the perceived advantage this affords the offeror. The ability to impose terms and back them up with a tight time limit may force the other side to capitulate or agree before it might otherwise have done so, increasing the value of the deal for the party making the offer. In many ways, the exploding offer is the ultimate hard-bargaining tactic: Party A makes a final offer and then threateningly says, "And that's good until noon tomorrow. After that, you can find another partner." In essence, the tactic defines an end to the negotiation process. An exploding offer is not only an offer in the traditional sense but is also the last offer. Rejection will automatically terminate the negotiation, and in some cases, the relationship as well.

   In terms of the vignettes mentioned earlier, it is easy to understand how exploding offers can serve the interest of the offeror. In Mary's case, the landlord wants to tie in the new tenant that very day. Perhaps the landlord is going away and wants to get the apartment filled. Or maybe he just thinks that Mary is the kind of tenant he wants in the building, and is trying to sweeten the deal. Perhaps the rent really is $850, and the landlord is disingenuously offering the $50 discount. Whatever the reason, it is worth $50 per month to the landlord to commit Mary that day, rather than undergoing the opportunity cost of continuing to search for other tenants.

   Similarly in John's case, the dealer may in fact be trying to meet the quota for the month, or he may be looking for a way to make a sweeter offer without undercutting the "going" price for that model car. In any event, having John leave the dealership is to be avoided at all costs, and the $500 exploding offer is an incentive for John to stay and make the deal.

In Pat's case, Company X is presumably interviewing several MBA students over the next several days. The company must pay to have the interviewer stay in a hotel until the process is concluded. During that time, the interviewer makes offers and waits for the students to pick among several offers; if rejected, the interviewer might make another offer and so on. How much simpler it is to tie up the first likely looking individual the interviewer meets, and go home.

There is also another reason why the exploding offer is used. It can be a sign of offeror weakness that might not be at all apparent to the recipient of the offer, but is almost always present.[1] Negotiators who use exploding offers may perceive themselves to be at a disadvantage relative to their competitors in terms of salary, conditions of sale, or the like. Or they may have severe time or budget constraints. Once again, the function of the exploding offer can be either to force a quick acceptance by ending the negotiation (and thus avoiding the necessity of sweetening the deal to an unacceptably high level) *or* to restrict the ability of the recipient to comparison shop, and therefore discover that the market was willing to pay at a significantly higher level.

Dealing with Exploding Offers: Try Being Reasonable First

In the tradition of *Getting to Yes* (Fisher and Ury 1981) and *Getting Past No* (Ury 1991), a number of possibilities exist for the individual faced with an exploding offer. Most of these involve getting away from positional stances in order to explore underlying interests and to look to create value via "principled negotiation" (Lax and Sebenius 1986). It is important to realize that exploding offers can be dealt with using these techniques, especially if there is some degree of goodwill in the interaction. An exploding offer is often made by a party that believes it stands to lose out in the negotiation or is unsure of its power. Building trust and appealing to reason can go a long way toward addressing this underlying concern, resulting in the exploding aspect of the offer being withdrawn.

For example, apartment hunter Mary might say, "I understand you'd like a check today. Let me be honest. I really like this place, and I want to take it for $850 per month. But I have to see a few other places. How about I call you in the morning, first thing?" This might suffice. Or in the automobile dealership case, John the customer could say, "I really appreciate the $500 reduction. But I need to think this over. What if I call you 9 a.m. Monday? Can we make the offer good until then?" The dealer can accept, in which case the deal is still alive, or reject the counteroffer, in which case John is faced with the same decision as he had before he made the suggestion. If the dealer really wants to make a quota, a sales agreement could be drawn up, dated that day, but requiring John's agreement on Monday before it goes forward (John should probably not pony up any money until Monday).

These are relatively easy situations to resolve. However, the classic exploding offer scenario, replete with elements of hard bargaining, cynicism, and coercion, is the job offer case involving Pat, the student. Here there needs to be a real addressing of interests.

My advice to students in Pat's situation is to have them point out to the organization that, since it wants its employees to be happy and productive, it is in the organization's interest to let the students feel that they have freely chosen this position as the most attractive option. The way to achieve this is to make the most attractive offer, not to constrain choice. Also, if the student is really the one that the organization wants, then the employer should be prepared to wait for that individual, rather than treating him or her like an interchangeable part.

The recipients of exploding offers should also be prepared to make sensible counteroffers. They should be able to say when they *would* be in a position to accept, and to explain why this date makes sense (as opposed to choosing an equally arbitrary future time such as a week or 10 days). I usually tell my students about my most enjoyable employment experience, when I was made an offer and told, in effect, "take your time deciding. You're the one we want, and we want you to do the thing that's right for you. We are here to help you make that decision in any way we can." The contrast between this kind of attitude and an exploding offer, both in terms of an individual's feelings and the likelihood of a good future relationship for the parties, should be obvious. I have academic friends who are tortured, years after accepting their jobs, with the question of what would have happened if their employers had allowed them the time to take one more interview, or await the decision of another school.

My first recommendation is, then, to engage in problem solving with respect to uncovering interests, generating and exploring options, moving to creative solutions, and emphasizing relationship issues. However, this can fail if the other party is unsympathetic or locked into a positional or cynical stance. In such an instance, particularly if one feels that the other side is behaving in an ethically questionable fashion, I recommend the "Farpoint Gambit."

Fighting Fire with Fire: The Farpoint Gambit

While I always recommend first attempting a "principled" or "integrative" solution, I believe that when such tactics prove untenable, more assertive steps need to be taken. Doing this successfully depends on understanding where the power of the exploding offer resides. Exploding offers pivot on a credible, inviolable deadline. If the deadline is violated and the negotiation continues, the credibility of the explosion (the removal of the offer) is destroyed. And if the other side has depended on this threat as a central tactic, their entire position may collapse, putting the recipient of the initial offer in a very advantageous position. The technique I recommend, which I call the "Farpoint Gambit," is from the catalog of "hoist-them-by-their-own-petard" tools, which sometimes makes it particularly satisfying to employ.

The Farpoint Gambit derives from an episode of the science fiction television show *Star Trek, The Next Generation,* in which the crew of the *Enterprise* (the spaceship from Earth) is put on trial by a powerful alien "for the crimes of humanity." (The episode is called "Encounter at Farpoint," hence the name of the technique.) The alien creates a kangaroo court with himself as judge, and the captain of the *Enterprise* (Jean-Luc Picard) defends the human race. At a certain point, the alien judge becomes piqued by the captain's spirited defense, and says to the bailiff, "Bailiff, if the next word out of the defendant's mouth is anything but guilty, kill him!" He then turns to Picard and asks, "Defendant, how do you plead?" Picard thinks for a moment as the bailiff menacingly points a weapon at him, them firmly announces, "Guilty." As the courtroom gasps (and after an inevitable television commercial break), he adds, "Provisionally." This is essentially the Farpoint Gambit.

The alien has presented Picard with the ultimate coercive offer: Say you're guilty or I'll kill you. Obviously, Picard doesn't think he's guilty, but he doesn't want to die. The power of the threat depends on getting Picard to admit that he's guilty—he does, but in such a way ("provisionally") that the alien judge is compelled to ask, "And what is the provision?" Picard then proceeds to talk his way out of the jam (as always happens with television heroes), and all is well. The point is that the alien is caught in his own trap: He's still arguing with Picard, who is still not guilty or dead. In the same way, an exploding offer can be defused by *embracing it,* using the Farpoint Gambit.

Consider again Pat's situation. Essentially, Company X is the alien, saying to Pat, "either the next words out of [your] mouth are 'I accept,' or it's no deal." Pat can attempt to reason with the company's representative, and if that does not work either walk away, accept, or use the Farpoint Gambit by saying, "I accept. Provisionally." The provision could be anything that takes the negotiation beyond that day, and might be things like "provided I can meet with the person I would be working for," or "provided my coworkers prove satisfactory," or even "provided I don't get a better offer from the companies I'm still waiting to hear from."

The key is to make requests that are completely reasonable, but which will eventually result in the deadline being violated, due to the need for further clarification, or the lack of authority of the negotiator making the offer. Once the deadline passes, the credibility of the threat is destroyed, and successive attempts to set arbitrary deadlines can be dealt with in exactly the same way. The recipient of the offer can accept at his or her leisure, or reject the offer based on an unsatisfactory resolution of the provisions of the original acceptance.

The Farpoint Gambit also works by leveraging off fractures in the other side or the imperfections in their informational strategies. Thus in Pat's case, the company's negotiator may not be authorized to offer moving and relocation expenses, or know what the policy is on day care for children. In such situations it is extremely easy to accept "pending satisfactory resolution of these issues" and then to continue to negotiate those and other issues.

The success of the Farpoint Gambit ultimately rests on the notion that the person receiving the exploding offer can eventually withdraw from the situation if no satisfactory resolution is forthcoming, without the offeror being able (or inclined) to sanction them for doing so. While this technique is about helping people get what they want from a coercive negotiating partner, it is *not* about helping people find a way to wriggle out of commitments given in good faith when they change their minds or get a better offer.

Inevitably, some negotiations, even those resuscitated by the Farpoint Gambit, are bound to fail. However, if conditions are attached to the acceptance—and these are not, by a reasonable assessment, met—then there really is not anything the company can do when the student withdraws, or the faculty candidate accepts an offer elsewhere, although possible reputational damage should still not be overlooked. It may be that each side has as much at stake as the other, which will help to keep both reasonable—no organization wants to get the reputation for strong-arming prospective employees with techniques of dubious morality. In other cases, there may be actual legal provisions that allow the individual to withdraw within a specified time limit after accepting, such as in the case of signing an agreement to purchase a car.

The Farpoint Gambit has a further advantage: It is nonescalative (Pruitt and Rubin 1986) and non-zero-sum in nature. Like the crew of the *Enterprise* in their endless quest for new frontiers, the Farpoint Gambit may force negotiators toward improved solutions at the "Pareto frontier" (e.g., see Raiffa 1982). It moves the parties in the "right" direction—that is, toward one another rather than apart. In this sense, the Farpoint Gambit is not as dangerous as techniques that require one side to call the other's bluff, or see who can hold out the longest. In these latter cases, someone frequently wins, and someone loses. The Farpoint Gambit is about both sides being able to take care of underlying interests, and thus able both to "win" and get what they want, with the offeror paying a fair price.

In Conclusion: When to Use—Or Not Use—The Gambit

I would strongly caution against using the Farpoint Gambit as a routine technique to gain advantage. Nothing is more frustrating and unacceptable than someone who makes a habit of taking a deal, and who then continues to impose conditions or introduce new issues. Indeed, this is the flip side of the reprehensible lowballing technique employed by shady salespersons. In pondering this, I have come up with some guidelines for situations in which I believe it is legitimate to employ the Farpoint Gambit.

Ideally, I would make sure that all three of these conditions were present before I would feel completely comfortable in using this tactic.

- The other side is perceived by the recipient of the exploding offer to be behaving unethically, and does not respond to appeals to reason.
- The recipient is truly interested in making a deal but needs more time to make a decision.
- There genuinely are issues that need clarification, which would make the difference between accepting or rejecting the deal.

The Farpoint Gambit is a technique that should not be used lightly, in a spirit of deception, or with a lack of good faith. However, in situations where the individual is trapped by the hardball tactics of an offeror who relies on an exploding offer, the Farpoint Gambit offers a means whereby the pressure applied by the other side can be turned against them, much as a judo expert can use a foe's momentum to provide the energy that leads to the latter's own undoing. To be sure, this is itself a hardball tactic (Schelling 1960; Deutsch 1973), and many might not feel comfortable using it. I offer the Farpoint Gambit as someone who has seen many friends, loved ones, and students put under enormous pressure, forced to make critical life decisions under unnecessarily difficult circumstances due to the callous use of power by people and institutions not operating in good faith.

Notes

The author would like to acknowledge the useful criticism he received on earlier drafts of this work from Professors Roy J. Lewicki of the Ohio State University; the late Jeffrey Z. Rubin of Tufts University; and Michael Wheeler of The Harvard Business School. Also significantly contributing to this work were members of the Program on Negotiation/Fletcher School of Law and Diplomacy "Tuesday Evening Reading Group."

1. Only in the case of a true monopolist, making an offer with many potential buyers, can one argue that the exploding offer is truly an act of self-serving arrogance and convenience on the part of the offeror.

References

Deutsch, M. 1973. *The resolution of conflict.* New Haven: Yale University Press.

Fisher, R., and W. L. Ury. 1981. *Getting to yes: Negotiating agreement without giving in.* Boston: Houghton Mifflin.

Lax, D. A., and J. K. Sebenius. 1986. *The manager as negotiator.* New York: Free Press.

Pruitt, D. G., and J. Z. Rubin. 1986. *Social conflict: Escalation, stalemate, and settlement.* New York: Random House.

Raiffa, H. 1982. *The art and science of negotiation.* Cambridge, MA: Harvard University Press.

Schelling, T. 1960. *The strategy of conflict.* Cambridge, MA: Harvard University Press.

Shell, G. R. 1991. When is it legal to lie in negotiations? *Sloan Management Review* 32, pp. 93–101.

Ury, W. 1991. *Getting past no: Negotiating your way from confrontation to cooperation.* New York: Bantam Books.

Implementing a Collaborative Strategy

Roy J. Lewicki
Alexander Hiam
Karen W. Olander

This chapter shows how to use the collaborative strategy. The word *collaboration* may sound strange to people who are used to viewing negotiation as competitive. But bargaining does not have to be a win–lose proposition—the pie does not have to be fixed. In many cases, conflict and competitiveness between the parties lead them to *believe* that there are only limited resources to be divided between the parties. It is often possible to find solutions to problems that will satisfy all parties by changing or growing the pie instead of fighting over it. The pie analogy, however, leads us to the principal challenge of a collaborative strategy: the parties must somehow learn how to work together. Collaboration, which is an open, sharing, creative process, does not come naturally when you are in a conflict situation or do not trust the other party. Collaboration is therefore difficult for many negotiators to master.

Some negotiators think they are collaborating when in fact all they have done is wrap their competitive strategy in a friendly package. Thus they put on the "image" of collaboration, only to move in for a competitive "grab" near the end of the negotiation. This is not collaboration—it is competitiveness in a collaborative disguise. True collaboration requires the parties to move beyond their initial concerns and positions and go on a joint quest for new, creative ways to maximize their individual and joint outcomes. Before we examine how the collaboration strategy works, let's see how a demonstration case can be adapted to this strategy. Here are Felice and Sara again this time taking a cooperative, win–win approach to setting up a partnership to develop their interior decorating business:

> "The bottom line is, we need $50,000 in cash, right now, if we want to do this right. I know you have the money—why are you hesitating to use it when we obviously need it?"
>
> "But Sara," Felice objected, "what's the rush? This is a big decision for me. What if things don't work out? I'd be taking all the financial risks and suffering most of the losses. Whatever happened to getting a bank loan?"
>
> "Well, I tried a few banks, but I didn't have any luck—my credit history isn't so great." Sara paused to offer some homemade cookies to Felice. "I'm sorry I'm being so pushy, I know this is something that you need to think through, and I'm not helping. It's just that I've already made some important contacts, and found promising offices for rent; I'm afraid if we don't get started soon, we'll never get going."
>
> Felice thought for a minute as she ate the cookie. "I understand your impatience, I'm impatient, too. I'm excited about working together and I don't want to waste more time. Maybe we're going about this in the wrong way. Let's just take a few minutes to go over our situation. We want to start an interior decorating business together. You have a lot of

Source: "Implementing a Collaborative Strategy," by Roy J. Lewicki, Alexander Hiam, and Karen W. Olander, from *Think before You Speak,* 1996, pp. 99–119. New York: John Wiley & Sons, Inc. Used with permission

experience, but no money to invest, and I have no experience but possibly a lot of money to invest. However, I'm reluctant to sink all my savings into something that may not work out, partly because I'd lose everything I have, but mostly because I'm afraid of ruining our friendship if it doesn't work out. I could probably get a bank loan, but then I'd still be responsible for all the finances, so it seems to me that we should consider bringing in a third party in some capacity."

"Hey—that's not a bad idea. But we would need someone who'd only help us financially—we still need to have control of the business," Sara absently picked crumbs off her sweater. "You know, that reminds me—an old friend of my dad is an architect in a very respected firm. I wonder if we could hook up with them somehow, maybe exchange the rent for an office in their building with a percentage of our business. They could refer customers to us, and eventually we could do the same for them. It's a beautiful old business—you'll love it. It would be a terrific showplace for our work. Do you think I should call him?"

"Well, let's think for a minute," said Felice, "What percentage would we offer them? How about 20 percent? That gives them enough to feel it's worthwhile without taking away our control. Then I could invest $20,000 in the business to get us started and we'll each keep 40 percent of the ownership."

"That sounds great! Let me try it—I'll call my dad right now and get the architect's phone number."

When Sara and Felice proposed the deal to the architect, he was very enthusiastic about their work and the potential for the fit with his business. He offered them office space in his building, and they moved into an office the following week. Within a month, they had landed several jobs that generated a cash flow and helped to establish their reputation as creative, reliable decorators. Over time, the business flourished. They eventually bought the 20 percent back from the architect (with a handsome profit), and their friendship remains strong.

Characteristics of the Collaborative Strategy

In the collaborative strategy both the relationship *and* the outcome are important to both parties. The two parties usually have long-term goals that they are willing to work for together. Both parties are committed to working toward a mutually acceptable agreement that preserves or strengthens the relationship. Because each party values the relationship, they will attempt to find a mutually satisfying solution for both parties. Working together effectively in a collaborative negotiation process can itself enhance the quality of the relationship. This approach is very different from the competitive strategy, where both sides want to win so badly that they pursue their goal at all costs and ignore all the factors that might allow a collaborative process.

In addition, in the collaborative model, intangibles are important and accounted for. These include such items as each party's reputation, pride, principles, and sense of fairness. Because these concerns are important, the negotiations must stay on a rational, reasonable, and fair level. If the parties get angry at each other, the collaborative atmosphere will degenerate into a competitive one. Allow for plenty of venting time if you or the other party begins to get irritated, and be sure to listen to complaints about your behavior with an open mind to avoid conflicts that can derail collaboration. There must be a great deal of trust, cooperation, openness, and communication between the parties to engage in effective problem solving.

Finally, the parties must be willing to make *concessions* to accomplish their goals. These concessions should be repaid with creative win–win solutions, but they represent a risk for each party that the other party must be careful not to abuse.

In the collaborative strategy, the constituency (if there is one) plays a very different role from that which it plays in competitive negotiations. Generally, the members of the constituency are supportive and will promote the relationship between the two parties.

The collaborative strategy relies on deadlines that are mutually determined and observed. They are not used for manipulation, as we found in the competitive strategy. Information flows freely and is not used to control the situation or guarded to maintain power. The objective is to find the best solution *for both sides.* Similarities between the two parties, not differences, are emphasized.

There are four major steps in carrying out a collaborative strategy: (1) identify the problem; (2) understand the problem; (3) generate alternative solutions; and (4) select a solution. We will examine each in detail.

Steps in the Collaborative Strategy

Identify the Problem

This may sound like a simple step, but in the collaborative model both sides are involved equally in the process, and both need to agree on what the problem is. When you were gathering information you focused on *your* point of view, but for the collaborative strategy to work, you will need to work closely with the other party to find a common view of the problem.[1]

When defining the problem, try to use neutral language and to keep it impersonal. For example, you might say "We are not able to get our work out on time" rather than "You are preventing us from doing our work and getting it out on time." It is important to define the obstacles to your goals without attacking other people.

Try to define the problem as a common goal. For example, in the Sara and Felice situation, they might say, "Our goal is to find a way to start our business without Felice having to assume too much financial risk." Keep the goal definition as simple as possible. Try not to load the situation with peripheral issues that are not really related to the central concern. Stick with the primary issues.

Each party needs to be assertive, but cooperative at the same time: You need to be clear about what you want to achieve, yet not at the expense of dominating the other side. Because the relationship is important, you need to see the problem from the other party's perspective—"to walk a mile in the other person's shoes" as much as possible. Understanding and empathy go a long way to finding the common issues.[2]

Watch out for a tendency to define solutions before you have fully defined the problem. In fact, you should avoid discussing solutions until you have thoroughly defined and understood the problem(s). And remember, the more creative the problem definition, the more likely you are to discover a new, beneficial win–win solution. Throw caution to the wind, brainstorm wildly, and hope for a creative insight that will make it fun and easy to solve the problem.

Understand the Problem

In this step, you try to get behind the issues to the underlying needs and interests.[3] As noted earlier, an *interest* is a broader perspective that each side has, which is usually "behind" their position. In our example, Felice's position is that she does not want to provide full financial backing for the new business; her interest is to minimize her financial risk while also helping to get the business started and into a profitable mode. You need to learn not only about the needs and interests of each party, but also about their fears and concerns. Felice's fear is that she will lose a large amount of her investment (and her savings) if the business goes bad. The reason for getting behind the positions is that they tend to be fixed and rigid; modifying them requires the parties to make concessions either toward or away from the target point. In contrast, interests define what the parties care about more broadly, and there are often multiple "roads to Rome," or several ways to resolve the conflict between these competing interests. In addition, a focus on interests tends to take some of the personal dimension out of the negotiation and shifts it to the underlying concerns.[4] Since there is bound to be a difference in thinking styles, people will approach even similar issues in different ways. Positions offer only one way to think about an issue; interests offer multiple ways to think about it. Thus you can find out "where they are coming from" more effectively by discussing interests than by stating positions.

Interests may reflect current or longer-term concerns. And parties are likely to have multiple interests. It is also important to realize that each party may have different interests. By using "why" questions, you can dig deeper into the reasons for each party's position. An interest is the why of a position.

Interests may be substantive,[5] as with concerns for prices, rates, and availability of resources. Interests may have to do with the process, as in how we will conduct the actual negotiation. This concern may, in turn, be based on how the process has been completed in the past, or on how we want to change and improve it for the future. Concerns may also center around sustaining and enjoying the relationship. Or a party may have a strong interest in principles. They may be concerned about what is fair or ethical, right or acceptable. For example, Felice and Sara have a number of interests at stake in addition to the substantive interest of their specific solution to funding their new business. Because they are starting a business in which they will work together actively, they are trying to get off on the right foot in the way they solve and deal with joint problems. Thus they want to establish a good problem-solving process, they want to preserve—and even enhance—their relationship with one another, and they probably care a great deal about principles, such as the precedent created by both the outcome and the process of this negotiation or the perceived fairness of their agreement. Felice and Sara have a lot riding on this deliberation, and it is most important that they work it out in a way that creates a good outcome and strengthens their working relationship.

Remember that even if you define interests carefully, they can change. Since the negotiation process is an evolving one, you may need to stop from time to time to reconsider interests. If the conversation begins to change in tone or the focus seems to shift, this may be a signal that interests have changed. Since the collaborative strategy is one of openness, the parties with changing interests should be encouraged to share their shifts in needs. The other party may facilitate this by being willing to expand resources,[6] extend the time frame, or change the details of the negotiation to accommodate the changed interests (we say more about some of these tactics in the next section). As Sara and Felice's business took off and prospered, their interests changed. As the business was successful, Felice was less worried that her financial investment would be seriously at risk. As the new decorating contracts were assured, she became more confident and trusted Sara more, and the two were eventually able to buy the 20 percent investment back from the architect. Both the changed nature of the business and the trust level between Sara and Felice had a lot to do with changing the interests of these two negotiators.

Generate Alternative Solutions

Once you have defined the issues to the satisfaction of both parties, you can begin to look for solutions. Notice that this is plural: *solutions.* You want to find a group of possible solutions, then select from among them the best solution for both parties.

There are two major ways to go about finding solutions. One is to redefine the problem so you can find win–win alternatives for what at first may have seemed to be a win–lose problem. The second is to take the problem at hand and generate a long list of options for solving it.

Redefining the Problem   To illustrate the different approaches, we will use an example suggested by Dean Pruitt, about a husband and wife who are trying to decide where to spend a two-week vacation.[7] He wants to go to the mountains for hiking, fishing, and some rest; she wants to go to the beach for sun, swimming, and night life. They have decided that spending one week in each place will not really be adequate for either person, because too much time is spent in packing, unpacking, and traveling between the two locations.

- *Expand the pie:* If the problem is based on scarce resources, the object would be to find a way to expand or reallocate the resources so that each party could obtain their desired end. Knowing the underlying interests can help in this endeavor. For example, the parties could take a four-week vacation and spend two weeks in each place. While this would require more time and money, each person would get a two-week vacation in the chosen spot.

- *Logroll:* If there are two issues in a negotiation and each party has a different priority for them, then one may be able to be traded off for the other. For example, if Problems A and B are common to both parties, but Party 1 cares most about Problem A and Party 2 cares most about Problem B, then a solution that solves both problems can provide each party with a happy resolution. "You get this and I get that." If there are multiple issues, it may take some trial and error to find what packages will satisfy each party. In our example, if the husband really wants to stay in an informal rustic mountain cabin, and the wife really wants to stay in a fancy hotel, then another resolution is for them to go to the mountains but stay in a fancy hotel (or an informal beach house at the shore).

- *Offer nonspecific compensation:* Another method is for one party to "pay off" the other for giving in on an issue. The "payoff" may not be monetary, and it may not even be related to the negotiation. The party paying off needs to know what it will take to keep the other party so happy that they won't care about the outcome of this negotiation. In a house sale negotiation, for example, the seller might include all window coverings (curtains, drapes, blinds) as part of the deal. The buyer may be so delighted that he decides not to ask for any other price break. In our vacation example, the wife might buy the husband a set of golf clubs, which will make him so happy that he will go anywhere she wants to go (since there are golf courses everywhere).

- *Cut costs:* In this method, one party accomplishes specific objectives and the other's costs are minimized by going along with the agreement. This differs from nonspecific compensation because in this method the other party can minimize costs and "suffering," whereas in the other method, the costs and suffering do not go away, but the party is somehow compensated for them. This method requires a clear understanding of the other party's needs and preferences, along with their costs. In our vacation example, the wife says to the husband, "What can I do to make going to the beach as painless as possible for you?" He tells her that he wants to stay in a beach house away from the big hotels, get some rest, and be near a golf course and near several places where he can go fishing. They both go down to their favorite travel agent and find a location that offers all these things.

- *Bridge:* In bridging, the parties invent new options that meet each other's needs. Again, both parties must be very familiar with the other party's interests and needs. When two business partners (Sara and Felice) bring in a third partner who can offer resources neither of them wanted to contribute, this is an effective example of bridging. In our vacation example, the husband and wife go to a travel agent and find a place that offers hiking, fishing, beaches, swimming, golf, privacy, and night life. They book a two-week vacation for Hawaii and have a wonderful time!

Generating a List of Solutions   The second approach to inventing solutions is to take the problem as defined and try to generate a list of possible solutions. The key to finding answers in this approach is to generate as many solutions as possible without evaluating them. The solutions should be general rather than party-specific—they should not favor one party over the other. At a later stage, each solution can then be evaluated to determine whether it adequately meets the needs and interests of both parties.

What is interesting in this process is that both parties engage in trying to solve the other party's problem as much as they do their own.[8] It is a cooperative endeavor. And, as you have probably heard many times before, two heads are better than one.

If you get to this stage, but the issues still seem murky, you may need to go back to the problem definition and rework that step. It should be easy to generate solutions if the problem is clearly stated in a way that does not bias solutions toward one party or the other. Otherwise, if you are comfortable with the definition of the problem, forge ahead.

There are a number of ways to generate ideas for solutions. Remember that you are only *generating* solutions in this step, not evaluating them or deciding whether to use them—yet. That will happen in the next step.

- *Brainstorming:* This common method for generating ideas usually works best in several small groups rather than one large one, depending on the number of people involved. Write down as many ideas as possible, without judging them. It is best to write or post the ideas on a flip chart, chalkboard, or similar display device, so that everyone can see them and keep track of what has been done. The key ground rule is that *ideas must not be evaluated as they are suggested.* Don't let anyone say, "Oh, that's a dumb idea!" or "That won't work!" Keep ideas flowing, keep focused on the problem and how to solve it, without associating people with the problem or the solutions.

    It often happens that people quickly think of a few possibilities, and then run out of ideas. At this point, it is easy to think you are done because you have a few solutions. Don't stop here—stick at it for a while longer. Otherwise you may miss some really good ideas, particularly creative ones that no one has considered before. Ask outsiders for ideas, too. Sometimes they bring a fresh approach to the problem.

- *Piggybacking* can be used in conjunction with brainstorming.[9] This technique is simply to build on someone else's idea to produce yet another idea. It's often done by working in a sequence order; one person starts with a brainstormed idea, then the next person has to "piggyback" until possible variations on the idea are exhausted.

- *Nominal groups:* In this method, each negotiator works with a small group— perhaps his or her constituency—and makes a list of possible solutions. These are discussed within the group, then considered, one at a time, by the group as a whole. They can be ranked in terms of preferences or likely effectiveness. The drawback of this method is that anyone not present at the session will miss offering input or helping to shape the solution.

- *Surveys:* Another useful method is to distribute a questionnaire stating the problem and asking respondents to list possible solutions. In this case, each person works alone on the survey, so people miss out on the synergy of working together. However, the advantage is that a number of people who have good ideas, but are normally reticent about getting into a group's conversation, can offer their thoughts and ideas without being attacked or critiqued. Another advantage is that this draws in the ideas of people who may not be able to attend the negotiation or formally participate in it.

Prioritize the Options and Reduce the List   Once you have a list of possible solutions, you can reduce it by rating the ideas. In communicating your priorities and preferences to the other party, it's important to maintain an attitude of "firm flexibility."[10] Be firm about achieving your interests, while remaining flexible about how those interests might be achieved. There are a number of tactics to keep the discussion collaborative while being clear and consistent about your preferences:

- Remember that you are only *prioritizing* the list, not yet deciding on the actual solution.

- Be assertive in defending and establishing your basic interests, but do not demand a particular solution.

- Signal to the other party your flexibility and willingness to hear the other party's interests by practicing your listening skills.

- Indicate your willingness to modify a position or have your interests met in an alternative way. Perhaps you will be able to trade one point for another. This will demonstrate your openness to suggestions and willingness to work together.

- Show ability and willingness to problem solve. Skill in problem solving is valuable here, especially if you get stuck on a particular point and need to find some way to resolve it to everyone's satisfaction. If you can settle this issue, it will help when you get to the next step and are actually deciding on the solution. You will have set the stage for collaboration.

- Keep lines of communication open. If tempers flare, take a break, and talk about it if need be. Also talk with the other party about how you can continue to work on the problem without getting angry or losing control. Make sure both parties feel that they are being heard. Steer discussion away from personalities, and concentrate on the issues: "Separate the people from the problem."[11]

- Underscore what is most important to you by saying, "This is what I need to accomplish," or "As long as I can accomplish _____, I'll be very happy." Resist the temptation to give in just to get a resolution. Giving in is an accommodating strategy that will not result in the best outcome for both parties.

- Reevaluate any points on which you disagree. Be sure that both sides agree on the adjusted prioritized list so that you will both feel comfortable as you move to the final step.

- Eliminate competitive tactics by identifying them and either confronting them or renegotiating the process. If the discussion becomes competitive, point out that this is happening. Then try to resolve the problem *before* the entire negotiation becomes competitive.

Select a Solution[12]

Using your prioritized list of potential solutions from the previous step, narrow the range of possibilities by focusing on the positive suggestions that people seemed to favor most. For example, one way to prioritize is to logroll (package each person's first choice together). If parties have the same first choice, but very different preferences for it, try to invent a way for both sides to "win" on this issue.

Try to change any negative ideas into positive ones,[13] or else eliminate them from the list. Stating alternatives as positives keeps the negotiation upbeat and on a positive note. Avoid attributing negative ideas to any particular person or side.

Evaluate the solutions on the basis of quality and acceptability. Consider the opinions of both parties. Do not require people to justify their preferences. People often do not know why they have a preference; they just do.

When you are preparing to select a solution, if you foresee any potential problems with this process, you may want to establish objective criteria for evaluation before you start the selection process.[14] In other words, before you move toward picking among prioritized options, work against a set of objective facts, figures, data, and criteria that were developed independently of the options. There are numerous examples. In our example between Felice and Sara, they might go to a small business assistance agency, such as a local bank or small business development group, to find out how other business partnerships have dealt with this situation. If a car owner and a garage mechanic are having a dispute about how much it should cost to repair a starter motor, there are books available that indicate the "standard" cost for parts and labor for this repair. Finally, if a group of people is trying to pick a job candidate from among a group who applied for the job, their work will be considerably facilitated if they spend time developing criteria by which to evaluate the applicants before they actually look at résumés and interview people. If you can't find objective criteria, another technique is to have a third party help you.

If necessary, use subgroups. These are helpful if the problem is complex or if the outcome will affect a large group. It may be more efficient to use several small groups than to use one large one. Be sure the subgroups contain representatives from each party.

Fairness and Other Intangibles   Intangibles are often operating in the decisions. For example, gaining recognition or looking strong to a constituency may be important factors in the selection of solutions. Acknowledge the importance of intangibles by building them into the decisions. For example, if the other party needs to maintain esteem with a constituency, they may be willing to settle on a lesser point that still allows them to appear in a favorable light. In fact, it will help them greatly if you work with them to determine how to make them look strong and capable to the constituency.

Fairness is usually one of the most important intangibles. In a win–win negotiation, both parties want to achieve a fair outcome, rather than maximize their outcome—which they might push for in a competitive negotiation. There are a number of ways to decide what is fair, but three common criteria often apply:[15]

- An outcome that gives each side *equal* outcomes. Thus it is not surprising that one of the most common ways to solve negotiation problems—particularly win–lose, competitive ones—is for the parties to agree to "divide it down the middle."

- An outcome that gives each side more or less based on *equity* (what it has earned or deserves, based on the time or energy committed). In this case, the side that puts in more should get out more. Equity is usually based on the ratio of outcome to input, so that the person who works harder, suffers more, and so on deserves a proportionally larger share of the results.

- An outcome that gives each side more or less, depending on what it *needs.* In this case, if one side can create a legitimate claim that it needs or deserves a better outcome, there may be a good case to be made for dividing up the resources so that those with greater needs actually gain more.

We can see how the equity versus equality arguments can easily come into play in the discussions between Felice and Sara. Sara—having no money but great creative skills—could argue that they should split all profits from the business equally. In essence, she is arguing that creative contribution and financial contribution to the business should be weighted equally. In contrast, Felice—having few creative skills but a lot of money to put toward the venture—could argue that they should split profits in proportion to the amount of money contributed during the start-up. If the two of them stuck to these positions strongly, they could have an intractable dispute over how to value financial and creative contributions, which would be a major block in their discussions.

Emotional Escalation   If emotions surface, or if people get angry, take a break. Give people an opportunity to discuss the reasons for their dissatisfaction. Be sure everyone has cooled off before you start again, and try to keep personalities out of the deliberations. If taking a break does not work, seek out a third party to help you.

Other Suggestions for Keeping the Decision-Making Process on Track   You can use logrolling to make combination options. You can also take advantage of risk preferences, differences in expectations, and differences in time preferences. For example, one party may prefer an option with low risk, while the other party is willing to accept an option with a much higher risk; you may be able to combine these so that each party gets its preferred outcome. Likewise, some options may satisfy only short-term concerns, but may be more important to one party than longer-term issues. These, too, can be traded off.

It is very important not to rush the process of selecting solutions, appealing as it may be to do so. If you get to the bottom line too quickly, you may miss some good potential options, and you may fail to ensure that both sides participate equally.[16] Collaborative efforts require the participation of both sides; they may also require time to mull over alternatives and think through all the consequences. Good collaborative negotiation requires time and cannot be rushed.

Remember that *everything is tentative until the very end.* During the solution-generating phase, some people may even object to writing anything down, as this may make them nervous. They may feel they are being railroaded into commitments they have not agreed to. Other than the "working documents" that you may create as you define the problem and invent options, you may want to begin to record decisions only when the group is close to consensus. That way, nothing is set in stone until the very end. This open, fluid approach makes it possible to share creative ideas and suggestions. The minute one party says, "But you said yesterday you'd be willing to . . . ," the collaboration starts to unravel as participants begin to worry about being held accountable for "positions." This difficult and critical rule is violated too often as people revert instinctively to a competitive style without realizing the impact on idea generation and sharing.

Once the parties have agreed on solutions and prepared a document to outline the agreement, it should be passed around for everyone to read. Some people have suggested that this may even be an excellent way to manage the entire prioritization and decision-making process. Start with a tentative draft of what people agree to, then continue to pass it around, sharpening language, clarifying words, and writing out agreements so that all agree with it and pledge to live by it. You may want to make a plan for implementing the agreement, and to set up a time frame in which the parties can try out the solution.[17] This again allows for all to fully participate and to become committed to the plan.

How to Be Successful with Collaborative Negotiation

Researchers have identified several keys to successful collaboration.[18] They are useful as a checklist for the strategic negotiator in planning and implementing a collaborative strategy.

Create Common Goals or Objectives

There may be three different ways the goals will be played out: All parties will share in the results equally; the parties will share a common end but receive different benefits; or the parties will have different goals, but share in a collective effort to accomplish them. In any of these cases, both parties believe that they can benefit by working together as opposed to working separately, and that the results will be better than they would be if each party worked separately.

Maintain Confidence in Your Own Ability to Solve Problems

This is more or less a matter of "If you think you can, you can." As we mentioned earlier, it helps to have a strong knowledge of the problem area, but lack of knowledge can be overcome if the desire is there. Probably the most important element is to develop skills in negotiating collaboratively, since it is a less common form of negotiation. The more you do it, the better you will become at doing it.

Value the Other Party's Opinion

Valuing the other party's point of view is difficult if you have been accustomed in the past to focusing only on your own position and maintaining it. In the collaborative strategy, you value the other party's position equally with your own.[19] You need good listening skills and openness to hear the other party's point of view.

Share the Motivation and Commitment to Working Together

In the collaborative strategy, you are not only committed to the idea of working together with the other party, you take actions to do so. You pursue both your own needs and those of the other party. This means each party must be explicit about their needs.

In collaborative negotiation, the parties strive to identify their similarities to each other and to downplay their differences. The differences are not ignored, they are simply recognized and accepted for what they are.

The parties are aware that they share a common fate, particularly if they expect to work together after this negotiation has been completed. They know they can gain more if they work jointly than if they work separately. To do this, they focus on outputs and results.[20]

Motivated, committed parties will control their behavior in a number of ways. Individuals will avoid being competitive, combative, evasive, defensive, or stubborn. They will work at being open and trusting, flexible, and willing to share information and not hoard it for their own use.

A Cautionary Note   Believe it or not, there is such a thing as too much collaboration! The two parties must not be so committed to each other that they do not look out for their own needs. If they begin to subordinate their needs to the other party, they will be moving toward the accommodating or lose–win strategies and will lose out on the benefits that the collaborative strategy can offer.

Trust

Because trust creates more trust—which is necessary to begin and sustain cooperation—it is important to make the opening moves in collaborative negotiation in a way that engenders trust.[21] Opening conversations may occur even before the formal negotiations begin, when the parties are just becoming acquainted. If one party finds a reason to mistrust the other party at this time, this may stifle any future efforts at collaboration.

If the parties are new to each other, or if they have been combative or competitive in the past, they will have to build trust. Each party will approach the negotiation with expectations based on the research they did on each other or on past history. Generally, we trust others if they appear to be similar to us, if they have a positive attitude toward us, or if they appear cooperative and trusting. We also tend to trust them if they are dependent on us. Likewise, making concessions appears to be a trusting gesture, so we are likely to respond in kind.

In contrast, it is easy to engender mistrust. This often begins either with a competitive, hostile action, or with an indication that one does not trust the other. Once mistrust gets started, it is very easy to build and escalate, and very difficult to change over to collaboration. Trust escalation and deescalation have often been compared with the children's game "Chutes and Ladders." In this analogy, it is easy to move down the "chute" of mistrust, rapidly sliding to the bottom, but much more difficult to climb back up the "ladder" that will restore and sustain good trust between parties.[22]

Clear, Accurate Communication

Communicating effectively is the bedrock of negotiation, no matter what form the bargaining strategy takes. In the collaborative strategy, precise and accurate communication is of the utmost importance. It is crucial to listen well so that you know what the other party wants and why they want it. This requires more than just superficial listening.

It is through communication that one party shares information with the other party.[23] This communication must be delivered in the most concrete of terms so there is no confusion or misinterpretation. Feedback and frequent questions can clarify the message if necessary.

Some of the communication in negotiation may be formal, based on procedural or other rules such as rules of order. Sometimes communication will be informal, as during breaks and after sessions. Or perhaps the entire undertaking will be informal, depending on the personal characteristics and styles of the participants.

Obstacles to Achieving Good Collaboration

Collaborative negotiation is a lot of work. But the rewards can be great. Sometimes, however, no matter how much you want to succeed, obstacles may prevent you from moving ahead with a collaborative strategy. One (or both) of the parties

- May not be able to do the required work.
- May have a win–lose attitude.
- May not be able to see the potential for collaboration.
- May be motivated to only achieve their own goals.
- May not be capable of establishing or maintaining productive working relationships.
- May be inhibited by biases.
- May have a constituency that is pressing for competitive behavior or quick outcomes.

Further, the situation may contain elements that require a mix of strategies. Then you need to separate the issues into the component parts and deal with each separately.

Sometimes you may feel that you do not have the time or energy to push forward with a collaborative strategy, especially if you encounter one or more of the preceding situations.

What If There Is a Breakdown?

If there is a conflict, try to move the discussion to a neutral point, and summarize where you are.[24] If there is a total breakdown in communication, and you just cannot get the negotiation back on track, you may need to resort to conflict resolution strategies or to third-party intervention. And also note that you and the other party can, at any point, reach a mutual agreement to abandon your collaboration and adopt another negotiating style. For instance, you might try collaborating, decide you don't like working together, and decide that you will "agree to disagree" and revert to a conventional competitive strategy—or toward a more expedient and simple outcome through compromising. Remember, however, that you will give up the relationship benefits, so do not advocate the competitive strategy unless you decide your initial estimation of relationship importance was too high. Also, since you will have shared much information through your collaboration attempt, it can now be used against you in a competitive negotiation. Therefore, the slide from collaboration to competition is not generally a happy or profitable one because some of the actions you undertook under the assumption that you could trust the other and work with them may now be used against you as weapons.

A Case Study: Negotiating Strategic Alliances

A business example of the use of negotiation is in the area of strategic alliances, which are gaining in importance worldwide, particularly in Europe. Global competition has intensified the scramble for access to markets, products, and technologies. Strategic alliances are one strategy that companies are using to survive or to keep up with the new developments in industry.

Negotiating a strategic alliance presents a challenge. "A bad negotiation tactic may do lasting damage; good negotiation tactics must be repeated a number of times before the partner accepts this as a pattern."[25] In a strategic alliance, the relationship concerns will be very important.

In 1985 Corning and Ciba-Geigy formed Ciba Corning Diagnostics, an alliance based in the United States, designed to enhance Corning's medical diagnostics business. Ciba-Geigy is a global pharmaceutical and chemical company based in Switzerland. Corning, based in New York, is a world leader in glass and ceramics technology. The alliance would combine the strengths of the two partners to develop innovative medical diagnostic tests.

There was synergy in what each partner could offer to the alliance. Negotiation went smoothly, as Ciba was willing to have Corning manage more extensively in the beginning. Corning's managers were willing to concede on points of strong interest to Ciba, and thus they were able to agree on a time line for their work. Each partner appointed its director of research and development to the board of the new alliance, which signaled to the other party a willingness to share technology, while garnering internal support for the alliance as well.

Each side had representatives to build consensus, improve communication, and obtain support for the parent organization, Ciba and Corning actively looked into ways for each partner to gain by opening up possibilities for broadening the product line, marketing, technology, and growth. They were able to negotiate any issues that arose because, as mutual trust grew, they were willing to discuss such problems clearly and openly.

A strategic alliance will not succeed if the two potential partners have conflicting underlying motives. If they are both leaders in their field, it may be difficult for them to collaborate. Likewise, if they have strongly differing views of which activities should take priority or what the time lines should be, the success of such an alliance would be questionable.

To create a successful alliance, each organization must be willing to support the efforts to create an alliance agreement. This means that political support must be generated within the organizations of the potential partners. Building support may take time. For example, the Japanese take a long time to complete this process (at least from the American point of view). Conversely, the Japanese see American firms as too pushy.

Negotiating with Your Boss

Since everyone has had some sort of experience dealing with a boss at one time or another, we will take a moment here to look at ways to negotiate collaboratively with a manager.[26] Although performance review, salary, and benefits are usually the major areas for discussion and possible conflict with one's manager, there are others that arise more often. For example, what if you are asked by your boss to do a project that you realize you cannot possibly complete without working overtime? If you do not mind staying late, go ahead. But if you find yourself doing this frequently and resenting it, maybe you need to consider negotiating about it the next time.

Negotiating with the boss is often viewed as a competitive, win–lose, or fixed-pie situation. It can also be viewed as a lose–win situation, in which it is better to accommodate and let the boss win all the time, rather than try to argue for a preferred outcome and have the boss be angry at your "assertiveness." But if you think about it, both parties might be able to gain something from collaborative negotiation.

Think about the steps in the collaborative strategy we covered earlier in the chapter. Look at your own needs, as well as those of your boss. Remember that the key to collaborative bargaining is to find a way to solve the other person's problem.

So in our hypothetical situation, your boss may have been asked by her boss to drop everything and get this project out, at any cost. (Your boss may have some bargaining of her own to do.) At any rate, your boss has to have this project done, and there is no way for you to complete it during normal hours, given the other work you have to do and the deadlines for those projects. Your boss could ask someone else to do it, but perhaps she knows you can do the job better and more quickly.

First, clarify the situation. Find out the circumstances from your boss. Be sure you understand the details of the project. Gather information you may need about what you are working on at the present time.

When it is time to discuss the project again, you will be prepared. Be sure your boss knows and understands the situation from your side. List what you are currently working on, and make sure she is willing for you to put those things aside to work on this rush project. Or does she prefer to have you give it only part of your attention? We knew one person who, when her boss piled new work on her desk, made a list of all the projects she was currently managing. Then she handed the list to her boss, and asked him to number the list in the order that he wanted things done. It made him decide what his priorities were.

You can make a number of suggestions for how to complete the project given the circumstances. (This means you will have brainstormed for ideas before you meet with her.) One option might be for the boss (perhaps with your help) to find more resources. Two people could perhaps help with the project, thus halving the time it will take to complete.

Another option would be for your boss to get an extension of the time allotted for the project. To do this, she would have to negotiate with her boss.

A third option might be to change the "specs" of the project (e.g., make it less detailed or more streamlined), which would allow you to complete it in less time.

You also could suggest, "If I stay late several nights to do this project, I would like to take compensating time off," or "If I do this project, then I need help to complete my other projects on time, or else an extension." These are compromising strategies.

This example illustrates that even an apparently simple negotiation can be more complex than we realize. In this case, it involves not just you and your boss, but her boss as well (and who knows who else?). In any situation, it helps to break down a problem into its component parts and try to get at the underlying needs.

Summary

In this chapter, we have outlined the collaborative strategy. When using this strategy, your objective is to both maximize your outcome on the substantive issues and sustain or enhance the quality of the relationship between you and the other side. To do so, you need to meet your outcome needs as well as the needs of the other party in a manner that strengthens the trust, mutuality, and productive problem-solving in the relationship.

Good collaboration is a wonderful thing to be able to create and sustain. But it is not an all-purpose panacea, and making it work well often requires a large commitment of time and energy. There are times when the parties might be just as well off to compromise, accommodate, or even avoid negotiations.

Endnotes

1. A. C. Filley, *Interpersonal Conflict Resolution* (Glenview, IL: Scott Foresman, 1975); G. F. Shea, *Creative Negotiating* (Boston: CBI Publishing, 1983).

2. A. Williams, "Managing Employee Conflict," *Hotels,* July 1992, p. 23.

3. R. Fisher and W. Ury, *Getting to Yes* (Boston: Houghton Mifflin, 1981); R. Fisher, W. Ury, and B, Patton, *Getting to Yes: Negotiating Agreement without Giving In,* 2nd ed. (New York: Penguin Books, 1991).

4. M. Freedman, *"Dealing Effectively with Difficult People," Nursing 93* (September 1993), pp. 97–102.

5. D. Lax and J. Sebenius, *The Manager as Negotiator: Bargaining for Cooperation and Competitive Gain* (New York: Free Press, 1986).

6. T. Gosselin, "Negotiating with Your Boss," *Training and Development,* May 1993, pp. 37–41.

7. D. G. Pruitt, "Achieving Integrative Agreements," in M. Bazerman and R. Lewicki (Eds.), *Negotiating in Organizations* (Beverly Hills, CA: Sage, 1983); R. J. Lewicki, J. Litterer, J. Minton, and D. A. Saunders, *Negotiation,* 2nd ed. (Burr Ridge, IL: Richard D. Irwin, 1994).

8. M. B. Grover, "Letting Both Sides Win," *Forbes,* September 30, 1991, p. 178.

9. G. F. Shea, "Learn How to Treasure Differences," *HR Magazine,* December 1992, pp. 34–37.

10. D. G. Pruitt, "Strategic Choice in Negotiation," *American Behavioral Scientist 27* (1983), pp. 167–194; Fisher, Ury, and Patton, *Getting to Yes: Negotiating Agreement without Giving In.*

11. Fisher and Ury, *Getting to Yes.*

12. Filley, *Interpersonal Conflict Resolution;* D. G. Pruitt and P. J. D. Carnevale, *Negotiation in Social Conflict* (Pacific Grove, CA: Brooks-Cole, 1993); Shea, *Creative Negotiating;* R. Walton and R. McKersie, *A Behavioral Theory of Labor Negotiations* (New York: McGraw-Hill, 1965).

13. Shea, "Learn How to Treasure Differences."

14. Fisher and Ury, *Getting to Yes.*

15. B. H. Sheppard, R. J. Lewicki, and J. Minton, *Organizational Justice* (New York: Free Press, 1992).

16. R. H. Mouritsen, "Client Involvement through Negotiation: A Key to Success," *The American Salesman,* August 1993, pp. 24–27.

17. A. Williams, "Managing Employee Conflict," *Hotels,* July 1992, p. 23.

18. Pruitt, "Strategic Choice in Negotiation"; D. G. Pruitt, *Negotiation Behavior* (New York: Academic Press, 1981); Filley, *Interpersonal Conflict Resolution.*

19. Fisher, Ury, and Patton, *Getting to Yes: Negotiating Agreement without Giving In.*

20. Freedman, "Dealing Effectively with Difficult People."

21. C. M. Crumbaugh and G. W. Evans, "Presentation Format, Other Persons' Strategies and Cooperative Behavior in the Prisoner's Dilemma," *Psychological Reports 20* (1967), pp. 895–902; R, L. Michelini, "Effects of Prior Interaction, Contact, Strategy, and Expectation of Meeting on Gain Behavior and Sentiment," *Journal of Conflict Resolution 15* (1971), pp. 97–103; S. Oksamp, "Effects of Programmed Initial Strategies in a Prisoner's Dilemma Game," *Psychometrics 19* (1970), pp. 195–196; V. Sermat and R. P. Gregovich, "The Effect of Experimental Manipulation on Cooperative Behavior in a Checkers Game," *Psychometric Science 4* (1966), pp. 435–436.

22. R. J. Lewicki and B. B. Bunker, "Trust in Relationships: A Model of Trust Development and Decline," in J. Z. Rubin and B. B. Bunker (Eds.), *Conflict, Cooperation and Justice* (San Francisco: Jossey-Bass, 1995).

23. M. Neale and M. H. Bazerman, *Cognition and Rationality in Negotiation* (New York: Free Press, 1991).

24. R. H. Mouritsen, "Client Involvement through Negotiation: A Key to Success."

25. Stephen Gates, "Alliance Management Guidelines," *Strategic Alliances: Guidelines for Successful Management* (New York: Conference Board, Report Number 1028, 1993).

26. T. Gosselin, "Negotiating with Your Boss"; M. B. Grover " Letting Both Sides Win."

Solve Joint Problems to Create and Claim Value
David A. Lax
James K. Sebenius

To solve your individual value-claiming "problem," your tactics must help you to learn accurately about the true *zone of possible agreement* (ZOPA) and to shape the other side's perceptions of the ZOPA in a manner favorable to you. Yet most negotiations are not purely about value claiming.

We now move to the table in search of tactics that *both* create and claim value, ideally on a long-term basis. At the end of the day, you want to create all possible value jointly, claim a full share of it, and prevent yourself from being exploited by a value-claimer. This can be a challenge, especially when the other side is playing a hardball, claiming game. Perhaps this stance is purely tactical or perhaps your counterparts simply don't see the potential for joint gains. Either way, this chapter offers a number of suggestions to push the negotiation in a productive direction.

Here's the essence of the joint problem that our tactics must solve. Creating value requires cooperation to elicit information—about interests, views, capabilities, and so on—and use that information to generate mutually beneficial options. This takes communication, trust, openness, and creativity. Yet those very qualities can open you up to exploitation by a determined value claimer. If you put all your cards on the table, while others play theirs close to the vest, you're likely to get nailed. And yet if everyone hides his or her cards, revealing little, and searching for openings to exploit, it becomes nearly impossible to come up with joint gains. You and your counterparts are likely to have a battle royal over a small pie.

Put otherwise, information in negotiation is a two-edged sword: essential to solve the joint problem and to create value, but also a source of vulnerability to a value-claimer on the other side. You can't easily separate the creating and claiming processes. It turns out that the way you create value affects how it gets divided. And the battle over dividing the pie often affects how much, if at all, it gets expanded. Managing this creating-claiming tension productively is the essence of successful negotiation. Problem-solving tactics, undertaken with a full understanding of the value-claiming aspect of negotiation, offer the best route to great outcomes.

Constructive negotiation processes, in which value is created as well as claimed, nevertheless tend to emphasize the joint nature of the problem to be solved. They stress:

- Reconciling the parties' real interests, rather than battling over their positions
- The future and mutual possibilities, rather than the past and who was right, wrong, and to blame for what happened before
- Factual discussions, rather [than] broad generalizations
- Joint problem solving, rather than adversarial posturing

Source: "Solve Joint Problems to Create and Claim Value," by David A. Lax and James K. Sebenius, from *3D Negotiation: Powerful Tools to Change the Game in Your Most Important Deals,* 2006, pp. 205–226. Boston, MA: Harvard Business School Publishing. Used with permission.

We can't hope to compress all of what's known about creating and claiming value at the table into a single chapter. But we will combine our own experience and the prescriptions of others to suggest some tactical guidelines that will make you more effective in a wide range of situations where there is the opportunity both to create and claim value.

Our tactical advice falls into four basic areas, which serve as the main sections of this chapter:

1. Ask, listen, and learn.
2. Divulge information strategically.
3. Foster an appealing and productive negotiation process.
4. Adopt a persuasive style.

Each class of tactics needs to be approached with a keen sense of productively managing both the creating and claiming aspects.

Ask, Listen, and Learn

At the table, you learn by listening and observing. You rarely learn much when you are talking!

Sales experts say that most salespeople talk 80 percent of the time and listen 20 percent of the time—but that the most *effective* salespeople listen 80 percent of the time and talk 20 percent of the time. One of the toughest things about negotiation is that it is hard to listen while you are talking. Even when the other side is talking, you tend to focus on what you are going to say next. So, actually listening to the other party, and processing what they're saying, requires extra effort. A few tactical suggestions follow.

Try Active Listening

Active listening, in which you play back to the other party what you just heard her say, helps you slow down and focus your attention on what she is saying. For example: "Let me just make sure that I understood you. You are concerned that if your bonus formula is tied to the projects you work on, and if the company decides to allocate more work to others, your compensation would go down even if allocating the work to others makes the company more profitable. If I understood you correctly, you'd like to have your bonus guaranteed at the level you received last year. Could you say a bit more about that?"

Even repeating back what you've heard without paraphrasing, followed by a pause, often prompts your counterpart to expand upon the point, and share more of his or her motivations in ways that may be helpful. It also may allow your counterpart to clarify her statement in a way that gracefully backs down from some aspects of the position or assertion. And, critically, when you keep testing your understanding, they *know* that you are listening.

Avoid Questions That Ask for a Yes or No Answer

Questions that elicit flat yes or no answers can be damaging. For example: "Do you mean you won't do a deal if it doesn't provide full indemnification for you and your team?" The answerer either has to undercut himself (unlikely) by saying "no," or by saying "yes" invest personal and perhaps organizational credibility in not backing down from the statement (in which case you're worse off having asked this yes-or-no question).

Ask Open-Ended Questions

In many cases, the most effective questions are open-ended. For example:

- "Why?" "Why not?"—as in, "You've said that your contracts people don't want to reimburse us for expenses that you have historically reimbursed us for. Can you say a little more about why this has become an issue at this point?" Or, "You say you can't agree to any price increases for two years. Could you tell us more about your situation and what's behind your thinking?"

- "What if we did it this way?"—as in, "What if we were to give you a bigger piece of our business? How would that affect your cost and sales situation? How much could you reduce the per unit price?"

- "How would that work from your perspective?"—as in, "How would it work from your standpoint if we were to raise fees on the following services, in the following circumstances?"

- "What kinds of problems would that create for you?"—as in, "If we were to reach agreement to provide the capital to fund the cash-calls that the partnership agreement requires you to make in return for a significant share of the returns you would get, what kind of pluses and minuses would that involve for you?"

And after you ask, *really listen.* When you start making proposals, listen to their objections. These objections may spotlight interests that they had not disclosed previously, and which, as a result, are not reflected in your proposals. Objections can enable you to shape new packages that better meet *your* interests, as well as theirs.

Bring a Designated Listener

When you bring a team to negotiate, it is helpful to include on the team a designated listener—someone whose role is not to talk, but carefully listen and take notes.

Divulge Information Strategically

Of course, you will be expected to do more than listen at the table; you will be expected to talk about your own needs and expectations. Here are some battle-tested ideas for revealing information in ways that also elicit information from the other side.

Begin with the End

A successful executive we know in the outsourcing industry begins his major negotiations by sitting down with his customer to write the positive press release that the two sides hope will result from the conclusion of a successful negotiation. By hashing out the joint ideal up front, he learns about key interests of his counterpart and also shares important interests. Both focus away from the barriers and on the opportunity, the "pot of gold" that could result from effective cooperation. At the same time, both sides may be gaining some psychological commitment to making a deal. When the negotiation hits a tough patch, the executive pulls out the release to reorient the effort.

Use the Norm of Reciprocity to Build Trust and Share/Gain Information

The concept of the "norm of reciprocity" leads us to want to reciprocate when someone does something that's helpful to us. It is a powerful psychological force, which you can tap into to gain information.

Share some low-cost information, and encourage the other side to share some information, as well. If your opposite numbers fail to reciprocate—or if, based on your prior research, they appear to be trying to mislead you—consider having an explicit discussion about what you have been trying to do: that is, to give and get enough information to enable you to jointly design a mutually beneficial deal. Sharing that information makes each of you vulnerable but is safer if both of you do it.

If they *do* reciprocate, provide additional information, and request more. In many negotiations, you can tap the power of the reciprocity norm to build trust over time. You may perform a personal favor, take your counterpart out for drinks or coffee, provide some helpful information outside of the negotiation, or in some other way do something positive. All of these moves are designed to build trust. The trust, in turn, will enable you and your counterpart to share information that will enable you both to create value.

Present Multiple Equivalent Offers

To learn more about your counterpart's interests and trade-offs, you can present her with a choice of two packages of equal value to you, and—without asking her to accept or reject either—ask her which package is better for her. If you have designed your packages carefully, you will learn something about her side's trade-offs, and move in a value-creating direction while revealing little about your preferences.

Similarly, if you are a buyer of a multifeatured product or service, you can ask the seller to price the product or service both with and without a certain feature. In this way, you can learn about the seller's trade-offs without revealing yours.

Sequence Issues Carefully and Negotiate Packages

We now turn to how sequencing the issues properly helps to create and claim value. Of course, to sequence issues properly, you need to understand your full set of interests associated with that issue and its relationship to other issues. For example, if you are negotiating the form of a transaction—merger, acquisition, or equity joint venture—there are powerful implications for the rest of the negotiation on how you settle that initial issue.

The most common advice about issue order is to settle the "easy issues first." On the positive side, this approach can help build trust, rapport, a sense that progress is possible, and momentum as you tackle harder issues. Getting easy issues out of the way can simplify the remaining negotiation.

Yet if you do settle the easy issues first, the only ones left at the end may require tough, value-claiming battles. This issue-by-issue approach may inadvertently transform a potentially cooperative deal into a highly competitive one, with real deadlock risks near the close. This often happens when everything but price is settled and the parties are far apart on this particular issue. Working out an overall, value-creating package for the endgame—in which nothing is settled until everything is settled, and there is mutual gain realized relative to no-deal options—can shift the dynamics in a much more positive direction.

When U.S. President Jimmy Carter was in the final stages of peace treaty negotiations between Egyptian President Sadat and Israeli Prime Minister Begin at Camp David, he confronted just such a situation: "The only serious problem was [Sadat's] desire to delete the entire paragraph on Jerusalem. I knew that the Israelis wanted the same thing, but I confess that I did not tell Sadat. I reserved that concession just in case I needed some bargaining points later on. Earlier in the process, Carter had packaged a classic easy issue—on which both Egyptians and Israelis wanted the identical outcome (to defer the status of Jerusalem)—with other, more contentious items. By doing this, Carter turned the ultimate package (minus Jerusalem) into more of a plus for each side, rather than setting up a much riskier, win–lose finale.

The negotiating dynamics involving easy issues can become complex. For example, faced with two main issues—one not too important to them and the other vital to them—some negotiators will fight hard on the vital one, then be flexible for the easier one, hoping to make up for any hard feelings. Other negotiators make a point of "giving in" first on the less key issue, hoping to generate some pressure for reciprocity from the other side on the remaining question. However, what is an easy issue for you to concede may in fact be the other side's most critical issue to get, or at least quite important to them. You may or may not realize this at the time you "give" on that issue. If you've already said yes to such an issue or issues, you may have little leverage left for your hardest topics when you later tackle them. This possibility amplifies the general wisdom of developing packages rather than settling issue-by-issue.

A further implication of this issue-sequencing logic affects agenda management. When negotiating large contracts, it is common to have one party's attorney make a list of unresolved issues and have the group work down the list one issue at a time, attempting to get closure on each before moving on to the next. While this method of agenda setting can help the parties to organize the remaining questions, it is almost guaranteed to leave unrealized value on the table for all parties. If the parties have opposing interests on each issue, they will typically reach mid-range settlements on each of the issues. Yet doing so fails to heed a basic principle of value creation. Specifically, for each side to do better, the party that places greatest weight on each issue should receive more favorable treatment on that issue in return for "compensation," such as giving the other(s) favorable treatment on the issues most important to them (providing the issues are of roughly similar importance). Thus, the agreement reached by finalizing one issue at a time is likely to be substantially worse for all parties than that reached by a process that is geared to look for differences in interest and thereby to facilitate trades. Although issue-by-issue agenda management is often the default procedure in many complex negotiations, we'd advise a focus on negotiating packages where possible.

Foster an Appealing and Productive Negotiation Process

Process matters

People tend to feel better about an agreement—and value it more highly—if it was reached by a process that they feel was fair. Conversely, they tend to reject offers, even economically attractive offers, if the process feels coercive.

We have found very useful negotiation process advice in *Getting Past No,* written by our friend and colleague Bill Ury. While it is framed as advice for dealing with difficult people, the book's advice works equally well in less adversarial settings. At its core is the notion that you should try to transform your negotiation process from one that is "face-to-face against each other" to "side by side against the problem." Don't think of the other side as "them" or as your adversaries; seek to align both your efforts against the problem of jointly craft agreements that meet each side's interests on a lasting basis, rather than glare at each other each other across the table.

The physical setup of the negotiations can play a role here. When both sides troop into a meeting room and position themselves on opposite sides of the conference table, this physical setup can almost function like a stage set, unconsciously cuing each side to fall into a well-worn script and adversarial roles. ("Ladies and gentlemen, this afternoon's production will be 'Face-to-Face Against Each Other.' ") We have seen negotiators break this unconscious mold by inviting both sides to set up on the same side of the table, together opposite a white board on which the "problem" was summarized. ("Instead, this afternoon's production will be 'Side by Side Against the Problem.' ") Would it surprise you that encounters of the second tend to be more productive?

In line with Ury's advice, we suggest that you relentlessly reframe your negotiation process in the following four directions.

Move from Positional to Interest-Based Conversations

Even when the discussion may seem to be narrowly focused, the interests that motivate the other side are often much richer than their bargaining positions.

Many tough negotiators are quick to stake out firm positions: "You have to cut your price by 5 percent per year if you want to keep our business." Our first advice is *not* to encourage this by, for example, starting or responding with "Here's my position. What's yours?" Although your counterpart may not be eager to engage in a collaborative process, consciously reframing away from bargaining positions to broader interests can help engage the other side in a more productive discussion. "I take it that you are trying to decrease your overall costs of manufacturing by 5 percent. What is the overall plan for doing this? What if we could figure out how to cut your manufacturing costs by 5 percent of what you pay us?" Often the kinds of questions we outlined above will help move past positions to interests.

The hard positional bargainer will likely require a lot of effort before engaging in a value-oriented discussion. But consciously focusing the discussion on how you can help the other side make more money—without cutting your prices!—can help engage a positional bargainer.

Move from Blaming and Past Actions to Problem Solving and the Future

When there have been problems in a relationship, they can infect the negotiations and turn the at-the-table interactions into a blame game. "You guys just can't perform. You set deadlines and don't meet them. You've introduced new features that don't work they way you said they would." And so on.

There's usually little advantage in arguing about who is to blame for what hasn't worked in the past, especially where the complaints have some validity. Your goal should be to learn from the past and push the focus to the future, by asking, "Let me get this straight. Which new features were you planning to use? How were you planning to use them? We need to make sure that the development group really understands what you are trying to accomplish." Instead of arguing about who's right and who's wrong, aggressively reframe to focus on to a joint quest to make the product do what they want. "I don't think the features you are using were meant to do what you intend, but I'm pretty confident that with a few modifications, we can enable the system to deliver what you want."

When there is a strong emotional content to your counterpart's presentation, you may need to acknowledge that emotion in a productive way, and then move toward problem solving—a subject that we'll return to below.

Move from High-Level Assertions to Fact-Based Statements

Negotiations can founder when they focus on high-level generalizations and assertions. This is especially true when the discussion degenerates into a "did not"/ "did so" interchange. For example, in a negotiation to renew a large outsourcing contract, a customer was convinced—and repeatedly asserted—that an outsourcer was overcharging them by significant amounts relative to their competitors in a highly competitive industry. The outsourcer protested strongly. The negative generalization cast a shadow over all of the substantive negotiations on the renewal of the contract: "How can we trust them on this issue if they've been screwing us for the last few years?"

We played a mediating role in this negotiation. To move from generalizations and assertions to facts, the parties agreed to our suggestion that we look on a confidential basis at how much the customer would have paid, given its usage, if it had been subject to the contracts of each of the comparable competitors also served by the outsourcer. Our analysis showed the customer actually enjoyed *better* contracts than all but one company. The outsourcer readily agreed to retroactively adjust the customer's contract so that it received the benefits of the one superior contract. The customer felt less aggrieved and greatly appreciated the outsourcer's gesture. By moving from assertions and counterassertions at high levels of generality to a more specific fact-based discussion, the two parties got their renewal negotiations back on track; in fact, they signed a several-hundred-million-dollar contract several months later.

Move from Price Haggling to Joint Problem Solving

Among the pitfalls of standard tactical negotiation is a relentless tug toward the kind of pure price negotiation. To maintain a productive climate, you may need to relentlessly reframe the negotiations away from that pure price focus, in favor of a fuller package of interests. For example: "I understand that you want to reduce costs of operation, and that the prices we charge you are important. We will respond to you on pricing. As we've discussed, price is only one part of what gives you a competitive advantage relative to your competitors, and we believe that we should focus not on price alone but on how we can help you maintain and strengthen your overall competitive position." If you've done a good job of understanding the other side's interests and situation—both from a business standpoint and from the personal standpoint of the individuals with whom you are negotiating—you can probably steer the conversation toward proposals that solve broader problems for your counterpart, rather than just reducing prices.

What if you can't? Then it's time to look for a way to appeal to the other side's stated interests, while still meeting your own. One of our clients—an engineering-oriented company, whose products include all the bells and whistles that its engineers could pack in—was losing ground to several Chinese firms that had begun offering a stripped-down version of the product for a fraction of our client's price. In negotiations with its customers, our client tried to explain that, as the customer grew, it would need to buy many more of the Chinese products. Because of the extra features, the customer would have to buy far fewer of our client's products to get the same functionality. This would mean lower total overall costs. The procurement vice president, who was clearly rewarded on minimizing total current outlay and not on lowering total lifetime outlay, continually demanded that our client match that low Chinese price and didn't want to budge from that position. In response, we advised our client to deactivate all the advanced features in their product, and sell it as a "stripped-down model" at a very low margin that would be cost-competitive with the Chinese models. When the customer grew and needed to expand its network, it would then have to purchase those advanced features—and would have to negotiate to get access to them at more attractive margins. But, at that point, purchasing these additional features even at high margins would be better than its no-deal option of purchasing another slew of the Chinese products.

In other words, our client turned the procurement VP's price-focused tactics *against* him by meeting his customer's interests of minimizing current cash outlays—while securing a higher-margin growth path for the long term. Our client followed this strategy with a number of customers, simultaneously increasing margins while becoming the market share leader in its product category.

Adopt a Persuasive Style

To work with your counterpart to create value—and at the same time to claim sufficient value for yourself—you should adopt a persuasive style. A persuasive negotiator:

- Understands the other side's story
- Is open to persuasion
- Is both empathetic and assertive
- Uses reciprocity to build trust
- Matches appeals to the other side's circumstances
- Recognizes how people process information

Let's look briefly at each of these points.

Understand Their Story

Different people interpret the same information or event differently. What set of facts, assumptions, and world view causes the other side to interpret things the way that they do? What are you missing?

Be Open to Persuasion

If you are not (or do not appear to be) open to persuasion, your counterparts very likely will sense that and adopt a similar stance. *Being open to persuasion is persuasive.*

Be Both Empathetic and Assertive

Robert Mnookin has identified two key dimensions of negotiation behavior: empathy and assertiveness. You are empathetic when you try to understand the interests and desires and motivations of the other side. You are assertive when you make your interests and demands clearly known to the other side. Many people feel that they must choose between being assertive and being empathetic—being "hard" or being "soft." But that's a false choice. Showing empathy about your counterpart's interests, perceptions, and constraints may make him or her more open to providing you with useful information. The more empathetically you understand your counterpart, the more effectively you can design value-creating deals and the better positioned you are to claim a full share of that value.

Frame Proposals in Terms of What They Care About

You are always more persuasive when you frame your proposals in terms of the values, beliefs, goals, and incentives of the recipient—and you deliver them in language used by the recipient. An associate of Rupert Murdoch remarked that, as a buyer, Murdoch "understands the seller—and, whatever the guy's trying to do, he crafts his offer that way."

For example, Paul Levy, CEO of Beth Israel Deaconess Medical Center in Boston, wanted his institution to be named the Official Hospital of Boston's immensely popular baseball team, the Red Sox. Before Levy had even heard about the opportunity, several other distinguished local hospitals had already made proposals to the Red Sox for this designation. Levy listened carefully to the new Red Sox management as it expressed a strong interest in being a good steward of a great franchise and actively participating in the life of the community. Accepting the baseline proposal for financial contributions by hospitals, Levy's team developed a detailed plan and presentation. Not only did this plan involve a financial relationship, but it also explained Beth Israel's own mission of community service and Levy's own role as a steward for an institution with a distinguished history. Against this backdrop, the presentation outlined several concrete steps through which Beth Israel and the Red Sox could jointly perform meaningful, visible service to their communities. Levy's suggestions included (1) a September 11th blood drive at Fenway Park (the team's stadium); (2) an Organ Donor Awareness Night at the stadium introduced by two players whose friend's wife survived as a result of a liver transplant; and (3) funding and managing a Red Sox Scholars Program, which annually established college scholarships for 25 academically talented but financially challenged middle-school students who would be mentored by Beth Israel doctors, and who would shadow key people in the club offices and at the hospital on "career days." The Red Sox were persuaded by this approach, adopting these and other initiatives within 18 months.

Seek Agreements that Feel Fair to Both Sides

At the end of the day, as noted earlier, most of us want to believe that the agreement we reached was both fair and reached by a fair process. So your preparations for negotiations should include: (1) developing compelling, fact-based arguments supporting your position; (2) identifying fairness rationales likely to be advanced by your counterpart; and (3) formulating counterarguments disputing the fairness of the counterpart's rationales. If the people on your side find it difficult to put themselves in your counterpart's shoes, consider bringing in someone who is not directly involved in the negotiation to try to think like the other side. Being seen as genuinely caring about fairness as well as making proposals that seem fair can both enhance your persuasiveness.

Persuade with Stories, as well as Analysis

Many businesspeople try to hammer away at those they're trying to persuade with compelling facts, logic, and analysis. But this may not be the most effective way to get people to act. In fact, psychologists have monitored subjects' brain activity during various kinds of persuasive appeals and have noted that many people's brains tend to "go dark" (i.e., show little brain activity) when presented with fact/logic-based appeals. In contrast, when people hear vivid stories or analogies, their brains light up, or become more active, and they tend to have much higher retention of the implications of what they've heard.

Inoculate Against Potentially Disadvantageous Arguments

If you can anticipate the counterarguments to your proposal that are likely to occur to your counterparts, you should acknowledge and deal with these counterarguments as part of your own approach. If you fail to raise the obvious counterarguments, they may reverberate inside the heads of the other side and weaken the persuasiveness of your overall appeal.

From a psychological standpoint, it doesn't matter much whether you address the counterarguments at the end or intersperse them throughout in your appeal. However, there are tactical considerations. For example, if you are presenting your argument in a context where you are likely to be interrupted and unable to complete the full argument, start with a clear presentation of your own complete argument before dealing with the counterarguments.

Build Both Substantive and Relationship Credibility

Building credibility along two dimensions—your knowledge and your relationships— can enhance your persuasiveness. You will be more persuasive on subjects in which you are perceived to have expertise. Thus, either be or bring a subject-matter expert. On the *relationship* level, establishing and continually strengthening your relationships with the other side will also go a long way toward making you more persuasive. If you don't have a strong relationship with your counterparts, look to bring in people who already have one. For example, a new key account manager might want to enlist the aid of her predecessor, if that predecessor had a good relationship with the executive on the other side. Where possible, *plan ahead.* Build relationships with the people on the other side *before* the negotiations get started.

Match Your Appeal to Where the Other Side Is

Our colleagues Doug Stone, Bruce Patton, and Sheila Heen argue that conversations take place on multiple levels: the rational, the emotional, and the "identity" level. The rational conversation is all about facts: What happened, and what should happen? Who said what, and who did what? Many negotiators try to operate only on the rational level and are uncomfortable about acknowledging feelings in the context of a professional negotiation. But the fact is, many meaningful negotiations raise *feelings,* and some raise strong feelings. Rather than denying that fact, acknowledge it, and tailor your approach to take account of emotional issues. And pay attention as well to identity issues—the most fundamental issues of self-image and who we are: good/bad, competent/incompetent, and so on.

Respond to the Emotion When Your Counterpart Displays Emotion

A counterpart who is angry, tense, or hurt is unlikely to react constructively to or even be able to hear a rational appeal. While you normally want to *move* to the rational level in the negotiation, you often have a *choice* about whether to respond to the substance or respond to the emotion. It is usually better to respond first to the emotion and its underlying basis: "It sounds like you are pretty unhappy. I imagine I would be unhappy too if I understood the situation as you did." But being empathetic does not mean that you have to accept responsibility for the other person's feelings or allow these feelings to serve as a basis for action. Remember: be both empathetic *and* assertive. Once your counterpart's feelings are better understood and acknowledged, he or she may be able to engage more effectively in substantive discussion.

Let's raise one important caveat here. There are negotiators who use anger and intimidation as bargaining tactics. We know a successful investment banker who, at critical moments on conference calls, sometimes reaches into his pocket for his "angry man pills." It often works; the recipients try to buy their way back into his good graces with concessions. In such cases, the attacker may pull back as soon as he is convinced that these tactics won't work. In some cases, blustering back may be exactly what is needed; in others, ignoring the outburst can be most effective. A great deal depends on the specific person. Learning about their history and style is vital to avoid a "blind" response.

Sometimes, however, you need to step back and negotiate explicitly about the process of negotiation: "We have to tell you that we are offended by what felt to us like accusations and insults. We don't think discourse of this kind is going to help us resolve the problems we jointly need to resolve. We are not interested in continuing this kind of discussion. Would you prefer to take a break for half an hour so that we can refocus, or would you prefer to reschedule at a later date?"

Deal with Your Feelings, Too

You have feelings, too, and these are likely to be engaged by a difficult negotiation. You will be more effective if your feelings don't seep out in the form of barbed comments, sarcastic questions, or the inability to listen. You need to find an effective way to express your feelings without asking the other side to take responsibility for your feelings.

One way to do this is to make "I" statements rather than "you" statements. Rather than saying, "You are untrustworthy," try, "When you make me a verbal offer and then follow up with a letter of intent that doesn't seem to match it, it becomes hard for me to trust you."

It's also important to disentangle the *impact* of your counterparts' actions from their *intent*. The fact that their actions had a negative impact on you does not mean that the impact was intended. After you have delved into their intent, it can make sense to explain how you experienced the impact of these actions.

Make Your Appeal Work Through Their Cultural Filters

Culture matters in negotiation. You and your counterparts may have very different cultural perspectives on the purpose of the negotiation, on communication, and on appropriate and constructive behavior. Is a long silence awkward, a sign of respectful consideration, or a tactic to get the other side to blurt out something of use? When your negotiation crosses national borders—or straddles other kinds of divides—a conscious focus on culture can be helpful to effectively create and claim value.

Bookstores are full of books focusing on cross-cultural negotiation, mostly with an emphasis on surface behavior and etiquette—to get to "yes," should you "kiss, bow, or shake hands"? Some of this advice is useful. But if you are not sure about how to avoid unintentionally offensive acts or gestures, we suggest any number of handbooks that go deeper than surface behavior or, better, getting local advice. The point is to avoid falling prey to national cultural stereotypes, most of which contain at least a grain of truth, but many of which can be dramatically off base. For example, in its approach to decision making, Sony is less like a traditional, consensus-driven Japanese firm and more like a Western company. Similarly, when negotiating with U.S. counterparts, it matters a great deal whether you are on Wall Street or in Kansas.

And culture is not merely geographically based. For example, we sometimes find greater similarities among engineering-oriented firms from different countries than we do among, say, between marketing- and engineering-oriented companies from the same country.

Culture (whether national, corporate, or professional) is embodied in *expectations* of more than surface behavior. Indeed, while surface behavior is the tip of the iceberg, deeper culturally based issues are like the invisible mass under the surface, far more likely to cause a deadly crash. Table 1 highlights a number of such negotiation-related expectations that are strongly influenced by culture. Think of it as a kind of checklist as you move into less familiar territory. If you aren't confident in a given category, seek advice.

If you are negotiating in a culture in which agreements follow from relationships, as is often the case, for example, in South America, you're generally well advised to

TABLE 1 | Cultural Expectations in Negotiation

Deeper Expectations	
Negotiation objective	Is the ultimate goal of negotiation more a signed contract or a relationship between the two sides?
Fundamental view of negotiation process	Is negotiation a process through which both sides can gain, or through which one side gains and the other loses?
Social unit	Is it an individualistic or group-oriented culture?
Power/decision making	Does the other side make decisions in an authoritarian fashion, with one key person? Is it a small group process? Is there a formal or informal hierarchy involved? Is consensus required?
Implementation	How likely and expected is literal implementation of the agreement? Or is the deal merely a starting point for further negotiation?
Surface and Process Expectations	
Team organization and representation	What level, type, and number of team members are expected?
Etiquette	Introductions, business cards, gifts, and socializing before substance of negotiation; expected deference, etc.
Formality level	How formally does a negotiator talk to others, use titles, dress, speak, and interact with other people?
Communication	Do negotiators place emphasis on direct and simple methods of communication, or do they rely on indirect and complex methods? Is persuasion, for example, fact-based and technical in nature, driven by deductive logic, argued from precedent, or a function of the status of the would-be persuader?
Emotional expression	Do negotiators show or hide their feelings; that is, do they exhibit a high or low degree of emotionalism?
Risk and uncertainty tolerance	Do participants have a high or low propensity to take risks and handle uncertainty while negotiating? In deals?
Sensitivity to time	How important is it to minimize the time spent negotiating? Do negotiators exhibit a high or low degree of impatience and urgency? Many or few interruptions? Long or short time horizon?
Building an agreement	Does an agreement begin from general principles and proceed to specific items, or does it begin with agreement on specifics and build "up" to an overall deal?
Form of agreement	Do negotiators prefer detailed contracts or agreement on general principles?

begin by developing relationships, rather than jumping into the details of the deal. If the other side expects agreement to follow from the development of general principles—as might be the case in France, for example—don't come into the first meeting with a detailed term sheet. Instead, be prepared to introduce general principles and work out the *conception* of the deal first.

We have found that negotiators tend to overattribute problems in negotiations to cultural differences. A U.K. CEO, for example, persisted in attributing his French counterpart's actions to French "arrogance," although upon further investigation, we found that the French negotiators were following an entirely rational, and almost obvious, strategy. That said, getting the right cultural filters in place—national or otherwise—is an important input to our method. How the other side sees its interests (both in substance and in the process of negotiation) and understands the game you are jointly playing—and what its expectations are of that game—should be key inputs into your tactical choices.

Can You Write Their Victory Speech?

Can you write the thirty-second, three-minute, and ten-minute versions of the your counterparts' "victory speech"—the speech they would give to their peers, bosses, and spouses about why the agreement they made with you is smart, fair, reasonable, and better than the alternatives? The point is not altruism; if you can't convincingly write such a speech, your proposal may not be persuasive and you probably need to learn more about the other party's situation, interests, and no-deal alternatives. Beyond serving as a rough diagnostic, the victory-speech exercise may also help you in framing proposals to the other side that "let them have your way" (for their reasons, not yours).

Finally, keep in mind that the potential to create value does not mean that claiming tactics go away or are somehow irrelevant. Many of the tactics we describe in this chapter are designed to help you create value, claim a full share of that value, and defend yourself against exploitation.

We'll end the chapter by returning to research we discussed on the importance of focusing on the opportunity and not the downside, even to the extent of committing a brief paragraph to paper on your positive aspirations for the deal. Negotiators who emphasize the outcomes and behaviors they want to promote, as opposed to those they want to avoid, tend to do better in the kinds of situations we've been discussing. Focusing on the opportunity—the possibilities of creating value and claiming a full share, on a long-term basis—is likely to cause you to reach and sustain attractive agreements in your negotiations.

- Effective tactics must productively manage the tension between the cooperative moves necessary to create value jointly and the competitive moves to claim it individually. This means eliciting enough information to generate good options while managing your vulnerability.

- Ask, listen, and learn:

  - Listen actively.

  - Ask open-ended questions rather than yes/no questions: "What if? Why? Why not? How would that work for you?"

  - Bring a designated listener.

- Divulge information strategically:

  - Begin with the end: At the beginning, jointly envision the pot of gold at the end of the rainbow, perhaps by writing a press release in advance on the hoped-for outcome that meets everyone's core interests.

- Use the norm of reciprocity to build trust and share/gain information: start by offering low-risk information and ratchet up.
- Present multiple equivalent offers.
- Sequence issues carefully and negotiate in packages.

- Foster an appealing, productive negotiation process by establishing a positive atmosphere:
  - Psychologically place the parties side by side against the problem rather than face-to-face against each other.
  - Focus on advancing interests rather than arguing positions.
  - Focus on the future instead of the past and on problem solving instead of blaming.
  - Focus on disaggregated fact-based communications rather than high-level assertions.

- Adopt a persuasive style.
  - Be open to persuasion.
  - Be both empathetic *and* assertive.
  - Tell stories as well as using facts and logic.
  - Inoculate against potentially disadvantageous arguments.
  - Match your appeal to where your counterparts are and how they process information.
  - Make your appeal work through their cultural filters.

- For the deal that "lets them have your way," write your counterparts' victory speech, showing their key audiences why accepting your proposal was a wise decision.

Even at Megastores, Hagglers Find No Price Is Set in Stone

Matt Richtel

San Francisco—Shoppers are discovering an upside to the down economy. They are getting price breaks by reviving an age-old retail strategy: haggling.

A bargaining culture once confined largely to car showrooms and jewelry stores is taking root in major stores like Best Buy, Circuit City and Home Depot, as well as mom-and-pop operations.

Savvy consumers, empowered by the Internet and encouraged by a slowing economy, are finding that they can dicker on prices, not just on clearance items or big-ticket products like televisions but also on lower-cost goods like cameras, audio speakers, couches, rugs, and even clothing.

The change is not particularly overt, and most store policies on bargaining are informal. Some major retailers, however, are quietly telling their salespeople that negotiating is acceptable.

"We want to work with the customer, and if that happens to mean negotiating a price, then we're willing to look at that," said Kathryn Gallagher, a spokeswoman for Home Depot.

In the last year, she said, the store has adopted an "entrepreneurial spirit" campaign to give salespeople and managers more latitude on prices in order to retain customers.

The sluggish economy is punctuating a cultural shift enabled by wired consumers accustomed to comparing prices and bargaining online, said Nancy F. Koehn, a retail historian at the Harvard Business School.

Haggling was once common before department stores began setting fixed prices in the 1850s. But the shift to bargaining in malls and on Main Street is a considerable change from even 10 years ago, Ms. Koehn said, when studies showed that consumers did not like to bargain and did not consider themselves good at it. "Call it the eBay phenomenon," Ms. Koehn said.

"The recession is helping to push these seedlings to the surface," she added. "It's a real turnabout on the part of the buyer and the seller."

John D. Morris, an apparel industry analyst for Wachovia, said that the ailing economy was not necessarily forcing all retailers to negotiate. But he says he believes that when there is an opportunity for negotiation, the shopper has the upper hand.

"This is one of the periods where the customer is empowered," Mr. Morris said. "The retailer knows that the customer is enduring tough times—and is more willing to be the one who blinks first in that stare-down match."

While tough times give people more incentive to change their behavior, it is the wealth of information about products made available on the Internet that gives consumers the know-how to try it. People now can quickly amass information on product availability and pricing, helping them develop strategies to get the best deal.

Source: "Even at Megastores, Hagglers Find No Price Is Set in Stone," by Matt Richtel, from *The New York Times,* March 23, 2008. PARS International. Used with Permission.

Michael Roskell, 33, a technology project manager from Jersey City, N.J., said he and a friend from high school periodically visit electronics stores. While Mr. Roskell expresses interest in buying an item, his friend acts as though he is dissatisfied with the price and threatens to leave.

"We play good cop, bad cop," Mr. Roskell said.

In February, he said, the friends got $20 off a pair of $250 speakers at 6th Avenue Electronics in the New York area. Earlier, he and the same friend negotiated to buy two 46-inch high-definition Sony televisions at P. C. Richard & Son, a New York-area electronics chain.

List price: $4,300. Price after negotiation: $3,305.50.

"My parents never did this," Mr. Roskell said. "But once you get it, you realize there's a whole economy built on this."

The strategy can even work when buying pants. At least it did for David Achee of Maplewood, N.J., who said he went to a Polo Ralph Lauren store in the SoHo neighborhood of Manhattan last month and became interested in a pair of pants on the clearance rack for $75. He told the salesperson that he had seen a similar pair on the Internet for $65, adding that he thought the pair on the rack looked worn (even though he did not really think so). He got the pants for around $50, he said.

Among his other tactics, he said, he sometimes threatens to walk out of a store and go to a competitor, as he did recently to get a price break on a drum set at a music store. But, mainly, he relies on researching prices and coming armed with information— prices he finds on the Internet and in ads from competitors.

"You can negotiate, but you have to do your research," said Mr. Achee, who works for the Port Authority of New York and New Jersey. "When I'm bargaining, I'm bargaining with information."

Information from the Internet helped Amber Kendall, 24, and her husband, Matt, when they shopped for a camera last October. The couple, who live in Boston, found the Canon camera they wanted online for $350, then used the Internet price to bargain with Ritz Camera, where the price was $400. Then they used the Ritz Camera offer to get the same price at Microcenter, where they preferred the warranty offer.

The technological influences are not just on the consumer side. Retail industry analysts said corporate retailers have begun using computer systems that let them do real-time pricing and profit analysis. Such systems tell a company what price it can set and still make money, and they illuminate the trade-off between lowering prices and raising sales volumes, said Andy Hargreaves, a retail industry analyst with Pacific Crest Securities.

Mr. Hargreaves did a little negotiating himself recently. At Best Buy last November, he bargained down the price of a 50-inch Samsung plasma television.

"They gave me a number. I gave them another number, and he gave me a final number," he said, noting that he got a $100 price break in addition to the $200 sale discount. "A lot of people don't realize you can go into Best Buy and ask them for a lower price."

Frederick Stinchfield, 23, was a Best Buy salesman in Minnetonka, Minn., until last January. He said about one-quarter of customers tried to bargain. Much of the time, he said, he was able to oblige them, particularly in circumstances where a customer buying electronics (like a camera) also bought an accessory (like a camera bag) with a higher markup. He said the cash registers at Best Buy were set up so that prices could be reset at checkout.

Salespeople and managers had the latitude to drop prices, though some were more likely to do so than others.

His advice for bargainer hunters? "If you get denied once, go looking for someone else who looks nice," said Mr. Stinchfield, who now works for the federal government in Washington, D.C. He added: "Come armed with information, and you will be rewarded."

Priya Raghubir, a marketing professor at the Haas School of Business at the University of California, Berkeley, said that retailers willing to haggle were making a calculated gamble that acceding to lower prices means establishing customer loyalty. The retail mantra is "customer lifetime value," meaning any single sale might not be that profitable, but an enduring relationship with a shopper would be.

There is just one problem with the theory, Ms. Raghubir said. It does not prove true over time.

Rather than retaining customers, the rise in haggling is making shoppers highly price-conscious and loyal ultimately to the least expensive offer, not to a brand or a retailer.

Home Depot, among others, begs to differ. Ms. Gallagher, the company spokes-woman, said that by allowing salespeople and store managers to make some pricing decisions, the company was creating a friendly environment that feels more like a local store than a monolithic corporate superstore. (She declined to say how much leeway individual salespeople or managers have.)

Ms. Raghubir says that retailers are realizing that customers are going to keep pressing them on price, because whatever reticence customers had about bargaining has evaporated.

"In the past, when you tried to get yourself a deal and it was an embarrassing thing—the kind of thing you did if you couldn't afford to pay," she said. "Now it's about being a smart shopper."

Negotiation Subprocesses

Reading 2.1

Negotiating Rationally: The Power and Impact of the Negotiator's Frame

Margaret A. Neale

Max H. Bazerman

Everyone negotiates. In its various forms, negotiation is a common mechanism for resolving differences and allocating resources. While many people perceive negotiation to be a specific interaction between a buyer and a seller, this process occurs with a wide variety of exchange partners, such as superiors, colleagues, spouses, children, neighbors, strangers, or even corporate entities and nations. Negotiation is a decision-making process among interdependent parties who do not share identical preferences. It is through negotiation that the parties decide what each will give and take in their relationship.

The aspect of negotiation that is most directly controllable by the negotiator is how he or she makes decisions. The parties, the issues, and the negotiation environment are often predetermined. Rather than trying to change the environment surrounding the negotiation or the parties or issues in the dispute, we believe that the greatest opportunity to improve negotiator performance lies in the negotiator's ability to make effective use of the information available about the issues in dispute as well as the likely behavior of an opponent to reach more rational agreements and make more rational decisions within the context of negotiation.

To this end, we offer advice on how a negotiator should make decisions. However, to follow this advice for analyzing negotiations rationally, a negotiator must understand the psychological forces that limit a negotiator's effectiveness. In addition, rational decisions require that we have an optimal way of evaluating behavior of the opponent. This requires a psychological perspective for anticipating the likely decisions and subsequent behavior of the other party. Information such as this not only can create a framework that predicts how a negotiator structures problems, processes information, frames the situation, and evaluates alternatives but also can identify the limitations of his or her ability to follow rational advice.

Rationality refers to making the decision that maximizes the negotiator's interests. Since negotiation is a decision-making process that involves other people that do not

Source: "Negotiating Rationally: The Power and Impact of the Negotiator's Frame," by Margaret A. Neale and Max H. Bazerman, from *The Academy of Management Executive, 6*, no. 3, 1992, pp. 42–51. Used with permission.

have the same desires or preferences, the goal of a negotiation is not simply reaching an agreement. The goal of negotiations is to reach a *good* agreement. In some cases, no agreement is better than reaching an agreement that is not in the negotiator's best interests. When negotiated agreements are based on biased decisions, the chances of getting the best possible outcome are significantly reduced, and the probabilities of reaching an agreement when an impasse would have left the negotiator relatively better off are significantly enhanced.

A central theme of our work is that our natural decision and negotiation processes contain biases that prevent us from acting rationally and getting as much as we can out of a negotiation. These biases are pervasive, destroying the opportunities available in competitive contexts, and preventing us from negotiating rationally. During the last 10 or so years, the work that we and our colleagues have done suggests that negotiators make the following common cognitive mistakes: (1) negotiators tend to be overly affected by the frame, or form of presentation, of information in a negotiation; (2) negotiators tend to nonrationally escalate commitment to a previously selected course of action when it is no longer the most reasonable alternative; (3) negotiators tend to assume that their gain must come at the expense of the other party and thereby miss opportunities for mutually beneficial trade-offs between the parties; (4) negotiator judgments tend to be anchored upon irrelevant information—such as an initial offer; (5) negotiators tend to rely on readily available information; (6) negotiators tend to fail to consider information that is available by focusing on the opponent's perspective; and (7) negotiators tend to be overconfident concerning the likelihood of attaining outcomes that favor the individual(s) involved.

Describing the impact of each of these biases on negotiator behavior is obviously beyond the scope of this article. What we will attempt to do, however, is to focus on one particular and important cognitive bias, *framing,* and consider the impact of this bias on the process and outcome of negotiation. The manner in which negotiators frame the options available in a dispute can have a significant impact on their willingness to reach an agreement as well as the value of that agreement. In this article, we will identify factors that influence the choice of frame in a negotiation.

The Framing of Negotiations

Consider the following situation adapted from Russo and Schoemaker:[1]

> You are in a store about to buy a new watch which costs $70. As you wait for the sales clerk, a friend of yours comes by and remarks that she has seen an identical watch on sale in another store two blocks away for $40. You know that the service and reliability of the other store are just as good as this one. Will you travel two blocks to save $30?

Now consider this similar situation:

> You are in a store about to buy a new video camera that costs $800. As you wait for the sales clerk, a friend of yours comes by and remarks that she has seen an identical camera on sale in another store two blocks away for $770. You know that the service and reliability of the other store are just as good as this one. Will you travel two blocks to save the $30?

In the first scenario, Russo and Shoemaker report that about 90 percent of the managers presented this problem reported that they would travel the two blocks. However, in the second scenario, only about 50 percent of the managers would make the trip. What is the difference between the two situations that makes the $30 so attractive in the first scenario and considerably less attractive in the second scenario? One difference is that a $30 discount on a $70 watch represents a very good deal; the $30 discount on an $800 video camera is not such a good deal. In evaluating our willingness to walk two blocks, we frame the options in terms of the percentage discount. However, the correct comparison is not whether a percentage discount is sufficiently motivating, but whether the savings obtained is greater than the expected value of the additional time we would have to invest to realize those savings. So if a $30 savings were sufficient to justify walking two blocks for the watch, an opportunity to save $30 on the video camera should also be worth an equivalent investment of time.

Richard Thaler illustrated the influence of frames when he presented the following two versions of another problem to participants of an executive development program.[2]

> You are lying on the beach on a hot day. All you have to drink is ice water. For the last hour you have been thinking about how much you would enjoy a nice cold bottle of your favorite brand of beer. A companion gets up to make a phone call and offers to bring back a beer from the only nearby place where beer is sold: a fancy resort hotel. She says that the beer might be expensive and asks how much you are willing to pay for the beer. She will buy the beer if it costs as much as or less than the price you state. But if it costs more than the price you state, she will not buy it. You trust your friend and there is no possibility of bargaining with the bartender. What price do you tell your friend you are willing to pay?

Now consider this version of the same story:

> You are lying on the beach on a hot day. All you have to drink is ice water. For the last hour you have been thinking about how much you would enjoy a nice cold bottle of your favorite brand of beer. A companion gets up to make a phone call and offers to bring back a beer from the only nearby place where beer is sold: a small, run-down grocery store. She says that the beer might be expensive and asks how much you are willing to pay for the beer. She will buy the beer if it costs as much as or less than the price you state. But if it costs more than the price you state, she will not buy it. You trust your friend and there is no possibility of bargaining with the store owner. What price do you tell your friend you are willing to pay?

In both versions of the story, the results are the same: you get the same beer and there is no negotiating with the seller. Also you will not be enjoying the resort's amenities since you will be drinking the beer on the beach. Recent responses of executives at a Kellogg executive training program indicated that they were willing to pay significantly more if the beer were purchased at a "fancy resort hotel" ($7.83) than if the beer were purchased at the "small, run-down grocery store" ($4.10). The difference in price the executives were willing to pay for the same beer was based upon the frame they imposed on this transaction. Paying over $5 for a beer is an expected annoyance at a fancy resort hotel; however, paying over $5 for a beer at a run-down grocery store is an obvious "rip-off." So even though the same beer is purchased and we enjoy none of the benefits of the fancy resort hotel, we are willing to pay almost a dollar more because of the way in which we frame the purchase. The converse of this situation is probably familiar to many of us. Have you ever purchased an item because "it was too good of a deal to pass up," even though you had no use for it? We seem to assign a greater value to the quality of the transaction over and above the issue of what we get for what we pay.

Both of these examples emphasize the importance of the particular frames we place on problems we have to solve or decisions we have to make. Managers are constantly being exposed to many different frames, some naturally occurring and others that are purposefully proposed. An important task of managers is to identify the appropriate frame by which employees and the organization, in general, should evaluate its performance and direct its effort.

The Framing of Risky Negotiations

The way in which information is framed (in terms of either potential gains or potential losses) to the negotiator can have a significant impact on his or her preference for risk, particularly when uncertainty about future events or outcomes is involved. For example, when offered the choice between gains of equal expected value—one for certain and the other a lottery—we strongly prefer to take the *certain* gain. However, when we are offered the choice between potential losses of equal expected value, we clearly and consistently eschew the loss for certain and prefer the risk inherent in the *lottery*.

There is substantial evidence to suggest that we are not indifferent toward risky situations and we should not necessarily trust our intuitions about risk. Negotiators routinely deviate from rationality because they do not typically appreciate the transient nature of their preference for risk; nor do they take into consideration the ability of a particular decision frame to influence that preference. Influencing our attitudes toward risk through the positive or negative frames associated with the problem is the result of evaluating an alternative from a particular referent point or base line. A referent point is the basis by which we evaluate whether what we are considering is viewed as a gain or a loss. The referent point that we choose determines the frame we impose on our options and, subsequently, our willingness to accept or reject those options.

Consider the high-performing employee who is expecting a significant increase in salary this year. He frames his expectations on the past behavior of the company. As such, he is expecting a raise of approximately $5,000. Because of the recession, he receives a $3,500 salary increase. He immediately confronts his manager, complaining that he has been unfairly treated. He is extremely disappointed in what his surprised manager saw as an exceptional raise because the employee's referent point is $1,500 higher. Had he known that the average salary increase was only $2,000 (and used that as a more realistic referent point), he would have perceived the same raise quite differently, and it may have had the motivating force that his manager had hoped to create.

The selection of which the relevant frame influences our behavior is a function of our selection of a base line by which we evaluate potential outcomes. The choice of one referent point over another may be the result of a visible anchor, the "status quo," or our expectations. Probably one of the most common referent points is what we perceive to be in our current inventory (our status quo)—what is ours already. We then evaluate offers or options in terms of whether they make us better off (a gain) or worse off (a loss) from what (we perceive to be) our current resource state.

Interestingly, what we include in our current resource state is surprisingly easy to modify. Consider the executive vice president of a large automobile manufacturer concern that has been hit by a number of economic difficulties because of the recession in the United States. It appears as if she will have to close down three plants, and the employee rolls will be trimmed by 6,000 individuals. In exploring ways to avoid this alternative, she has identified two plans that might ameliorate the situation. If she selects the first plan, she will be able to save 2,000 jobs and one of the three plants. If she implements the second plan, there is a one-third probability that she can save all three plants and all 6,000 jobs, but there is a two-thirds probability that this plan will end up saving none of the plants and none of the jobs. If you were this vice president, which plan would you select? Plan 1 or Plan 2?

Now consider the same options (Plan 1 or Plan 2) framed as losses: If the vice president implements Plan 1, two of the three plants will be shut down and 4,000 jobs will be lost. If she implements Plan 2, then there is a two-thirds probability of losing all three plants and all 6,000 jobs, but there is a one-third probability of losing no plants and no jobs. If you were presented with these two plans, which would be more attractive? Plan 1 or Plan 2?

It is obvious that from a purely economic perspective, there is no difference between the two choices. Yet managers offered the plans framed in terms of gains select the first plan about 76 percent of the time. However, managers offered the choice between the plans framed in terms of losses select the first plan only about 22 percent of the time. When confronted with potential losses, the lottery represented by Plan 2 becomes relatively much more attractive.

An important point for managers to consider is that the way in which the problem is framed, or presented, can dramatically alter the perceived value or acceptability of alternative courses of action. In negotiation, for example, the more risk-averse course of action is to accept an offered settlement; the more risk-seeking course of action is to hold out for future, potential concessions. In translating the influence of the framing bias to negotiation, we must realize that the selection of a particular referent point or base line determines whether a negotiator will frame his or her decision as positive or negative.

Specifically, consider any recurring contract negotiation. As the representative of Company A, the offer from Company B can be viewed in two ways, depending on the referent point I use. If my referent point were the current contract, Company B's offer can be evaluated in terms of the "gains" Company A can expect relative to the previous contract. However, if the referent point for Company A is an initial offer on the issues under current consideration, then Company A is more likely to evaluate Company B's offers as losses to be incurred if the contract as proposed is accepted. Viewing options as losses or as gains will have considerable impact on the negotiator's willingness to accept side B's position—even though the same options may be offered in both cases.

Likewise, the referent points available to an individual negotiating his salary for a new position in the company include (1) his current salary; (2) the company's initial offer; (3) the least he is willing to accept; (4) his estimate of the most the company is willing to pay; or (5) his initial salary request. As his referent moves from 1 to 5, he progresses from a positive to a negative frame in the negotiation. What is a modest *gain* compared to his current wage is perceived as a loss when compared to what he would like to receive. Along these same lines, employees currently making $15/hour and demanding an increase of $4/hour can view a proposed increase of $2/hour as a $2/hour gain in comparison to last year's wage (Referent 1) or as a $2/hour loss in comparison to their stated or initial proposal of $19/hour (Referent 5). Consequently, the location of the referent point is critical to whether the decision is positively or negatively framed and affects the resulting risk preference of the decision maker.

In a study of the impact of framing on collective bargaining outcomes, we used a five-issue negotiation with participants playing the roles of management or labor negotiators.[3] Each negotiator's frame was manipulated by adjusting his or her referent point. Half of the negotiators were told that any concessions they make from their initial offers represented losses to their constituencies (i.e., a negative frame). The other half were told that any agreements they were able to reach that were better than the current contract were gains to their constituencies (i.e., the positive frame). In analyzing the results of their negotiations, we found that negatively framed negotiators were less concessionary and reached fewer agreements than positively framed negotiators. In addition, negotiators who had positive frames perceived the negotiated outcomes as more fair than those who had negative frames.

In another study, we posed the following problem to negotiators:

> You are a wholesaler of refrigerators. Corporate policy does not allow any flexibility in pricing. However, flexibility does exist in terms of expenses that you can incur (shipping, financing terms, etc.), which have a direct effect on the profitability of the transaction. These expenses can all be viewed in dollar value terms. You are negotiating an $8,000 sale. The buyer wants you to pay $2,000 in expenses. You want to pay less expenses. When you negotiate the exchange, do you try to minimize your expenses (reduce them from $2,000) or maximize net profit, i.e., price less expenses (increase the net profit from $6,000)?

From an objective standpoint, the choice you make to reduce expenses or maximize profit should be irrelevant. Because the choice objectively is between two identical options, selecting one or the other should have no impact on the outcome of the negotiation. What we did find, in contrast, is that the frame that buyers and sellers take into the negotiation can systematically affect their behavior.[4]

In one study, negotiators were led to view transactions in terms of either (1) net profit or (2) total expenses deducted from gross profits. These two situations were objectively identical. Managers can think about maximizing their profits (i.e., gains) or minimizing their expenses (i.e., losses). These choices are linked: If one starts from the same set of revenues, then one way to maximize profits is to minimize expenses; and if one is successful at minimizing expenses, the outcome is that profit may be maximized. That is, there is an obvious relationship between profits and expenses. So objectively, there is no reason to believe that an individual should behave differently if given the instructions to minimize expenses or to maximize profits. However, those negotiators told to maximize profit (i.e., a positive frame) were more concessionary. In addition, positively framed negotiators completed significantly more transactions than their negatively framed (those told to minimize expenses) counterparts. Because they completed more transactions, their overall profitability in the market was higher, although negatively framed negotiators completed transactions of greater mean profit.[5]

The Endowment Effect

The ease with which we can alter our referent points was illustrated in a series of studies conducted by Daniel Kahneman, Jack Knetsch, and Richard Thaler.[6] In any exchange between a buyer and a seller, the buyer must be willing to pay at least the minimum amount the seller is willing to accept for a trade to take place. In determining the worth of an object, its value to the seller may, on occasion, be determined by some objective third party such as an economic market. However, in a large number of transactions, the seller places a value on the item—a value that may include not only the market value of the item but also a component for an emotional attachment to or unique appreciation of the item. What impact might such an attachment have on the framing of the transaction?

Let's imagine that you have just received a coffee mug.[7] (In the actual demonstration, coffee mugs were placed before one-third of the participants, the "sellers," in the study.) After receiving the mug, you are told that in fact you "own the object (coffee mug) in your possession. You have the option of selling it if a price, to be determined later, is acceptable to you." Next you are given a list (see Exhibit 1) of possible selling prices, ranging from $.50 to $9.50, and are told for each of the possible prices, you should indicate whether you would (*a*) sell the mug and receive that amount in return, or (*b*) keep the object and take it home with you. What is your selling price for the mug?

Another third of the group (the "buyers") were told that they would be receiving a sum of money and they could choose to keep the money or use it to buy a mug. They

---

EXHIBIT 1 | The Coffee Mug Questionnaire

For each price listed below, indicate whether you would be willing to sell the coffee mug for that price or keep the mug.

If the price is $0.50, I will sell _____ ; I will keep the mug _____.
If the price is $1.00, I will sell _____ ; I will keep the mug _____.
If the price is $1.50, I will sell _____ ; I will keep the mug _____.
If the price is $2.00, I will sell _____ ; I will keep the mug _____.
If the price is $2.50, I will sell _____ ; I will keep the mug _____.
If the price is $3.00, I will sell _____ ; I will keep the mug _____.
If the price is $3.50, I will sell _____ ; I will keep the mug _____.
If the price is $4.00, I will sell _____ ; I will keep the mug _____.
If the price is $4.50, I will sell _____ ; I will keep the mug _____.
If the price is $5.00, I will sell _____ ; I will keep the mug _____.
If the price is $5.50, I will sell _____ ; I will keep the mug _____.
If the price is $6.00, I will sell _____ ; I will keep the mug _____.
If the price is $6.50, I will sell _____ ; I will keep the mug _____.
If the price is $7.00, I will sell _____ ; I will keep the mug _____.
If the price is $7.50, I will sell _____ ; I will keep the mug _____.
If the price is $8.00, I will sell _____ ; I will keep the mug _____.
If the price is $8.50, I will sell _____ ; I will keep the mug _____.
If the price is $9.00, I will sell _____ ; I will keep the mug _____.
If the price is $9.50, I will sell _____ ; I will keep the mug _____.

were also asked to indicate their preferences between a mug and sums of money ranging from $.50 to $9.50. Finally, the last third of the participants (the "choosers") were given a questionnaire indicating that they would later be given an option of receiving either a mug or a sum of money to be determined later. They indicated their preferences between the mug and sums of money between $.50 and $9.50. All of the participants were told that their answers would not influence either the predetermined price of the mug or the amount of money to be received in lieu of the mug.

The sellers reported a median value of $7.12 for the mug; the buyers valued the mug at $2.88; and the choosers valued the mug at $3.12. It is interesting that in this exercise, being a buyer or a chooser resulted in very similar evaluations of worth of the mug. However, owning the mug (the sellers) created a much greater sense of the mug's worth. In this case, it was approximately 40 percent greater than the market (or retail) value of the mug.

The explanation for this disparity lies in the fact that different roles (buyer, seller, or chooser) created different referent points. In fact, what seems to happen in such situations is that owning something changes the nature of the owner's relationship to the commodity. Giving up that item is now perceived as loss, and in valuing the item, the owner may include a dollar value to offset his or her perceived loss. If we consider this discrepancy in the value of an item common, then the simple act of "owning" an item, however briefly, can increase one's personal attachment to an item—and typically, its perceived value. After such an attachment is formed, the cost of breaking that attachment is greater and is reflected in the higher price the sellers demand to part with their mugs as compared to the value the buyers or the choosers place on the exact same commodity. In addition, we would expect that the endowment effect intensifies to the extent that the value of the commodity of interest is ambiguous or subjective, or the commodity itself is unique or not easily substitutable in the marketplace.

Framing, Negotiator Bias, and Strategic Behavior

In the previous discussion, we described the negotiator behaviors that may arise from positive and negative frames within the context of the interaction. In this section, we identify some of the techniques for strategically manipulating framing to direct negotiator performance.

Framing has important implications for negotiator tactics. Using the framing effect to induce a negotiating opponent to concede requires that the negotiator create referents that lead the opposition to a positive frame by couching the proposal in terms of their potential gain. In addition, the negotiator should emphasize the inherent risk in the negotiation situation and the opportunity for a sure gain. As our research suggests, simply posing problems as choices among potential gains rather than choices among potential losses can significantly influence the negotiator's preferences for specific outcomes.

Framing can also have important implications for how managers choose to intervene in dispute among their peers or subordinates. Managers, of course, have a wide range of options to implement when deciding to intervene in disputes in which they are not active principals. If the manager's goal is to get the parties to reach an agreement rather than having the manager decide what the solution to the dispute will be, he or she may wish to facilitate both parties' viewing the negotiation from a positive frame. This is tricky, however, since the same referent that will lead to a positive frame for one negotiator is likely to lead to a negative frame for the other negotiator if presented simultaneously to the parties. Making use of the effects of framing may be most appropriate when a manager can meet with each side separately. He or she may present different perspectives to each party to create a positive frame (and the subsequent risk-averse behavior associated with such a frame) for parties on both sides of the dispute. Again, if the manager is to affect the frame of the problem in such a way to encourage agreement, he or she may also emphasize the possible losses inherent in continuing the dispute. Combining these two strategies may facilitate both sides' preference for the certainty of a settlement.

Being in the role of buyer or seller can be a naturally occurring frame that can influence negotiator behavior in systematic ways. Consider the curious, consistent, and robust finding in a number of studies that buyers tend to outperform sellers in market settings in which the balance of power is equal.[8] Given the artificial context of the laboratory settings and the symmetry of the design of these field and laboratory markets, there is no logical reason why buyers should do better than sellers. One explanation for this observed difference may be that when the commodity is anonymous (or completely substitutable in a market sense), sellers may think about the transaction in terms of the dollars exchanged. That is, sellers may conceptualize the process of selling as gaining resources (e.g., how many dollars do I gain by selling the commodity); whereas buyers may view the transaction in terms of loss of dollars (e.g., how many dollars do I have to give up). If the dollars are the primary focus of the participants' attention, then buyers would tend to be risk seeking and sellers risk averse in the exchange.

When a risk-averse party (i.e., the seller, in this example) negotiates with a risk-seeking party (i.e., the buyer), the buyer is more willing to risk the potential agreement by demanding more or being less concessionary. To reach agreement, the seller must make additional concessions to induce the buyer, because of his or her risk-seeking propensity, to accept the agreement. Thus in situations where the relative achievements of buyers and seller can be directly compared, buyers would benefit from their negative frame (and subsequent risk-averse behavior). The critical issue is that these naturally occurring frames such as the role demands of being a "buyer" or "seller" can easily influence the way in which the disputed issues are framed—even without the conscious intervention of one or more of the parties.

It is easy to see that the frames of negotiators can result in the difference between impasse and reaching an important agreement. Both sides in negotiations typically talk in terms of a certain wage, price, or outcome that they must get—setting a high referent point against which gains and losses are measured. If this occurs, any compromise below (or above) that point represents a loss. This perceived loss may lead negotiators to adopt a negative frame to all proposals, exhibit risk-seeking behaviors, and be less likely to reach settlement. Thus negotiators, similar to the early example involving the beach and the beer, may end up with no beer (or no agreement) because of the frame (the amount of money I will pay for a beer from a run-down grocery store) that is placed on the choices rather than an objective assessment of what the beer is worth to the individual.

In addition, framing has important implications for the tactics that negotiators use. The framing effect suggests that to induce concessionary behavior from an opponent, a negotiator should always create anchors or emphasize referents that lead the opposition to a positive frame and couch the negotiation in terms of what the other side has to gain.

In addition, the negotiator should make the inherent risk salient to the opposition while the opponent is in a risky situation. If the sure gain that is being proposed is rejected, there is no certainty about the quality of the next offer. Simultaneously, the negotiator should also not be persuaded by similar arguments from opponents. Maintaining a risk-neutral or risk-seeking perspective in evaluating an opponent's proposals may, in the worst case, reduce the probability of reaching an agreement; however, if agreements are reached, the outcomes are more likely to be of greater value to the negotiator.

An important component in creating good negotiated agreements is to avoid the pitfalls of being framed while, simultaneously, understanding the impact of positively and negatively framing your negotiating opponent. However, framing is just one of a series of cognitive biases that can have a significant negative impact on the performance of negotiators. The purpose of this article was to describe the impact of one of these cognitive biases on negotiator behavior by considering the available research on the topic and to explore ways to reduce the problems associated with framing. By increasing our understanding of the subtle ways in which these cognitive biases can reduce the effectiveness of our negotiations, managers can begin to not only improve the quality of agreements for themselves but also fashion agreements that more efficiently allocate the available resources—leaving both parties and the communities of which they are a part better off.

Notes

This article is based on the book by M. H. Bazerman, and M. A. Neale, *Negotiating Rationally* (New York: Free Press, 1992).

1. Adapted from J. E. Russo and P. J. Schoemaker, *Decision Traps* (New York: Doubleday, 1989).

2. R. Thaler, "Using Mental Accounting in a Theory of Purchasing Behavior," *Marketing-Science 4* (1985), pp. 12–13.

3. M. A. Neale and M. H. Bazerman, "The Effects of Framing and Negotiator Overconfidence," *Academy of Management Journal 28* (1985), pp. 34–49.

4. M. H. Bazerman, T. Magliozzi, and M. A. Neale, "The Acquisition of an Integrative Response in a Competitive Market Simulation," *Organizational Behavior and Human Performance 34* (1985), pp. 294–313.

5. See, for example, Bazerman, Magliozzi, and Neale (1985); Neale and Bazerman, (1985); M. A. Neale and G. B. Northcraft, "Experts, Amateurs, and Refrigerators: Comparing Expert and Amateur Decision Making on a Novel Task," *Organizational Behavior and Human Decision Processes 38* (1986), pp. 305–17; M. A. Neale, V. L. Huber, and G. B. Northcraft, "The Framing of Negotiations: Context versus Task Frames," *Organizational Behavior and Human Decision Processes 39* (1987), pp. 228–41.

6. D. Kahneman, J. L. Knetsch, and R. Thaler, "Experimental Tests of the Endowment Effect and Coarse Theorem," *Journal of Political Economy* (1990).

7. The coffee mugs were valued at approximately $5.00.

8. Bazerman et al., (1985); M. A. Neale, V. L. Huber, and G. B. Northcraft, (1987).

Managers and Their Not-So Rational Decisions

S. Trevis Certo
Brian L. Connelly
Laszlo Tihanyi

Today's corporate environment requires managers to be excellent decision makers. Their ability to make fast, widely supported, and effective decisions will, in large part, shape the performance of their firms. In this article, we describe two cognitive systems that influence decision making. System 1 refers to a process that is fast, effortless, and intuitive. System 2 is a slow, controlled, and rule-governed decision-making process. Both are important to a wide variety of managerial decisions, and they interact with each other. There are, however, a number of forces at work that hinder the effectiveness of these processes. For example, we know from prospect theory that managers are unwilling to incur loss, so much so that they often make irrational decisions based on a small probability that they could avoid such loss. Another example, the escalation of commitment, explains why managers may continue to dedicate resources to failed projects. We describe these and other biases, with a view toward helping managers better understand the problems of decision making and improve the effectiveness of their decisions.

Managerial Decision Making

Each day, practicing managers around the globe make decisions, some of which are more important than others. Based on the prominence of decision making in everyday life, researchers in various disciplines—both within and outside of business schools—have examined the ways in which individuals make decisions. That various disciplines within business schools have studied decision making should come as no surprise, as managers make decisions that span the various business functions.

Webster's Dictionary defines decision as "the act of making up one's mind." Hastie (2001) suggests that decisions involve three main components: courses of action (i.e., alternatives), beliefs about objective states and processes (including outcome states), and desires (i.e., utilities) that correspond to the outcomes associated with each potential action–event combination. Stated more simply, Hastie suggests that good decisions are those which link decision-makers' utilities with decision outcomes.

In business settings, managers make various types of decisions. Managers may make relatively minor decisions that are primarily operational or tactical in nature. For example, a manager may need to decide which type of napkins to stock in a restaurant. In contrast, managers may make more strategic decisions that involve larger outlays of capital. Such strategic decisions may include, for example, potential acquisition targets or host countries for foreign direct investment.

A decision implies that an individual has access to two or more alternatives. Some decisions may involve many alternatives, such as "Which country should we enter

Source: "Managers and their not-so rational decisions," by S. Trevis Certo, Brian L. Connelly, and Laszlo Tihanyi, from *Business Horizons, 51,* no. 2, March–April 2008, pp. 113–119. Kelley School of Business. Used with permission.

to begin our globalization effort?" In contrast, other decisions may involve only two alternatives (i.e., "yes/no" decisions), such as "Should I hire this individual to work in our department?" In fact, Henry Mintzberg studied the decision-making processes used by executives and found most decisions that executives faced were yes/no decisions (Mintzberg, 1975).

The decisions managers make vary in risk and uncertainty. Although some managers use these two terms interchangeably, they are, in fact, distinct. Frank Knight (1921) suggested long ago that *risk* refers to situations in which statistical probabilities can be assigned to alternative potential outcomes. The probabilities associated with the outcomes of roulette, for example, are known to individuals in advance. In contrast, *uncertainty* refers to situations whereby the probability that a particular outcome will occur cannot be determined in advance. A manager, for instance, may be unable articulate the probability that R&D expenditures will increase a firm's sales in five years.

It is important to note, though, that risk and uncertainty are not always objective standards. Specifically, two managers may ascribe differing levels of uncertainty or risk to the same decision. To this end, scholars have examined the role of perceptions in understanding how these characteristics may influence decisions (e.g., Weber, Anderson, & Birnbaum, 1992).

How Managers Make Decisions

There exists a sizeable literature—descriptive and normative—related to decision making. Perhaps the most prominent assumption in this body of literature is that decision makers are rational. Among scholars working in this arena, decision makers are understood to vary with respect to their beliefs, opinions, and preferences, but rationality deals with the notion that these should cohere in a defensible fashion (Shafir & LeBoeuf, 2002). This explanation complements the assertion by Eisenhardt and Zbaracki (1992, p. 18) that "In its most basic form, the rational model of choice follows the everyday assumption that human behavior has some purpose." Summarizing the decision-making literature and the role of rationality, Shafir and LeBoeuf (2002, p. 492) suggest that "the rationality assumption has come to constitute perhaps the most common and pivotal assumption underlying theoretical accounts of human behavior in various disciplines."

Despite the dominant stronghold of rationality in decision-making research, some scholars have questioned this assumption. Herbert Simon (1957) introduced the concept of bounded rationality, which suggests that managers make imperfect decisions due to a variety of factors including lack of information, inadequate time, and cognitive limitations. Simon's work suggests that managers could make better decisions, if only they could access the necessary resources. Instead, though, managers are often forced to make decisions without the resources necessary to ensure decision-making success. Simon labeled this process of making decisions that are suboptimal yet "good enough" as *satisficing*.

Decision-Making Processes

As decision-making research progressed, scholars began to question whether or not a single process properly described decision making. Stanovich and West (2002) summarized this research by suggesting that two cognitive systems, which they labeled as

System 1 and System 2, influence decision making. According to their framework, System 1 refers to a process that is described as fast, automatic, effortless, and often emotional. Kahneman (2003) suggests that this system relies, to some extent, on habit and is difficult to break. Some scholars roughly equate this system to a decision-maker's intuition or instincts (see also Miller & Ireland, 2005).

In contrast, System 2 is described as slow, controlled, requiring effort, rule-governed, and flexible (Kahneman, 2003). This system is often typified as a more "rational" decision-making process. Bazerman (2006) describes, for example, a rational decision-making process that includes steps such as defining the problem, identifying relevant criteria, weighting these criteria, generating alternatives, rating alternatives on each criterion, and computing the optimal decisions.[1] Some scholars propose that System 1 is less developed, while System 2 has evolved over time (for a synopsis, see Morse, 2006). This line of reasoning is consistent with Evans' (2003) assertion that humans and animals share System 1 processes, but System 2 is believed to have evolved more recently and is uniquely human.

Both System 1 and System 2 processes are important to managerial decision making, and one is not inherently preferred over the other. For most people, these two processes work together in such a way that System 2 monitors the activities of System 1, either confirming or denying intuitive decisions. It would be impossible for managers to operate using comprehensive System 2 processes for every decision they face, so they often rely on System 1 processes wherever it is sufficient and practical (Chugh, 2004). In fact, skilled decision makers may actually make higher-quality decisions when they rely on their intuition rather than relying on purely economic utility functions. For example, a manager who has a hunch about hard-to-quantify potential synergies in a proposed acquisition may be operating under System 1 processes, but the manager would later confirm these hunches through the System 2 process of due diligence.

While both processes may work in tandem, they are also susceptible to biases that interfere with our ability to make good decisions. Most people are aware that biases can create false impressions and distort intuitive judgment, but biases also affect System 2 processes, causing managers to make irrational decisions. In the remainder of this article, we describe some of the most significant biases and how they affect managerial decision making.

Decision-Making Biases

Daniel Kahneman, the 2002 Nobel Laureate in economics, made many important contributions to rational decision-making theory in conjunction with Amos Tversky. Prospect theory, as their collective ideas came to be known, describes several potential systematic biases derived from laboratory experiments.[2] The results of these experiments cast doubt on the rational choices executives make.

Framing and Loss Aversion

One of the most common biases in decision making involves framing. When executives make decisions, they may frame the potential outcomes of their decisions differently relative to an earlier status quo. For example, some executives of a firm may consider a takeover or a buyout offer as the ideal solution to the firm's problems. Others within the firm may believe that the same transaction is destructive. Whether an option is framed as a gain or as a loss can lead to systematic differences in decision-makers' preferences, and may result in different outcomes for the firms involved.

When options are framed as potential for loss, prospect theory describes how managers may be irrationally unwilling to incur loss. The idea behind loss aversion is an observed asymmetry between perceived gains and losses. Results of several experiments suggest that decision makers are approximately twice more likely to try to avoid losses than favor gains; that is, their "value function" is twice as steep when they consider losses than when they consider gains. The perception that losses appear larger than equal-size gains forms the basis of the endowment effect in economics. Thaler (1980) found that individuals value their own goods that they consider selling more than they value goods that they consider buying. One practical implication of loss aversion was described by Odean (1998) in a study on investor behavior. This work suggests that investors hold on to their losing stocks too long, but sell their winning investments too soon.

Avoiding such loss aversion bias is nearly impossible, but being aware of its existence can help managers make better decisions. Furthermore, anticipation of loss aversion by competitors, buyers, or suppliers can improve the effectiveness of decision making. A recent article by Mercer (2005) lists several examples of the loss aversion bias from political science. Because the examples described above are from field settings rather than laboratory studies, they are more readily applicable to competitive conditions, the environment whereby many managerial decisions are made.

Risk Seeking

In contrast to loss aversion, prospect theory researchers have also observed that decision makers irrationally seek risk. Risk-seeking behavior works in two different ways. First, individuals will take irrational risks when the alternative is a certain loss, despite the fact that System 2 processes should lead them to the opposite conclusion. This is actually the other side of the loss aversion coin, because it suggests that individuals strongly prefer risks that might possibly mitigate a loss. For example, managers may prefer a product development project with a high probability of large loss over a development project with a certain, but much smaller, loss. Second, individuals will take irrational risks when the potential payoff is unusually large. An example of this is evident in lottery jackpot events, whereby individuals are willing to bet for a large prize, despite its associated small probability. Here again, there appears to be a bias toward the potentially large payoff that distorts System 2 decision making.

Contrary to the principles of rationality, risk-seeking preferences also tend to be nonlinear. That is, when the probability of an event increases by the same rate but may lead to a different outcome, people make their decisions differently. For example, a .01 increase in the probability of an event occurring appears to be different for decision makers if this increase is added to an earlier low probability (e.g., .25) as compared to an earlier high probability (e.g., .99).

We see an example of risk seeking in the recent decisions made by Jeroen van der Veer. After taking the helm as CEO of Royal Dutch Shell PLC, van der Veer abolished the old board structure, streamlined decision making, and effectively concentrated power in the CEO position. The new structure facilitated risk-seeking behavior and was followed by a series of high-risk investments. Rather than maintain the long-held and stable portfolio of traditional oil-development deals, van der Veer placed big bets on multi-billion dollar projects in places such as Qatar and Russia's Far East. *The Wall Street Journal* calls the strategy a gamble that is paying off for now, but, as van der Veer admits, it is still too early to deem the project an outright success (Cummins & Chazan, 2007).

Source Dependence

Source dependence is based on the observation that decision makers often consider the source of an uncertain event, in addition to its level. For example, people may prefer to bet on a familiar sporting event, such as the NCAA Basketball March Madness, than on a matched chance event (e.g., a coin toss), regardless of the clearer probability in the chance event. Source dependence bias may explain failed acquisitions in seemingly related industries or failed investments in stocks of well-known but risky firms, in the areas of technology, communication, and entertainment.

The problem of source dependence was likely a contributing factor to the recent collapse of the sub-prime mortgage industry. Banks and lenders are familiar with both mortgages and the underlying housing market. As housing prices boomed, they felt comfortable offering progressively easier and riskier lending terms. The number of no- or low-documentation loans increased three-fold from 2001 to 2006, placing lenders in a highly risky position. It is unlikely that they would have placed such high-risk bets in other, less familiar industries. When housing prices slumped nationwide, their position was exposed and delinquencies skyrocketed.

Escalation of Commitment

Calvin Coolidge famously noted the importance of perseverance when he declared, "persistence and determination alone are omnipotent." While there are virtues associated with trying again in the face of failure, problems arise when executives remain committed to a course of action despite mounting evidence that the action is not paying off. In fact, research suggests that decision makers are likely to allocate more funds to an investment project when feedback shows that the project is failing than when the project is succeeding (Staw & Ross, 1989). Perhaps owing to personal responsibility or ego, decision makers seem to interpret negative feedback as a signal that they should commit additional resources in order to save a project to which they were initially committed. Even though the initial decision was made on a rational System 2 basis, subsequent decisions may be irrational as they involve continued, and escalating, investment in a failing course of action.

History is replete with decisions that appear to have been influenced by irrational escalation of commitment. For example, the tunnel mega-project commonly known as "the Big Dig" was conceived, designed, and undertaken to relieve congestion of Boston's tangled historical streets. The project, initially estimated at a cost of $2.6 billion, was plagued with a wide variety of implementation, environmental, and human resource problems from the beginning. Learning of serious problems at various stages of construction, turnpike officials and politicians continued to allocate additional funding. The Big Dig was completed in 2006, with expenses totaling over $15 billion. Once the plans were in place and unexpected problems arose, a process of escalating commitment began that would have been very difficult to reverse.

Escalation of commitment may affect a broad array of business decisions. Shimizu and Hitt (2005), for example, found that many firms retained unprofitable business units with steadily mounting losses for years without divesting them. In several cases the arrival of outside executives, who were not involved in the initial acquisition decision, was needed to hasten divestiture of the failing division. Others have found evidence of this bias in the new product development process. Schmidt and Calantone (2002), for instance, found that managers who initiated a new product were less likely to perceive it as failing and were more likely to continue funding the project despite evidence of failure than those who assumed leadership after the product was launched. Escalation of commitment often occurs for another common business decision: information technology (IT) investment. Many internal IT projects become "runaways" that continue to receive funding in excess of their benefits (Nulden, 1996). Together, these findings suggest that simply giving managers more information wilt not necessarily lead to better decisions. Instead, organizational, social, and psychological factors combine such that those who were involved in an initial decision may interpret negative incoming information differently than those who arrive later.

Overconfidence

There exists a substantial literature highlighting the egos of business executives (Hiller & Hambrick, 2005). This literature reflects a natural tendency to overestimate our abilities and perceived chances of success. This bias is sometimes called the Lake Wobegon effect, named for Garrison Keillor's humorous musings on the human condition as he describes the people of Lake Wobegon, "where all the women are strong, all the men are good-looking, and all the children are above average." Although assessments of self-competence vary based on the task being performed, overconfidence may span across multiple contexts. If individuals reassessed their behaviors, attributes, and abilities in light of changing tasks, they might avoid forming inflated estimates. This often does not happen, though, because past success becomes the primary influence in forming future beliefs. Falsely assuming that prior patterns of successful behavior will continue to work under new conditions, people overestimate their ability to succeed at tasks under new and changing requirements.

William Smithburg, CEO of Quaker, displayed such hubris and serves as an apt illustration. Renowned for his highly successful and almost impulsive acquisition of Gatorade, Smithburg purchased the brand for $220 million and grew its worth to several billion dollars, representing nearly half of Quaker's sales. This success in hand, Smithburg embarked on an acquisition of Snapple for $1.4 billion. Industry analysts voiced concern because Snapple was outside the mass-market arena, did not have manufacturing or distribution synergies with Gatorade, and was carrying obsolete material due to poor inventory management (Nutt, 2004). Despite these apprehensions, Smithburg was confident that he could succeed where others had failed in turning the Snapple brand into a money maker; unfortunately, the overconfidence effect potentially distorted his estimation of the problems associated with the Snapple brand. The disastrous result was summarized well by an April 1997 headline, which read: "$1.4 billion mistake costs CEO his job" (Millman, 1997, p. 1).

The overconfidence effect is likely to influence managers at many different levels of the organization. Malmendier and Tate (2003) saw evidence of such a bias at the highest levels, finding that overconfident CEOs invested a greater percentage of cash back into the firm rather than releasing the cash as dividends. These CEOs likely overestimated their ability to produce success and, as a result, ended up investing in many projects that they should have avoided. Others have found that overconfidence leads to dysfunctional strategic persistence among samples of both executives and students (Audia, Locke, & Smith, 2000). The problem of strategic persistence often arises because individuals who are successful at a task are more likely to believe, mistakenly, that they will continue to be successful under new conditions. Entrepreneurs may be particularly susceptible to this bias. Statistics abound which point to the low chances of success for new ventures. Entrepreneurs, however, generally feel that they will succeed where others typically fail. One study finds that 8 out of 10 entrepreneurs estimate their chances of success to be about 70 percent, and fully one-third believe their chances of success are completely certain (Cooper, Woo, & Dunkelberg, 1988). Although this may be more prevalent in some people than others or for some decisions as compared to others, it appears that people overestimate their abilities and chances of success with some degree of regularity.

Closing Observations

Summarizing the research on decision making represents a daunting challenge. Herein, we outlined the basic processes that individuals employ to make decisions, and we reviewed a number of biases that may interfere with these processes. Although we believe it is important to understand these processes and biases, it is imperative to note that our review only scratches the surface of the vast decision-making literature. In the process of writing this article, for example, we entered the term *decision making* in a prominent search engine for academic research pieces, and the search returned over 32,000 relevant articles.

In our view, this academic work is important, and we seldom reflect on the significance of decision making in our lives. Herein, we have reviewed several different examples of decision making in the context of business. It is easy to forget, though, how many relatively simple decisions we make each day: Which clothes should I wear? Which way should I drive to work? Should I pick up my dry cleaning before or after work? What will I eat for lunch? In contrast, we make many other decisions that are less simplistic: Should I entertain another job offer? How should I manage my relationship with a difficult co-worker? In which neighborhood should I buy a new house? Simply stated, decision making pervades our lives; as such, it is important to understand how we make decisions.

We have described a number of specific cognitive biases that affect managers' judgment; we expect most people's experience and everyday observations will confirm the presence of these biases in their own work environment. However, we would like to offer two caveats. First, we reviewed only a small number of decision-making biases. In fact, researchers have uncovered many other biases which we were unable to include in our review.[3]

Second, it is relatively straightforward to demonstrate that biases exist and apply to the general populace, but it is much more difficult for individuals to recognize the effect that these same biases have in governing their own judgments and inferences. There is a perceived asymmetry in susceptibility to biases that causes us to believe our own judgments are less prone to distortion than those of others (Ehrlinger, Gilovich, & Ross, 2005). In other words, people perceive themselves to be better-than-average in a wide variety of domains, and the decision-making context is no exception.

Another explanation for "bias blind spots" is that we assess susceptibility to bias differently, for ourselves than we do for others. When examining ourselves, we rely on introspection and look for detectable traces of the influence of bias, but in most cases such traces are hard to find or do not exist. When evaluating others, however, we are more likely to consult our own abstract theories about biases and objectively apply them to the situation at hand. In this sense, we hope that our article has not armed readers with new theories to explain the faulty decisions of others without also turning these theories inward and applying them to one's own decision-making processes. Another phenomenon that brings about a bias blind spot is that people are more inclined to understand that they may be guilty of bias in the abstract, but less willing to admit susceptibility in specific instances.

In closing, then, we suggest that it is not enough to simply understand how managers make decisions and how biases might affect those decisions. It is also important to take the difficult final step of acknowledging that the same biases apply to ourselves and to our specific decisions. Hopefully, by better understanding the processes and biases involved in decision making, we might all make better decisions.

Endnotes

1. Hammond, Keeney, and Raiffa (1999) provide a slightly different rational decision-making model.

2. For notable examples of their influential work, see: Kahneman, Slovic, and Tversky (1982), Kahneman and Tversky (1979).

3. For an excellent review of these biases, see Gilovich, Griffin, and Kahneman (2002).

References

Audia, P. G., Locke, E. A., & Smith, K. G. (2000). The paradox of success: An archival and a laboratory study of strategic persistence following radical environmental change. *Academy of Management Journal, 43*(5), 837–853.

Bazerman, M. H. (2006). *Judgment in managerial decision making.* Hoboken, NJ: John Wiley & Sons.

Chugh, D. (2004). Societal and managerial implications of implicit social cognition: Why milliseconds matter. *Social Justice Research, 17*(2), 203–222.

Cooper, A. C., Woo, C. Y., & Dunkelberg, W. C. (1988). Entrepreneurs' perceived chances for success. *Journal of Business Venturing, 3*(2), 97–108.

Cummins, C., & Chazan, G. (2007, March 29). Risk-taking Shell CEO stays in race. *The Wall Street Journal,* p. B1.

Ehrlinger, J., Gilovich, T., & Ross, L. (2005). Peering into the bias blind spot: People's assessments of bias in themselves and others. *Personality and Social Psychology Bulletin, 31*(5), 680–692.

Eisenhardt, K. M., & Zbaracki, M. J. (1992). Strategic decision making. *Strategic Management Journal, 13*(8), 17–37.

Evans, J. St. B. T. (2003). In two minds: Dual-process accounts of reasoning. *Trends in Cognitive Sciences, 7*(10), 454–459.

Gilovich, T., Griffin, D., & Kahneman, D. (2002). *Heuristics and biases: The psychology of intuitive judgment.* Cambridge, UK: Cambridge University Press.

Hammond, J. S., Keeney, R. L., & Raiffa, H. (1999). *Smart choices: A practical guide to making better decisions.* Boston: Harvard Business School Press.

Hastie, R. (2001). Problems for judgment and decision making. *Annual Review of Psychology, 52*(1), 653–683.

Hiller, N. J., & Hambrick, D. C. (2005). Conceptualizing executive hubris: The role of (hyper-)core self-evaluations in strategic decision-making. *Strategic Management Journal, 26*(4), 297–319.

Kahneman, D. (2003). Maps of bounded rationality: Psychology for behavioral economics. *American Economic Review, 93*(5), 1449–1475.

Kahneman, D., Slovic, P., & Tversky, A. (1982). *Judgment under uncertainty: Heuristics and biases.* Cambridge, UK: Cambridge University Press.

Kahneman, D., & Tversky, A. (1979). Prospect theory: An analysis of decision under risk. *Econometrica, 47*(2), 263–292.

Knight, F. H. (1921). *Risk, uncertainty, and profit.* Boston: Houghton Mifflin.

Malmendier, U., & Tate, G. (2003). CEO overconfidence andcorporate investment. *Journal of Finance, 60*(6), 2661–2700.

Mercer, J. (2005). Prospect theory and political science. *Annual Review of Political Science, 8*(1), 1–21.

Miller, C. C., & Ireland, R. D. (2005). Intuition in strategic decision making: Friend or foe in the fast-paced 21st century? *Academy of Management Executive, 19*(1), 19–30.

Millman, N. (1997). $1.4 billion mistake costs CEO his job: Snapple snafu finally too much to swallow. *Chicago Tribune,* p. 1.

Mintzberg, H. A. (1975). The manager's job: Folklore and fact. *Harvard Business Review, 53*(4), 49–61.

Morse, G. (2006). Decisions and desire. *Harvard Business Review, 84*(1), 42–51.

Nulden, U. (1996). Escalation in IT projects: Can we afford to quit or do we have to continue? *Proceeding of the IEEE Computer Society Information Systems Conference* (pp. 136–142). Palmerston North, New Zealand: IEEE Computer Society Press.

Nutt, P. (2004). Expanding the search for alternatives during strategic decision-making. *Academy of Management Executive, 18*(4), 13–28.

Odean, T. (1998). Are investors reluctant to realize their losses? *Journal of Finance, 53*(5), 1775–1798.

Schmidt, J. B., & Calantone, R. J. (2002). Escalation of commitment during new product development. *Journal of the Academy of Marketing Science, 30*(2), 103–118.

Shafir, E., & LeBoeuf, R. A. (2002). Rationality. *Annual Review of Psychology, 53*(1), 491–517.

Shimizu, K., & Hitt, M. A. (2005). What constrains or facilitates divestitures of formerly acquired firms? The effects of organizational inertia. *Journal of Management, 31*(1), 50–72.

Simon, H. A. (1957). *Models of man: Social and rational.* New York: Wiley.

Stanovich, K. E., & West, R. F. (2002). Individual differences in reasoning: Implications for the rationality debate? In T. Gilovich, D. Griffin, & D. Kahneman (Eds.), *Heuristics and biases: The psychology of intuitive judgment.* Cambridge, UK: Cambridge University Press.

Staw, B. M., & Ross, J. (1989). Understanding behavior in escalation situations. *Science, 246,* 216–220.

Thaler, R. H. (1980). Toward a positive theory of consumer choice. *Journal of Economic Behavior and Organization, 1*(1), 39–60.

Weber, E. U., Anderson, C. J., & Birnbaum, M. H. (1992). A theory of perceived risk and attractiveness. *Organizational Behavior and Human Decision Processes, 52*(3), 492–523.

When Your Thoughts Work Against You

Even the most educated and experienced negotiators succumb to predictable cognitive biases. Here's how to improve your decision making—and your results.

In 2000, 18-year-old Matt Harrington was widely considered the most promising pitcher in the Major League Baseball (MLB) draft. The Colorado Rockies chose him as their seventh pick and then sweetened the pot after Harrington, his parents, and his agent, Tommy Tanzer, rejected the team's first offer. On behalf of his client, Tanzer turned down the Rockies' final offer of $4 million over two years, though it was a typical offer for a seventh-pick player.

After a disappointing season in the independent leagues, Harrington entered the 2001 MLB draft, where the San Diego Padres made him the 58th overall selection. On the advice of his new agent, Scott Boras, Harrington rejected an offer of $1.25 million over four years and a $300,000 signing bonus.

In 2002, following another lackluster season in the independent leagues, Harrington did poorly in the MLB draft and turned down less than $100,000 from the Tampa Bay Devil Rays.

In 2003, the Cincinnati Reds drafted Harrington in the 24th round and offered him little more than the opportunity to play; again talks fell through. In 2004, the New York Yankees drafted Harrington in the 36th round but passed on making him an offer.

After failing to receive any offer in the 2005 draft, Harrington became a free agent. In 2006, he received a minor-league contract from the Chicago Cubs, but he was released before the 2007 season began. He continues to play for independent-league teams, earning about $1,000 per month, and works other jobs during the off-season.

Matt Harrington holds the dubious distinction of being the longest holdout in the history of the MLB draft. His string of botched negotiations ensured that his career ended before it could even begin.

The mistakes Harrington and his negotiating team made are spectacular as a whole, but considered one by one, they are not unique. In their book, *Judgment in Managerial Decision Making* (Wiley, seventh edition, 2008), professors Max H. Bazerman of Harvard Business School and Don A. Moore of Carnegie Mellon University present Harrington's thwarted baseball career as a cautionary tale to illustrate the decision-making errors that affect virtually all negotiators.

In negotiation, we unwittingly operate under a number of systematic and predictable cognitive biases on a regular basis. Many of these errors in thinking result from our tendency to put too much trust in our intuition. Here we present five of the most common mistakes that Bazerman and Moore have identified and suggest a number of ways to keep this faulty thinking from ruining your most important talks.

Source: "When Your Thoughts Work Against You" from the *Program on Negotiation* newsletter at the Harvard Law School (www.pon.harvard.edu), October 2008, Vol. 11, No. 10, pp. 1–5. Used with permission.

Mistake No. 1: Viewing Negotiation as a Fixed Pie

Negotiators often falsely assume that their interests are directly opposed to those of their counterparts. The prevalence of competition in our society, ranging from sports to university admissions to corporate promotion systems, can lead us to view many other situations as win–lose. For example, too many negotiators assume that the pie of resources is fixed in size when, in fact, opportunities exist to expand the pie by creating value.

What's more, researchers have found that the belief in a fixed pie causes negotiators to devalue any concession their "adversary" makes. Unfortunately, Matt Harrington and his agents succumbed to the tendency to view the other side's alleged best offer with too much suspicion. They also neglected to explore the possibility of a value-creating trade, such as accepting the salary offered and negotiating performance-based bonuses if Harrington played as well as he expected.

Solution: Share Information

The simplest way to break through the fixed-pie mindset in a negotiation is to disclose information to your counterpart. In particular, try to provide information that could lead to wise tradeoffs. If a customer complains about your prices, break down your costs for her and ask whether she is willing to make concessions on delivery time or other issues in return for lower prices. Typically, the discoveries you reach jointly will outweigh the risk that the other side will take advantage of the information you disclose.

Mistake No. 2: Anchoring on the First Offer

Harrington and his family fell victim to another common cognitive bias: they were overly affected by the first number that entered the negotiation. Harrington's first agent, Tommy Tanzer, told MLB teams with high draft choices that Harrington would require at least a $4.95 million first-year signing bonus—an unrealistic amount that scared off seven teams in the draft. This high anchor created expectations in the minds of Harrington and his family that could not be supported.

Initially, the Harringtons stood by Tanzer's hard bargaining. Only later did they come to understand that they had hired an inexperienced agent—and filed a lawsuit against him for botching the deal.

Solution: Reject Anchors

Unprepared negotiators are far more likely to fall into traps, such as inappropriate anchors, than their prepared counterparts. When you come to the table unprepared, you put yourself at a distinct disadvantage. Set concrete goals for the negotiation in advance so you won't be swayed by others' influence tactics and vivid stories.

In addition, keep in mind that your thinking will tend to be more intuitive and less rational when you're pressed to make snap decisions. Don't allow other negotiators to force you to give an answer right away. Instead, schedule breaks between negotiating sessions that give you time to think and evaluate.

Mistake No. 3: Escalating Commitment

After wising up about Tanzer, why did the Harringtons make the same mistake year after year—rejecting decent offers in favor of much worse alternatives?

When Tanzer urged his 18-year-old client to turn down the Rockies' multimillion-dollar deal, he unwittingly set up his client for a string of failed negotiations. According to Bazerman and Moore, negotiators have a tendency toward irrational *escalation of commitment*—a strong psychological need to justify their prior decisions and behaviors, both to themselves and to others. After you've invested a great deal of time and energy in a course of action, it's difficult to know when to quit.

Many of us would rather remain committed to a losing strategy than admit we're throwing good money after bad. As for Harrington, by turning down one disappointing draft offer after another, he committed himself more deeply to doing better the next year, even as the odds of that happening dropped out of sight.

Solution: Don't Dwell on the Past

Thoughts about the "sunk costs" you've invested can keep you plodding forward long after you should quit a negotiation or settle for a disappointing deal. Yet economists tell us that past investments should rarely affect our decisions about the future. At each decision point during your talks, make sure you have a sound basis for escalating your commitment to a deal.

Mistake No. 4: Feeling Too Confident

Harrington's refusal to give up the chase for a huge MLB salary package probably meshed with yet another cognitive bias: overconfidence in his ability to eventually meet his goal. Each year, the pitcher slipped lower in the draft, yet he stuck doggedly to his aspiration of winning the type of contract that much more valuable players were receiving.

Overestimating the chances that your counterpart will meet your demands is a common and potentially devastating negotiation error. Just like Harrington, job seekers are often overconfident about what the other side will offer them to join an organization. Negotiators who fail to reach agreement after overestimating their value may find they've squandered rare opportunities.

Solution: Consider the Opposite

Before you negotiate, reflect on the possibility that your expectations are incorrect—and actively seek out information that might prove you wrong. During this evaluation process, a trusted outside party, whether an expert within your organization, a consultant, or some other adviser, could be your best resource. Outsiders are likely to offer a more objective view of the negotiation than you could ever manage.

Next, be willing to listen openly to difficult feedback and follow through on it. By accepting your own uncertainty about the future and the other side's interests, you put yourself in a position to make proposals that satisfy everyone. If the Harringtons had consulted with baseball experts, they might have realized that Matt's agent was in over his head.

Mistake No. 5: Focusing Too Narrowly on the Issues

The ability to focus closely on a person or task can be invaluable in many areas of life, including test taking, artistic pursuits, and relationships. Yet in negotiation, an overly narrow focus on the issues at stake can be a detriment, according to Bazerman and Moore. In particular, negotiators err by focusing too closely on short-term concerns, on their own desires, and on obvious issues at the expense of new ones.

Bazerman tells the story of two firms that pushed forward a joint venture to market a new product without addressing a number of ambiguities. To date, the companies have spent more than $350 million arguing over which side owns which share of the market. Greater focus on long-term implementation could have staved off this battle. Similarly, Matt Harrington and his advocates focused too narrowly on the goal of securing a high offer in the MLB draft—and failed to think about how the young man and his family would be affected if they failed to get a deal.

Solution: Ask Questions and Make Multiple Offers

By asking the other party lots of questions about his positions and interests, you'll gain a more realistic sense of your chances of getting what you want, now and in the future. In addition, put forth several different offers that you value equally. The other side's reactions to the various proposals will help you identify trade-off and reformulate packages that show your flexibility and commitment to making a deal.

Reading 2.4

Untapped Power: Emotions in Negotiation
Daniel L. Shapiro

Editors' Note: To many negotiators and mediators an "emotional issue" sounds like one with no real substance to it, yet one that's liable to damage the situation at any moment. Shapiro shows how unsophisticated that view is. Emotions, recognized and unrecognized, regularly trap professional negotiators as well as clients, when these emotions can be anticipated and dealt with constructively. Not only that, but there are positive uses of emotion in negotiation.

> *"We don't experience the world as it is. We experience the world as we are."*
> *Anaïs Nin*

Two lawyers meet for the first time to negotiate a settlement. To the unaware observer, their greeting is perhaps notable for its uneventfulness. They shake hands, sit down, introduce themselves, and begin talking about the concerns of their respective clients. Each wants to negotiate this small case quickly in order to move on to big, lucrative cases waiting in the docket. And each knows that an agreement can easily be created to meet the interests of their current clients.

Under the surface, however, each lawyer experiences a world of emotions. "He's much older than I expected," thinks the one lawyer. She worries that he might try to control the whole negotiation process, and she calls to mind possible statements she could say to assert her professional status in the interaction. Meanwhile, the older lawyer looks at this younger negotiator and recalls an image of his ex-wife. He feels instantly repelled, but feigns cordial professionalism. Not surprisingly, then, neither listens very well to the other during the meeting; neither learns the other's interests nor shares their own; and neither brainstorms options that might lead to mutual gains. They merely haggle over how much money the one client will pay the other. Each side firmly entrenches in a monetary position; and they close the meeting at impasse.

Are emotions a barrier to a wise agreement? Is it best for negotiators like these two lawyers to toss their emotions aside and to focus purely on the "important" substantive matters, like money? In this brief essay, I suggest reasons why emotions constitute a risk to negotiator efficacy. I then explain that emotions are unavoidable in a negotiation and propose ways in which emotions actually can be *helpful* in reaching a wise agreement.

Emotions Can Obstruct a Negotiated Agreement

There are a number of ways in which emotions can hinder the ability of negotiators to reach a wise agreement in a fair and amicable way.[1] First, emotions may divert our attention from substantive matters. If we or others are angry or upset, both of us will

Source: "Untapped Power: Emotions in Negotiation," by Daniel L. Shapiro, from *The Negotiator's Fieldbook*, with Andrea Kupfer Schneider and Christopher Honeyman (Eds.), 2006, pp. 263–269. American Bar Association. Used by permission.

have to deal with the hassle of emotions. Whether we decide to yell back, to sit quietly and ignore the outburst, or to storm out of the room, somehow we will need to respond.

Second, revelation of emotions can open us up to being manipulated. If we blush with embarrassment or flinch with surprise, these observable reactions offer the other party hints about our "true" concerns. A careful observer of our emotional reactions may learn which issues we value most and least—and could use that information to try to extract concessions from us.

For example, John and Mary, a husband and wife, shopped for an anniversary ring in New York City. After hours of shopping, they entered a small store with a sign in the window that read, "Lowest price in town." Mary spotted a sapphire ring in the corner of the main display case. She looked at John, looked at the ring, and smiled in excitement. A jeweler approached them and took the ring out of the display case. John inquired about the asking price. The jeweler named his "rock bottom" price. John was surprised, but not only because of its cost. Moments earlier, he had overheard the jeweler offering another couple that same ring for $400 less. John suspected that the jeweler had raised the asking price after seeing Mary's excitement about the ring. The couple decided to buy a ring elsewhere.

Third, thinking may take a subordinate role to feeling. Emotions are desirable for falling in love, but they make it difficult to think precisely in a negotiation. Because we cannot easily quantify or measure emotions, talking about emotions reduces the role of hard data, facts, and logic. It makes little sense to try to negotiate quantitatively over emotions: "I'll give you 10 percent more respect if you give me 20 percent less resentment."

Fourth, unless we are careful, emotions will take charge of us. They may cause us to lose our temper, to stumble anxiously over our words, or to sulk uncontrollably in self-pity. We may neglect even our own substantive goals. In anger, we may reject an agreement that is superior to our alternatives.[2] Or we may focus not on our substantive goals at all, but rather on hurting the negotiator whose actions triggered our anger.[3]

Thus, it is not surprising that a negotiator may fear the power of emotions. They are dangerous and can be destructive. However, this analysis is only a partial picture of the role that emotions play in a negotiation.

Get Rid of Emotions?

Folk wisdom offers clear advice about how to deal with emotions in negotiation: Do not get emotional. Negotiators commonly are encouraged to "Swallow your pride," "Do not worry," and "Keep a straight face." For a negotiator, emotions are seen as an impediment to avoid at all costs. However, this advice is untenable and often makes things worse.

Emotions Are Unavoidable

Human beings are in a state of "perpetual emotion."[4] Whether negotiating with another lawyer or with a friend, we constantly experience affective states of some type or another, such as anger, boredom, nostalgia, or anxiety.[5] Emotions are stimulated by the context surrounding us (e.g., walking into another lawyer's office), by our own actions, feelings, and thoughts (e.g., worrying about one's junior status), and by the actions of the other negotiator toward us (e.g., their demeaning behavior toward us).

Negotiators can be personally affected in many different ways, including by impulses, emotions, moods, and attitudes.[6] An *impulse* is a strong desire to do a particular behavior now, without much thought about possible consequences. If the young lawyer experiences feelings of mistreatment by the older lawyer, she may have an impulse to storm out of the room, ruining the possibility of a negotiated agreement.

Negotiators often feel the more generalized pushes and pulls of *emotions,* which are positive or negative reactions to matters of personal significance. In contrast to impulses, which propel us to do a *particular* behavior now, such as to tear up the "biased" proposal drafted by the other side, emotions motivate us toward general kinds of behavior, such as to attack the other party in *some way* for their self-serving behavior. An important part of most emotions is the action tendency,[7] which is the type of behavioral urge associated with that emotion. In anger, for example, the action tendency is to strike out or attack. In guilt, the action tendency is to repent. Of course, a person may not act upon the action tendency; that is why it is called a tendency and not an actuality.

Moods are low intensity affective states, background music to our thoughts and actions. Whether we experience a positive mood due to our pay raise or a negative mood due to the rainy weather, our moods may have an effect on our negotiating behavior.[8]

Attitudes are positive or negative evaluations of a person, institution, policy, or event.[9] If the young lawyer learns that her counterpart is deceiving her, she may develop a negative attitude toward him.

Suppressing Emotions Can Make Things Worse

It is not possible to suppress one's actual feelings. We feel some particular emotion, and then we come to realize the emotion which we are experiencing. It is possible, however, to suppress the expression of those feelings.[10] A negotiator may feel angry toward another without expressing that anger through words, tone of voice, or body language.

Suppressing resentment, anger, or other strong emotions can debilitate a negotiator's cognitive and behavioral functioning in several ways.[11] First, the negative emotional experience remains, leaving the negotiator in an internal state of tension. This agitated state may motivate us to act in ways that do not serve our short- or long-term interests.[12] A negotiator may hide her anger toward a colleague, then explode weeks later at a trivial behavior conducted by the colleague. Second, the effort to suppress the display of emotions consumes important cognitive energy. People are limited in their cognitive capacity to process information,[13] so additional cognitive tasks decrease a negotiator's ability to think about important substantive or process issues. Third, a negotiator who suppresses his or her emotions may be more likely to stereotype that counterpart as an "adversary," leading to competitive behavior. There is evidence that the act of suppressing emotions increases physiological arousal both personally and in one's negotiating counterpart.[14] With heightened physiological arousal, each negotiator has a reduced attentional capacity, making stereotypical thinking more likely.[15]

Emotions Can Help You Reach Your Negotiation Goals

Emotions affect our ability to reach negotiation goals. In most negotiations, each party has two goals: affective satisfaction and instrumental satisfaction.[16] The ability to deal effectively with emotions increases the likelihood of attaining those goals.

Affective satisfaction is our general level of satisfaction with the emotions experienced during an interaction. Affective satisfaction focuses on our feelings about our feelings—our "meta-emotions" for short.[17] How do we feel about the feelings we experienced in the negotiation? In reflecting upon our interaction with the other party, do we generally feel satisfied with our emotional experience, or do we feel angry, upset, and dissatisfied?

A second goal focuses on instrumental satisfaction, the extent to which substantive work requirements are fulfilled. If two lawyers walk away from a weeklong negotiation with plenty of good feelings but no new ideas about how to deal effectively with their differences, the meeting might be considered an affective success but an instrumental failure.

Using Emotions to Move You toward Your Negotiation Goals

Negotiators are not merely victim to the dangers of emotions. In fact, interest-based negotiators can reap great benefit by understanding the information communicated via emotions and by enlisting positive emotions into their interactions.

Understanding the Information Communicated by Emotions

The emotion theorist Sylvin Tompkins suggested that emotions amplify motivation.[18] They signal the importance of issues to us and let us know about what we care. They bring personally important goals into the forefront of attention and give them urgency. The goals may be instrumental or affective in nature.

Hence, awareness of emotions, one's own and those of others, provides a negotiator with an understanding of the importance of each person's interests and concerns. A negotiator may come to realize the extent to which she wants a particular object (instrumental satisfaction) or a particular kind of treatment and deference (affective satisfaction). With expanded information about the relative importance of interests, parties are more capable of devising options for mutual gain.

Emotions are not only internal; they have a communicative function.[19] If the other negotiator says something that offends you, the look on your face may change. Your eyebrows may furrow and your lips may pucker. Your voice may become deeper, and the rhythm of your speech may turn more abrupt. Through these behaviors, you are communicating to the other negotiator that you are angry. By expressing your emotion, you provide the other with important information about how you want to be treated.

Even if you suppress the expression of your own emotions, they are still communicating information to at least one person: you. The feeling of butterflies in your stomach signals to you that you may be anxious. The feeling of heaviness throughout your body signals that you may be disappointed. Although some negotiators are very good at hiding the expression of their "true" feelings from others, it is much more complicated to hide your own feelings from yourself.

Because emotions communicate information, an observant negotiator may try to exploit that information. Some negotiators try to stimulate an emotion—positive or negative—in others for strategic gain.[20] A car salesperson may try to build a positive affiliation with the customer to encourage the sale of a car on his car lot ("You have kids? Me, too! This car is great for taking the kids on vacation.") Or the salesperson may feign surprise at a customer's "outrageously low" asking price for the car.

Does emotional manipulation work? Sometimes. Negotiators may be exploited if they are unaware that their emotions are being manipulated. However, putting aside ethical and moral questions, the exploitive use of emotions is not foolproof.[21] First, negotiators who use exploitive tactics may get caught. A customer may learn that the car salesperson does *not* actually have children and may decide to take her business elsewhere. Second, the tactics of a manipulative negotiator may backfire. A salesperson's feigned surprise at a customer's "outrageously low" asking price may cause the customer *not* to feel ashamed at her asking price, but rather to feel annoyed at the salesperson's comment and to shop elsewhere.

Exploiting emotions runs the additional risk of damaging long-term relationships. Many negotiations involve people who have ongoing relationships with one another and who are in close and consistent contact. Lawyers, politicians, diplomats, and organizational employees tend to interact with a small and stable network of colleagues. Emotional exploitation may work to one negotiator's advantage in the short term, but over the course of time others may become aware of the manipulation, become angry, and subvert the exploitation through overt or covert retaliation.[22] Even in situations of asymmetric power, the less powerful person may use subtle tactics to retaliate against the exploitation. ("Sorry boss, but I forgot to send out the package on time yesterday.")

Negative Emotions Have Downfalls in a Negotiation

Negative emotions are not completely useless in a negotiation. Consider a simple distributive negotiation. If two boys argue over who should get the last cookie in the cookie jar, the child who expresses more anger—yelling louder and making more credible threats to hurt the other—may be at an advantage. The expression of anger communicates a willingness to go to extremes, even if that means getting in trouble or foregoing a better alternative.

Yet negative emotions have serious downfalls in a negotiation. The angry boys do not explore value-creating options, such as asking a parent if they can go to the store to buy more cookies. And once the conflict over the cookie is resolved, emotional residue may become the seeds of future conflict.[23] The boy who did not get the cookie may feel resentment, which easily may fuel future disagreement.

Enlisting Positive Emotions to Motivate Collaboration

A growing body of research suggests that positive emotions increase the likelihood that negotiators will satisfy their instrumental and affective goals. Compared to those in a neutral mood, negotiators in a positive mood achieve more optimally integrative outcomes, use fewer aggressive behaviors, and report higher enjoyment of their interaction.[24] As parties build affiliation with one another and develop fulfilling roles, they become more engaged in their negotiation tasks and experience a state of "flow," a peak motivational experience that is intrinsically and personally rewarding.[25]

Positive emotions contribute to the long-term sustainability of each party's commitments. Negotiators may experience positive emotions toward one another due to joint participation in the negotiation process, joint brainstorming on the agreement, or a positive emotional connection with one another. The power of positive emotions toward the agreement and toward the other can override the temptation for parties to dishonor their commitments.

Positive emotions also foster cognitive expansion. Positive emotions can aid negotiators' attempts to problem-solve creative options to satisfy their interests.[26] Positive emotions trigger the release of a neurochemical called dopamine, which in turn fosters improved cognitive ability for a negotiator to think creatively. These findings are consistent with the research of Barbara Fredrickson,[27] who proposes that certain positive emotions—including joy, interest, contentment, and pride—all share the ability to broaden attentional, cognitive, and behavioral ability. This theory is supported by a tremendous amount of research conducted by Alice Isen and colleagues.[28] Isen's research suggests that people experiencing positive affect demonstrate thinking that is flexible, creative, integrative, and efficient. Each of these characteristics is important for an interest-based negotiator, who is trying to brainstorm creative options that satisfy each party's interests.

Some of the motivational benefit's of positive emotions can be reaped whether one is a hard bargainer or interest-based negotiator. In either case, each party needs the other to create a joint agreement. That is the essence of negotiation. Hence, the parties must co-manage the negotiation process, and the collaborative inclinations fostered by positive emotions can improve the efficiency of that process. Even parties in a single, nonrepeat negotiation must co-manage the negotiation process. The stimulation of positive emotions, as well as the consequent eliciting of collaborative behaviors, can facilitate the efficiency of the negotiation.

Conclusion

While it is true that emotions can be a barrier to a value-maximizing agreement, the common advice to "get rid of emotions" is infeasible and unwise. On the contrary, research suggests that negotiators can improve the efficiency and effectiveness of a negotiation by gaining an understanding of the information communicated by emotions, their own and those of others, and enlisting positive emotions into the negotiation.

Endnotes

1. The ideas in this section are drawn primarily from: Roger Fisher and Daniel Shapiro, *Beyond Reason: Using Emotions as You Negotiate* (New York: Penguin, 2005).

2. Max Bazerman, et al., "The Death and Rebirth of the Social Psychology of Negotiations," in *Blackwell Handbook of Social Psychology,* eds. Garth Fletcher and Margaret Clark (New York: Wiley-Blackwell, 2000); Modal Pillutla and J. Keith Murnighan, "Unfairness, Anger and Spite: Emotional Rejections of Ultimatum Offers," *Organizational Behavior and Human Decision Processes* 68 (1996), pp. 208–24.

3. Joseph Daly, "The Effects of Anger on Negotiations Over Mergers and Acquisitions," *Negotiation Journal* 7 (1991), pp. 31–39.

4. Daniel Shapiro, "A Negotiator's Guide to Emotions: Four 'Laws' to Effective Practice," *Dispute Resolution Magazine* (Winter 2001), pp. 3–8.

5. David Watson and Lee Anna Clark, "Emotions, Moods, Traits, and Temperaments: Conceptual Distinctions and Empirical Findings," in *The Nature of Emotions: Fundamental Questions,* eds. Paul Ekman and Richard Davidson (New York: Oxford University Press, 1994).

6. Shapiro, "A Negotiator's Guide to Emotions: Four 'Laws' to Effective Practice."

7. Nico Frijada, *The Emotions* (New York: Cambridge University Press, 1986).

8. Alice Isen, "Positive Affect and Decision Making," in *Handbook of Emotions,* 2nd ed., eds. Jeannette Haviland-Jones and Michael Lewis (New York: Guilford Press, 2000).

9. Icek Ajzen, *Attitudes, Personality, and Behavior* (London: Taylor & Francis, 1988).

10. I do acknowledge evidence suggesting that it may not be possible to suppress the microexpressions that occur immediately upon experiencing a particular emotion. *See* Mark G. Frank and Paul Ekman, "The Ability to Detect Deceit Generalizes Across Different Types of Highstake Lies, *Journal of Personality and Social Psychology* 72 (1997), p. 1429.

11. James Gross, "Emotion Regulation: Affective Cognitive and Social Consequences," *Psychophysiology* 39 (2002), pp. 281–91.

12. James Averill, "Emotions Are Many Splendored Things," in *The Nature of Emotions: Fundamental Questions,* eds. Paul Ekman and Richard Davidson (New York: Oxford University Press, 1994), pp. 99–102.

13. Susan Fiske and Shelley Taylor, *Social Cognition,* 2nd ed. (New York: McGraw-Hill, 1991).

14. Gross, "Emotion Regulation: Affective, Congnitive and Social Consequences."

15. Delroy Paulhus et al., "Some Effects of Arousal on Sex Stereotyping," *Personality and Social Psychology Bulletin* 18 (1992), pp. 325–30.

16. Daniel Shapiro, "Negotiation Residuals: The Impact of Affective Satisfaction on Long-Term Relationship Quality," *Program on Negotiation Papers,* 2000, WP00-3, pp. 1–19. Daniel Shapiro, "Negotiating Emotions," *Conflict Resolution Quarterly* 20 (2002), p. 68.

17. John Gottman, et al., *Meta-Emotion: How Families Communicate Emotionally* (Mahwah, NJ: Lawrence Erlbaum, 1997).

18. Silvan Tomkins, "Affect as the Primary Motivational System," in *Feelings and Emotions: The Loyola Symposium,* ed. Megda Arnold (New York: Academic Press, 1970), pp. 101–10.

19. Robert Levenson, "Human Emotion: A Functional View," in *The Nature of Emotions: Fundamental Questions,* eds. Paul Ekman and Richard Davidson (New York: Oxford University Press, 1994), pp. 123–26.

20. Bruce Barry, "The Tactical Use of Emotion in Negotiation," in *Research on Negotiation in Organizations,* eds. Robert Bies et al. (Greenwich, CT; Jai Press, 1999), pp. 93–121.

21. Robert Axelrod, *The Evolution of Cooperation* (New York: Basic Books, 1984).

22. Keith Allred et al., "The Influence of Positive Affect and Visual Access on the Discovery of integrative solution in Bilateral Negotiation," *Organizational Behavior and Human Decision Processes* 37 (1997), pp. 175–187.

23. Shapiro, "Negotiation Residuals: The Impact of Affective Satisfaction on Long-Term Relationship Quality."

24. Peter Carnevale and Alice Isen, "The Influence of Positive Affect and Visual Access on the Discovery of Integrative Solutions in Bilateral Negotiation," *Organizational Behavior and Human Decision Processes* 70 (1997), pp. 175–187.

25. Mihaly Csikszentmihalyi, *Flow: The Psychology of Optimal Experience* (New York: Harper Perennial, 1990).

26. Joseph Forgas, "On Feeling Good and Getting Your Way: Mood Effects on the Negotiator Cognition and Bargaining Strategies," *Journal of Personality and Social Psychology* 72 (1998), pp. 565–77; Isen, "Positive Affect and Decision Making."

27. Barbara Fredrickson, "The Role of Positive Emotions in Positive Psychology: the Broaden-and-Build Theory of Positive Emotions," *American Psychologist* 56 (2001), pp. 218–226.

28. Isen, "Positive Affect and Decision Making."

Staying with No

Holly Weeks

It's hard to say no. It's harder still to stay with the no in the face of your counterpart's disappointment or anger. Here is how to be heard and respected without damaging relationships.

Roger Fisher, negotiation expert and coauthor of the widely influential book *Getting to Yes,* used to tell his law students that sometimes he wished he had written a book about getting to no. He didn't have trouble saying no, he said, but he had trouble staying with the no: when family members were disappointed or associates pressed him, he would give up, and give in—even to things he didn't want to do.

Like Fisher, most of us want to be agreeable; we want to accommodate people. For one thing, people generally like us better when we say yes to them than when we say no. For another, saying no can be unpleasant—sometimes very much so. Particularly when we are saying no—to someone senior—we feel considerable tension between our desire to stay with no and our desire to stay out of trouble.

The people to whom we say no rarely like hearing it, and it's no wonder. Our saying no signals rejection—of their ideas, of their wishes, of their priorities. Consequently, most people will try to get us to change the no to a yes. That means we have to work to defuse emotion on both sides: our discomfort at staying with an unpopular no and our counterpart's irritation, disappointment, or anger at hearing it.

We could, of course, cut the Gordian knot by giving in. But in the end, the consequences of not staying with no can cause much more damage—to our self-confidence, to our relationship with the other person, and to our credibility and effectiveness as a professional.

If we want to reduce the tension around staying with no, we will do better to think not about *whether* to stay with no, but *how.*

Many Reasons for the Other's Resistance

First, however, it helps to recognize why your counterparts want to "yes the no" and readjust your own emotional response to their efforts.

Business Culture

It isn't inherently insulting to you that the other person wants you to back off your no—it's part of our business climate to try to yes the no. If you want to keep the emotional temperature cool, don't read her challenging your no as an affront to your dignity or credibility.

Source: "Staying with No," by Holly Weeks, from the *Harvard Management Communication Letter* at the Harvard Business School 1, October 1, 2004, Vol. 1, No. 4. Used with permission.

Personal Experience and Expectations

Your counterpart's personal experience and expectations rather than the interpersonal relations between you may be the strongest determinant of how he responds to your no. He may be argumentative, wheedling, stunned, or angry because that's how he always handles hearing no.

I was staying with no in a conversation with a lawyer until I was eventually persuaded to his view. After I agreed, however, he kept right on hammering me to change my mind. Finally I laughed and said, "But Peter, I'm agreeing with you."

He paused and said, "Mostly people don't."

Context

There may be something about your staying with no—maybe something interpersonal, maybe not—that makes your no particularly difficult to accept. It's not unusual, for example, for someone who might be able to hear a no privately to be embarrassed to consent to it publicly. She may want you to back down so she can save face.

Not all of the friction between the effort to stay with no and the effort to yes the no is bad, but some of it is. Bad friction turns into a contest of wills, with one side winning and the other caving in or backing down. That's hard on relationships and often leads to payback.

Your Own Resistance

While your counterpart's resistance to your no can be hard to take, part of the problem may lie on your side, even if it doesn't feel that way. Far more people are coached to yes the no than to stay with no. Anyone who simply picks up a general interest magazine is instructed never to take no for an answer; in contrast, those of us who are trying to stay with no get very little guidance. So without practiced techniques to fall back on, we respond emotionally.

Staying with no puts us in two different predicaments. On the one hand, we don't like to be negative. On the other, we don't like to be pushed. If you especially don't like to be negative, you probably tend to soften your no. It feels natural to you to try to stay with no gently. But this may result in your no not getting heard.

If you especially don't like to be pushed, you likely tend to become combative as you stay with no. For you, the natural thing is to get the conversation over with, not stretch it out. The problem with this strategy is that it may require you to spend a lot of time on after-the-fact damage control.

The solution in both cases is to change how you say no—that's the piece you can control. You need to acquire the skill of saying and staying with no neutrally—to say no simply, clearly, and directly, using arguments that are not easily weakened by your counterpart.

The Neutral No

A neutral no is steady, uninflected, and clear. It's mostly illustrated by what it's not. It's not harsh, it's not pugnacious or apologetic, it's not reluctant or heavily buffered, and it's not overly nice. Neutral and nice are not the same. Even if you're nice, use neutral to stay with no.

By sticking with neutral, you're concentrating on the business end of no, not the personal. If your first no is tentative, your second is brusque, and your third is caustic, I don't necessarily hear your intentions, whatever they may be. It's not my job to read intentions. I hear that first you give me hope and then you lose your temper. That's hard on relationships and on your reputation.

You want a referee's manner. A ref just says what he says—good news for some, bad news for others—regardless of the strong feelings on both sides that his message may inspire. His job is to give his message neutrally and stay with it neutrally if challenged.

A neutral manner doesn't prevent you from speaking directly about the friction between staying with no and trying to yes the no. "It's hard for me to tell you no; it must be hard for you to hear" is consistent with neutral. Use your own language here, but check that what you say is neutrally spoken:

- If you know or suspect why your counterpart is resisting your no, acknowledge his concern honestly but without giving hope. "You have a lot invested in what you're asking, and it looks like I'm personally blocking you." Give a reason or justification for your no. "I see my job as balancing valid, but competing, needs. I'm focusing on that." Aren't you just creating an opening for an argument there? Sometimes, yes. But the objective of staying with no is not necessarily to terminate this conversation with a monosyllable.

- If your reason is well chosen and neutrally spoken, stay with it. Don't volley different arguments with your counterpart. Changing an argument is not necessarily an improvement over repetition.

- In some cases, you may want to tell your counterpart what you could say yes to. That's not a foundation of staying with no, it's an option and the beginning of a negotiation. If you're open to that, you don't have to wait for the counterpart to ask.

Dos and Don'ts

Keep Your Eye on the Issue, Not the Personal

You see your job as staying with no; I see my job as yessing that no. No one is doing anything wrong—we just don't want the same outcome here. It helps to think of the push–pull between us as an honest disagreement about how the tension should be resolved. It does not help to think of my resistance to your no as disrespect for you.

Know Your Triggers

Your counterpart may be trying out different tactics to get you to yes your no. The tactic the counterpart uses matters only if you're vulnerable to it. Which arguments are you most susceptible to? Which tactics? Does an ominous suggestion that the union will hear about this roll off or rattle you? Do tears move you to offer a tissue or to fold? Most of us know where we're vulnerable. If, for example, you are undermined by a counterpart who says she is disappointed in you and personally let down because you stay with no, you have probably been vulnerable to that sense of falling short of expectations before.

Don't Give Them Too Much to Read

It is very hard to pick out what part of a message to read if, first, the message is mixed and, second, there's an emotional flare in it. A harsh no that offends or angers people makes them stick to their guns, even if all you wanted to do was get the conversation over with. On the other hand, people who are uncomfortable staying with no often overdo the apologetic nature of their no—they say no, express their regret for it, and ask to be forgiven for staying with no, all at the same time. The message surrounding the no seems to be, "I want to stay with no and yet have you like me." That's hard to read, but more important, if I don't want to hear the no, it's very easy for me to overlook it.

Don't Weaken Your No

Curiously, many people do this backward. They start saying no using lightweight reasons, holding back the real, heavyweight reason. And the counterpart swats away the little reasons because they aren't very persuasive. To limit the frustration on both sides, give reasons with good weight up front.

An executive assistant had been helping out a colleague by taking on work that was not his responsibility. Now he needed to curtail his tendency to say yes all the time because he was swamped. The next time his colleague asked for his customary help with photocopying, he said, "I have to say no, and it's really my fault because I don't seem to be managing my time very well." His colleague disagreed that he wasn't managing his time well—in fact, she praised how well he managed his time. And, not accepting that the executive assistant had a time-management fault, the colleague also didn't accept his no.

He had offered a self-criticism with his no because he wanted to head off the potential criticism that he wasn't being very helpful. But he weakened his no by doing so.

Beware Misguided Empathy

Most of us genuinely regret it if our counterpart is disappointed when we stay with no. But be careful and clear about what you can legitimately claim to share.

A newly married couple was surprised and upset to have their mortgage application declined by their new bank. The mortgage officer agreed that it was disappointing. She listened to their protests and arguments, making suggestions while staying with no. But as the couple was leaving her office, she said, "Believe me, I feel as bad about this as you do." The young wife turned to her, stiff with new indignation, and said, "No. You don't."

The mortgage officer undermined her good no by claiming that her pain was as great as theirs. That will almost never feel right to those who must accept the no.

Avoid a Battlefront Attitude: "I Won't Give In; You Lose"

Not everyone tries to soften her no. Some of us say no combatively, and treat staying with no as escalating warfare. This could be you if you find a battle of wills stimulating. When staying with no feels like a triumph of the will, good outcomes—and good judgment—are in jeopardy.

Don't Give False Hope

Staying with no tentatively, or with a show of reluctance, makes it easy for your counterpart to hope you will change your no—and hard for him to accept the no. It sounds like your no is on the edge of tipping over into yes, so your counterpart is encouraged to keep pushing. Try the positive approaches suggested here to break a pattern of giving in, instead of falling back on a manner of saying no that suggests you are about to give in.

Practice Staying with No; Don't Avoid It

If you want to get better at staying with no in the face of the arguments and tactics that trigger you, it makes sense to practice with someone who will play the part of your worst nightmare in a protected setting. That's better than waiting until a real situation arises, when a lot is on the line.

You want to practice for four reasons: (1) so you'll stay with your message, (2) so you won't edit it on your feet, (3) so you'll know what it's going to feel like to say it, and (4) so you can see whether you really want to stay with this no—or whether you should yes it.

Reading 2.6

Risks of E-Mail

Anita D. Bhappu
Zoe I. Barsness

Editors' Note: *It's increasingly likely that you will find yourself conducting negotiations by e-mail, if only as one aspect of the process. The authors discuss how e-mail changes both what is discussed and how it's discussed, and they have some salutary warnings for you. Using e-mail it turns out, can distort what you're trying to say, and may also affect your perception of what* they *are trying to say.*

> *For the first time in human history, mass cooperation across time and space is suddenly economical. "There's a fundamental shift in power happening," says Pierre Omidyar, founder and chairman of the online marketplace eBay Inc. "Everywhere, people are getting together and, using the Internet, disrupting whatever activities they're involved in."*[*]

Negotiations are not immune from the disruptive effects of technology. After all, the communication media that negotiators use can influence not only what information they share and how that information is communicated, but also what information they attend to and how they interpret it. Certain information is easy to communicate face to face but difficult to describe in an e-mail. For example, emotional appeals are more challenging to make over e-mail than logical arguments. The exchange of nuanced information can also be constrained by e-mail technology because its structure limits the breadth and depth of information that can be exchanged. Finally, people pay attention to different things and are influenced by different people to varying degrees when using e-mail than face-to-face communication. The social distance imposed by electronic communication may encourage negotiators to engage in more confrontational behavior, or to focus so strongly on their own interests they reduce consideration of the other party's needs. This self-absorption and corresponding lack of other-awareness can make it difficult for electronic negotiators to assess differential preferences and identify potential joint gains. On the other hand, the minimization of status differences that occurs when negotiators communicate electronically may enhance the negotiation process by encouraging lower status negotiators to work harder to achieve their negotiating goals, thus preventing the premature closure of negotiations. In sum, negotiators interacting electronically not only face challenges, they enjoy unique opportunities. In this chapter, we discuss some of the ways in which e-mail alters the information-sharing processes and power dynamics during negotiation that have important ramifications for information exchange and the generation of joint gains. We also discuss useful information-sharing strategies and tactics that negotiators might adopt when interacting electronically to overcome the obstacles and exploit the opportunities that electronic communication presents negotiators.

Source: "Risks of E-Mail," by Anita D. Bhappu and Zoe I. Barsness, from *The Negotiator's Fieldbook,* with Andrea Kupfer Schneider and Christopher Honeyman (Eds.), 2006, pp. 395–400. American Bar Association. Used by permission.

Lack of Media Richness in E-Mail

Media richness is one of two characteristics of e-mail that are particularly relevant to negotiation. Media richness is the capacity of a communication medium to transmit visual and verbal cues, enabling it to support a variety of languages (e.g., body, paralanguage, and natural), provide more immediate feedback, and facilitate communication of personal information.[1] E-mail is considered a lean medium because it transmits neither visual nor verbal cues, whereas face-to-face communication is considered a rich medium because it transmits both. The lack of media richness in electronic communication contexts reduces the social presence of others and increases the perceived social distance among negotiators who are physically separated and communicating by computer.[2] Thus, negotiators' social awareness of each other's personal situation or emotional state, for example, may be seriously diminished. Negotiators may also engage more heavily in self-interested behavior when using e-mail rather than in face-to-face communication because they neither see nor hear one another. Furthermore, they may fail to elicit from the other party—or simply ignore—important information about his or her interests and priorities. E-mail usage may, therefore, accentuate a self-interest schema (i.e., the extent to which a negotiator emphasizes his or her own rather than collective interests) and its attendant behaviors.[3]

On the other hand, e-mail usage may limit the leverage of status-based power and encourage more candid information sharing because reduced social cues lower the salience of social group differences and social status. Indeed, the lack of social cues in e-mail causes people to be more direct and confrontational in their communications.[4] Such confrontational behavior can be further exacerbated by the diminished social presence of others and by feelings of anonymity associated with e-mail.[5]

Finally, negotiators are more likely to focus on the content rather than the context of their messages when using e-mail.[6] Given that a significant proportion of a message's meaning comes from its associated visual and verbal cues such as facial expressions, body language, and tone of voice, the inability to transmit these cues when using e-mail may cause negotiators to rely more heavily on logical argumentation and the presentation of facts rather than on emotional or personal appeals. Research suggests, for instance, that communication styles in e-mail are more task-oriented and depersonalized than in face-to-face interactions.[7] Reduced contextual information may, however, impede the negotiator's ability to interpret message meaning. Information exchanged in e-mail tends to be less nuanced than information exchanged face to face in the same situation because back channel and clarifying information, such as speech acknowledgements (e.g., "mmm" or "huh?") and reactive body language (e.g., head nods) are reduced.[8] Indeed, much of such clarifying information is simply lost when using e-mail because the information processing costs associated with translating this type of information into purely textual form are significant and sufficiently prohibitive.

In short, e-mail constrains information exchange, diminishing negotiators' ability to accurately assess differential preferences and identify potential joint gains. Indeed, one examination comparing face-to-face and computer-mediated negotiations revealed that negotiators interacting electronically were less accurate in judging the other party's interests.[9] E-mail interaction may also promote the use of distributive tactics because it encourages direct and confrontational communications, leading to conflict spirals that result in lower joint gains or even impasse. Some researchers, for example, have demonstrated a higher incidence of impasse and less integrative outcomes in e-mail than face-to-face negotiations.[10] These findings may reflect the difficulty of establishing rapport when using e-mail because it limits visual access to the nonverbal behavior that enables relational development. The development of rapport has been shown to foster more mutually beneficial settlements, especially in lean media contexts, perhaps because rapport engenders greater social awareness and connection among negotiators.[11]

The effects of electronically mediated communication on negotiation process and outcomes are not entirely detrimental, however. E-mail may facilitate better processing of social conflict because lean media do not transmit visual and verbal cues. The visible presence of others can induce arousal that leads to more aggressive behavioral responses. The absence of visual and verbal cues in e-mail, however, may defuse such triggers.[12] It may also reduce the salience of social group differences, which prevents coalition formation. In addition, because negotiators are physically isolated and the social presence of others is diminished, they can take time to "step out" of the discussion and thoughtfully respond rather than merely react to the other party's behavior, limiting escalation of social conflict even further.[13]

Lastly, e-mail may promote more equal participation among negotiators. The salience of social group differences and social status is reduced in lean media because there are fewer social context cues,[14] encouraging lower status individuals to participate more and reducing social influence bias among negotiators.[15] Rather than discounting or ignoring information provided by lower status individuals, as they might in face-to-face communication, negotiators may be influenced more by this information when using e-mail. Thus, even though less nuanced information is communicated between negotiators, more diverse information may actually be received. Attention to this "new" information may subsequently enable negotiators to identify optimal trades and create more integrative agreements.

Interactivity in E-Mail

Interactivity is the other characteristic of e-mail that is particularly relevant to negotiation. Interactivity is the potential of a communication medium to sustain a seamless flow of information between two or more negotiators.[16] Interactivity has two dimensions. The first, a temporal dimension, captures the synchronicity of interactions. Face-to-face communication is synchronous because all negotiators are co-temporal and each party receives an utterance just as it is produced; as a result, speaking turns tend to occur sequentially. E-mail is typically asynchronous because negotiators can read and respond to others' messages whenever they desire and not necessarily sequentially. Parallel processing, the second dimension of interactivity, describes the ability of the medium to enable two or more negotiators to simultaneously submit messages. Parallel processing is common in threaded e-mail discussions, such as during a multi-party, online negotiation.

Asynchronous media like e-mail impose high "understanding costs" on negotiators because they provide little "grounding" to participants in the communication exchange.[17] Grounding is the process by which two parties in an interaction develop a shared sense of understanding about a communication and a shared sense of participation in the conversation. Without the clues provided by shared surroundings, nonverbal behavior, tone of voice, or the timing and sequence of the information exchange typically found in face-to-face communication, negotiators may find it challenging to accurately decode the messages that they receive electronically. Information and context are, therefore, parsed differently in asynchronous and synchronous media, which will certainly influence the way that negotiators construct messages as well as their ability to interpret the messages that are sent via e-mail.

Research suggests, for instance, that negotiators using asynchronous e-mail exchange very long comments that include multiple points all in one "bundle."[18] Since the receiver's opportunity to respond to or clarify points that the sender is attempting to make is reduced when using e-mail, the sender is inclined to outline his or her arguments in one e-mail message that is also likely to be more task-oriented and depersonalized.[19] Argument bundling may facilitate the identification of integrative agreements by encouraging negotiators to link issues together and consider them simultaneously rather than sequentially, but such an approach can also place higher demands on the receiver's information processing capabilities.[20] Negotiators may, therefore, have more difficulty establishing meaning and managing feedback in asynchronous e-mail exchanges, further hindering their efforts to successfully elicit and integrate the information that is required to construct a mutually beneficial agreement.

Although asynchronous e-mail exchange is the most common, e-mail can be nearly synchronous if negotiators are all online simultaneously. In this latter case, parallel processing may actually encourage individuals to share more information than in face-to-face communication because it allows negotiators to voice their different perspectives simultaneously.[21] Parallel processing can also undermine existing power dynamics and encourage direct confrontation because it prevents any one individual from suppressing the views of others by seizing control of the discussion.[22] Face-to-face communication, on the other hand, does not support parallel processing and instead constrains negotiators to sequential turn taking. Therefore, the parallel processing dimension of e-mail, which is absent in face-to-face communication, may further support the simultaneous consideration of multiple issues during negotiation. Coupled with the greater diversity of information exchange among parties encouraged by the reduction of power differentials, parallel processing in e-mail is likely to promote the search for joint gains and thus potentially enhance integrative outcomes.

E-Mail and Information Exchange

Previous research suggests that at least two distinct information-processing modes are manifest during negotiations: an analytical-rational mode and an intuitive-experiential mode.[23] Individuals who adopt an analytical-rational mode rely more heavily on logic and deductive thinking and their associated tactics (e.g., development of positions and limits, use of logical argumentation, and the presentation of facts), while individuals who adopt an intuitive-experiential mode rely more heavily on intuition and experience and *their* associated tactics (e.g., appeals to emotion, the presentation of concrete personal stories, and the use of metaphors).[24] These two different information-processing styles, however, are not equally suited to the electronic context.

Reduced visual and verbal cues in e-mail may lead negotiators to use more rational-analytical communication tactics (e.g., logical argumentation and the presentation of facts). Such an effect is likely to favor negotiators who value logic and deductive thinking and are more adept at the use of these tactics. Heuristic and error search, where negotiators find their way to agreement through the exchange of alternative proposals, is likely to adapt *well* to the e-mail context since it supports issue packaging and argument bundling. However, the intermittent and often overlapping nature of most e-mail exchanges is likely to severely inhibit direct information-sharing approaches that rely on sequential turn-taking and reciprocal question and answer exchange. Negotiators who generally adopt a direct information-sharing strategy may, therefore, find e-mail *ill-suited* to their preferred information-sharing strategy. Indeed, the simultaneous consideration of multiple issues is likely to favor negotiators who rely more heavily on intuitive-experiential thinking styles and tactics.[25] Negotiators with a preference for indirect information-sharing strategies, because they must regularly infer meaning both from what is said (e.g., explicit offers) and what is implied (e.g., proposals entertained), may be more skilled at interpreting the meaning of multi-issue proposals and subsequently more adept at using what they have learned to develop better integrative agreements in e-mail.

Conclusion

People are increasingly relying on e-mail to negotiate deals and transactions, which may save them time, reduce their costs, and increase their convenience. However, the effectiveness of using e-mail to negotiate and the ultimate value that individuals are able to derive from such negotiations depend on communication norms of the negotiators in question. In particular, individuals need to be sensitive to the effects of communication media on social influence and information-sharing processes, which influence information exchange during negotiations. As our discussion suggests, the use of e-mail can both hinder and ameliorate the negotiation process depending on the specific schemas and behaviors enacted by the involved parties. A first step to minimizing the obstacles and enhancing the benefits associated with electronically mediated negotiations is to heighten individuals' awareness of these potential pitfalls and benefits. In doing so, we hope that this discussion will enable negotiators to better manage the negotiation process and reap greater joint gains.

Endnotes

*   Robert D. Hof, "The Power of Us: Mass Collaboration on the Internet Is Shaking Up Business," *Business Week*, June 20, 2005, 75–82.

1.   Richard L. Daft and Robert H. Lengel, "Information Richness: A New Approach to Managerial Behavior and Organizational Design," *Research in Organizational Behavior* 6 (1984), p. 191.

2.   John Short et al., *The Social Psychology of Telecommunications* (New York: John Wiley & Sons, 1976); Lee Sproull and Sara Kiesler, "Reducing Social Context Clues: Electronic Mail in Organizational Communication," *Management Science* 32 (1986), p. 1492.

3.   Zoe I. Barsness and Anita D. Bhappu, "At the Crossroads of Technology and Culture: Social Influence, Information Sharing, and Sense-Making Processes During Negotiations," in *Negotiation Theoretical Advances and Cross-Cultural Perspectives*, eds. Michelle Gelfand and Jeanne Brett (Stanford, CA: Stanford University Press, 2004).

4.   Sara Kiesler and Lee Sproull, "Group-Decision Making and Communication Technology," *Organizational Behavior and Human Decision Processes* 52 (1992), p. 96.

5.   Terri L. Griffith and Gregory B. Northcraft, "Distinguishing between the Forest and the Trees: Media, Features, and Methodology in Electronic Communication Research," *Organizational Science* 5 (1994), p. 272.

6.   Rosalie J. Ocker and Gayle J. Yaverbaum, "Asynchronous Computer-Mediated Communication versus Face-to-Face Collaboration: Results on Student Learning," *Group Decision and Negotiations* 8 (1999), p. 427.

7.   Nigel J. Kemp and Derek R. Rutter, "Cuelessness and the Content and Style of Conversation," *British Journal of Social Psychology* 21 (1982), p. 43.

8.   Raymond A. Friedman and Steve C. Currall, "Conflict Escalation: Dispute Exacerbating Elements of E-Mail Communication," *Human Relations* 56 (2003), p. 1325; Kathleen L. Valley et al., "A Matter of Trust: Effects of Communication on the Efficiency and Distribution of Outcomes," *Journal of Economic Behavior and Organization* 34 (1998), p. 211.

9.   Vairam Arunachalam and William N. Dilla, "Judgment Accuracy and Outcomes in Negotiations: A Casual Modeling Analysis of Decision-Aiding Effects," *Organizational Behavior and Human Decision Processes* 61 (1995), p. 289.

10.   Rachel Croson, "Look at Me When You Say That: An Electronic Negotiation Simulation," *Simulation Gaming* 30 (1999), p. 23; Arunachalam and Dilla, "Judgment Accuracy and Outcomes in Negotiations: A Casual Modeling Analysis of Decision-Aiding Effects"; Valley et al.," A Matter of Trust: Effects of Communication on the Efficiency and Distribution of Outcomes."

11.   Aimee L. Drolet and Michael W. Morris, "Rapport in Conflict Resolution: Accounting for How Face-to-Face Contact Fosters Mutual Cooperation in Mixed-Motive Conflicts," *Journal of Experimental Social Psychology* 36 (2000), p. 26; Don A. Moore et al., "Long and Short Routes to Success in Electronically Mediated Negotiations: Group Affiliations and Good Vibrations," *Organizational Behavior and Human Decision Processes* 77 (1999), p. 22.

12.   Peter J. Carnevale et al., "Looking and Competing: Accountability and Visual Access in Integrative Bargaining," *Journal of Personality and Social Psychology* 40 (1981), p. 111.

13.   Linda M. Harasim, "Networlds: Networks as a Social Space," in *Global Networks: Computers and International Communication*, ed. Linda M. Harasim (Cambridge, MA: MIT Press, 1993), p. 15–34.

14.   Lee Sproull and Sara Kiesler, *Connections: New Ways of Working in the Networked Organization* (Cambridge, MA: MIT Press, 1991).

15.   Jane Siegel et al., "Group Processes in Computer-Mediated Communication," *Organizational Behavior and Human Decision Processes* 37 (1986), p. 157; Anita D. Bhappu et al., "Media Effects and Communication Bias in Diverse Groups," *Organizational Behavior and Human Decision Processes* 70 (1997), p. 199.

16.   Robert E. Kraut et al., "Task Requirements and Media Choice in Collaborative Writing," *Human Computer Interactions* 7 (1992), p. 375.

17.   Herbert Clark and Susan Brennan, "Grounding in Communication," in *Perspectives on Socially Shared Cognition*, eds. Lauren Resnick et al., (Washington, DC: American Psychological Association, 1991); Friedman and Currall, "Conflict Escalation: Dispute Exacerbating Elements of E-Mail Communication."

18.   Friedman and Currall, "Conflict Escalation: Dispute Exacerbating Elements of E-Mail Communication;" Ashley S. Rosette et al., "The Influence of E-Mail on Hong Kong and U.S. Intra-Cultural Negotiations" (paper presented at the Annual Meetings of the International Association for Conflict Management, 2001.)

19.   Kemp and Rutter, "Cuelessness and the Content and Style of Conversation."

20.   Barsness and Bhappu, "At the Crossroads of Technology and Culture: Social Influence, Information Sharing, and Sense-Making Processes During Negotiations."

21.   Simon S. K. Kam and John Schaubroeck, "Improving Group Decisions by Better Pooling Information: A Comparative Advantage of Group Decision Support Systems," *Journal of Applied Psychology* 85 (2000), pp. 565–573.

22.   Jay F. Nunamaker et al., "Information Technology for Negotiating Groups: Generating Options for Mutual Gain," *Management Science* 37 (1991), p. 1325.

23.   Seymour Epstein et al., "Individual Differences in Intuitive-Experimental and Analytical Rational Thinking Styles," *Journal of Personality and Social Psychology* 71 (1996), p. 390.

24.   Michelle J. Gelfand and Naomi Dyer, "A Cultural Perspective on Negotiation: Progress, Pitfalls, and Prospects, *Applied Psychology: An International Review* 49 (2000), p. 62.

25.   Ibid.

Reading 2.7

Where Does Power Come From?
Jeffrey Pfeffer

Long-term studies of companies in numerous industries ranging from glass and cement manufacturing to the minicomputer industry "show that the most successful firms maintain a workable equilibrium for several years . . . but are also able to initiate and carry out sharp, widespread changes . . . when their environments shift."[1] These so-called discontinuous or frame-breaking changes always alter the distribution of power. Consequently, organizational innovation often if not inevitably involves obtaining the power and influence necessary to overcome resistance.

To be successful in this process, we need to understand where power comes from. It is critical to be able to diagnose the power of other players, including potential allies and possible opponents. We need to know what we are up against. Knowing where power comes from also helps us to build our own power and thereby increase our capacity to take action. It is useful to know that getting a new product introduced may involve power and politics, and to understand the pattern of interdependence and the points of view of various participants. But to be effective, we also need to know how to develop sources of power and how to employ that power strategically and tactically.

We all have implicit theories of where power comes from, and we occasionally act on these theories. For instance, we may read and follow the advice of books on "power dressing," pondering issues such as whether yellow ties are in or out and whether suspenders are a signal of power. The cosmetic surgery business is booming, in part, at least, because some executives are worried that the signs of aging may make them appear to be less powerful and dynamic. People attend courses in assertiveness training, go through psychotherapy, and take programs in public speaking for numerous reasons, but among them is the desire to be more powerful, dynamic, and effective.

Many of our theories about the origins of power emphasize the importance of personal attributes and characteristics—which are very difficult to alter, at least without herculean efforts. We sometimes overlook the importance of situational factors over which we may have more direct influence. If we are going to be effective in organizations, we need to be skillful in evaluating our theories of the sources of power, as well as sensitive to various cognitive biases. This chapter briefly outlines some issues to think about as we observe the world and try to diagnose the sources of power. It also sets the stage for the consideration of personal characteristics and situational factors as sources of power.

Personal Attributes as Sources of Power

When we walk into an organization, we see people first, not situations. People are talking, moving around, and doing things. People have personalities, idiosyncrasies, and mannerisms that engage our attention and hold our interest. Our preoccupation with the

Source: "Where Does Power Come From?" by Jeffrey Pfeffer from *Managing with Power: Politics and Influence in Organizations,* 1992, Harvard Business School Publishing, pp. 71–81. Used by permission.

vividness of the people we meet leads to what some psychologists have called "the fundamental attribution error"—our tendency to overemphasize the causal importance of people and their characteristics, and underemphasize the importance of situational factors.[2] The phenomenon is pervasive, and there are many examples. One striking manifestation of the tendency to ignore situational factors in evaluating people is provided in an experimental study done by a colleague.[3] The study entailed assessing the performance of a speaker—a situation not dissimilar to assessing the power of someone we encounter in an organization. In the study, evaluators asked questions that were either positively or negatively biased—and moreover, they were aware of the bias when asked about it later. Nevertheless, evaluators were themselves affected by the answers they elicited through their biased questions. They "underestimated the potential effect of their own behavior (the situation) in drawing conclusions based on potentially constrained answers."[4] Instead of discounting the diagnostic value of the behavior they had affected, evaluators used that information in making assessments both of the performance and (in other studies) of the attitudes of others. In other words, even when we know that the behavior we observe is strongly affected by situational factors, we readily make attributions and evaluations about others based on that behavior.

Not only do we overattribute power to personal characteristics, but often the characteristics we believe to be sources of power are almost as plausibly the consequence of power instead. Interviews with 87 managerial personnel (including 30 chief executive officers, 28 high-level staff managers, and 29 supervisors) in 30 Southern California electronics firms assessed beliefs about the personal characteristics of people thought to be most effective in the use of organizational politics and in wielding power.[5] The percentages of all respondents mentioning various characteristics are displayed in Table 1.

Without, for the moment, denying that these characteristics are associated with being powerful and politically effective, consider the possibility that at least some of them result from the experience of being in power. Are we likely to be more articulate and

TABLE 1 | Personal Traits Characterizing Effective Political Actors

Personal Characteristic	Percentage Mentioning
Articulate	29.9
Sensitive	29.9
Socially adept	19.5
Competent	17.2
Popular	17.2
Extroverted	16.1
Self-confident	16.1
Aggressive	16.1
Ambitious	16.1

Source: From Robert W. Allen et al., "Organizational Politics: Tactics and Characteristics of Its Actors, "*California Management Review* 22 (1979), p. 80. Reprinted by permission of The Regents of the University of California.

poised when we are more powerful? Are we likely to be more popular? Isn't it plausible that power causes us to be extroverted, as much as extroversion makes us powerful? Aren't more powerful and politically effective people likely to be perceived as more competent? Certainly power and political skill can produce more self-confident and even aggressive behavior. And considering that people usually adjust their ambitions to what is feasible, people who are more powerful are probably going to be more ambitious, and to be viewed as such.

Why is the causal ordering of more than academic interest? The answer is that we may try to develop attributes to help us attain power, and if those attributes are ineffective or dysfunctional, we can get into trouble. Most of us can recall people who "acted out the role" and behaved as if they were more powerful and important than they were. This behavior typically only erodes support and makes one ineffective, even if the same behavior, exhibited by someone holding power, is accepted and enhances that person's effectiveness.

A third problem in drawing inferences from personal attributes lies in the fact that people are seldom randomly assigned to their situations. External factors often have a direct bearing on the success or failure of an individual, and yet many studies of power fail to take account of such factors. Consider David Winter's study of the effect of three individual dispositions—the power motive, the need for achievement, and the affiliation–intimacy motive—on various indicators of leader effectiveness, including one measure closely related to a common definition of power: the ability to get one's way in terms of appointments or initiatives.[6]

Winter's sample is the U.S. presidents, a nonrandom sample if ever there was one. Each president's personality traits were assessed by scoring the first inaugural address for imagery that represents the underlying motive. Winter's results are correlations between presidential scores on the three traits and several outcome measures such as being re-elected, having court and cabinet appointments approved, and avoiding or entering war.[7] The analysis does not consider the possibility that the type of person elected to office is not independent of the times and conditions that bracket the election, and that perhaps these factors, not just motive profiles, help explain outcomes such as avoiding or entering war.

Errors of this type are made routinely. For instance, in evaluating own-recognizance bail programs, studies often don't account for the fact that the people are not randomly released on their own recognizance; only the less dangerous prisoners are likely to be released.[8] Thus the tendency of those released without bail to not commit crimes does not necessarily mean that if the program were extended to all prisoners the same results would hold. The wider point here is that we need to understand and account for how people wind up in various situations, and to use this information in evaluating their power and their effectiveness. In general, we need to be thoughtful when we analyze personal characteristics as sources of power, particularly if we intend to take action based on those insights.

Structural Sources of Power

Structural perspectives on power argue that power is derived from where each person stands in the division of labor and the communication system of the organization. The division of labor in an organization creates subunits and differentiated roles, and each subunit and position develops specialized interests and responsibilities. Further, each subunit or position makes claims on the organization's resources.[9] In the contest for resources, those who do well succeed on the basis of the resources they possess or control as well as the ties they can form with people who influence allocations.[10] Control over resources, and the importance of the unit in the organization, are derived from the division of labor, which gives some positions or groups more control over critical tasks and more access to resources than others.[11] Power, then, comes from the control over resources, from the ties one has to powerful others, and from the formal authority one obtains because of one's position in the hierarchy.

For instance, in a study of 33 purchase decisions, the most frequently mentioned characteristic of those perceived to have influence over the decision was that the choice would affect them:

> . . . in a company which makes musical instruments, the choice of a tractor truck was said by one informant to have been influenced most by the traffic supervisor. "He lives with the situation, so he must have the choice," he said.[12]

Who is affected by a decision is determined, obviously, by the division of labor. According to those interviewed in the study, people with formal responsibility for the unit where the product was to be used, or with responsibility for the performance or output of the product, were also viewed as influential. Although interviewees were asked to judge who had the most influence "regardless of who had the final authority," authority and responsibility were often-mentioned sources of influence in these purchase situations.[13] Authority and responsibility, too, are conveyed by one's position in the formal structure of the organization.

Or consider the power sometimes possessed by purchasing agents.[14] They stand between engineering, production scheduling, and marketing on the one hand, and outside vendors on the other. Some purchasing agents were able to use this intermediary position to obtain substantial influence over other departments that, in many instances, possessed more formal status and authority than they did. By relying on purchasing rules and procedures (which they often had developed themselves), the agents made it necessary for other departments to accede to their power—as is evidenced by the willingness of other departments to provide favors to those in purchasing in exchange for preferential treatment.

The point about situational sources of power is that one possesses power simply by being in the right place—by being in a position of authority, in a place to resolve uncertainty, in a position to broker among various subunits and external vendors—almost regardless of one's individual characteristics. Authority and responsibility are vested in positions, and one's ability to broker is affected significantly by where one sits in the structure of interaction. Of course, not all people in the same situations are able to do equally well. Some purchasing agents, for instance, were much more successful than others in raising the power and status of their departments, in spite of the fact that virtually all wanted to do so, and some of this difference resulted from variations in political skill among the purchasing agents in the various companies. This suggests that while situations are important, one's ability to capitalize on the situation also has decisive implications.

The Fit between Situational Requirements and Personal Traits

An important source of power is the match between style, skill, and capacities and what is required by the situation. For instance, in a study of influence at a research and development laboratory of 304 professionals, the participants were questioned about influence in their organization. Was influence primarily related to being (1) an internal communication star, someone who had extensive contacts within the laboratory but who was not linked to external sources of information; (2) an external communication star, someone linked primarily to external information and not well connected in his own unit; or (3) a boundary spanner, someone linked both to others within his own unit and to external sources of information?[15] Influence was measured with respect to technical, budgetary, and personnel decisions. The principal finding was that the type of person who was influential depended on the nature of the project: in technical service projects, with less task uncertainty, internal communication stars were most influential, while in applied research units, boundary spanners carried the most weight.

Another illustration of the contingency between situations and the characteristics that provide influence comes from a study of 17 organizations that had recently purchased a piece of offset printing equipment.[16] For some organizations, the purchase was new and therefore totally unfamiliar; for others, it involved the replacement of an existing piece of equipment; and for still others, it involved adding a piece of equipment. Clearly, the amount of uncertainty differed, it being greatest for those buying offset printing equipment for the first time, and posing the smallest problem for those firms that were merely acquiring another piece of the same equipment they already had. Individual experience was most highly related to influence in the case of purchasing an additional piece of equipment. Internal communication and the number of different sources of information consulted were most strongly related to influence in the case of new purchase decisions. Those who were able to affect perceptions of need were most influential in adding a piece of equipment, while those who gathered external information were more influential in the situation in which new equipment was being purchased. These two studies, as well as other research, strongly suggest that

> The influence of a subunit or individual on a decision is a function of (1) the kind of uncertainty faced by an organization, (2) the particular characteristic or capability which enables reducing organizational uncertainty, and (3) the degree to which a particular subunit [or individual] possesses this characteristic. As decision-making contexts vary, so do the sources of organizational uncertainty, and consequently, the bases for influence in organizational decision making.[17]

The necessity of matching personal characteristics to the situation can be seen in politics as well as in business. Ronald Reagan, the former movie actor and U.S. president, came to office at a time in which mass communication, through the medium of television, was essential. Reagan had no skill in dealing with details, but was a "great communicator." Lyndon Johnson rose to power at a time when television was less important and party organizations were stronger. The ability to pay attention to small details and the willingness to do favors for colleagues and constituents were critical. Had Reagan and Johnson been able to exchange decades, it is likely that neither one would have been elected president. Johnson's difficulty in responding to the rise of the media in his administration shows his inability to flourish in an era of mass communication. And Reagan would have been unsuited for the continual attention to detail that was required of old-style party politicians. Not only are particular kinds of knowledge and skill differentially critical across time and settings, but personal attributes also become more or less important, depending on the setting.

Can Charisma Be Transferred?

Charisma is perhaps the best illustration of the fit between situations and personal attributes. The concept of charisma came into social science from theology, where it means "endowment with the gift of divine grace."[18] Charismatic leaders often emerge in times of stress or crisis. They create an emotional (rather than purely instrumental) bond with others; they take on heroic proportions and appeal to the ideological values of followers.[19] President John Kennedy, Martin Luther King, and Gandhi were all charismatic figures.

Some have asserted that charisma is a characteristic of the individual, based on the person's need for power, achievement, and affiliation, as well as on his inhibitions in using power.[20] Moreover, charisma and personality are said to explain the effectiveness of leaders—for instance, that of U.S. presidents.[21] A careful longitudinal study of a school superintendent in Minnesota provides some interesting evidence on the interaction between charismatic properties and situational constraints.[22]

While serving in a large, suburban school district in Minnesota, the superintendent exhibited both charisma and effectiveness. Her work drew attention in the media and the legislature. She "gained wide acclaim for her massive grassroots program to cut $2.4 million from the budget while at the same time successfully avoiding the 'bloodletting' of retrenchment."[23] School personnel described her in interviews as "a mover, a shaker, a visionary . . . who had made a dramatic, unprecedented impact on the district. People believed that she had extraordinary talents."[24] She developed an extremely loyal following, unlike the superintendents who had preceded her. She involved many people in the process of change in the district, forming task forces to investigate district policy and budget problems, hiring consultants to conduct workshops to develop a vision of the future, and redesigning jobs and the administrative structure of the district office. Her effect on the district was striking:

> Budget reductions were scheduled without acrimonious debate. The school board unanimously approved the superintendent's budget reductions after only a brief discussion. Teachers awarded her a standing ovation, despite her recommendations to cut support jobs and program funding. Innovative ideas poured in from district personnel. . . . At the end of her two years as superintendent, the district had cataloged over 300 suggestions for innovative ventures.[25]

Then she was appointed by the governor of Minnesota to be the head of the state Department of Education. She brought to this new position the same modus operandi she had used as district superintendent: "Begin with a mission and a vision that outline where one wants to go; generate enthusiasm and support for the vision at the grassroots level; . . . create a structure for change at the Department of Education that will serve to channel the interest and energy into innovative programs."[26] During her first year in her new job, she personally visited almost every one of the 435 school districts in the state. She initiated town meetings held in 388 public school districts, which drew about 15,000 citizens. She sponsored public opinion polls. She replaced the top five assistant commissioners with her own team of nine people, all formerly outsiders to the Department of Education.[27] And what were the results of all of these efforts?

As one might imagine, efforts to restaff and restructure the Department of Education were immediately opposed by those already well served by the existing structure. Five of the new assistants were either fired or resigned from office within the first year.[28] The press soon heard of morale problems, departures of key middle managers, and confusion over routine tasks and job assignments. Instead of being able to focus on long-term change, she now found herself "embroiled in the day-to-day details of established bureaucratic order."[29] Charisma, so evident at the school district level, clearly did not transfer to her new position at the state level, nor could it be created at will.

The administrator had more success in her role as superintendent because it gave her more control and more autonomy over educational matters. She was also able to have closer, more personal relationships with those she wanted to influence when she operated at the local level. As the governor's political appointee, she had to worry about what her actions would mean for him. As head of a large state department, she "was embedded in a much more complex web of relations among the legislature, state executive departments, constituents, interest groups and networks, and state and national educational communities."[30] Her freedom of action was constrained, and her personal contacts were worth much less; in short, she needed to rely more on bureaucratic politics and less on emotional appeal than she had been accustomed to.

As situational factors change, the attributes required to be influential and effective change as well. That is why it is important not only to find positions with the political demands that match our skills and interests, but also to tailor our actions to the circumstances we confront. In any event, we can probably best understand the sources of power as deriving from individual characteristics, from advantages the situation provides, and from the match between ourselves and our settings.

Endnotes

1. Michael L. Tushman, William H. Newman, and Elaine Romanelli, "Convergence and Upheaval: Managing the Unsteady Pace of Organizational Evolution," *California Management Review* 29 (1986), pp. 29–44.

2. R. E. Nisbett and L. Ross, *Human Inferences: Strategies and Shortcomings of Social Judgment* (Englewood Cliffs, NJ: Prentice Hall, 1980).

3. Linda E. Ginzel, "The Impact of Biased Feedback Strategies on Performance Judgments," Research Paper #1102 (Palo Alto, CA: Graduate School of Business, Stanford University, 1990).

4. Ibid., p. 26.

5. Robert W. Allen et al., "Organizational Politics: Tactics and Characteristics of Its Actors," *California Management Review* 22 (1979), pp. 77–83.

6. David G. Winter, "Leader Appeal, Leader Performance, and the Motive Profiles of Leaders and Followers: A Study of American Presidents and Elections," *Journal of Personality and Social Psychology* 52 (1987), pp. 196–202.

7. Ibid., p. 200.

8. Christopher H. Achen, *The Statistical Analysis of Quasi-Experiments* (Berkeley: University of California Press, 1986).

9. Andrew M. Pettigrew, *Politics of Organizational Decision-Making* (London: Tavistock, 1973), p. 17.

10. Ibid., p. 31.

11. D. J. Hickson et al., "A Strategic Contingencies' Theory of Intraorganizational Power," *Administrative Science Quarterly* 16 (1971), pp. 216–29.

12. Martin Patchen, "The Locus and Basis of Influence in Organizational Decisions," *Organizational Behavior and Human Performance* 11 (1974), p. 209.

13. Ibid. p. 213.

14. George Strauss, "Tactics of Lateral Relationship: The Purchasing Agent," *Administrative Science Quarterly* 7 (1962), pp. 161–86.

15. Michael L. Tushman and Elaine Romanelli, "Uncertainty, Social Location and Influence in Decision Making: A Sociometric Analysis," *Management Science* 29 (1983), pp. 12–23.

16. Gerald R. Salancik, Jeffrey Pfeffer, and J. Patrick Kelly, "A Contingency Model of Influence in Organizational Decision Making," *Pacific Sociological Review* 21 (1978), pp. 239–56.

17. Ibid., p. 253.

18. Bernard M. Bass, "Evolving Perspectives on Charismatic Leadership," *Charismatic Leadership,* eds. Jay A. Conger, Rabindra N. Kanungo, and Associates (San Francisco: Jossey-Bass, 1988), pp. 40–77.

19. Robert J. House, William D. Spangler, and James Woycke, "Personality and Charisma in the U.S. Presidency: A Psychological Theory of Leadership Effectiveness," unpublished, Wharton School, University of Pennsylvania, 1989.

20. Ibid.; Robert J. House, "A 1976 Theory of Charismatic Leadership," *Leadership: The Cutting Edge,* eds. J. G. Hunt and L. L. Larson (Carbondale: Southern Illinois University Press, 1977).

21. House, Spangler, and Woycke, "Personality and Charisma."

22. Nancy C. Roberts and Raymond Trevor Bradley, "Limits of Charisma," *Charismatic Leadership,* eds. Jay A. Conger, Rabindra N. Kanungo and Associates (San Francisco: Jossey-Bass, 1988), pp. 253–75.

23. Ibid., p. 254.

24. Ibid., p. 260.

25. Ibid., p. 263.

26. Ibid.

27. Ibid., p. 264.

28. Ibid., p. 269.

29. Ibid.

30. Ibid., p. 268.

Reading 2.8

Harnessing the Science of Persuasion
Robert B. Cialdini

A lucky few have it; most of us do not. A handful of gifted "naturals" simply know how to capture an audience, sway the undecided, and convert the opposition. Watching these masters of persuasion work their magic is at once impressive and frustrating. What's impressive is not just the easy way they use charisma and eloquence to convince others to do as they ask. It's also how eager those others are to do what's requested of them, as if the persuasion itself were a favor they couldn't wait to repay.

The frustrating part of the experience is that these born persuaders are often unable to account for their remarkable skill or pass it on to others. Their way with people is an art, and artists as a rule are far better at doing than at explaining. Most of them can't offer much help to those of us who possess no more than the ordinary quotient of charisma and eloquence but who still have to wrestle with leadership's fundamental challenge: getting things done through others. That challenge is painfully familiar to corporate executives, who every day have to figure out how to motivate and direct a highly individualistic workforce. Playing the "Because I'm the boss" card is out. Even if it weren't demeaning and demoralizing for all concerned, it would be out of place in a world where cross-functional teams, joint ventures, and intercompany partnerships have blurred the lines of authority. In such an environment, persuasion skills exert far greater influence over others' behavior than formal power structures do.

Which brings us back to where we started. Persuasion skills may be more necessary than ever, but how can executives acquire them if the most talented practitioners can't pass them along? By looking to science. For the past five decades, behavioral scientists have conducted experiments that shed considerable light on the way certain interactions lead people to concede, comply, or change. This research shows that persuasion works by appealing to a limited set of deeply rooted human drives and needs, and it does so in predictable ways. Persuasion, in other words, is governed by basic principles that can be taught, learned, and applied. By mastering these principles, executives can bring scientific rigor to the business of securing consensus, cutting deals, and winning concessions. In the pages that follow, I describe six fundamental principles of persuasion and suggest a few ways that executives can apply them in their own organizations.

The Principle of Liking: People Like Those Who Like Them
The Application: Uncover Real Similarities and Offer Genuine Praise

The retailing phenomenon known as the Tupperware party is a vivid illustration of this principle in action. The demonstration party for Tupperware products is hosted by an individual, almost always a woman, who invites to her home an array of friends, neighbors, and relatives. The guests' affection for their hostess predisposes them to buy from

Source: "Harnessing the Science of Persuasion" by Robert B. Cialdini, from the *Harvard Business Review,* October 2001, pp 72–79. Harvard Business School Publishing. Used with permission.

her, a dynamic that was confirmed by a 1990 study of purchase decisions made at demonstration parties. The researchers, Jonathan Frenzen and Harry Davis, writing in the *Journal of Consumer Research,* found that the guests' fondness for their hostess weighed twice as heavily in their purchase decisions as their regard for the products they bought. So when guests at a Tupperware party buy something, they aren't just buying to please themselves. They're buying to please their hostess as well.

What's true at Tupperware parties is true for business in general: If you want to influence people, win friends. How? Controlled research has identified several factors that reliably increase liking, but two stand out as especially compelling—similarity and praise. Similarity literally draws people together. In one experiment, reported in a 1968 article in the *Journal of Personality,* participants stood physically closer to one another after learning that they shared political beliefs and social values. And in a 1963 article in *American Behavioral Scientists,* researcher F. B. Evans used demographic data from insurance company records to demonstrate that prospects were more willing to purchase a policy from a salesperson who was akin to them in age, religion, politics, or even cigarette-smoking habits.

Managers can use similarities to create bonds with a recent hire, the head of another department, or even a new boss. Informal conversations during the workday create an ideal opportunity to discover at least one common area of enjoyment, be it a hobby, a college basketball team, or reruns of *Seinfeld.* The important thing is to establish the bond early because it creates a presumption of goodwill and trustworthiness in every subsequent encounter. It's much easier to build support for a new project when the people you're trying to persuade are already inclined in your favor.

Praise, the other reliable generator of affection, both charms and disarms. Sometimes the praise doesn't even have to be merited. Researchers at the University of North Carolina writing in the *Journal of Experimental Social Psychology* found that men felt the greatest regard for an individual who flattered them unstintingly even if the comments were untrue. And in their book *Interpersonal Attraction* (Addison-Wesley, 1978), Ellen Berscheid and Elaine Hatfield Walster presented experimental data showing that positive remarks about another person's traits, attitude, or performance reliably generate liking in return, as well as willing compliance with the wishes of the person offering the praise.

Along with cultivating a fruitful relationship, adroit managers can also use praise to repair one that's damaged or unproductive. Imagine you're the manager of a good-sized unit within your organization. Your work frequently brings you into contact with another manager—call him Dan—whom you have come to dislike. No matter how much you do for him, it's not enough. Worse, he never seems to believe that you're doing the best you can for him. Resenting his attitude and his obvious lack of trust in your abilities and in your good faith, you don't spend as much time with him as you know you should; in consequence, the performance of both his unit and yours is deteriorating.

The research on praise points toward a strategy for fixing the relationship. It may be hard to find, but there has to be something about Dan you can sincerely admire, whether it's his concern for the people in his department, his devotion to his family, or simply his work ethic. In your next encounter with him, make an appreciative comment about that trait. Make it clear that in this case at least, you value what he values. I predict that Dan will relax his relentless negativity and give you an opening to convince him of your competence and good intentions.

The Principle of Reciprocity: People Repay in Kind

The Application: Give What You Want to Receive

Praise is likely to have a warming and softening effect on Dan because, ornery as he is, he is still human and subject to the universal human tendency to treat people the way they treat him. If you have ever caught yourself smiling at a coworker just because he or she smiled first, you know how this principle works.

Charities rely on reciprocity to help them raise funds. For years, for instance, the Disabled American Veterans organization, using only a well-crafted fund-raising letter, garnered a very respectable 18 percent rate of response to its appeals. But when the group started enclosing a small gift in the envelope, the response rate nearly doubled to 35 percent. The gift—personalized address labels—was extremely modest, but it wasn't what prospective donors received that made the difference. It was that they had gotten anything at all.

What works in that letter works at the office, too. It's more than an effusion of seasonal spirit, of course, that impels suppliers to shower gifts on purchasing departments at holiday time. In 1996, purchasing managers admitted to an interviewer from *Inc.* magazine that after having accepted a gift from a supplier, they were willing to purchase products and services they would have otherwise declined. Gifts also have a startling effect on retention. I have encouraged readers of my book to send me examples of the principles of influence at work in their own lives. One reader, an employee of the state of Oregon, sent a letter in which she offered these reasons for her commitment to her supervisor:

> He gives me and my son gifts for Christmas and gives me presents on my birthday. There is no promotion for the type of job I have, and my only choice for one is to move to another department. But I find myself resisting trying to move. My boss is reaching retirement age, and I am thinking I will be able to move out after he retires. . . . [F]or now, I feel obligated to stay since he has been so nice to me.

Ultimately, though, gift giving is one of the cruder applications of the rule of reciprocity. In its more sophisticated uses, it confers a genuine first-mover advantage on any manager who is trying to foster positive attitudes and productive personal relationships in the office: Managers can elicit the desired behavior from coworkers and employees by displaying it first. Whether it's a sense of trust, a spirit of cooperation, or a pleasant demeanor, leaders should model the behavior they want to see from others.

The same holds true for managers faced with issues of information delivery and resource allocation. If you lend a member of your staff to a colleague who is shorthanded and staring at a fast-approaching deadline, you will significantly increase your chances of getting help when you need it. Your odds will improve even more if you say, when your colleague thanks you for the assistance, something like, "Sure, glad to help. I know how important it is for me to count on your help when I need it."

The Principle of Social Proof: People Follow the Lead of Similar Others

The Application: Use Peer Power Whenever It's Available

Social creatures that they are, human beings rely heavily on the people around them for cues on how to think, feel, and act. We know this intuitively, but intuition has also been confirmed by experiments, such as the one first described in 1982 in the *Journal of Applied Psychology.* A group of researchers went door-to-door in Columbia, South Carolina, soliciting donations for a charity campaign and displaying a list of neighborhood residents who had already donated to the cause. The researchers found that the longer the donor list was, the more likely those solicited would be to donate as well.

To the people being solicited, the friends' and neighbors' names on the list were a form of social evidence about how they should respond. But the evidence would not have been nearly as compelling had the names been those of random strangers. In an experiment from the 1960s, first described in the *Journal of Personality and Social Psychology,* residents of New York City were asked to return a lost wallet to its owner. They were highly likely to attempt to return the wallet when they learned that another New Yorker had previously attempted to do so. But learning that someone from a foreign country had tried to return the wallet didn't sway their decision one way or the other.

The lesson for executives from these two experiments is that persuasion can be extremely effective when it comes from peers. The science supports what most sales professionals already know: Testimonials from satisfied customers work best when the satisfied customer and the prospective customer share similar circumstances. That lesson can help a manager faced with the task of selling a new corporate initiative. Imagine that you're trying to streamline your department's work processes. A group of veteran employees is resisting. Rather than try to convince the employees of the move's merits yourself, ask an old-timer who supports the initiative to speak up for it at a team meeting. The compatriot's testimony stands a much better chance of convincing the group than yet another speech from the boss. Stated simply, influence is often best exerted horizontally rather than vertically.

The Principle of Consistency: People Align with Their Clear Commitments

The Application: Make Their Commitments Active, Public, and Voluntary

Liking is a powerful force, but the work of persuasion involves more than simply making people feel warmly toward you, your idea, or your product. People need not only to like you but to feel committed to what you want them to do. Good turns are one reliable way to make people feel obligated to you. Another is to win a public commitment from them.

My own research has demonstrated that most people, once they take a stand or go on record in favor of a position, prefer to stick to it. Other studies reinforce that finding and go on to show how even a small, seemingly trivial commitment can have a powerful effect on future actions. Israeli researchers writing in 1983 in the *Personality and Social*

Psychology Bulletin recounted how they asked half the residents of a large apartment complex to sign a petition favoring the establishment of a recreation center for the handicapped. The cause was good and the request was small, so almost everyone who was asked agreed to sign. Two weeks later, on National Collection Day for the Handicapped, all residents of the complex were approached at home and asked to give to the cause. A little more than half of those who were not asked to sign the petition made a contribution. But an astounding 92 percent of those who did sign donated money. The residents of the apartment complex felt obligated to live up to their commitments because those commitments were active, public, and voluntary. These three features are worth considering separately.

There's strong empirical evidence to show that a choice made actively—one that's spoken out loud or written down or otherwise made explicit—is considerably more likely to direct someone's future conduct than the same choice left unspoken. Writing in 1996 in the *Personality and Social Psychology Bulletin,* Delia Cioffi and Randy Garner described an experiment in which college students in one group were asked to fill out a printed form saying they wished to volunteer for an AIDS education project in the public schools. Students in another group volunteered for the same project by leaving blank a form stating that they didn't want to participate. A few days later, when the volunteers reported for duty, 74 percent of those who showed up were students from the group that signaled their commitment by filling out the form.

The implications are clear for a manager who wants to persuade a subordinate to follow some particular course of action: Get it in writing. Let's suppose you want your employee to submit reports in a more timely fashion. Once you believe you've won agreement, ask him to summarize the decision in a memo and send it to you. By doing so, you'll have greatly increased the odds that he'll fulfill the commitment because, as a rule, people live up to what they have written down.

Research into the social dimensions of commitment suggests that written statements become even more powerful when they're made public. In a classic experiment, described in 1955 in the *Journal of Abnormal and Social Psychology,* college students were asked to estimate the length of lines projected on a screen. Some students were asked to write down their choices on a piece of paper, sign it, and hand the paper to the experimenter. Others wrote their choices on an erasable slate, then erased the slate immediately. Still others were instructed to keep their decisions to themselves.

The experimenters then presented all three groups with evidence that their initial choices may have been wrong. Those who had merely kept their decisions in their heads were the most likely to reconsider their original estimates. More loyal to their first guesses were the students in the group that had written them down and immediately erased them. But by a wide margin, the ones most reluctant to shift from their original choices were those who had signed and handed them to the researcher.

This experiment highlights how much most people wish to appear consistent to others. Consider again the matter of the employee who has been submitting late reports. Recognizing the power of this desire, you should, once you've successfully convinced him of the need to be more timely, reinforce the commitment by making sure it gets a public airing. One way to do that would be to send the employee an e-mail that reads, "I think your plan is just what we need. I showed it to Diane in manufacturing and Phil in shipping, and they thought it was right on target, too." Whatever way such commitments are formalized, they should never be like the New Year's resolutions people privately make and then abandon with no one the wiser. They should be publicly made and visibly posted.

More than 300 years ago, Samuel Butler wrote a couplet that explains succinctly why commitments must be voluntary to be lasting and effective: "He that complies against his will/Is of his own opinion still." If an undertaking is forced, coerced, or imposed from the outside, it's not a commitment; it's an unwelcome burden. Think how you would react if your boss pressured you to donate to the campaign of a political candidate. Would that make you more apt to opt for that candidate in the privacy of a voting booth? Not likely. In fact, in their 1981 book *Psychological Reactance* (Academic Press), Sharon S. Brehm and Jack W. Brehm present data that suggest you'd vote the opposite way just to express your resentment of the boss's coercion.

This kind of backlash can occur in the office, too. Let's return again to that tardy employee. If you want to produce an enduring change in his behavior, you should avoid using threats or pressure tactics to gain his compliance. He'd likely view any change in his behavior as the result of intimidation rather than a personal commitment to change. A better approach would be to identify something that the employee genuinely values in the workplace—high-quality workmanship, perhaps, or team spirit—and then describe how timely reports are consistent with those values. That gives the employee reasons for improvement that he can own. And because he owns them, they'll continue to guide his behavior even when you're not watching.

The Principle of Authority: People Defer to Experts

The Application: Expose Your Expertise; Don't Assume It's Self-Evident

Two thousand years ago, the Roman poet Virgil offered this simple counsel to those seeking to choose correctly: "Believe an expert." That may or may not be good advice, but as a description of what people actually do, it can't be beaten. For instance, when the news media present an acknowledged expert's views on a topic, the effect on public opinion is dramatic. A single expert-opinion news story in *The New York Times* is associated with a 2 percent shift in public opinion nationwide, according to a 1993 study described in the *Public Opinion Quarterly.* And researchers writing in the *American Political Science Review* in 1987 found that when the expert's view was aired on national television, public opinion shifted as much as 4 percent. A cynic might argue that these findings only illustrate the docile submissiveness of the public. But a fairer explanation is that, amid the teeming complexity of contemporary life, a well-selected expert offers a valuable and efficient shortcut to good decisions. Indeed, some questions, be they legal, financial, medical, or technological, require so much specialized knowledge to answer, we have no choice but to rely on experts.

Since there's good reason to defer to experts, executives should take pains to ensure that they establish their own expertise before they attempt to exert influence. Surprisingly often, people mistakenly assume that others recognize and appreciate their experience. That's what happened at a hospital where some colleagues and I were consulting. The physical therapy staffers were frustrated because so many of their stroke patients abandoned their exercise routines as soon as they left the hospital. No matter how often the staff emphasized the importance of regular home exercise—it is, in fact, crucial to the process of regaining independent function—the message just didn't sink in.

Interviews with some of the patients helped us pinpoint the problem. They were familiar with the background and training of their physicians, but the patients knew little about the credentials of the physical therapists who were urging them to exercise. It was a simple matter to remedy that lack of information: We merely asked the therapy director to display all the awards, diplomas, and certifications of her staff on the walls of the therapy rooms. The result was startling: Exercise compliance jumped 34 percent and has never dropped since.

What we found immensely gratifying was not just how much we increased compliance, but how. We didn't fool or browbeat any of the patients. We *informed* them into compliance. Nothing had to be invented; no time or resources had to be spent in the process. The staff's expertise was real—all we had to do was make it more visible.

The task for managers who want to establish their claims to expertise is somewhat more difficult. They can't simply nail their diplomas to the wall and wait for everyone to notice. A little subtlety is called for. Outside the United States, it is customary for people to spend time interacting socially before getting down to business for the first time. Frequently they gather for dinner the night before their meeting or negotiation. These get-togethers can make discussions easier and help blunt disagreements—remember the findings about liking and similarity—and they can also provide an opportunity to establish expertise. Perhaps it's a matter of telling an anecdote about successfully solving a problem similar to the one that's on the agenda at the next day's meeting. Or perhaps dinner is the time to describe years spent mastering a complex discipline—not in a boastful way but as part of the ordinary give-and-take of conversation.

Granted, there's not always time for lengthy introductory sessions. But even in the course of the preliminary conversation that precedes most meetings, there is almost always an opportunity to touch lightly on your relevant background and experience as a natural part of a sociable exchange. This initial disclosure of personal information gives you a chance to establish expertise early in the game, so that when the discussion turns to the business at hand, what you have to say will be accorded the respect it deserves.

The Principle of Scarcity: People Want More of What They Can Have Less of

The Application: Highlight Unique Benefits and Exclusive Information

Study after study shows that items and opportunities are seen to be more valuable as they become less available. That's a tremendously useful piece of information for managers. They can harness the scarcity principle with the organizational equivalents of limited-time, limited-supply, and one-of-a-kind offers. Honestly informing a coworker of a closing window of opportunity—the chance to get the boss's ear before she leaves for an extended vacation, perhaps—can mobilize action dramatically.

Managers can learn from retailers how to frame their offers not in terms of what people stand to gain but in terms of what they stand to lose if they don't act on the information. The power of "loss language" was demonstrated in a 1988 study of California home owners written up in the *Journal of Applied Psychology.* Half were told that if they fully insulated their homes, they would save a certain amount of money each day. The other half were told that if they failed to insulate, they would lose that amount each day. Significantly more people insulated their homes when exposed to the loss language. The same phenomenon occurs in business. According to a 1994 study in the journal *Organizational Behavior and Human Decision Processes,* potential losses figure far more heavily in managers' decision making than potential gains.

In framing their offers, executives should also remember that exclusive information is more persuasive than widely available data. A doctoral student of mine, Amram Knishinsky, wrote his 1982 dissertation on the purchase decisions of wholesale beef buyers. He observed that they more than doubled their orders when they were told that, because of certain weather conditions overseas, there was likely to be a scarcity of foreign beef in the near future. But their orders increased 600 percent when they were informed that no one else had that information yet.

The persuasive power of exclusivity can be harnessed by any manager who comes into possession of information that's not broadly available and that supports an idea or initiative he or she would like the organization to adopt. The next time that kind of information crosses your desk, round up your organization's key players. The information itself may seem dull, but exclusivity will give it a special sheen. Push it across your desk and say, "I just got this report today. It won't be distributed until next week, but I want to give you an early look at what it shows." Then watch your listeners lean forward.

Allow me to stress here a point that should be obvious. No offer of exclusive information, no exhortation to act now or miss this opportunity forever should be made unless it is genuine. Deceiving colleagues into compliance is not only ethically objectionable, it's foolhardy. If the deception is detected—and it certainly will be—it will snuff out any enthusiasm the offer originally kindled. It will also invite dishonesty toward the deceiver. Remember the rule of reciprocity.

Putting It All Together

There's nothing abstruse or obscure about these six principles of persuasion. Indeed, they neatly codify our intuitive understanding of the ways people evaluate information and form decisions. As a result, the principles are easy for most people to grasp, even those with no formal education in psychology. But in the seminars and workshops I conduct, I have learned that two points bear repeated emphasis.

First, although the six principles and their applications can be discussed separately for the sake of clarity, they should be applied in combination to compound their impact. For instance, in discussing the importance of expertise, I suggested that managers use informal, social conversations to establish their credentials. But that conversation affords an opportunity to gain information as well as convey it. While you're showing your dinner companion that you have the skills and experience your business problem demands, you can also learn about your companion's background, likes, and dislikes—information that will help you locate genuine similarities and give sincere compliments. By letting your expertise surface and also establishing rapport, you double your persuasive power.

And if you succeed in bringing your dinner partner on board, you may encourage other people to sign on as well, thanks to the persuasive power of social evidence.

The other point I wish to emphasize is that the rules of ethics apply to the science of social influence just as they do to any other technology. Not only is it ethically wrong to trick or trap others into assent, it's ill-advised in practical terms. Dishonest or high-pressure tactics work only in the short run, if at all. Their long-term effects are malignant, especially within an organization, which can't function properly without a bedrock level of trust and cooperation.

That point is made vividly in the following account, which a department head for a large textile manufacturer related at a training workshop I conducted. She described a vice president in her company who wrung public commitments from department heads in a highly manipulative manner. Instead of giving his subordinates time to talk or think through his proposals carefully, he would approach them individually at the busiest moment of their workday and describe the benefits of his plan in exhaustive, patience-straining detail. Then he would move in for the kill. "It's very important for me to see you as being on my team on this," he would say. "Can I count on your support?" Intimidated, frazzled, eager to chase the man from their offices so they could get back to work, the department heads would invariably go along with his request. But because the commitments never felt voluntary, the department heads never followed through, and as a result the vice president's initiatives all blew up or petered out.

This story had a deep impact on the other participants in the workshop. Some gulped in shock as they recognized their own manipulative behavior. But what stopped everyone cold was the expression on the department head's face as she recounted the damaging collapse of her superior's proposals. She was smiling.

Nothing I could say would more effectively make the point that the deceptive or coercive use of the principles of social influence is ethically wrong and pragmatically wrongheaded. Yet the same principles, if applied appropriately, can steer decisions correctly. Legitimate expertise, genuine obligations, authentic similarities, real social proof, exclusive news, and freely made commitments can produce choices that are likely to benefit both parties. And any approach that works to everyone's mutual benefit is good business, don't you think? Of course, I don't want to press you into it, but, if you agree, I would love it if you could just jot me a memo to that effect.

The Six Channels of Persuasion

G. Richard Shell
Mario Moussa

Extensive research on how people influence one another in work settings has revealed that they return over and over to a relatively discrete number of persuasion moves. Although communication scholars have labeled as many as sixteen separate and identifiable strategies (including such things as issuing threats, giving simple orders, and making requests), we think six main persuasion channels dominate when people are selling ideas.

You can test our six-channels hypothesis in the laboratory of your own experience. Next time you step onto an airplane, notice the persuasion messages surrounding you as you board, buckle up, and take off. Here is what a typical plane ride might reveal.

Channel #1: Interest-Based Persuasion

As you reach your seat, you may notice some deal making going on. We were on a plane recently and asked a young businesswoman who was about to take her aisle seat nearby to switch for one of our aisle seats. We explained that a switch would enable us to get some work done together. "Sure." she replied, "if one of you could help me get my bag into this overhead."

Interest-based persuasion takes place every time someone frames a sales pitch in terms of the other party's self-interest. A simple example might be: "Accepting my idea will help you on your next performance evaluation." But, as the airplane example shows, interests are also the bases for negotiations, both inside and outside the organization. In negotiation, each side has something the other side wants or could use—capabilities, resources, status, pieces of information, or authority to take some action—and they make a trade. The trade can be explicit, as it was in the airline example above, or it can be implicit, as happens when you ask someone to cover a client call for you and mentally note that you owe that person a reciprocal favor at some point in the future (more on this when we discuss relationships below).

Interestingly, many executives tell us that they do not think of themselves as negotiating at work even though they are appealing to people's interests and trading a variety of subtle psychological currencies day in and day out. That is fine with us. The essence of this persuasion channel is inducement, not trading. Thus, *you are engaged in interest-based persuasion whenever you pitch your idea as addressing the other party's underlying needs.*

Channel #2: Authority

The airplane seat belt sign blinks on: authority-based persuasion. We recognize this signal and obey without giving the matter another thought. On a plane, most people are tuned to the "authority" channel because their safety depends on it.

Source: "The Six Channels of Persuasion," by G. Richard Shell and Mario Moussa, from *The Art of Woo: Using Strategic Persuasion to Sell Your Ideas,* 2007, pp. 32–41. New York: Penguin. Used with permission.

Authority is the most commonly used influence tool in most work settings. The authority channel is usually used in "top-down" situations, when someone gives an order to someone lower in a hierarchy. But even a secretary can use this channel if he or she has jurisdiction over expense accounts or other procedures.

In the airplane example, we tend to defer to authority automatically because the seat belt sign is credible, routine, and inherently reasonable. Social science research reveals that authority triggers a deep stimulus–response reaction when the right situational cues are in place. This accounts for the myriad occasions in everyone's working day when a superior makes a request, and a subordinate compiles without questioning in any way the order's merits or wisdom.

In the early 1960s, in one of the most famous psychological experiments ever run, Yale University professor Stanley Milgram tested to see if he could figure out how otherwise peace-loving German citizens had succumbed to the Nazi regime under Hitler. His results were remarkable: He was able to persuade ordinary subjects from New Haven, Connecticut, to deliver what they honestly thought were a series of painful, high-voltage electric shocks (they were actually harmless) to other people. He did this by dressing his psychology lab assistants in white lab coats and styling his exercise in the language and rituals of science. His New Haven subjects had agreed to obey the orders of the assistants—the surrounding circumstances suggested a high level of legitimacy for the proceedings—and were constantly reassured that the responsibility for the outcomes of the experiment resided solely with the experimenters.

Just how far were these randomly selected citizens willing to go? Twenty-seven of the forty-one people who participated (over 67 percent) continued giving the shocks up to what they were told was the lethal level. *Psychology Today* reported in 2002 that a meta-analysis of all experiments of this type revealed a stable finding: roughly 60 percent of people presented with these authoritative—but not coercive—conditions can be counted on to obey authoritative orders rather than "rock the boat" and protest. This is admittedly an extreme example of unthinking, habitual deference to authority, but Milgram's experiment illustrates a basic truth. Most people are susceptible to assertive displays of positional authority—which explains why your formal position is such a vital part of your credibility in presenting ideas.

Nevertheless, Milgram's experiments did *not* reveal that people will do anything for others who are in authority. What they showed was that people will defer to authority when it is presented to them in a certain way, under extremely well-crafted conditions, and when the orders do not involve a direct violation of *their own* interests. Had Milgram asked his subjects to administer a series of painful shocks to themselves, he would have heard quite a bit more protest.

You are using authority-based persuasion *whenever you appeal to your formal position or authoritative rules or policies as a means of getting others to agree with your proposal.* But when selling important ideas in most organizations, you should not expect Milgram-like, automatic deference. Rather, effective appeals using authority are almost always accompanied by independent justifications and explanations to help persuade the audience that the exercise of authority is *legitimate and consistent with the audience's core interests* under the particular circumstances.

Channel #3: Politics

Back on the plane, a nearby elderly passenger is hot and wants to complain about the lack of cool air circulating as the plane fills up. She fiddles with the air vent and nothing seems to happen. First move: build a coalition (a key skill in organizational politics). "Are you feeling a little stuffy?" she asks you. You politely nod. "Let's ask them to turn up the air conditioning." She pushes the attendant button. A stewardess appears. "We're feeling pretty warm here," she says on behalf of the newly formed "We Want Cooler Air" movement. "I'll see what I can do," replies the attendant, and then adds soothingly: "It will cool down quickly once we get into the air."

Social scientists define politics as processes by which individuals, usually working in groups, try to exert influence over the actions of a larger organization. As political theorist Hannah Arendt put it, "Political power corresponds to the human ability not just to act but to act in concert." We won't be discussing politics in the traditional sense, that is, the dynamics of elections and political parties. But the use of coalitions, pressure tactics, and power moves is not limited to government. People act in political ways inside many groups—from families to business firms.

A study of nearly five hundred organizations by two Swedish management scholars published in 2004 found that "some" political activity took place in nearly all (95 percent) of the surveyed organizations. A small number of firms (6 percent) had a "great deal" of politics and an equally small number (5 percent) had none at all. The balance of the sample was split roughly equally between those having politics to "a fair extent" and to "a fairly low extent." The kinds of activities reported most frequently included covert, informal decision-making processes (77 percent of organizations) and lobbying (75 percent). The activity reported least often was the use of passive resistance to frustrate change initiatives (60 percent). Other political behaviors included important people saying one thing and doing another (71 percent) and subgroups using bureaucratic procedures to frustrate change (64 percent).

If even the egalitarian Swedes have this much political activity at work, the authors note, it is a good bet that companies in other cultures face similar challenges. But many in both the academic and business communities refuse to acknowledge politics in organizational behavior because politics is seen as illegitimate. We consider ourselves realists in this regard. The issue is not whether there is politics in your organization; the issue is how skillfully you deal with it as part of your campaign to advance your ideas.

When most people use the words "organizational politics," they are thinking of its darker sides: egos, turf wars, and backstabbing. But politics has a light side, as well. When an organization faces up to politics and handles it well, different points of view and interest groups are acknowledged, forums exist to air these differences, and representatives of groups meet and argue openly for their interests—all in the service of the overall corporate good. In other words, healthy and productive political debate recognizes that many issues can be seen from multiple perspectives. Political considerations such as injured pride and the need for status are simply part of the environment most people work in.

Thus, dark side or light, *you are using the political persuasion channel whenever you acknowledge that appearances may be as important as substance in your idea-selling strategy, work through coalitions and alliances, or make use of back channels and lobbying.* This channel naturally overlaps with, and cuts across, all the other channels. A given political move may incorporate interests, authority, relationships, values, and evidence-based persuasion.

Channel #4: Rationality

As your plane taxis to take off, a video comes on telling you what to do in the "unlikely event of an emergency"—the seat cushion that can be used as a flotation device, and so forth. You know the video. The mode here is rational persuasion. You are not persuaded. First, you have heard the pitch so many times that you tune it out. Second, you have never heard of anyone actually surviving a plane crash by using the seat cushion as a flotation device. The video is full of detailed, specific information, but it lacks overall credibility.

We define rationality-based persuasion as *trying to influence someone's attitudes, beliefs, or actions by offering reasons and/or evidence to justify a proposal on its merits.* As the airplane example makes clear, the audience holds the keys to success in using this mode. If the audience is willing to listen to reason, you have a chance of influencing them. If not, no amount of data or logical persuasion will get them on your side.

Every organization gives at least lip service to the rationality mode and many are genuinely dedicated to making decisions based on the best arguments and evidence available. Thus, you almost always need to gather the best evidence and arguments you can as part of an idea-selling campaign.

IBM's legendary president, Tom Watson Sr., believed so thoroughly in a rational, thoughtful approach to business that he created one of the most famous corporate slogans of the twentieth century: THINK. The idea was born one day when Watson was working at the National Cash Register Company. Finding himself at a meeting where nobody was challenging anything being said, Watson burst out, "The trouble with everyone [here] is that we don't think enough." The following day he created a sign with five huge, all-capital letters on it and placed it at the podium where presentations were being made. The sign said "THINK."

At IBM, Watson's THINK sign could be found on every desk and in every conference room. But what, exactly, did Watson mean by it? He once explained it this way: "By THINK, I mean *take everything into consideration* [emphasis added]. . . . [But] we're not interested in a logic course."

Watson's slogan sent a strong message to his employees about the culture he wanted to instill at IBM. It was a culture based on rational thought. But, as Watson insisted, logic alone seldom dictates a given result. In using the rationality channel to persuade, you must be prepared to engage in debate. Different people come to very different conclusions about the same evidence based on their respective needs and biases. In addition, you (or your evidence) may lack credibility in your audience's eyes and, like the passengers on the airplane listening to the flotation device lecture, the audience will tune you out. Thus, rationality in persuasion usually pivots on what philosophers call "practical reason." You need to get all the evidence on the table (or, as Watson said, "take everything into consideration"), and then you must encourage people to apply their professional judgment and experience.

Channel #5: Inspiration and Emotion—The Vision Channel

You reach for the airline magazine to pass the time. It opens to a double-page advertisement for a luxury car that, if purchased, will transform you into someone who looks like James Bond (or dates him) and is vacationing at an expensive, well-known resort. This is what we call "visionary" persuasion: attempts to evoke emotions such as hope, desire, or team spirit to motivate you to adopt an attitude or to take a particular action. Once again, the attempt is unsuccessful. You are not the Bond (or Bond's) type. You like your dependable, five-year-old Honda.

At the deepest levels of human motivation lie people's feelings, beliefs, identities, spiritual roots, cultural ties, and life stories. Visionary devices such as stories and images help persuaders to access these levels, appealing directly to the audience's intuitions. As one persuasion expert has put it, "People make their decisions based on what the facts mean to them, not on the facts themselves."

You don't have to be a charismatic leader with a plan to rid the world of disease to become a skilled user of visionary persuasion tools. Beliefs and purposes come in many forms and cover all areas of life and work. An audience's everyday commitment to being a good citizen, a good professional, or a good parent is an excellent foundation for visionary persuasion.

When we speak of the visionary influence channel, therefore, we include *any appeal to an audience's overriding sense of purpose, values, or beliefs as the foundation for selling your idea.* Visionary persuasion thus often takes the form of a special type of reason-based argument in which your justifications relate to the higher aspirations and purposes embraced by your listeners. When you present an idea in such a way that it prompts an audience to say, "Supporting this proposal will help me become the type of person I want to be," or "Adopting this idea will help us feel that we belong to the type of organization people respect and admire," you are working in this channel.

Channel #6: Relationships

Back on the plane, a young boy across the aisle is lobbying for a cookie from his father. "I told you the cookies were for later," says the dad. "Aw, Dad, I was really good in the airport. Can't I have half of one now?" Out comes a cookie and some deal making ensues over how to divide it.

It is hard to overstate the importance of relationships. A positive relationship favorably predisposes an audience toward your message. In the words of psychologist Robert Cialdini, "We prefer to say 'yes' to people we know and like." A negative relationship, meanwhile, distorts almost everything an idea seller says.

The research on how rapport and relationships work to facilitate (or block) communication is deep and wide. In an early study on selling insurance, researchers discovered that the best insurance salesmen were no different from the average in product knowledge, number of sales calls, or even number and type of questions asked. The only difference was in how quickly and authentically the best salesmen put their customers at ease by finding some common experience or affiliation the salesmen and customers shared—some similarity.

The world inside organizations is no different. Research shows that the longer people at work know one another, the more their relationships tend to harden into positive and negative patterns. When people at work first meet, the basis for rapport or trust is very shallow, built mainly on demographic similarities such as age and gender. As the relationships lengthen, people rely on actual experiences with each other to form opinions about trust and credibility. Finally, for the longest running relationships, trust is based on similarity of perspective on a range of issues. Demographic similarity fades out as a factor and there is much less monitoring of actual behavior—because the other person has "passed the test."

Working relationships are also characterized by reciprocity, linking this channel to the interest-based persuasion channel discussed earlier. Within relationships, a host of subtle items can be exchanged. In the airplane example, the young boy appealed to his earlier good behavior in the airport as the basis for rewarding him now with the cookie. The currencies of exchange in relationships—both at home and at work—are endless: past or promised favors, information, gossip, access, temporary relief from company rules or policy, self-esteem stroking, opportunities for advancement, griping privileges, secrets, and on and on.

To sum up, you are accessing the relationship channel *whenever you use similarity, liking, rapport, and reciprocity, or rely on your existing network of contacts and friends, to open doors as part of an idea-selling strategy.*

Conclusion

The world of the airplane is not that different from your world at work. In fact, for pilots and flight attendants, it *is* a world of work. And people depend on these professionals to be effectively persuasive every time a plane takes off. Moreover, as the discussion of the six channels makes clear, selling ideas is not a matter of forcing or coercing people to do things, though this is all too often the default persuasion system in many organizations. Persuasion is about working hard to properly align interests, values, and relationships—and sending messages to others on channels they are tuned to.

Negotiating with Liars

Robert S. Adler

One of the enduring truths about human beings is that we lie—frequently and often quite casually. In fact, if one believes the recent claims of many psychologists, the impulse to deceive resides deep within our genes, a central feature of our common humanity. As one scholar of deception puts it, "Lying is not exceptional; it is normal, and more often spontaneous and unconscious than cynical and coldly analytical. Our minds and bodies secrete deceit."[1]

Numerous studies confirm that few people can make it through a typical day without lying.[2] In one, subjects asked to keep diaries of their conversations reported that they told lies anywhere from 30 percent to 50 percent of the time on topics including their feelings, their actions and their plans and whereabouts.[3] Some 60 percent of newly introduced individuals lie to one another within minutes simply to create a favorable impression,[4] and dating couples apparently lie to each other even more.[5] According to the most conservative estimates of human resource managers, 25 percent of all résumés contain significant lies.[6] Moreover, lying behaviors start early—typically at age three or four.[7]

It should not be surprising, then, that when it comes to negotiation, the process is often strewn with falsehoods and deception. In fact, many observers find it difficult to imagine negotiating without some element of deception. Professor James White, an expert in the field, writes:

On one hand the negotiator must be fair and truthful; on the other he must mislead his opponent. Like the poker player, a negotiator hopes that his opponent will overestimate the value of his hand. . . . The critical difference between those who are successful negotiators and those who are not lies in this capacity both to mislead and not to be misled.[8]

The Morality and Legality of Lying

The pervasiveness or lying may cause some negotiators to become overly casual about the truth. The unspoken, and perhaps unconscious, thought is that if everyone lies, why is it so bad? In a widely read and frequently cited 1991 article in *Sloan Management Review,* Richard Shell, a legal studies and business ethics professor at the Wharton School of the University of Pennsylvania, voiced a spirited objection to the notion that we should adopt a relaxed attitude toward lying in negotiation settings: "[W]hat moralists would often consider merely 'unethical' behavior in negotiations turns out to be precisely what the courts consider illegal behavior."[9] To illustrate the point, Shell reviews numerous legal precedents to make the case that law and morality overlap substantially in outlawing false representations in bargaining situations. Common law fraud requires five simple elements: (1) a false representation of a material feet, (2) knowledge or belief as to its falsity, (3) an intent to induce the other party to rely on the representation,

Source: "Negotiating with Liars" by Robert S. Adler, from the *MIT Sloan Management Review* 48, no. 4, Summer 2007. Used with permission.

(4) justifiable reliance by the injured party, and (5) damage or injury to the innocent party.[10] Based on these elements, Shell concludes that "unethical bargaining practices are, as, often as not, illegal or become so after they are brought to light."[11] In other words, it's not just wrong; it's usually illegal to lie when bargaining.

Not All Deceptions Are Lies

To be sure, one should note that Shell's argument has limits. Notwithstanding his objections to negotiators' lies, he acknowledges that attempts to mislead are a fairly standard part of negotiations—something all negotiators need to be cognizant of.[12] No one should expect full disclosure at a flea market or used-car lot.

In fact, Shell does not argue that people who make misleading statements have necessarily committed an immoral or illegal act. That would mean that negotiators have a fiduciary relationship, imposing the highest duty of honesty and disclosure. At some point, the courts require people to mind the principle of caveat auditor ("let the listener beware").[13] Sales talk, for example, notoriously walks a fine line between legally binding factual statements and mere gratuitous praise, commonly known as "puffing."[14] Technically, the courts hold parties to the truth of their representations, yet they forgive puffs. The challenge is distinguishing legally binding statements from nonbinding ones. Consider, for example, one court's determination that when a sales agent referred to a building as "superb," "super fine" and "one of the finest little properties" in the city, he was simply puffing and not saying anything meaningful about the property's condition.[15] Contrast this with another court's ruling that a salesperson who described a computer as "first class" did make a representation that constituted a legally binding warranty,[16] or another court requiring a car dealer to stand behind an auto he said was in "good running condition."[17] How one is supposed to tease out a consistent "bright line" distinction from these rulings lies beyond the skill of our finest legal minds.[18]

It is also possible to gain advantage over an opponent (and without legal consequence) by not disclosing information that the other party ideally would like to know. For example, a farmer would be thrilled to hear that the party seeking to buy his land represented an oil company that wanted to exploit the mineral reserves. Similarly, a property owner would want to know that the person negotiating to buy his property represented one of the world's largest resort and entertainment companies.[19] Yet, for a variety of public policy reasons, the courts do not typically require companies to volunteer this kind of information.[20] Only if the nondisclosure strikes a court as particularly oppressive or unfair have courts required affirmative disclosure.[21]

Further, the courts rarely punish parties simply for being evasive. As viewers who watch politicians and public officials on Sunday morning interview shows can attest, there is a real art to responding to questions by changing the subject or answering questions that have not been asked.[22] Finally, it is often possible to avoid liability by using misleading behaviors that make no representations, but which seem to. Immanuel Kant famously offered the example of A deceiving B into believing that he is headed on a journey by conspicuously packing a suitcase, hoping that B would draw the intended conclusion.[23]

In light of the moral and legal ambiguity of lying, negotiators need to brace themselves for bargaining deception. They need to understand how they can detect lies and establish safeguards. As critical as this area is, few academic scholars have explored them beyond noting the importance of taking care when one bargains. This article examines the next steps to determine whether one can know when his or her opponent is lying and, if so, what one can do for protection.

Can We Detect Lies?

Everyone seems to have a favorite method for determining when someone is lying. Among the presumed "giveaways" are averting eye contact, pulling on one's ear, sweating, changing vocal pitch, increased (or decreased) smiling, long pauses between answers, rubbing one's arm or fingers, and heavy breathing. The list is long and often inconsistent: Someone blinks—or doesn't blink—and people insist that that person is lying. Many people claim that their test is reliable, and they recount personal experiences as evidence.

However, research shows that most people are quite incompetent as lie detectors. Liars are not easy to spot.[24] Indeed, according to most experiments, the odds of detecting whether someone is lying rarely exceed random chance.[25] For example, the popular notion that liars avert their gaze has been debunked.[26] Other indicators have been similarly discredited: that liars shift posture, move their heads in particular ways, smile inappropriately, make incriminating gestures and reveal falsehoods through specific foot or leg movements.[27] In fact, accomplished liars, knowing what observers look for as signals of deceit, can do an excellent job of controlling those behaviors. If anything, looking for such cues can interfere with an accurate assessment of truth telling. In one study, students were better able to detect lies by reading a transcript than by watching a videotape.[28]

Further evidence of how difficult it is to identify liars comes from a field study of suspects interrogated by the British police. In contrast to laboratory studies (where the only negative fallout from having one's lies detected might be the loss of a cash bonus), this study focused on individuals who faced lengthy incarceration if they lied unsuccessfully.[29] Through a careful winnowing process, the researchers obtained a number of taped interviews in which the suspects both told the truth and lied during an interrogation. (For confirmation that the suspects actually lied, the authors insisted on irrefutable evidence, such as verifiable confessions, after initial denials of wrongdoing.) The authors then asked independent observers to view the tapes and track a broad variety of behaviors, such as gaze aversion, head movement, blinking, head shaking, body scratching, speech disturbances, frequency of saying "ah" or "um," and verbal pauses. The authors then compared these behaviors to the known instances of lying in the tapes. Based on these observations, the authors reached several important conclusions. First, they debunked the notion that there is a typical indicator of deceptive behavior.[30] Second, the most reliable indicators of deception were stunningly minor: Most suspects paused longer and blinked less when lying.[31] Given how subtle these indicators are, it is fair to conclude that there is no universal—or easily readable—telltale sign of lying.

Equally sobering is the growing body of evidence showing that trained professionals—law enforcement officials, judges, psychiatrists, polygraph examiners, CIA agents or other skilled interrogators—rarely do better than lay observers in detecting lies under controlled experimental conditions.[32] Although they may exhibit high levels of confidence in their ability to detect lies, their certitude is not backed by data.[33]

Concerns Over Lie Detection Technologies

Over the years, scientists have developed a variety of technologies and techniques for detecting lies, most of which remain highly controversial. Topping the list are polygraph machines, often called lie detectors, which relate changes in heart rate, blood pressure and electro-dermal reactivity to a subject's truthfulness. Widely used by law enforcement agencies and businesses, lie detectors have increasingly come under critical scrutiny. The skepticism prompted Congress to enact legislation in 1988 banning the use of polygraph machines in most routine business settings and limiting their use to cases of national security.[34] In 2002, a National Academy of Sciences panel reviewed data from several decades of polygraphs and concluded that there was "little basis for the expectation that a polygraph test could have extremely high accuracy."[35] In fact, the panel estimated that if polygraphs were administered to a group of 10,000 people that included 10 spies, nearly 1,600 innocent people would fail the test—and two of the spies would pass.[36]

In recent years, other technologies have been proposed as alternatives to the polygraph. One of the most highly publicized methods has been described in a number of studies by Paul Ekman.[37] Ekman claims that when people lie, they involuntarily display fleeting facial expressions that give away their deception. He asserts that trained practitioners are able to use his method to detect lies with high degrees of accuracy.[38] However, a measure of skepticism is justified. Given the fleeting nature of microexpressions (and how minor and confusing many of the signals are), it is difficult to see how they can be interpreted with much accuracy in business negotiations.

There are similar doubts about other new technologies, including voice-stress analyzers, magnetic resonance imaging machines and advanced thermal-imaging technology. In recent years, as concerns about terrorism have spread, such tools have been touted for their accuracy in detecting lies. Yet sorting out claims about their effectiveness has become a challenge for law enforcement and defense experts. To date, most experts remain skeptical, and the likelihood that any of these techniques will be useful in the immediate future for businesspeople is remote.[39]

Protecting Against Deception

Given the challenges in detecting lies, one might be tempted to conclude that there are no realistic protections. However, this would be an overreaction. Indeed, one can greatly minimize the risk of lies in bargaining through a series of steps designed either to expose lies and liars before negotiations begin or to provide protection from lies.

Before the Bargaining Begins

Every negotiation expert worth his or her salt offers the same advice: prepare, prepare, prepare. Preparation is particularly critical when facing opponents for the first time and the stakes are high. There are two parts: researching the other side's character and bona fides, and anticipating scenarios that might play out in the negotiation.

Research Background and Bona Fides   At a minimum, one should check available sources of public information—the Better Business Bureau, the Federal Trade Commission, state and local consumer protection offices—to see whether the other side has run afoul of the law or good business practices.[40] Perhaps the quickest way to begin is to run a search through Google, Yahoo! or one of the other Internet search engines. If suspicions arise about the other side's bona fides or good faith, asking that person to disclose credentials, credit record or personal history forces the individual to prove his or her legitimacy as a bargaining partner. Some negotiators are uneasy about asking for this information since it indicates that they do not trust the other side. It depends on how you ask. Asking politely, with reassurances that you are trying to establish trust, will usually offset any negative reaction from an honest opponent.

Set Special Ground Rules for Bargaining   Under the law, most contracts are negotiated at "arm's length," meaning that the parties have no special duty of disclosure, and each side is acting in his or her own interest. Although the two sides are not free to lie to each other, they generally do not have any duty to disclose secret, material information. This means that an agent bargaining on behalf of the oil company or the amusement park builder to buy land has no obligation to share what they intend to do with the acquired property. However, some experts have argued that parties (especially lawyers) should consider entering into pre-negotiation agreements whereby they commit themselves to negotiate according to higher standards; specifically, they might agree to disclose all material information, abstain from unreasonable delays and abstain from imposing hardships on the other party to force favorable settlements.[41] At a minimum, this would provide reasonable guarantees that a negotiator was not withholding critical information (such as the existence of oil on one's property). Moreover, one side's refusal to enter into a "good faith in negotiation" agreement might act as a tip-off that he or she plans to withhold vital information.

During the Bargaining Process

Once bargaining is under way, there are a variety of tools to detect lies. Even when lies can't be detected, one can still build in safeguards against them.

Look for Potential Signs of Deception   Despite evidence that there are no reliable behavioral "giveaways" of lying, the reality is that some individuals are incompetent liars. One should carefully observe the other party to determine if this is so, particularly by monitoring his or her baseline demeanor.[42] If an animated person suddenly becomes shy or a calm person begins to fidget, it is important to pay attention to what they are saying and take additional protective measures.

Ask Questions in Different Ways   People who wish to deceive do not necessarily resort to outright lies, which can lead to charges of fraud. Instead, they dodge, duck, bob and weave around the truth, assuming that their statements will be misconstrued or not challenged. For example, if Tom is trying to contact Suzy and asks John for her phone number, John—who has her e-mail address but not her phone number—might be technically correct in saying that he doesn't have her number. To avoid such a narrow response, Tom should ask John whether he knows of any way to contact Suzy.

Similarly, if Mary asks Sam if he has ever been arrested or convicted of fraud or theft, Sam might respond indignantly: "I've never been convicted of anything like those crimes." The reply might gloss over the fact that he had been charged with fraud but never convicted. Without pushing him to respond to her question about previous arrests, Mary may be misled; whether a court would find that Sam led Mary astray is debatable. Some courts might, but many jurisdictions would probably rule in Sam's favor, believing that it was Mary's job to ask follow-up questions.[43]

If the questioner isn't convinced that the complete story is forthcoming, he or she can try another approach. The questioner can try to summarize the point at issue in his or her own words and demand that the other side answer with a "yes" or "no." If the person responds with words other than yes or no, the negotiator would be well advised to continue grilling the opponent. Conversely, the negotiator might infer something negative from an opponent's refusal to answer questions about a hidden ownership in land and say, "Since I can't get you to answer the question directly, I am going to assume that you do have an undisclosed interest in the property."

Ask the Opponent to "Come Clean"   In any setting where one feels that the other side is not being forthcoming, one should push the other party to reveal all relevant information. To do that, one needs to ask whether there are any material facts that have not been disclosed—in effect, to come clean about knowledge. For example, Sherry strongly suspects that Brad has a hidden reason for wanting to buy her house, but she can't get him to go beyond saying that he sees "strong commercial possibilities." At some point, Sherry might try a different approach and ask, "Is there something important that you know about this deal that you haven't told me?" If Brad denies any knowledge and Sherry later discovers that Brad knows that a highway is slated to go through the area, Sherry might have a strong legal case based on Brad's false representation to her. Although Brad might not have a legal duty to volunteer this information, by denying that he is withholding anything, he exposes himself to possible legal damages for fraudulent nondisclosure.[44]

Ask Questions to which You Already Know the Answer   A well-known way to test veracity is to probe areas where you know the answer. If the other side responds with a lie, you know that there is an issue of trustworthiness. A famous example of this approach can be found in the 1962 Cuban Missile Crisis. At a meeting with Soviet Foreign Minister Andrei Gromyko, President John F. Kennedy, armed with photographs, asked Gromyko to admit that the Russians had located the missiles in Cuba. Gromyko repeatedly denied that this was the case, whereupon Kennedy angrily ordered a blockade of Cuba and demanded that the missiles be removed.

Take Notes During Negotiations   When disputes arise after a deal has been struck, one of the difficulties of holding the other side accountable is establishing what was actually stated in the discussion leading up to the agreement. Expert negotiators typically take good notes on critical points to remove any potential ambiguity. Some read the other side's words back to them and ask them to confirm it for accuracy. Others go so far as to bring another party in as a witness to the discussion.

Include Written Claims as Part of the Final Agreement   In cases where the other party's representations about facts are fundamental to making the deal acceptable, it makes sense to insist that the relevant representation be included in the written terms of the deal. For example, Acme Manufacturing Co. might be reluctant to purchase a widget supplier because it is nervous about future demand for widgets. To reassure Acme, the seller might provide a multiyear purchase commitment from a major customer. However, as a condition of the deal, Acme should insist on getting a reference to the commitment in writing.

Use Contingent Agreements for Protection   Sometimes merely stating an intention to include the other party's statements in the written agreement triggers a more honest discussion. If, however, the other side insists that its original representation is correct, a skilled negotiator can take the next step: Insist on a "contingency" provision in the contract that provides specific protection should the representation turn out to be false. In contingency agreements, the parties agree in advance on consequences and remedies (including monetary damages) if and when certain events unfold.[45]

Trust but Verify   Many people will remember President Ronald Reagan's negotiations with Soviet Premier Mikhail Gorbachev in 1987 over the Intermediate Nuclear Forces Treaty, where Reagan used a line attributed to Lenin: "Trust, but verify." The reality is that parties are more likely to trust each other when they have a means of determining whether the other party's representations are accurate. Society has developed a number of legal and regulatory tools (including performance bonds and escrow agents) to help provide protections against dishonesty and bad faith in bargaining. Depending on the circumstances, negotiators should always consider whether such mechanisms are appropriate for achieving their objectives.

Former U.S. Ambassador Clare Booth Luce once remarked, "Lying increases the creative faculties, expands the ego and lessens the frictions of social contacts." Because lying serves so many "useful" purposes, it is no surprise that it is so popular with humans. Knowing this, negotiators need to guard themselves against being exploited when they bargain. As H. L. Mencken noted, "It is hard to believe that a man is telling the truth when you know that you would lie if you were in his place." Fortunately, there are steps you can take to protect yourself against lies and lying liars.

Endnotes

1. D. L. Smith, *Why We Lie: The Evolutionary Roots of Deception and the Unconscious Mind* (New York: St. Martin's Press, 2004), 15. For additional discussion of the psychology of lying, see R. Wright, *The Moral Animal: Why We Are the Way We Are: The New Science of Evolutionary Psychology* (New York: Pantheon Books, 1994), 324–325.

2. See B. M. DePaulo, S. E. Kirkendol, D. A. Kashy, M. M. Wyer and J. A. Epstein, "Lying in Everyday Life," *Journal of Personality and Social Psychology* 70, no. 5 (May 1996): 979–995; Smith, *Why We Lie,* 9–16; and A. Kornet, "The Truth About Lying," *Psychology Today* (May–June 1997), 52–58. The seminal work on lying is S. Bok, *Lying: Moral Choice in Public and Private Life* (New York: Vintage, 1978).

3.   DePaulo, *Lying in Everyday Life,* 990.

4.   R. S. Feldman, J. A. Forrest and B. R. Happ, "Self-Presentation and Verbal Deception: Do Self-Presenters Lie More?" *Basic and Applied Social Psychology* 24, no. 2 (2002): 163–170.

5.   Kornet, "The Truth About Lying," 53 (citing studies by B. M. DePaulo).

6.   T. Prater and S. B. Kiser, "Lies, Lies and More Lies," *SAM Advanced Management Journal* 67 (Spring 2002): 9–16.

7.   See M. Lewis, "The Development of Deception" in *Lying and Deception in Everyday Life,* eds. M. Lewis and C. Saami (New York: Guilford Press, 1993), 90–105.

8.   J. J. White, "Machiavelli and the Bar: Ethical Limitations On Lying in Negotiation," *American Bar Foundation Research Journal* 5, no. 4 (autumn 1980): 926–938, 928. Scholars have repeatedly noted the propensity of negotiators to lie. See, for example, M. Schweitzer, "Negotiators Lie," *Negotiation* 8, no. 12 (December 2005): 1.

9.   G. R. Shell, "When Is It Legal to Lie in Negotiations?" *Sloan Management Review* 43, no. 1 (spring 1991): 93–101.

10.   Ibid., 94–98. See also W. P. Keeton, D. B. Dobbs, R. E. Keeton and D. G. Owen, *Prosser and Keeton on the Law of Torts,* 5th ed. (St. Paul, Minnesota: West Publishing, 1984), 107–109, 737.

11.   Shell, "When Is It Legal to Lie in Negotiations?" 99.

12.   "Commercial negotiations seem to require a talent for deception." Ibid., 93.

13.   S. P. Green, "Lying, Misleading and Falsely Denying: How Moral Concepts Inform the Law of Perjury, Fraud and False Statements," *Hastings Law Journal* 53 (2001): 157–212, 160.

14.   Section 2-313 of the Uniform Commercial Code provides that an express warranty is created "by any affirmation of fact or promise made by the seller to the buyer which relates to the goods and becomes part of the 'basis of the bargain.'" Section 2-312(2) provides, however, that "an affirmation merely of the value of the goods or a statement purporting to be merely the seller's opinion or commendation of the goods does not create a warranty." These latter affirmations are commonly referred to as "puffs."

15.   *Ed Miller & Sons Inc. v. Earl,* 502 N.W. 2d 444 (Nebraska 1993).

16.   *Ellmer v. Delaware Mini-Computer Sys. Inc.,* 665 S.W. 2d 158 (Texas App.1983).

17.   *Melotz v. Schecls,* 801 P. 2d 593 (Montana 1990).

18.   Two of the most well-known commentators in the law of sales have thrown in the towel. See J. J. White and R. S. Summers, *Uniform Commercial Code,* 4th ed. (St. Paul, Minnesota: West Publishing, 1995), 9.4,335. They state that "anyone who says he can tell a 'puff' from a warranty is a fool or a liar."

19.   To avoid speculators driving up the cost of land for Disney World, the Disney Corp., in 1964, purchased 27,400 acres in Orange and Osceola Counties in Florida through the use of dummy corporations and confidential agents operating under such names as the Latin-America Development and Management Corp. and the Reedy Creek Ranch Corp. See http://en.wikipedia.org/wiki/DisneyWorld.

20.   The most frequently cited reason is that forcing parties with superior knowledge to share information that they have painstakingly and expensively acquired would undermine their incentive to seek and gather such information, thus imposing serious efficiency costs on the public. As Professor Donald Langevoort states: "Though the law of nondisclosure is

fluid and fuzzy, there is widespread recognition that parties to a negotiation are privileged to withhold at least some crucial information from the other, lest there be a disincentive to the socially beneficial production or discovery of that sort of information." See D. C. Longevoort, "Half-Truths: Protecting Mistaken Inferences By Investors and Others," *Stanford Law Review* 52 (1999): 87–125, 89–90.

21. The courts have required affirmative disclosure in at least four circumstances: (1) when the nondisclosing party makes a partial disclosure that is or becomes misleading in light of all the facts, (2) when the parties stand in a fiduciary relationship to one another, (3) when the nondisclosing party has "superior information" vital to the transaction that is not accessible to the other side and (4) when special transactions are at issue, such as insurance contracts. Shell, "When Is It Legal To Lie in Negotiations?" 95.

22. On this point, Shell states, "there is no commandment in negotiation that says 'Thou shalt answer every question that is asked.' And as an aspiring idealist, I have found it useful to follow this rule: Whenever you are tempted to lie about something, stop, think for a moment, and then find something—anything—to tell the truth about." See G. R. Shell, *Bargaining For Advantage: Negotiation Strategies For Reasonable People* (New York: Penguin Books, 1999), 228.

23. I. Kant, "Lectures on Ethics 226," trans. L. Infield (1963), in Green, *Lying, Misleading and Falsely Denying,* 159.

24. See, for example, G. S. Goodman, T. L. Luten, R. S. Edelstein and P. Ekman, "Detecting Lies in Children and Adults," *Law and Human Behavior* 30, no. 1 (May 2006): 1–10 (noting that, on average, people's accuracy in detecting adults' lies rarely exceeds chance guesses); P. Ekman and M. O'Sullivan, "Who Can Catch a Liar?" *American Psychologist* 46, no. 9 (1991): 913–920; C. Lock, "Deception Detection: Psychologists Try to Learn How to Spot a Liar," *Science News* 166, no. 5 (July 31,2004): 72–73; and R. M. Henig, "Looking For the Lie," *New York Times Sunday Magazine*, February 5, 2006, sec. 6, p. 47.

25. That is, one choosing randomly between "truth" or "falsity" would have a 50–50 chance of getting the correct answer. Few test subjects get more than 50 percent of their guesses right when they seek to determine whether a person is telling the truth in a controlled experiment. See S. Kassin, "On the Psychology of Confessions: Does Innocence Put Innocents At Risk?" *American Psychologist* 60, no. 3 (April 2005): 215–228, 217.

26. S. Mann, A. Vrij and R. Bull, "Suspects, Lies and Videotape: An Analysis of Authentic High-Stake Liars," *Law and Human Behavior* 26, no. 3 (June 2002): 365–376; B. M. DePaulo, J. I. Stone and G. D. Lassiter, "Deceiving and Detecting Deceit," in *The Self and Social Life,* ed. B. R. Schlenker (New York: McGraw-Hill, 1985), 323–370; and A. Vrij, *Detecting Lies and Deceit: The Psychology of Lying and Its Implications For Professional Practice* (Chichester, United Kingdom: Wiley, 2000). Vrij reviews more than 40 studies about liars' behavior.

27. DePaulo et al., "Deceiving and Detecting Deceit," 340, Table 12–4.

28. J.E. Hocking et al., "Detecting Deceptive Communication From Verbal, Visual and Paralinguistic Cues," *Human Communication Research* 6, no. 1 (fall 1979): 33–46.

29. Mann "Suspects, Lies and Videotape," 366.

30. Ibid, 371.

31. Ibid.

32. For a review of studies that have examined skilled professionals' accuracy in controlled experiments and have demonstrated no greater skill in detecting lies than untrained laypeople, see Ekman, "Who Can Catch a Liar?" 913; and Kassin, "On the Psychology of Confessions," 217.

33. B. M. DePaulo and R. L. Pfeifer, "On-the-Job Experience and Skill at Detecting Deception," *Journal of Applied Social Psychology* 16, no. 3 (1986): 249–267; and Ekman, "Who Can Catch a Liar?" 919.

34. *Employee Polygraph Protection Act of 1988,* P.L. 100-347, 29 U.S.C. §§2001-09 (1988).

35. Board on Behavioral, Cognitive and Sensory Sciences and Education, National Academy of Sciences, *The Polygraph and Lie Detection,* www.nap.edu/books/0309084369/html.

36. D. Eggen and S. Vedantam, "Polygraph Results Often in Question," *Washington Post,* May 1, 2006, sec. A, p. 1.

37. Ekman, "Who Can Catch a Liar?" 914. See also P. Ekman and W. V. Friesen, "Detecting Deception from the Body or Face," *Journal of Personality and Social Psychology* 29, no. 3 (1974): 288–298; and P. Ekman, W. V. Friesen and M. O'Sullivan, "Smiles When Lying," *Journal of Personality and Social Psychology* 54, no. 3 (1988): 414–420.

38. Ibid.

39. See P. R. Wolpe, K. R. Foster and D. D. Langeleben, "Emerging Neuro technologies for Lie-Detection: Promises and Perils," *American Journal of Bioethics* 5, no. 2 (2005): 39–49; R. Willing, "Terrorism Lends Urgency to Hunt For Better Lie Detector," *USA Today,* Nov. 4, 2003; D. Wagner, "Arguments Rage Over Voice-Stress Lie Detector," *Arizona Republic*, Oct. 10, 2005; and M. Hansen, "Truth Sleuth or Faulty Detector?" *ABA Journal* 85 (May 1999): 16.

40. P. C. Cramton and J. G. Dees, "Promoting Honesty in Negotiation: An Exercise in Practical Ethics," *Business Ethics Quarterly* 3, no. 4 (1993): 359–394.

41. S. R. Peppet, "Lawyers' Bargaining Ethics, Contract and Collaboration: The End of the Legal Profession and the Beginning of Professional Pluralism," *Iowa Law Review* 90 (2005): 475–538.

42. Mann, "Suspects, Lies and Videotape," 372.

43. Langevoort cites a variety of circumstances that affect court rulings in this area of fraud law: the precise words used, the relative sophistication of the parties, whether the parties are bargaining face to face and so on. Langevoort, "Half-Truths," 102–109.

44. The elements of common law fraud for omission or failure to disclose facts are: (1) an omission to state or disclose, (2) material facts, (3) when there is a duty to do so, (4) with intent to deceive or mislead, (5) causing justifiable reliance on the part of the victim and (6) which is the proximate cause of injury. See N. W. Palmieri, "Good Faith Disclosures Required During Precontractual Negotiations," *Seton Hall Law Review* 24 (1993): 70–213,142. See also, *Henry v. Office of Thrift Supervision,* 43 F. 3d 507 (10th Cir. 1994).

45. Contingent agreements are often used in circumstances in which the parties have different and irreconcilable visions of the future. Rather than argue endlessly about what the future holds, the parties can simply put a contingency in the agreement that provides different outcomes depending on which version of the future proves accurate. See M. H. Bazerman and J. J. Gillespie, "Betting On the Future: The Virtues of Contingent Agreements," *Harvard Business Review* 77, no. 5 (September–October 1999): 155–160.

Negotiation Ethics
Charles B. Craver

When I teach negotiation courses to attorneys and business people, I often begin by indicating that I have rarely participated in professional negotiations during which both sides did not lie, yet I have encountered very few negotiators I thought were dishonest. How can negotiators lie without being dishonest? They misrepresent matters they are not expected to discuss truthfully.

Two people get together to negotiate. One is authorized to accept any amount over $100,000, while the other is authorized to pay up to $130,000. They thus have a $30,000 settlement range between their respective bottom lines. They initially exchange small talk, then begin to explore the substantive issues of their exchange. The person who hopes to obtain money states that he cannot accept anything below $150,000, while the person willing to pay money indicates that she cannot go a penny over $75,000. They are pleased to have begun their interaction successfully, yet both have begun with bold-faced lies.

Model Rule 4.1, which regulates the ethics of lawyers, provides that an attorney "shall not knowingly make a false statement of material fact or law to a third person." This unequivocally indicates that lawyers may not lie. When is a lie not a lie, when it's by a lawyer! When this rule was being drafted, people who teach negotiation skills pointed out that if all lies were forbidden, when attorneys negotiated most would be subject to discipline because of what is euphemistically characterized as "puffing." As a result, a reporter's comment was included with Rule 4.1 indicating that different expectations are involved when attorneys are negotiating.

> Whether a particular statement should be regarded as one of fact can depend on the circumstances. Under generally accepted conventions in negotiation, certain types of statements ordinarily are not taken as statements of material fact. Estimates of price or value placed on the subject of a transaction and a party's intentions as to an acceptable settlement of a claim are in this category.

As a result, if one party offered to pay the other $115,000, the offer recipient could ethically indicate that this sum was unacceptable to his side even though he knew it was perfectly acceptable. If the other side requested a non-admission provision indicating that her side wished to disclaim any admission of legal responsibility for what was being resolved, the first party could vehemently oppose such a provision even though he knows that his client doesn't care about such a provision. He does this in an effort to obtain more money for his client in exchange for the non-admission clause the other side values. Both of these statements are considered "puffing" since they pertain to non-material information.

I have no difficulty with the reporter's comment indicating that statements concerning one's actual settlement intentions and the subjective value placed on items being

Source: "Negotiation Ethics," by Charles B. Craver, from *The Negotiator Magazine,* December 2005. Used by permission of the author.

exchanged do not have to be truthful. They pertain to "puffing" and do not involve matters one expects to be discussed with complete candor. On the other hand, I find it odd to state that these matters do not concern "material fact." When we negotiate, the factual, legal, economic, and political issues underlying the instant transaction are really secondary. What parties have to determine through the negotiation process is how the other side values the items being exchanged and how much of each must be offered to induce the other side to enter into an agreement. Nonetheless, I do expect such "puffing" and am not offended by persons who over or under state the value of items for strategic purposes or who are not forthright regarding their true settlement intentions.

The principal difficulty professional organizations have regulating the behavior of negotiators concerns the unique circumstances in which most bargaining interactions are conducted. They are usually done on a one-on-one basis in person or over the telephone. If one person is a lying scoundrel and they are accused of dishonesty by another party, they lie to the disciplinary authority. It is extremely difficult for such a body to determine which side is telling the truth. What really regulates this area is the market place. If persons behave in a questionable manner, their reputations will be quickly tarnished. When someone encounters others who will lie about what they have the right to know, they usually tell their friends and associates. Those deceivers begin to encounter difficulties when they negotiate. Individuals don't trust them. Their statements have to be independently verified, and their agreements have to be reduced to writing. Their negotiations become more cumbersome and less efficient. If they try to regain reputations for honesty, they discover how difficult it is to overcome stories about their past. Any negotiator who contemplates improper behavior during bargaining interactions should appreciate the substantial risks involved. A short-term gain may easily become a long-term stumbling block to future deals.

The three basic areas of misrepresentations concern affirmative misrepresentations, truthful statements that are incomplete and misleading, and the failure to disclose information necessary to prevent misunderstandings by the other side.

I. Affirmative Misrepresentations

Suppose my client is thinking of selling her company and another party has approached us to discuss their possible purchase of this firm. Assume that the corporate owner has told her negotiator that she would like to get at least $50 million, but might go as low as $45 million if necessary. The prospective buyer asks how much it would take to buy this firm. Can I ethically suggest $60 million? Clearly the answer is yes, because this pertains to non-material information—our settlement intentions—and is considered acceptable "puffing." They then offer $35 million and I ask if they would consider going higher. Could they ethically suggest an unwillingness to increase their offer? Again yes, since this is still "puffing."

If no one else has indicated an interest in my client's business, could I ethically indicate that other bidders are involved? Although I have had a few attorneys suggest that this type of statement is mere "puffing," I don't agree. I think this is highly material fact information that must be discussed honestly if it is mentioned at all. As a result, if I state that other prospective buyers are in the picture, I have to convey truthful information. If several other parties have expressed an interest in the same firm and have offered us $40 million, could I ethically state that we have been offered $50 million? Since I consider this to be material fact information this possible buyer has the right to rely upon, I don't believe I can make such a misrepresentation. I might, however, be able to avoid the ethical dilemma by indicating that other parties are interested in our firm and stating that someone will have to pay $50 million if they wish to purchase the company. I am not disclosing what offers have actually been received, but am only indicating—truthfully—that some offers have been tendered. Without disclosing the actual amounts involved, I am merely stating that it will take $50 million to buy the company. Even if my client is willing to sell for less, this is nonmaterial "puffing."

To what degree may I overstate the true value of the company my client is selling? May I suggest it has a rosy future, even if that is not entirely clear? May I say we are on the verge of an important product development when that is incorrect? May I indicate that we have accounts receivable of $540,000, when those accounts total only $150,000? The first statement of a wholly subjective nature is probably acceptable if I don't embellish too greatly. The other two would be improper, because they concern material fact information the other party has the right to know truthfully. While I may have no affirmative obligation to disclose these facts, if I choose to discuss them I must do so honestly.

II. Partially True Statements

Some seemingly truthful statements can be misleading. A famous legal case involves a person injured in an automobile accident. His ribs are cracked and he suffers soft tissue injuries. With the passage of time, the ribs and the affected tissue heal. The defense lawyer sends the plaintiff to a physician who will be used as an expert for the defense at trial. That doctor verifies that the ribs have healed, but finds a life-threatening aneurism on that person's aorta. If asked by the claimant's attorney about the examining physician's findings, could the defense lawyer respond that everything is fine? Clearly not, because this would be a misrepresentation of material fact. What if that lawyer merely states that "the ribs have healed nicely?" Would this truthful statement be acceptable, or does it deceitfully imply that nothing else has been discovered? The vast majority of lawyers asked this question suggest that this would be an impermissible misrepresentation—despite the truth of what is being said—due to the fact the person making the statement knows that the listener is likely to misinterpret what is being said to mean that everything has healed. Ethical opinions have held that truthful statements may constitute actionable misrepresentations when they are made under circumstances in which the person making the statements knows the other party is misinterpreting what is being conveyed. While the defense lawyer may not have to answer the question about the doctor's findings, she should not be permitted to say something she knows will be misleading.

A similar issue might arise when someone is thinking of purchasing a house that suffered substantial damage in a hurricane but seems to have been repaired. What if the prospective purchaser asks if the storm damage has been repaired? Could the seller truthfully indicate that the roof has been completely replaced, but say nothing about the fact the eaves under the roof still leak when it rains? Since it should be apparent that the person hearing this representation would be likely to assume that the storm damage has been entirely repaired, the seller should either have to remain silent or include information indicating that additional leaks exist. In many states requiring house sellers to disclose known defects of a serious nature, the seller would be obliged to disclose the leaking eaves even if they are not specifically asked about this issue.

When negotiators are asked about delicate issues or decide to raise those matters on their own, their statements should be phrased in a manner that conveys—both explicitly and implicitly—truthful information. They should not use half-truths they know are likely to induce listeners to misunderstand the actual circumstances. If they are not sure what to say, they may remain silent. If they choose to speak, however, they must do so in a way that is not misleading.

III. Impermissible Omissions

In many business and legal interactions the basic rule is caveat emptor—buyer beware. If the buyer does not ask the right questions and the seller makes no affirmative misrepresentations, the buyer has no recourse if he subsequently discovers problems. When might seller silence give rise to legal liability? Whenever the law imposes an affirmative duty to disclose. As noted above, the laws in many states require home sellers to disclose known defects of a serious nature. Sellers who fail to satisfy this duty may be sued for the damages caused by the undisclosed defects.

Similar affirmative duties are imposed upon stock and bond sellers by securities laws. Before selling stock or bonds to buyers, owners are required to provide prospectuses that include detailed financial information. If they fail to include relevant positive and negative information, they can be held liable for their omissions.

What about the defense lawyer who knows about the aortic aneurism. When that actual case arose, the defense attorney was not only under no obligation to disclose the negative information—he was under an ethical duty not to volunteer that information because of the confidential nature of the medical news obtained from his own expert witness. Several years ago, the American Bar Association modified Model Rule 1.6 covering confidentiality to indicate that lawyers *may*—but are still not required to—disclose confidential information when such disclosure is necessary to prevent death or serious bodily injury. Although some people thought this modification should have required disclosure in such circumstances, mandatory disclosure was rejected. While defense attorneys possessing such negative information cannot ethically misrepresent the operative facts—either directly or through partially truthful statements they know are misleading—they still don't have to volunteer that information. I personally would have preferred a rule that required such disclosure, both because of the moral implications involved and to avoid possible economic harm to attorneys who do the right thing and lose business to lawyers who promise not to disclose such information unless specifically directed to do so by their clients.

IV. Conclusion

Although some misrepresentations are considered acceptable "puffing," others are clearly inappropriate. It is not always easy to draw the line between statements the other side does not have the right to rely upon and those they may consider sacrosanct. When my students ask about the proper demarcation, I tell them to ask how they would feel if their opponent were to make the misrepresentation they are contemplating. If they would consider their opponent dishonest then they should refrain from such conduct themselves. I like to leave them with a quote from Mark Twain: "Always do right. This will gratify some people and astonish the rest."

Three Schools of Bargaining Ethics
G. Richard Shell

The three schools of bargaining ethics I want to introduce for your consideration are (1) the "It's a game" Poker School, (2) the "Do the right thing even if it hurts" Idealist School, and (3) the "What goes around, comes around" Pragmatist School.

Let's look at each one in turn. As I describe these schools, try to decide which aspects of them best reflect your own attitudes. After you figure out where you stand today, take a moment and see if that is where you ought to be. My advice is to aim as high as you can, consistent with your genuinely held beliefs about bargaining. In the pressured world of practice, people tend to slide down rather than climb up when it comes to ethical standards.

The "It's a Game" Poker School

The Poker School of ethics sees negotiation as a "game" with certain rules. The rules are defined by the law. Conduct within the rules is ethical. Conduct outside the rules is unethical.

The modern founder of the Poker School was Albert Z. Carr, a former special consultant to President Harry Truman. Carr wrote a book in the 1960s called, appropriately enough, *Business as a Game.* In a related article that appeared in the *Harvard Business Review,* Carr argued that bluffing and other misleading but lawful negotiating tactics are "an integral part of the [bargaining] game, and the executive who does not master [these] techniques is not likely to accumulate much money or power."

People who adhere to the Poker School readily admit that bargaining and poker are not exactly the same. But they point out that deception is essential to effective play in both arenas. Moreover, skilled players in both poker and bargaining exhibit a robust and realistic distrust of the other fellow. Carr argues that good players should ignore the "claims of friendship" and engage in "cunning deception and concealment" in fair, hard-bargaining encounters. When the game is over, members of the Poker School do not think less of a fellow player just because that person successfully deceived them. In fact, assuming the tactic was legal, they may admire the deceiver and vow to be better prepared (and less trusting) next time.

We know how to play poker, but how exactly does one play the bargaining "game"? Stripped to its core, it looks like this: Someone opens, and then people take turns proposing terms to each other. Arguments supporting your preferred terms are allowed. You can play or pass in each round. The goal is to get the other side to agree to terms that are as close as possible to your last proposal.

In the bargaining game, it is understood that both sides might be bluffing. Bluffs disguise a weak bargaining hand—that is, the limited or unattractive alternatives you

Source: "Three Schools of Bargaining Ethics," by G. Richard Shell, from *Bargaining for Advantage: Negotiating Strategies for Reasonable People,* 1999, pp. 215–222. New York: Penguin Books. Used with Permission.

have away from the table, your inability to affect the other side's alternatives, and the arguments you have to support your demands. Unlike poker players, negotiators always attempt to disclose a good hand if they have one in the bargaining game. So the most effective bluffs are realistic, attractive, difficult-to-check (but false) alternatives or authoritative (but false) supporting standards. Experienced players know this, so one of the key skills in the bargaining game is judging when the other party's alternatives or arguments are really as good as he or she says. If the other side calls you on your bargaining bluff by walking away or giving you a credible ultimatum, you lose. Either there will be no deal when there should have been one, or the final price will be nearer to their last offer than to yours.

As mentioned, the Poker School believes in the rule of law. In poker, you are not allowed to hide cards, collude with other players, or renege on your bets. But you are expected to deceive others about your hand. The best plays come when you win the pot with a weak hand or fool the other players into betting heavily when your hand is strong. In bargaining, you must not commit outright, actionable fraud, but negotiators must be on guard for anything short of fraud.

The Poker School has three main problems as I see it. First, the Poker School presumes that everyone treats bargaining as a game. Unfortunately, it is an empirical fact that people disagree on this. For a start, neither the idealists nor the pragmatists (more on these next) think bargaining is a game. This problem does not deter the Poker School, which holds that the rules permit its members to play even when the other party disagrees about this premise.

Second, everyone is supposed to know the rules cold. But this is impossible, given that legal rules are applied differently in different industries and regions of the world.

Finally, the law is far from certain even within a single jurisdiction. So you often need a sharp lawyer to help you decide what to do.

The "Do the Right Thing Even If It Hurts" Idealist School

The Idealist School says that bargaining is an aspect of social life, not a special activity with its own unique set of rules. The same ethics that apply in the home should carry over directly into the realm of negotiation. If it is wrong to lie or mislead in normal social encounters, it is wrong to do so in negotiations. If it is OK to lie in special situations (such as to protect another person's feelings), it is also OK to lie in negotiations when those special conditions apply.

Idealists do not entirely rule out deception in negotiation. For example, if the other party assumes you have a lot of leverage and never asks you directly about the situation as you see it, you do not necessarily have to volunteer information weakening your position. And the idealist can decline to answer questions. But such exceptions are uncomfortable moments. Members of the Idealist School prefer to be candid and honest at the bargaining table even if it means giving up a certain amount of strategic advantage.

The Idealist School draws its strength from philosophy and religion. For example, Immanuel Kant said that we should all follow the ethical rules that we would wish others to follow. Kant argued that if everyone lied all the time, social life would be chaos.

Hence you should not lie. Kant also disapproved of treating other people merely as the means to achieve your own personal ends. Lies in negotiation are selfish acts designed to achieve personal gain. This form of conduct is therefore unethical—period. Many religions also teach adherents not to lie for personal advantage.

Idealists admit that deception in negotiation rarely arouses moral indignation unless the lies breach a trust between friends, violate a fiduciary responsibility, or exploit people such as the sick or elderly, who lack the ability to protect themselves. And if the only way you can prevent some terrible harm like a murder is by lying, go ahead and lie. But the lack of moral outrage and the fact that sometimes lying can be defended do not make deception in negotiations right.

Idealists strongly reject the idea that negotiations should be viewed as "games." Negotiations, they feel, are serious, consequential communication acts. People negotiate to resolve their differences so social life will work for the benefit of all. People must be held responsible for all their actions, including the way they negotiate, under universal standards.

Idealists think that the members of the Poker School are predatory and selfish. For its part, the Poker School thinks that idealists are naive and even a little silly. When members of the two schools meet at the bargaining table, tempers can flare.

Some members of the Idealist School have recently been trying to find a philosophical justification for bluffs about bottom lines. There is no agreement yet on whether these efforts have succeeded in ethical terms. But it is clear that outright lies such as fictitious other offers and better prices are unethical practices under idealist principles.

The big problem for the idealists is obvious: Their standards sometimes make it difficult to proceed in a realistic way at the bargaining table. Also, unless adherence to the Idealist School is coupled with a healthy skepticism about the way other people will negotiate, idealism leaves its members open to exploitation by people with standards other than their own. These limitations are especially troublesome when idealists must represent others' interests at the bargaining table.

Despite its limitations, I like the Idealist School. Perhaps because I am an academic, I genuinely believe that the different parts of my life are, in fact, a whole. I aspire to ethical standards that I can apply consistently. I will admit that I sometimes fall short of idealism's strict code, but by aiming high I hope I am leaving myself somewhere to fall that maintains my basic sense of personal integrity.

I confess my preference for the Idealist School so you will know where I am coming from in this discussion. But I realize that your experience and work environment may preclude idealism as an ethical option. That's OK. As I hope I am making clear, idealism is not the only way to think about negotiation in ethical terms.

The "What Goes Around Comes Around" Pragmatist School

The final school of bargaining ethics, the Pragmatist School, includes some original elements as well as some attributes of the previous two. In common with the Poker School, this approach views deception as a necessary part of the negotiation process. Unlike the Poker School, however, it prefers not to use misleading statements and overt lies if there is a serviceable, practical alternative. Uniquely, the Pragmatist School displays concern for the potential negative effects of deceptive conduct on present and future relationships. Thus lying and other questionable tactics are bad not so much because they are "wrong" as because they cost the user more in the long run than they gain in the short run.

As my last comment suggests, people adhere to this school more for prudential than idealistic reasons. Lies and misleading conduct can cause serious injury to one's credibility. And credibility is an important asset for effective negotiators both to preserve working relationships and to protect one's reputation in a market or community. This latter concern is summed up in what I would call the pragmatist's credo: What goes around comes around. The Poker School is less mindful of reputation and more focused on winning each bargaining encounter within the rules of the "game."

What separates the Pragmatist School from the Idealist School? To put it bluntly, a pragmatist will lie a bit more often than will an idealist. For example, pragmatists sometimes draw fine distinctions between lies about hard-core facts of a transaction, which are always imprudent (and often illegal), and misleading statements about such things as the rationales used to justify a position. A pragmatic car salesman considers it highly unethical to lie about anything large or small relating to the mechanical condition of a used car he is selling. But this same salesman might not have a problem saying "My manager won't let me sell this car for less than $10,000" even though he knows the manager would sell the car for $9,500. False justification and rationales are marginally acceptable because they are usually less important to the transaction and much harder to detect as falsehoods than are core facts about the object being bought and sold.

Pragmatists are also somewhat looser within the truth when using so-called blocking techniques—tactics to avoid answering questions that threaten to expose a weak bargaining position. For example, can you ethically answer "I don't know" when asked about something you *do* know that hurts your position? An idealist would refuse to answer the question or try to change the subject, not lie by saying "I don't know." A pragmatist would go ahead and say "I don't know" if his actual state of knowledge is hard to trace and the lie poses little risk to his relationships.

The Ethical Schools in Action

As a test of ethical thinking, let's take a simple example. Assume you are negotiating to sell a commercial building and the other party asks you whether you have another offer. In fact, you do not have any such offers. What would the three schools recommend you do?

A Poker School adherent might suggest a lie. Both parties are sophisticated businesspeople in this deal, so a lie about alternatives is probably legally "immaterial." But a member of the Poker School would want to know the answers to two questions before making his move.

First, could the lie be easily found out? If so, it would be a bad play because it wouldn't work and might put the other side on guard with respect to other lies he might want to tell. Second, is a lie about alternatives the best way to leverage the buyer into making a bid? Perhaps a lie about something else—a deadline, for example—might be a better choice.

Assuming the lie is undetectable and will work, how might the conversation sound?

BUYER: Do you have another offer?

POKER SCHOOL SELLER: Yes. A Saudi Arabian firm presented us with an offer for $_____ this morning, and we have only 48 hours to get back to it with an answer. Confidentiality forbids us from showing you the Saudi offer, but rest assured that it is real. What would you like to do?

How would an idealist handle this situation? There are several idealist responses, but none would involve a lie. One response would be the following:

BUYER: Do you have another offer?

IDEALIST SELLER 1: An interesting question—and one I refuse to answer.

Of course, that refusal speaks volumes to the buyer. Another approach would be to adopt a policy on "other buyer" questions:

BUYER: Do you have another offer?

IDEALIST SELLER 2: An interesting question, and one I receive quite often. Let me answer you this way. The property's value to you is something for you to decide based on your needs and your own sense of the market. However, I treat all offers with the greatest confidence. I will not discuss an offer you make to me with another buyer, and I would not discuss any offer I received from someone else with you. Will you be bidding?

Of course, this will work for an idealist only if he or she really and truly has such a policy—a costly one when there is another attractive offer he or she would like to reveal.

A final idealist approach would be to offer an honest, straightforward answer. An idealist cannot lie or deliberately mislead, but he is allowed to put the best face he can on the situation that is consistent with the plain truth:

BUYER: Do you have another offer?

IDEALIST SELLER 3: To be honest, we have no offers at this time. However, we are hopeful that we will receive other offers soon. It might be in your interest to bid now and take the property before competition drives the price up.

How about the pragmatists? They would suggest using somewhat more sophisticated, perhaps even deceptive, blocking techniques. These techniques would protect their leverage in ways that were consistent with maintaining working relationships. Once again, assume that the buyer has asked the "other offer" question and there are no other offers. Here are five ways a pragmatist might suggest you block this question to avoid an out-and-out factual lie about other offers while minimizing the damage to your leverage. Some of these blocking techniques would work for idealists, too:

- *Declare the question out of bounds:* "Company policy forbids any discussion of other offers in situations like this"—note that, if untrue, this is a lie, but it is one that carries less risk to your reputation because it is hard to confirm. If there really is such a company policy, an idealist could also use this move to block the question.

- *Answer a different question:* "We will not be keeping the property on the market much longer because the market is moving and our plans are changing." Again, if untrue, this statement is a mere lie about a "rationale" that troubles pragmatists less than idealists.

- *Dodge the question:* "The more important question is whether we are going to get an offer from you—and when."

- *Ask a question of your own:* "What alternatives are you examining at this time?"

- *Change the subject:* "We are late for our next meeting already. Are you bidding today or not?"

Blocking techniques of this sort serve a utilitarian purpose. They preserve some leverage (though not as much as the Poker School) while reducing the risk of acquiring a reputation for deception. Relationships and reputations matter. If there is even a remote chance of a lie coming back to haunt you in a future negotiation with either the person you lie to or someone he may interact with, the pragmatists argue that you should not do it.

So—which school do you belong to? Or do you belong to a school of your own such as "pragmatic idealism?" To repeat: My advice is to aim high. The pressure of real bargaining often makes ethical compromisers of us all. When you fall below the standard of the Poker School, you are at serious risk of legal and even criminal liability.

Reading 2.13

A Painful Close

Leonard Greenhalgh

Phase 6: The Close

PHASE 1	PHASE 2	PHASE 3	PHASE 4	PHASE 5	PHASE 6	PHASE 7
Preparation	Relationship building	Information gathering	Information using	Bidding	Closing the deal	Implementing the agreement

At the conclusion of the bidding process, the negotiators will have arrived at an outcome that they've tentatively agreed upon. Now it's time to close the deal.

A simplistic view of the closing process involves getting the other party to actually sign the agreement. But really good negotiators know that getting a signature is the least important aspect of concluding the negotiation—that there's something much more important to attend to.

The basic objective in closing the deal is to build commitment to the agreement. When the parties finish the bidding, the agreement they have is still *tentative.* They've repeatedly taken positions and then abandoned them. The negotiated outcome is nothing more than the last position they took, so they need to become committed to it. Without commitment, they may not honor the agreement when it comes time to implement it.

The most important factor that holds negotiators back from making a commitment is anxiety. Thus, during the closing process it's important to separately consider what people are *saying* and how they're *feeling.* A major source of anxiety is worrying about whether the other party has taken advantage of you. Here again the relationship you've created will make a difference. If the relationship has been competitive, you'll be more worried about being exploited. If there's high trust and a sense of alliance in the relationship, you'll worry less.

Even in positive relationships, anxiety arises from postpurchase dissonance (also known as "buyer's remorse," or "the winner's curse"). This is where we second-guess ourselves: "Why is the other party happy with the deal? Did I not gather enough information to know what's a fair deal? Did I settle for too little? Am I leaving money on the table?" The bigger the decision, the more stressful it is.

For example, people are both happiest *and* most miserable when they buy their first house. Let's say you found "the perfect house" but the real-estate agent had listed it at a price that was high for the local market. So you made a counteroffer 20 percent below

Source: "A Painful Close," by Leonard Greenhalgh, from *Managing Strategic Relationships: The Key to Business Success,* 2001, Chapter 6, pp. 210–218. New York: The Free Press, an imprint of Simon & Schuster. Used with permission.

the asking price. That put you below the price of comparable properties, but you had the funds to come up a little in subsequent rounds of bidding. You were surprised when the owner immediately snapped up this offer.

Objectively, you got the perfect house at a price below what you were willing to pay. So why did you end up feeling miserable? Because the close was a poor one. The realtor got in the way of forming a relationship with the owner. This prevented you from gathering information about the owner's needs, and what the owner's alternatives were if she or he didn't make a deal with you. So you were in the dark. You didn't know whether the owner was desperate to sell and gave you a super deal, or whether the owner was thinking, "There's a sucker born every minute." The seller, by the way, would have been just as upset if you had immediately agreed to the full asking price.

A general point here is that the *process* of negotiation tends to make people feel anxious when the bidding comes to a conclusion. The real-estate agent was running an impersonal, faceless process. You were spending more money than you'd ever spent in your life, and you were denied all the assurances that you and the seller were equally satisfied with the outcome. You'd have been spared all that stress if you'd been able to meet with the seller and learn why he or she had accepted your counteroffer. You needed reassurance. (See "A Painful Close" below.)

A Painful Close

I have a bad history of making purchase decisions that don't make total sense to my wife. Her diagnosis is that I have low impulse control, especially when there's an opportunity to acquire an adult toy. I, on the other hand, have always viewed myself as finding creative ways to meet family needs. Take, for example, the lawn situation. We have a very large lawn at our summer home on the coast of Maine. In August, the grass dries out and turns to straw because the fog and drizzle of early summer give way to a month of drought. But the lawn is on the shore of a lake. So here I am, looking at the lawn here and the water there, figuring out what would be the most efficient way to sprinkle water on the lawn without running our well dry.

To make a long story short, one day I went out with my friend Fred and came home with two fire engines. I got a fabulous deal because I bought the pair—a volume discount of sorts. Readers with lawns should note that if you shoot a fire hose straight up into the air, you can make it rain on your lawn. It's really fun. You can even water flower beds with a fire hose after a little practice. (The first flower bed was blown into the neighbor's yard: I used too much pressure. You also have to be careful when washing windows with it. They break pretty easily, and the dining room can get ankle deep in water within seconds. That doesn't go over big in any household.)

But my wife wasn't impressed with the wisdom of this purchase. Maybe it was driving up to the front of the house with lights flashing and sirens wailing that got us off to a bad start. Whatever the reason, she never was convinced that I had bought legitimate irrigation equipment rather than two more toys. Here's where my history reduced my credibility. She didn't think I really needed more than five motorcycles. Or a 1922 Indianapolis racer to drive to the office during good weather. The result of this history is that I'm not allowed to make any purchases without adult supervision.

OK, that's the context. Now here's the situation. We'd been paying a local contractor to do some shoreline landscaping for us. The workman was using a very large (twenty-ton) excavator to move dirt around. I sat and watched him work for a couple of hours. It's amazing how much work you can do with one of those large machines, especially if you're used to moving soil with a spade and a wheelbarrow.

As he was leaving to take a lunch break, the workman commented on my apparent interest and asked me if I wanted to operate the excavator while he was at lunch. Of course I did! But I was concerned. The machine was huge and immensely powerful, and could obviously do a lot of damage. I said to him, "What if I screw something up?" His response was honest, if not comforting. He said, "What do I care? It's *your* property." So I got into the machine and after a few minutes of instruction, ran it for an hour. That was *really* fun.

Turn the clock ahead eight months. I came across this flyer announcing an auction. Featured at the top of the flyer was a picture of the biggest, most beautiful excavator I've ever seen. A large contractor was going bankrupt and all of his equipment was being sold off to the highest bidder, I took the flyer home. As soon as I put it on the table—before I opened my mouth—my wife said, "No!" using that same tone of voice she uses when the kitten is about to climb the curtains to stalk a fly.

An hour later, I meekly asked, "Can we at least talk about it?" This brought on a stern lecture about the "toys" I already owned—a tractor (well, three, if you count the antique and the log skidder), a bulldozer, a backhoe, a skid-steer loader, a dump truck (well, OK, two, if you count the smaller one, which hasn't been sold yet, and the two pickup trucks don't count because they aren't dump trucks), a giant wood chipper, and a few more gardening tools—big ones, admittedly, but this is a thirty-acre property. And I did eventually sell the two fire engines, most of the motorcycles, and the 1922 Indy car. Plus the boat. Sometimes you have to make sacrifices to make room for more toys.

The next morning, I announced that I could probably make a business case for buying the excavator. We had a budget of $20,000 to pay contractors to do major earthmoving. (Our 30 acres is actually a wildlife refuge, and we've been digging ponds for waterfowl, otters, and beavers, as well as undoing the damage that had been done by strip-mining in the mid-1900s.) Creating and restoring wildlife habitat is a big undertaking. So I argued that we should be indifferent between paying that much to a contractor and buying the machine, doing the work ourselves, and then reselling the machine. Eventually she consented to let me go to the auction. I had to agree to an absolute $20,000 limit, that she'd accompany me, and Fred would stay home.

So we showed up at this auction. I knew I was out of my league right away. Everyone except me was a construction-company owner. They were going from machine to machine, making insightful comments about this and that, talking about what each one was worth. (I was clueless.) They even looked different. I was the only one *not* wearing one of those baseball hats with a logo on it—John Deere, Detroit Diesel, Caterpillar, Budweiser. I had just come from the office and was dressed like an Ivy League professor. And my wife was the only woman there.

But nevertheless, I was prepared. I had done some research on the excavator. It was a Caterpillar 235, which had an industry reputation as the best large excavator in its class. The dealer offered to sell me a new one for around $350,000, and said prices for used ones were all over the map, depending on the machine's condition, the state of the used-equipment market, who else was bidding that day, etc. He was skeptical that it could be bought for $20,000. They'd be looking for at least $50,000. But then he added, "Hey, you never know. An auction's an auction."

The excavator was the last item being sold that day. This means I had to keep quiet while they sold off all this *beautiful* equipment that we really could have put to good use had I not been threatened with bodily injury if I opened my mouth. So I really had an appetite when the excavator lumbered forward in front of the crowd. It was magnificent, I thought. It's too big, my wife pointed out. OK, so it weighed fifty tons and was bigger than our house. And it was too large to move over public roads without those silly pickup trucks with the flashing lights that go in front of and behind a huge tractor trailer. But it would do a lot of earthwork, very fast . . .

The auctioneer started out, "Here we have the last item to be sold today. It's a Caterpillar 235, the Rolls-Royce of excavators. You all know what it's worth, so who'll start the bidding at $50,000?" I was crestfallen. The Caterpillar dealer was right. This machine really was out of my range. But there was silence in the room, and more than 100 construction-company owners were shuffling about, talking quietly.

The auctioneer resumed, "All right, who'll give me $35,000?" Again there was silence. Next he said, "OK, who'll give me *anything* for this Caterpillar 235?" Sensing opportunity, I blurted out, "I'll give you five thousand." The auctioneer peered at me, as if in disbelief, then said, "OK. We have to start somewhere. Who'll give me ten?" The man next to me looked me over, curiously, and then said, "I'll give you six." Someone else said, "Seven." So I said "Eight" in a resolute tone, hoping to signal that it was pointless bidding against me. But someone else said "Nine" and the man next to me bid "Ten."

Two minutes later, the man next to me had bid "Nineteen" and I had one chip left to play. I jumped in with "Twenty" before someone else did. My wife's grip on my arm had crossed the threshold of pain. She isn't always subtle when communicating with me. There'd be no latitude on the $20,000 limit I had agreed to, and I already had welts developing.

But a curious thing happened. There was silence in the room. The auctioneer said, "OK, we're at twenty. Who'll give me twenty-one?" After more silence, he said, "Come *on*, people. This is a Cat 235. Who'll give me twenty-one?" After more silence, he repeated, "I can't believe this. Who'll give me twenty-one?"

Well, I couldn't believe it either. The experience had become surreal.

I was having a panic reaction. The color had drained from my face, my mouth had become dry, my hands cold and sweaty. I hoped this was a bad dream. The auctioneer's voice sounded distant as he said "Going once . . . going twice . . ." I was hoping the ground would swallow me up, or that I could magically turn back the clock and start the day again. I was suddenly rescued from the depths of my despair by a brilliant idea. The man next to me had bid $19,000. Why not give him $1,100 so he could outbid me?

But before I could make the offer, the gavel came down, and the auctioneer said, "Sold! To the gentleman in the tweed jacket. Thank you for coming, folks. The next auction is in two weeks at . . ."

I didn't hear anything else. I was in shock. It had dawned on me that here I was, a rank amateur, who was willing to pay more than everyone else in the room—people who knew the construction business and the market for used heavy equipment. In a daze, I paid for the

excavator. As I walked through the parking lot, my panic attack blossomed into clinical depression. It lasted for two days.

Now let's look at what the problem was. It was *the close.* Instead of just saying
"Sold!" the auctioneer could have said, "Sir, you just got yourself a hell of a deal. The
only reason you paid so little for this machine is that the construction industry is currently in recession. You bought the best machine in the world at a fraction of its true
value. If all you do is park this and then sell it when the recession's over, you'll make a
lot of money. You're lucky to have had $20,000 to *invest* today." But he didn't. Auction-
eers don't close deals. They simply terminate the bidding process. They really ought to
think about the close as a means of providing greater value to buyers.

The point here is that postpurchase dissonance is so powerful that you're not immune to it even if you expect it and understand it. Hey, I *teach* this stuff. And I treat
people who suffer from anxiety and depression. But I couldn't help myself. Objectively
the purchase was a bargain, but still I couldn't help reacting to the heartless close.

We should note that postbidding dissonance arises primarily in isolated transactions. There's less anxiety if the current negotiation is one event within a longer series
of interactions, because you usually have less to worry about. Even the least-ethical
competitive-type negotiator is going to be hesitant to exploit you if it risks retaliation.
And if you're engaged in *serial negotiations,* the norms of reciprocity will give you
some protection: if you get a really bad deal this time, the other party will be obliged
to make it up to you in subsequent dealings. In short, your worst fears arise when you
know you may never see the other party again. Thus, a strong ongoing relationship is
your greatest comfort.

Reassurance Tactics

With this understanding of how postbidding anxiety arises, let's now return to the process
of closing the negotiation. Your objective is to reassure the other party that her or his anxiety is unfounded. You can actually say that you got less from the deal than you hoped for,
or expected. You can say that she or he negotiated well when dealing with you. You can
draw comparisons to other negotiations to provide reassuring external benchmarks. Almost anything you say along these lines will be better than total silence.

The best reassurance tactic is to restate specifically why it's a good deal for both
parties. Your ability to do this will depend on how good a job you did of information
gathering. You have to really know whether it's a good deal to be credible in persuading
the other party that it meets his or her underlying needs.

The importance of the relationship-building phase is very obvious when it comes
time to close the deal. The relationship that has developed will influence how vulnerable the other person feels. If she or he feels a strong bond and trusts you, confidence in
the constraining effect of relational ethics will reduce anxiety about being exploited.

A useful reassurance tactic is to emphasize continuity of the relationship. Anxiety
is highest in isolated transactions. So it can be helpful to make the deal seem less
isolated in time and space. An executive can say, for example, "Hey, we're both in this
industry together, and everybody knows everybody. You and I both have reputations to

maintain, and both of us will look back and be proud of what we agreed on today. We've done our best to come up with a package that seems to make the most sense for both of us. What more can we do?"

There's also a piece of advice for negotiators who have competitive personalities. *Never gloat about how well you did, even long after the negotiation is over.* This is obvious to most people, but people who like to compete sometimes go beyond simply doing better than the other party: they point out that they won and the other party lost. This degradation ritual may be acceptable in certain macho sports contests, but it's the *worst* way to close a negotiation. Not only does the other party feel bad about settling for too little, she or he also has to endure humiliation. In business dealings, the result can be disastrous, because the other party will avoid doing business with you in the future, seek revenge, or find excuses not to implement the agreement.

Thus far, we've discussed how you use reassurance tactics to alleviate anxiety in the other party. You may also need to alleviate your own anxiety. You won't always be lucky enough to be dealing with someone who's sensitive enough to understand the problem and use a reassuring process. But you can usually take someone with you who will make you feel good about your decisions. Many people do this instinctually. They invite a friend to accompany them on shopping expeditions (where they may buy nonroutine items). The motive to seek companionship is obvious; the motive to seek reassurance is less obvious but often more powerful.

Phase 7: Implementing the Agreement

It's a big mistake to assume that the negotiation is over and done with after the contract is signed. The negotiation isn't really complete until the agreement has been put into effect. If the process has been a good one, the negotiators are more likely to follow through on what has been agreed to. If the process has been a bad one, they'll have little personal commitment to making the deal a reality.

The implementation problem is very obvious in U.S. labor negotiations, where contract negotiations are seen as different from contract administration (what we're calling implementation). If contract negotiations have been bad, contract administration will be a nightmare. The union will contest every questionable action by managers and will flood management with grievances—protests that need to be addressed by means of a formal conflict-resolution process. The costs are very high: grievances consume managers' time, cost money to arbitrate if the union won't accept management's proposed resolutions, and impede work flow.

U.S. labor negotiations usually founder at the relationship-building phase. The parties maintain an adversarial stance toward each other, and this influences all of the negotiation process. The agreement therefore usually ends up being a reluctant compromise that union members are resentful about. Not surprisingly, they have a stronger motive to be a nuisance to management than to ensure that work proceeds in the best interests of the company.

Or think about negotiating a pay raise. The most favorable time for you to bring up the issue may be when you're approaching a deadline in delivering a project to a client. Let's say you did most of the work, and at this point in time, your input is crucial to finishing the project on time. If you demand a 10 percent raise, you may get it. But your ultimatum may haunt you during the implementation phase. Your boss may give you less responsibility in the future, for fear of being so dependent on you. You also may be denied promotion opportunities, and given poor assignments and low performance ratings. Remember that human beings are emotional creatures, and they react in emotional ways.

Negotiation Contexts

Reading 3.1

Staying in the Game or Changing It: An Analysis of *Moves* and *Turns* in Negotiation
Deborah M. Kolb

As parties bargain over the terms of an agreement, they are concurrently negotiating their relationship. In this parallel negotiation, parties seek to position themselves to advantage by using a variety of strategic moves. In so doing the other party can be put into a defensive position making it difficult to advocate effectively. Turns, such as interrupting, correcting, questioning, naming, and diverting, challenge these moves. Turns can be used restoratively to move out of a defensive position or participatively, to engage the other in collaboration. Anticipating strategic moves and having turns in mind is part of preparing to negotiate.

Negotiation strategy and tactics typically cover how negotiators deal with the substantive dimensions of the issues in dispute. And it is convention to distinguish strategies and tactics that apply in distributive from those in integrative and mutual gains. In distributive negotiations, strategic thinking covers such matters as opening offers, the pattern of concessions, and the use of threats and commitments. Integrative negotiating strategy centers on learning about interests and needs, looking for opportunities for trades, and developing creative options (Fisher, Ury, and Patton 1991; Pruitt and Carnevale 1993).

In a field where the lure of prescription is strong, the strategic advice on how to manage the process vis-à-vis the substantive issues can be very useful. However, our research with women suggests that it is an incomplete picture of the strategic repertoire a negotiator needs—incomplete because it ignores the issues of power and position so central to most negotiated interactions. Consider the following examples:

> A self-employed consultant negotiates a contract renewal with a valued client, who claims that the consultant's rates are out of line with what he delivers and threatens to hire a different provider.

Source: "Staying in the Game or Changing It: An Analysis of *Moves* and *Turns* in Negotiation," by Deborah M. Kolb, from the *Negotiation Journal,* 20, no. 2, April 2004, pp. 256–268. Used with permission.

The vice president of global ventures is in negotiation with the vice president of European operations to close down a nonperforming subsidiary. They agree that the VP of operations will take care of it, but nothing happens. When the VP of global ventures questions him about the status, he tells her that she is overreacting and to calm down.

A director of marketing schedules a meeting to negotiate salary and bonus with her boss based on a profitable year and the extra work she has picked up in the face of increased turnover. Her boss reminds her that times are tight and that, in fact, she is lucky to still have a job. He asks her not to raise salary issues at this time and says he knows that she can be counted on to do this favor.

In each of these examples, one party is seeking to control the negotiation by challenging the other's claims to legitimacy and credibility. In a defensive position, it is difficult for the challenged party to advocate for his or her own interests and concerns. Contrary to best practice assumptions, mutual gain solutions are unlikely to be achieved in these situations. These are examples of strategic moves, actions taken by a negotiator to position him or herself in an advantageous light. These moves can have the effect, even though not necessarily intentionally, of putting the other party in a defensive or down position. Turns are the ways that negotiators can challenge a move.

The notion of moves and turns began with our interest in gender (Kolb and Williams 2003). As we were doing the research for the book *Everyday Negotiation: Navigating the Hidden Agendas of Bargaining,* women told us about some rather horrific experiences in negotiation. A travel agent had to keep her cool in a negotiation with a corporate travel planner who yelled at her when she refused to give him a rebate. "Look bitch," he shouted, "either you give me a rebate or the deal is off!" A labor negotiator had her proposal rejected when her counterpart said, "You think this is all a Zen experience; you can't really speak for the management group." A consultant, in negotiation with a client, was told to "take the deal back to your boss."

These women were being diminished and demeaned in their negotiations in ways that made it almost impossible for them to use the prescriptive advice about strategies and tactics no matter what type of negotiation it was. What these examples suggested was that positioning in the negotiation was critically related to how competent and credible the negotiator was perceived. For a host of structural and cultural reasons having to do with race, class, status, and hierarchical position, negotiators can find themselves in a down position. Indeed, even people who hold power and influence in some contexts can find themselves challenged in others. It is important to emphasize, therefore, that these incidents are not just experienced by women.

Positioning is central to the idea of moves and turns, and indeed, to the notion of the shadow negotiation. In the first section of this essay, I will discuss the idea of positioning and root it in a number of different intellectual traditions. In the next section, I will concentrate on the concept of the shadow negotiation and how moves and turns fit within that framework. I want to suggest that moves and turns constitute critical moments in negotiation. They can be critical in a number of different respects. The next section proposes a typology of moves and turns and how each type can function as a critical moment. In putting forth these ideas, I will draw from a variety of case examples, my own and those of others.

Positioning in Negotiation

In the recent past, the negotiation field has been dominated by several perspectives: economic decision analysis (Raiffa 1982; Lax and Sebenius 1986); social psychology (Rubin, Pruitt, and Kim 1994; Thompson 2001); and cognitive psychology (Neale and Bazerman 1994). These perspectives focus on individual actors (as either principals or agents) engaged in transactional deal making. The best outcomes are achieved through the rational analysis of the game and the required strategy. In so doing, these rather technical negotiation models ignore the very social and political processes that make the kind of deal making they espouse possible. To focus, for example, on cognition and analytic prowess as major barriers to agreement minimizes the connection between how a negotiator is positioned (and continually positioning) in the process and his or her ability to engage the substantive issues in the ways the models suggest. For they presume a party has agency in the process, in the sense that she is positioned to advocate for herself, and that that agency is credited (Kolb and Putnam 1997). I suggest that agency is more problematic and is an ongoing accomplishment in the process.

The notion of social positioning is not a new one in the field, but it has not been central to either theorizing or prescriptive work in negotiation. For the most part, the perspective has been most developed in mediation and disputing scholarship (Mather and Yngvesson 1980–81; Silbey and Merry 1986; Cobb 1993) that draws on theories of social construction (Berger and Luckman 1966; Blumer 1969). This work views people as engaged in constructing their roles and identities in social interaction subject to expectations and the constraints of the social structure they find there. This focus on the interaction as the nexus of analysis encourages us to see roles and the display of identity as quite fluid. Indeed, *role negotiation* is often a term that is used to describe these processes (Gerson and Preiss 1985).

In my work on mediation, I have argued that the roles mediators play shape how they see the process and its demands. The roles they play are very much negotiated and created in the context of the relationships they have with significant others—namely the professionals in labor relations with whom they work. Through the actions the mediators take, they seek to control and frame the process in such a way that they can effectively act within it (Kolb 1983). Managing impressions of their role is part of this process as well.

Translating these ideas to the negotiation context suggests that agency, a concept so central to the dominant paradigms in the field, is not a given, but rather is socially constructed in an interactive context. By focusing on these interactions, we must attend to the ways parties present themselves and their positions in ways that make them feel (and appear) competent and in control. This is the *face* they present in negotiations. To have these presentations challenged can, to a greater or lesser degree, undermine a negotiator's face, sense of herself (Wilson 1992), and ultimately the agency that she claims in advocating for her interests.

Discourse analysis nests these ideas in conversation. Rather than see a negotiator's strategy and tactics as a manifestation of a self-interested individual negotiator, a discourse perspective locates these ideas in an interactive conversation. The notion of position is central to this perspective (Davies and Harre 1990). Gherardi (1995) describes position as "what is created in and through a conversation as speakers and hearers construct themselves as persons: it creates a location through which social relations and actions are mediated."

Negotiators are concerned with constructing legitimate social positions for themselves (and others) in order for them to both create and claim value. From a delegitimated or defensive position, it is difficult to do either (Cobb 1993). Therefore, one way to look at *moves* and *turns* in negotiation is to see them as the cocreation of structure or moral order in which the process can play out.[1]

A discourse perspective underlies one way that feminist scholars look at gender. Although it is still pretty common to conceptualize gender in terms of binary categories— that is, to compare men and women and how they act—this essentialist and static conception is increasingly being challenged (Flax 1990; Gherardi 1995; Calas and Smircich 1996; Fletcher 1999). In the negotiation field, for example, studies of the differences between women and men have only two outcomes—women are either different from or the same as men. What this work does is generally highlight women's deficiencies. It fails to take into account how social structures and the very knowledge base of negotiation may create these deficiencies. More recent work seeks to understand the conditions under which gender differences would occur, but they still take a rather static view of differences between men and women (Riley 2001; Gelfand et al. 2002; Babcock and Laschever 2003).

Feminists, who work from a postmodern perspective, highlight the fluid and contextual character of gender relations. By embracing discourse, these scholars shift from a focus on the rational, self-interested subject to looking at how subjective and objective positions are produced in language and conversations (Weedon 1987). Part of that project focuses on disciplinary knowledge and how it shapes power relations (Weedon 1987; Calas and Smircich 1996). Others, however, focus more on interactive settings where meanings about gender are produced. So when feminist scholars talk about positioning, they are interested in how women define themselves and are defined within a particular context.

Lorber (1994) describes the various ways that women in workplace interactions can have their positions undercut through, among other means, condescending chivalry, supportive discouragement, radiant devaluation, considerate domination, and collegial exclusion. While it is expected in such interactions that women will passively accept these positions, that men will do dominance and women deference, these choices are not inevitable. When Alcoff (1988) defines the concept of *positionality,* she highlights how women can actively utilize their location to construct new meanings about gender roles and relations rather than simply take up ones that are assigned. This perspective highlights two things: that women have choices in the positions they take up in discourse and that predetermined positions can be resisted. While expectations might suggest that women take up a one-down position, a position that is consistent with gender identity, these expectations can be disrupted and destabilized (Gherardi 1995). And from such destabilization, new meanings about role and position can be constructed.

Another perspective that helps inform this work concerns different ways of looking at power. In negotiation, the dominant model of power has been Emerson's: the power of A to get B to do something that B would rather not do. Determinants of power in negotiation typically focus on degrees of dependence and independence (Bacharach and Lawler 1981). Thus negotiators with good BATNAs are presumably in more powerful positions in negotiation. Obviously, other dimensions of power are also relevant—access to resources, hierarchical position, and access to influential others. However, as Lax and Sebenius (1986) note, positional power achieved in any of these manners is not determining—witness weaker parties who come out ahead. Scott (1987) calls these successful—and often low-profile actions—the *weapons of the weak*.

Power is exerted in more nuanced ways in social interactions. Following the work of Michel Foucault, scholars observe how knowledge and accepted truths, which appear natural and neutral, serve to discipline action. Certain discourses become dominant and hold sway in ways actors do not necessarily recognize as exercises of power. Elsewhere we have argued that in the negotiation field, the discourse of individual psychology and economic decision making privileges certain ways of being and marginalizes others, and this contributes to gender inequities (Kolb and Putnam 1997; Putnam and Kolb 2000; Kolb 2003). Feminist scholars have embraced this perspective with some important caveats.

The focus on the dispersion of power and its multiple modes of functioning has helped scholars focus on the microprocesses that construct gender in the workplace (Martin and Meyerson 1998; Fletcher 1999). It also serves to empower people in workplace interactions to resist these exercises of power (Meyerson 2001). By recognizing the ways social structures operate through microprocesses of power in commonplace interactions, individuals can act individually and collectively to change narratives that position them to disadvantage (Ewick and Silbey 1995).

In sum, this work on positioning suggests an alternative, yet complementary, perspective on how to describe what is occurring in a negotiated interaction. Although parties are focused on the issues, they are engaged in an interactive process. Elements of that process have been theorized and studied—the use of threats and bluffs for example or the challenges of dealing with difficult situations (Schelling 1960; Ury 1990; Stone, Patton, and Heen 1999; McGinn and Keros 2002). The concept of positioning in the negotiation gives coherence to these disparate approaches. It is that concept that the notion of the *shadow negotiation* attempts to capture.

Moves and Turns in the Shadow Negotiation

The *shadow negotiation* refers to the complementary and parallel dynamic that occurs as parties work on the issues that separate them. Our identities as negotiators, the legitimacy of our positions, the power and authority we claim, the import of gender and race, are always part of what is being negotiated while we are negotiating over the substantive issues. Of course, they are intimately connected. Establishing and maintaining visible presence and credibility are intended to influence how the other responds to our demands. The distinctions are not neat: At the same time as parties are focused on their issues— learning about them, putting out proposals and arguments, and making concessions— they are engaged in a shadow negotiation that is about relative positioning.

It is not that these two processes are separable, but rather that we can look at what is occurring from these two perspectives. We can focus on how parties are dealing with their issues and working (or not) toward agreement and at the same time, pay attention to how what they say and do also represents a process of positioning (or challenges/ acceptance of it). To look at negotiations from the perspective of the shadow negotiation is to attend to how parties manage impressions of themselves, how they claim and maintain legitimacy and credibility, how they assert what power and influence they have, and how they shape perceptions of what is possible (Kolb and Williams 2003). Central to the shadow negotiation is the idea of moves and turns.

Moves

Goffman (1969) developed the idea of a *move* in his application of game theory to social interaction: "A move, analytically speaking, is not a thought or decision or expression, or anything else that goes on in the mind of a player; it is a course of action which involves real consequences."

Goffman specifically does not define a *move* too precisely (1981). Rather, he uses it as a vehicle to capture streams of interaction and how they play out in various expression games. As Pentland (1992) observes, "Moves have the desirable properties of being meaningful to the interactants, related to structural properties of the situation, and yet under the willful control of the interactants." In other words, moves need to be looked at in terms of the action itself, how others respond ("ratifying" is how Goffman puts it), and their role in the overall game.

How do we look at moves in the negotiation game? Strategic moves are actions negotiators take to position themselves (and others) in the negotiation process. In making these moves, negotiators want to position themselves as competent and legitimate in order to be credible advocates for themselves and their interests. In making their moves, negotiators try to project an image of themselves and what they want in the best possible light.

As part of the normal byplay of negotiations, negotiators use *strategic moves* to enhance their position.[2] These moves can have the effect of undermining or delegitimizing the other party (Kolb and Williams 2003). Negotiators are most credible when they are positioned to advocate for their interests. When a party is challenged in ways that put them in a one-down (sometimes a gendered) position, they have a more difficult time pressing for what they need.

Moves that challenge a party's positioning potentially cover a wide spectrum of action. One type discussed widely in the literature are the so-called "dirty tricks" where negotiators employ some familiar tactics, such as good cop–bad cop, in order to throw the other negotiator off (Fisher, Ury, and Patton 1991). There are other forms of action that are so demeaning of a person that they verge on harassment (Kolb and Williams 2003). Undoubtedly these moves do occur; however, we are more interested in more routine, normal moves that stem from one party's efforts to advocate for him or herself.

In moving to put oneself into a good position, the effect of this type of advocacy is to challenge some aspect of the position the other negotiator is claiming. These are part of the normal interactive byplay of negotiation. The moves that are of interest are ones that challenge a negotiator's own presentation of self and/or put him/her on the defensive so that s/he finds it hard to advocate credibly. Several of the most common moves are listed below:

> *Challenging competence or expertise:* With these moves, claims of experience and expertise are called into question. In the contract negotiation mentioned earlier, the move—"your fees are way out of line with what you deliver"—calls into question the value of the product/service. The implication is that asking for higher fees is not possible.

Demeaning ideas: With these moves, the ideas themselves are attacked in ways that give the proponent little room to respond. Saying something like "you can't be serious about this proposal" makes the idea and the proponent sound ridiculous. Obviously, these moves make it difficult to argue for what might otherwise be a reasonable idea.

Criticizing style: Using phrases like "don't get so upset," the person—who he or she is, and how he or she acts—becomes the subject of the move. To be challenged as overreacting or inconsiderate positions a negotiator as an irrational person who cannot be reasoned with, or who is selfish or not nice. This move can call forth unfortunate stereotypes such as the hysterical female (Gherardi 1995). These moves can be unsettling as few of us think of ourselves as unreasonable or difficult.

Making threats: Threats are used to try to force a choice on a negotiator: "Cut your rates or there is no deal." As assertions of power, these moves can back a negotiator into a corner, making it risky to propose some other solution.

Appealing for sympathy or flattery: The moves described thus far have been critical of the person and his or her ideas. But in everyday negotiation in the workplace, appeals for sympathy and flattery also can be quite powerful. When people say, "I know you won't let me down" or "I really need your help on this," they are counting on the move to silence you, to make it difficult for you to advocate and press for what you want.

Strategic moves like these five (and there are likely variants) can be seen as situated exercises of power meant to put a person in his or her place. In the interactive byplay, these moves are intended to position the negotiator in a one-down, defensive position. To have one's competence, motives, ideas, legitimacy, and style challenged as the other party presses for advantage not only challenges the potential argument or claim a negotiator wants to make, it can also undermine the negotiator's sense of self-competence and confidence. In a one-down position, the other negotiator can have the advantage. Strategic moves present the recipient with a choice. She can make a defensive countermove or she can *turn* it.

Moves can be responded to with *reactive countermoves,* which are comebacks in kind. For example, when somebody says, "Don't get so upset" a reactive countermove would be to respond, "I am not upset." Although such a reactive countermove is quite common, it is clear that it tends to reinforce the previous move. That is, the recipient of the move stays in the original, defensive position. One of the reasons that reactive countermoves are so common is because negotiators do not recognize that a move is being used as a tactic and so they respond emotionally and defensively.

Strategic moves can also be ignored. In a sales negotiation, for example, when the buyer of advertising from a TV station mentions the poor ratings of a show under discussion, the seller can just ignore the aspersion. Of course the move has been made and it sits there. It is not clear whether the seller agrees or not. When seriously demeaning moves are made about sex or race, to ignore them is potentially to collude in that positioning (Gherardi 1995; Kolb and Williams 2003). Remaining silent implicitly reinforces racist or sexist aspersions.

Moves can be resisted through the use of *turns.* Again we draw on Goffman who introduced the idea of a turn (1969). But his use of *turn* refers to the idea of *turn taking;* in other words, when it is your turn in the game, you can choose to make a move. We extend Goffman's idea of *turn* in a number of different ways.

First, turns are responses to moves. They are the moments of potential resistance, where the recipient of the move refuses to take up the defensive position in which she is placed (Gherardi 1995). Second, turns change meaning and so reposition the person. Turns shift the meaning of the move: They resist the positioning and reframe it. When meanings are unstable, as they are in an unfolding negotiation where two or more interpretations exist at any given moment, these indirect methods or turns can reframe how parties are viewed (Ferguson 1991; Gherardi 1995). A repertoire of turns, such as interrupting the action, naming a challenge, questioning the move, correcting impressions, and diverting to the problem, are means a negotiator can use to resist the positioning.[3]

Turns

Turns are actions negotiators take in response to strategic moves, moves that put them in a one-down or defensive position. The argument is that to accept that definition of oneself hampers the negotiator's credibility and sense of agency, giving some advantage to the mover. Turns are an effort to restore some parity to positioning. In my work, I have identified five turns:

- *Interruption:* Interrupting the action disrupts the move. Even the shortest break means that people are not in precisely the same position after it.

- *Naming:* To name a move signals recognition of what is occurring. It suggests that the negotiator is not taken in. The turner, in other words, rejects the positioning.

- *Questioning:* Questioning suggests something puzzling about a move. Rather than directly naming a move, to question it is to throw it back to the mover—implying one is not sure what prompted it.

- *Correcting:* A correcting turn substitutes a different version or motivation to the one the move implied. Rather than just rejecting the positioning, a correcting turn constructs a different positioning for the turner that can neutralize the move.

- *Diverting:* A diverting turn shifts the focus to the problem itself. It is a way of ignoring the implication of the move but also has the negotiator take control of the process.

There are some important points to make about turns before we analyze them in terms of critical moments. With the exception of interruption, I have emphasized the verbal. However, nonverbal actions, such as laughing off a comment or turning away, can also have the effect of turning a situation.

In a turn, tone of voice is as important as what is said. The use of humor, sarcasm, and irony can be most effective in naming or correcting a move. Gherardi (1995) uses a wonderful example to make this point in a kind of everyday negotiation. After returning from a conference, one of her senior male colleagues went to open the door for her: "Do you want me to open the door for you or will you react as if I'd grabbed your arse?"

Gherardi observes that she was put in a position of either a hysterical feminist or a sweet and docile lady who knew her place in academia as well as society. "I decided on sarcasm and told him emphatically that I formally authorized him to open that door and all the other doors and obstacles that might stand in my way."

Gherardi's turn points up another dimension of moves and turns, the degree to which they are accomplished in the moment or occur over time. The challenge of thinking on one's feet to be prepared for a move can be daunting. We have argued that it is often possible to anticipate moves as one plays out several scenarios in preparing for a negotiation (Kolb and Williams 2003). However, such preparation can never be complete, and one can always be caught unawares. It is here that interruption can be useful.

But moves can also be turned over time. Meyerson (2001) describes how people in everyday negotiation in the workplace pick their time to turn moves that previously happened. When a move is made in a public space, like a meeting, the target may judge that it is risky to raise the issue in the moment. Under those circumstances, it is more likely that the other will hear the turn and learn from it later in a more private setting.

Finally, it is important to note, that recognizing a move as such and acting to turn it is not always clear-cut. I have observed how overtures intended to uncover interests and learn more about a party's situation can often be read as a move. For example, in a buyer–seller negotiation, one can ask about the success of the seller's product or service or what her aspirations are for how it will do in the future. This kind of inquiry can lead to the creation of contingent agreements (Bazerman and Gillespie 1999). However, it can also be read as a move to discredit the seller's service. Rather than being forthcoming about aspirations (a good thing), the seller gets into a defensive mode or tries to turn what they misread as a move (a bad thing).

How Turns Can Work: Implications for Critical Shifts

The concept of *moves* and *turns* gives us a lens into the political dimensions of the negotiation process. As such, moves and turns are critical moments in negotiation. But they can function differently. In this section, I want to take a preliminary look at how moves and turns might function as restorative and participative moments in negotiation.

Restorative Turns

Up to this point, I have used *moves* and *turns* in one particular way, as a means to create or restore some kind of equity in the process. For some time, I have been concerned with how negotiators (particularly women) who find themselves in a one-down or defensive position can turn moves to get themselves into a more proactive, agentic position. From that proactive position, they can more credibly advocate for themselves. All the examples I have used so far exemplify this restorative dimension of turns. Thus, when competence, ideas, or style are challenged, the negotiator turns the move in order to try to level the playing field.

Restorative turns are important from two perspectives.[4] Restoring one's position to be in a more credible role is important to the progress of the negotiation. Without a negotiator who is equally able to advocate for her own self, there is little incentive for the other party to engage in the work of mutual gains negotiation or to claim value in distributive bargaining (Rubin et al. 1994). That is, the other party needs a credible advocate, not a defensive wimp, in order to engage.

Restorative turns are a means to promote mutual interdependence in negotiation. Moves that serve to disempower or put a party on the defensive can be seen as an action by the mover to assert power and control in the process. These moves signal that the mover sees herself in a one-up position and hence less dependent on the outcome of the negotiation. What follows is that the target of the move is seen in a one-down position and more dependent. By turning such moves, the target resists this definition. By turning the move, the turner encourages the mover to reconsider; they are more interdependent than the mover might want to acknowledge. In this way, restorative turns are about how parties negotiate their relative power in the process. Returning to our earlier scenarios,

> The self-employed consultant *turned* the move that challenged his competence. The client claimed that his rates were out of line with what was delivered. The consultant *corrected* the move by bringing in the fee schedules of other like firms. In response to the threat of using another provider, the consultant *named* the move, "You and I both know that will mean more work for you," implying that the threat was not taken seriously.
>
> The VP of global ventures likewise *corrected* the move that positioned her as overreacting by saying, "This is serious. You know Jim (CEO) is looking very carefully at this. We are both under the gun." In turning this move, the VP of global operations reframed the position she was put in—not out of control, but responding to legitimate pressure from the CEO.

Restorative turns are important because negotiators cannot effectively advocate if their legitimacy or credibility is being challenged. Restorative turns also disrupt the assertion of control by one party over the range of possible agreements. If the consultant stays anchored by the statement "your fees are out of line," it will be difficult for him to advocate for a fee schedule more to his liking. Restorative turns are most likely to occur in the early phases of a negotiation when parties are posturing for each other and testing the range of what is possible. As such they tend to restore the balance of power that existed; naming and correcting turns are most likely to accomplish this.

Participative Turns

Participative turns are intended to engage the other party. Whereas restorative turns can put the other party on the defensive, *participative turns* position the other party more as a partner. Turns are participative when they are phrased in such a way that they leave space for the other person to talk from her own legitimate, not defensive, position. Looking back at an earlier scenario, for example,

> In her negotiation over salary, the director can turn the *appeal for sympathy* move, a move that could silence her, with a *correcting* turn: "I know you are in a difficult position and I'd like to do what I can" or with a *questioning* turn: "I wonder how you could respond in my situation?" Or she could *divert* the move: "I know things are tight, but I want to explore some other ideas with you."

These turns acknowledge the problem but open up the possibility that both can talk about the situation. They can shift the negotiation from blaming and defending to an exploration of what may be possible in the circumstances. Notice that the turns in this example work differently from the earlier restorative examples. In the fee negotiation, the correcting turn shows that the other person is mistaken. Although it restores the credibility of the consultant, it could result in a defensive response from the client. Likewise in the subsidiary example, the VP of global ventures invokes the CEO to correct the move, which could invite backlash. In the salary example, the director talks about intentions and invites the boss to work with her. Participative turns not only resist the move, but do so in a way that has the potential to open up the dialogue in ways that restorative turns are not likely to do.

In an interesting example from the world stage, in trade negotiations between U.S. Trade Representative Charlene Barshefsky and her Chinese counterpart over intellectual property, Barshefsky used interruption and diverting turns participatively in response to a threat.

> Menacingly, he (Chinese negotiator) leaned forward across the table toward Barshefsky and said flatly, "It's take it or leave it." Barshefsky, taken aback by the harsh tone, surprised, her counterpart by sitting quietly. She waited 30–40 seconds—an eternity given the intensity of the negotiation—and came back with a measured reply: "If the choice is take or leave it, of course I'll leave it. But I can't imagine that's what you meant. I think what you mean is that you'd like me to think over your last offer and that we can continue tomorrow."[5]

Barshefsky's participative turns of the threat disrupted it and resulted in a major compromise the next morning. The interruption (her silence) was important; it enabled her to reassert control. Further, her diverting turn signaled her intention to revise the Chinese negotiator's offer, but did it in a way that gave him space to back down. In this case, her turning a threat signaled that this tactic would not work and pushed the mover to reconsider.

Both restorative and participative turns have the potential to be critical in shifting a negotiation. Restorative turns can involve each party testing the other's mettle. Such posturing can move the negotiations along. Of course, it is also possible that this kind of posturing can result in backlash and impasse. Participative turns seem to be more likely to lead to positive transitions and even the possibility that some forms of transformation might occur.

Meyerson (2001) has used the concept of moves and turns in her work on tempered radicals. These are people who are successful in existing systems, but negotiate change, especially around identity group issues. Meyerson argues that turns can be moments of learning and transformation. Responding to a move, a negotiator can make a turn that does more than restore a balance or shift the discussion: It actually causes the mover to reflect on his or her action. And in so doing, the turn has potential as a moment of learning for the individual mover and to advance the relationship between the mover and turner and may lead the negotiation in directions that could not be predicted (Putnam 2004).

Conclusion

This essay attempts to lay out some new ways of thinking about the negotiation process. Based on a number of different literatures in the social sciences—especially feminist postmodern work—I have suggested that negotiators are negotiating about their positions in the process while they are engaging their issues. *Moves* and *turns* is a framework

I propose that can begin to unpack what is occurring in the positional byplay of the process. Finally, I suggest that moves and turns can function as different types of critical moments.

This essay raises more questions than it answers. First, the repertoire of moves and turns comes from our research on women (primarily) in the workplace and generally from their descriptions of what occurred. This limitation suggests several directions for future work, including looking at moves and turns in other domains and having access to actual scripts of the process. Second, moves and turns as separable actions is a fairly rudimentary approach to the process. Indeed, Goffman (1981) proposes that moves describe a course of action. Thus a promising approach would be to try to identify various streams of moves and turns. Looking at restorative and participative turns might be an interesting beginning.

Finally, there is the issue of prescription. If moves and turns happen in the moment, how can we help negotiators become more adept at the "mindfulness" (Wheeler 2002) it takes to manage this complexity? I know from my students and from executive workshops I have given that having confidence in one's ability to both make moves and to turn them is a skill many want to enhance.

Endnotes

1. Kathleen McGinn's work focuses, in part, on how a conjoint or shared moral order is constructed in negotiations.

2. There are also situations where negotiators use appreciative moves that position the other party as legitimate and credible. From such mutual positioning, collaboration is more likely.

3. These are examples of what Sylvia Gherardi calls the *postmodern tools of resistance*. "This is a paradoxical form of communication, but it is quite normal in handling interaction situations comprising a double-bind and requiring, simultaneously, a ritualistic form of communication which is 'supportive' of the symbolic order of gender, one that is 'restitutive' of the violation of that order, and one that is 'resistant' to the domination it expresses." (Gherardi 1995: 139).

4. I recognize that *restorative* may be a problematic term because it implies that there was some preexisting situation. I use the term just to indicate that negotiators want to restore a face in the interaction that might be challenged.

5. *Charlene Barshefsky (B),* Harvard Business School Case, 9-801-422 (Sebenius and Hulse 2001).

References

Alcoff, L. 1988. Cultural feminism versus post-structuralism: The identity crisis in feminist theory. *Signs* 13(3), pp. 405–436.

Babcock, L., and S. Laschever. 2003. *Women don't ask: Negotiation and the gender divide.* Princeton, NJ: Princeton University Press.

Bacharach, S., and E. Lawler. 1981. *Bargaining.* San Francisco: Jossey-Bass.

Bazerman, M. H., and J. J. Gillespie. 1999. Betting on the future: The virtues of contingent contracts. *Harvard Business Review,* September–October, pp. 155–60.

Berger, P., and T. Luckman. 1966. *The social construction of reality: A treatise in the sociology of knowledge.* New York: Doubleday.

Blumer, H. 1969. *Symbolic interaction.* Englewood Cliffs, NJ: Prentice-Hall.

Calas, M., and L. Smircich. 1996. From a woman's point of view: Feminist approaches to organization studies. In *Handbook of organization studies,* ed. S. Clegg, C. Hardy, and W. Nord. Newbury Park, CA: Sage.

Cobb, S. 1993. Empowerment and mediation: A narrative perspective. *Negotiation Journal* 9(3), pp. 245–59.

———. 1994. A narrative perspective on mediation: Toward the materialization of the "story-telling" metaphor. In *New directions in mediation,* ed. J. P. Folger and T. S. Jones. Thousand Oaks, CA: Sage.

Davies, B., and R. Harre. 1990. Positioning: The discursive production of selves. *Journal of the Theory of Social Behavior* 1, pp. 43–63.

Ewick, P., and S. S. Silbey. 1995. Subversive stories and hegemonic tales: Toward a sociology of narrative. *Law and Society Review* 29, pp. 197–226.

Ferguson, K. 1991. Interpretation and genealogy in feminism. *Signs* 16, pp. 322–39.

Fisher, R., W. Ury, and B. Patton. 1991. *Getting to YES: Negotiating agreement without giving in,* 1st ed., 2d ed. Boston: Houghton Mifflin.

Flax, J. 1990. *Thinking fragments: Psychoanalysis, feminism, and postmodernism in the contemporary west.* Berkeley, CA: University of California Press.

Fletcher, J. 1999. *Disappearing acts: Gender, power, and relational practice at work.* Cambridge, MA: MIT Press.

Gelfand, M., V. Smith Major, J. L. Raver, L. H. Hishi, and K. O'Brien. 2002. *Dynamic theory of gender and negotiation.* Unpublished paper, University of Maryland.

Gerson, J. M., and K. Preiss. 1985. Boundaries, negotiation, consciousness: Reconceptualizing gender relations. *Social Problems* 32(4), pp. 317–31.

Gherardi, S. 1995. *Gender, symbolism, and organizational culture.* Newbury Park, CA: Sage.

Goffman, E. 1969. *Strategic interaction.* Philadelphia: University of Pennsylvania Press.

———. 1981. *Forms of talk.* Philadelphia: University of Pennsylvania Press.

Kolb, D. 1983. *The mediators.* Cambridge, MA: MIT Press.

Kolb, D. M. 2003. Gender and negotiation. In *Gender, work, and organizations,* ed. R. Ely, E. Foldy, and M. Scully. London: Blackwell Publishers.

Kolb, D. M., and L. L. Putnam. 1997. Through the looking glass: Negotiation theory refracted through the lens of gender. In *Frontiers in dispute resolution in industrial relations and human resources,* ed. S. Gleason. Ann Arbor, MI: Michigan State University Press.

Kolb, D. M., and J. Williams. 2003. *Everyday negotiation: Navigating the hidden agendas of bargaining.* San Francisco, CA: Jossey-Bass/John Wiley.

Lax, D., and J. Sebenius. 1986. *The manager as negotiator.* New York: The Free Press.

Lorber, J. 1994. *The paradoxes of gender.* New Haven: Yale University Press.

Martin, J., and D. Meyerson. 1998. Women and power. In *Power and influence in organizations,* ed. R. Kramer and M. Neale. Thousand Oaks, CA: Sage.

Mather, L., and B. Yngvesson. 1980–1981. Language, audience, and the transformation of disputes. *Law and Society Review* 15, pp. 775–821.

McGinn, K. L., and A. Keros. 2002. Improvisation and the logic of exchange in embedded negotiations. *Administrative Science Quarterly* 47(3), pp. 442–73.

Meyerson, D. 2001. *Tempered radicals.* Cambridge, MA: Harvard University Press.

Neale, M., and M. Bazerman. 1994. *Cognition and rationality in negotiation.* New York: The Free Press.

Pentland, B. T. 1992. Organizing moves in software support hot lines. *Administrative Science Quarterly* 37, pp. 527–48.

Pruitt, D. G., and P. J. Carnevale. 1993. *Negotiation in social conflict.* Buckingham, England: Open University Press.

Putnam, L. L. 2004. Transformations and critical moments in Negotiations. *Negotiation Journal* 20(2), pp. 275–95.

Putnam, L. L., and D. M. Kolb. 2000. Rethinking negotiation: Feminist views of communication and exchange. In *Rethinking organizational communication from feminist perspectives,* ed. P. Buzannell. Newburg Park, CA: Sage Publications.

Raiffa, H. 1982. *The art and science of negotiation.* Cambridge, MA: Harvard University Press.

Riley, H. 2001. *When does gender matter in negotiations? The case of distributive bargaining.* Unpublished dissertation, Harvard University.

Rubin, J., D. G. Pruitt, and S. H. Kim. 1994. *Social conflict: Escalation, stalemate and settlement.* New York: McGraw Hill.

Schelling, T. 1960. *The strategy of conflict.* Cambridge, MA: Harvard University Press.

Scott, J. 1987. *Weapons of the weak.* New Haven: Yale University Press.

Sebenius, J. and R. Hulse. 2001, *Charlene Barshefsky (B).* Cambridge, MA: Harvard Business School Case.

Silbey, S. S., and S. Merry. 1986. Mediator settlement strategies. *Law and Policy* 8, pp. 7–32.

Stone, D., B. Patton, and S. Heen. 1999. *Difficult conversations.* New York: Viking.

Thompson, L. 2001. *The mind and heart of the negotiator.* Englewood Cliffs, NJ: Prentice-Hall.

Ury, W. 1990. *Getting past no.* New York: Bantam.

Weedon, C. 1987. *Feminist practice and poststructuralist theory.* Oxford: Blackwell.

Wheeler, M. 2002. *Presence of mind.* Harvard Business School Note, 9-903-009.

Wilson, S. R. 1992. Face and face work in negotiation. In *Communication and negotiation,* ed. L. Putnam and M. E. Roloff. Newbury Park, CA: Sage.

The Soft Sell

Chuck Salter

Sure, the folks at CDW will sell you a computer. But first they want to talk about your kids, your pets, and your favorite team.

If you're one of Ron Kelly's regular customers, you probably know that he's 35 and has a wife named Michelle, a 9-year-old son named Andrew, and a German Shepherd named Bones. You know that he majored in journalism and poly sci at SIU (that's Southern Illinois University) and was supposed to attend Northwestern's law school, but instead came to work at CDW (that's Computer Discount Warehouse). You know that he bleeds red and black for the Chicago Blackhawks.

You also know that he knows as much, if not more, about you.

Kelly, an affable account manager, is a master at relationship-based selling, which is CDW's specialty. It's the nonsales sales call: two friends catching up before eventually turning to a little business. Customers love it. "He's my sales rep, but he's also my friend," says Todd Greenwald, director of operations for Heartland Computers, which sells bar-code scanners. "Most of the time we don't even talk about price. I trust Ron."

Despite competing in a highly volatile industry against thousands of local rivals, CDW has managed to become a high-tech heavyweight in the 20 years since founder Michael Krasny started the business at his kitchen table. The company, based in Vernon Hills, Illinois, outside Chicago, now sells around $5 billion worth of computer equipment and services a year.

CDW is a middleman. It buys from the likes of HP, Microsoft, IBM, Apple, and Sony (pretty much everyone but Dell), and sells primarily to corporations but also to schools and government agencies. Those customers could buy directly from a manufacturer themselves or shop around and find a better price. But CDW wins them over with selection, speed, and service. It offers more than 80,000 products, ships more than 90 percent of its orders the same day, and acts as the de facto IT department for many of its 400,000-plus small-business clients.

While sales have been growing steadily, this is a grueling business: IT prices continue to drop, margins continue to narrow, and finding and keeping customers is more important than ever. The sales philosophy at CDW grew out of Krasny's belief that "people do business with people they like," as posters throughout the company remind the 1,880-member sales force. Plenty of sales organizations preach this truism. But CDW acts on it as few organizations do, particularly ones this big. In surveys, its customers consistently give CDW top marks and say they see it as a long-term partner. The number-one reason for such loyalty? The one-on-one relationships with account managers, customers say. Heartland's Greenwald even cites CDW as a model for his company's sales staff. "They're not just selling but getting into people's lives," he says.

Source: "The Soft Sell," by Chuck Salter, from *Fast Company,* January 2005. pp. 72–73. Used with permission.

What's particularly impressive is that, for the most part, the interaction occurs over the phone. Despite the lack of face time, CDW account managers forge close ties. One customer invited his CDW contact to his wedding. Kelly and Greenwald share Blackhawks season tickets. It's not uncommon to find customers and reps whose partnership has outlasted job changes, budget cuts, and marriages. "I've had customers who have been laid off who still call me at home," says Hayden Beadle, an account manager for nine years.

Of course, these relationships don't just happen. "There's a methodology," says Harry Harczak, executive vice president of sales. CDW's customer-management software, compensation, training, and culture are designed to encourage unusually close and long-lasting partnerships with clients. John Edwardson, the CEO of CDW and the former head of United Airlines, likes to point out that account managers get more training than some pilots: six weeks of orientation, then six months of sales training in CDW Academy, then another year of monthly training sessions in the "masters' program."

New hires start with the basics, the traits that make account managers successful: enthusiasm, empathy, and responsiveness, to name a few. They eavesdrop on calls and learn unwritten dos (use the customer's name frequently) and don'ts (don't lead with price). But there is no script. "We never say, 'This is what you want to say,'" says Tom Jay, a sales trainer at CDW Academy. "We say, 'This is the principle. Use your own touch.'"

New account managers are reminded to be patient yet persistent. They hear about salespeople who courted customers for months before making the first sale that unlocked a multimillion-dollar account. "It takes a while to build a relationship with people," says Jay. "It takes getting on the phone every day, not because it'll pay off tomorrow, but six months from now."

Edwardson says the key is letting account managers "own the business." They decide the tone, the pace, even the profit margin, since they have some leeway to set prices. The approach lets them entice new customers with low prices and gradually make up the difference over time as they gain a greater percentage of the IT budget.

The relationship isn't based solely on being likable. It's grounded in helping customers succeed. Account managers think like the customer and try to anticipate problems. For instance, before storms rocked Florida last summer, some account managers emailed clients there with battery and backup-storage solutions. "It's easy to fall into the trap of being an order taker in sales," says Shelly Troka, who runs orientation training. "Instead of just sending a purchase order, we want to ask, 'Why are you buying the router?' That's how you identify customers' needs."

But ultimately, the business revolves around lots and lots of phone calls, like one in early October between CDW's Beadle and Deborah Neff, an IT administrator at American Municipal Power-Ohio. The business part of the call—details about digital cameras that Neff was considering—could wait while Neff regaled Beadle with a story of how her PDA recently broke.

Three years ago, when Beadle tackled the AMPO account, Neff had a longtime local vendor, but she wanted a backup. She began testing Beadle with small orders. He came across as genuine and patient, not slick or pushy. He asked insightful questions. He was a good listener. He heard about the car Neff bought over eBay and about her sick cat. Because he proved himself to be conscientious and reliable with a sliver of her IT needs, he earned her trust, and consequently got more and more orders—color printers, laptops, a $10,000 plotter. What was once a $10,000-a-year account has grown more than tenfold. Beadle and CDW have replaced the old vendor. "Sometimes I'll present a problem I'm having: 'This is driving me nuts, Hayden. Got any ideas?' " says Neff. "And he always does." Does Neff think of him as a salesman anymore? "Never," she says. "He's my business partner." That's a leap any sales rep would love to make.

CDW's Keys to a Lasting Relationship

- *Update your little black book:* To help account managers keep track of dozens of calls a day. CDW developed software to capture details about each call and each customer. Another feature ranks contacts within a company by power and influence to help navigate the network behind IT purchases.

- *No cheesy pickup lines:* Forget selling ice to an Eskimo. You don't earn customers' trust by selling them things they don't need. Better just to ask, "What can I do to make your job easier?" It's a question that never gets old.

- *Avoid blind dates:* CDW interacts with customers primarily over the phone, but its Intranet alts for customer displays photos of account managers. Next to each picture is a green or red indicator showing who's in the office and who's out.

- *Don't be afraid to say the three most difficult words:* They are, of course, "I don't know." CDW's account managers can't possibly know everything about their 80,000 products. But there's no need to panic or bluff. They call in an expert: one of the manufacturer-certified specialists the company has added in recent years.

- *It's all about give and take:* If a customer shares something personal, such as an unwavering passion for the Cubs, take it as a sign of trust and reciprocate. It makes business less impersonal. Remember CDW founder Michael Krasny's motto: People do business with people they like.

Bargaining in the Shadow of the Tribe
John H. Wade

Editors' Note: The negotiations have gone on for hours or months or years. A deal is at hand. And now, the other side mentions for the first time that the approval of some previously unrecognized person is required, or there is no deal. Could you have prepared for this? Do you have options at this point? Are you, perhaps, the negotiator making the dread announcement that you must respond to a higher power before a deal's a deal? Here, Wade meticulously deconstructs the circumstances that lead to "shadow of the tribe" negotiations, and suggests what you can do.

It is rare for an individual present at a negotiation or mediation to have "unlimited" authority to settle or make decisions. Even the most rugged individualist usually has someone looking over his/her shoulder. This may be a spouse, child, business partner, CEO, board of directors, shareholders, head office in Chicago, club, or church members. We are all part of some "system" or "network" of influences. These people in the background, sometimes in the shadows, can be described as supporters, influences, bosses, stakeholders, third parties, constituents, outsiders, armchair critics, bush lawyers, sticky beaks, nosey parkers,[1] ratifiers, destabilizers, tribal members, intermeddlers, cheersquads, principals, hawks, doves, or moderates.[2] Here in this article, the terminology of "the tribe" will often be used.

The visible negotiator can be labeled an agent, representative, spokesperson, mouth-piece, pawn, victim, channel, or go between.

Christopher Moore characterizes constituent groups as either "bureaucratic" or "horizontal." Bureaucratic constituents are the hierarchy of decision makers in companies, government agencies, tribes, schools, and many other institutions. "Horizontal" constituents are friends, relatives, and co-workers whom a disputant feels obliged to consult and listen to.[3] The following case study illustrates the discovery of a powerful horizontal constituent, namely a spouse.

Case Study 1—Ambushed by a Powerful Spouse

A cotton factory owner contracted with an expert factory designer and builder to renovate sections of his mill for $2 million. When the renovations were complete the owner was disappointed as the promised rate of production did not occur until three months thereafter. The new machinery often did not work during the first three months. The factory experienced repetitive "down-time." Accordingly, the factory owner withheld the last payment of $250,000 to the renovator. Incensed, the renovator commenced court

Source: "Bargaining in the Shadow of the Tribe," by John H. Wade from *The Negotiator's Fieldbook*, with Andrea Kupfer Schneider and Christopher Honeyman (Eds.), 2006, pp. 475–484. American Bar Association. Used with permission.

action in one state (the state of the contract) to recover the last installment. Predictably, the factory owner cross-claimed, in the state where the factory was actually constructed, for three months of diminished profits, being around $1 million. The entrenched parties and lawyers were required to attend mandatory mediation.

After lengthy and sometimes vitriolic negotiation between the two teams at the table (11 people in total), the mediator took the two CEOs for a walk down the street. Standing under a tree for an hour with the mediator reframing and asking "what if" questions, led to a settlement between the two CEOs. However, the tough renovator CEO suddenly announced, "Of course I will not be able to settle this today. I will have to run this all past my wife".

The mediator reframed, placated the other irate CEO and retreated with the renovator CEO in order to phone his wife. In a carefully orchestrated conversation, the mediator spoke to the wife (with the husband present) and praised the husband, explained what progress had been made, empathized with her suffering and loss, and brainstormed on the risks of other options. The wife spoke to her renovator husband (with the mediator still present), and in a short time confirmed the grateful husband's decision to settle.

Obviously, some negotiators do not disclose that they will need to convince influential outsiders about any outcome.[4] They lie, or are embarrassed, or overestimate their own influence over their constituents. At a later stage of preparation, or at the joint negotiation meetings, more direct questions may unearth the outsiders in the shadows, ever-present in spirit, though absent in the flesh:

- "How will Mary, the head of your department, feel about that sort of result?"
- "Your wife appears to have suffered a lot as your business struggled. How does she feel about this meeting?"
- "Most insurers I meet have an authorized range, but then need to make phone calls once the recommended result is outside that range. I assume that is also true for you?"
- "You will go through blood, sweat, and tears at the negotiation. That will change your perspectives. Are there any club/church/party members sitting calmly back home ready to criticize your efforts?"

Despite all this tactful investigation, no one may know until the fateful request by one party to make a phone call at the "end" of the negotiation. The other negotiators may meanwhile live with ignorance or suspicions.

How to Manage Any Influential Outsiders

If key tribal members are identified (or suspected) during the routine preparation, or at any subsequent time during a mediation or negotiation, how many ways are there for a negotiator to respond to this information? Set out below are standard responses to add to the toolbox.[5] All have advantages and disadvantages.

- Refuse to negotiate.
- Adjourn until authority figures are "present."
- Carry on regardless.

- Normalize.
- Ask a ritualistic "authority" question.
- Insist on written authority within the subjective range or objective range of "fairness."
- Agree to use the best endeavors to sell the agreement.
- Seek the opinion of an evaluative mediator or expert.
- Consult with the outside authority/influence before negotiation.
- Consult with outside influences before the negotiation and arrange a decision-making process.
- Have selected "reporting" team members explain the settlement and progress to outside authorities before anyone else.
- Warn of the dangers of reneging—"What if . . . ?"
- Throw a tantrum.

Refuse to Negotiate

The first response to knowledge or suspicion about influential outsiders is to refuse to negotiate or mediate. "I am not willing to waste time and money talking to some middle manager, lackey, puppet, or person without authority to settle." This refusal to negotiate may lead to further conflicts or litigation, subsequent lying about authority to settle, or the emergence of the influencers from the shadows.

Adjourn Until Authority Figures Are "Present"

The second response follows normally from the first. That is, one or more disputants may refuse to negotiate or mediate on major questions, unless and until key authority figures are "present" in person or are available on the phone or teleconferencing facility during the mediation or negotiation.

In many conflicts, such brinkmanship is futile as those with persuasive or legal power are too many, too distant, too expensive, or too busy to appear. Nevertheless, many mediations and negotiations are organized creatively to enable:

- An auditorium of constituents and families to be present, witness, speak and vote.
- A CEO from overseas to be "present" via teleconferencing, or telephone.
- Travel of key family or board members to an all day (and sometimes all-night) meeting in a convenient central location.

The presence of numerous influential people creates constant logistical challenges of expense and coordinating calendars. However, once these logistical difficulties are overcome, they provide helpful pressures to "find a solution now that all of us are here." One possible method to manage time is to encourage many people to attend, on the express condition that the number of speakers will be limited to those who are nominated representatives, or to those given the microphone or some other "talking symbol" by a chairperson. This method has been used effectively in large town hall meetings between angry residents and local councils.

Nevertheless, this solution of "adjourn until" will be opposed strongly by middle managers and family members who fear the presence of their own bosses or family during the meeting. These outside authorities may be resentful for the inconvenience of attending; critical of the disputant for "being unable to sort this out by yourself;" and dangerously judgmental of their own tribal representative if too many skeletons come out of the closet during the negotiation.

Additional opposition to this "adjourn until X can be present" option will some-times come from the *other* disputants. That is, one set of disputants objects to "interfer-ence" and "delays" due to the proposed presence of the other disputant's "officious boss," "nosey brother," "pushy husband," "aggressive union member," or "opinionated accountant." These legitimate objections and perceptions can usually be reframed ("So you would like X to work alone/independently?" or "So you are worried about the dy-namics if X is present?"). The objector can then be challenged by questions such as: "If Y does not attend, will X ever settle?" "How will you feel if X wants Y to check any deal you reach?" "How can you ensure that the brother/boss/accountant/wife gives an informed opinion, rather than an ignorant reaction?"

The writer as mediator regularly uses similar questions to persuade disputants that they should consent to and welcome the presence of an "appropriate" influential spouse, accountant, or wise friend to "help" another disputant. Despite sometimes initial resistance, the persuasion has always succeeded on the basis that it is "better to have a visible influence, than someone whiteanting in the background."[6] This exercise always involves a further task of trying to find "extra helpers" to equalize numbers present for each faction at the mediation/negotiation.

With a few notable exceptions, the presence of the outside influence has been essential, or at least helpful in order to find a resolution.

Children as Powerful "Outside Influencers"   One common group of powerful influ-encers who are often not "present" at negotiations and mediations, are children. Parents have legal power to make decisions about their children but sometimes have limited per-suasive power, particularly over teenagers in industrialized societies.

Carry on Regardless

The third response to suspicions or knowledge of key influencers, or absence of "com-plete authority to settle," is to say nothing and continue the process.

Some negotiators may decide that even opening the questions of "Do you both have authority to settle?" or "How shall we identify and manage influential outsiders?" is so inflammatory, complex, and time-consuming that it is better not discussed. Arguably, the topic will remain safely buried, either because no substantive resolution is reached or recommended (so no telephone calls need to be made); or the settlement is within the "agent's" range (again, so no telephone calls need to be made); or it is so routine for cer-tain disputants (e.g., middle managers, some insurers) to make phone calls, that it is not necessary to discuss what is normal. Moreover, if a settlement is reached and approval is then sought from an outsider, and this procedural ambush causes offense to the other party, then in those (statistically few?) cases, the negotiations can be "managed" at that stage. Why clumsily anticipate what may not turn into a problem?

Others have seen many negotiations stumble and fail due to the influence of tribal members. These scarred negotiators may be reluctant to "carry on regardless" or "wait and see what happens" in relation to these hovering armchair critics.

Normalize

The fourth response to the perceived pressure from outsiders is for the negotiator to give one or more "normalizing" speeches. The aim of these speeches is to attempt to convince one of the negotiators that the need for outside ratification is "normal;" is not devious; is not normally part of a good cop–bad cop negotiation tactic (though it could be that!); that competent negotiators do not fuss over this procedural step; and that progress can be made despite the need for outside approval. For example, "Jill, in my experience it is normal for middle managers in large businesses or government to seek approval for the agreement you hope to reach today. They cannot risk their jobs by settling without higher level approval. If you insist on them having full authority to settle, their easiest escape is to leave the decision to a judge; then they will avoid being blamed for the outcome."

These kinds of speeches by a team member may assist a disputant to persist with the negotiation/mediation, rather than prematurely choose option one—namely, refuse to negotiate.

Ask a Ritualistic "Authority" Question

The fifth possible response to the knowledge or suspicion that one or more of the disputants will need to consult an outsider before signing any settlement, is for the negotiator to ask ritualistically, "Do you have authority to settle this dispute?" This question can be asked in writing in the preparation documents required to be completed by each negotiator. Alternatively, this question can be asked or re-asked at both private and joint meetings. Presumably, some negotiators are hoping for a confident or mumbled "yes" as an answer.

The mumble or the body language may suggest a lie or more complex motives. A more precise and tactical answer could be: "Yes, I have complete authority to negotiate or to settle so long as the outcome is fair/reasonable/in the range. If it is an unusual settlement, or one out of the normal range, then obviously I will have to consult my superiors/constituents/family. I assume that you would have to do likewise if you were in my position."

Whatever answer is given, it leaves the parties with some unresolved tensions. A confident affirmative answer may well be a lie or a mask to complexity; a mumbled affirmative answer will raise suspicions; and a "correct" tactical and qualified affirmative may open a detailed discussion of the meaning of "reasonable"; and a negative answer may lead to option one—a refusal to negotiate.

Insist on Written Authority to Settle Within the Subjective Range or Objective Range of "Fairness"

The sixth possible response is for a negotiator to insist that some or all of the negotiators produce a written (and irrevocable) authority to settle. This written step may appear to provide more certainty than the ritualistic oral assurances set out in the previous response.

However, in reality, those who draft such written authorities know that they provide little certainty that the alleged agent will act upon the apparent authority. Why?

This is because an authority can be drafted in one of two ways—subjectively or objectively. A subjective written authority gives the agent the power to enter into such agreement as the agent believes is "reasonable," "fair," "appropriate," or "reflecting common commercial practices." All these words leave the agent with such a broad discretion that if he believes that the outcome is anything other than "advantageous," he may want to consult with the influential constituents anyhow (to protect his/her job or reputation or safety). That is, the representative's broad "legal" authority is qualified by his or her certain knowledge that he has limited "persuasive" authority.

An objective written authority supposedly gives the agent more certainty and less discretion. For example, "My lawyer is hereby given irrevocable authority by me to settle this dispute for an amount not less than $400,000."

However, such an objective authority to settle, is no panacea. First, by defining outcomes only in dollars, it restricts creative packaging. Second, the existence of such a key piece of information, namely the "reservation" or "walk-away," creates the risk that it may be leaked to the other side. Third, the authority may specify a false and flexible figure which can be "accidentally leaked" to the other side. Fourth, the authority does not prevent real or theatrical consultation taking place anyhow.

Agree to Use the Best Endeavors to Sell the Agreement

The seventh possible response to the negotiator's knowledge or suspicion that one or more of the negotiators will need to consult with influential outsiders before reaching agreement is to negotiate for the agent to use his or her "best endeavors" to sell the outcome to the constituents.

This option may seem weak. However, the writer and other colleagues have used it successfully on a variety of occasions.

This response anticipates a standard type of conversation between the negotiator (N) and his or her constituents (C) after a mediation or negotiation. For example:

C: "How did the mediation/negotiation go last night?"

N: "Well, we reached agreement. It is not all that you hoped for."

C: "What did you agree to?"

N: "Well, there are four basic provisions as follows . . ."

C: "That doesn't seem very fair. Why did we get so little? Are you happy with that outcome?"

N: "Well, I am not happy, but in the circumstances . . ."

C: "If you are not happy, why did you agree to it?"

N: "Well, it was the best I (we) could do. The mediator put us under some pressure to be realistic."

C: "We will need some time to reconsider this. It is very disappointing. I certainly will not sign/ratify. They must be laughing about . . ."

This standard disclose, disappoint, defend, and blame language is clearly foreseeable between some agents and tribes. Many representatives at mediations are in an unenviable position of martyrdom by the awaiting tribal hawks.[7]

This predictable pattern may encourage a wary mediator or negotiator to go through the following steps. First, ask each negotiator (privately and perhaps publicly) "What if you reach an agreement which you believe is satisfactory but which disappoints your constituents/members/family?" Second, the mediator asks "What if the post-settlement conversation with your constituents is as follows . . ." (mimics the disclose, disappoint, defend and blame language)? In the writer's experience, the representatives tend to nod glumly.

Third, the mediator asks, "Would you (each) be prepared to return to your club/constituents and highly recommend the outcome you reach (tomorrow, next week, next month, etc.)? There is no point working hard for an agreement if you then allow that routine and undermining conversation to occur. You might as well abandon the meeting now."

The negotiators can usually be persuaded to agree orally or in writing as follows:

"If we reach an agreement after working hard through a range of possibilities, we will not report back to X in a half-hearted fashion. We will unanimously report back to X about the issues and the options. We will unanimously and enthusiastically recommend the outcome we reach as satisfactory, workable, and the best option available. We will endeavor to 'sell' the outcome to our constituents."

Seek the Opinion of an Evaluative Mediator or Expert

Following the previous response, there is an eighth method to help the representative save face, job, and safety; and to create doubt for any angry hawks lurking among the constituents.

This involves hiring an evaluative mediator who is respected in the field in which the disputants are negotiating; and/or bringing to the mediation or negotiation an expert in the field as an observer and commentator. An oral or written statement from an attending expert, such as, "This negotiated outcome is, in my opinion, within the range of predictable results in court/the marketplace." usually gives the nervous negotiators some welcome ammunition against the outside critics.

Consult with the Outside Authority/Influence Before Negotiation

The ninth possible response of a negotiator to the real or suspected existence of an influential outsider is to consult with that outsider before the joint sessions begin.

The writer uses this method in the majority of his negotiations and mediations. A negotiator asks his or her own constituents, and then secretly or openly any accessible supporters behind the "opposition," a series of routine diagnostic questions about causes of conflict, interventions, glitches, risks if the conflict continues, and possible substantive outcomes. These questions often produce important benefits including new perspectives and hypotheses for both the negotiators and the outsiders, and a sense of inclusion and respect from those constituents.

Consult with Outside Influences Before the Negotiation and Arrange a Decision-Making Process

There is a tenth important response that every mediator and negotiator needs to have in his or her conceptual and linguistic repertoire when outside tribal members are obvious or unearthed. This response is to insist upon and organize a "decision rule" within each group of constituents.[8]

> There is a variety of methods by which groups can decide to make decisions. In decision-making groups, the dominant view is to assume that majority rules and at some point take a vote of all members, assuming that any settlement option that receives more than 50 percent of the votes will be the one adopted. Obviously, this is not the only option. Groups can make decisions by dictatorship (one person decides), oligarchy (a small but dominant minority coalition decides), simple majority (one more person than half the group), two-thirds majority, broad consensus most of the group agrees, and those who dissent agree not to protest or raise objections, and true unanimity (everyone agrees). Understanding what decision rule a group will use before deliberations begin will also significantly affect the group process. For example, if a simple majority will make the decision in a five-person group, then only three people need to agree. Thus, any three people can get together and form a coalition—during the meeting or even prior to the meeting. In contrast, if the rule will be consensus and unanimity, then the group must meet and work hard enough to assure that all parties' interests are raised, discussed, and incorporated into the group decision.[9]

That is, during preparation for negotiation *between* parties, representatives from each group are required to facilitate discussions *within* each of the parties' tribes on the key question—"By what process will the group make a decision?"

For example, a negotiator (or mediator) can typically go through the following steps described below.

Brinkmanship and Doubt Creation   "I am not willing to negotiate unless both groups decide clearly on how they will vote to approve or disapprove their respective representatives' recommendations."

"No group can agree unanimously on what day of the week it is; so don't come back to me with a unanimity rule."

"I am also not willing to accept a 'wait and see' or 'we will work it out later' voting process. That is a recipe for failure and embarrassment for me as your representative. We all know that some of you will be disappointed with the outcome, and some will be able to live with that same outcome."

Facilitate Agreement on Each Group's 'Decision Rule'   "If you wish, I can meet with my group to develop an answer to this key question 'How will we make a decision as a group at the end of the negotiation?'"

"If you wish, I can tell you a range of ways other groups like you have made decisions. You can add those to your list of possibilities before deciding."

Write Out and Publicize the 'Decision Rule' of Each Group Before the Joint Mediation or Negotiation Begins   This third step is helpful as it reduces the chances of a whole group later reneging on their decision rule; and encourages negotiators who can see that the decision-rules may be a way of controlling hawks on their own team, or on the opposition's team. Without a visible decision rule in place, a skilled hawk can exploit the inevitable post-recommendation or post-settlement regrets within a group, and organize rejection of many negotiated or recommended agreements. [Wade & Honeyman, *Lasting Agreement*] The following case example illustrates the use of a pre-determined intra-team decision-making process.

Case Study 2—Face Saving Decision Rule

A mediation occurred between two factions of a church. Both wanted to acquire the church property and exclude the other for a host of alleged miscommunications, misdemeanors, and personality defects. Vitriolic litigation had commenced to appoint a trustee for sale of the church.

The two factions were represented at the mediation by seven and eight elders respectively. One lawyer took the mediator aside and said that his group of seven could never agree to any outcome as two ("hawks") of the seven had paid all his legal fees; were deeply hurt; and wanted victory as a "matter of principle."

The grateful mediator sent each faction away to determine "How to make a decision at the end of the mediation?" The seven decided upon a 5-to-2 majority decision; the eight upon a 5-to-3 majority decision. This was publicly announced.

Eight hours later, a group of two from each faction reached a recommended outcome which they agreed to "sell" hard to their colleagues. They succeeded. The faction of seven predictably voted 5 to 2 in favor of the recommended package with the two hawks dissenting.

The pre-existing decision rule then enabled both hawks to make speeches that they did not like the outcome, but they were men of honor, and would comply with the agreed majority vote by their friends.

Have Selected "Reporting" Team Members Explain the Settlement and Progress to Outside Authorities Before Anyone Else

This is another vital response that every negotiator needs to add to his/her toolbox in order to deal with armchair critics who are eagerly awaiting the outcome of a negotiation.

This practice can helpfully complement the previous two responses, namely consulting with outsiders and organizing a decision-rule *before* the negotiation (or mediation). After each negotiation session, an appointed reporting negotiator strives to report to the influential constituents *before* or at the same time as other team members do so. This can be done by phone, fax, or email with copies being given simultaneously to the team members on one or both sides. This enables the team of negotiators to build upon the interpretation and language adopted in the report. It will also reduce the predictable dilemma for the other team members of reporting, disappointing, defending, and blaming.

The aims of this response are to:

- Protect the negotiating team from hostile outsiders.

- Create doubt for the armchair critics.

- Give the negotiating team and the critics a new set of words, metaphors, and expressions to describe the historical events at the negotiation. These words can profoundly influence simmering hostile perceptions and emotions.

- Avoid a defensive negotiator from too readily "blaming" another team member, a perceived hawk or dove, or the negotiation process for the outcome.

- Develop further trust in the reporting negotiators who ideally model transparency and problem-solving skills.

The writer uses this practice regularly when organizing negotiations which involve influential outsiders. It sometimes requires persuasion to convince all team members of the potential benefits to them when a diplomatic "reporting negotiator" provides the first feedback to the waiting constituents. Of course, sometimes hawks break the "reporting" agreement by leaking their own loaded versions about negotiation progress to the press or to their own constituents.

Warn of the Dangers of Reneging—"What If . . . ?"

Negotiators usually have a range of phrases to exhort their own team and the other disputants to perform their agreements, despite pressures from outsiders to renege.

These may have the effect of preparing the disputants for such pressures, and giving them a practiced repertoire of language when placed under such pressures to renege. For example:

- "What will you do in the next week when some of our supporters criticize us for reaching this agreement?"

- "How will you respond when some of our fellow committee members say, "You should have obtained a better deal?"

- "Should we practice that speech now so that we gain confidence and consistency?"

This preparation is particularly important in those disputes where there is a necessary gap in time between agreement and ratification of the agreement by constituents or a court. For example, in family, native title, environmental, succession, and human rights disputes, it is normal for a mediated or negotiated agreement to require court approval before the agreement becomes legally binding. As many lawyers can nervously testify, this pause provides a dangerous gap of days or weeks when one or more parties can be pressured by constituents or self-doubt to renege.

Throw a Tantrum

This response involves a mild-mannered negotiator expressing strong and theatrical disapproval when one party suddenly suggests that he needs to consult with an influential outsider. The theatrical negotiator has the goal of pressuring the wavering negotiator into signing immediately, rather than passing responsibility to outsiders.

A negotiator's exhortations might be as follows:

- "I can't believe that at this stage of the meeting, you want to make a phone call! What kind of message will that send to my team? They are likely to walk out angrily and not come back."
- "We have all put in so much work to reach this agreement. And now you want to risk it all with a break so that you can talk to your relatives?"
- "You can't do this Mary! Your reputation as a negotiator will be in tatters. In the future, our firm will insist on negotiating with anyone but you."

The writer has not used the fake tantrum in these circumstances, but has anecdotally heard of others trying this intervention. It obviously has many risks for a negotiator, including allegations of bullying, cultural clumsiness, or ignorance of other more suitable interventions, or a walk-out.

Conclusion

This article has identified and systematized 13 possible responses to influential tribes and outsiders before, during, and after negotiations. There are probably other responses or hybrids that could be added from the repertoires of experienced mediators and negotiators. Obviously, each response has advantages and disadvantages.

In the writer's opinion, this is another common hurdle in negotiations where mediators can add value to "unassisted" negotiations.[10] First, the mediator can question strategically in order to identify influential outsiders; second, pose a neutral problem-solving question (e.g., "how to respond to influential outsiders?"); and third, be aware of and, if possible practiced in, the 13 responses to this question. These three steps can be mastered by expert negotiators. However, a master negotiator may often (rightly?) be suspected by the opposition of strategic manipulation of the process. Less suspicion of bias may fall upon a respected mediator who is employed by all parties to manage negotiation dynamics including the unruly behavior of hawks, doves, and moderates in the background.

This analysis raises challenges for the systematic training of mediators and negotiators: questions for research on the actual behavior of mediators and negotiators in relation to managing the influence of outsiders; questions about the rate of use of each of these responses in different areas of conflict and culture; and questions about what evidence, if any, can be collected to measure and predict the rate of "success" of each response to ubiquitous outside influences.

Endnotes

Adapted from John H. Wade, "Bargaining in the Shadow of the Tribe and Limited Authority to Settle," *Bond Law Review* 15 (2003), p. 115.

1. A "sticky beak" is an inquisitive, prying person"; and a "nosey parker" is a "person who continually pries, a meddler," from *The Macquarie Dictionary of Australian Colloquialisms* (McMahons Point, New South Wales: Macquarie Library, 1984), pp. 220 and 299.

2. A "hawk" is a competitive member of a group who has a clear solution as a goal that is perceived as "winning," and who is prepared to engage in contentious tactics, sometimes including violence, in order to "win" in the short term. A "dove" is a person whose major goal is peace and nonviolence, achieved by peaceful methods including yielding, even if achieved at short-term costs. A "moderate" is a person whose goal is to find a solution acceptable to all disputants and interest groups, by a combination of mild contentious tactics, negotiation, face-saving, and compromise.

3. Christopher W. Moore, *The Mediation Process* (New York: John Wiley & Sons, 2003), pp. 438–41.

4. John H. Wade, *Representing Clients at Mediation and Negotiation* (Queensland, Bond University, 2000), pp. 118–24. *See* Janet R. Johnston and Linda E. G. Campbell, *Impasses of Divorce* (New York: Free Press, 1988), where they suggest that pressure from relatives is one of the three primary causes for sustaining conflict between highly conflicted couples.

5. *See* John H. Wade, "Tools for a Mediator's Toolbox: Reflections on Matrimonial Property Disputes," *Australian Dispute Resolution Journal* 7 (1996), p. 93.

6. A "whiteant" is a termite that eats timber in houses leaving a veneer of strength, which however collapses under the slightest pressure.

7. *See* Dean G. Pruitt and Sung Hee Kim, *Social Conflict-Escalation, Stalemate and Settlement* (New York: McGraw-Hill, 2003) for an analysis of changes to social structures and psychology that tend to perpetuate conflict.

8. *See* Roy J. Lewicki et al., *Negotiation,* 5th ed. (New York: McGraw-Hill, 2005).

9. Ibid., p. 367.

10. For discussions of various standard hurdles see Lewicki, *Negotiation*, chapter 17; John S. Hammond et al., *Smart Choices: A Practical Guide to Making Better Decisions* (Cambridge, MA: Harvard Business Publishing, 1999); Rober Mnookin, ed., *Barriers to Conflict Resolution* (New York: W. W. Norton & Company, 1995); and John H. Wade, "The Last Gap in Negotiations—Why Is It Important? How Can It Be Crossed?" *Australian Dispute Resolution Journal* 6 (1995), p. 93.

Reading 3.4

The Fine Art of Making Concessions
Deepak Malhotra

Most people understand that negotiation is a matter of give and take: You have to be willing to make concessions to get concessions in return. But the process of making concessions is easier said than done. Consider how events unfolded in the following management-union negotiation, adapted from Richard E. Walton and Robert B. McKersie's book *A Behavioral Theory of Labor Negotiations: An Analysis of a Social Interaction System* (ILR Press, 1991).

The head of a manufacturing firm was preparing to initiate talks with the leadership of the employees' union. The biggest issue on the table was a wage increase. The union was asking for a 4 percent increase, while management wanted to raise salaries by only 1 percent.

The executive considered the situation. During past negotiations, weeks were lost as each side jockeyed for position, feigned willingness to walk away, and eventually compromised on an unsurprising outcome. In this case, a deal at 2.5 percent, the midpoint of the two parties' opening positions, seemed likely to be agreeable to both sides.

This time things would be different, he resolved. He would save everyone hassle and delay by making concessions early. Against the advice of the mediator, he opened discussions by announcing that the eventual outcome was obvious and that he was prepared to make a final offer: 3 percent, the most he could have offered. The union's leadership was pleased by this offer—yet they did not accept it. If the firm could offer so much at the outset, they reasoned, perhaps they had set their sights too low. As the union's aspirations rose to unrealistic levels, a promising negotiation unraveled and culminated in a strike.

Concessions are often necessary in negotiation. But, as this story shows, they often go unappreciated and unreciprocated. In this article, I present four strategies to help you maximize the likelihood that others will acknowledge your gestures of goodwill and reciprocate in kind.

1. Label Your Concessions

In negotiation, don't assume that your actions will speak for themselves. Your counterparts will be motivated to overlook, ignore, or downplay your concessions. Why? To avoid the strong social obligation to reciprocate. As a result, it is your responsibility to label your concessions and make them salient to the other party—a responsibility that the manufacturer in the introductory example neglected.

When it comes to labeling, there are a few rules to follow. First, let it be known that what you have given up (or what you have stopped demanding) is costly to you. By doing so, you clarify that a concession was, in fact, made. For example, the manufacturer could

Source: "The Fine Art of Making Concessions" by Deepak Malhotra from the *Program on Negotiation* newsletter at the Harvard Law School (www.pon.harvard.edu), January 2006, Vol. 9, No. 1, pp. 9–11. Used by permission.

have explained the effect of a 3 percent wage increase on his firm's bottom line or discussed how difficult it would be for him to justify it to his board of directors.

Second, emphasize the benefits to the other side. My own research suggests that negotiators reciprocate concessions based on the benefits they receive, while tending to ignore how much others are sacrificing. One way for the manufacturer to highlight the benefits he was providing to the union would be to contrast his offer with those made by similar firms (assuming they were lower).

Third, don't give up on your original demands too hastily. If the other side considers your first offer to be frivolous, your willingness to move away from it will not be seen as concessionary behavior. By contrast, your concessions will be more powerful when your counterpart views your initial demands as serious and reasonable. Accordingly, spend time legitimating your original offer and then use it as a reference point when labeling your concession. The manufacturer, for example, would have been wise to make concessions slowly. Eventually, he could point out that his final offer was closer to the union's original demands than it was to his own.

2. Demand and Define Reciprocity

Labeling your concessions helps trigger an obligation to reciprocate, but sometimes your counterpart will be slow to act on that obligation. To increase the likelihood that you get something in return for your concession, try to explicitly—but diplomatically—demand reciprocity.

For example, consider the following negotiation between an IT services firm and a client. The client suggests that the IT firm's cost estimates are unreasonably high; the IT firm's project manager believes that the cost estimates are accurate (and perhaps conservative) given the complexity of the project and the short deadline. If the project manager is willing to make a concession, she might say: "This isn't easy for us, but we've made some adjustments on price to accommodate your concerns. We expect that you are now in a better position to make some changes to the project deadlines. An extra month for each milestone would help us immeasurably."

Notice that this statement achieves three goals. First, it labels the concession ("This isn't easy for us, but we've made some adjustments . . ."). Second, it tactfully demands reciprocity ("We expect that you are now in a better position to make some changes . . ."). Third, it also begins to define the precise form that reciprocity should take ("An extra month for each milestone . . ."). While each of these elements is critical, negotiators often overlook the need to define reciprocity. Remember that no one understands what you value better than you do. If you don't speak up, you're going to get what your counterpart thinks you value or, worse, what is most convenient for your counterpart to give.

The strategy of demanding and defining reciprocity plays out in a variety of contexts; those who understand how to use it can profit from it immensely. A great example is a tactic consultants and contractors use. When a client praises her work, a smart consultant will quickly point out that the person who would really love to hear this praise is her boss (or other potential customers). In this way, she defines for the appreciative customer how best to reciprocate.

3. Make Contingent Concessions

One hallmark of a good working relationship is that parties don't nickel-and-dime each other for concessions. Rather, each side learns about the interests and concerns of the other and makes good-faith efforts toward achieving joint gains.

Unfortunately, while fostering such norms is desirable, it is not always possible. Recently, one of my students in an executive education class explained that while he would be more than happy to engage in mutual give-and-take during his negotiations, he often has trouble doing so with his contractors and customers. Some are clearly untrustworthy or entirely self-interested. Such negotiators are likely to exploit his goodwill by refusing to reciprocate at all, much less in the way he has defined.

My advice to the executive: When trust is low or when you're engaged in a one-shot negotiation, consider making *contingent concessions*. A concession is contingent when you state that you can make it only if the other party agrees to make a specified concession in return. For example, if the executive was renegotiating a service contract with a customer, he might suggest that a requested concession is impossible given the current contract but possible under certain conditions. He might say, "We can provide additional support but only if you agree to purchase some of the following additional services," or, "This is literally the best we can do on price right now. But if you can adjust some of your demands, we might be able to reopen the price issue."

Contingent concessions are almost risk-free. They allow you to signal to the other party that while you have room to make more concessions, it may be impossible for you to budge if reciprocity is not guaranteed. Keep in mind, however, that an over-reliance on contingent concessions can interfere with building trust. If you demand immediate compensation every time you make a concession, your behavior will be seen as self-serving rather than oriented toward achieving mutual satisfaction.

4. Make Concessions in Installments

Which of these scenarios would make you happier?

Scenario A:
While walking down the street, you find a $20 bill.
Scenario B:
While walking down the street, you find a $10 bill. The next day, on a different street, you find another $10 bill.

The total amount of money found is the same in each scenario—yet the vast majority of people report that Scenario B would make them happier. More generally, extensive research (beginning with the work of the late Stanford University professor Amos Tversky and the Princeton University professor and Nobel laureate Daniel Kahneman in the 1970s) demonstrates that while most of us prefer to get bad news all at once, we prefer to get good news in installments.

This finding suggests that the same concession will be more positively received if it is broken into installments. For example, imagine that you are negotiating the purchase of a house and that a wide gap exists between your initial offer and the seller's asking price. You are willing to increase your offer by a maximum of $40,000. You will be more effective if you make two smaller concessions, such as $30,000 followed by $10,000, than if you make one $40,000 concession.

There are other reasons to make concessions in installments. First, most negotiators expect that they will trade offers back and forth several times, with each side making multiple concessions before the deal is done. If you give away everything in your first offer, the other party may think that you're holding back even though you've been as generous as you can be. The manufacturer who offered a 3 percent wage increase to the employees' union up front faced exactly this problem.

Installments may also lead you to discover that you don't have to make as large a concession as you thought. When you give away a little at a time, you might get everything you want in return before using up your entire concession-making capacity. Whatever is left over is yours to keep—or to use to induce further reciprocity. In the real estate example, you might discover that the initial $30,000 increase in your offer was all that you needed to sign the deal!

Finally, making multiple, small concessions tells the other party that you are flexible and willing to listen to his needs. Each time you make a concession, you have the opportunity to label it and extract goodwill in return.

All of the above strategies are aimed at guaranteeing that the concessions you make are not ignored or exploited. It is important to note, however, that when someone refuses to reciprocate, the refusal often hurts her as much as the party who made the concession. Nonreciprocity sours the relationship, making it difficult for negotiators to trust each other or risk further concessions. Thus, effective negotiators ensure not only that their own concessions are reciprocated but also that they acknowledge and reciprocate the concessions of others.

Reading 3.5

The High Cost of Low Trust
Keith G. Allred

Counteracting misperception and mistrust at the beginning of a negotiation can help negotiators avoid vicious cycles and sustain virtuous ones.

For decades, Hormel Foods and its employees enjoyed one of the most cooperative and productive labor–management relationships in the processed foods industry. But beginning in the late 1970s, when Hormel pushed for wage concessions, the company's relationship with its workforce began to deteriorate, especially at the plant in Austin, Minnesota, the quiet "company town" where Hormel was founded.

By the time the labor contract with the local union was up for renegotiation in 1985, each side in the Austin dispute had decided to take an aggressive approach, convinced of the other side's hostility and unreasonableness. Contract negotiations concluded in 1986 only after a bitter nine-month employee strike and after the vast majority of unionized employees had been fired, forced to take early retirement, or placed on recall lists. In the process, neighbors in Austin turned against one another, and the fabric of the community was torn to shreds.

Such stories of relationships gone bad are unfortunately common in the business world. In negotiation, as in the business world at large, relationships are key. Those that become contentious and suspicious are liable to result in frustrating and costly outcomes. By contrast, relationships that are cooperative and trusting tend to foster negotiation success.

How do suspicion and retaliation—or, by contrast, trust and cooperation—become embedded in a relationship? Decades of social science research confirm the strength of the *norm of reciprocity*—the human tendency to respond to the actions of others with similar actions. If we're treated with respect and cooperation, we tend to respond with respect and cooperation. What's more, a single round of action followed by a reciprocal response can work itself into an ongoing cycle. A cooperative interaction often initiates a virtuous cycle in which cooperation sustains itself, while a hostile interaction tends to perpetuate a vicious cycle of contention and suspicion.

Building on others' research into the particular triggers of such vicious and virtuous cycles, I've identified the triggers most likely to help managers avoid vicious cycles and sustain virtuous ones. In my studies, hundreds of executives were each rated by between 4 and 10 of their colleagues on a range of items. Here I'll show how my findings and those of other social scientists can help you replace vicious cycles with the virtuous cycles you need to improve your negotiations and your ongoing business relationships.

Source: "The High Cost of Low Trust" by Keith G. Allred, from the *Program on Negotiation* newsletter at the Harvard Law School (www.pon.harvard.edu), June 2004, Vol. 7, No. 7, pp. 1–4. Used with permission.

Vicious Cycle Triggers

Vicious cycles frequently grow out of the widespread human tendency to take an exaggerated view of others' perceived hostility or unreasonable behavior. This exaggeration leads us to reciprocate with negative behavior of our own. Although based on an initial misperception, our own hostility creates a self-fulfilling prophecy—the other side is likely to respond negatively in return. Taking this genuinely hostile response as confirmation of our earlier perceptions, we fail to recognize that our own actions created exactly what we feared. Here are some particularly potent triggers of this vicious cycle.

Naive Realism

Most people tend to assume that their view of the world reflects reality. Researchers Rob Robinson, Dacher Keltner, Andrew Ward, and Lee Ross describe three aspects of this phenomenon, known as *naive realism.* First, when confronting a problem, we typically think that we're reasonable and objective. Second, we assume that anyone looking at the same evidence would draw the same conclusions we do. Third, when others reach different conclusions, we suspect they're unreasonable or driven by dubious motives. This last inference triggers vicious cycles: differences of opinion firm up our belief that, given the other side's unreasonableness, extreme measures are our only option. Often these perceptions are painfully symmetric, with each side convinced of the other's obstinacy and unaware of the other's view. As each side escalates accordingly, costs mount and relationships are destroyed.

The Confirmatory Bias

In negotiation, we're also likely to fall victim to the *confirmatory bias*—the tendency to seek out information that verifies our preexisting beliefs and to ignore or find flaws with disconfirming information. Although it's counterintuitive, providing the same information to two opposing parties can further polarize their beliefs. Charles Lord, Lee Ross, and Mark Lepper studied this effect by examining the views of activists on both sides of the capital punishment debate. After giving their views on the issue, the activists read two articles from law journals, one in favor of capital punishment and one opposed. The researchers then measured changes in the activists' views.

The Sincerity Gap

I've seen organizations try to manipulate fairness perceptions with disastrous results. An aerospace company implemented a "quality circle" program aimed at generating employee feedback. When the company failed to respond to any of the employees' concerns, workers were infuriated. "It was fine that the company didn't care what I thought," one employee told me, "but it was truly insulting to ask for my views and then ignore them." There's a simple rule of thumb here. If you're not genuinely interested in the other side's perspective, don't ask for it.

Despite the fact that they had all read the same articles, pro–capital punishment activists felt even more strongly about their position, and anti–capital punishment activists were also more convinced that they were right. When reading the articles, each side sought out evidence to support their opinions and found fault with the disconfirming information. Because both sides thought they were being reasonable and objective, they were baffled by the other side's inability to see the "facts." The result? A vicious cycle of polarization.

Accuser and Excuser Biases

How we assign responsibility for harmful behavior also triggers vicious cycles. In our research, my colleagues and I found an *accuser bias:* when someone does something that causes us harm, we tend to hold him or her excessively responsible. Suppose that Lisa, a development director for a nonprofit agency, needs a report from Ron, the agency's marketing director, for a grant application she's writing. If Ron fails to deliver the report on time, Lisa is likely to blame the hardship caused by the missed deadline on factors within Ron's control, perhaps condemning him as irresponsible. She's also likely to underestimate the extent to which factors beyond Ron's control, such as another urgent task handed to him at the last minute by their boss, explain the harmful behavior. The accuser bias fosters anger and hostility, which foster the impulse to retaliate.

While we're liable to blame others for harmful behaviors, our studies show that people are likely to let themselves off the hook for the harm that they cause. The *excuser bias* describes the tendency to focus on factors beyond our control to explain away our behavior, while turning a blind eye toward factors within our control. Ron is likely to claim to Lisa that their boss's urgent request is responsible for his tardiness, while overlooking the fact that he was already far behind schedule and probably would have missed the deadline anyway.

Winning Traits

In my studies, the managers and executives who were most successful in avoiding contentious relationships were rated by their colleagues as (1) above average in their ability to recognize that reasonable people could come to different conclusions and (2) slow to blame others and willing to accept personal responsibility for problems. Similarly, professionals rated effective at listening to, understanding, and respecting others' perspectives were best able to sustain cooperative and trusting relations.

Whether colleagues, departments, organizations, or countries are negotiating, the pernicious interplay of the accuser and excuser biases can snowball into a vicious cycle. Suppose Lisa blows up at Ron for the missed deadline. He's likely to fall victim to the accuser bias himself, attributing Lisa's "unjustified" attack to her hostile personality. The stage is set for a relationship fraught with bitterness and retaliation.

Virtuous Cycle Triggers

We've seen how vicious cycles get started, but what about their opposite, virtuous cycles? My research found that a particularly powerful trigger of virtuous relationships is *fairness perceptions.* Researchers have long understood the importance of people's perceptions of the fairness of a negotiation outcome. More recently, it's been discovered that we also attend closely to whether the negotiation *process* was itself fair. We tend to judge a negotiation to have been fair when we ourselves had ample opportunity to voice our point of view. Our sense of fairness increases the more we sense that the other side has genuinely considered our perspective.

Fairness perceptions have strong implications for those seeking to build strong relationships. First, the more fairly we feel we've been treated, the greater our satisfaction with the outcome, even if it isn't what we wanted. Second, we're more willing to abide by agreements reached through a process that felt fair than we are to comply with agreements reached through a process that didn't feel fair. Third, the more fairly we feel we've been treated, the more likely we are to trust the other side and cooperate with them. Studies indicate that the sense of being carefully listened to is more likely to inspire cooperation and trust in negotiation than are substantive concessions.

Avoiding Vicious Cycles, Promoting Virtuous Cycles

It would be far easier to overcome vicious cycles if they were always rooted in misperception. But while most people reciprocate cooperative moves, others will try to take advantage. How can you distinguish your misperceptions of hostility from genuine ill will? The first thing to do is to test your assumptions. Before mounting an aggressive response to the other side's perceived unreasonable behavior, check your perspective with others who don't have a stake in the issue. If others are more understanding of a view that strikes you as wholly unreasonable, it may be that you and your negotiating partner have honest and reasonable differences of opinion. Before assuming ill intent, look for extenuating circumstances that might provide an alternative explanation. Better yet, ask the other party to explain her behavior.

As you're working to promote a virtuous cycle, keep in mind that having a close and positive relationship with the other party is no guarantee that a negotiation will result in a mutually beneficial outcome. As Harvard Business School professor Kathleen McGinn has found in her research, negotiating partners who share a high regard don't necessarily succeed in finding mutually beneficial solutions. Sometimes negotiators can become so concerned about each other's outcomes that they overlook their own best interests. Good will should always be combined with the active pursuit of joint gains.

Reading 3.6

Consequences of Principal and Agent

Jayne Seminare Docherty
Marcia Caton Campbell

Editors' Note: What's going on away from the negotiating table? How does the relationship between your counterpart and her principals impact you? Docherty and Caton Campbell explain how the structure of the agency relationship, for you and for the other side, can dramatically impact negotiation behaviors and outcomes. This chapter is related to Nolan-Haley's on Informed Consent, but also relates to chapters on team negotiations, particularly Bellman's on internal discord within a team.

This chapter assumes that becoming a creative, reflective practitioner of negotiation requires more than mastering negotiation techniques or strategies. We think it highly likely that a professional negotiator will encounter negotiation situations where the parties differ in type—for example, an individual negotiating with a corporation or a corporation negotiating with a local community group. It is also highly likely that a professional negotiator will encounter situations where back table negotiations between the principal party and the agent representing that party disrupt the primary negotiation. There is no way to equip negotiators with a set of discrete skills for managing these kinds of challenges. Instead, negotiators need to understand the structure of the negotiations operating at the same time as the conflicts being addressed by negotiations. This chapter offers some tools for analyzing both the conflict and the negotiation process when it involves agents negotiating on behalf of others.

Negotiation courses usually focus their primary attention on the interactions among the parties involved in the actual negotiation. Such courses also tend either to isolate the negotiation process from the social context within which it is embedded, or to assume that negotiators need only know about one small piece of the social context (e.g., the legal system or the business world). Negotiators should be encouraged to step back from the negotiation process and think more broadly about the social context within which they are operating. To this end, it is useful to consider how the structure of the larger social conflict or social problem affects the negotiation process. Some students of negotiation will protest that they are not dealing with *conflicts;* they are helping people address problems or differences. We would counter that the difference between a conflict and a dispute or "mere problem" can be quite small. It is often a matter of the perceptions of the parties; therefore, it is useful for all students of negotiation to understand the way the nature of the conflict—including its relative intensity—affects a negotiation process.

What do we mean by "social context" and "structure of the larger social conflict?" Negotiation is a process for managing or resolving conflicts that emerge in a particular

Source: "Consequences of Principal and Agent," by Jayne Seminare Docherty and Marcia Caton Campbell, from *The Negotiator's Fieldbook* with Andrea Kupfer Schneider and Christopher Honeyman (Eds.), 2006, pp. 497–504. American Bar Association. Used by permission.

social context.[1] For example, a negotiation may take place in a corporate setting, in a family, in the legal system, or in an institutional, governmental, or community setting. In each of these cases, the context or setting of the conflict carries certain norms, rules, and expectations—some formal and some informal—about how a negotiation process will be managed. Who needs to be at the table? What kinds of issues are negotiable and what kinds of issues may the parties not even raise in negotiation? How will the parties comport themselves during the negotiation?

Every social conflict, no matter the context within which it emerges, can also be said to have a structure. The structure of a conflict should not be confused with the structure of negotiation, as described by Korobkin,[2] which is also an important issue to be considered in educating negotiators. When we talk about the structure of a conflict, we are referring to features of the conflict such as the number and nature of the parties and the quality of their relationships. This contrasts with the dynamics of a conflict, which looks at changes in the parties' relationships and interactions over time. Think of the "structure of a conflict" as a still photograph of the actors and their relationships taken at a given moment and the "dynamics of a conflict" as a film of their interactions. The structure of a conflict can change as a conflict progresses so structural analysis needs to be done in an iterative manner. Conflict structure includes the *number of parties* involved. Is this a two party conflict or a multi-party conflict? Structure also includes *the nature of the parties*. Are the parties in the conflict individuals or corporate entities? If they are corporate entities, are they tightly or loosely organized? The number of parties and their nature are only two aspects of conflict structure, but we can use them to illustrate why negotiators should learn to think about the relationship between the structure of a conflict and the negotiation process.

> Negotiation is defined as an interactive communication process by which two or more parties who lack identical interests attempt to find a way to coordinate their behavior or allocate scarce resources in a way that will make them better off than they could be if they were to act alone.[3]

This definition of negotiation references the basic elements of negotiation—parties, issues, goals, and interactions. Like many commonly used definitions of negotiation, it does not address the context of the negotiation encounter, but it is a useful place to start.

When thinking about a negotiation process in the abstract—negotiation as an ideal type—we usually think of two parties even though we know that real life often presents us with multi-party negotiations. We are also inclined to think of parties as negotiating on their own behalf. Again, in real life, we know that parties may be represented by others who negotiate on their behalf. In some contexts, particularly when working with multi-party, community-level negotiations, professionals talk about parties and their representatives. In other settings, particularly law or business, the literature refers to the parties as *principals* and their representatives as *agents*. This chapter will use both sets of terms.

Because negotiation is a process driven by communication, any increase in the number of persons involved—adding more parties or involving agents acting on behalf of principals—complicates the process. We all know what happens in the game of telephone; the more a message gets passed around, the more likely it is to be distorted. When messages must go from principal A to agent A; from agent A to agent B; from

FIGURE 1 | Interconnected or "Embedded" Negotiations

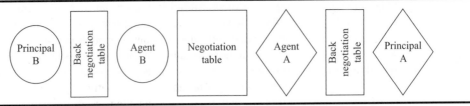

agent B to principal B and back again, we have more places where messages can get distorted. If we throw in principal C and agent C, or even more parties and their agents, the communication problems become daunting indeed. Figure 1 diagrams a relatively simple negotiation with two parties represented by agents.[4]

When teaching students the art of negotiating on behalf of others, we can focus on the problems that might arise between agents and principals and give them skills to prevent or overcome those problems. Thus, noting that an agent who does not understand her client's interests and positions might miss opportunities for an integrative agreement, we can make our students practice interviewing skills that will help them uncover the client's interests. Noting the serious problem of poor communication between principal and agent, we can teach active listening, clear presentation, and other communication techniques. We can emphasize the need for establishing informed consent between the negotiator and the client (Nolan-Haley, *Informed Consent*). Similarly, recognizing that the interests of the agent and the principal sometimes differ, we can familiarize negotiators with the ethical and professional standards regulating their relationship with clients.[5]

These are all valid parts of a good negotiation curriculum, but they are not enough to develop highly skilled reflective practitioners of negotiation. Negotiators also need to learn that introducing principal-agent relationships into a negotiation establishes a set of interconnected negotiations. Principal A and agent A have a set of "back table negotiations" and so do principal B and agent B. The negotiations at the table intersect with and affect the negotiations behind the table and vice versa. Put another way, conflicts between principals and their agents impact the conflicts between the parties to the central conflict and vice versa.

Sometimes agents and their principals use this structure of interconnected negotiations for strategic purposes. Parties can buy time in the primary negotiation by dragging out their back table negotiations. The agent can also use an absent principal as an excuse for taking actions ("My client made me say this.") or for declining offers from the other party ("I'm sorry, but my client won't let me accept this offer."). On the other hand, there are times when problems with the back table negotiations actually jeopardize the central negotiation (Wade, *Tribe*). Highly skilled negotiators need to understand why this happens and how they can work with these problems.

The back table negotiations are difficult enough when the agent is representing a single individual (say, one spouse in a divorce negotiation). They become extremely complicated when the parties are collective entities (say, corporations, community groups, warring militias, or unions). Yet, efficiency and cost-saving concerns dictate that most negotiations involving collective entities are carried out through representatives.

This is one place it really pays to understand the structure of the larger conflict, because structural factors help determine just how difficult the back table negotiations are likely to become. We have already alluded to the regulatory mechanisms that govern (more or less formally) some principal-agent relationships. However, in many cases these controls do not exist, because representatives of parties are selected through political processes. Their roles as agents in a negotiation are socially and politically negotiated, as is the evaluation it their performance, their ability to continue in the role of agent for a sustained period, and their ability to deliver on any negotiated agreements.

For example, in the book *What's in a Frame?* we described a case in which a city proposed a highway extension right through an area considered sacred ground by a local Native American tribe (Caton Campbell and Docherty, *Framing*). Using the same example here, we might convene a multi-party negotiation involving a coalition of five Native American tribes, elected officials from the city and adjacent counties, developers, a variety of activist groups (including environmentalists, Native American rights groups, and anti-sprawl groups), the state's congressional delegation, and a large federal agency. Obviously, these parties will need to send representatives to negotiate on their behalf, and the negotiation process will need, to be designed to accommodate multiple back table negotiations. In a case this complicated, a facilitator or mediator (or a team of facilitators and mediators) may be hired to help manage the negotiation. However, good negotiators should not rely solely on a facilitator or mediator to help them navigate a complex, multi-party negotiation process. Party representatives can be far more effective if they understand why back table negotiations are so important and why those negotiations might stymie the primary negotiation.[6]

Two structural factors can increase or decrease the possibility that conflicts between parties and their representatives will negatively affect the main negotiation. Negotiators should learn to ask the following questions about each representative in a negotiation:

- How formal and structured is the relationship between the principal and the agent?
- How much legitimacy does the agent have?

Some principal-agent relationships are contractual and regulated. An agent is hired to negotiate on behalf of party A. Party A may fire the agent at will, and may also be able to hold the agent accountable for his performance according to the contractual agreement. Party A may also be able to file a complaint against the agent with a professional body, and/or sue the agent. For his part, the agent may quit as representative for party A and may have rights to sue if party A fails to meet contractual obligations. The relationship is professional, not personal; it is contractual, not political. In other words, it is formal and highly structured.

In other cases, however, representatives may be selected through a variety of political processes, ranging in formality from voting to volunteering. A union representative is elected. She must keep a close eye on her constituency lest she not be re-elected, and there are formal mechanisms for recalling her if the rank-and-file members feel that she is not representing their interests. This is a formal and structured process, but it is messier than a contractual relationship. Even less formal and structured are relationships between parties and representatives when the parties are loose coalitions or voluntary membership groups. In these cases, representatives often volunteer to speak for the group or they may be selected based on their personal charisma. If the group is informal and voluntary, the membership of the group may be subject to fluctuations so that the representative may have difficulty presenting a coherent position. Furthermore, there are few if any formal mechanisms for the group to remove a volunteer from the negotiation table.

This leads to the problem of reliability. Can any given agent "deliver" on a negotiated agreement? How accurately is any given agent representing the interests and positions of the parties? Will the back table negotiations—which may take the form of a vote in the case of a union or may be a lot messier and more difficult to track in the case of ad-hoc voluntary organizations—support the agreement reached at the negotiation table? It is usually, but not always, safe to assume that an agent representing a party through a contractual relationship has checked carefully with the party before affirming any agreement. In more political relationships between a party and its representative, it is much harder to predict whether the back table negotiations will support the agreements reached at the main negotiation table.

The more political a relationship is between representative and party, the more others involved in the negotiation need to focus on the question of legitimacy. Legitimacy enters into a negotiation at several points. Each person involved in the negotiation must be seen as a legitimate negotiating partner by the other negotiators, otherwise negotiations cannot proceed. In the case of agents negotiating on behalf of principals, there is an added legitimacy question: does Party A accept the agent representing Party A at the table as a valid representative? Thus, looking at a multi-party negotiation involving representatives of larger parties we can ask: how legitimate is any given representative at any given moment?

Legitimacy or the lack thereof may be related to the way the agent was chosen. If, in the case described above, the Bureau of Indian Affairs appoints representatives for the coalition of five tribes, those representatives will probably have low legitimacy. They may even need to take much more hard-line positions in the negotiation to compensate for their "tainted" appointment. That does not mean we can assume the tribal representatives will have high legitimacy if they are selected from within. Internal conflicts within and among the tribes may distort the selection process. Furthermore, the legitimacy of any representative may change over time and may be affected by the negotiation process. An agent may gain legitimacy by succeeding in the negotiation or lose legitimacy by failing.

Taken together, the formality of the agent-principal relationship and the agent's legitimacy with the party help determine whether agent-principal conflicts (problems with the back table negotiations) are more or less likely to disrupt interparty negotiations. We can use the formality/informality continuum and the low legitimacy/high legitimacy continuum to create a model that illustrates the likelihood that conflicts between a party and its representative will derail a negotiation (Figure 2).

In addition to the legitimacy of other representatives and the formality of their relationship with their respective parties, good negotiators should have some understanding

FIGURE 2 | Legitimacy and Formality of Principal-Agent Relationship

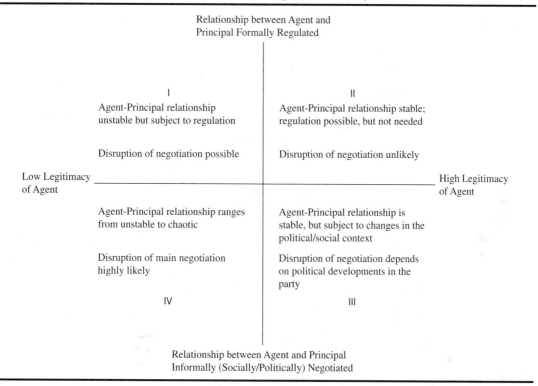

Relationship between Agent and
Principal Formally Regulated

I
Agent-Principal relationship
unstable but subject to regulation

Disruption of negotiation possible

II
Agent-Principal relationship stable;
regulation possible, but not needed

Disruption of negotiation unlikely

Low Legitimacy
of Agent

High Legitimacy
of Agent

Agent-Principal relationship ranges
from unstable to chaotic

Disruption of main negotiation
highly likely

IV

Agent-Principal relationship is
stable, but subject to changes in the
political/social context

Disruption of negotiation depends
on political developments in the
party

III

Relationship between Agent and Principal
Informally (Socially/Politically) Negotiated

of the way the *nature* of the party impacts their back table negotiations. Some parties can move quickly, while others need significantly more time to validate or reject proposed agreements. This is not *always* a stalling tactic; it may be an honest reflection of the complexity of the party's internal organization, or a reflection of the party's culture (Kelly, *Indigenous Experience*).

For example, non-native representatives will probably see a Native American representative in our case as potentially able to deliver constituents, but the tribal representative will almost always disavow the ability to speak for anyone but himself as an individual. It is common to hear tribal representatives say something like, "I represent the X people, but I speak only for myself." A tribal representative's ability to deliver constituents depends on extensive and lengthy back table discussions with tribal members, some of which can take months. This is something that non-native negotiators have great difficulty with since temporal efficiency is a hallmark of "good" negotiations in the Western business, legal, and administrative worlds.

Developing a chart such as the following can help a negotiator pay attention to the structural factors that shape back table negotiations between a representative and his party. A blank version of this chart can be filled in for a particular case. The negotiator should also always remember to map her own party on this diagram so that she examines the structural factors that are shaping her own back table negotiation.

Type of Party	Nature of Structure	Speed with which it can act	Coherence of goals
Corporation	Highly organized Hierarchical	Quick—once the necessary component parts become involved	Very coherent—clear, widely shared standards for measuring success (i.e., bottom line)
Government agency	Hierarchical Organized, but may have some incoherence in the system because of competing mandates and the influence of political actors on policies and standard operating procedures	Slow compared to corporations Quick compared to community organizations and other political groups	May be confused by competing mandates and shifting political scene
Community organization—e.g., neighborhood association	Semi-structured Democratic and therefore open to change	Relatively slow—needs time to build consensus through democratic processes	May not be fully coherent and may lack shared standards for measuring success
Native American tribe	Frequently subject to internal conflicts between "progressive" and "traditional" factions Culturally more likely to work by consensus rather than majority vote	May be very slow, particularly if tribe works by consensus and deliberation	May be difficult to discern because of internal conflicts

There are many negotiations that do not require the level of analysis outlined in this chapter. However, when faced with a complex negotiation involving different types of parties using representatives, looking at the structure of the larger conflict and the nature of the parties can be a very helpful process. It assists a negotiator in setting realistic expectations about such basic factors as how long a negotiation will probably take and the likelihood of ratification of an agreement reached at the primary negotiation table. A negotiator who understands the pressures and opportunities created by a counterpart's back table negotiations can also craft more creative proposals by incorporating the needs and interests of the agent and her principals into each round of discussion.

Endnotes

1. Among the contextual features that negotiators should learn to assess is the relative stability or turbulence of the environment in which they are negotiating. For more on this issue, *see* Jayne Seminare Docherty, *The Little Book of Strategic Negotiation: Negotiating during Turbulent Times* (Intercourse, PA: Good Books, 2005).

2. Russell Korobkin, *Negotiation Theory and Strategy* (2002), pp. 33–220.

3. Ibid., p. 1.

4. This diagram and many of the ideas in this chapter were greatly enriched by Jayne Seminare Docherty's conversations with Ron Kraybil (Eastern Mennonite University), Frank Blechman (independent consultant), and Carol Gowler (Conflict Transformation Program, Eastern Mennonite University).

5. For attorneys, this would include a working knowledge of, among other things, *The Modern Rules of Professional Conduct* (2004).

6. Multi-party negotiations can be greatly enhanced by the type of pre-negotiation work described in Jayne Seminare Docherty, "One Tool Among Many," in *The Negotiator's Fieldbook,* eds. Andrea Kupfer Schneider and Christopher Honeyman (Chicago: American Bar Association, 2006), chapter 65. Interveners may offer parties training in negotiating, as well as engaging in data gathering and fact-finding to help parties arrive at a coherent picture of which issues will be covered in the negotiations and what will not. Also see Bernard Mayer, "Allies in Negotiation," in *The Negotiator's Fieldbook,* eds. Andrea Kupfer Schneider and Christopher Honeyman (Chicago: American Bar Association, 2006), chapter 69.

Reading 3.7

The Tension between Principals and Agents
Robert H. Mnookin
Scott R. Peppet
Andrew S. Tulumello

Sam Walsh is about to sell his house and move to Arizona to retire. He bought the house eight years ago when the real estate market was in a slump. The market is booming now, and some of his friends have recommended that he sell his home without a real estate agent. Sam has seen books that describe how to advertise a house, how to conduct a successful open house, and how to negotiate with a potential buyer through the process of offer and acceptance, purchase and sale, and closing. And of course the Internet now offers new possibilities for listing one's home. Given all these resources and a booming market, Sam thinks perhaps he could sell his house fairly quickly and for a good price by himself, without paying an agent's 6 percent commission.

But Sam isn't so sure that the savings are worth all that effort and anxiety. Granted, real estate agents are expensive, but what if selling independently doesn't go well? And it seems like an awful hassle. Wouldn't it be easier to let an agent handle all the details? And more comfortable not to have to do all that negotiating with the buyer?

Sam calls a family friend who recently bought property in the neighborhood and asks her whether she liked her real estate agent. "Sure," the friend says. "She's a great agent—her name is Betty Ortiz. Give her a call. She'll help you out."

The Goal: Reaping the Full Benefits of Hiring an Agent

Sam wonders whether hiring a real estate agent will provide a net benefit in the sale of his home. On the one hand, maybe an agent will sell his home more quickly and for more money than he could otherwise get. If he doesn't use an agent, maybe his home will sit unsold for months. But on the other hand, maybe the agent won't earn her commission and will end up *costing* Sam money. How should Sam decide what to do? How will his decision about hiring an agent affect the sale of his home? Moreover, if he hires an agent, how should he negotiate the terms of that relationship?

Agency relationships are everywhere. We constantly delegate authority to others so that they may act in our place. We ask lawyers to represent us; we give money managers authority to make our investments; we ask doctors to take responsibility for our medical care; we depend on employees to do the work we assign; and we elect public officials to legislate on our behalf. Indeed, it is hard to imagine how society could function at all without agents acting on behalf of principals—diplomats on behalf of nations; labor

Source: "The Tension between Principals and Agents," from *Beyond Winning: Negotiating to Create Value in Deals and Disputes,* by Robert H. Mnookin, Scott R. Peppet, and Andrew S. Tulumello, 2000, pp. 69–82. Cambridge, MA: Belknap Press. Used by permission.

leaders on behalf of unions; sports agents on behalf of players; literary agents on behalf of authors.

When a principal hires an agent to act on his behalf in negotiations across the table with another party, he may expect—naively—that the agent will be motivated solely to serve the principal's interests. This is how principal-agent relations would work ideally. But in the real world, agents always have interests of their own. As a result, the principal-agent relationship is rife with potential conflicts that demand skillful management behind the table.

For example, a client and his lawyer may need to negotiate how the lawyer will be paid; how the other side will be approached; what information will be sought from or disclosed to the other side; at what point to accept the other side's offer, and so on. If these issues are left unacknowledged and unaddressed, they can adversely affect the negotiation across the table. For all of these reasons, effective negotiation requires a good understanding of the benefits and risks of the agency relationship and how it can best be managed.

Agency Benefits

Why are agency relationships so pervasive in negotiation? Because an agent can provide significant benefits to her principal. These benefits derive from four sources:

- **Knowledge:** An agent may have specialized knowledge—that the principal lacks—about market conditions, formal or informal norms, or relevant risks and opportunities. An investment banker will know potential buyers for her client's company, for example, and may be better able to price the deal.

- **Resources:** An agent, by reason of his reputation and relationships, may be able to provide access and opportunities that would otherwise be unavailable. For example, a well-known literary agent can get a publisher to read a new author's manuscript, and later negotiate favorable deal terms, because of the agent's reputation for having good judgment.

- **Skills:** An agent may be a better negotiator than the principal, whether owing to experience, training, or natural ability. A client may hire an attorney to negotiate a settlement or a deal, for example, because the client believes that the lawyer will be more effective.

- **Strategic advantages:** An agent may be able to use negotiation tactics on behalf of the principal in a way that insulates the principal from their full impact. The principal can remain the "good cop" while the agent plays the bad cop. For example, a sports agent can engage in hard-bargaining tactics with the team's general manager while the player remains on good terms with the team. Conversely, a collaborative agent may be able to settle a dispute with an agent on the other side even if the principals are in conflict.

In many cases, the agent will be able to do things the principal could never do on his own, and the possibility for both the principal and agent to benefit from trade between them is clear. The agent may have an absolute advantage over the principal with respect to those activities. In Sam and Betty's case, Betty may have skills, knowledge, and resources that Sam lacks. But economic theory suggests that even if Sam knows as much—or more—about selling residential real estate as Betty, that doesn't necessarily mean that he should sell his house himself. The economic principle of *comparative advantage* dictates that there can be gains from trade when each party (whether a person, firm, or country) specializes in the production of goods and services for which that party's opportunity cost is lower. If Sam's opportunity costs are high, it may be more efficient for Sam to hire Betty as his agent and spend his time doing what he does best.

Imagine that Sam has decided to talk to Betty about whether to hire her. They meet at his home on a Saturday afternoon. Betty walks through the house, noting approvingly many of the details and features that might raise the selling price. As Sam gives Betty a tour, she asks him all sorts of questions—about the square footage of the house, when he purchased it and what he paid for it, the age of the appliances and heating system, the condition of the roof, any electrical work or other upgrading he might have done. By the time they sit down to talk, Betty has a fair picture of the investment that Sam has made.

> **BETTY:** Well, it's a beautiful property. You obviously care a great deal about your home. The kitchen is lovely—you made a wise choice to remodel there. I think you should do very well, given the way houses are selling this season. The first thing we would need to do is agree on a listing price and a date to put the house on the market. I'd suggest sooner rather than later. As for a price, I've brought some information we can look at.

> **SAM:** That's great. But before we get into the numbers, I wondered if we could talk about your services. To be honest, I'm still trying to decide whether to retain an agent at all, rather than sell the house myself.

> **BETTY:** Oh, sure. No problem. I would definitely go with an agent, but then I'm biased. But let me tell you the sorts of advantages having an agent brings.

In describing the role she will play for Sam in the transaction, Betty emphasizes the sorts of benefits described above. First, Betty says she can help Sam get the best possible price for his house. "Setting the right asking price is critical," Betty says. "I know the market." She's brought lots of information showing recent sales in his neighborhood and town, recent trends in the market, and detailed comparables that she would use to justify whatever price they arrive at. "It's not easy setting just the right price," Betty says. "Too low and it's easy to sell but you don't get full value. Too high and you can scare off potential buyers. Or if you do find one, the bank won't finance their mortgage."

Betty then describes her approach to marketing and shows Sam a few sample brochures of other houses she has sold recently. She also emphasizes how her relationships might benefit Sam. "I have some clients of my own who might be interested, and I know every important broker in town," she explains. She tells Sam that after putting his house on the market she would first bring a caravan of other real estate brokers through in order to expose the house to those working in the area. Then she would invite brokers to bring their own clients for a few days before hosting the first open house on a Sunday afternoon. "That's a big draw," Betty says. Brokers who have seen the house already will try to get their clients back before the open house. And then the open house should attract lots of casual lookers and those clients who weren't able to make it during the week. After the initial open house, Betty explains, she would hold open houses for two more weekends. "I can also save you from what would otherwise be a real nuisance. I'll be responsible for showing your house, and I'll be sure that we set these open houses and other visits at times that are convenient for you."

SAM: That would be great. The less hassle, the better.

BETTY: Last but not least, I've had lots of experience at negotiating home sales. Not only can I help you get the best price, I can help you figure out which offers to take seriously, how best to make counteroffers, and what secondary terms are reasonable. In my experience it's best if the seller doesn't have to deal directly with the buyer or the buyer's agent. You'll find it a lot more comfortable to hold out for the good price if you don't have to deal directly with the other side.

SAM: What about after I've accepted an offer?

BETTY: Well, I'll take care of moving toward a formal purchase and sale agreement. I'll make sure any necessary inspections get done, and sometimes I even help the buyers get their mortgage.

Betty and Sam keep talking, and Sam sees the advantages that Betty will confer in terms of skills, resources, and knowledge. She has access to clients and other brokers, she knows the market, and she has lots of time to invest in selling his house. He decides that he'll use an agent, and he feels comfortable with using Betty. She seems open and easy to talk to, and not too pushy.

SAM: OK, but what about fees? What would your commission be on a sale?

BETTY: My commission is the standard 6 percent of the sale price. You pay nothing unless we sell the house. Actually, the fee is normally split with the buyer's agent, assuming there is one. But whether or not the buyer has an agent, the fee is 6 points.

SAM: Hmm. What happens if you sell the house very quickly? Is the fee still 6 percent?

BETTY: Yep, if we sell it quickly, isn't that a good thing? That's what we want, right?

SAM: Sure, I guess. But the quicker the sale, the less work you have to do, right? And what if there *isn't* a buyer's agent? What if a random buyer just walks in to the first open house and plunks down my asking price? Is the fee still 6 percent?

BETTY: Yes, it is.

The Problem: Agency Costs

Sam sees the advantages of hiring Betty. But there's a nagging question in his mind: Are these fees really worth it? What if she sells the house without much effort? Or what if she doesn't work hard enough? How will Sam know? Despite Betty's upbeat attitude and optimism about working together to sell his house, Sam fears there may be problems down the road. At this point, however, he's not sure exactly what those might be.

Hiring an agent is not a simple matter. Bringing an agent into a negotiation introduces a third tension: between the principal and the agent. Because agents often have expert knowledge, substantial experience, and special resources that the principal lacks, the relationship can create value. At the same time, however, because the agent's interests may not align with those of the principal, a number of unique and intensely stubborn problems can arise. The literature on this subject is vast, largely because these problems are so pervasive and cut across so many activities.[1] Here, we introduce some of the central issues.

The Sources of the Tension

Agency costs are not limited to the amount of money that a principal pays an agent as compensation for doing the job. They also include the money and time the principal spends trying to ensure that the agent does not exploit him but instead serves his interests well. To understand why agency costs exist, consider that principals and agents may differ in three general ways:[2]

- Preferences
- Incentives
- Information

Different Preferences   First, the preferences, or interests, of an agent are rarely identical to those of the principal. Consider their economic interests. Betty's primary economic interest is in her own earnings as a real estate agent. In this transaction, Sam's primary economic interest is in the net sale price for his house. Betty may have other interests as well. She has a strong interest in her reputation and in securing future clients. She has an interest in maintaining good relationships with other agents, banks, home inspectors, and insurance agencies. Betty is a repeat player in this game, while Sam, particularly if he intends to leave the community, is a one-shot player who might be more than willing to sacrifice Betty's reputation in order to get a better deal for himself. Conversely, Betty may be reluctant to bargain hard for certain advantages for Sam because of her desire to maintain a congenial relationship with the buyer's agent, who may be a source of future client referrals.

Different Incentives   Agency problems may also arise because the *incentives* of the principal and the agent are imperfectly aligned. The culprit is typically the agent's fee structure, which may create perverse incentives for the agent to act contrary to the principal's interests. This discrepancy is sometimes called an incentive gap.

For example, Sam wants an arrangement that maximizes his expected net sale proceeds after her fee. Betty, on the other hand, wants a fee structure that yields her the highest expected return *for her time spent*. If they agree to a percentage fee, Betty may prefer a quick and easy sale at a lower price to a difficult sale at a higher price because with the former she will get more return for hours spent working. Indeed, a recent study suggests that when realtors put their *own* homes on the market, they tend to get higher-than-average prices, because they get the entire benefit of their additional hours of work, not just 6 percent of it.[3]

Different Information   The information available to the principal and the agent may differ. We are speaking here of kinds of information that either side may have an incentive to keep to itself. Betty may know that market conditions are improving, for example, but she may be reluctant to share this with Sam for fear of inflating his expectations. Similarly, it may be difficult to know how much effort an agent is actually putting in on the principal's behalf. Because the principal cannot readily discover this information, the agent might shirk her responsibilities and earn pay without expending effort.

Management Mechanisms and Their Limitations

These potential conflicts can be controlled somewhat, through three basic management mechanisms:

- Incentive contracts
- Monitoring systems
- Bonding

Incentive Contracts   Incentives can be built into contracts between principals and agents to better align their interests. For example, instead of paying employees an hourly wage, a manufacturing firm might choose to pay its workers by the piece, thereby tying compensation of these agents directly to volume. Or a distributor might pay its sales-people on a commission basis, compensating them only to the extent that their sales efforts boost the bottom line. Similarly, farm workers are often paid by the amount of produce harvested instead of by the hour, to minimize slacking, and waiters are paid through tips, to encourage more attentive service.

Many different incentive structures exist, including:

- Percentage compensation
- Hourly fees
- Fixed fees
- Bonuses or penalties

These methods can minimize the principal-agent tension, but no incentive structure can ever completely resolve it. To see why, consider our real estate example. Real estate agents are commonly paid a commission only if a sale is completed. This is an incentive contract: the agent's reward depends on successful performance. Such contracts have both benefits and drawbacks. On the one hand, Betty profits—and Sam incurs agency-related costs—only if Betty manages to sell his house. On the other hand, as we have seen, this incentive may induce Betty to pressure Sam to accept a deal that is not optimal for Sam but which guarantees Betty a quick profit in comparison to her efforts. To be *perfectly* aligned, Betty's incentives vis-à-vis the sale would have to be identical to Sam's. But for this to occur, Betty would have to buy the house herself and resell it; only then would she have a 100 percent stake in the sale, as Sam does. This, of course, would transform her into the principal stakeholder and eliminate the agency relationship altogether.

Because Betty does not have as great a stake in the sale as Sam does, Betty and Sam may face conflicting incentives at various points in the transaction. Suppose that with very little effort, maybe 25 hours of work, Betty could sell Sam's house for $250,000. With a 6 percent commission, this would generate a $15,000 fee—$600 an hour. Assume that with a great deal of effort, perhaps 100 hours of work, the house could be sold for $275,000. Sam would pay Betty an additional fee of $1,500 on the extra $25,000. From Betty's perspective, the marginal effort may not be worthwhile. She works 75 extra hours for only $1,500—which works out to $20 an hour. Even if Betty could sell the house for $300,000 with only 50 extra hours of work, she might still decide that it was not worth the extra $3,000 fee at $60 per hour. She might feel that her 50 hours would be better spent selling someone else's house at a much higher hourly rate—even though Sam would almost *surely* feel that an extra $47,000 in *his* pocket justified the additional time on Betty's part.

Uncertainty about the housing market will further complicate Sam and Betty's task. Neither of them knows what will happen if Sam turns down an offer of $250,000 and Betty puts in additional effort in the hope of receiving $275,000 or $300,000. Most likely, however, Betty will have more information on this point than Sam. Can he trust her to reveal this information candidly, when it might be in her interest for him to accept the lower offer?

Consider the homeowner's dilemma at an even earlier stage of the transaction, before the house goes on the market. After thinking about these problems, Sam might realize that Betty has an incentive to set a low selling price for his home so that it could be sold quickly and with little effort. Reaching for the stars isn't in Betty's interest. It might not be in Sam's interest either, but he wants to be sure that Betty is giving him information candidly. He might thus decide to ask a number of agents for competing estimate recommendations. Although this could provide him with some reassurance, competition of this sort is not a complete solution. Instead, such competition may encourage agents to make unrealistically high estimates in the hopes of securing an exclusive listing. After the listing is secured, an agent might put the house on the market for the high price but then expend little effort trying to market the house. After some period of time, the agent might then approach the owner and indicate the necessity of lowering the price to increase the chances of a sale. In the end, the homeowner may end up *worse* off for having initially set an unrealistically high price, particularly if a record of large unilateral price concessions is taken by prospective buyers to indicate that the house is of questionable value. Again, information disparities make it difficult for the principal to align the agent's incentives with his own. The homeowner may be unable to monitor the agent's efforts or the accuracy of a single agent's estimates.

Why doesn't Sam just pay Betty by the hour? Many professionals—including lawyers and accountants—have traditionally been compensated in this way. At first glance, this may seem a straightforward way to guarantee that the agent expends the needed effort to get a good price. In reality, however, compensation by the hour creates an incentive for an agent to put in *more* time than may be necessary to get a good price. To earn a large commission on the sale of Sam's house, Betty will necessarily have to invest a great deal of time. A quick sale with little effort will be less profitable for her than a sale that takes longer. Other things being equal, of course, Sam would prefer a sale sooner rather than later. Betty's incentive to put in extra time doesn't necessarily meet Sam's needs.

An hourly fee also creates monitoring problems. How does Sam know the number of hours Betty is actually putting in? And how does he know whether those hours are being spent efficiently, in a way that most benefits Sam? Is she diligently pursuing buyers, contacting other agents, and creating attractive brochures and ads to market the property? Or is she just holding open houses over and over again so that she can bill Sam for the set-up and break-down time? Sam might have reason to fear that Betty will not use her time most productively under an hourly fee arrangement.

Sam could also offer to pay Betty a fixed fee for her work. Assume that Sam expects to list the house for $250,000. He and Betty know that if the house sells for this amount she'll earn a commission of $15,000. But neither knows what the actual sale price will be. The market is hot. Maybe Sam will receive offers above his asking price—it's been known to happen in his neighborhood. Or maybe no buyer will come along and he'll have to drop the price to $230,000, or even lower. If Sam believes that the hot market will work to his advantage, he might offer to pay Betty $15,000, regardless of the sale price. He would thus insure against the possibility of a greater fee, at the risk that he would over-compensate Betty in the event the market failed him and the price had to be lowered.

Fixed fees have certain advantages. They encourage the agent to get the job done within the cost parameters set by the fixed fee. However, fixed fees can create perverse incentives of their own. If Betty will receive $15,000 regardless of her effort or the sale price, why should she put in the time required to sell the house at $250,000, as long as she sells it at *some* price?

What about a percentage fee with a clause to reduce the percentage if the house sells very quickly? Sam has already expressed concern that the house might sell in just a few days with minimal effort on Betty's part. If that's the case, why should Betty get her full 6 percent commission? Sam might propose that if the house sells within seven days of listing, Betty's commission will be reduced to 4 percent. Even if Betty agrees to this fee structure, however, it creates a new set of incentive problems. Now Betty has an incentive to delay. Why sell the house on day five if on day eight she'll make an additional 2 percent?

What about some hybrid of a percentage fee and an hourly fee? After all, Sam's real concern is that Betty will slack off if the house *doesn't* sell quickly. It's on day fifty that he needs Betty to work at selling the house, not on days one and two. Thus, Sam might suggest a lower percentage fee—perhaps 5 percent—plus an hourly bonus for work performed after day fourteen. In this way, he might hope to inspire Betty to put effort in when he needs it most. But from Betty's perspective, this arrangement forces her to put effort into trying to sell a house that's not priced right for the market. Why should she bear the burden in such a situation? Why shouldn't Sam lower the price and thus generate more sales interest? And why should she work toward an early sale—which Sam, too, would prefer—if it just means that she'll get a lower percentage fee?

Monitoring Systems   If incentive contracts don't completely solve the problem, why can't a principal just watch over his agent and ensure that the agent performs satisfactorily? This is the second management mechanism: monitoring. If Sam knows which marketing activities are most likely to result in the sale of his house, he can simply follow Betty around and see whether she engages in those activities. This mechanism is often used by employers, who monitor their employees and compensate them based, in part, on how well they perform.

The problem with monitoring, however, is that it is expensive and it doesn't always tell the principal what he needs to know. In order to determine whether an agent has performed appropriately, the principal must be able both to observe the agent's behavior, which is often impossible, and to distinguish desirable from undesirable behavior, which is often beyond the principal's expertise. Sam, for example, can't watch Betty's every move. To do so would waste the time he is saving by hiring her in the first place. In addition, even if he did watch her closely, he might not be able to distinguish between high-quality and low-quality work. If only three people attend his first open house, should he blame Betty? Were her marketing efforts substandard compared to what other agents would have done? Sam is unlikely to know.

Perhaps Sam could employ another specialist or expert to monitor Betty. This approach is not uncommon. For example, a corporation's in-house lawyers often monitor the efforts of the corporation's outside lawyers, who work for private firms. Similarly, outside corporate directors often monitor the efforts of management. It should be obvious, however, that this is hardly an ideal solution. Hiring yet another professional to provide services is expensive—and the compensation arrangement for this other professional may *in itself* create distorting incentives. Moreover, a conspiracy of sorts may develop between the agents. In the corporate world, management is often responsible for selecting their monitors—the outside or "independent" directors. This inevitably raises concerns about informal collusion. In a general sense, such collusion results from the fact that similarly situated agents have more frequent contact with each other than principals and agents do. To the extent that agents expect to have repeat dealings with one another, this may well affect their behavior—sometimes in ways that may benefit the principal, but other times in ways that do not.

Bonding   Principal-agent differences can also be dampened by requiring the agent to post a bond, usually in the form of money, at the start of the agency relationship, which he must forfeit if he acts in a way that conflicts with the principal's interests. In the construction industry, a contractor may post a bond underwritten by an insurance company that can be used to complete the job for the owner if the contractor goes broke during the project. Pensions are sometimes considered such a bond: throughout their careers employees are induced to act in their employers' best interests for fear of losing their pension's large financial rewards. Similarly, compensation that is above market rates can be considered a form of principal-agent bond: if an employee is found acting contrary to the employer's interests and is fired, he forfeits the market surplus that he has enjoyed up to that point.

An agent's concern for her reputation can also serve as a bond to protect her principal.[4] Even if Betty has an economic incentive not to spend extra time working for a sale price above $250,000, and even if she knows that Sam cannot effectively monitor her shirking, Betty might still work diligently in order to keep her professional reputation intact. Real estate agents often acquire clients through word of mouth. Without recommendations from previous clients like Sam, Betty is unlikely to succeed in her business.

While in some circumstances the principal may be able to affect the agent's reputation, this is generally an imperfect solution to agency problems.[5] It may be difficult to observe or verify that a particular outcome—success or failure—is attributable to the agent's actions.

In addition, principals can exploit agents as well as the other way around. For example, a homeowner might use an agent to acquire valuable information about the home's expected value, and even to begin testing the house on the market, but then exclude some friend or acquaintance from the agency contract and subsequently sell the house directly to this third party. By doing so, the buyer and seller could share in the savings of the agent's fee, while the agent would be left uncompensated for her efforts.

For our purposes, one major lesson emerges: although these management mechanisms can reduce principal-agent differences, none of them eliminates the tension completely, alone or in combination. Our third tension is inescapable: there are always agency costs. In a particular context, some mechanisms will obviously be better than others. But reputational markets are never perfect. Monitoring is always costly. And any compensation scheme creates incentives that can be perverse in some circumstances. In a relatively simple transaction such as a real estate sale, the parties may not find it worthwhile to expend resources writing elaborate agency contracts. To do so would just further shrink the pie. In addition, trying to exert control over an agent can have paradoxically *negative* consequences on the agency relationship: in part, agents are value-creating for their principals *because* they are independent decision-makers, not puppets.

Endnotes

1. This chapter draws on important intellectual contributions from the new "institutional economics." This new field flows from research by Ronald Coase, Oliver Williamson, Michael Spence, Richard Zeckhauser, and many others. See generally Ronald H. Coase, *The Firm, the Market, and the Law* (Chicago: University of Chicago Press, 1988); Ronald H. Coase, "The Nature of the Firm," *Economica* 4 (1937), p. 386; Ronald H. Coase, "The Problem of Social Cost," *Journal of Law and Economics* 3 (1960), p. 1; Oliver E. Williamson, *The Economic Institutions of Capitalism; Firms, Markets, Relational Contracting* (New York: Free Press, 1985); A. Michael Spence, *Market Signaling: Informational Transfer in Hiring and Related Screening Processes* (Cambridge, MA: Harvard University Press, 1974); John W. Prett and Richard J. Zeckhauser, *Principals and Agents: The Structure of Business* (Cambridge, MA: Harvard Business School Press, 1985), pp. 1–35. For a recent series of essays on agency and negotiation, with an annotated bibliography, see Robert H. Mnookin and Lawrence E. Susskind, eds., *Negotiating on Behalf of Others: Advice to Lawyers, Business Executives, Sports Agents, Diplomats, Politicians, and Everyone Else* (Thousand Oaks, CA: Sage Publications, 1999).

2. Zeckhauser has called these three types of differences "the golden triangle." Richard J. Zeckhauser, "The Strategy of Choice" in *Strategy and Choice,* ed. Richard J. Zeckhauser (Cambridge, MA: MIT Press, 1991). (We have used the label "preferences" in lieu of his label "valuation.")

3. *See* Ronald C. Rutherford, Thomas M. Springer, and Abdullah Yavas, "Conflicts between Principals and Agents: Evidence from Residential Brokerage," (unpublished manuscript on file with authors, March 1999). (Suggesting that brokers sell their own homes for an average of 3 percent more than the price they get for their clients' homes.) *See also* Dinah Wisenberg Brin, "Real-Estate Brokers Get a Higher Price When Selling Own Homes, Study Finds," *Wall Street Journal*, April 19, 1999, p. B3.

4. *See* Ronald J. Gilson and Robert H. Mnookin, "Disputing through Agents: Cooperation and Conflict between Lawyers in Litigation," *Columbia Law Review* 94 (1994), p. 509.

5. *See*, e.g., Geoffrey P. Miller, "Some Agency Problems in Settlement," *Journal of Legal Studies* 16 (1987), pp. 189 and 210; Benjamin Klein and Keith B. Leffler, "The Role of Market Forces in Assuring Contractual Performance," *Journal of Political Economy* 89 (1981), p. 615; David Charny, "Non-Legal Sanctions in Commercial Relationships," *Harvard Law Review* 104 (1990), pp. 375, 391–394.

When a Contract Isn't Enough: How to Be Sure Your Agent Gets You the Best Deal

James K. Sebenius

Negotiation is often handled by an agent or representative. Here's some advice on managing this potentially double-edged relationship.

When selling your house or company, working out terms with your publisher, or handling a lawsuit, you often engage an agent. Lawyers, investment bankers, literary agents, and others who negotiate on your behalf may help you in many ways: They may have greater specialized expertise than you do, they may be better bargainers, they may have superior access to the other side, they may serve as a useful buffer, and they may save your time. (In "When You Shouldn't Go It Alone," an article in the March issue of *Negotiation,* my colleague Lawrence Susskind delves into some of the advantages of relying on agents and offers good advice on how to use them effectively.)

With the benefits of employing an agent, however, come certain risks. A faulty contract, for instance, can set the stage for disaster by failing to properly align her incentives and provide for appropriate monitoring of her work. (See the sidebar "The Pitfalls of Faulty Contracts.") Even experienced negotiators who take great care in constructing agent contracts may unexpectedly find themselves facing agent incentive and monitoring problems. These issues, which often arise from factors that fall heavily *outside* the structure of the contract, can lead to three kinds of problem agents.

In this article, I describe the telltale signs of *faulty agents, free agents,* and *double agents.* If you fail to look out for these problem agents, your interests may suffer in negotiation.

1. Faulty Agents

A *Wall Street Journal* article tells the story of top executive pay attorney Joseph Bachelder, who was representing a client who'd just been chosen as a company's next CEO. After a first session with the board's representative to hammer out a compensation package, Bachelder took his client aside and informed him that he would get everything he wanted from the negotiation.

Why was Bachelder so confident of total victory? Because, he explained, the board had put the firm's well-regarded general counsel in charge of the negotiations. Why was this a mistake? "When this is over, you're going to be that guy's boss," Bachelder happily informed his client. "He knows that. He can't fight you too hard on anything."

Source: "When a Contract Isn't Enough: How to Be Sure Your Agent Gets You the Best Deal" by James K. Sebenius, from the *Program on Negotiation* newsletter at the Harvard Law School (www.pon.harvard.edu), July 2004, pp. 3–5. Used with permission.

The board picked a *faulty agent* for this negotiation—one whose underlying incentives conflicted with the board's best interests. The general counsel's dominant interest was to lay the groundwork for a good relationship with the future CEO. As its representative in these critical talks, the board should have instead hired an outside specialist with properly aligned interests.

The faulty agent problem often shows up in Pentagon contracting. Procurement officers are charged with representing the public interest when negotiating with defense contractors. Yet some of these officers quietly make plans to leave the civil service and join one of these defense contractors—at a far higher salary. While still representing the Pentagon, such agents are likely to go much easier on the other side than they should.

While an overriding self-interest in a future relationship with a negotiation counterpart may create a faulty agent, so may the *lack* of any meaningful future concern. Consider a company that is negotiating an alliance or acquisition through a heavily price-driven process with a strong legalistic component. In such instances, it's common for one internal team, such as the business development unit, to act as the company's agent. When the team's job is done—often after a nasty, adversarial process—the company's operational management unit inherits the unenviable job of making the arrangement work.

Jerry Kaplan, founder of GO Corporation, an early pen computing firm, criticized the process by which IBM invested in his firm. In his book *Startup* (reprint ed., Penguin, 1996), Kaplan writes, "Rather than empowering the responsible party to make the deal, IBM assigns a professional negotiator, who usually knows or cares little for the substance of the agreement but has absolute authority. . . . The negotiator begins by assembling a list of interested internal constituents, all of whom are free to add new requirements . . . or block some minor concession."

When a faulty agent leads a negotiation, it's unlikely the right minds will converge on a productive arrangement. Similarly, while the top management of two companies in a supply chain may speak glowingly of the strength and quality of their partnership, the buyer's procurement agent may be motivated by monthly targets and penny-pinching while overlooking broader concerns. A fanatical focus on getting the best price may be due in part to how the agent is evaluated by her superior, but also may derive from the organization's culture.

When suppliers seek advice on dealing with faulty agents, they might be told to listen actively, to improve their body language, and to decide who should make the first offer. Another strategy is to nurture an internal champion on the other side who truly benefits from your added quality and service—and who will pressure the agent on your behalf.

2. Free Agents

Supposedly a negotiator who works faithfully on behalf of his principal's real interests, a free agent has incentives and control over the process that effectively lead him to act independently. Investment bankers or other deal makers with a powerful interest in closing a deal can function as free agents. For example, when Matsushita Electric Industrial Co.

paid $6.59 billion in 1990 for MCA, the owner of Universal Pictures and several record companies and theme parks, its rationale was to ensure a steady flow of "creative software" for its global hardware businesses. Senior MCA management agreed to the acquisition largely with the expectation that its new, cash-rich Japanese parent could provide capital for entertainment businesses needed to make MCA competitive with rivals such as Disney and Cap Cities/ABC.

Matsushita chose Mike Ovitz, a former Hollywood talent agent with a burning ambition to become a corporate matchmaker, to represent it at the bargaining table. Ovitz masterminded an intricate set of maneuvers that kept the two parties mostly *apart* during the process, managing the information flow and both sides' expectations until the deal was virtually closed.

Both Matsushita and MCA developed a distorted perception of the other's real intentions, leading to postdeal friction and the sale of MCA five years later to

---

The Pitfalls of Faulty Contracts

Some of the trickier aspects of designing the right contract with your agent include properly aligning her incentives and monitoring her work. Supervising your agent can be especially hard when she knows more than you do about the area of work. For example, hiring an agent who's a lawyer and paying her on an hourly basis may induce her to spend more time than you think necessary—at your expense. She might become a literary perfectionist, spending hours crafting and polishing an offer letter to the other side when, as far as you're concerned, the second draft would have done just fine. To prevent her from running up needless hours, you might opt instead for a fixed-fee engagement. Then, however, she may cut corners, doing just enough to reach her fee.

Contingent contracts that grant higher agent fees as your outcome improves may superficially align both your interests. Yet here, too, conflicts may lurk. For example, as a negotiation unfolds, if your agent believes that the odds that the deal will close are falling, he may reduce his effort, and the no-deal outcome may become self-fulfilling. By contrast, once a profitable agreement seems very likely, your agent, unbeknownst to you, may take excessive negotiating risks on your behalf, hoping for a much better outcome or even a "trophy deal" to burnish his reputation. In short, even when both you and your agent have incentives to reach a strong deal, your appetites for risk may radically differ.

These pitfalls suggest the need for awareness and clarity when drawing up a contract with an agent. Specifically, you should work to design the financial arrangement most suited to your situation, align incentives and monitor the agent's work as well as possible, and engage either someone you've worked with successfully or someone who has a solid reputation for efficiency, effectiveness, and faithful representation.

For more on this topic, see *Beyond Winning: Negotiating to Create Value in Deals and Disputes* by Robert H. Mnookin et al. (Harvard University Press, 2000) and *Negotiating on Behalf of Others,* ed. by Robert H. Mnookin and Lawrence E. Susskind (Sage, 1999).

Seagram, at a substantial loss to Matsushita both in terms of face and money—¥165 billion, or about $1.6 billion. In part due to the cultural chasms dividing old-line industrial Japan, creative Hollywood, and the New York financial community, neither side truly probed the other's underlying expectations until it was too late. But even more than culture, a free agent with a dominant interest in forging a deal—almost any deal—was a key factor, as was the substantial freedom he was given to act on that interest.

3. Double Agents

When their incentives are wrong enough and their control over the negotiation process is high, merely faulty agents can morph into *double agents.* Many buyers of real estate and of companies can wryly testify how standard financial arrangements can unwittingly produce this result. Consider the common practice of compensating the real estate agents or investment bankers on both sides with a percentage of the sale price. What tacit alignments do such arrangements create? Just like the seller and his agent, the buyer's agent now benefits from a high-priced deal. Pity the hapless buyer, the sole player looking for a bargain.

Beyond faulty contracts, other factors can produce double agents. After a small business suffered a fire, for example, its owner hired an experienced consultant to negotiate damage claims with his insurance company. The consultant was promised a fixed fee for success, plus a sliding bonus based on the settlement amount. The consultant very quickly negotiated an adequate settlement, but the owner soon became disenchanted with the outcome. Why? Because he learned that his agent, after dealing for years with the same small set of insurance companies, had fallen into a pattern of rapid but relatively modest claims settlements. If he had bargained harder for his client, the consultant might have gained an incremental incentive fee but would have risked retaliation from the insurance company. In effect, the business owner was a one-time bit player in a long-term game that powerfully aligned the interests of the insurance company with those of the consultant.

Here's a more unusual instance of a double agent. *New York Times* columnist Nicholas Kristof was reporting from Iraq when he was summoned to a government ministry to account for an "outrageous" article he'd written detailing the Saddam Hussein regime's brutal torture of a Muslim leader. Included in the meeting was Kristof's official Iraqi government minder. In a 2003 column, Kristof describes the experience of being "menacingly denounced by two of Saddam's henchmen":

> Neither man could speak English and they hadn't actually read the offending column . . . my government minder took my column and translated it for them. I saw my life flash before my eyes. But my minder's job was to spy on me, and he worried that my tough column would reflect badly on his spying. Plus, he was charging me $100 a day, and he would lose a fortune if I was expelled, or worse. So he translated my column very selectively. There was no mention of burning beards or nails in heads. He left out whole paragraphs. When he finished, the two senior officials shrugged and let me off scot-free.

Kristof was fortunate indeed that the incentives of this Iraqi government representative—just like those of double agents in more benign settings—were dramatically misaligned from those of his superiors. Contrary interests plus the capacity to control and shape the information that he passes along is a common trait of a double agent.

How can you avoid becoming the next victim of a faulty agent (wrong interests), a free agent (wrong interests plus control of the process and information), or a double agent (an extreme version of faulty and free)? When evaluating and engaging a potential agent, you need to focus on more than just designing a contract that aligns your financial incentives. To keep a problem agent at bay, fix a penetrating eye on her present and future relationships, her full set of interests, and the extent to which she will be able to filter information and control the negotiating process.

This Is Not a Game: Top Sports Agents Share Their Negotiating Secrets

Alix Stuart

From the sidelines, professional athletes have leverage that corporate negotiators can only dream of. Endowed with unmatchable skills and advised by top agents, stars like Alex Rodriguez, LeBron James, and Maria Sharapova can just name their price, threaten to walk, and receive untold riches, right?

Not quite. For anyone who has followed the saga of Terrell Owens, All-Pro wide receiver for the Philadelphia Eagles, it's clear that even a star needs to play by certain rules. When Owens's agent, Drew "The Shark" Rosenhaus, fumbled an attempt to secure a better contract for him, Owens vented his displeasure by insulting his teammates and was effectively terminated.

While Owens's situation is an extreme example of how aggressiveness can backfire, other top agents say they are just as restricted by basic negotiation principles as the next guy. "There has to be some resolute willingness to push the envelope," says sports agent Leigh Steinberg, head of Leigh Steinberg Enterprises and the inspiration for the character Jerry Maguire in the 1996 movie of the same name, but "you need to remember that all humans have ego and pride, so the key is to try and avoid confrontation."

Can the intricacies of sports negotiation offer any lessons for finance executives? Sure, signing All-Star pitcher Roger Clemens to another year is much more glamorous than brokering a better compensation package, selling off a business, or quelling employee dissatisfaction. But the similarities outweigh the differences. Deal-making in the corporate world involves "the same dynamics" as negotiating sports contracts, says Peter Carfagna, who oversaw contracts for the likes of Tiger Woods while he was chief legal officer at International Management Group and now teaches negotiation strategy at Case Western Reserve University. Even when you have a good deal of leverage, he adds, "you have to use it selectively, so you develop a reputation for being reasonable."

Make a List, Check It Twice

The first step, say many agents, is to catalog what you want. The longer and more varied your wish list, the better. "You should itemize a whole litany of requests, which become bargaining chips," says Bill Duffy, agent for National Basketball Association stars like Yao Ming and Drew Gooden. That strategy essentially means padding your must-haves with nice-to-haves and not disclosing which are which. "You may have things that you're willing to throw away, but your opponent doesn't know that," says Duffy.

Knowing the priorities ahead of time makes it easier to concentrate on the things that matter most to your client, says Lon S. Babby, agent for the NBA's Grant Hill and Ray Allen. He gives clients a list and asks them to rank about 15 criteria, from salaries

Source: "This Is Not a Game: Top Sports Agents Share Their Negotiating Secrets," by Alix Stuart, from *CFO Magazine*, January 1, 2006. Used with permission.

and incentives to state income-tax considerations. Such lists are just as critical in corporate deals, although they may not appear until the later stages of a negotiation. "A lot of people think it's just about price, but it's often more subtle," says Peter Falvey, managing director at Revolution Partners, a Boston-based investment bank. In his experience, concerns like liquidity and employee provisions often take precedence.

The question then becomes whether to tackle the most or least important issue first—and how transparent to make the ranking. Carfagna says that while at IMG he used an "inside-out strategy," starting with the most important issues, "because I wanted to know if we had a deal before getting to the peripheral issues." In the corporate world, some deal-makers, like John J. Leahy, CFO of Boston-based technology consultancy Keane Inc., believe in dealing with the low-hanging fruit first. "The more things you can agree to, the more psychological momentum you get, and the further along you are to getting the deal done," he says.

In most corporate deals, a letter of intent spells out core terms like price and time frame, so there is a defined starting point. Finance chiefs say that makes the process more efficient. Duffy, on the other hand, prefers to have the other side make the first offer, because "you certainly wouldn't want to underbid." Either way, the key to a successful deal is to engineer the back-and-forth so that "you get what you want, but you have the other side offer it," says Babby.

Head Games

Once you know what you want, the next step is to "inhabit the reality" of the person with whom you are negotiating, says Steinberg. "You've got to understand what the pressures are on that person," he adds. His first step is to research the negotiation history of a team's general manager, running through questions like: Is this someone who will make a first offer and stick with it, or does he play a high-low negotiation game? Is this someone who has real authority, or will he need to run the deal by his boss?

Such due diligence, as CFOs would call it, is much like that advocated by negotiation guru Roger Fisher in his landmark book *Getting to Yes,* and it recently helped Steinberg land a giant salary for Pittsburgh Steelers quarterback Ben Roethlisberger. When Steinberg negotiated the first-round draft pick's initial contract with the Steelers in 2004, he knew the team was "philosophically opposed" to clauses known as escalators—incentives that enhance base salary in a deal's latter years. For his part, though, Roethlisberger wanted the opportunity to earn more for performance and to keep pace with other quarterbacks over time.

So Steinberg did some creative term-setting, and in the end Roethlisberger agreed to take the lowest possible base salary in his starting year in exchange for a $9 million signing bonus and a six-year contract filled with incentives based on playing time that could make it worth as much as $40 million over that time. "Had we insisted on an escalator, he might still be holding out," says Steinberg.

On the corporate side, Keane CFO Leahy has recognized that one of his first steps in deals with privately held, owner-run companies is to get sellers "past the emotional hurdle" of letting go. Since sellers are typically concerned with the fate of their customers and employees, Leahy says that he tries to make the case that merging with Keane will be best for all involved. Without promising too much, he tries to get owners comfortable with "the role current employees will play in the combined company, or demonstrate the type of investments we're willing to make."

Perception Is Reality

Of course, what both sides want ultimately ends up second to what the market will bear. Consequently, in sports negotiations—as in many CEO and CFO compensation contracts—a major component of external due diligence is a peer review. That often means making a case that a particular athlete exceeds the competition—as the agent defines it. "The question in these negotiations is often whose definition of performance and value will prevail," says Steinberg.

Setting such terms is especially important when marketing somewhat damaged goods. Last season, Tom O'Connell, head of Tampa-based Legends Management Group, represented a minor-league third baseman who was struggling after a "tremendous" previous season. By isolating the source of his poor performance—a switch to the American League after seven years in the National League—O'Connell could then go back to some of the National League teams that had courted him to "rekindle the fire." And in the end, O'Connell secured a deal in a more familiar environment; one that he believes offers the player a greater opportunity to make the majors. The trick, says O'Connell, is selling potential: "It's very easy to ride a thoroughbred, but Seabiscuit is a whole different animal," he explains.

Similarly, what the jockeying Guidant recently did to rejuvenate its acquisition by Johnson & Johnson is a case study in emphasizing potential. When Guidant announced last fall that some of its pacemakers and defibrillators had been recalled, J&J tried to renege on its $25 billion offer, on the grounds that conditions had materially changed. Rather than rolling over and playing dead, however, Guidant filed a lawsuit against J&J for breach of contract, maintaining that its share price was still strong and that it would soon have the lawsuits behind it. Ultimately, the two parties agreed on a discounted price—about 15 percent below the original offer. (At press time, however, another suitor—Boston Scientific Corp.—had trumped the J&J bid for Guidant and the deal was uncertain.)

Some agents have struck gold for their clients by thinking outside the peer group. That was how former tennis player Anna Kournikova earned a reported $20 million in endorsements in 1999, more than any other female tennis player, even though she was hardly a top-ranked player. "We posited that the marketplace for Anna Kournikova was not the tennis marketplace, but the celebrity and entertainment marketplace," says Kournikova's agent at the time, Octagon's Phil de Picciotto. "Essentially the argument is, 'Yes, you're paying more than you ever thought you would. But we're going to deliver more than you could ever imagine.'"

Executive-compensation consultants are hard-pressed to name a CFO with that kind of star power, but there are ways to stand apart. "Some CFOs are more valuable than others, either because they have depth in a certain area of finance expertise or breadth in areas beyond finance," says Jan Koors, managing director of Pearl Meyer & Partners. One advantage enjoyed by those in the business world is that, unlike athletes, executives typically enhance their skills with age. An athlete, says Babby, may be "the nicest guy in the city, but if he can't play anymore, it's a cold business."

Resolve and Patience

Many athletes get the best deals when they have alternatives. That's why free agency, or being able to field offers from multiple teams, is so often at the heart of the deal in professional sports.

That fact was perfectly illustrated by Ray Allen's most recent negotiations with the Seattle SuperSonics, says Babby. The agent started by approaching the team a year ahead of the contract expiration to offer it first dibs on "a franchise icon," but found the team unwilling to pay. Not until a year later did the team re-sign Allen at the salary he wanted—after his contract expired and he had other offers. "We saw the market one way, they saw it another way, and ultimately we couldn't get it resolved until [Allen] could go out and prove his value," the agent says.

Still, for the ultimate alternative—walking away—to work, says Carfagna, "you have to be willing to make good on your threat." Such resolve is probably why the Minnesota Vikings' Bryant McKinnie eventually got a better deal than the team wanted to give. The seventh draft pick in 2002 asked to be paid more than the player ranked behind him, but the team refused to meet that condition. In response, McKinnie held out eight weeks into the regular season, losing out on any salary he would have been paid if he had been signed in a timely fashion. Finally, as the November 1 deadline by which Minnesota had to sign or lose him drew near, the team owners caved and paid McKinnie for a full five years, despite the half season he'd missed. "He was able to resist the temptation of signing an inferior deal," says McKinnie's agent, SFX Sports Group's Jim Steiner.

When such strong-arm tactics would be counterproductive, agents say that relying on performance-based contingencies—and patience—can be the best way to get a deal done. When the San Francisco 49ers released Jerry Rice in 2001 at age 39, for example, Steiner, his agent, admits that "we had only a certain amount of leverage, because there were only two teams interested, [the Oakland Raiders and the Detroit Lions,] and Detroit was willing to go only so far." In that case, he and Rice accepted a relatively low seven-figure salary, and then renegotiated for a better deal after Rice exceeded expectations and went to the Pro Bowl.

Similarly, earnout structures used in deals when an unproven product is at stake can reward future value. Murraysville, Pennsylvania-based medical-device maker Respironics Inc., for example, agreed to buy a product line from SpectRx Inc. back in 2003 for $5 million in cash and an additional $6.25 million over the next two years, contingent on the business's performance. In November, SpectRx got the last of its checks from the buyer, ending up with a grand total of $9.5 million for the product line. Says CFO Dan Bevevino: Earnouts are "a good way to bridge any difference in valuation perspectives," while ensuring that the buyer pays only for what it gets.

Be Nice

In all negotiations, however, sports agents agree that the tenor must be professional, courteous, and ethical. As soft as it sounds, many agents say building good relationships is what is most critical to getting the best deals. "It's a small world, and what goes around comes around," says Duffy.

Such an attitude paid off in spades for agent Mark Bartelstein when client Darius Songaila's contract with the Sacramento Kings came up for renewal last year. Bartelstein could have secured a release by working up a three-year deal with another NBA team that the Kings could not have matched, but Songaila's preference was an offer the Kings easily could have topped—a shorter contract from the Chicago Bulls.

So, with nothing to offer, Bartelstein went to the King's operating chief, whom he considers a friend, and asked for a favor. "I went to Jeff [Petrie] and said, 'Would you do the right thing for Darius?'" Bartelstein recalls, at which point Petrie backed off the negotiations. Bartelstein believes the implicit agreement was that he would remember the goodwill in the future when it came to marketing the Kings to clients. "He knows I'm not going to forget he did something for me," says Bartelstein.

The ultimate prize for a CFO in any negotiation, however, may be the personal satisfaction that comes from a battle well fought, regardless of the final terms. If a CFO won't argue for what he really wants, says Steinberg, he will be consigned to "that great mass of people who walk through life with a terrible roiling sense in their gut, feeling underappreciated and trod on." And, of course, if you can show shareholders the money, you may just feel like a star.

You Had Me at Percentage: How Sports Deals Get Done

Anna Kournikova

Tennis

Her Deal: Despite not having won any major tennis tournaments, Kournikova was able to garner a reported $20 million in endorsements in 1999. How? Her agents marketed her as a category killer, thanks to her good looks and charismatic personality.

Darius Songaila

Basketball

His Deal: Songaila was bound to the Sacramento Kings unless he could find a deal the Kings couldn't match. His preferred option, though, was an easily topped two-year contract from the Chicago Bulls. So his agent, Mark Bartelstein, used his longtime relationship with the Kings to ask for a favor—the release of Songaila—and got it.

Jerry Rice

Football

His Deal: When the San Francisco 49ers released Rice in 2001, only two teams were interested in him, leaving him little leverage. So Rice accepted a relatively low salary, and then renegotiated for a better deal after he exceeded expectations and went to the Pro Bowl.

Reading 3.10

The New Boss
Matt Bai

Andy Stern, who leads the largest and fastest-growing union in the country, is determined to save the American worker.
    And he's willing to tear apart the labor movement—and perhaps the Democratic Party as well—in order to do it.

Purple is the color of Andrew Stern's life. He wears, almost exclusively, purple shirts, purple jackets, and purple caps. He carries a purple duffel bag and drinks bottled water with a purple label, emblazoned with the purple logo of the Service Employees International Union, of which Stern is president. There are union halls in America where a man could get himself hurt wearing a lilac shirt, but the SEIU is a different kind of union, rooted in the new service economy. Its members aren't truck drivers or assembly-line workers but janitors and nurses and home health care aides, roughly a third of whom are black, Asian, or Latino. While the old-line industrial unions have been shrinking every year, Stern's union has been organizing low-wage workers, many of whom have never belonged to a union, at a torrid pace, to the point where the SEIU is now the largest and fastest-growing trade union in North America. Once a movement of rust brown and steel gray, Big Labor is increasingly represented, at rallies and political conventions, by a rising sea of purple.

All of this makes Andy Stern—a charismatic 54-year-old former social service worker—a very powerful man in labor, and also in Democratic politics. The job of running a union in America, even the biggest union around, isn't what it once was. The age of automation and globalization, with its "race to the bottom" among companies searching for lower wages overseas, has savaged organized labor. Fifty years ago, a third of workers in the United States carried union cards in their wallets; now it's barely 1 in 10. An estimated 21 million service industry workers have never belonged to a union, and between most employers' antipathy to unions and federal laws that discourage workers from demanding one, chances are that the vast majority of them never will.

Over the years, union bosses have grown comfortable blaming everyone else— timid politicians, corrupt CEOs, greedy shareholders—for their inexorable decline. But last year, Andy Stern did something heretical: He started pointing the finger back at his fellow union leaders. Of course workers had been punished by forces outside their control, Stern said. But what had big labor done to adapt? Union bosses, Stern scolded, had been too busy flying around with senators and riding around in chauffeur-driven cars to figure out how to counter the effects of globalization, which have cost millions of Americans their jobs and their pensions. Faced with declining union rolls, the bosses made things worse by raiding one another's industries, which only diluted the power of

Source: "The New Boss," by Matt Bai, from *The New York Times Magazine,* January 30, 2005, pp. 38–45. Used with permission.

their workers. The nation's flight attendants, for instance, are now divided among several different unions, making it difficult, if not impossible, for them to wield any leverage over an entire industry.

Stern put the union movement's eroding stature in business terms: if any other $6.5 billion corporation had insisted on clinging to the same decades-old business plan despite losing customers every year, its executives would have been fired long ago.

"Our movement is going out of existence, and yet too many labor leaders go and shake their heads and say they'll do something, and then they go back and do the same thing the next day," Stern told me recently. He is a lean, compact man with thinning white hair, and when he reclines in the purple chair in his Washington office and crosses one leg over the other, he could easily pass for a psychiatrist or a math professor. He added, "I don't have a lot of time to mince words, because I don't think workers in our country have a lot of time left if we don't change."

A week after the election in November, Stern delivered a proposal to the AFL–CIO that sounded more like an ultimatum. He demanded that the federation, the umbrella organization of the labor movement, embrace a top-to-bottom reform, beginning with a plan to merge its 58 unions into 20, for the purpose of consolidating power. If the other bosses wouldn't budge, Stern threatened to take his 1.8 million members and bolt the federation—effectively blowing up the AFL–CIO on the eve of its 50th anniversary. Stern's critics say all of this is simply an excuse to grab power. "What Andy's doing now with his compadres is what Vladimir Putin is trying to do to the former Communist bloc countries," says Tom Buffenbarger, president of the union that represents machinists and aerospace workers. "He's trying to implement dictatorial rule."

Stern says he is done caring what the other bosses think. "If I don't have the courage to do what my members put me here to do, then how do I ask a janitor or a child care worker to go in and see a private-sector employer and say, 'We want to have a union in this place'?" Stern asks. "What's my risk? That some people won't like me? *Their* risk is that they lose their jobs."

The implications of Stern's crusade stretch well beyond the narrow world of organized labor and into the heart of the nation's politics. The stale and paralyzed political dialogue in Washington right now is a direct result of the deterioration of industrial America, followed by the rise of the Wal-Mart economy. Lacking any real solutions to the growing anxiety of working-class families, the two parties have instead become entrenched in a cynical battle over who or what is at fault. Republicans have made an art form of blaming the declining fortunes of the middle class on taxes and social programs; if government would simply get out of the way, they suggest, businesses would magically provide all the well-paying jobs we need. Democrats, meanwhile, cling to the mythology of the factory age, blaming Republican greed and "Benedict Arnold CEOs"—to use John Kerry's phrase—for the historical shift toward globalization; if only Washington would close a few tax loopholes, they seem to be saying, the American worker could again live happily in 1950.

About the last place you might expect to find a more thoughtful and compelling vision for the global age is in the fossilized, dogmatic leadership of organized labor. But Andy Stern is a different kind of labor chief. He intends to create a new, more dynamic kind of movement around the workers of the 21st century. And if some old friends in labor and the Democratic Party get their feelings hurt in the process, that's all right with him.

The Old Boss

Earlier this month, Tom Buffenbarger invited me down to the machinists' union's training facility on the Patuxent River in southern Maryland, about a 90-minute drive from Washington. The little campus features 87 hotel rooms, a library, a theater, and a dockside dining room. There was no training going on that week, and as I wandered the empty halls, I peered into glass cases containing some of the products made by the heavy machine operators and plant workers who make up much of the union's rank and file: a parking meter, aluminum soda cans, a Winchester rifle, a box of animal crackers. There were black-and-white photos of the union's past presidents with Harry Truman, Hubert Humphrey, and Ted Kennedy. I glimpsed an exhibit meant to celebrate what the machinists apparently considered a triumphant moment: the Eastern Airlines strike that began in 1989 and ended, two years later, with the destruction of the company. It was as if I had wandered into the industrial economy's version of Jurassic Park: "Welcome to Laborland, U.S.A., and please be careful—there are actual union leaders wandering around."

At its zenith, in 1969, the machinists' union was about a million strong, but that was before robots supplanted assembly-line workers and Chinese factories began replacing a lot of American plants. The union now has some 380,000 active, dues-paying members. Buffenbarger told me that the union had lost more than 100,000 members in the last four years alone—members whose jobs were eliminated or moved overseas—for which he placed the blame squarely on free-trade deals and the Bush administration. Buffenbarger looks like what you would probably imagine a union boss to look like. He is a big, fleshy man with a bald crown and ursine hands. He began his career, decades ago, as a tool-and-dye apprentice. Now he flies around in the union's very own Lear jet. "We couldn't do what we do without it," he explained unapologetically.

Buffenbarger said that Andy Stern is wrong in his central point about the labor movement; in fact, unions have as much power as ever. The problem, as Buffenbarger sees it, is one of public relations and messaging. All the unions need to do to reverse their fortunes, Buffenbarger said, is to speak up louder. To that end, Buffenbarger has proposed that the AFL–CIO spend $188 million to create, among other things, a Labor News Network on cable TV. "There is no bigger organization than the collective labor movement," he told me. "Even the NRA doesn't have 13 million members. But they act like they do, and I think that's where we fall down. We need to act like we do."

In a speech earlier that morning, Buffenbarger took on Stern, portraying him as an arrogant usurper and comparing him to "a rather small peacock." Buffenbarger, of course, stands to lose clout if the AFL–CIO meets Stern's demands, since the machinists might well be forced to merge with other unions, some of whom might not see the need for a private jet. But I sensed a reason for his resentment that went beyond simple self-interest; underneath his rhetoric, you could detect the fault line between an industrial economy and a service economy, between old labor and new. Buffenbarger sneered at Stern's Ivy League education—Stern got his degree from the University of Pennsylvania, where he spent his freshman year studying business—and mocked him for setting up a blog. What Buffenbarger didn't like about Stern is that he looked and sounded so much like management.

"He's trying to corporatize the labor movement," Buffenbarger said. "When you listen to him talk, it's all about market share. It's about loss and gain. It's about *producers* and *consumers*." He wrinkled his face when he said this, as if the words themselves tasted sour in his mouth. "I think he's enamored of all the glitz and hype of the Wall Street types. He must be a fan of Donald Trump. I think he wants his own TV show."

Reengineering the Union

Stern, it's true, is about as far from a tool-and-dye man as you can get. His father built a profitable legal practice in northern New Jersey by catering to small Jewish businesses, helping their owners make the jump from corner store to full-service retailer. After college, where, by his own account, he mostly avoided thinking about classes or the future, an aimless Stern took a job with the Pennsylvania welfare department, compiling case histories for aid recipients. The department's social service workers had just won the right to collective bargaining, and a group of young idealists, Stern included, seized control of the local union.

Nothing in Stern's prototypically suburban background made him a natural candidate for organized labor—for many affluent college kids of his generation, the notion of unions brought to mind images of dank social halls and cigar-chewing thugs—but this was the early 1970s, and when you had a genuine chance to scream truth to power, you took it. Soon he went to work full-time for the union. Stern and his cadre got the pay increases and better benefits they demanded—and went on strike anyway. "Most of us were just playing union," he says now, laughing. "We'd watched enough movies so we could figure it out."

Unlike most union bosses, who rise up through the administrative ranks, ploddingly building alliances and dispatching their enemies, Stern spent most of his career as an organizer in the field, taking on recalcitrant employers and bargaining contracts. In 1984 John Sweeney, then the president of the SEIU, summoned Stern to Washington to coordinate a national organizing drive. When Sweeney ran for president of the entire AFL–CIO in 1995, Stern helped run his campaign; after Sweeney won, the brash and ambitious Stern maneuvered to replace him as head of the SEIU. The ensuing drama was a classic of labor politics. Before an election could be held, Sweeney left the union in the hands of a top lieutenant, who wasted no time in firing Stern and having him escorted from the building. As Stern tells the story, he vowed that he wouldn't set foot back in the L Street headquarters unless he was moving into the president's fifth-floor office. Six weeks later, his reform-minded allies in the locals helped get him elected, and he became, at 45, the youngest president in the union's history.

Having grown up around his father's small business clients, and having spent much of his adult life at bargaining tables, Stern had learned a few things about the way business works. He came to embrace a philosophy that ran counter to the most basic assumptions of the besieged labor movement: the popular image of greedy corporations that want to treat their workers like slaves, Stern believed, was in most cases just wrong. The truth was that companies in the global age, under intense pressure to lower costs, were simply doing what they thought they had to do to survive, and if you wanted them to behave better, you had to make good behavior viable for them.

Stern's favorite example concerns the more than 10,000 janitors who clean the office buildings in the cities and suburbs of northern New Jersey. Five years ago, only a fraction of them were unionized, and they were making $10 less per hour than their counterparts across the river in Manhattan. Stern and his team say they were convinced from talking to employers in the fast-growing area that the employers didn't like the low wages and poor benefits much more than the union did. Cleaning companies complained that they had trouble retaining workers, and the workers they did keep were less productive. The problem was that for any one company to offer better wages would have been tantamount to an army unilaterally disarming in the middle of a war, cheaper competitors would immediately overrun its business.

The traditional way for a union to attack this problem would be to pick the most vulnerable employer in the market, pressure it to accept a union, and then try to expand from there. Instead, Stern set out to organize the entire market at once, which he did by promising employers that the union contract wouldn't kick in unless more than half of them signed it. (Getting the first companies to enter into the agreement took some old-fashioned organizing tactics, including picket lines.) The SEIU ended up representing close to 70 percent of the janitors in the area, doubling their pay in many cases; from minimum wage to more than $11 an hour. Stern found that by bringing all of the main employers in an industry to the table at one time, rather than one after the other, he was able to effectively regulate an entire market.

Stern talks about giving "added value" to employers, some of whom have come to view him, warily, as a partner. At about the time Stern took over the union, his locals in several states were at war with Beverly Health and Rehabilitation Services, an Arkansas-based nursing home chain. The company complained that cuts in state aid were making it all but impossible to pay workers more while operating their facilities at a profit. Stern and his team proposed an unusual alliance: If Beverly would allow its workers to organize, the SEIU's members would use their political clout in state legislatures to deliver more money. It worked. "I do believe Andy's a stand-up guy," says Beverly Health's COO Dave Devereaux.

At the same time Stern was employing inventive labor tactics to work with business, he was also using new-age business theory to remake the culture of his union. When Stern came into power, the SEIU represented a disparate coalition of local unions that identified themselves by different names and maintained separate identities. This was the way it had always been, which was fine in an era when employers and unions were confined to individual markets. To Stern, however, this was now a problem. If his members were going to go up against national and global companies, they were going to have to convey the size and stature of a national union. "You know your employer is powerful, so you want to believe you're part of something powerful as well" is the way he explained it to me.

Stern hired a corporate consulting firm versed in the jargon of the new economy and undertook a campaign to "rebrand" the union. He used financial incentives to get all the local branches of the union to begin using the SEIU name, its new logo and, of course, its new color. In some respects, the SEIU now feels very much like a *Fortune* 500 company.

In the lobby of its headquarters, a flat-screen TV plays an endless video of smiling members along with inspirational quotes from Stern, as if he were Jack Welch or Bill Gates. The union sold more than $1 million worth of purple merchandise through its gift catalog last year, including watches, sports bras, temporary tattoos, and its very own line of jeans. (The catalog itself features poetry from members and their children paying tribute to the union, along with recipes like Andy Stern's Chocolate Cake with Peanut-Butter Frosting.)

In all of this, Stern's critics in other unions see a strange little cult of personality. Another way to look at it, though, is that Stern understands the psychology of a movement; workers in the union want to feel as if someone is looking out for them. When he and I walked into the SEIU campaign office in Miami shortly before the presidential election, the union's activists greeted him with hugs or shy smiles. Stern took a moment to chat with each member. "I got to have my picture taken with you once before, you know," one man told him proudly. "You mean *I* got to have my picture taken with *you*," Stern replied with the timing of a politician.

As the SEIU was soaring in membership and strength during the late 1990s, much of big labor was seeing its influence further erode. And there were those who thought the SEIU wasn't doing enough for the movement as a whole. Cecil Roberts, president of the mineworkers, personally challenged Stern to follow the example of the mineworkers' legendary leader John L. Lewis, who helped build up the entire labor movement in the 1930s. But Stern demurred. Just running the union was taking all of his time, and what was left he wanted to spend with his son, Matt, and his daughter, Cassie. There would be time later, when his children were older, to think about reshaping the future of American labor.

Then, all at once, Stern's personal world collapsed. A little more than two years ago, Cassie, 14, who was born unusually small and with poor muscle tone, became ill after returning home from a routine operation, stopped breathing in her father's arms, and died. In the aftermath, Stern's 23-year marriage to Jane Perkins, a liberal advocate, unraveled. He rented an apartment in northwest Washington and shed most of his furniture, hurling himself into his work at the union. He is very close to his 18-year-old son, but his son splits his time between his parents' homes. On weeks when Stern is alone, he told me, he looks forward to stopping by the Dancing Crab, a local bar, to eat dinner alone and read the paper. "I'm in a very transitional moment of life," he says.

Often, when Stern talks about his daughter, he wanders off, without really meaning to, into a story about a union member he has met somewhere who reminds him of Cassie, or whose own daughter—"someone else's Cassie"—is stuck in a failing school. The recollections bring him to the brink of tears. It is as if he can't help conflating the fate of workers with the fate of his daughter. Time has become a paradox for him; on one hand, he has more of it than ever before, and yet he can't escape the panicky feeling that time is running out.

"When Cassie died," Stern said, "it was like: 'I'm 52 years old. How many more years am I really going to do this? Why am I so scared to say what I really think?'" If he were a religious man, Stern told me, he might think that it was not a coincidence that he was given, through his loss, so much free time and clarity at the very moment when organized labor was in crisis. He says it would be comforting to believe he has been chosen for a mission. It is clear, from the way he says this, that part of him believes it anyway.

Big Labor's Big Brawl

Stern's plan to rescue the American worker begins with restructuring the AFL–CIO. Since the 1960s, a lot of struggling unions have chosen to merge rather than perish, to the point where there are half as many unions in the federation today as there were at its height. Stern argues that this Darwinian process, so lamented by labor leaders, is in fact healthy and hasn't gone far enough. Unions, he says, work best when they're large enough to organize new workers at the same time as they fight battles on behalf of old ones, and when they represent a large concentration of the workers in any one industry. Smaller unions lack the muscle to organize entire markets the way that the SEIU has been able to do with janitors and home health care workers. At the same time, some unions have desperately scrambled to maintain or increase their memberships—and thus their revenue—by signing up workers well outside their core areas. So the United Auto Workers ends up representing graduate students, and the machinists represent park rangers. This is self-defeating, Stern argues; all it does is divide labor's strength.

Stern's 10-point plan would essentially tear down the industrial-age framework of the House of Labor and rebuild it. The AFI–CIO, he says, would consist of 20 large unions, and each union would be devoted to a single sector of the 21st-century economy, like health care or airlines. Ever the apostle of field organizing, Stern wants these restructured unions to put more time and resources into recruiting new members in fast-growing exurban areas—in the South and the West especially—where a new generation of workers has never belonged to a union. His plan would slash the amount that each union pays in dues to the AFL–CIO by half, provided that those unions put some of the money back into local organizing. This is not a small idea; it would, essentially, take resources away from the federation's headquarters, which uses it for policy studies and training programs, and give it back to the guys who set up picket lines and rallies.

The basic strategy is to take the same principles Stern demonstrated organizing New Jersey's janitors and make them the model for the entire American labor movement. If only two or three large unions represented all the nation's health care workers, they could go into a growing market—Reno, say, or Albuquerque—and bargain with all the hospitals at the same time. Labor would be able to focus on setting standards for entire industries, as opposed to battling one employer at a time.

Stern's plan has incited fury within a lot of smaller unions, whose members don't seem to think the movement needs a self-appointed savior. The proposed reorganization would sweep away a lot of small unions as if they were debris on the factory floor. "Andy is impatient, and he sprang this on his peers without any discussion," says John Sweeney, Stern's former mentor. "I think he needs to stand still for a minute and listen to what other people think, and learn from other experiences as well."

You would imagine, given how often Stern's critics have called him arrogant, that he'd be used to it by now, but clearly the word still stings him. He is a man who prides himself on his emotional connection with janitors and nursing aides, and he almost cannot bear the suggestion that he thinks he's smarter than everyone else. Stern prefers to see himself as a man who gets along with all kinds of people, whether they drive the limousine or ride in the back. ("I actually was the most popular person in my high school class," he once told me.)

During an airport layover, I saw him open his laptop and peruse the Unite to Win blog. (Stern actually contributes from time to time to three separate blogs, including Purpleocean.org, an SEIU site designed for like-minded people who aren't even in a union.) Stern established the online forum so that everyone in the labor movement— whether supportive of his plan or opposed to it—could tell him exactly what they thought of his ideas. They haven't held back. "Sometimes I really hate this," he said in the airport lounge, wincing slightly. "I don't like seeing my name there and people calling me an arrogant idiot."

Even Stern's allies admit that his ultimatum to big labor is a little high-handed. John Wilhelm, copresident of the union that represents hotel, restaurant, and garment workers, is supportive of Stern, and Wilhelm is said to be considering a challenge to Sweeney when he runs for another term as AFl–CIO president this year. But he said he disagrees with Stern's idea of merging unions against their will. Because Stern's union is so powerful, Wilhelm told me, Stern doesn't always feel the need to tread as softly as he might. "Frankly, he doesn't have to be as diplomatic as others do," Wilhelm said. "There's a thin and perhaps indiscernible line between a person who comes across as arrogant and a person who tries to tell the truth even when it's unpleasant. And the truth about our labor movement is unpleasant."

When I first started talking to Stern about his controversial plan last summer, he seemed to regard it more as a provocation to big labor than as a proposal that might actually be adopted. He talked as if he were resigned to the idea that the SEIU would ultimately break from the federation. But as the next meeting of the AFL–CIO executive board in March draws near, there seems to be in union headquarters around the nation the faintest stirrings of a revolt. Stern's ideas have become the basis for an entirely new debate about the future of labor, and now several unions have offered their own, more modest versions of a reform plan in response. The biggest surprise came in December, when James P. Hoffa, president of the famously old-school Teamsters, weighed in with a set of recommendations quite similar to Stern's.

Increasingly the question for Stern is not whether he is prepared to leave the AFL–CIO, but how much of his plan has to be enacted in order for the SEIU to stay. It is a question he evades. "What I won't do," he said, "is pretend we made change. It's not worth having this fight or discussion if, in the end, you can't look people in the eye and say we really have taken a big step forward."

Workers of the World, Globalize?

Even if big labor eventually does come to be made up of bigger unions, Stern sees a larger challenge: can you build a multinational labor movement to counter the leverage of multinational giants whose tentacles reach across oceans and continents? The emblem of this new kind of behemoth, of course, is Wal-Mart, the nation's largest employer. Wal-Mart has, in a sense, turned the American retail model inside out. It used to be that a manufacturer made, say, a clock radio, determined its price and the wages of the employees who made it, and then sold the radio to a retail outlet at a profit. Wal-Mart's power is such that the process now works in reverse: In practice, Wal-Mart sets the price for that clock radio, and the manufacturer, very likely located overseas, figures out how low wages will have to be in order to make it profitable to produce it. In this way, Wal-Mart not only resists unions in its stores with unwavering ferocity but also drives down the wages of its manufacturers—all in the service of bringing consumers the lowest possible price.

"What was good for GM ended up being good for the country," Stern says. "What's good for Wal-Mart ends up being good for five families"—the heirs to the Walton fortune. Stern's reform plan for the AFL–CIO includes a $25 million fund to organize Wal-Mart's workers. But as a retail outlet, Wal-Mart doesn't really fall within the SEIU's purview. What Stern says he is deeply worried about is what he sees as the next generation of Wal-Marts, which *are* on his turf: French, British, and Scandinavian companies whose entry into the American market threatens to drive down wages in service industries, which are often less visible than retail. "While we were invading Iraq, the Europeans invaded us," Stern says. Most of these companies have no objection to unionizing in Europe, where organized labor is the norm. But when they come to the United States, they immediately follow the Wal-Mart model, undercutting their competitors by shutting out unions and squeezing paychecks.

Take, for instance, the case of Sodexho, a French company that provides all the services necessary to operate corporate buildings, from catering the food to guarding the lobby. In Europe, Sodexho is considered a responsible employer that works with unions and compensates its employees fairly. In the United States and Canada, where the company employs more than 100,000 workers, Sodexho's policy is to discourage its employees from joining unions. As a maneuver to get Sodexho to the bargaining table, last year the SEIU resorted to taking out ads in French newspapers, shaming the company's executives in their own country, where the idea of scorning unions is considerably less chic. Stern says Sodexho has started negotiating.

Stern's big idea for coping with this new kind of multinational nemesis is to build a federation of unions, similar to the AFL–CIO except that its member unions would come from all over the world. As Stern explained it, a French company might not be so brazen about bullying American workers if it had to worry about a French union protesting back home. The point, he said, is to force companies like Sodexho to adhere to the same business standards in New York and Chicago as it does in Paris, by building a labor alliance that is every bit as global as modern capital.

At first, this global vision sounded a little dreamy to me, as if Stern might have been watching too many *Superfriends* reruns. Then he invited me, just before Christmas, on a one-day trip to Birmingham, England. The occasion was a meeting of Britain's reform-minded transportation union. Tony Woodley, the union's general secretary, flashed a broad smile and threw his arm around Stern when Stern arrived, after flying all night, to give the keynote address. Two SEIU employees were already on hand; it turned out that Stern had dispatched them to London temporarily to help Woodley set up an organizing program.

As we drank coffee backstage, Stern and Woodley told me about the case of First Student, a company that in the last few years had become the largest, most aggressive private school bus company in the United States. The company had become a target of SEIU locals in several cities because it wouldn't let its drivers unionize. "We keep seeing these things about them in the union newsletter," Stern said. "And it starts nibbling at your brain. I said, 'Who are these people, First Student? What's going on here?' And then we do a little research, and we find out what idiots we are. This is a major multinational company. They're 80 percent unionized in the United Kingdom. So we write a letter to the union here, and we say, 'Can you help us?'"

Woodley sent British bus drivers to Chicago to meet with their American counterparts. Then the American bus drivers went to London, and lobbyists for the British union took them to see members of Parliament. They also held a joint demonstration outside the company's annual meeting. Woodley told me that First Student—known as First Group in Britain—was now making a bid for rail contracts there, and his union intended to lobby against it unless the company sat down with its American counterparts in Florida and Illinois.

I asked Woodley, who looks like Rudy Giuliani with more hair, why he would use his own union's political capital to help the SEIU. He nodded quickly, in a way that suggested that there were a lot of people who didn't yet understand this. He explained that it worked both ways; his union was suffering at the hands of multinationals, too, and Stern would be able to return the favor by pressuring American companies doing business in Britain. Moreover, Woodley went on to say, if European companies get used to operating without unions in America, it might be only a matter of time before they tried to export that same mentality back to Europe. "I don't expect miracles," Woodley said. "I don't expect international solidarity to bring huge companies to their knees overnight. But we've got to do a damn sight more than we're doing."

Stern invited the top executives of about a dozen unions from Europe and Australia to a meeting in London this April, which will be the maiden gathering of what he says he hopes will become a formalized global federation. He recently met with union leaders in Beijing too. Most labor experts assume that the Chinese unions are tools of the business-friendly government, but Stern says he came away believing that they are as jolted by the global economy as workers in America. "You have to understand, they're just seeing something new," he says. "These are public unions that are used to health benefits and real discussions, and suddenly they're meeting these huge corporations—like Wal-Mart—that, because the executives can make a phone call to someone in the local government, won't even talk to them. It's all new."

There are, however, painful questions inherent in globalizing the labor movement. At a recent meeting with his executive board, Stern mused out loud about the possibility of conducting a fact-finding mission to India, along with executives from one of the companies outsourcing its jobs there. Perhaps that could be a first step, he thought, toward raising the pay of Indian workers who have inherited American jobs.

Then Stern stopped himself and considered a problem. Sure, there was an obvious logic to unionizing foreign phone operators or machinists: American workers won't be able to compete fairly for jobs until companies have to pay higher wages in countries like China and India. But how would it look to workers in America? How would you avoid the appearance that you were more worried about the guy answering the phone in Bangalore than you were about the guy he replaced in Iowa? John Kerry and other

Democrats had been railing against the CEOs who outsourced American jobs—and here was Andy Stern, considering joining forces with those very same CEOs to make sure their Indian workers were making enough money.

"The truth is that as the living standard in China goes up, the living standard in Ohio goes down," Stern said. "What do you do about that? Are we a global union or an American union? This is a hard question for me to answer. Because I'm not comfortable with the living standard here going down. This is a question I think we need to think about going forward, but I don't think that means we should be scared."

The idea of a global union isn't entirely new. But the concept has never been translated into a formal alliance, and experts who study labor think Stern may be onto something important. I realized during our brief time in Birmingham why Stern seemed ambivalent about whether the AFL–CIO approved his reform plan, or whether his union even stayed in the federation. In a sense, no matter how the conversation is resolved, it is bound to lag a full generation behind the reality of the problem; it is as if the unions are arguing against upgrading from LPs to compact discs while the rest of the world has moved on to digital downloads. Even if the leaders of big labor do kill off half their unions and reorganize the rest, all they will have done, at long last, is create a truly national labor movement—at exactly the moment that capital has become a more sprawling and more obstinate force than any one nation could hope to contain.

Reengineering the Party

The more Andy Stern looks at organized labor and the Democratic Party, the more he sees the parallels between them. Like big labor, the modern Democratic Party was brought into being by imaginative liberal thinkers in the 1930s and reached its apex during the prosperity of the postwar industrial boom. Like the union bosses, Democratic leaders grew complacent in their success; they failed to keep pace with changing circumstances in American life and didn't notice that their numbers were steadily eroding. Now, Stern says, Democrats and the unions both find themselves mired in the mind-set of a bygone moment, lacking the will or perhaps the capacity to innovate or adapt. What you see in both cases, Stern told me borrowing from the new-age language of business theory, is "the change pattern of a dying institution."

The big conversation going on in Democratic Washington at the moment, at dinner parties and luncheons and think-tank symposia, revolves around how to save the party. The participants generally fall into two camps of unequal size. On one side, there is the majority of Democrats, who believe that the party's failure has primarily been one of communication and tactics. By this thinking, the Democratic agenda itself (no to tax cuts and school vouchers and Social Security privatization; yes to national health care and affirmative action) remains as relevant as ever to modern workers. The real problem, goes this line of thinking, is that the party has allowed ruthless Republicans to control the debate and has failed to sufficiently mobilize its voters. A much smaller group of prominent Democrats argues that the party's problems run deeper—that it suffers, in fact, from a lack of imagination, and that its core ideas are more an echo of government as it was than government as it ought to be.

Virtually everyone in the upper echelons of organized labor belongs solidly to the first camp. Stern has his feet firmly planted in the second. The economic policy of the Democratic Party, he says, "is basically being opposed to Republicans and protecting the New Deal. It makes me realize how vibrant the Republicans are in creating 21st-century ideas, and how sad it is that we're defending 60-year-old ideas." Like big labor, Stern says, the party needs to challenge its orthodoxy—and its interest groups—if it wants to put forward a program that makes sense for new-economy workers. Could it be that the Social Security system devised in the 1930s isn't, in fact, the only good national retirement program for today's wage earner? Is it possible that competition is the best way to rescue an imperiled public school system?

"I'm not convinced that you can do this from the inside," Stern told me at one point. Just as he is willing to strike out from the AFL–CIO, he doesn't rule out a split from the Democratic Party. "I feel like we have to do everything we can within our power to get both the labor movement and the parties in this country to represent workers the way they should," he said. "And if we can't, then we have to decide what our strategy is. Do we spend all our money running ballot initiatives and forget about candidates? Do we look for people to create an independent worker party? I don't know."

Stern isn't the only Democrat in Washington making this case—but he may be the most powerful and connected. Among his friends and allies he counts at least two billionaires: the financier George Soros and the philanthropist Eli Broad, who is talking with Stern about ideas to reform Los Angeles schools. Stern was one of the founding members of America Coming Together, the largest private get-out-the-vote effort ever assembled. His top political aide, Anna Burger, who is the SEIU's secretary treasurer, recently took a seat on the board of the Democracy Alliance, a network of wealthy liberal donors. How Stern wields this influence—and his union's money—can have a real impact on the direction of the party.

Other union leaders can spend their money on Buffenbarger's news network if they want, but Stern seems bent on leveraging his money against the party establishment. Last year, while he campaigned as many as six days a week for Kerry and other Democrats, Stern nevertheless undertook a series of actions that infuriated party leaders. First, with his encouragement, the SEIU's locals voted to endorse Howard Dean before the primaries. Then Stern gave more than $500,000 to the Republican Governors Association because, he said, some of the GOP's gubernatorial candidates had better positions for workers. As if that wasn't provocative enough a signal, Stern chose the moment of the Democratic convention in Boston to remark publicly, in an interview with *The Washington Post,* that it might be better for the party and the unions if John Kerry lost the election.

Stern told me he had been partly inspired, oddly enough, by the example of Stephen Moore, the arch-conservative ideologue who, until recently, ran the Club for Growth. The club, which is anathema to both Democrats and moderate Republicans in Washington, raises millions from corporate antitax crusaders, then spends it not only against Democrats (Tom Daschle was a prime target) but also against Republican incumbents who aren't deemed sufficiently conservative. Moore has infuriated some Republican leaders, who say he divides the party, but the Club for Growth has helped push the party to the right, putting moderates on the defensive and making Republicans think twice before they cast a vote against a tax cut.

Stern invited Moore to speak at an SEIU meeting in Chicago a few years ago—which is roughly the equivalent of Michael Moore being asked over to the National Rifle Association for lunch. Now Stern has begun to emulate the club's model; last year, the SEIU ran its own candidate, a union ally, against the Democratic House speaker in Washington State, because the speaker voted against a health benefits package for home health care workers. The union's challenger lost—but only by about 500 votes. "I think we need to spend more time running candidates against Democrats," Stern says matter-of-factly.

This approach holds some risk for a union boss. Most of Stern's members, after all, are lifelong Democrats. Will they be OK with a leader who's willing to entertain an overhaul of Social Security? Would they support Stern if he crossed the teachers' unions and came out for school vouchers? Stern seems convinced that his members want new solutions to these problems, not dogmatic answers, and he is betting that they're more loyal to him and the union than they are to the party. He seems poised to fill a space—between the world of organized labor and the world of social and economic policy—that hasn't been filled since Walter Reuther, the head of the United Auto Workers, advised the Kennedys and Lyndon Johnson on civil rights. "There's been no analog to Andy in the last 30 or 40 years in America," says Simon Rosenberg, who heads the New Democrat Network and is running for Democratic Party chairman. "There's been no labor leader who has emerged as a thought leader as well."

This spring, Stern plans to convene an eclectic group of Democrats to begin outlining a new economic agenda. "We don't want it to be the same old people," Stern told me. "We want people who might say, for example, 'Maybe privatization isn't such a terrible thing for people,' even if that's not what the Democratic Party thinks. Or, for example, 'Wal-Mart isn't the worst thing for the economy after all.'" He laughed heartily at that one. "We need to shock people out of their comfort zone and make them think."

The Big Questions

Stern is not the first giant of the labor movement to talk about breaking up big labor or the Democratic Party. Reuther and the United Auto Workers stormed out of the AFL–CIO in 1968 and formed a new alliance with the Teamsters. A few labor leaders, furious at Harry Truman's treatment of workers, followed Henry Wallace out of the Democratic Party in 1948. Neither venture lasted long enough for anyone to remember much about it. Reuther died suddenly in 1970, and the new alliance barely outlived him; Wallace's Progressive Party finished fourth in the 1948 election, behind the Dixiecrats, and faded away. Arguably, the lesson of these and other rebellions is that the threat of building new workers' institutions usually proves more potent than the reality.

The question that Stern's detractors ask is this: What is Andy Stern really after? Does he long to be the Reuther of his day, phoning presidents and holding forth to rooms full of reporters?

"I don't like politics," Stern said more than once. "After the last election, a lot of people called me and said everything from 'You should run for president' to 'You should be chairman of the DNC.' And neither of them had the slightest bit of reality or held any interest for me." That Stern can mention this casually—that someone suggested he not

merely phone a president, but run for president—would indicate that he is as susceptible to self-glorification as the next guy, and maybe more so. But if what Stern really
wanted was to run the world, he could surely spend his nights in more powerful company than that of the bartender at the Dancing Crab. When I asked what he envisioned
himself doing in his 60s, Stern said, "I hope I find someone to fall in love with and travel
with and watch my son have grandkids."

His adversaries will say this is disingenuous, but, as so often happens in public life,
they may be misunderstanding the human factor that compels Andy Stern. Everyone
who knows him well will tell you that he is driven by an authentic passion for workers.
And yet, at the same time, it doesn't take a psychology degree to see that he lives these
days in a state of suspended agony. Stern gives the impression of having been shaken
loose from conformity by the death of his daughter and the end of his marriage; nothing
can hurt him more than he has already been hurt, which breeds in him the kind of abandon
that can be dangerous to the status quo.

This is how history often changes; it's the people who are running from something
worse who are willing to hurl themselves into walls that others won't scale. The facts of
our time are clear enough: A ruthless kind of globalized economy is upon us, and it
is not going away. Many American industries are bound to be surpassed by leaner
competitors, and the workers left behind by this tectonic shift have little power to influence
the decisions of corporate barons whose interests know no national boundaries. More
Americans now hold stock—often in a 401(k)—than are members of a union. And the
institutions that have, for the last century, protected the ideal of the American worker—
organized labor and the Democratic Party—are clinging mightily to structures and programs born in the era of coal and steel, perhaps out of fear that innovation would
somehow discredit the things they have worked for all these years, or perhaps for the
simple reason that no one knows what to do next.

The visionary men who built big labor and the modern Democratic Party met the
challenges specific to their moment. What Andy Stern is doing, in his own way, is
provoking an argument more relevant to our moment. Can American workers ever be secure in a global market? Can a service economy sustain the nation's middle class? And
are we brave enough to have the conversation?

Can't Beat Them? Then Join a Coalition

In 2006, representatives of wind-energy developers started knocking on the doors of Wyoming ranchers. They were seeking to persuade the ranchers to sell the rights to build wind turbines on their land, reporter Addie Goss recounted on National Public Radio. Typically, the developers build wind farms by leasing large blocks of land from many different landowners in western states. In Wyoming, ranchers began signing leases without knowing the true value of the wind sweeping across their land.

U.S. Department of Agriculture program coordinator Grant Stumbough heard about the wind developers crisscrossing Wyoming and had a brainstorm: by working together, the ranchers might be able to get better deals.

Stumbough formed a "wind association" model in which ranchers and farmers pool as much as 100,000 acres of their land, negotiate leasing rights with wind developers as a group, and divide the profits. Eight wind associations now exist in Wyoming alone, and the model is catching on in other western states.

Rather than waiting passively for an offer from a single developer, wind associations market their land rights to dozens of companies, sometimes triggering bidding wars in the process. Royalties from a wind project could potentially generate hundreds of thousands of dollars annually for a rancher, Stumbough told NPR—a gold mine for those who are struggling to stay afloat in a depressed cattle market.

As a negotiator, what should you do when you're in over your head? In our last issue, we discussed a number of strategies for boosting your bargaining power at times when your position seems hopelessly weak. Carefully assessing your own outside alternatives and those of your counterpart, trying to change the rules of the game when they work against you, creating a strategy for your entire portfolio of negotiations, and appealing to the other side's sense of fairness are a few techniques you can use to increase your strength at the table.

As some Wyoming ranchers have learned, you can also gain leverage and improve your results by banding together in a coalition with other relatively weak parties. As a member of a coalition, you can harness the resources you need to face a tough opponent.

How Coalitions Work

In certain situations, negotiators are unqualified to bargain on their own behalf. Lawyers, agents, and other third parties can provide the expert negotiation guidance needed to prosper in situations as wide-ranging as a divorce settlement, a book sale, or a corporate merger.

Source: "Can't Beat Them? Then Join a Coalition" from the *Program on Negotiation* newsletter at the Harvard Law School (www.pon.harvard.edu), March 2009, Vol. 12, No. 3, pp. 1–4. Used with permission.

A negotiating coalition takes the "Don't go it alone" strategy a step further. Rather than (or in addition to) hiring one or more advisers to negotiate for you, a number of weak parties who might otherwise be in competition with one another join forces to negotiate in a collective, organized manner with one or more stronger parties.

Labor unions may be the most obvious example of a negotiating coalition. When a company negotiates with an employee individually, it could threaten to hire someone else in the face of the employee's demands. By contrast, when employees bargain collectively through a union, they avoid the need to compete against one another (at least on certain issues) and typically achieve a more competitive compensation and benefits package than they would have negotiated on their own.

Why Join a Coalition?

Returning to our Wyoming story, a rancher who negotiates individually with a wind developer over leasing rights risks being coerced into accepting a lowball offer. After all, both sides understand that the developer could walk away and talk with the rancher's neighbor instead. By contrast, when ranchers join wind associations, they become part of an organized, informed group. The coalition has the power and ability to negotiate with multiple developers over the lease of a much larger, and thus much more attractive, piece of land.

Coalitions bring several benefits to weak parties. First, when weak parties join a coalition, they avoid destructive competition with one another and, by pooling their resources, gain strength in negotiations with stronger parties. In addition, a coalition defuses a common adversary's ability to pit one weak party against another or to credibly threaten to walk away.

Coalitions can bring advantages to the party across the table as well. Susan Williams Sloan, who works for the American Wind Energy Association, a wind industry trade group, pointed out to NPR's Goss that wind associations offer developers a "one-stop shop." She also noted that landowners who belong to associations tend to be better informed about the issues at stake in their leasing negotiations. Although the developers may end up paying a higher per-acre lease price to an association than they would to individual ranchers, the developers typically prefer to work with landowners who understand their contracts, according to Sloan.

In sum, a coalition is likely to lead to a more efficient negotiation process that could benefit everyone involved, including consumers and other constituents who may be affected by the outcome.

Joining the Pack

When should you negotiate as a coalition rather than on your own? How can you ensure that your coalition functions productively? Here are three tips:

1. Recognize coalition opportunities   Coalitions are often a possibility when you're one of numerous weak parties facing one or more stronger parties. Coalitions can operate as large, highly structured, and long-term organizations, or they can be groups that unite informally around a single issue.

Your organization might try to temporarily coordinate sales tactics with those of your competitors if you believe clients are taking advantage of the market. For example, companies facing a profit-destroying e-auction could agree to insist on negotiation instead. Similarly, a small-business owner might sign on to a cooperative that negotiates collectively with insurance companies to lower the costs of providing health insurance to employees.

2. Weigh the pros and cons of joining a coalition   Before signing up with a coalition, take time to meet with your potential partners to discuss the potential benefits and costs of joining, advises Massachusetts Institute of Technology professor Lawrence Susskind. Don't tie yourself down to a coalition before you've asked and answered key questions such as these to your satisfaction:

- Is the coalition well organized to negotiate with the other side?
- How much will I have to pay, if anything, to join and remain a member of the coalition? What costs might we face down the road?
- Does the coalition have a good ethical reputation and a track record for success?
- Does the coalition understand the value of collaborative negotiation?
- What consequences might we face if a negotiation doesn't go well?
- Do the benefits of a successful deal outweigh these risks?
- If we succeed, how will the coalition allocate the value it creates?

Costly labor strikes, consumer boycotts, and long-term damage to members' reputations are a few of the hazards coalitions face when they limit themselves to competitive strategies and underestimate their counterparts' strength and tolerance. To prevent such pitfalls, avoid groups that rely on hardball negotiation tactics as a matter of course.

3. Manage group interactions   If you decide to form a new coalition on your own, Susskind advises you to collect relatively firm commitments from potential partners while retaining the flexibility to switch allegiance. As the group comes together, appoint or hire a manager to prepare an agenda. Then, working together, make time to establish your ground rules, assign research tasks, and summarize your conclusions. You also need a lead negotiator and, in the case of high-profile negotiations, a spokesperson to communicate your agenda to the outside world.

During the negotiation process itself, it's important to identify and address disagreements quickly and correct miscommunication away from the table, says Susskind. And when it comes time to make a decision, strive for unanimity but be willing to settle for near-complete agreement.

---

3 Truths for Potential Coalition Members

1. If a common adversary is pitting weak parties against each other, it may be time to form a coalition.
2. Coalitional bargaining can improve the quality of the offers you receive and make talks more efficient.
3. You'll likely be dissatisfied with a coalition if its agenda and philosophy clash with yours.

Building and Maintaining Coalitions and Allegiances throughout Negotiations

Lisa Bracken

Allegiances and coalitions can provide incredibly powerful leverage in negotiations. They are usually comprised of members with complimentary interests and, through their numbers, can collar the attentions of public officials and members of the media even when other efforts have failed to produce results. As helpful as they can be in negotiation, you'll want to be wary, however, of certain inherent aspects of coalition building and their maintenance that can become challenging under certain circumstances, and find ways of hedging against such occurrences. This article examines the dynamics of coalition building and offers tips on ways to start strong, stay strong, and position yourself in a manner which preserves your influence within an alliance.

Thinking of Building or Joining a Coalition? Consider These Six Essential Aspects First

In deciding whether to build, lead, or simply participate in a coalition, the following six considerations can help guide your decision-making process, clarify your position within the coalition, and manage the factors that drive coalition objectives.

1. Identify the Common Objective

Does there appear to be a compelling and therefore, driving force behind the coalition which can act to unify its components as it moves forward toward its collective goal? Do you share in this objective? Do you share in the means and methods to achieve it? These can be points of contention among participating members, so isolating these issues and providing potential solutions for them in the beginning can help assure long-range success.

2. Determine How Much Influence You Will Have within the Coalition

When your stake in the outcome of coalition objectives is high, you will want to exercise as much influence as possible, while participating in a cooperative manner and maintaining an objective perspective. This can be a difficult balancing act; yet, establishing yourself as a cornerstone whenever possible can make your participation in a coalition that much more valuable in negotiations. As a cornerstone, you will represent an anchoring and stabilizing presence within your coalition, and your participation will likely be consequential to any eventual outcome.

Source: "Building and Maintaining Coalitions and Allegiances throughout Negotiations," by Lisa Bracken, from *The Negotiator Magazine,* March 2006. Used with permission of the author.

3. Will You Lead the Charge, or Are Others Willing to Trumpet the Common Cause?

Even if you have built or lead the coalition, and even if you are a cornerstone presence, to make it an effective power you must participate as a member and encourage others to bring their ideas, concerns, actions, and resources to the process. This helps veil outside focus upon your involvement, which may be desirable in a high-profile situation. Further, mobilizing others behind a common ideal increases others' investment and participation in the group. To function effectively, coalitions must have real workers mobilized and active.

4. Will You Recognize if Other Participants Have Retreated Behind You?

By over-playing the role of cornerstone, you may fail to recognize when other members of the coalition have effectively edged you out or moved on without you. A failure to realize you are leading an army of one could be not only embarrassing but devastating to your negotiation position, and it's a development you definitely don't want to learn from your adversary. Although potentially fruitful time commitments, coalitions, nonetheless, require careful management to stay on target and remain effective.

5. How Will You Control the Communication of Information?

In all coalition meetings, it's wise to prepare for disclosed information to find its way into the media within 24 hours. If you have any information that is highly sensitive to public exposure, a coalition meeting is probably not the best place to disclose it. Determine initially what information is expected to be shared and judiciously manage it.

6. Appreciating the Coalition as a Fragile and Imperfect Design

Coalitions are by their natures bound only by a few mutual objectives, and because individuals possess many interests and complex motives, it can be difficult to predict when unity has begun to weaken. Never depend upon a coalition to sustain cohesion. They have a habit of disintegrating at precisely the most personally vulnerable moment. If you know this at the outset, you can better prepare for the eventuality.

When the Greater Good Ceases to Be Good for You Also . . . It's Time to Restructure Your Relationship

If you attempt to create or join a coalition, examine your reasons for doing so—and examine the motives of those who comprise the coalition. Unless other participants perceive they may be impacted equally by the results of coalition action, they are not necessarily truly aligned. Some, in fact, may find themselves believing they can benefit from your injustice, or aim to further their own cause rather than that of the alliance. This situation may be acceptable as long as the relationship matrix remains one of mutual benefit.

As a member of a coalition, I once grappled with the complexities of compromising my own interests in an effort to aid others. Seeing my obvious discomfort, a friend offered this profound advice: "Remember that their objectives can be very different than yours.

If it came down to choosing between your family's wellbeing or this group—who cannot even decide where to sit around the table, let alone what is really important—how civic-minded do you want to be?"

You need to ask yourself if you are willing to throw away whatever may make you whole for the benefit of those who may squander your gift for their own selfish objectives. Few people are willing to truly give something for nothing. If you are one of these, you are noble. But realize, you may fight the fight and, in the end, win something so elusive that others may neither appreciate nor benefit from those efforts. And worse, you may not even recognize your own victory.

Coalitions, therefore, require that you keep who and what you're fighting for front and center at all times. When the greater good ceases to be good for you also, or acts to compromise your objective, it's time to restructure your relationship.

Guard against the potential of allies shifting their internal allegiances in order to swing the balance of power in their own favor. This is one reason why learning a perceived ally's motive to join an allegiance is so important. Be wary, at all times, of coalition dynamics where there may exist the potential for a power cluster, particularly one that may come to outweigh or undermine your issue in the eyes of your adversary.

If you position yourself as a cornerstone—most easily achieved by possessing the greatest damage, organizing and managing the coalition, and bringing greater resources to bear including multiple sources of information—you will maintain greater influence over the vitality of the coalition. You will also, by design, bear the greatest risk. This places you in a position of being able to leverage the coalition to your advantage. Be mindful, however, that this advantage can quickly wane or altogether disappear within the mobile parameters that conceived it.

Be cautious of allying with those whose objectives are counter in the long or short run to yours. They will reflect upon you and could taint your adversary's perception of you or allow your adversary to capitalize on this perception by wrongly exposing or taking you out of context to the pubic.

Strengthening the Adhesion of a Coalition

Beyond the possession of a common goal, **there are four more important ways you can strengthen coalition adhesion:**

1. Try and Show Mutual Benefit through Both Short-Term as Well as Long-Term Goals

Progress towards the end goal needs to be regularly commemorated by acknowledging even small advancements in that direction. Member commitment to coalitions needs continual reinforcement and reassurance.

Members need to know, for example, why resources may be concentrated in such a manner that one member appears to benefit more than others. It is helpful at the outset to clarify the relative damages or gains and involvement of each member of the coalition, so that if resources appear unevenly distributed there is explanation for it and expectations are in line. These and other reasons can work in dynamic concert to jeopardize the cohesion of any coalition at any given time, leading to the possibility of an individual or a cluster of influential persons attempting to turn the tide in their favor, strike out independently, or form their own union.

A cost-sharing arrangement within a coalition may enable the group to retain attorneys and data-collection professionals otherwise beyond the capabilities of an individual. Even without cost-sharing abilities, a well-organized coalition committed to group objectives may encourage the interest of these experts on a contingency basis. Of course, this coveted advantage is not without risk. You will want a back-up plan in the event the coalition fails before a solution is accomplished and you find yourself holding a handful of bills and negotiating with your adversary on a one-on-one basis.

2. Communication Is an Important Element of Coalition Strength

Everyone should be thinking and behaving as a single unit. In order to achieve and help sustain this mindset, you will want to establish a network within which you can keep the coalition abreast of developments. Hosting regular meetings may be necessary—but know that convenient venues require careful security management.

If you find yourself, either by design or default, leading your coalition, be prepared to explain how developments may affect individual members and the group as a whole Unless your group is exclusive, well controlled, and practically sequestered, it will be virtually impossible to keep information quiet in such an environment, so there will be times you'll have to weigh individual interest against disclosure. Never rule out that an adversary representative may be positioned within the organization. Even if you trust the individuals within the group to handle information with care, they will probably feel likewise about others outside the group who may actually possess other, more self-serving motives. At times, you may benefit by turning this natural phenomenon to your favor when you'd perhaps like your adversary to be a little more aware of your future plans.

3. Demonstrate True Leadership

Effective leaders don't lead—they inspire others to follow. A coalition represents many of the challenges and advantages of a true democratic process. By maintaining objectivity in your opinions; encouraging individual participation; avoiding favoritism among members; presenting sound, balanced solutions together with credible information; participating in group solution-seeking; and soliciting resources useful to the group, you will increase your chances of winning and maintaining coalition favor through leading by example.

4. You Can Help Assure Your Own Success

Coalitions possess the potential for both risk and benefit. Before you construct or elect to participate in a coalition, devote time and attention to considering the coalition's innate instabilities, and account for the appropriate design and level of management required to sustain it. These advance measures can fortify an inherently fragile design, keep it strong and viable throughout your negotiations process, and provide a uniquely formidable lever in structuring your success.

The Surprising Benefits of Conflict in Negotiating Teams

In December 2008, incoming U.S. President Barack Obama created a stir by appointing Senator Hillary Clinton, his bitter opponent for the Democratic nomination, to be his secretary of state. Could Obama expect loyalty from someone he had traded barbs with for months? Would the risky choice be vindicated, or would it backfire?

Some compared Obama's choice to Abraham Lincoln's decision, following his hard-fought election in 1860, to appoint all three of his rivals for the Republican nomination to his cabinet. In her book *Team of Rivals: The Political Genius of Abraham Lincoln* (Simon & Schuster, 2005), Doris Kearns Goodwin maintains that Lincoln was largely able to inspire his former opponents to overcome their differences and rally around him. But in an op-ed piece in *The New York Times,* historian James Oakes argues that Lincoln was a successful president *despite* the "contentious, envious and often dysfunctional collection of prima donnas" in his cabinet, not because of them.

In the realm of negotiation, the question as to whether rivalries and differences of opinion harm or help teams is a critical one. Here we examine what negotiation research reveals about team harmony and cohesion.

The Pros and Cons of Teamwork

When a negotiation is a complex one that requires a broad set of knowledge, skills, and experience, gathering a team can be a smarter choice than trying to go it alone, according to Professor Elizabeth Mannix of Cornell University. Negotiation research supports the notion that teams are more effective than individuals in many situations. Yet without adequate coordination and planning, teams are unlikely to meet their full potential, and the results can be disappointing.

What determines whether team negotiations succeed or fail? In interviews with experienced team negotiators, Kristin Behfar (University of California, Irvine), Ray Friedman (Vanderbilt University), and Jeanne Brett (Northwestern University) found that the degree to which teams effectively meet their unique challenges with appropriate strategies depends on how well they manage their internal dynamics.

Notably, the researchers found that the *type* of disputes that occur within teams can have very different effects on performance. When teams face disagreements that center on substantive issues related to the negotiation task, such as those related to interests, priorities, and goals, the resolution of such conflicts can actually spur better outcomes.

Source: "The Surprising Benefits of Conflict in Negotiating Teams" from the *Program on Negotiation* newsletter at the Harvard Law School (www.pon.harvard.edu), February 2009, pp. 5–7. Used with permission.

By contrast, when conflicts get personal—deteriorating into bitter denunciations and criticism, for example—team performance may suffer.

How Your Team Can Thrive Amid Conflict

The following three suggestions can help you foster productive rather than debilitating conflict within your negotiating team:

1. Seek Familiarity, Not Friendship. In their research, Deborah Gruenfeld and Margaret Neale of Stanford University, Katherine Philips of Northwestern University, and Elizabeth Mannix found that team members who had not worked together before were unable to pool the information necessary to solve a problem. By contrast, teams of individuals who were familiar with one another easily pooled information and solved the same problem. Familiarity enables team members to share information and engage in the constructive conflict needed to find a solution, according to Mannix.

This doesn't mean that teams should be built around close friendships. On the contrary, because friendship networks tend to spring up based on similar interests and skills, teams of friends may lack the diversity of knowledge and experience that's needed to tackle a difficult negotiation. Thus, the best team may be one made up of people with diverse skills who have worked together before (and even clashed from time to time), rather than teams of close, like-minded individuals.

2. Discuss Differences in Advance. To prevent conflicts among diverse, strong-minded team members from overshadowing group goals, Mannix advises negotiation teams to spend at least twice as much time preparing for upcoming talks as they expect to spend at the table. Because the other side will be ready and willing to exploit any chinks in your team's armor, it's important to hash out your differences in advance.

Start by encouraging the team to brainstorm and debate the issues to be discussed during talks. Spend time debating goals, the team's best alternatives to the present agreement, and your reservation point—the worst outcome you, as a team, will accept. Then, spend just as much time exploring the other side's likely goals, background, alternatives, and reservation point. Having trouble coming to agreement on the facts? Teams sometimes resolve substantive differences by bringing in experts for guidance on areas of confusion, Behfar and colleagues found in their research.

What about personality conflicts? In the Behfar study, some negotiators described the particular problem of coping with highly confrontational or emotional group members. Teams that overcame this difficulty did so by practicing their negotiation script in advance with the goal of directing and controlling the behavior of volatile members. To avoid conveying weakness to the other side, rather than calling for a break at the first sign of trouble, some teams devised secret signals they could use to bring wayward members in line—for instance, someone might stretch out her arms to communicate to another member that he's getting off track.

3. Assign Roles and Responsibilities. Before negotiating, teams should also discuss how to take advantage of members' different skills, suggests Mannix. Which member has the best listening skills? This person could be put in charge of watching and reading members of the other team and reporting his observations to his own team during breaks. Which team member has the most negotiation experience? This person could be appointed the team leader—the chief decision maker who corrals the rest of the group. Who is the best communicator? The team spokesperson should be a calm, articulate individual who is willing to follow the leader and the teams negotiation plan.

In addition to brainstorming different scenarios that could occur at the table and role-playing how you will respond, your team should discuss the decision rules you will use when you confer privately to weigh the various offers on the table. Because unanimity can be difficult to achieve, you might opt for a majority-decision rule that allows most parties to get what they need from a deal.

By dividing up key responsibilities, debating differences of opinion before negotiating, and keeping talks respectful, your team will be in a strong position to capitalize on its differences. As for the Obama administration, can Hillary Clinton and other cabinet members look beyond their individual interests and negotiate effectively on behalf of the president and the American people? Stay tuned.

---

3 Guidelines for Teams Facing Negotiations

1.   When choosing teams, diversity of experience should trump friendship.

2.   Debate substantive differences and defuse personality issues.

3.   Assign roles, brainstorm possible scenarios, and choose a decision rule.

Individual Differences

Reading 4.1

Women Don't Ask
Linda Babcock
Sara Laschever

A few years ago, when Linda (one of the authors of this piece) was serving as the director of the PhD program at her school, a delegation of women graduate students came to her office. Many of the male graduate students were teaching courses of their own, the women explained, while most of the female graduate students had been assigned to work as teaching assistants to regular faculty. Linda agreed that this didn't sound fair, and that afternoon she asked the associate dean who handled teaching assignments about the women's complaint. She received a simple answer: "I try to find teaching opportunities for any student who approaches me with a good idea for a course, the ability to teach, and a reasonable offer about what it will cost," he explained. "More men ask. The women just don't ask."

The women just don't ask. This incident and the associate dean's explanation suggested to Linda the existence of a more pervasive problem. Could it be that women don't get more of the things they want in life in part because they don't think to ask for them? Are there external pressures that discourage women from asking as much as men do—and even keep them from realizing that they can ask? Are women really less likely than men to ask for what they want?

To explore this question, Linda conducted a study that looked at the starting salaries of students graduating from Carnegie Mellon University with their master's degrees.[1] When Linda looked exclusively at gender, the difference was fairly large: The starting salaries of the men were 7.6 percent or almost $4,000 higher on average than those of the women. Trying to explain this difference, Linda looked next at who had negotiated his or her salary (who had asked for more money) and who had simply accepted the initial offer he or she had received. It turned out that only 7 percent of the female students had negotiated but 57 percent (eight times as many) of the men had asked for more money. Linda was particularly surprised to find such a dramatic difference between men and women at Carnegie Mellon because graduating students are strongly advised by the school's Career Services department to negotiate their job offers. Nonetheless, hardly any of the women had done so. The most striking finding,

Source: "Women Don't Ask," by Linda Babcock and Sara Laschever, from *Women Don't Ask: Negotiation and the Gender Divide,* 2003, pp.1–16 Princeton, NJ: Princeton University Press. Used with permission.

however, was that the students who had negotiated (most of them men) were able to increase their starting salaries by 7.4 percent on average, or $4,053—almost exactly the difference between men's and women's average starting pay. This suggests that the salary differences between the men and the women might have been eliminated if the women had negotiated their offers.

Spurred on by this finding, Linda and two colleagues, Deborah Small and Michele Gelfand, designed another study to look at the propensity of men and women to ask for more than they are offered.[2] They recruited students at Carnegie Mellon for an experiment and told them that they would be paid between $3 and $10 for playing Boggle™, a game by Milton Bradley. In *Boggle,* players shake a cube of tile letters until all the letters fall into a grid at the bottom of the cube. They must then identify words that can be formed from the letters vertically, horizontally, or diagonally. Each research subject was asked to play four rounds of the game, and then an experimenter handed him or her $3 and said, "Here's $3. Is $3 okay?" If a subject asked for more money, the experimenters would pay that participant $10, but they would not give anyone more money if he or she just complained about the compensation (an indirect method of asking). The results were striking— almost *nine times* as many male as female subjects asked for more money.[3] Both male and female subjects rated how well they'd played the game about equally, meaning that women didn't feel they should be paid less or should accept less because they'd played poorly. There were also no gender differences in how much men and women complained about the compensation (there was plenty of complaining all around). The significant factor seemed to be that for men, unhappiness with what they were offered was more likely to make them try to fix their unhappiness—by asking for more.

In a much larger study, Linda, Michele Gelfand, Deborah Small, and another colleague, Heidi Stayn, conducted a survey of several hundred people with access to the Internet (subjects were paid $10 to log on to a website and answer a series of questions).[4] The survey asked respondents about the most recent negotiations they'd attempted or initiated (as opposed to negotiations they'd participated in that had been prompted or initiated by others). For the men, the most recent negotiation they'd initiated themselves had occurred two weeks earlier on average, while for the women the most recent negotiation they'd initiated had occurred a full month before. Averages for the second most recent negotiations attempted or initiated were about 7 weeks earlier for men and 24 weeks earlier for women.

These results suggest that men are asking for things they want and initiating negotiations much more often than women—two to three times as often.[5] Linda and her colleagues wanted to be sure that this discrepancy was not produced simply by memory lapses, however, so the survey also asked people about the *next* negotiation they planned to initiate. In keeping with the earlier findings, the negotiations planned by the women were much further in the future than those being planned by the men—one month ahead for the women but only one week ahead for the men. This means that men may be initiating *four* times as many negotiations as women. The sheer magnitude of this difference is dramatic, especially since respondents to the survey included people of all ages, from a wide range of professions, and with varied levels of education. It confirms that men really do take a more active approach than women to getting what they want by asking for it.

The more than 100 interviews we conducted—with men and women from a range of professions (including full-time mothers) and from Britain and Europe as well as the United States—supported these findings.[6] When asked to identify the last negotiation in which they had participated, the majority of the women we talked to named an event several months in the past and described a recognized type of structured negotiation, such as buying a car. (The exceptions were women with small children, who uniformly said, "I negotiate with my kids all the time.") The majority of the men described an event that had occurred within the preceding week, and frequently identified more informal transactions, such as negotiating with a spouse over who would take the kids to soccer practice, with a boss to pay for a larger-size rental car because of a strained back, or with a colleague about which parts of a joint project each team member would undertake. Men were also more likely to mention more ambiguous situations—situations that could be construed as negotiations but might not be by many people. For the most part, the men we talked to saw negotiation as a bigger part of their lives and a more common event than the women did.

One particularly striking aspect of our findings was how they broke down by age. The changes brought about by the women's movement over the last 40 years had led us to expect greater differences between older men and women than between their younger counterparts. And indeed when we discussed the ideas with younger women they often suggested that the problems we were studying were "boomer" problems, afflicting older women but not themselves. To our surprise, however, when we looked exclusively at respondents to the Web survey who were in their twenties and early thirties, the gender differences in how often they initiated negotiations were similar to or slightly *larger* than the differences in older cohorts (with men attempting many more negotiations than women).[7] In addition, both the starting salary study and the *Boggle* study used subjects who were in their twenties. This persuaded us that the tendency among women to accept what they're offered and not ask for more is far from just a "boomer" problem.

The Asking Advantage

But just because women don't ask for things as often as men do, is that necessarily a problem? Perhaps directly negotiating for advantage—asking for what you want—is a male strategy, and women simply employ other equally effective strategies to get what they want. This is an important point, but only partly accurate. Women often worry more than men about the impact their actions will have on their relationships. This can prompt them to change their behavior to protect personal connections, sometimes by asking for things indirectly, sometimes by asking for less than they really want, and sometimes simply by trying to be more deserving of what they want (say, by working harder) so they'll be given what they want without asking. Women also frequently take a more collaborative approach to problem solving than men take, trying to find solutions that benefit both parties or trying to align their own requests with shared goals. In many situations, women's methods can be superior to those typically employed by men. Unfortunately, however, in our largely male-defined work culture, women's strategies can often be misinterpreted and can leave them operating from a position of weakness. And in many cases, the only way to get something is to ask for it directly.

So let's look at the importance of asking.

First, consider the situation of the graduating students at Carnegie Mellon, in which eight times as many men as women negotiated their starting salaries. The women who did not negotiate started out not just behind their male peers, but behind where they could and should have been. With every future raise predicated on this starting point, they could be paying for this error for a long time—perhaps for the rest of their careers.

Liliane, now 46, is an electrical engineer and a successful software designer in New England's competitive high-tech industry. Although she earned excellent grades in college, she was so insecure when she started out in her field that she felt she didn't even deserve to be interviewed for an engineering job—she was only "faking it." Despite her doubts, she quickly received an offer from a highly regarded company. When the company's personnel manager asked her what kind of salary she was looking for, she said, "I don't care what you pay me as long as you give me a job." A big smile spread across the personnel manager's face, she remembers. She later learned that he gave her the absolute bottom of the range for her position, which was 10 to 20 percent less than her peers were earning. It took her 10 years to fix this inequity, and she only did so, finally, by changing jobs.

Quantifying—in terms of dollars and cents—the loss to Liliane and women like her from not negotiating their salaries produces sobering results. Take the following example. Suppose that at age 22 an equally qualified man and woman receive job offers for $25,000 a year. The man negotiates and gets his offer raised to $30,000. The woman does not negotiate and accepts the job for $25,000. Even if each of them receives identical 3 percent raises every year throughout their careers (which is unlikely, given their different propensity to negotiate and other research showing that women's achievements tend to be under-valued), by the time they reach age 60 the gap between their salaries will have widened to more than $15,000 a year, with the man earning $92,243 and the woman only $76,870. While that may not seem like an enormous spread, remember that the man will have been making more all along, with his extra earnings over the 38 years totaling $361,171. If the man had simply banked the difference every year in a savings account earning 3 percent interest, by age 60 he would have $568,834 more than the woman—enough to underwrite a comfortable retirement nest egg, purchase a second home, or pay for the college education of a few children. This is an enormous "return on investment" for a *one-time* negotiation. It can mean a higher standard of living throughout one's working years, financial security in old age, or a top-flight education for one's kids.

The impact of neglecting to negotiate in this one instance—when starting a new job—is so substantial and difficult to overcome that some researchers who study the persistence of the wage gap between men and women speculate that much of the disparity can be traced to differences in entering salaries rather than differences in raises.[8]

Another estimate of a woman's potential lost earnings from not negotiating appears in the book *Get Paid What You're Worth* by two professors of management, Robin L. Pinkley and Gregory B. Northcraft. They estimate that a woman who routinely negotiates her salary increases will earn over $1 million more by the time she retires than a woman who accepts what she's offered every time without asking for more. And that figure doesn't include the interest on the extra amount earned.[9] Even in such a small matter as the *Boggle* experiment, the gains to asking were great. Everyone who asked for more money received $10, more than three times as much as those who didn't ask and received only $3.

We all know that few employers will pay us any more than they need to. They're prepared to spend extra to get an applicant they want, but happy to pay less if they can. Assuming applicants will negotiate, they routinely offer less than they're able to pay.[10] But if we fail to ask for more, it's a rare employer who will insist that we're not being paid enough. A recent study shows that this is true even at institutions with a committed policy against discriminating between men and women. This study describes a man and a woman with equivalent credentials who were offered assistant professorships by the same large university. Shortly after the two were hired, a male administrator noticed that the man's salary was significantly higher than the woman's. Looking into it, he learned that both were offered the same starting salary. The man negotiated for more, but the woman accepted what she was offered. Satisfied, the administrator let the matter drop. He didn't try to adjust the discrepancy or alert the female professor to her mistake. The university was saving money and enjoying the benefits of a talented woman's hard work and expertise. He didn't see the long-term damage to his institution and to society from not correcting such inequities, and she didn't know how much she had sacrificed by not negotiating the offer she'd received.[11]

More than Money

The penalties for not negotiating extend far beyond the merely monetary, too. As Pinkley and Northcraft demonstrate,

> Applicants with identical experience and performance records but different salary histories are rated differently by employers. If your compensation record is better than others, employers will assume that your performance is better too. . . . Accepting less will imply that you have less value than other new hires.[12]

In many cases, employers actually respect candidates more for pushing to get paid what they're worth. This means that women don't merely sacrifice additional income when they don't push to be paid more, they may sacrifice some of their employers' regard too. The experience of Hope, a business school professor, tells this story clearly. When she completed graduate school, Hope was offered a job at a prestigious management consulting firm. Not wanting to "start off on the wrong foot," she accepted the firm's initial salary offer without asking for more. Although she feared that negotiating her salary would damage her new bosses' impression of her, the opposite occurred: She later learned that her failure to negotiate almost convinced the senior management team that they'd made a mistake in hiring her.

Similarly, Ellen, 44, a senior partner at a large law firm, was checking the references of an experienced paralegal named Lucy whom she wanted to hire. One of Lucy's former supervisors described a long list of Lucy's strengths and recommended her highly. But when Ellen asked about Lucy's weaknesses, the supervisor said that Lucy could be more assertive. Ellen asked if she meant Lucy needed to be more assertive on behalf of the firm's clients. The supervisor said no, Lucy was terrific at tracking down any information that could benefit a client's case. What she meant, the supervisor explained, was that Lucy needed to be more assertive on her own behalf. "She could be a lot more assertive when it comes to her own professional needs and rewards," the woman explained. This supervisor felt that not asking for more on her own behalf was a professional weakness in Lucy—and a serious enough weakness that she mentioned it when providing an otherwise glowing reference.

Women also make sacrifices in their personal lives by not asking for what they need more of the time. Miriam, 46, an architect, is also married to an architect. But whereas her husband works for an internationally known firm and travels regularly for his job, Miriam works for herself. And because they have two children, she restricts herself to residential projects in her home state. When her children were small, her husband was out of town two to five days a week, and she was taking care of the children pretty much by herself. Although she enjoyed a lot of artistic freedom in her work and built up a successful practice constructing $2–3 million houses (houses that won awards and were featured in design magazines), the demands of her family life felt crushing. "I just felt like this is the way that life is for me and there is not anything that I can do about this." Now she wonders "if there would have been ways of asking for more help" instead of "working and working until I fell apart." The problem was that "asking didn't really seem like a possibility, but I'm sure that it was."

Missing the Chance

Besides not realizing that asking is possible, many women avoid negotiating even in situations in which they know that negotiation is appropriate and expected (like the female students in the starting salary study). In another one of Linda's studies, 20 percent of the women polled said that they never negotiate at all.[13] Although this seems unlikely (perhaps these women think of their negotiations as something else, such as "problem-solving" or "compromising" or even "going along to get along"), their statement conveys a strong antipathy toward negotiating among a huge number of women. (In the United States alone, 20 percent of the female adult population equals 22 million people.)

That many women feel uncomfortable using negotiation to advance their interests—and feel more uncomfortable on average than men—was confirmed by a section of Linda's Internet survey. This part of the survey asked respondents to consider various scenarios and indicate whether they thought negotiation would be appropriate in the situations described. In situations in which they thought negotiation was appropriate, respondents were also asked to report how likely they would be to negotiate in that situation. Particularly around work scenarios, such as thinking they were due for a promotion or a salary increase, women as a group were less likely to try to negotiate than men—even though they recognized that negotiation was appropriate and probably even necessary.[14]

These findings are momentous because until now research on negotiation has mostly ignored the issue of when and why people attempt to negotiate, focusing instead on tactics that are successful once a negotiation is under way—what kinds of offers to make, when to concede, and which strategies are most effective in different types of negotiations.[15] With few exceptions, researchers have ignored the crucial fact that the most important step in any negotiation process must be deciding to negotiate in the first place.[16] Asking for what you want is the essential first step that "kicks off" a negotiation. If you miss your chance to negotiate, the best negotiation advice in the world isn't going to help you much. And women simply aren't "asking" at the same rate as men.

Endnotes

1. Babcock 2002.

2. Small, Babcock, and Gelfand 2003.

3. Only 2.5 percent of the female subjects but 23 percent of the male subjects asked for more.

4. Babcock, Gelfand, Small, and Stayn 2002. The survey was hosted by Jonathan Baron's website at the University of Pennsylvania.

5. Another interpretation is possible, however. Men may not really be doing more negotiating than women; men and women may behave in the same ways but label or describe their behavior differently. That is, what a man calls a negotiation, a woman calls something else. This interpretation seems less plausible because it suggests that men and women define a common word in our language differently. But even if it is true, it still has implications for behavior. If women aren't calling their interactions negotiations and men are, women may not be viewing those encounters as strategically and instrumentally as men do and may therefore gain less from them in significant ways.

6. Although we strove to make our sample as representative as possible of the full diversity of women in Western culture, we use the interviews only to illustrate the ideas in the book and did not try to ensure that our sample exactly matched current demographic patterns in the population. We also interviewed far more women than men.

7. Babcock, Gelfand, Small, and Stayn 2002.

8. Gerhart 1990.

9. Pinkley and Northcraft 2000. Example is from page 6.

10. Ibid.

11. Janoff-Bulman and Wade 1996.

12. Pinkley and Northcraft 2000. Quotation is from page 6.

13. Babcock, Gelfand, Small, and Stayn 2002.

14. Ibid.

15. For good texts that summarize negotiation research, see Thompson 1998; Raiffa 1982; Lewicki, Saunders, and Minton 1997; Neale and Bazerman 1991.

16. Janoff-Bulman and Wade 1996; Gerhart and Rynes 1991; Kaman and Hartel 1994.

References

Babcock, L. 2002. Do graduate students negotiate their job offers? Carnegie Mellon University. Unpublished report.

Babcock, L., M. Gelfand, D. Small, and H. Stayn. 2002. Propensity to initiate negotiations: A new look at gender variation in negotiation behavior. Carnegie Mellon University. Unpublished manuscript.

Gerhart, B. 1990. Gender differences in current and starting salaries: The role of performance, college major, and job title. *Industrial and Labor Relations Review* 43(4):418–433.

Gerhart, B., and S. Rynes. 1991. Determinants and consequences of salary negotiations by male and female MBA graduates. *Journal of Applied Psychology* 76:256–262.

Janoff-Bulman, R., and M. B. Wade. 1996. The dilemma of self-advocacy for women: Another case of blaming the victim? *Journal of Social and Clinical Psychology* 15(2):143–152.

Kaman, V. S., and C. E. Hartel. 1994. Gender differences in anticipated pay negotiation strategies and outcomes. *Journal of Business and Psychology* 9(2):183–197.

Lewicki, R., D. Saunders, and J. Minton. 1997. *Essentials of negotiation.* Boston: McGraw-Hill/Irwin.

Neale, M. A., and M. H. Bazerman. 1991. *Cognition and rationality in negotiation.* New York: Free Press.

Pinkley, R. L., and G. B. Northcraft. 2000. *Get paid what you're worth.* New York: St. Martin's Press.

Raiffa, H. 1982. *The art and science of negotiation.* Cambridge, MA: Harvard University Press.

Small, D., L. Babcock, and M. Gelfand. 2003. Why don't women ask? Carnegie Mellon University. Unpublished manuscript.

Thompson, L. 1998. *The mind and heart of the negotiator.* Upper Saddle River, NJ: Prentice Hall.

Become a Master Negotiator

Michael Benoliel
Linda Cashdan

"How many of you consider yourselves effective negotiators?" I often ask students and managers at the beginning of my negotiation courses. Most of them raise their hands. It is not surprising. Untrained negotiators often have an overblown sense of their own capabilities because they have a misconception of what it takes to be a master negotiator. They are trapped in a self-serving illusion of competency because they believe that the ability to negotiate is a "natural skill" you are either born with or without. In fact, negotiating is an acquired competency that requires both training and a complex set of intelligences, attitudes, and skills.

Negotiators' Intelligence

In Western society, which is dominated by science and technology, cognitive intelligence has long been elevated to a supreme status. Achievement tests developed during the twentieth century used a formula based on the ratio between a person's age and his mental capabilities (based on his test answers) to determine that person's "intelligence quotient" (IQ). Schools use the IQ measures for student placements, and the military uses them to classify soldiers into different roles.

A negotiator must have cognitive intelligence to comprehend complex ideas, to reason based on facts, to plan a course of action, to solve problems, and to make rational decisions. Some researchers have argued that cognitive intelligence can play a decisive role in complex negotiations with multiple parties that are extended over a long period of time. Moreover, by having cognitive abilities and negotiating rationally, negotiators are more likely to avoid costly psychological traps, like an irrational commitment to escalation (pursuing a failing course of action) or basing a judgment on irrelevant information.

Effective negotiators use their cognitive abilities to master the substance—the issues—of the negotiation, plan well in advance, and develop a sound negotiating strategy. They often deal with a vast amount of information, which has to be analyzed and synthesized, and which makes the negotiating task both intellectually challenging and satisfying.

Eric Benhamou, the former CEO of Palm and 3Com, likes to negotiate because, he says, it enables him to plan systematically, assess goals in advance, and build the kind of convincing arguments that will make his case. Former U.S. Trade Representative Charlene Barshefsky is also a rational negotiator. As a trained lawyer, she values advanced preparation, mastery of the substance, and developing convincing and winning arguments.

Source: "Become a Master Negotiator," by Michael Benoliel with Linda Cashdan, from *Done Deal: Insights from Interviews with the World's Best Negotiators,* 2005, Chapter XI, pp. 217–238. Avon, MA: Platinum Press, an Imprint of Adams Media. Used with permission.

Emotional Intelligence

Cognitive abilities are necessary in negotiating, but not sufficient. To negotiate effectively, you must also possess emotional intelligence. Studies on the effect of emotions in negotiations show that negotiators in a positive mood process information more effectively, are more creative, and thus are more innovative in solving problems. In addition, positive emotions make the parties less contentious and more optimistic about the future, which, in turn, increases the chances they will search for multiple alternatives and find a better integrative—win–win—agreement.

In his book *Emotional Intelligence* (1995), Daniel Goleman popularized the concept of multiple intelligences and defined emotional intelligence as "the extent to which a person is attuned to his or her own feelings and to the feelings of others." Emotional intelligence consists of self-awareness, self-regulation, self-motivation, patience, and empathy—each of which is a characteristic that a successful negotiator must possess.

Self-Awareness

Self-awareness means being cognizant of your own thoughts, moods, impulses, and behavior, how they affect you, and how they may affect the people with whom you are negotiating. As the chairman of the peace talks in Northern Ireland in 1996, former Senate Majority Leader George Mitchell demonstrated this ability. After meeting for a year and a half, and listening for hundreds and hundreds of hours to the same arguments, he looked inward and reflected upon his feelings. "I felt frustrated and angry," he wrote. "I worked hard not to let my anger show. . . . I was very angry and considered letting it all out," he continued, because he thought "[p]erhaps an emotional outburst would shock them all out." But, Mitchell concluded, "It was too late. Nothing I said now could produce an agreement . . . I had to look to the future. . . . Once again, I would have to be upbeat."

Self-Regulation

The importance of restraining and regulating emotions in negotiations was recognized centuries ago. "A man who is naturally violent and easily carried away is ill fitted for the conduct of negotiation," French diplomat François de Callières wrote in his 1716 book *On the Manner of Negotiation with Princes*.

Self-regulation is not about masking all feelings; it is about channeling emotions into behavior that is appropriate to the situation. It is about mastering emotions so that you can repress extreme anger when it is important to do so, and let it fly when it is an equally strategic move.

Unskilled negotiators tend to negotiate combatively, driven by their emotions. Harvard University professor Jay O. Light often hears such negotiators say, "If the other guy thinks he can get the best of me, he has another thing coming. When it comes to negotiating, I'm not one to mess around with. The other guy will learn soon enough I don't crack easily and that when I want something, I get it."

Former Secretary of State James Baker recounts how his negotiations with Hafez al-Assad, president of Syria, were grueling, protracted, exasperating, and often emotional.

But, in most cases, Baker was able to monitor and regulate his strong emotions. Baker, furious in one session, when Assad suddenly reopened issues for negotiation that he had already assured Baker were a done deal, consciously modulated his irritation, and referred to Assad's calculated reversal as a misunderstanding.

But, at the same time, when Baker felt a display of emotion might advance the negotiating agenda, he exploded. In the midst of one particularly frustrating session with Assad, which had lasted nine hours and forty-five minutes without a break, Baker intentionally slammed his briefcase shut with force and let the Syrian leader know how angry he was.

Baker's rare theatrical drama was the result of emotional exhaustion brought on by a long and frustrating effort to get a done deal. In this instance, Baker used the drama to send a signal as to how far the other side could push him. The action was especially effective because it was so out of character.

Self-Motivation

Self-motivation is the quality that enables you to pursue your goals with persistence and energy in the face of difficulties and frustrations, and to focus like a laser beam on what you want to achieve.

Studies on Olympic athletes, world-class musicians, and chess grand masters show that they all share a common trait—the ability to push themselves and to rise above difficulties and disappointments.

Many point to President Jimmy Carter's self-motivation as the central force of the extraordinary success of the 1978 Camp David Summit between Israel and Egypt, which resulted in the historical peace accord. President Carter not only displayed command of the substantive issues and impressive social skills during the two weeks of the summit; he also had stamina. In one of the most intense negotiations between Prime Minister Menachem Begin of Israel and President Anwar el-Sadat of Egypt, Carter's faith, optimism, and dogged determination pushed him to creatively find compromises where others might have willingly relented.

Self-motivation may be difficult to maintain in high-stakes negotiations, especially between parties who have been involved in a decades-long protracted and violent conflict. But Shimon Peres, former prime minister of Israel, says having seen wars and peace between Egypt, Jordan, and Israel has taught him that what was an impossibility yesterday is a possibility today. "I am an optimist," he says, "and when I get a 'no' as an answer, I am not angry. I don't lose my patience. I don't lose my persistence."

Patience

Indeed, *patience* may be a key to maintaining self-motivation. Wide gaps between parties take time to resolve. In labor-management negotiations, the give and take can be protracted and the desired goal may take a long time. As AFL–CIO Secretary-Treasurer Richard Trumka says, "You just keep working your way through that." It is the virtue of patience that propels you. "If you expect to come and have everything fall into place in two hours and then go to dinner," Trumka says, "then probably you are not suited to be a negotiator. Sometimes it takes weeks, sometimes longer—months and years."

It took, for example, 14 years to negotiate the Panama Canal treaty. It took two years and 575 meetings to negotiate an end to the Korean War. The direct Israeli-Palestinian negotiations have been going on and off since 1993, so far without a satisfactory resolution.

"You can't go into negotiations and expect a very rapid resolution of differences," former President Gerald Ford said. "The differences are often very valid. They require gradual movement."

Empathy

Empathy is the fifth component of emotional intelligence. It is built on self-awareness, and is about understanding the feelings of others and taking their views into account in formulating trade-offs and offers. It is the ability to read emotions through verbal messages and nonverbal cues like tone of voice, gestures, and facial expressions.

Palestinian Chief Negotiator Sa'eb Erekat believes respect is a stepping stone to empathy. "Respect the other side," he advises. "Don't ever undermine his or her concerns. Try to understand his or her point of view, whether you agree or disagree with it. Try to feel what the other side is feeling."

It is the custom each year in Israel on Holocaust Memorial Day that an evening siren sounds all over the country for two minutes, and all activities come to a halt. Traffic stops, and people stand silent. Erekat has lived under Israeli occupation for more than 36 years, since he was a boy of 12. Nonetheless, he says, when he was negotiating with the Israelis in Tel Aviv one Holocaust Memorial Day and the siren went off, he stood up silently beside the Israeli negotiators.

The dimensions of emotional intelligence—self-awareness, self-regulation, self-motivation, patience, and empathy—are all necessary and important qualities for managing emotions—yours and the other side's.

Interpersonal Intelligence

In his influential 1983 book, *Frames of Mind,* Howard Gardner challenged the importance of the IQ test and suggested instead that individuals possess a wide spectrum of intelligences. These include the spatial intelligence of artists and architects; the kinesthetic intelligence of dancers and athletes; the musical intelligence of composers, musicians, and singers; and the interpersonal intelligence of successful diplomats, salespeople, lawyers, mediators, and teachers.

Interpersonal intelligence—or social intelligence—is the ability to understand other people, what motivates them, and how to work cooperatively with them. Socially intelligent negotiators know how to build relationships, are good listeners, and enjoy interactions. They also tend to be good at organizing groups—coordinating activities, and leading them. They excel in finding mutually acceptable solutions. They are social analysts—perceptive, attentive, and able to detect what motivates people and what their concerns are.

Triple Competency

You must possess cognitive, emotional, and interpersonal intelligences in order to develop the triple competency that is essential for a master negotiator. Among the many important skills a negotiator needs to develop in order to be effective are three paramount negotiating capabilities: mastering the substance, building relationships and trust, and managing the negotiation process.

Cognitive intelligence is central to being able to master the substance and the issues, and emotional and interpersonal intelligences are central to being able to build relationships and trust. Managing the negotiation process requires a combination of all three of these intelligences.

The triple competency negotiation model is, in contrast to other models, a dynamic model because it includes a time dimension. The behaviors of effective negotiators and the decisions they make are always in the context of time. You may, for example, enter a negotiation knowing that if it doesn't work you have an attractive alternative deal waiting in the wings—a BATNA (best alternative to a negotiated agreement). But while you are negotiating, the party waiting in the wings may fly away.

The emphasis as to which of the triple competencies is most important varies as negotiators move from one negotiation stage to another. In the prenegotiation phase, negotiators focus mostly on research and preparation—mastery of the substance—and not on building relationships with their counterparts. At this stage not much is invested in managing the process as it has not begun, except in preliminary moves to design the architecture of the negotiations (planning the sequencing of issues, designing teams, etc.), which could determine how the process will take place.

As the negotiation begins, the focus shifts from substance mastery to building relationships and managing the process. As negotiators build strong relationships and trust gradually increases, there is a tendency to focus less on substantive research because the parties may be willing to accept more of what their now-trusted counterparts say at face value. The focus here shifts more and more to managing the process.

The implication of the triple competency negotiation model is that negotiators have to use their multiple intelligences to operate effectively and simultaneously in the three areas.

Essential Qualities of Master Negotiators

In addition to the triple competencies—mastering the substance, building relationships and trust, and managing the process—there are other important qualities for effective negotiation.

Harmony

Unskilled negotiators focus exclusively on their self-interests and needs. Master negotiators, in contrast, see the situation through multiple perspectives, incorporating both their own interests and others' interests into their negotiation behavior.

That's because the secret of negotiation, as François de Callières wrote in 1716, is "to harmonize the interests of the parties concerned"—to create reciprocal advantage, where both parties benefit. An agreement not advantageous to both sides, Callières warned, will contain the seeds of its own dissolution.

In order to create reciprocal advantage, you have to know what you want to accomplish, says Christie Hefner, CEO of Playboy Enterprises. "But an equally clear perspective," she points out, "should be on the concerns and needs of the other side. What I am always trying to do is sense things from the other side's perspective."

It doesn't mean you agree with "others." Rather, it means that you develop the ability to look at the world through their eyes and not just your own, because only then can you figure out a way to harmonize their interests with your own.

Pragmatism

In March of 1995, when sports agent Leigh Steinberg negotiated Drew Bledsoe's multi-year contract for the first time with Bob Kraft, the owner of the New England Patriots, Kraft proposed $29 million over seven years. Steinberg immediately countered with $51 million. Kraft, disappointed and angry, shook his head, then got up and left the chaotic lobby of the Arizona Biltmore Hotel in Phoenix, where the NFL was holding its annual meeting. Bledsoe doesn't want to do anything with my team, Kraft told himself. He wants to be a free agent.

It would take six months for Steinberg to call Kraft and invite him for dinner at an Italian restaurant near the waterfront in Boston where they could negotiate quietly. Aware of how emotionally charged the case was, Steinberg let Kraft vent his anger and frustration and assured him that Bledsoe would prefer to stay with the Patriots. Leaving was not an issue, Steinberg assured Kraft.

After a conversation that lasted well past midnight, they made a deal. The next morning they met again to refine the deal—a seven-year $42 million package that included an $11.5 million signing bonus, the largest in the league's history.

It was a successful resolution because Steinberg focused on the goal rather than his ego and was pragmatic about how to achieve it. "My clients," he says, "have a short career span, especially if they get injured. So I cannot allow anything to impact my clients' careers."

Effective negotiators set high but realistic goals. They are motivated by practical considerations and do not let themselves become entangled in abstract ideological principles. When necessary, they negotiate with villains. In the early and mid-1990s, Ambassador Richard Holbrooke dealt with Balkan leaders, whom he described as thugs and murderers.

Yitzhak Rabin, the late prime minister of Israel, used a pragmatic business model and "did business" in 1993 with Yasir Arafat, someone he had previously called a terrorist and murderer. Arafat was the only leader, Rabin believed, who could deliver on his promises. A matter of calculated national interest prompted Rabin to disconnect from his feelings.

Innovation

Effective negotiators are creative and flexible, says Eric Benhamou, former CEO of Palm and 3Com, especially when it appears that the parties are deadlocked. Then they come up with creative ideas to unlock the deadlock. This kind of negotiation, he says, "leaves you with the most satisfaction. Just when you thought you were headed to a brick wall, toward a no-deal, some other angle is revealed, and you find a way to accomplish your objectives and also meet the objectives of the other side without giving up much."

Creative ability is learned. Creative negotiators must have the courage to defy the crowd and think differently, and the perseverance to try a new course in the face of obstacles. "When it comes to a creative negotiator," says Leigh Steinberg, "there is a fellow named Carmen A. Policy, the president and CEO of the Cleveland Browns [football team] who has a critical quality—resilience. He has the ability to come back from the most frustrating negotiation situation, which seems completely inexplicable, so contorted that there is no way that it will ever be resolved. And yet, he comes back with a fresh approach to fight another day."

Creative solutions arise from thinking "outside of the box," when negotiators are fully attached (immersed in what is going on), yet capable of detaching themselves from the existing order, and flexible enough to open up to new information and ideas and adopt them.

Creativity is a skill as well as a mindset. There are three types of negotiating creativity. One is modifying something that exists—changing a proposal or expanding on an option. The second is combining something by putting together two previously unrelated proposals or options into one (bundling unrelated issues into one set). The third type of creativity is coming up with something completely new, thinking up a new option or a new trade-off, or redefining (reframing) an issue from a completely new angle.

Creativity is a function of professional conditioning. Lawyers, for example, are trained to be advocates and therefore tend to subscribe to the combative, win/lose approach of the legal system. Their adoption of the adversarial style, instead of a repertoire of styles—competition, cooperation, and competition-cooperation—inhibits creativity. Research and development scientists, on the other hand, are conditioned to explore multiple ways of tackling a subject. Experimentation and collaboration are the ingredients of their creativity and technological and scientific innovations.

Creativity, it has been suggested, can be learned by using relaxation techniques like meditation, listening to music, or taking walks in the park. It can be fostered also by "working out" your mind using (individual and collective) brainstorming techniques.

Be a Visionary

Negotiators create the future. Whether they resolve a protracted conflict or negotiate a successful business deal, they create a new and hopefully better reality.

The visionary negotiator has an idealized goal that proposes something better than the status quo. Negotiators like Shimon Peres in politics and Sumner Redstone in business, will tell you that they are optimists. They believe in a better future—either political or economic—and know how to articulate it and sell it. Furthermore, their vision is not an abstract idea but an agenda for action to which they are wholeheartedly committed—trying to build conflict-free societies, or a prosperous business enterprise.

As visionaries, negotiators are risk takers, not gamblers. They are first-movers, seeing possibilities others don't see. Yet, they are also realistic—connected to their reality but not trapped by it.

Be a Strategist

Effective negotiators always have a strategy that is tailored to the specific case they are negotiating. They know that what worked successfully in one case may not always work in other cases. As former Zenith Corporation Chairman Jerry Pearlman points out, every case is different: "Someone who has successfully negotiated three mergers might make a mess of the fourth."

Summary

Negotiation mastery may be inborn for some, but for most it is a learned and practiced skill. Effective negotiators are endowed with multiple intelligences—cognitive, emotional, and social—and use them to various degrees before, during, and after the negotiation.

Those multiple intelligences are the foundations on which negotiation competencies are built. Your core competency is the "triple competency" (mastery of the substance, building relationships, and managing the process), which enables you to harmonize the interests of the parties involved, approach the negotiation pragmatically as a problem-solving venture, innovate, create a vision as to where and how the negotiation should end, and develop a planned, yet flexible, strategy. To become a master negotiator, you must stay flexible and attentive enough to operate in several arenas at the same time. You must build and maintain the vision in your mind of how things will be at the end of the successful negotiation.

Negotiating is a stressful, time consuming, sometimes frustrating, often exhausting process. Ambassador Dennis Ross vividly recalls one week during the Hebron negotiations in 1997 when he negotiated all night, every night for six nights in a row. "We would end about seven in the morning," he says. "I'd go back to the hotel, take a shower, take a nap, and then go back to work."

But Ross and other master negotiators will readily tell you negotiating is also an exciting, energizing, unusually satisfying mental activity. Many enjoy the process itself—not just completing the deal. James Baker loves "interacting with other human beings at a very high intellectual level." Scott Smith, president and publisher of the *Chicago Tribune,* finds negotiating is "a stimulating blend of interpersonal and analytical dynamics."

Others, like former Senator Bill Bradley, are more fascinated by what the process allows them to accomplish. "I like to negotiate when I feel there is something important at stake," he says. Whether the final accomplishment is a new company, a new law, a new treaty, or a new contract that satisfies both sides, most master negotiators say negotiating enables them to walk away with the satisfaction of having created something of value in the process.

Should You Be a Negotiator?

Ray Friedman
Bruce Barry

For decades, researchers have tried to find if there were any connections between individual characteristics and bargaining outcomes. These researchers studied an array of personality measures—including "Machiavellianism," "authoritarianism," and "interpersonal orientation"—but the results were contradictory and inconclusive. We decided to conduct a more comprehensive and careful study of individual differences and negotiations. The results were surprising.

We began by building upon recent advances in the study of personality. Instead of hundreds of idiosyncratic personality types, psychologists have identified five overarching elements of personality and developed better ways to measure these elements. Three of them, we thought, might relate to negotiations. A person who is "extroverted" is sociable, talkative, and excitable. An "agreeable" person tends to be generous, cooperative and flexible. And a "conscientious" person is organized, persevering, and planful. In addition to these three personality factors or traits, we examined how general intelligence affects the outcome of negotiating situations.

For win–lose negotiations, such as haggling over a used car, we thought those who were agreeable would tend to be more easily influenced by their opponent and more uncomfortable with the conflict. They would be less aggressive in opening offers, more easily anchored by their opponent's opening offer, and more likely to give in to the other side. We thought those who were extroverted would be more likely to reveal secret information and more influenced by opponent opening offers, since they were more socially engaged with the opponent. Those who were conscientious would plan better for negotiations, we thought, and be better able to counter opponent tactics. Similarly, we assumed general intelligence helps negotiators, making it easier to understand what tactics make sense.

To test these predictions, we put hundreds of students through a simulated business negotiation involving a simple win–lose premise: a supplier and a manufacturer negotiating over the price of a single component. We had these same students fill out personality tests, and we consulted their standardized academic test scores as a measure of intelligence. (Tests like the SAT and the GMAT are well accepted as pretty good measures of what psychologists call "general cognitive ability," or general intelligence.)

To our surprise, conscientiousness and intelligence had no effects. (In other studies of employee accomplishments these were usually the most important factors predicting success.) Agreeableness and extroversion, however, did impact bargaining outcomes and in the ways we predicted.

Those who were extroverted tended more than others to raise their opening offers when their opponent started high. In other words, extroverts were likely to be swayed by

Source: "Should You Be a Negotiator?" by Ray Friedman and Bruce Barry, from *Owen Manager,* Summer 1999, pp. 8–9. Owen Graduate School of Management, Vanderbilt University. Used with permission.

an opponent's extreme first offer (for example, thinking "hmm, she's asking a very high price—perhaps those widgets are worth more than I thought"). Those who were agreeable had the same problem and in the end came away with lower results for themselves.

Thus, for this type of win–lose negotiation, how you tend to engage socially with the opponent makes a difference, but intelligence and planning do not. The implication: If you are extroverted or agreeable, be aware that your personality may undermine your ability to do well in this kind of bargaining encounter. You may be easily influenced by an opponent's tactics in win–lose bargaining. Perhaps you should not be the one to negotiate these types of deals.

We did, however, find one silver lining that may help people high in extroversion or agreeableness overcome these risks. The effects of these traits were less pronounced among those who entered our simulated negotiations with high expectations for themselves. A robust principle, confirmed by many research studies, is that negotiators who come to the bargaining table with high aspirations generally do better for themselves. People with high aspirations seem to pay more attention to the dynamics of the situation and bargain more aggressively.

So if you are high in these traits of extroversion or agreeableness, and have to or want to be at the bargaining table, make sure you set high aspirations for yourself. Although this may seem like good commonsense advice, the fact is many negotiators, especially inexperienced ones, don't take the time to think seriously in advance about what they hope to gain from an encounter. And those who do may have relatively little confidence in their ability to do well, and as a result carry into the encounter rather modest expectations. The research tells us that high expectations often translate into better outcomes, and this may be particularly true for individuals whose personalities otherwise work against them.

We also studied a very different type of negotiation—one that allows for the creation of mutual gain through creative problem solving. There are many situations like the previous one in this article, where negotiating is just a pure haggle over a single issue, like the price of an object for sale. But other situations are far more complex, with negotiators trying to sort their way through several issues—some of which involve shared interests and some of which involve divergent interests. The challenge in these situations is to figure out where agreements can benefit both parties and where compromises have to be made—all while juggling a variety of concerns and issues. These types of encounters, sometimes called "mixed motive" situations, are more likely to be found in complex business negotiations, political disputes, and the like. To the extent that bargainers can successfully find common ground and produce a settlement that pleases both parties, these situations are also sometimes referred to as "win–win" bargaining encounters.

For these negotiations we had different predictions. We expected those who were agreeable and extroverted to do better, since information sharing and cooperation help problem solving. We also expected intelligence to be a plus, since cognitive ability helps negotiators develop creative solutions to complex problems. We tested these predictions by, again, having students participate in a bargaining simulation. But this time, the simulation was more complex—a negotiation between a shopping mall developer and a potential retail tenant. Price was not the issue; rather, bargainers had to hammer out a contractual agreement regarding several issues related to the use, potential subletting, and assignment of the leased property. We evaluated and coded these agreements in order to test our predictions about how personality and intelligence would affect who does well and whether both parties can benefit from the individual characteristics of bargainers.

To our surprise, agreeableness and extroversion had no effects. How one interacts socially with the other side did not affect the results of this type of "win–win" negotiation. Intelligence, however, did yield the results we expected. The smarter the negotiators were, the more they were able to produce creative, well-structured solutions to difficult bargaining problems. The smarter the negotiators were, the bigger the pie that was split between the two sides.

In one twist to this story, we examined whether one side or the other captured for themselves a bigger share of the increased value from joint gains. In other words, if bargaining pairs featuring at least one "smarter" person were able to generate a bigger pie to split, who got how much of the pie? You might assume that the smarter of the two individuals would grab the bigger share of whatever is at stake. But surprisingly, it turned out that those who bargained with a smarter opponent did better for themselves. The moral of the story: In negotiations where there is a need for creative problem solving, try to negotiate with the smartest opponent you can. In these kinds of complex situations, the real gains come not necessarily from crushing the other person with aggressiveness, but from finding creative ways to solve problems that add value for both parties. Our study suggests that more smarts at the bargaining table—whether yours or the other person's—increases the chances that creative solutions benefiting both parties can be discovered.

Stepping back to look at both of our studies, the results were intriguing. For win–lose negotiations, personality matters but intelligence does not matter. For win–win negotiations, personality does not matter, but intelligence does matter. There is no one overall best person to do all negotiations; rather, who is best for negotiation depends on the type of negotiation. Whether you are the right person to negotiate depends on the situation.

The challenge is to know yourself and what type of negotiation you are facing. Many people assume that success in bargaining is a simple matter of nerve and tactical aggressiveness. Our research tells a different and more complicated story. Different types of bargaining situations call for different types of tactics and quite possibly different types of negotiators. Personality traits that help you in one kind of situation may undermine your success in another. Much of our teaching covers exactly these points—what are your tendencies when you negotiate, and how can you tell if a negotiation has the potential for mutual gains? Effective negotiators are apt to have a thoughtful response to both of these questions.

Negotiation across Cultures

Reading 5.1

Culture and Negotiation
Jeanne M. Brett

Joe Romano found out on a business trip to Taiwan how close a one-syllable slip of the tongue can come to torpedoing a deal. . . . Mr. Romano, a partner of High Ground, Inc., an emerging technology-marketing company in Boston, has been traveling to Asia for 10 years and speaks fluent Mandarin and Taiwanese. Or so he thought, until he nearly blew an important deal when he met the chief executive of a major Taiwanese manufacturer. "You're supposed to say 'Au-ban,' which means basically, 'Hello, No. 1 Boss,'" Mr. Romano explained. "But being nervous, I slipped and said 'Lau-ban ya,' which means, 'Hello, wife of the boss.' So I basically called him a woman in front of 20 senior Taiwanese executives, who all laughed," he said. "He looked at me like he was going to kill me because in Asia, guys are hung up on being seen as very manly. I had to keep asking them to forgive 'the stupid American' before the CEO would accept my apologies."

Language mistakes and violations of local protocol are difficult to avoid when negotiating globally, but they are seldom deal breakers. As Mr. Romano learned, a groveling apology can go a long way toward mending relationships.

The real cultural deal breakers are embedded in failures to take culture into account at two critical points: when planning the negotiation and when choosing strategy. Three of my students discovered this for themselves in the course of researching Lafarge's first and second attempts to establish a foothold as a major cement manufacturer in Yunnan province in China. Lafarge, a French company, is the world leader in building materials, holding top positions in each of four areas: cement, aggregates and concrete, roofing, and gypsum.

Lafarge's planning gaffe involved a failure to understand the Chinese government's interests. Lafarge wanted to enter the Yunnan market profitably and quickly by taking full ownership of two state-owned cement manufacturers. Lafarge assumed the government would be willing to sell, if the price was right. But Lafarge was wrong. The government's interests were less in money than in access to Lafarge's state of the art cement-manufacturing processes. In 2004, the time of this negotiation, the Chinese

Source: "Culture and Negotiation," by Jeanne M. Brett, from *Negotiating Globally: How to Negotiate Deals, Resolve Disputes, and Make Decisions Across Cultural Boundaries*, 2nd ed., 2007, Chapter 2, pp. 25–52. San Francisco: Jossey-Bass, a Wiley Imprint. Used with permission.

government had plenty of foreign capital; what it needed was a means of upgrading its inefficient construction manufacturing industry, while maintaining jobs and ensuring a steady supply of construction materials. The government also knew that transferring state-owned entities to local interests would be viewed more favorably from a public relations perspective than would a direct sale to a foreign company.

Lafarge's *strategic* gaffe involved the choice of whom to send to Yunnan to negotiate. Lafarge initially sent two fairly junior members of their investment team to talk to the heads of the two Yunnan cement companies. Although Lafarge may have thought that they were simply engaging in some due diligence research—were these the right companies to buy—the Chinese were miffed that a potential business partner would send analysts to talk to business directors. According to Sanjeev Krishna (investment officer for emerging markets at Health Sciences, International Finance Corporation—World Bank) the due diligence process in China is far different than in the West. In China, he advises, one needs to develop a solid relationship before embarking on the due diligence process. In the West typically a lot of due diligence is conducted prior to an entity even deciding to develop a relationship.

The end of this story is that Lafarge is in Yunnan province and technical know-how is being transferred to the Chinese cement companies, but the ultimate deal was not quite what Lafarge had envisioned. Lafarge formed a joint venture with a Hong Kong company to purchase 80 percent of the Yunnan cement business. As a result, Lafarge's ultimate share was only half of that (40 percent), not the 100 percent it initially sought.

This chapter is about how culture affects negotiation. It begins with an introduction to ways of characterizing different dimensions and types of cultures. It goes on to describe a general framework that illustrates how culture affects negotiation.

Although it is filled with examples of negotiating in different parts of the world, keep in mind that the chapter is not about protocol and not about how to negotiate in individual specific places, such as China. The reason for this will be explained more thoroughly in the section on cultural prototypes and cultural stereotypes. But in brief the reason is that even experience within a culture does not guarantee future negotiating success. Mr. Romano had 10 years of experience negotiating in Asia. Lafarge started doing business in China in 1994. Ten years later, when Lafarge opened negotiations in Yunnan province it already had cement operations in Sichuan province. To adequately integrate cultural knowledge into negotiation strategy requires more than experience; it requires an understanding of how and why culture affects negotiations.

What Is Culture?

Culture is the distinct character of a social group. It emerges from the patterned ways that people in a group respond to the fundamental problems of social interaction.

A useful metaphor for describing culture is an iceberg. Just like with an iceberg there is more to culture below the surface than above, and just like an iceberg, culture is not static, it drifts and shifts. Figure 1 illustrates the cultural iceberg. Visible above the squiggly "waterline" of the cultural iceberg are behaviors and institutions. Below the waterline are two deeper, psychological levels. Each of the following sections examines one level.

FIGURE 1 | Culture as an Iceberg

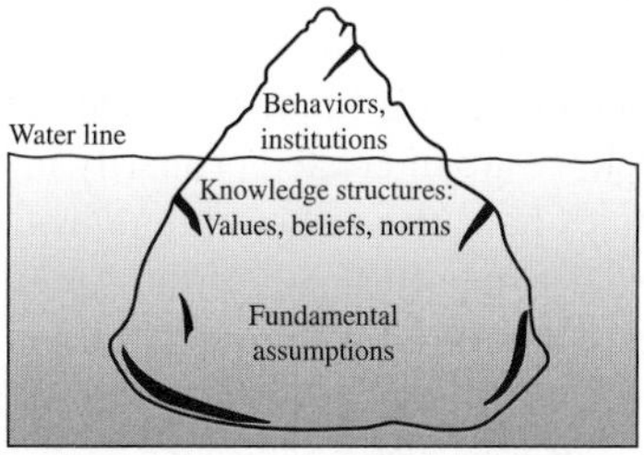

Behaviors and Institutions

Above the iceberg's waterline are the characteristic *behavior* patterns of cultural members, as well as the culture's overt institutions. Some of the most obvious cultural behavioral differences are differences in greetings. For example, in Japan people bow; in India they may press hands together in *namaste*; in Latin America they grab each other's upper arms; and in France, Italy, and Spain they kiss on the cheeks. Although it is always polite to respect another culture's greeting protocols, and there are many websites with good advice about what to do in Rome and so on, it is not always necessary to engage in them when negotiating cross culturally. You are after all a cultural outsider. Even with significant cultural experience you will probably never get the inclination of the Japanese bow right, because the degree of inclination depends on the status of the person you are bowing to.

Interpreting the behaviors that you may see at the negotiation table is of greater importance. The risk is that you will jeopardize the negotiation by interpreting these behaviors through the lens of your own culture. For example, the first time I watched a class of Indian managers negotiate, I was startled by their side-to-side head movements. Side-to-side head movements in U.S. culture mean no, no, no! I thought negotiations were not going well, and I was really upset when many in the class continued this behavior during my debriefing. I asked my host professor, "What went wrong, they hated the class, how can we fix it for tomorrow?" He replied, "Why do you think that?" I said, "They shook their heads no, no, no all afternoon." "Oh," he said, "That means 'I'm listening.'"

I cannot anticipate all the behaviors that you are likely to encounter across the negotiation table. I can assure you that it is normal to interpret those behaviors through the lens of your own culture, and that such interpretation is frequently erroneous and may affect negotiation relationships and ultimately outcomes. To avoid these cultural biases when negotiating globally, you need a cultural interpreter, someone who not only knows the language but also can interpret the body language and the strategic behavior being exhibited across the table. Your cultural expert should also be able to help you understand the cultural context of the negotiation, for example, the institutional environment in which the negotiation is embedded.

Institutions on the iceberg figure stands for economic, social, political, legal, religious institutional environments that may affect the negotiation. Culture is manifested in institutional choices, such as whether there is a free-market economy or a communist political system, and it is embedded in the institutions' *ideologies*—the set of principles and precepts underlying institutional choices.

These cultural institutions provide social structures for nation-states, which is why in this book we are interested primarily in culture contained within national boundaries. Nation-states have their own unique institutional cultures that negotiators must navigate. Consider the aftermath of the Arcelor acquisition by Mittal. Ultimately, Arcelor shareholders preferred selling to Mittal, a company registered in Rotterdam, incorporated within EU laws, and run by an Indian living in London, rather than selling to Severstal, a Russian company lead by a Russian oligarch, Alexsei Mordashov. Why? Mittal's EU-based political, legal, and economic environment apparently was viewed by shareholders as much less risky than Severstal's.

Another reason to be concerned with the institutional structure of nation-states is that governments have interests that derive from their institutional ideologies and are reflected in their approach to negotiations. As we saw in the Lafarge example, the Chinese government, although encouraging foreign investment, nevertheless had strong institutional interests that included maintaining some local ownership, acquiring state-of-the-art technology, maintaining employment, and availability of construction materials.

In fact, one of the most important realities about negotiating globally is that governments are frequently at or close to the table. Western and Eastern companies alike, regardless of their negotiation experience, too frequently stumble badly when they try to do business in a new cultural environment. A recent example is China National Offshore Oil Company's 2005 failed bid for Unocal, which was ultimately bought domestically by Chevron. CNOOC failed to take into account the risk that their acquisition could be blocked by the U.S. Congress. When Congressional approval appeared to be unlikely, CNOOC let Chevron outbid them for Unocal. Failing to understand the institutional environment in which the negotiation is occurring can sabotage negotiations.

Cultural Values, Beliefs, Norms, and Knowledge Structures

The behaviors and institutions that one can see above the cultural iceberg's waterline are supported underwater by a culturally shared psychology of values, beliefs, norms, and knowledge structures. It is convenient to characterize a culture by its values or norms, but there are two important traps to avoid when doing so.

The first trap to avoid is confounding a cultural *prototype* (a central tendency) with a cultural *stereotype* (the idea that everyone in a culture is the same; that there is no distribution around the mean). Keep in mind this distinction between prototypes and stereotypes. There is always variance within a culture.

The second trap is failing to understand that cultures are characterized by features measured at the individual level but then aggregated (averaged across cultural group members) to create a cultural prototype. It is at the cultural group level that we are most likely to find relationships between group-level psychological elements of culture and negotiation behaviors and outcomes. Individual-level cultural values seldom explain individual-level negotiation behavior or outcomes.

FIGURE 2 | Cultural Prototypes and Cultural Stereotypes

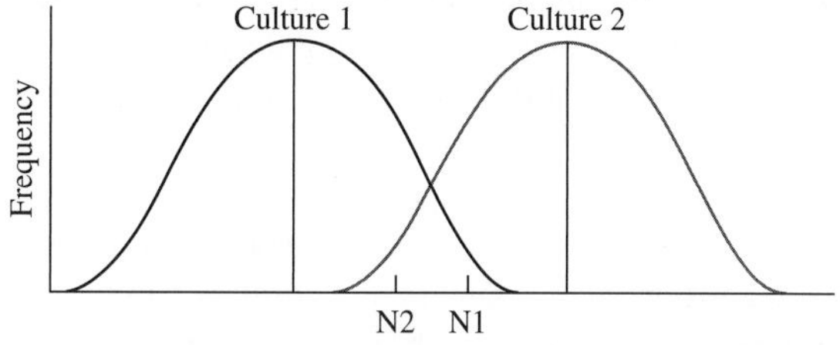

Figure 2 may help you to visualize the meaning of each of the traps. Each bell curve in Figure 2 illustrates a different culture's distribution on a psychological characteristic. The lines dropped from the height of the curve illustrate the cultural prototype. Note that there is a distribution around each culture's prototype and each distribution has "tails." Also notice that there are plenty of members from both cultures in the central, overlapping region of the curves. Not everyone in Culture 2 is more extreme on the cultural variable than everyone in Culture 1. In fact, N1, a negotiator from Culture 1, is actually closer to the Culture 2 prototype than N2, a negotiator from Culture 2. These cultural overlaps help explain why psychological elements of culture measured at the individual level do not predict negotiation behaviors or other types of outcomes.

So why bother studying psychological characteristics of culture if you cannot see them, if they do not characterize everyone in the culture, and if, at least at the individual level, they do not predict negotiation outcomes very well, if at all? Even though psychological characteristics are below the surface of the cultural iceberg, you often can see them reflected in the culture's institutional ideology and in the patterns of behavior characteristic of people from that culture. Even though not every cultural member is going to be like the cultural prototype, because of the nature of the bell curve, more cultural members will fall under the central bell than in the tails of the curve. This means that unless a culture is extremely heterogeneous (the curve is very flat), anyone you negotiate with is more likely to come from the cultural center than from the tails. In addition, knowing cultural prototypes helps you anticipate the other party's interests as you prepare your planning document. It also helps you anticipate their likely strategic behaviors as you make your own strategic choices.

Cultural Values

A *value* is a judgment of what is important in social interaction. A cultural value is a judgment shared by a group. National cultures differ in terms of shared values. Two such differences seem particularly important for negotiations: individualism versus collectivism and hierarchy versus egalitarianism. (However, other value continuums—such as a focus on traditional ways versus openness to change—may account for national cultural differences in particular negotiations.)

Individualism versus Collectivism   The continuum *individualism versus collectivism* distinguishes between cultures that generally place individuals' interests above those of the collective and cultures that generally place collective needs above those of individuals.

In individualist cultures social, economic, and legal institutions promote the autonomy of individuals, reward individual accomplishment, and protect individual rights. In collective cultures institutions promote interdependency of individuals with the others in their families, work establishments, and communities by emphasizing social obligations. Individual accomplishment reflects back on others with whom the individual is interdependent. Legal institutions support collective interests above individual interests.

Research generally categorizes nations in North America (excluding Mexico) and Western Europe as individualist cultures and pretty much the rest of the world as more or less collective, especially East Asia and Latin America. No one has studied Africa.

Coming from a culture that is high on individualism or high on collectivism may affect negotiators' interests, goals, and so on—elements of their planning as well as their strategic choices. For example, individualistic cultures promote and condone self-interest, which may be reflected in negotiators' targets and their strategic use of argument; collective cultures' emphasis on social obligations may be reflected in negotiators' choices for indirect confrontation and face saving.

An example illustrates that there are cultural differences in negotiation strategy even between cultures that are in many ways similar. A U.S. software engineer working on a project for an Israeli client reported how much he was challenged by the different ways of approaching issues and discussing them: "There is something pretty common to the Israeli culture, they like to argue. I tend to try and collaborate more, and it got very stressful for me until I figured out how to kind of merge the cultures."

According to my own research, Israeli managers are more likely to have individualistic social motives than are managers from any other culture I have studied.

However, you may find much less in this book about individualism versus collectivism than you might have expected, considering that this is the cultural value most widely studied by psychologists. Although some commentators claim that the difference between individualism and collectivism influences basic psychological processes, these same commentators admit "the empirical basis for this conclusion is not as firm as might be desired." Even in the 2004 *Handbook of Negotiation and Culture* (edited by Michele Gelfand and yours truly), individualism versus collectivism dominates the chapters on culture. But a review of the research cited in these chapters attempting to link individualism versus collectivism to negotiation processes and outcomes is disappointing. In the negotiation contexts of deal making, dispute resolution, and negotiating decisions in multicultural teams, I simply do not see evidence of a link, beyond a possible difference in the level of self-interest and concern for relationships. Only in the negotiation context of social dilemmas is there clear research evidence of an effect associated with individualistic versus collective cultural differences. In social dilemmas, people from collective cultures *are* more cooperative than those from individualist cultures.

In sum, the cultural value of considering individualism versus collectivism does not give us a great deal of leverage in understanding culture's effects on negotiation. This may be because individualism and collectivism do not act in isolation from other elements of culture. Psychological culture is an amalgam of values, beliefs, norms, and knowledge structures. Just knowing that a culture is more or less individualistic does not tell us enough to do more than make very general statements about likely behavior in negotiations. We have to look at more elements of culture.

Hierarchy versus Egalitarianism   The continuum *hierarchy versus egalitarianism* distinguishes between cultures that are differentiated into closed and inflexible social ranks and cultures in which social structure is relatively flat, open, and malleable. In hierarchical cultures, social status determines social power, and social power generally transfers across situations. In egalitarian cultures, social boundaries are more permeable, and social status may be both short-lived and variable across situations.

Western cultures, especially Northern European nations, tend to be egalitarian. As you move south in Europe and on to Africa and south from North America to Central and South America, culture tends to be more hierarchical. Asian cultures are usually classified as hierarchical.

In a study of multicultural teams, Kristin Behfar, Mary Kern, and I found that hierarchical-egalitarian value differences were a pervasive challenge, in some cases limiting some team members' participation in negotiating team decisions. A manager reared in India told us about being on a team that was trying to standardize a process across a U.S. company's sites in Belgium, Mexico, Canada, and the United States. He said, "In India, if you had a senior business person [on the team], just by age you would give them more respect and the reporting relationships [would stay] pretty much intact [even when on a team together]. You don't call your director by his first name. You usually refer to him as Sir XYZ. And I think the people in Mexico are also like that to a large extent. I felt like they also watch very carefully what they say in terms of who they address and how they say it and how forceful they are. . . . But I think that's asking a little too much of the Americans. . . . their reporting relationships are still there, but when you're in a meeting they usually consider everybody as an equal. . . ."

In hierarchical cultures, the reluctance to confront higher-status people may stem from concern for maintaining and using social hierarchies. When conflict does occur in hierarchical cultures, the conflict is more likely to be handled indirectly by a social superior than by direct confrontation. When a higher-status third party gets involved in a dispute, that party's decision reinforces its authority without one party having to concede to the other, hence losing social status. In contrast, in an egalitarian culture, success in *direct* negotiations can lead to differentiated status, but not likely to *permanent* changes in social status, since a negotiated agreement in an egalitarian culture is unlikely to be an avenue for setting precedents.

Within hierarchical cultures, social relations are bound by a web of responsibilities and obligations that are mostly absent from egalitarian cultures. For example, in hierarchical cultures, social inferiors are expected to defer to social superiors, who in return for the power and privilege conferred on them by right of their status have an obligation to look out for the well-being of lower-status parties. No such obligations exist in egalitarian cultures. In the 1990s, for example, Rubbermaid (now Newell Rubbermaid) was the leading brand-name maker of plastic kitchenware and household items such as laundry baskets, yet definitely of lower business status than Wal-Mart. When the price for the main component in its products, resin, more than tripled between 1994 and 1996, Wal-Mart (Rubbermaid's biggest customer) balked at paying increased prices. When Rubbermaid insisted, Wal-Mart relegated the manufacturer's items to undesirable shelf space and used its market power to promote a Rubbermaid rival.

The web of responsibility and obligation that engulfs social relationships in hierarchical cultures reflects a rather fixed distribution of power in those cultures. The concept of BATNA is not unheard of in hierarchical cultures, but it is much less important than determining parties' relative status, which then translates to responsibilities and obligations and the distribution of resources in a negotiated agreement.

How negotiators from hierarchical cultures determine power is sometimes lost on Western culture negotiators. A Brazilian manager working for a Latin American division of a U.S. company that sources a lot of products in Asia told us about a negotiation he attended on the buyer's side along with his U.S. boss. On the seller's side sat four Koreans. He says, "In the meetings . . . the Koreans were trying to put things very carefully in an ornate manner. And this guy (the U.S. boss) didn't want to know the introductions or the small issues. He wanted the issues that were really going to close or make or break the business. The Koreans were shocked, as they wanted to go through the small stuff to warm up the negotiation first." No doubt underneath the "small stuff" in this warm-up to the negotiation was information about the company and the products that the Koreans thought were important in order to establish their status in the negotiation.

In contrast, the concept of BATNA fits well with the conceptualization of power in egalitarian cultures. BATNAs are situational and flexible. If a negotiator is unhappy with his or her BATNA, he or she may be able to improve it.

Beliefs

A *belief* is an expectation. Culture has the very nice effect of helping cultural members navigate social life without having to negotiate every move. If I'm in Great Britain, Japan, or Australia with my friend Mara, she drives. Mara is Australian, she knows the rules of the road for left-side driving, and, more important, she believes that the other drivers on those roads also know the rules. Mara's beliefs allow her to anticipate other drivers' actions and get us safely to our destination. In the United States, Europe, or North Africa, I drive. In China and India, we take taxis.

Beliefs permeate negotiations: beliefs about the other party's interests and priorities; beliefs about their power, be it from status or BATNA; beliefs about their reservation price and about the strategic choices they are likely to make.

Beliefs about trust are very important in negotiations because they underlie the strategic choice of negotiating distributively or integratively. Without trust, negotiators are not likely to share information about interests and priorities that is necessary for high net-value integrative agreements. *Trust* in negotiation is the willingness to make yourself vulnerable to the other party, usually by sharing information. *Quick trust* is the belief that the other party is trustworthy until he or she proves to be untrustworthy. Quick trust is characteristic of U.S. negotiators. In contrast, *slow trust* is characteristic of negotiators who wish to build strong relationships prior to sharing information in a negotiation that might make them vulnerable to the other party. Slow trust is the belief that the other party has to prove that he or she is trustworthy. In slow-trust cultures, trust and trustworthiness are qualities that are held in great esteem and not easily earned, but rather must be built gradually.

A French lawyer working for an American company told me about her company's interest in developing business in Morocco. The company's area managers identified a Tunisian partner and began developing a relationship with him. He wanted assurance that the American company was serious, so the area managers arranged to bring in the regional European head for a meeting. However, the regional manager's expectations about what was going to be accomplished at the meeting were very different from those of the potential Moroccan partner. The Moroccan partner greeted the regional manager upon arrival, engaged him in social conversation, then departed with him for a lunch that took three hours and pushed the regional manager up against a flight deadline. He was furious; he had come to Morocco to talk business. From his perspective, nothing had been accomplished. But the French observer speculates that the Moroccan partner was *also* disappointed in the meeting because no relationship was built with the high-status regional manager.

Negotiators from Western cultures may believe that engaging in small talk at the beginning of a new negotiation relationship is a waste of time. But negotiators from relationship-oriented cultures such as Tunisia, an Arabic-speaking, Muslim culture, may use such conversation to consolidate knowledge about the extent to which the other party is to be trusted. Recall the earlier example about the Brazilian observing his American boss trying to get negotiations started with the Koreans; small talk may contain important information about power and status that a party is trying to convey. If the recipient of the small talk does not understand the subtext, perhaps the listener is not worthy of trust.

Norms for Directness of Communication

Norms are standards of appropriate and inappropriate behavior in a cultural context. Norms are functional because they reduce the number of choices people have to make about how to behave. And, like beliefs, norms that provide guidance about how you should behave also provide insight into how others in the culture are likely to behave.

Norms regarding directness or indirectness of communication are important when negotiating globally. When people communicate indirectly, the same words take on different meanings depending on the context in which they are spoken. People in indirect-communication cultures (also called *high-context cultures*) understand each other because they share the social context with the speaker. In high-context cultures, people interpret words together with the context in which the words were conveyed. It's no surprise then that these indirect-communication cultures tend also to be collective cultures in which people share common social contexts. By contrast, in direct-communication cultures information is communicated explicitly; meaning is on the surface of the message, not embedded in its context. People in direct-communication cultures (also called *low-context cultures*) understand each other because they share a vocabulary. Although they, too, share a social context, they do not need to pay attention to that context to interpret a communication. Direct communication cultures also tend to be individualistic.

The research by Edward T. Hall and others indicates pretty clearly that non-Western cultures (for example Japanese, Russian, and Arab cultures) use indirect communication more than Western cultures, such as Germany, the United States, and Switzerland.

Negotiators with experience in Japan know that a Japanese "yes" *(hai)* doesn't necessarily mean "yes." An Indian manager working out of Singapore for a Fortune 500 company on an eBusiness project learned this the hard way. He told us about negotiating with team members who were in Japan:

> So . . . we would fly in there and . . . say, "Okay, this is what . . . the businesses priority [is] across Asia, and do the projects in Japan align with the same priorities?" . . . and so on . . . What would typically happen is . . . we would pretty much get a "yes," [and] on the face of it we would feel that we got a consensus, [and that] they bought into the priorities of the projects and . . . where [the dollars] should be spent on these projects. . . . [W]e thought we achieved a lot . . . However, in terms of their actions, we would . . . not see the same, . . . and their projects would still be focused on things which we believed . . . the Japan team felt were high priority for them. Their spending on the projects would continue in the same way. So what we were seeing was that we would walk into this meeting, we would have a consensus, they would say yes, [but] when we would come back [to Singapore] it would not be reflected in their actions."

Determining whether or not parties had an agreement was a major challenge that surfaced when Kristin Behfar, Mary Kern, and I interviewed members of multicultural teams about the challenges they faced. Parties from high-context cultures are frequently simply reluctant to say "no," and parties from low-context cultures that want a "yes" are very good at hearing what they want to hear and not very good at interpreting a high-context "yes."

Interpreting high- and low-context communication in negotiations goes beyond understanding when yes means no. If negotiators are going to reach integrative agreements, they need to share information about interests and priorities.

The latest research shows that negotiators from low- and high-context cultures negotiate in rather different ways. Low-context-culture negotiators generally use a questioning strategy that culminates rather far into the negotiation with a settlement offer that links the issues. They ask the other party questions about interests and priorities, assume that the party is telling the truth, and reciprocate with information about their own interests and priorities. As this process unfolds during the first half to two-thirds of the negotiation, low-context-culture negotiators slowly build an understanding of the trade-offs possible in negotiations, then they start using this information to make offers to capture the trade-offs. In contrast, high-context-culture negotiators use a more indirect strategy to gain information about the other side's interests and priorities. The strategy is to make and receive both single- and multi-issue offers. On the surface, this negotiation strategy seems pretty direct: I tell you what I want, and you tell me what you want. But the information about interests and priorities is not on the surface of the offers; instead, it is embedded *between* them. I slowly build an understanding of your interests and priorities by drawing inferences about them from the way you change my offer.

Low- versus high-context cultural norms not only predispose negotiators to use either the questioning or the offer strategy, they also may inhibit full understanding of the other party's interests and priorities. The high-context-culture negotiator should be able to understand the direct communications of the low-context negotiator, but the low-context negotiator may not be sufficiently experienced with high-context communication to draw inferences about interests and priorities from a pattern of offers and counteroffers. This may be particularly true when issues are offered one at a time, rather than in a package.

Regardless of the research showing that low- and high-context cultures respectively favor the questioning and offer strategies, in principle, negotiators from low-context cultures should be able to use the offer strategy and negotiators from high-context cultures should be able to use the questioning strategy. Some psychologists argue that all human behaviors are available to people in all cultures, it's just that characteristics of different cultures cue different means of fulfilling a social function, such as negotiation. But cultural psychologists are just beginning to study when culturally normative behavior occurs and when it does not.

Knowledge Structures

A *knowledge structure* is a cognitive construction. It is an implicit theory, a mental model, an actor's script for a specific domain of thought or action. Knowledge structures are important because they guide judgments and decisions, and direct actions in specific domains such as negotiation. Negotiators' knowledge structures contain the answer to the question, What does a person like me do in a situation like this?

It is useful to address knowledge structures at this point of our inquiry into culture and negotiation because knowledge structures integrate cultural values, beliefs, and norms that are relevant to a particular context of negotiation. The question has two parts: "What does *a person like me* do in *a situation like this?*" Both parts rely on culture. A *person like me* is defined by the context of the psychological elements of the values, beliefs, and norms of one's cultural identity group. A *situation like this* is likewise viewed through a normative cultural lens: "What is appropriate behavior in this situation?"

Using cultural values to predict negotiation behavior is pretty simple: if you know the value prototype of a culture, you can make a straightforward prediction, for example, that the culture is individualistic and therefore the negotiator will only care about his or her own interests. (Except, of course, as we discussed previously, such predictions are frequently off the mark.) Using knowledge structures to predict negotiation behavior is not at all simple. It requires knowing something about the person's cultural background *and* about the negotiation situation and how people in a culture react to different situations. For example, in a study of managers acting as third parties in dispute resolution, U.S. and Japanese third parties acted pretty much as one might predict given knowledge that the U.S. culture tends to be egalitarian and the Japanese culture to be hierarchical. U.S. third parties tended to involve the disputants in the decision to resolve the dispute regardless of whether they were bosses or peers. Japanese third parties tended to make the decision to resolve the dispute themselves. But Chinese third parties intervened very differently depending on their role as boss or peer. When the Chinese were in the role of boss, they acted like the Japanese. When the Chinese were in the role of peer, they acted like the Americans.

Despite being hard to use to make predictions, knowledge structures are extremely useful because they integrate multiple influences of culture and they take into account characteristics of the negotiation contexts in which we find ourselves. Knowledge structures help us plan our global negotiations and make strategic choices.

Cultural Assumptions

An *assumption* is an unproven supposition. Assumptions form the broad base of our cultural iceberg (Figure 1). They are linked to cultural members' knowledge structures and the ideologies underlying cultural institutions.

Cultural assumptions are widely held by members of a culture. Yet many times people are unaware of the assumptions that guide their own behavior, only realizing what those assumptions are when they try negotiating with someone whose assumptions are different. The assumptions in Table 1 were articulated by a Japanese software engineer to be used as part of a cultural training program for his company, Infosys, a global leader in IT and business consulting.

Recognizing differences in fundamental cultural assumptions is the first step toward developing a working relationship that respects and uses those differences. A multicultural team member told us what happened when the members of the U.K.–U.S. financial services team began working together. He said that the U.S. approach to problem solving was to *forge ahead and start trying to rip apart things and let's do this and that,* whereas the U.K. members of the team took a more pragmatic approach: *let's not hurry up, let's think about this.* At first these different approaches to problem solving generated conflict, but when they didn't go away, the group not only learned to live with their differences but also realized that their cultural differences provided good checks and balances for teamwork.

We label the teams' negotiated decision-making process *fusion* (like fusion cooking, in which chefs may substitute a spice or sauce or cooking technique from an Asian culture in a French or Italian recipe). Fusion allows for the coexistence of both culture's approaches. Fusion is being discussed seriously now by political scientists and government officials who are faced with multicultural populations that desire to protect their cultural differences rather than integrate or assimilate. Perhaps one of the reasons why Infosys has become "one of the jewels of the Indian information technology world" is that the company is willing to recognize, confront, and negotiate cultural differences in order to get work done!

A Model of How Culture Affects Negotiation

Figure 3 illustrates how culture affects a two-party negotiation.

The exhibit shows that negotiators from each culture come to the negotiating table with interests and priorities that are culturally based. In the negotiation between the Chinese government and Lafarge, the Chinese government had three interests: local control, updating technology, and uninterrupted delivery of cement. These interests and the high priority placed on them compared with simply attracting more foreign investment illustrate how culture affects interests. Despite rapid economic

TABLE 1 | Assumptions of Indian and Japanese Software Engineers

Assumption	Indian Engineer	Japanese Engineer
Self-concept	I am superior.	I am inferior.
Customer	Customer is a partner, an adult	Customer is God or a child
Words	Words are not final. Some are less important.	Words are final. They are commitment.
Commitment	I cannot say I do not know.	I cannot say I know.
Communication	I talk.	I listen.
Expertise	I am an expert after 10 days.	I am an expert after 10 years.
Teamwork	The team is there for me.	I am here for the team.
Decision making	I make a decision.	The team makes a decision.
Time	I value my time.	I value your time.
Negotiation	I convince you. I present my position.	I sympathize with you. I represent your position.
Silence	Silence is emptiness of the mind. (weakness)	Silence is consolidation of the mind. (strength)
Comprehension	I focus on the big picture.	I focus on the details.
Rules	Rule can be applicable. Some are less important.	Rule is a rule. No exception. All are important.
Suggestion	No. This is a better way. I will give you solution.	Yes but . . . Maybe, this is a better way. How do you think?
Risk	Risk is to be managed.	Risk is to be avoided.
Emotion	Emotion is to share.	Emotion is to hide, or explode.
Quality	I achieve the goal. 90 percent is completed.	I achieve the goal. 120 percent is completed.
Relationship	I spoke to him once. He is a friend of mine.	I spoke to him 10 times. I just know him.
Schedule	It takes five days. Therefore, it takes a week.	It takes five days. Therefore, it does not take a week.
Explanation	It is information.	It is an excuse.
Hierarchy	I obey my boss and act accordingly.	I obey my boss, but may act differently.
Arguing	It adds values. It is enjoyable.	It damages the relationship. It is uncomfortable.
Information	I share any information. I like quantitative info.	I share necessary information only. I like qualitative info.

Source: Used with permission of Junichi Yoshida and Infosys.

growth and membership in the World Trade Organization, China remains a planned economy; in the case of Lafarge, economic planning took precedence over foreign investment. Lafarge had two interests entering the Yunnan market: speed and profitability. These interests, too, were cultural. Lafarge is a for-profit enterprise. Its investments in China are motivated by its desire to make money for its shareholders. Lafarge was interested in bringing new cement technology to these plants in Yunnan province not because it is altruistic but because with new technology, production would be more profitable. Note that neither the Chinese government nor Lafarge's interests required that Lafarge own 100 percent of the cement plants, even though Lafarge set out to do so. The fit between negotiators' priorities and interests is what generates potential.

Culture also may affect negotiators' strategic behavior: their confrontational style, their social motivation, and their integrative or distributive strategic approach to negotiation. We know a little about strategic behavior in the Lafarge negotiation. Lafarge's initial confrontational strategy was direct, motivated by its goal to accumulate economic capital. It sent financial analysts to Yunnan Province to do due diligence, collecting information that would allow Lafarge to develop a target price that would ensure profitability. In contrast, leadership of the Chinese cement companies no doubt preferred a less direct strategy that engaged first in relationship-building with high-level peers from Lafarge. They probably were concerned for their jobs. Financial analysts could not provide the relationship assurances they were likely seeking.

Figure 3 shows that negotiators' strategies generate a pattern of interaction in negotiation. That interaction can be functional and facilitate capturing the potential for an agreement; or, as in the Lafarge negotiation in Yunnan province, it can be dysfunctional and lead to an impasse.

FIGURE 3 | Culture in a Two-Party Negotiation

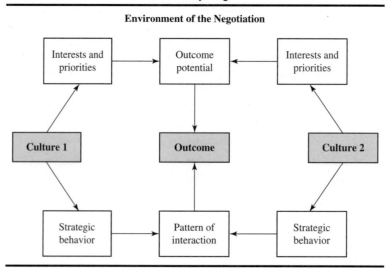

Figure 3 illustrates one more important aspect of negotiating globally: the environment in which the negotiation is embedded. Environment refers to the context of negotiation and encompasses all the pressures and parties who are not at the table but nevertheless have an impact on negotiation. In Lafarge's case, the negotiation environment included the fact that China had a communist government, that China was engaged in a period of rapid growth and development of infrastructure (for example, constructing roads and buildings that require cement), and that the commitment to market economics was not uniform throughout China.

Culture and the Negotiation Planning Document

Now that we know more about culture, we can expand planning for a negotiation to include culture.

We have already discussed how institutional and psychological culture affect parties' interests and priorities. Analysis of cultural bases for interests and priorities can be incorporated directly into the Negotiation Planning Document.

Incorporating Cultural Parties   The Negotiation Planning Document can be extended as illustrated in Table 2 by adding columns to represent multiple parties. In the previous section, the Chinese party in the Lafarge negotiation was represented as the directors of the two Yunnan province cement companies, but it would be more correct to represent the Chinese party with three faces: the company directors, the Yunnan province government, and the central Chinese government. It also may be that the two directors have different interests and should be separated for the purpose of planning. By adding a column for each party and analyzing each of the parties' positions, interests, and priorities, we incorporate culture into planning for negotiation.

Incorporating Cultural BATNAs   BATNAs too may be cultural. Consider Lafarge's BATNA to buying 100 percent of the Yunnan cement plants. This was China. Buying land and building one's own plant was not an option, but there was the option of entering into a rather complex joint venture agreement with a third party from Hong Kong. The joint venture ultimately bought 80 percent of the cement plants. There are lots of corporate strategic reasons for entering into joint ventures. In this case, those reasons had to do with the economic and political environment of the negotiation.

Negotiation Strategy and Culture

Culture should also be on your mind as you make choices about negotiation strategy. There is plenty of discussion, but not much formal research, concerning cultural differences in direct versus indirect confrontation. Negotiators from cultures that are collective—and that engage in slow-trust and high-context communication—tend to prefer relationship-building prior to substantive negotiating. Since this pattern covers a large part of the world, it may be wise to plan to build relationships early when negotiating globally. Lafarge will never know whether the structure of its ultimate deal might have been better if the company had sent high-level managers to Yunnan province to build relationships with the directors of the cement companies, and possibly also with local officials.

TABLE 2 | Negotiation Planning Document for Lafarge

Issue	Lafarge			Company Directors			Yunnan Province Government			Chinese Central Government		
Example	Priority	Position	Interests	Priority	Position	Interests	Priority	Position	Interests	Priority	Position	Interests
Price	1	Low	Make money	4	Indifferent	Not owners	2	High	Owners	4	High	Precedent
Speed	2	Rapid	Make money	3	Slow	Retain control	5	Slow	Manage employment	5	Medium	Manage employment, production, gain technology
Local Control and Jobs	5	No	Manage productively	1	Yes	Retain jobs	1	Yes	Retain prestige, employment	3	Some	Manage employment, gain technology
Technology	3	Yes	Efficiency	2	Yes, but	Threatened, don't know how to manage with Lafarge technology	3	Yes, but	Not cause a loss of jobs	2	Yes	And train locals to use it
Uninterrupted Delivery of Cement	4	Yes	Make money	5	Don't care	Not their job	4	Yes	Do not want to slow down local projects	1	Yes	Meet national needs
BATNA		Joint venture			Keep running the plants			Sell to another buyer			Sell to another buyer	

Research does not support the idea that negotiators from some cultures primarily use integrative strategy and those in other cultures primarily use distributive strategy. There are three reasons: first, although negotiators themselves may have a preferred strategy, research indicates that they systematically alternate distributive and integrative strategies during negotiations. Second, there is substantial variation within cultures in the ability to use integrative strategy (and variation in how it is used). Third, savvy integrative negotiators can direct even diehard distributive negotiators to high joint-net-gain outcomes. How to do all these things is covered thoroughly in Chapters Three and Four. Here, however, let's look a bit further at what's involved in setting aside one's own culturally dominant negotiation strategies in the interest of getting an agreement. Let's ask, What are the risks in conceding to the other party's *micro-level strategy?*

Micro-level strategy refers to procedural issues such as where the negotiation takes place; whether the issues are discussed in a one-at-a-time agenda format; who is at the table; and what the negotiating medium is, for example, face-to-face, conference call, or e-mail. In a negotiation between a U.S. company and a Saudi company in which messengers were employed, Darren Wee pointed out that in his previous experience, his company had never before negotiated with agents with no authority to make commitments. He said, "The Saudis wanted a list of questions and points that we wanted to cover and they would get back to us preapproving some questions and indicating others were not approved. They even dictated the seating chart at each meeting and wanted names and positions of all participants. . . ." "We had to concede all the process, and a significant amount of value to do the deal." Ultimately, Darren Wee's company reached an agreement with the Saudis with margins that were acceptable to top management. Should they have conceded "all the process"? Would they have reached agreement if they had not?

Does making concessions on the micro-level process signal weakness? It certainly does signal flexibility and interest in the negotiation. It may help build relationships— "Okay, let's try it your way." However, it may also signal weakness in a hierarchical culture in which it may be taken as evidence of deference to a more powerful party— deference that would be expected to generalize across process and outcome. In contrast, the innate flexibility of an egalitarian culture implies that being flexible about the process should not necessarily signal substantive weakness.

A Complex Link

It would be helpful if the relationships between culture and negotiation were simple and straightforward, if one could say when in Rome use this strategy, when in Beijing use that one. The research to date indicates quite clearly that the link between culture and negotiation is complex. Look back at Figure 2 to see again the two reasons why this link between culture and negotiation is not straightforward: not all members of a culture behave like the cultural prototype, and cultural profiles overlap.

A third reason for the complexity of relationship between culture and negotiation is that cultures are not composed of single features. Cultures have profiles of features. Single cultural features may be more or less important, depending on the profile in which they are embedded. Given the state of the research, we can make only general statements about single cultural features and negotiation strategy.

A fourth reason why negotiation strategy is not perfectly related to culture is that knowledge structures that encompass cultural effects are nevertheless contextually cued: *What does a person like me do in a situation like this?*

Fifth and finally, there is the influence of the other negotiators at the table. Negotiators are quite likely to reciprocate each other's strategies. When all negotiators are from the same culture, reciprocity reinforces culturally normative negotiation behaviors. When negotiators are from different cultures, reciprocity may help negotiators adjust their strategies to each other, but the resulting negotiation process may be a fusion of culturally different strategies.

Anticipating cultural differences at the negotiation table helps negotiators make sense of those differences when they appear and adjust their own behaviors to reinforce or to block the other party's strategy. Excellent global negotiators proceed slowly, testing their assumptions about what strategy will be effective with the other party. They are willing to adjust their use of negotiation strategy to achieve their interests.

Intercultural Negotiation in International Business

Jeswald W. Salacuse

Introduction

Although negotiating a purely domestic business deal and negotiating an international transaction have much in common, the factor that is almost always present in an international negotiation and generally absent from a domestic negotiation is a difference in culture among the parties. In international business, transactions not only cross borders, they also cross cultures. Culture profoundly influences how people think, communicate, and behave, and it also affects the kinds of deals they make and the way they make them. Differences in culture among business executives (for example, between a Chinese public-sector plant manager in Shanghai and an American division head of a family company in Cleveland) can therefore create barriers that impede or completely stymie the negotiating process. The purpose of this article is to examine the effect of differences in culture on international business negotiations and to suggest ways to overcome problems encountered in intercultural dealings.

The Nature of Culture

Definitions of culture are as numerous and often as vague as definitions of negotiation itself (Moran and Stripp 1991, pp. 43–56; Zartman 1993, p. 19). Some scholars would confine the concept of culture to the realm of ideas, feeling, and thoughts. For example, one working definition offered by two negotiation experts is that "Culture is a set of shared and enduring meanings, values, and beliefs that characterize national, ethnic, and other groups and orient their behavior" (Faure and Sjostedt 1993, p. 3). Others would have culture also encompass behavior patterns and institutions common to a given group or community. E. Adamson Hoebel, a noted anthropologist, defined culture as "the integrated system of learned behavior patterns which are characteristic of the members of a society and which are not the result of biological inheritance" (Hoebel 1972, p. 7). While the essence of culture may reside in the mind, it must be pointed out that persons gain their understanding of their and others' cultures primarily, if not exclusively, from observing the behavior and institutions of a particular group.

For purposes of this paper, culture is defined as the socially transmitted behavior patterns, norms, beliefs, and values of a given community (Salacuse 1991, p. 45). Persons from that community use the elements of their culture to interpret their surroundings and guide their interactions with other persons. So when an executive from a corporation in Dallas, Texas, sits down to negotiate a business deal with a manager from a Houston company, the two negotiators rely on their common culture to interpret each other's statements and actions. But when persons from two different cultures—for example an executive from Texas and a manager from Japan—meet for

Source: "Intercultural Negotiation in International Business," by Jeswald W. Salacuse, from *Group Decision and Negotiation* 8, no. 3, May 1999, pp. 217–236. Kluwer Academic Publishers. Used with permission.

the first time, they usually do not share a common pool of information and assumptions to interpret each others' statements, actions, and intentions. Culture can therefore be seen as a language, a "silent language," which the parties need in addition to the language they are speaking if they are truly to communicate and arrive at a genuine understanding (Hall 1959). Like any language, the elements of culture form a system, which has been variously characterized as a "system for creating, sending, storing, and processing information" (Hall and Hall 1990, p. 179) and a "group problem-solving tool that enables individuals to survive in a particular environment" (Moran and Stripp 1991, p. 43). Culture serves as a kind of glue—a social adhesive—that binds a group of people together and gives them a distinct identity as a community. It may also give them a sense that they are a community different and separate from other communities.

This article is concerned primarily with national cultures, cultures identified with a particular country. But culture and nationality are not always the same thing. Within Nigeria, for example, the culture of the Ibos of the largely Christian southeastern part of the country and the Hausas of the mainly Muslim north are different and distinct. Similarly, individual corporations and professions may have their own distinct organizational or professional cultures whose norms and behavior patterns may predominate in certain respects over the ethnic or national cultures of their professions' members. For example, a continuing concern in the current wave of mergers and acquisitions in the United States is the problem of blending the cultures of two organizations, such as Morgan Stanley and Dean Witter, after the deal has been signed (Lublin and O'Brian, 1997). But while cultural values, attitudes, and behavior patterns may appear permanently embedded in a group, particularly in the context of an encounter between two different cultures, in fact culture is dynamic. It is constantly changing (Bohannan 1995).

And finally, in considering the role of culture in international business negotiation and relationships, it is important to remember that the world has a staggering diversity of cultures. For example, while certain observers speak of "Asian culture" as if it were a homogeneous set of values, beliefs, and behavior patterns followed by all Asians (Mahbubani 1995), in reality Asia has many different and distinct cultures from India to Laos, from Korea to Indonesia. Each has its own values and practices that may differ markedly from those prevailing in another country—or indeed in another part of the same country. The negotiating style of Koreans, for example, is not the same as that of the Lao. And even within countries that from outward appearances seem to have a fairly uniform cultural identity, like the French and the Germans, significant differences may nonetheless exist between regions—such as the difference between the business community in Paris and that of the *midi* in southern France.

The Elements of Culture

One may conceive of the four cultural elements mentioned in the previous definition—behavior, attitudes, norms, and values—as forming a series of concentric circles, like the layers of an onion, illustrated by Figure 1.

FIGURE 1 | Culture as an Onion

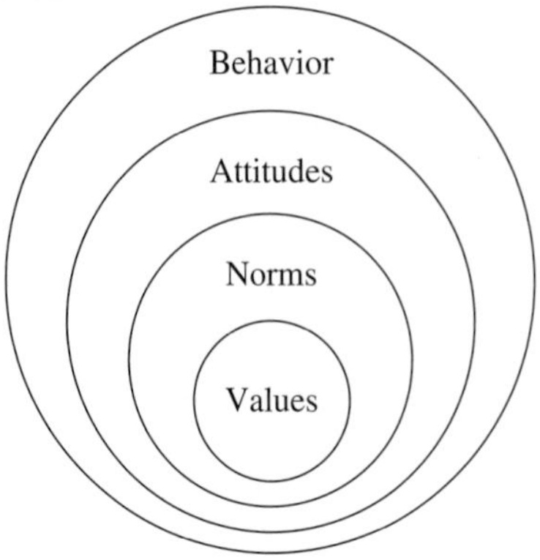

The process of understanding the culture of a counterpart in a negotiation is similar to peeling an onion. The outermost layer of the onion is behavior, the words and actions of one's counterpart. It is this layer which a negotiator first perceives in an intercultural negotiation. A second inner layer consists of attitudes of persons from that culture toward specific events and phenomena—for example, attitudes about beginning meetings punctually or the appropriate format of presentations. Attitudes may become evident to a counterpart in an intercultural negotiation only after protracted discussions. Next are norms, the rules to be followed in specific situations. Here, for example, a negotiator may come to realize that his or her counterpart's seemly rigid insistence on punctuality is not merely a personal idiosyncrasy but is based on a firm rule derived from his or her culture.

The innermost layer—the core—consists of values. Norms about the way meetings are conducted, representatives chosen, or persons rewarded are usually based on certain values that are important to that culture. Such differences in values are often the most difficult for negotiators to detect and understand. Indeed, the parties to an international negotiation may discover their value differences only after they have signed the contract and begun to work together. Such differences in cultural values between partners in an international joint venture, for example, may lead to severe conflict and ultimately the failure of their enterprise, a factor that may explain why many international ventures have a short life.

In their valuable book *The Seven Cultures of Capitalism,* based on extensive survey research among thousands of executives from throughout the world, Hampden-Turner and Trompenaars (1993) found sharp differences that could be explained only by different cultural values to such basic management tasks as group decision making, hiring, rewarding employees, and making and applying rules. For example, with respect to group decision making, wide variations among cultural groups existed in answering the following question:

What is the better way to choose a person to represent a group?

A. All members of the group should meet and discuss candidates until almost everybody agrees on the same person; or

B.   The group members should meet, nominate persons, vote, and choose the person with a majority of the votes even if several people are against the person.

In this question, according to the authors, the values of adversarial democracy and consensual democracy were in tension. While 84.4 percent of the Japanese opted for Answer A (consensual democracy), only 37.7 percent of the Americans did so. It is interesting to note that there were differences among Asians on this question. For example, unlike the Japanese, only 39.4 percent of the Singaporeans chose Answer A, exhibiting an aversion to consensual democracy that is perhaps reflected in Singapore's authoritarian political system. One can imagine that this difference in cultural values about decision making between Japanese and American executives in a joint venture might lead to serious conflict between the joint venture partners. Other kinds of value conflicts may arise, for example, between individualism prized by Americans and communitarianism embodied in many Asian cultures; about whether in hiring an employee it is more important to consider individual talent or the ability to fit into the organization; or about whether to reward persons on the basis of group performance or by individual achievement only.

Differences in cultural values can present themselves in international business transactions and relationships time after time and day after day, and they may ultimately turn what appeared to be a harmonious negotiation or business relationship into a continuing source of conflict between the parties. Once the conflict surfaces, it may be exacerbated by the way the parties try to cope with it. One unfortunate tendency is for each of the parties to extol their own cultural values but to denigrate those of their business or negotiating partner. For example, Americans, with their high store on individualism, will tend to see their value system positively: as for individual rights and human freedom, as putting the individual above the tyranny of the group, as knowing that a group prospers only when individuals prosper, and as efficient. Persons coming from cultures where communitarian values are prized will see themselves as unselfish, humane, for group interests and rights, and knowing that individuals prosper only when the group prospers. Yet Americans, when confronted with a communitarian culture, may tend to ascribe to only its negative characteristics. So Americans, reacting to Japanese values in a decision to retain a 15-year employee whose performance has declined, might consider their Japanese counterparts as tolerant of freeloaders, giving in to the tyranny of the group, weak, and inefficient. On the other hand, the Japanese would probably characterize the Americans as ignoring the contributions and needs of the group, lacking in loyalty, inhumane, and selfish.

It is important therefore for business executives in a negotiation to understand the values inherent in the culture of their counterparts and not to characterize those values in a negative way.

The Effect of Cultural Differences on Negotiation

Differences in culture between deal makers can obstruct negotiations in many ways. First, they can create misunderstandings in communication. If one American executive responds to another American's proposal by saying, "That's difficult," the response, interpreted against American culture and business practice, probably means that the door is still open for further discussion, that perhaps the other side should sweeten its offer. In some other cultures, for example in Asia, persons may be reluctant to say a direct and emphatic no, even when that is their intent. So when a Japanese negotiator, in response to a proposal, says, "That is difficult," he is clearly indicating that the proposal is unacceptable. "It is difficult" means "no" to the Japanese, but to the American it means "maybe."

Second, cultural differences create difficulties not only in understanding words, but also in interpreting actions. For example, most Westerners expect a prompt answer when they make a statement or ask a question. Japanese, on the other hand, tend to take longer to respond. As a result, negotiations with Japanese are sometimes punctuated with periods of silence that seem excruciating to an American. For the Japanese, the period of silence is normal, an appropriate time to reflect on what has been said. The fact that they may not be speaking in their native language lengthens even more the time needed to respond.

From their own cultural perspective, Americans may interpret Japanese silence as rudeness, lack of understanding, or a cunning tactic to get the Americans to reveal themselves. Rather than wait for a response, the American tendency is to fill the void with words by asking questions, offering further explanations, or merely repeating what they have already said. This response to silence may confuse the Japanese, who are made to feel that they are being bombarded by questions and proposals without being given adequate time to respond to any of them.

On the other hand, Latin Americans, who place a high value on verbal agility, have a tendency to respond quickly. Indeed, they may answer a point once they have understood it even though the other side has not finished speaking. While inexperienced American negotiators are sometimes confused by Japanese delays in responding, they can become equally agitated in negotiations with Brazilians by what Americans consider constant interruptions.

Third, cultural considerations also influence the form and substance of the deal you are trying to make. For example, in many parts of the Muslim world, where Islamic law prohibits the taking of interest on loans, one may need to restructure or relabel finance charges in a deal as "administrative fees" in order to gain acceptance at the negotiating table. More substantively, differences in culture will invariably require changes in products, management systems, and personnel practices. For example, in Thailand, the relationship between manager and employee is more hierarchical than it is in the United States. Workers are motivated by a desire to please the manager, but they in turn expect and want their managers to sense their personal problems and be ready to help with them. In other cultures, such as in Australia, employees neither expect nor want managers to become involved with employees' personal problems. Thus an Australian project in Thailand would need to change its concept of employee relations because of the local culture (Hughes and Sheehan 1993).

And finally, culture can influence "negotiating style," the way persons from different cultures conduct themselves in negotiating sessions. Research indicates fairly clearly that negotiation practices differ from culture to culture (Weiss 1994, p. 51). Indeed, culture may influence how persons conceive of the very nature and function of negotiation itself. Studies of negotiating styles are abundant (e.g., Binnendijk 1987; Fisher 1980; Graham et al. 1988; Campbell et al. 1988). Some seek to focus on describing and analyzing the negotiating styles of particular groups. Indeed, the practitioner's fascination with cultural negotiating styles seems to have spawned a distinct literary genre: the "Negotiating with . . ." literature. Numerous books and articles bearing such titles as "Negotiating with the Japanese," "Negotiating with the Arabs," and "Negotiating with the Chinese" seek to lead the novice through the intricacies of negotiating in specific cultures (for a bibliography of such literature, see Salacuse 1991, pp. 174–83). Another approach to studying negotiating style is cross-cultural and comparative. It seeks to identify certain basic elements in negotiating style and to determine how they are reflected in various cultures. It is this approach which the next part of this article will adopt.

Culture and Negotiating Styles: Ten Factors in Deal Making

The great diversity of the world's cultures makes it impossible for any negotiator, no matter how skilled and experienced, to understand fully all the cultures that he or she may encounter. How then should an executive prepare to cope with culture in making deals in Singapore this week and Seoul the next? One approach is to identify important areas where cultural differences may arise during the negotiation process. A knowledge of those factors may help an international business negotiator to understand a counterpart and to anticipate possible misunderstandings. Toward this end, scholars have developed a variety of frameworks and checklists that may be applied cross-culturally (e.g., Weiss 1985; Moran and Stripp 1991; Salacuse 1991). Based on a review of the literature as well as interviews with practitioners, the author, in an earlier work (Salacuse 1991), identified 10 factors that seemed to be the most problematic. These 10 factors, each of which consisted of two poles, were (1) negotiating goals (contract or relationship?); (2) attitudes to the negotiating process (win–win or win–lose?); (3) personal styles (formal or informal?); (4) styles of communication (direct or indirect?); (5) time sensitivity (high or low?); (6) emotionalism (high or low?); (7) agreement form (specific or general?); (8) agreement-building process (bottom up or top down?); (9) negotiating team organization (one leader or consensus?); and (10) risk taking (high or low?). Negotiating styles, like personalities, display a wide range of variation. The 10 negotiating traits listed here can be placed on a spectrum or continuum as illustrated in Figure 2.

FIGURE 2 | The Impact of Culture on Negotiation

Trait			
Goal	Contract	↔	Relationship
Attitudes	Win–lose	↔	Win–win
Personal styles	Informal	↔	Formal
Communications	Direct	↔	Indirect
Time sensitivity	High	↔	Low
Emotionalism	High	↔	Low
Agreement form	Specific	↔	General
Agreement building	Bottom up	↔	Top down
Team organization	One leader	↔	Consensus
Risk taking	High	↔	Low

The purpose of the matrix in Figure 2 is to identify specific negotiating traits affected by culture and to show the possible variation that each trait or factor may take. With this knowledge, an international business negotiator may be able to understand better the negotiating styles and approaches of his counterparts from other cultures. Equally important, it may help negotiators determine how their own styles appear to those same counterparts on the other side of the bargaining table.

In order to test this approach to understanding negotiating style, the matrix was translated into a survey questionnaire and administered to 310 business executives, lawyers, and graduate business students (many of whom had substantial work experience) from all continents at various sites in North America, Latin America, and Europe. The respondents came from 12 countries: the United States, the United Kingdom, France, Germany, Spain, Mexico, Argentina, Brazil, Nigeria, India, China, and Japan. After receiving an explanation of the matrix and questionnaire, respondents were asked to rate their own attitudes anonymously toward each of these negotiating traits on a five-point scale. In general, as will be seen, the survey revealed significant correlations between the respondents' assessment of certain traits of their negotiating styles and the national cultures from which they came.

The results of the survey must be read with several caveats. First, the answers that the respondents gave reflected only how they saw themselves (or would like others to see them) rather than their negotiating styles and behavior in actual negotiations. The results can be read only as indicating a certain predisposition of individual cultures toward certain factors affecting the negotiation process. Second, negotiating style in a given negotiation may be influenced by numerous factors besides culture, including personality, bureaucracy, business experience, and the nature of the transactions under negotiation. For example, an executive who is predisposed to approach a business negotiation as a problem-solving, integrative process (win–win) may behave in a distributive, confrontational way (win–lose) when confronted by a hostile counterpart at the negotiating table. Third, all the respondents spoke English, completed the survey in English, had substantial international experience, and were participating in graduate university education or advanced executive seminars, also conducted in the English language. As a result, they may not be representative of most business executives in their cultures. On the other hand, they are fairly representative of the kinds of persons who conduct international negotiations on behalf of companies. Fourth, the meaning of key terms in the survey, such as *direct, indirect, risk, general,* and *specific,* were not strictly defined but instead were interpreted by each respondent according to his or her own subjective interpretation, a factor obviously influenced by culture. Fifth, both the size of the sample and the number of cultures surveyed were limited.

Negotiating Goal: Contract or Relationship?

Different cultures may view the very purpose of a business negotiation differently. For many American executives, the goal of a business negotiation, first and foremost, is often to arrive at a signed contract between the parties. Americans consider a signed contract as a definitive set of rights and duties that strictly binds the two sides, an attitude succinctly summed up in the statement "a deal is a deal."

Japanese, Chinese, and other cultural groups in Asia, it is said, often consider that the goal of a negotiation is not a signed contract, but the creation of a relationship between the two sides (e.g., Pye 1982). Although the written contract describes the relationship, the essence of the deal is the relationship itself. For Americans, signing a contract is closing a deal; for many Asians, signing a contract might more appropriately be called opening a relationship. This difference in view may explain why Asians tend to give more time and effort to prenegotiation, while Americans want to rush through this first phase in deal making. The activities of prenegotiation, whereby the parties seek to get to know one another thoroughly, are a crucial foundation for a good business relationship. They may seem less important when the goal is merely a contract.

The results of the survey showed significant differences among the cultures surveyed with respect to the negotiating goals of contract and relationship. Thus only 26 percent of the Spanish respondents claimed that their primary goal in a negotiation was a relationship compared to 66 percent of the Indians. On the other hand, the preference for a relationship was not as pronounced among the Chinese (54.5 percent) as one might have expected from the literature, and the Japanese appeared almost evenly divided on the question, with a slight preference for a contract as a negotiating goal. Table 1 summarizes the survey results on this issue.

Negotiating Attitude: Win–Lose or Win–Win?

Because of differences in culture or personality, or both, businesspersons appear to approach deal making with one of two basic attitudes: that a negotiation is either a process in which both can gain (win–win) or a struggle in which of necessity, one side wins and the other side loses (win–lose). Win–win negotiators see deal making as a collaborative and problem-solving process; win–lose negotiators see it as confrontational. In a reflection of this dichotomy, negotiation scholars have concluded that these approaches represented two basic paradigms of the negotiation process: (1) distributive bargaining (i.e., win–lose) and (2) integrative bargaining or problem solving (i.e., win–win) (e.g., Hoppman 1995; Lewicki et al. 1993). In the former situation, the parties see their goals as incompatible, while in the latter they consider themselves to have compatible goals.

For example, developing country officials often view negotiations with multinational corporations as win–lose competitions. In negotiating investment contracts, they often consider profits earned by the investor as automatic losses to the host country. As a result, they may focus their efforts in the negotiation fixedly on limiting investor profit in contrast to discovering how to maximize benefits from the project for both the investor and the country. It is interesting to note that those same officials might approach negotiations in their home villages with members of their ethnic group or clans on a win–win basis.

TABLE 1 | Goal: Contract or Relationship?

Contract:	Spn.	Fr.	Braz.	Jpn.	USA	Ger.	UK	Nig.	Arg.	Chi.	Mex.	Ind.
Percentage:	73.7	70	66.7	54.5	53.7	54.5	47.1	46.7	46.2	45.5	41.7	33.3

TABLE 2 | Negotiating Attitude: Win–Win or Win–Lose?

Win–Win:	Jpn.	Chi.	Arg.	Fr.	Ind.	USA	UK	Mex.	Ger.	Nig.	Braz.	Sp.
Percentage:	100	81.8	80.8	80	77.8	70.7	58.8	50	54.5	46.7	44.4	36.8

The survey conducted by the author found wide differences among the cultures represented in the survey on this question. Whereas 100 percent of the Japanese viewed business negotiation as a win–win process, only 36.8 percent of the Spanish were so inclined. The Chinese and Indians, the other two Asian cultures represented in the survey, also claimed that negotiation was for them win–win, and the French, alone among Europeans, took a similarly pronounced position on the question. Table 2 summarizes the results of all groups surveyed with respect to this attitude toward negotiation.

Personal Style: Informal or Formal?

Personal style concerns the way a negotiator talks to others, uses titles, dresses, speaks, and interacts with other persons. Culture strongly influences the personal style of negotiators. It has been observed, for example, that Germans have a more formal style than Americans (Hall and Hall 1990, p. 48). A negotiator with a formal style insists on addressing counterparts by their titles, avoids personal anecdotes, and refrains from questions touching on the private or family life of members of the other negotiating team. An informal-style negotiator tries to start the discussion on a first-name basis, quickly seeks to develop a personal, friendly relationship with the other team, and may take off his jacket and roll up his sleeves when deal making begins in earnest. Each culture has its own formalities, which have special meaning within that culture. They are another means of communication among the persons sharing that culture, another form of adhesive that binds them together as a community. Negotiators in foreign cultures must respect appropriate formalities. As a general rule, it is always safer to adopt a formal posture and move to an informal stance, if the situation warrants it, than to assume an informal style too quickly.

On the other hand, an encounter between negotiators having different personal styles can sometimes lead to conflict that impedes a negotiation. For an American or an Australian, calling someone by his or her first name is an act of friendship and therefore a good thing. For a Japanese or an Egyptian, the use of the first name at a first meeting is an act of disrespect and therefore a bad thing.

Except for the Nigerians, a majority of the respondents within each of the 12 groups surveyed claimed to have an informal negotiating style; however, the strength of this view varied considerably. While nearly 83 percent of the Americans considered themselves to have an informal negotiating style, only 54 percent of the Chinese, 52 percent of the Spanish, and 58 percent of the Mexicans were similarly inclined. Among the four European national cultures surveyed, the French were the strongest in claiming an informal style. Although both the Germans and Japanese have a reputation for formality, only slightly more than one-quarter of the respondents in these two groups believed they had a formal negotiating style. Differences in cultures with respect to the meaning of the terms *formal* and *informal* may have influenced this result. The survey's findings on this negotiating trait are summarized in Table 3.

TABLE 3 | Personal Style: Formal or Informal?

Formal:	Nig.	Spn.	Chi.	Mex.	UK	Arg.	Ger.	Jpn.	Ind.	Braz.	Fr.	USA
Percentage:	53	47.4	45.5	41.7	35.3	34.6	27.3	27.3	22.2	22.2	20	17.1

Communication: Direct or Indirect?

Methods of communication vary among cultures. Some place emphasis on direct and simple methods of communication; others rely heavily on indirect and complex methods. It has been observed, for example, that whereas Germans and Americans are direct, the French and the Japanese are indirect (Hall and Hall 1990, p. 102). Persons with an indirect style of communication often make assumptions about the level of knowledge possessed by their counterparts and to a significant extent communicate with oblique references, circumlocutions, vague allusions, figurative forms of speech, facial expressions, gestures, and other kinds of body language. In a culture that values directness such as the American or the Israeli, one can expect to receive a clear and definite response to proposals and questions. In cultures that rely on indirect communication, such as the Japanese, reaction to proposals may be gained by interpreting seemingly indefinite comments, gestures, and other signs.

The confrontation of these styles of communication in the same negotiation can lead to friction. For example, the indirect ways Japanese negotiators express disapproval have often led foreign business executives to believe that their proposals were still under consideration when they had in fact been rejected by the Japanese side. In the Camp David negotiations, the Israeli preference for direct forms of communication and the Egyptian tendency to favor indirect forms sometimes exacerbated relations between the two sides. The Egyptians interpreted Israeli directness as aggressiveness and, therefore, an insult. The Israelis viewed Egyptian indirectness with impatience and suspected them of insincerity, of not saying what they meant.

In the survey, respondents in all cultural groups by a high margin claimed to have a direct form of communication. Here too the organizational culture of the participants and their international experience may have strongly influenced their responses to the questionnaire. It is worth noting, however, that the two cultural groups with the largest percentage of persons claiming an indirect style were the Japanese and the French. Table 4 summarizes the results on this issue.

Sensitivity to Time: High or Low?

Discussions of national negotiating styles invariably treat a particular culture's attitudes toward time. So it is said that Germans are always punctual, Latins are habitually late,

TABLE 4 | Communication: Direct or Indirect?

Indirect:	Jpn.	Fr.	Chi.	UK	Braz.	Ind.	Ger.	USA	Arg.	Spn.	Mex.	Nig.
Percentage:	27.3	20	18.2	11.8	11.1	11.1	9.1	4.9	3.8	0	0	0

Japanese negotiate slowly, and Americans are quick to make a deal. Commentators sometimes claim that some cultures "value" time more than others, but this may not be an accurate characterization of the situation. Rather they may value differently the amount of time devoted to and measured against the goal pursued. For Americans, the deal is a signed contract and "time is money," so they want to make a deal quickly. Americans therefore try to reduce formalities to a minimum and get down to business quickly. Japanese and other Asians, whose goal is to create a relationship rather than simply sign a contract, will need to invest time in the negotiating process so that the parties can get to know one another well and determine whether they wish to embark on a long-term relationship. They may view aggressive attempts to shorten the negotiating time with suspicion as efforts to hide something.

As a general rule, Asians tend to devote more time and attention to the prenegotiation phase of deal making than do Americans. Whereas American executives and lawyers generally want to "dispense with the preliminaries" and "to get down to cases," most Asians view prenegotiation as an essential foundation to any business relationship; consequently, they recognize the need to conduct prenegotiation with care before actually making a decision to undertake substantive negotiations of a deal. One of the consequences of this difference in approach is that Americans sometimes assume that discussions with Asian counterparts have passed from prenegotiation to a subsequent stage when in fact they have not because the Asians have not yet decided to undertake substantive negotiations. This type of misunderstanding can lead to suspicions of bad faith, resulting ultimately in total failure of the talks. Negotiators need to be sure that they and their counterparts are always in the same phase of the deal-making process. One way of making sure is by using written agendas, memoranda, and letters of intent to mark the various phases.

The survey did not reveal significant divergences with respect to time. A majority of the respondents from all cultural groups surveyed claimed to have a high sensitivity to time; however, the strength of the minority view on this question varied considerably among the groups. The Indians, French, and Germans included a substantial percentage of respondents asserting a low sensitivity to time. Table 5 summarizes the results.

These survey results on this question could have been affected by the organizational cultures of the respondents, as well as by variations in the way that respondents interpreted the term *time sensitivity*. Cultural discussions about time in negotiations often refer to two elements: promptness is meeting deadlines and the amount of time devoted to a negotiation. Thus Germans, it has been observed, are highly time sensitive with regard to promptness but less so with respect to their willingness to devote large amounts of time to a negotiation (Hall and Hall 1990, p. 37). Thus they are punctual (high time sensitivity) but slow to negotiate and make decisions (low time sensitivity).

TABLE 5 | Sensitivity to Time: High or Low?

Low:	*Ind.*	*Fr.*	*Ger.*	*Mex.*	*Spn.*	*Arg.*	*US*	*Jpn.*	*Chi.*	*Nig.*	*UK*	*Braz.*
Percentage:	44.4	40	36.4	33.3	21.1	15.4	14.6	9.1	9.1	6.7	5.9	0

Emotionalism: High or Low?

Accounts of negotiating behavior in other cultures almost always point to a particular group's tendency or lack thereof to act emotionally. According to the stereotype, Latin Americans show their emotions at the negotiating table, while Japanese and many other Asians hide their feelings. Obviously, individual personality plays a role here. There are passive Latins and hotheaded Japanese. Nonetheless, various cultures have different rules as to the appropriateness and form of displaying emotions, and these rules are brought to the negotiating table as well.

In the survey conducted by the author, Latin Americans and the Spanish were the cultural groups that ranked themselves highest with respect to emotionalism in a clearly statistically significant fashion. Among Europeans, the Germans and English ranked as least emotional, while among Asians the Japanese held that position, but to a lesser degree than the two European groups. Table 6 summarizes the results with regard to emotionalism.

Form of Agreement: General or Specific?

Cultural factors also influence the form of the written agreement that parties try to make. Generally, Americans prefer very detailed contracts that attempt to anticipate all possible circumstances and eventualities, no matter how unlikely. Why? Because the "deal" is the contract itself, and one must refer to the contract to handle new situations that may arise in the future. Other cultures, such as the Chinese, prefer a contract in the form of general principles rather than detailed rules. Why? Because it is claimed that the essence of the deal is the relationship between the parties. If unexpected circumstances arise, the parties should look to their relationship, not the contract, to solve the problem. So in some cases, a Chinese may interpret the American drive to stipulate all contingencies as evidence of lack of confidence in the stability of the underlying relationship.

Some practitioners argue that differences over the form of an agreement are caused more by unequal bargaining power than by culture. In a situation of unequal bargaining power, the stronger party usually seeks a detailed agreement to "lock up the deal" in all its possible dimensions, while the weaker party prefers a general agreement to give it room to "wiggle out" of adverse circumstances that are bound to occur. So a Chinese commune as the weaker party in a negotiation with a multinational corporation will seek a general agreement as a way of protecting itself against an uncertain future. According to this view, it is context, not culture, that determines this negotiating trait.

The survey showed that a majority of respondents in each cultural group preferred specific agreements over general agreements. This result may be attributed in part to the relatively large number of lawyers among the respondents, as well as to the fact that multinational corporate practice favors specific agreements and many of the respondents,

TABLE 6 | Emotionalism: High or Low?

Low:	Ger.	UK	Jpn.	Ind.	Fr.	Nig.	USA	Chi.	Spn.	Mex.	Arg.	Braz.
Percentage:	63.6	52.9	45.5	44.4	40	40	36.6	27.3	21.1	16.7	15.4	11.1

TABLE 7 | Agreement Form: General or Specific?

General:	Jpn.	Ger.	Ind.	Fr.	Chi.	Arg.	Braz.	USA	Nig.	Mex.	Spn	UK
Percentage:	45.5	45.4	44.4	30	27.3	26.9	22.2	22	20	16.7	15.8	11.8

regardless of nationality, had experience with such firms. The survey responses on this point may have been a case where professional or organizational culture dominated over national cultural traits. On the other hand, the degree of intensity of responses on the question varied considerably among cultural groups. While only 11 percent of the British favored general agreements, 45.5 percent of the Japanese and of the Germans claimed to do so. Table 7 sets out the survey results with respect to agreement form.

Building an Agreement: Bottom Up or Top Down?

Related to the form of the agreement is the question of whether negotiating a business deal is an inductive or a deductive process. Does it start from agreement on general principles and proceed to specific items, or does it begin with agreement on specifics, such as price, delivery date, and product quality, the sum total of which becomes the contract? Different cultures tend to emphasize one approach over the other.

Some observers believe that the French prefer to begin with agreement on general principles, while Americans tend to seek agreement first on specifics. For Americans, negotiating a deal is basically making a series of compromises and trade-offs on a long list of particulars. For the French, the essence is to agree on basic principles that will guide and indeed determine the negotiation process afterward. The agreed-upon general principles become the framework, the skeleton, upon which the contract is built.

A further difference in negotiating style is seen in the dichotomy between "the building-down approach" and the "building-up approach." In the building-down approach, the negotiator begins by presenting the maximum deal if the other side accepts all the stated conditions. In the building-up approach, one side begins by proposing a minimum deal that can be broadened and increased as the other party accepts additional conditions. According to many observers, Americans tend to favor the building-down approach, while the Japanese tend to prefer the building-up style of negotiating a contract.

The survey did not reveal significant cultural trends on this issue among Americans, Germans, and Nigerians, since the respondents from these three groups were relatively evenly divided on the question. On the other hand, the French, Argentineans, and Indians tended to view deal making as a top-down (deductive) process, while Japanese, Mexicans, and Brazilians tended to see it as a bottom-up (inductive) process. Table 8 summarizes the results on the question.

TABLE 8 | Building an Agreement: Bottom Up or Top Down?

Top down:	Ind.	Arg.	Fr.	UK	Chi.	Ger.	USA	Nig.	Spn.	Jpn.	Braz.	Mex.
Percentage:	66.7	61.5	60	58.8	54.5	54.5	53.7	53.3	52.6	36.4	33.3	33.3

Team Organization: One Leader or Group Consensus?

In any international business negotiation, it is important to know how the other side is organized, who has the authority to make commitments, and how decisions are made. Culture is one important factor that affects how executives and lawyers organize themselves to negotiate a deal. Some cultures emphasize the individual while others stress the group. These values may influence the organization of each side to a negotiation. One extreme is the negotiating team with a supreme leader who has complete authority to decide all matters. Many American teams tend to follow this approach, which has been labeled the "John Wayne style of negotiations" (Graham and Herberger 1983, p. 160). Other cultures, notably the Japanese, stress team negotiation and consensus decision making. When you negotiate with such a team, it may not be apparent who is the leader and who has authority to commit the side. In the first type, the negotiating team is usually small; in the second it is often large. For example, in negotiations in China on a major deal, it would not be uncommon for the Americans to arrive at the table with 3 persons and for the Chinese to show up with 10. Similarly, the one-leader team is usually prepared to make commitments and decisions more quickly than a negotiating team organized on the basis of consensus. As a result, the consensus type of organization usually takes more time to negotiate a deal.

The survey on negotiating styles revealed differences in preference among respondents, depending on culture. The group with the strongest preference for a consensus organization were the French. French individualism has been noted in many studies (Hall and Hall 1990), and perhaps a consensus arrangement in French eyes is the best way to protect that individualism. Despite the Japanese reputation for consensus arrangements, only 45 percent of the Japanese respondents claimed to prefer a negotiating team based on consensus. The Brazilians, the Chinese, and Mexicans, to a far greater degree than any other groups, preferred one-person leadership, a reflection perhaps of the political traditions in those countries. The results of the survey on this point are summarized in Table 9.

Risk Taking: High or Low?

Research supports the conclusion that certain cultures are more risk averse than others (Hofstede 1980). In deal making, the culture of the negotiators can affect the willingness of one side to take "risks" in the negotiation—to divulge information, try new approaches, or tolerate uncertainties in a proposed course of action. A negotiator who senses that the other side is risk averse needs to focus efforts on proposing rules and mechanisms that will reduce the apparent risks in the deal for them.

The Japanese, with their emphasis on requiring large amounts of information and their intricate group decision-making process, tend to be risk averse, a fact affirmed by the author's survey, which found Japanese respondents to be the most risk averse of all

TABLE 9 | Team Organization: One Leader or Consensus?

One Leader:	Braz.	Chi.	Mex.	UK	USA	Spn.	Arg.	Ger.	Jpn.	Ind.	Nig.	Fr.
Percentage:	100	90.9	90.9	64.7	63.4	57.7	57.7	54.5	54.5	44.4	40	40

TABLE 10 | Risk Taking: High or Low?

Low:	Fr.	Ind.	UK	Chi.	USA	Nig.	Arg.	Ger.	Braz.	Mex.	Spn.	Jpn.
Percentage:	90	88.9	88.2	81.8	78	73.3	73.1	72	55.6	50	47.4	18.2

countries covered in the survey. Americans in the survey, by comparison, considered themselves to be risk takers, but an even higher percentage of French, British, and Indians claimed to be risk takers. Table 10 summarizes the survey results with respect to risk.

Coping with Culture

In view of the importance of cultural differences in international business negotiations, how should negotiators seek to cope with them? The following are a few simple rules.

Rule 1: Learn the Other Side's Culture

In any international business dealing, it is important for a negotiator to learn something about the other side's culture. The degree to which such learning takes place depends on a number of factors, including the nature and importance of the transaction, the experience of the negotiators, the time available for learning, and the similarities or lack thereof between the cultures represented in the negotiation. For example, the negotiation of a simple, one-time export sale may demand less cultural knowledge than the negotiation of a long-term strategic alliance, which may require the parties to audit each other's culture as well as their financial assets.

Ideally, learning another's culture can require several years of study, mastery of a foreign language, and prolonged residence in the country of that culture. An American faced with the task of negotiating a strategic alliance with a Thai company in Bangkok in two weeks' time cannot, of course, master Thai culture that fast. At best, he or she can learn enough to cope with some of the principal effects that Thai culture may have on making the deal. Important sources of information on Thai culture would include histories of the country, consultation with persons having business experience in the country, local lawyers and consultants, anthropological and ethnographic studies, reports on the current political situation, and accounts, if any, on negotiating with the Thais. As Weiss quite correctly points out, the degree of a negotiator's cultural knowledge will influence strategies and tactics during the negotiation (Weiss 1994, p. 53). For example, a person with strong familiarity with the counterpart's language and culture may use the negotiation style and approach of his counterpart's culture, while a person with less familiarity may choose, as a strategy, to employ an agent or mediator from that culture to assist in the negotiations.

As international business transactions increasingly take the form of long-term relationships—what Gomes-Casseres (1996) has termed the "alliance revolution"—it is equally important to recognize that cultural learning continues long after the contract is signed. In effect, the dynamics of such long-term relationships between the parties are very much a continuing negotiation as the alliance partners shape the rules and practices of their business relationship.

Rule 2: Don't Stereotype

If rule one in international negotiation is "know the other side's culture," rule two is "avoid overreliance on that knowledge." As the survey indicates, not all Japanese evade giving a direct negative answer. Not all Germans will tell a counterpart specifically what they think of a proposal. In short, the negotiator who enters a foreign culture should be careful not to allow cultural stereotypes to determine his or her relations with local businesspersons. Foreign business executives and lawyers will be offended if they feel their counterparts are not treating them as individuals, but rather as cultural robots. In addition to giving offense, cultural stereotypes can be misleading. Many times the other side simply does not run true to the negotiating form suggested by books, articles, and consultants. The reason, of course, is that other forces besides culture may influence a person's negotiating behavior. Specifically, these forces may include the negotiator's personality, the organization he or she represents, and the context of the particular negotiation in question.

Rule 3: Find Ways to Bridge the Culture Gap

Generally, executives and lawyers who confront a culture different from their own in a negotiation tend to view it in one of three ways: as an obstacle, a weapon, or a fortress (Salacuse 1993). At the operational level, cultural differences are hardly ever seen as positive.

The conventional view among most American executives is that cultural differences are an obstacle to agreement and effective joint action. They therefore search for ways to overcome the obstacle. But a different culture in a business setting can become more than an obstacle; it can be seen as a weapon, particularly when a dominant party tries to impose its culture on the other side. For example, American lawyers' insistence on structuring a transaction "the way we do it in the United States" may be considered by their foreign counterparts as the use of American culture as a weapon.

Faced with a culture that it perceives as a weapon, a party to a business deal may become defensive and try to use its own culture as a fortress to protect itself from what it perceives as a cultural onslaught. The Japanese have often adopted this approach when confronted with American demands to open their markets. France's drive to limit the use of English in advertising is a defensive response to what it considered to be the weapon of "Anglo-Saxon" culture.

It may be helpful to try to think of cultural differences in yet another way. Differences in cultures tend to isolate individuals and groups from each other. In short, cultural differences create a gap between persons and organizations. Often the action that people take when confronted with cultural differences serves only to widen the gap—as, for example, when one side denigrates the other side's cultural practices.

Remembering the words of the English poet Philip Larkin, "Always it is by bridges that we live," effective international business negotiators should seek to find ways to bridge the gap caused by cultural difference. One way to build that bridge is by using culture itself. If culture is indeed the glue that binds together a particular group of people, the creative use of culture between persons of different cultures is often a way to link those on opposite sides of the culture gap. Basically, there are four types of cultural bridge building that one may consider when confronted with a culture gap in a negotiation:

1. *Bridge the gap using the other side's culture:* One technique for bridging the gap is for a negotiator or manager to try to assume some or all of the cultural values and characteristics of the foreign persons with whom he or she is dealing. In international business, negotiators often try to use or identify with the other side's culture in order to build a relationship. For example, when President Sadat of Egypt negotiated with Sudanese officials, he always made a point of telling them that his mother had been born in the Sudan. He was thus using a common cultural thread to build a relationship with his counterparts. In effect, he was saying, "Like you, I am Sudanese, so we have common cultural ties. I understand you and I value your culture. Therefore you can trust me." Similarly, an African American managing a joint venture in Nigeria stressed his African heritage to build relationships with Nigerian counterparts. And an Italian American negotiating a sales contract in Rome emphasized his Italian background as a way of bridging the cultural gap that he perceived.

2. *Bridge the gap using your own culture:* A second general approach to bridging the culture gap is to persuade or induce the other side to adopt elements of your culture. To implement this approach successfully requires time and education. For example, in order to give a common culture to a joint venture, an American partner incurred significant cost by sending executives of its foreign partner to schools and executive training programs in the United States and then assigning them for short periods to the U.S. partner's own operations.

3. *Bridge with some combination of both cultures:* A third approach to dealing with the culture gap is to build a bridge using elements from cultures of both sides. In effect, cultural bridging takes place on both sides of the gap and, with luck, results in the construction of a solid integrated structure. The challenge in this approach is to identify the most important elements of each culture and to find ways of blending them into a consistent, harmonious whole that will allow business to be done effectively. Sometimes a third person in the form of mediator or consultant can help in the process.

4. *Bridge with a third culture:* A final method of dealing with the culture gap is to build a bridge by relying on a third culture that belongs to neither of the parties. Thus, for example, in a difficult negotiation between an American executive and a Chinese manager, both discovered that they had a great appreciation of French culture since they had both studied in France in their youth. They began to converse in French, and their common love of France enabled them to build a strong personal relationship. They used a third culture to bridge the cultural gap between China and America. Similarly, negotiators from two different national cultures may use elements of their common professional cultures, as lawyers or as engineers, to bridge the gap between them.

Conclusion

Cultural bridging, like bridge construction, requires the cooperation of the parties at both ends of the divide. No negotiator will permit a bridge to be built if he or she feels threatened or sees the bridge as a long-term danger to security. Consequently, negotiators who want to build a bridge across the cultural divide to their counterpart must be concerned to strengthen the other side's sense of security, not weaken it as happens all too often in international business relationships.

References

Binnendijk, H. (ed.). (1987). *National Negotiating Styles.* Washington, DC: U.S. Department of State.

Bohannan, P. (1995). *How Culture Works.* New York: Free Press.

Campbell, N. C. G., et al. (1998). "Marketing Negotiations in France, Germany, the United Kingdom, and the United States," *Journal of Marketing* 52, pp. 49–62.

Faure, G. O., and G. Sjostedt. (1993). "Culture and Negotiation: An Introduction," in G.O. Faure and J. Z. Rubin (eds.), *Culture and Negotiation.* Newbury Park, CA: Sage Publications.

Fisher, G. (1980). *International Negotiation: A Cross-Cultural Perspective.* Yarmouth, ME: Intercultural Press.

Gomes-Casseres, B. (1996). *The Alliance Revolution.* Cambridge, MA: Harvard University Press.

Graham, J. L., et al. (1988). "Buyer–Seller Negotiations around the Pacific Rim: Differences in Fundamental Exchange Processes," *Journal of Consumer Research* 15, pp. 48–54.

Graham J. L., and R. A. Herberger. (1983). "Negotiators Abroad—Don't Shoot from the Hip: Cross-Cultural Business Negotiations," *Harvard Business Review* 61, pp. 160–83.

Hall, E. T. (1959). *The Silent Language.* New York: Doubleday.

Hall, E. T., and M. Reed Hall. (1990). *Understanding Cultural Differences.* Yarmouth, ME: Intercultural Press.

Hampden-Turner, C., and A. Trompenaars. (1993). *The Seven Cultures of Capitalism.* New York: Doubleday.

Hoebel, E. A. (1972). *Anthropology: The Study of Man* (4th ed.) New York: McGraw-Hill.

Hofstede, G. (1980). *Culture's Consequences: International Differences in Work-Related Values.* Newbury Park, CA: Sage Publications.

Hoppman, T. (1995). "Two Paradigms of Negotiation: Bargaining and Problem Solving," *Annals, AAPSS* 542, pp. 24–47.

Hughes, P., and B. Sheehan. (1993). "Business Cultures: The Transfer of Managerial Policies and Practices from One Culture to Another," *Business and the Contemporary World* 5, pp. 153–70.

Lewicki, R., et al. (1993). *Negotiation—Readings, Exercises, and Cases.* Burr Ridge, IL: McGraw-Hill.

Lublin, J. S., and B. O'Brian. (1997). "Merged Firms Often Face Culture Clash," *Wall Street Journal,* February 14, 1997, p. A9A.

Mahbubani, K. (1995). "The Pacific Way," *Foreign Affairs* 74, pp. 100–11.

Moran, R. T., and W. G. Stripp. (1991). *Successful International Business Negotiations.* Houston: Gulf Publishing Company.

Pye, L. (1982). *Chinese Negotiating Style.* Cambridge, MA: Oelgeschlager, Gunn and Hain.

Salacuse, J. W. (1991). *Making Global Deals—Negotiating in the International Market Place.* Boston: Houghton Mifflin.

Salacuse, J. W. (1993). "Implications for Practitioners," in G. O. Faure and J. Z. Rubin (eds.), *Culture and Negotiation.* Newbury Park, CA: Sage Publications.

Weiss, S. E. (1994). "Negotiating with Romans," (parts 1 and 2), *Sloan Management Review* 35, pp. 51, 85.

Zartman, I. W. (1993). "A Skeptic's View," in G. O. Faure and J. Z. Rubin (eds.), *Culture and Negotiation.* Newbury Park, CA: Sage Publications.

American Strengths and Weaknesses

Tommy T. B. Koh

American Strengths and Qualities

Two caveats are appropriate for any discussion of national negotiating styles. First, there may not necessarily be a definable negotiating style for each country or people. Good and effective negotiators, irrespective of their national or cultural background, have certain common skills. Second, although it is probably possible to say impressionistically that the American people possess certain character and personality traits, there are many exceptions to the rule, and a person's negotiating style is inevitably affected by his character, temperament, and attitude toward people.

American negotiators have many strengths and qualities. If distance makes the heart grow fonder, my perception of Americans may be unrealistically favorable and idealized, since Singapore is located 12,000 miles away from the United States.

First, U.S. negotiators are usually well prepared. They arrive at negotiations with their homework completed, and they are armed with facts, figures, maps, and charts. They usually know what their national interests are and what their negotiating objectives are. This is not always the case among Third World negotiators.

Second, American negotiators tend to speak clearly and plainly. As someone who was educated in the Anglo-Saxon legal tradition, I regard this as a virtue, not a liability. However, the American preference for plain speaking can sometimes cause unintended offense to other negotiators whose national culture prefers indirectness, subtlety, and avoidance of confrontation. There are, of course, exceptions to this rule.

Third, U.S. negotiators tend to be more pragmatic than doctrinaire. They focus on advancing their country's interests rather than principles that they cherish. The Reagan administration, however, was a clear exception to this rule, and at the Third U.N. Conference on the Law of the Sea decided, for rational and arguable reasons, that principles were more important than interests.

Fourth, American negotiators generally do not regard negotiations as a zero-sum game. A good U.S. negotiator is even prepared to put himself in the place of his negotiating adversary. A good U.S. negotiator is prepared to admit that his adversary, like himself, has certain irreducible, minimum national interests. A good U.S. negotiator is prepared to engage in a process of give and take, and he believes that the successful outcome of a negotiation is not one in which he wins everything and his adversary loses everything, but rather one in which there is a mutuality of benefits and losses, in which each side has a stake in honoring and maintaining the agreement.

Fifth, a U.S. negotiator's opening position is never his final position. He expects his opponent to make a counterproposal or a counteroffer. He is anxious to reach an agreement and will, therefore, make concessions to his opponent, expecting—not unreasonably—that

Source: "American Strengths and Weaknesses," by Tommy T. B. Koh, from *International Negotiation* 1, no. 2., 1996, pp. 313–317. Brill Academic Press. Used with permission.

his adversary will behave in like manner. Americans are sometimes completely exasperated at international forums when their adversaries do not behave as they do.

Sixth, the American people are very candid and straightforward, and this is reflected in their negotiating style. Americans are not usually perceived as cunning or devious. In only one incident have I found American negotiators to be devious, and that was shocking. This incident occurred in July 1981 when the United Nations sponsored an international conference on Cambodia. The conference was initiated by the ASEAN (Association of Southeast Asian Nations) countries, which proposed a framework for the resolution of the Cambodian situation. All Cambodian factions were invited to participate in the conference, including, of course, the Khmer Rouge. Vietnam was invited, but boycotted the meeting. At the conference General Alexander Haig, then U.S. Secretary of State, staged a dramatic walkout, accompanied by the entire U.S. delegation, when the Khmer Rouge leader approached the rostrum to speak. The picture of this walkout appeared on the front page of *The New York Times*.

On a subsequent day, the ASEAN countries and the People's Republic of China (PRC) were locked in a ferocious confrontation over the future role of the Khmer Rouge in any postsettlement Cambodia. The ASEAN countries argued that in light of the massacres and atrocities that the Khmer Rouge had committed, it would be morally and legally impermissible to allow them to return to power. We demanded a public election to be organized and supervised by the United Nations. To ensure free elections, we insisted that all armed elements be disarmed or sequestered in camp. The Chinese fought against all these points. The negotiating group was composed of 25 delegations, but the dynamics of the discussions revolved around the PRC, the ASEAN countries, and Pakistan as a middleman. Pakistan, however, was not an honest broker and basically submitted a series of amendments to dilute the ASEAN position. I assumed that Pakistan, because of its proximity to the PRC, was "fronting" for the Chinese, and was shocked to learn later that they were actually fronting for the Americans. Although the American delegation had publicly walked out of the negotiations, they were privately supporting China for geostrategic reasons. This is the only example of devious behavior by American negotiators of which I am aware, but I will remember it.

Weaknesses and Idiosyncrasies

One problem in negotiating with Americans is that American delegations usually suffer from serious interagency rivalries. During the U.N. Law of the Sea Conference the American delegation met every morning, and sometimes their internal meetings lasted longer than the other meetings in the conference.

A second problem in negotiating with the United States is the separation of power between the administration and the Congress. One has to be very careful if one is negotiating an agreement that is subject to ratification by the U.S. Senate. It is important to always keep in touch with U.S. senators as the negotiating process continues in order to obtain their independent inputs, be aware of their sensitivities, and recognize vested domestic interests and blocking constituencies.

A third special characteristic is the influence of the U.S. private sector and private interest groups on negotiations. During the Law of the Sea Conference I made it a point to meet not only with the official U.S. delegation and members of the Congress, but also to meet with representatives from the seabed mining industry, the petroleum industry, the fishing industry, the marine scientific community, the environmental lobby, and individuals who have an affection for marine mammals. The reality of political life in America is that even one of these many lobbies can block ratification of a treaty. Foreign negotiators must understand the domestic political process in the United States and must, in some way, interfere in American internal affairs to ensure the success of their mission.

A fourth problem—the role of U.S. media—is a problem more for U.S. negotiators than for their counterparts. This is a problem because somehow the good nature of Americans and their propensity to candor makes it very difficult even for negotiators to keep confidences. And in the midst of a sensitive negotiation it is sometimes very counterproductive for the media to report on issues that are under negotiation. In a speech to the House Foreign Affairs Committee, former Secretary of States George Shultz recounted with great frustration an occasion when the United States and U.S.S.R. were engaged in bilateral negotiations. The negotiation had reached a critical point, and he had that day drafted a cable giving his final instructions. He said he found to his horror at breakfast the next morning that *The New York Times* had reported the content of his cable. Members of the U.S. media should be asked whether they should exercise more discretion and self-restraint. Do they not feel an allegiance as American citizens to the advancement and protection of American national interests? Should not the right of the public to know and the freedom of the press sometimes be modulated by competing and larger interests? The extent to which the United States exposes its flank makes it easier for others to win at the negotiating table.

A fifth weakness is impatience. Americans suffer from an "instant-coffee complex." They do not have time, as Europeans and Asians do, to buy coffee beans, grind them every day, brew the coffee, enjoy the aroma, and savor every sip. Americans are always in a rush and are extremely frustrated when there is a lack of progress. Americans are result-oriented. Jeane Kirkpatrick had a shock several years ago when she visited the ASEAN capitals and met the foreign ministers of the six ASEAN countries. To each she asked, "Do you think there are prospects for settling the Cambodian conflict?" All six ASEAN foreign ministers said yes. She said, "Do you think it will be soon?" They all said, "Oh yes, very soon." She said, "Well, how soon?" They said, "Oh, about five years' time." She was shocked because to an American five years' time is certainly not soon.

A sixth weakness is cultural insensitivity. Everyone is guilty of this, not only Americans. Everyone assumes that others have similar cultures, customs, and manners. Singaporeans are "the barbarians of Southeast Asia." We are "the least sensitive and least subtle people in the region." But if one is a professional negotiator, then part of the preparation for an effective negotiation is to learn enough about the culture of one's adversary to at least avoid simple errors of behavior, attribution, and body language.

Finally, it is surprising that in many recent multilateral forums the United States has been represented by amateur rather than professional negotiators. Given that the United States is so rich in human resources and has a foreign service studded by superstars, it is amazing how inadequately the United States is represented at important international negotiations.

Conclusion

In conclusion, a good negotiator, whether an Indian, an American, a Canadian, English, Ghanian, or whoever, is a person with certain definable skills, aptitudes, and temperaments. His character and personality have an impact on his effectiveness. Some American negotiators put people off; others readily win people's confidence. In choosing a negotiator, select someone who does not bristle like a porcupine but who can win the trust and confidence of his negotiating partners. What are these qualities that attract people's confidence and trust? These are moral qualities, qualities of leadership. If a negotiator is a leader, a person who acquires a reputation for competence, reliability, and trustworthiness, then others will trust him with leadership roles. The word *charisma* is not useful because it does not accurately portray the quality that bestows leadership on certain negotiators and not others. Henry Kissinger is not charismatic; he is dominating and impassive and has an exceptional intellect and a monotonous voice. In 1976, when the Law of Sea Conference was deadlocked between industrialized and developing countries, Kissinger, who was then secretary of state and had no background in the law of the sea and knew nothing about seabed mining, spent one morning in New York meeting with the U.S. delegation. In the afternoon he met with other leaders of the Group of 77, and by the end of the day presented an innovative scheme for reconciling the competing ambitions and claims of the different countries.

There probably is an American negotiating style, and this partakes of the qualities, attitudes, customs, conventions, and reflexes that have come down through U.S. history, culture, and political institutions. On the whole, American negotiators have very positive qualities, being well prepared, reasonable, competent, and honorable. Even more than this, some, like Elliott Richardson, will take it upon themselves to be an honest broker and help to settle a conflict between two other groups in which they are a totally disinterested party. This graciousness and willingness to help are positive attributes as well.

Resolving Differences

Reading 6.1

Doing Things Collaboratively: Realizing the Advantage or Succumbing to Inertia?

Chris Huxham
Siv Vangen

The project has worked out, but oh boy, it has caused pain.
> —Senior health promotion officer, health promotion partnership

Decisions are made by the alliance executive, but they keep procrastinating over big decisions . . . you can't afford to procrastinate over spending a million pounds.
> —Information manager, retail property development alliance

Multi-agency work is very slow . . . trying to get people moving collectively rather than alone is difficult.
> —Project officer, young offender community organization

I am under partnership attack from my colleagues.
> —Operations manager, engineering supply chain

The long catalog of failed JVs—Icatel/Sharp, Sony/Qualcomm, Lucent/Philips—demonstrates the enormous difficulties in pulling companies like these together.
> —A Gartner analyst quoted in the *Financial Times,* December 10, 2002, p. 8

Not everyone who works daily in collaborative alliances, partnerships, or networks reports such negative experiences as these. Indeed the *Financial Times* (June 24, 2003, p. 14) reports a Nokia executive as saying that their linkages are paying off. Others talk similarly enthusiastically about their partnership experiences:

> When it works well you feel inspired . . . you can feel the collaborative energy.

However, very many do express frustration. There has been much rhetoric about the value of strategic alliances, industry networks, public service delivery partnerships, and many other collaborative forms, but reports of unmitigated success are not common. In this article we explore the nature of *the practice of collaboration,* focusing in particular on some of the reasons why collaborative initiatives tend to challenge those involved.

Source: "Doing Things Collaboratively: Realizing the Advantage or Succumbing to Inertia?" by Chris Huxham and Six Vangen, from *Organizational Dynamics* 33, no. 2, 2004, pp. 190–201. Elsevier. Used with permission.

Two concepts are central to this exploration. The first is *collaborative advantage.* This captures the synergy argument: To gain real *advantage* from collaboration, something has to be achieved that could not have been achieved by any one of the organizations acting alone. This concept provides a useful "guiding light" for the purpose of collaboration. The second concept, *collaborative inertia,* captures what happens very frequently in practice: The output from a collaborative arrangement is negligible, the rate of output is extremely slow, or stories of pain and hard grind are integral to successes achieved.

Clearly there is a dilemma between advantage and inertia. The key question seems to be this:

> If achievement of collaborative advantage is the goal for those who initiate collaborative arrangements, why is collaborative inertia so often the outcome?

To address this question, and the question of what managers can do about it, we will present a set of seven overlapping perspectives on collaborative management. This is extracted from the theory of collaborative advantage, which has derived from extensive action research over 15 years. We have worked with practitioners of collaboration, in the capacity of facilitators, consultants, and trainers, in a wide variety of collaborative situations. We have kept detailed records about the challenges and dilemmas faced by managers, and of comments they make in the course of enacting their collaborative endeavors. Many such statements are reproduced as illustrative examples in this article.

Perspective 1: We Must Have Common Aims But We Cannot Agree on Them

Agreement on aims is an appropriate starting point because it is raised consistently as an issue. *Common wisdom* suggests that it is necessary to be clear about the aims of joint working if partners are to work together to operationalize policies.

Typically individuals argue for common (or at least compatible), agreed, or clear sets of aims as a starting point in collaboration. *Common practice,* however, appears to be that the variety of organizational and individual agendas that are present in collaborative situations makes reaching agreement difficult. For example, a board member of an alliance of 120 charities commented on the difficulty of reconciling members' interests. Invariably someone would call to say, "We don't want you to do that."

The reasons behind the struggles for agreement may not be obvious. Organizations come together bringing different resources and expertise to the table, which in turn creates the potential for collaborative advantage. Yet organizations also have different reasons for being involved, and their representatives seek to achieve different outputs from their involvement. Sometimes these different organizational aims lead to conflicts of interest. Furthermore, for some organizations the joint purpose for the collaboration is perceived as central to achieving organizational purposes, whereas others are less interested and perhaps only involved (reluctantly) as a result of external pressure. Tensions often arise, therefore, because some organizations are very interested in influencing and controlling the joint agenda, and some are reluctant to commit resources to it, and so on. Similarly, individuals too will join the collaboration with different expectations, aspirations, and understandings of what is to be achieved jointly. It follows that while at first glance it may appear that partners need be concerned only with the joint aims for the collaboration, in reality organizational and individual aims can prevent agreement because they cause confusion, misunderstanding, and conflicts of interest. In addition, while some of these various aims may be explicit, many will be taken for granted (assumed) by one partner but not necessarily recognized by another, and many will be deliberately hidden:

> My company is really most interested in having access to, and experience of, the Chinese business environment and cares little for the formally declared purpose of the alliance.

On reflection then it is not so surprising that reaching agreement can be very difficult.

Managing Aims in Practice

Figure 1 is a simplified version of a framework of aims in collaborative situations. Its purpose is to facilitate a better understanding of the motivations of those involved, and the ways in which multiple and (sometimes even) conflicting aims can prevent agreement and block progress. In turn, this sort of understanding can help in finding ways of addressing the concerns of all involved. The framework distinguishes between the various types of aims mentioned and emphasizes that some aims will be assumed rather than explicitly acknowledged, and many will be deliberately hidden.

This framework can be used as an effective tool for gaining insight about the motivations of members of a collaboration—even of one's own! Obviously it is not possible to know others' hidden agendas, but it is possible to speculate on the possibility that they might have some—and even guess at what they might be. Trying to "fill in" each of the cells of the framework for each other partner can be enlightening, whether it is done quickly, "back of an envelope" style, or as a major investigative exercise. Gaining this kind of insight into partners' expectations and aspirations can be very helpful in understanding and judging how best to work with them.

At the general level, the obvious conclusion to be drawn from the framework is that it is rarely going to be easy in practice to satisfy fully the common wisdom. Therein lies the dilemmas—clarity of purpose provides much needed direction, yet open discussion

FIGURE 1 | A Framework for Understanding Aims in Collaboration

(One Participant's Perspective)	Explicit	Assumed	Hidden
Collaboration Aims	The purpose of the collaboration.		By definition these are perceptions of joint aims and so cannot be hidden.
Organization Aims	What each organization hopes to gain for itself via the collaboration.		
Individual Aims	What each individual hopes to gain for him/herself via the collaboration.		

can unearth irreconcilable differences! Difficulties that arise out of the need to communicate across different professional and natural languages and different organizational and professional cultures are unlikely to assist the negotiation process. Likewise, concerns about accountability of participants to their own organizations or to other constituents are unlikely to make it easy for individuals to make compromises. Often the only practical way forward is to get started on some action without fully agreeing on the aims. In the words of the manager of an urban regeneration partnership engaged in writing a bid for funding, the task for managers can be to

> find a way of stating the aims so that none of the parties can disagree.

Perspective 2: Sharing Power Is Important, But People Behave As If It's All in the Purse Strings

As with the previous perspective, the "pain" associated with issues of power is often raised by practitioners of collaboration. *Common wisdom* is that "the power is in the purse strings," which suggests that those who do not have control of the financial resource are automatically deprived of power. Viewed dispassionately, these perceptions quite often seem at odds with "reality" since most parties do, minimally, have at least the "power of exit." A manager in an automotive industry joint venture commented,

> The balance of power was seemingly with the U.K. company, who had a majority shareholding; but in reality it was with the U.S. company, who knew how closely the investment analysts were watching the joint venture. The threat of pulling out was always in the background.

However, the *common practice,* unsurprisingly, is that people act as though their perceptions are real and often display defensiveness and aggression.

Looking more closely at where power is actually used to influence the way in which collaborative activities are negotiated and carried out, it is possible to identify different *points of power.* Many of these occur at a micro level in the collaboration, and would often not be particularly obvious to those involved. One example of a point of power is the naming of the collaboration, since this is likely to influence what it does. Those who are involved in the naming process are therefore in a powerful position at that time. Other examples concern invitations to join a collaboration; those who choose whom to involve are obviously powerful, but those who choose the process of whom to involve are even more so.

Many points of power relate to communication media and processes. One set of examples concerns the arrangements for meetings. Clearly, any person taking the role of chair or facilitator in a meeting is in a position of power while the meeting is in place, but those who get to choose which facilitator to appoint are more subtly and perhaps more significantly powerful. Those who choose the location of a meeting may be in a powerful position, particularly in terms of determining whether it will be on the premises of one of the participants. Those who choose the timing of the meeting are also powerful. It is possible to identify many more points of power that typically are present during collaborative activities.

An important characteristic of points of power is that they are not static. In collaborative situations, power continually shifts. At the macro level, for example, in a pre–start-up phase, those who get to draw up contracts, write bids for funding, or have direct access to a customer may be powerful. In a start-up phase, however, once money is available, those who are given the task of administering the collaboration may be highly powerful in determining many parameters concerned with direction and ways of working. It may be only at later stages that the actual members become active and have the chance to exert power.

Less obvious, but very significant, are the continuous shifts of power at a micro level during all phases. For example, network managers are often in powerful positions between meetings because they are the only people formally employed by the network—and hence the only people who have its agenda as their main concern. They may also have access to the network funds. During meetings, however, members can shift many of the points of power in significant ways, often determining new members, times, and locations of meetings as well as influencing agreements about action. Those less centrally involved, such as facilitators or consultants, can be in powerful positions for short periods of time. External influences, such as those from government, can sometimes be extremely powerful in a short-term way as they make demands for reports or responses to initiatives.

Managing Power in Practice

Issues concerned with control of purse strings are significant, but there are many other points at which power is, in practice, enacted in collaborative settings. All participants have power at one time or another and may frequently have the option to empower themselves. Understanding and exploring the points of power can enable assessment of where and when others are unwittingly or consciously exerting power, and where and when others may view them as exerting power. It also allows for consideration of how and when deliberately to exert power. Responding to these insights, however, requires a willingness to accept that manipulative behavior is appropriate, which some would argue is against the spirit of collaborative working. We will return to this point later.

Perspective 3: Trust Is Necessary for Successful Collaboration, But We Are Suspicious of Each Other

Issues relating to trust are also commonly raised by participants. The *common wisdom* seems to be that trust is a precondition for successful collaboration. However, while the existence of trusting relationships between partners probably would be an ideal situation, the *common practice* appears to be that suspicion, rather than trust, is the starting point. Often participants do not have the luxury to choose their partners. Either imposed (e.g., government) policy dictates who the partners must be or, as expressed by the business development manager of the Far East operation of a major oil producer, the pragmatics of the situation dictate that partners are needed where trust is weak:

> You may have to jump into bed with someone you don't like in order to prevent a competitor coming into the market.

This suggests that it is appropriate to pay attention to trust *building* between partners.

One way of thinking about trust building is through the loop depicted in Figure 2. This argues that two factors are important in getting started in a trusting relationship. The first is concerned with the formation of expectations about the future of the collaboration; these will be based either on reputation or past behavior, or on more formal contracts and agreements. Given the earlier remarks about the difficulty of agreeing on aims in collaborative settings, this in itself is a nontrivial starting point. The second starting point involves risk taking. The argument is that partners need to trust each other *enough* to allow them to take a risk to initiate the collaboration. If both of these initiators are possible, then the loop argues that trust can gradually be built through starting with some modest but realistic aims that are likely to be successfully realized. This reinforces trusting attitudes between partners and provides a basis for more ambitious collaboration.

Managing Trust in Practice

The practical conclusion from the trust-building loop is very similar to that concerning the management of aims: Sometimes it is better to get started on some small but tangible action and then to allow trust to develop slowly. This incremental approach to trust building would obviously not be relevant if an immediate need to attain a major objective is paramount. In those situations, expectation forming and risk taking would have to be managed simultaneously and alongside other trust-building activities. However, in other situations building trust incrementally is, in principle, appealing. We shall return to it later.

Perspective 4: We Are Partnership-Fatigued and Tired of Being Pulled in All Directions

In this perspective it is not so much the common wisdom but the *taken for granted assumptions* that are to be challenged. One of the most surprising observations about collaborative situations is the frequency with which clarity about who the collaborators

FIGURE 2 | The Trust Building Loop

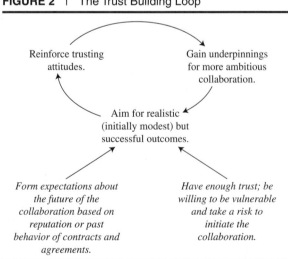

are is lacking. Different members often list different partners from each other, and staff who are very centrally involved in managing collaborations often cannot name partners without referring to formal documentation. Reasons for this include the different statuses or commitment that people or organizations have with regard to the network

> They were only involved to provide the financial support . . . (rather than as a proper member).

and ambiguity about whether people are involved as individuals or on behalf of their organizations:

> Members were invited to join because of their ethnic background, but the organizations they worked in (which were not specifically concerned with ethnicity issues) then became partners.

The lack of clarity about who partners are is often compounded by the complexity of collaborative arrangements in practice. The sheer scale of networking activities is one aspect of this. Many organizations are involved in multiple alliances. One major electronics manufacturer, for example, is said to be involved in around 400 strategic alliances. Clearly, even with the most coherent alliance management practices, no individual manager is likely to know which partner organizations are involved. Clearly also, multiple alliances must pull the organization in a variety of different directions. As one senior manager in a division of a multinational computer hardware manufacturer put it,

> We have separate alliances with two companies (worldwide operating system providers) that are in direct competition with each other . . . there is a lot of conflict within the company over these alliances . . . the people involved try to raise the importance of theirs.

The same issue arises in the public-sector context, with ever increasing numbers of partnerships and interagency initiatives appearing in localities. In this case, however, the problem that is most commonly voiced is "partnership fatigue," with individuals often regularly attending meetings of five or six collaborative schemes. More extreme cases occur in this sector too. For example, a manager from a community-based career guidance organization commented,

> When I heard of the person attending meetings of five partnerships, I thought "Is that all?!" . . . My organization is involved in 56 partnerships.

There are many other consequences of these multiple initiatives apart from fatigue. One is that some participants try to link agendas across the initiatives; but the links they see relate to the particular combinations of initiatives that they are involved in, which generally do not overlap precisely, if at all, with involvements of other members. Another is that it is hard for any individual to judge when another is inputting the views of their employing organization or bringing an agenda from another partnership.

In addition to the volume of relationships, there is frequently complexity in the networks of relationships between organizations. For example, the complexity of interacting supply chain networks—in which every supplier has multiple customers, every customer has multiple suppliers, and suppliers have suppliers and customers have customers—is potentially infinite. Many networks of collaborations are, in addition, hierarchical in the sense that collaborations are members of other collaborations. For example, a local government organization may be a member of a regeneration partnership but also a member of several community collaborations, which are in turn members of a community "umbrella group," which is in turn a member of the regeneration partnership. Similarly, joint ventures may be members of strategic alliances, trade associations may represent their members in policy networks, and so on.

Managing Ambiguity and Complexity in Practice

Clearly, it is hard for managers to agree on aims, build mutual understanding, and manage trust and power relationships with partners if they do not unambiguously know who their partners are. Equally, it is difficult to manage collaborative working in complex systems in which different elements must be affecting each other but there is little clarity on the nature of the interrelationships.

Diagramming techniques can help in mapping the structure of partnerships. Figure 3 provides two possible ways of doing this. Obviously this cannot remove the ambiguity and uncertainty completely, but it is generally enlightening at the point of construction and useful as a long-term reminder. As with the aims framework, this exercise can be done in more or less detail.

At a general level, learning how to identify, live with, and progress despite ambiguity and complexity is probably the key challenge of this perspective. A careful approach to nurturing relationships must be an essential aspect of this.

Perspective 5: Everything Keeps Changing

Collaborative structures are commonly talked about as though stability of membership can be *taken for granted,* at least for a tangible period. The ambiguity and complexity indicated in the previous section would be difficult enough for participants to cope with if that were the case. In practice, however, policy influences, which may be internal but are frequently imposed externally, often generate restructuring of member organizations. Mergers and demergers, new start-ups and closures, acquisitions and sell-offs, and restructurings are all commonplace. In turn, these imply a necessary restructuring of any collaboration in which they participated.

Equally, policy changes in the individual organizations or the collaboration affect the purpose of the collaboration. These may be generated internally—for example, as the result of a revision of strategic direction. Or they may be generated externally—for example, as a result of government policy or major market disturbances. Either way, this in turn implies a shift in the relevance of the collaboration to its members. New members may join and others may leave, and sometimes such changes are imposed:

> The problem isn't that their collaboration is not working, but that because of the new policy we are asking them to work differently, which means breaking up established successful and effective working relationships and building new ones.

FIGURE 3 | Example Diagramming Methods for Mapping the Complexity of Collaborative Structures

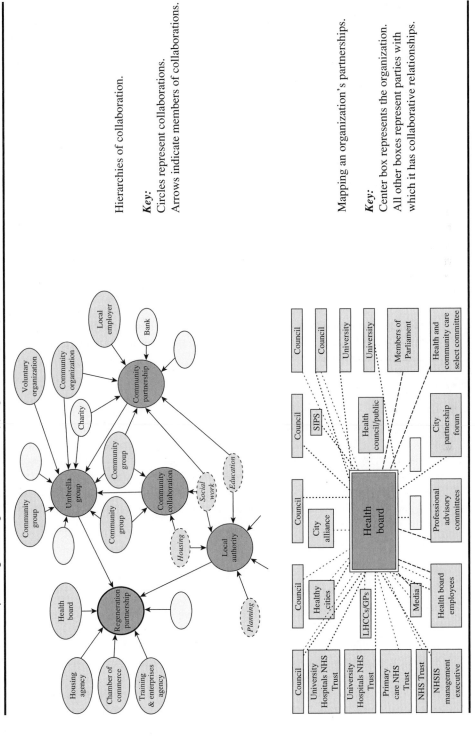

Hierarchies of collaboration.

Key:
Circles represent collaborations.
Arrows indicate members of collaborations.

Mapping an organization's partnerships.

Key:
Center box represents the organization.
All other boxes represent parties with
which it has collaborative relationships.

Another source of dynamic change comes with individual movements. The manager of a company that was delivering a major service for an alliance partner, for example, commented that the relationship with the partner organization had been both helped and hindered because

> ... the chief executive in the partner organization was, until recently, my boss in my own organization.

The relationships between individual participants in collaborations are often fundamental to getting things done. This makes collaborations highly sensitive to changes in individuals' employment, even if these are simply role changes within one of the participating organizations. Finally, even if all of these factors stood still there is often an inherent dynamic. If an initial collaborative purpose is achieved, there will usually be a need to move to new collaborative agendas, and these are likely to imply different membership requirements.

All organizations are dynamic to the extent that they will gradually transform. However, collaborations are sensitive to transformations in *each of* the partner organizations and therefore may change very quickly. In one example, a collaborative group with an ambiguous structure involving many partners went through three identifiable reincarnations over a three-year period and ended up as a very controlled partnership between two organizations. Its final stated purpose was related to, but definitely not the same as, the original one. It would be reasonable to argue that the final partnership was a different one from the original collaborative group, but it is possible to trace a clear lineage from one to the other.

Managing Collaborative Dynamics in Practice

One obvious conclusion that derives from recognition of the dynamic nature of collaborations is that the appealing trust-building loop (Figure 2) is inherently extremely fragile. Effort put into building mutual understanding and developing trust can be shattered, for example, by a change in the structure of a key organization or the job change of a key individual. A practical conclusion, therefore, for those who want to make collaboration work is that *the nurturing process must be continuous and permanent.* No sooner will gains be made than a disturbance, in the form of a change to one of the partners, will shatter many of them.

Perspective 6: Leadership Is Not Always in the Hands of Members

Given the inherent difficulties with collaborative forms that have been discussed so far, the issue of leadership seems highly relevant. Because traditional hierarchies do not exist in collaborative settings, it is appropriate to consider leadership in a general sense, rather than as specifically the realm of senior executives or prominent public figures. Here we consider leadership as being concerned with *the mechanisms that lead to the actual outcomes of a collaboration.* Put simply, we are concerned with what "*makes things happen*" in a collaboration. More formally, this concern is with the formation and implementation of the collaboration's policy and activity agenda.

Looked at from this perspective, leadership, interestingly, becomes something that is not enacted only by people. Structures and processes are as important in leading agendas as are the participants involved in the collaboration. Thus, for example, a structure in which only two organizations are involved in partnership should allow both organizations good access to the agenda, but clearly excludes others. To take an extreme contrast, a collaboration in which any organization that wants to be a member may send a representative allows wide access to the agenda in principle, but it can be difficult for any individual to have much influence in practice. Similarly, in the context of collaborative processes, a collaboration for which a major form of communication is through open meetings is going to allow a very different form of access to the agenda from one whose principal mode of communication is through e-mail and/or telephone. Thus agendas may be led by the type of structure that is in place and the type of processes used. Once again, this challenges a *taken for granted* presumption about the nature of leadership. Agendas can, of course, also be led by participants, though generally these are emergent, informal leaders rather than those who lead from a position of authority.

Structures, processes, and participants can be thought of as different *media* through which collaborative leadership is, in practice, enacted. An important point about these media is that all three are largely not controlled by *members* of the collaboration. Structures and processes are sometimes imposed externally—for example, by government, a corporate headquarters, or a funding body. Even if this is not the case, they often emerge out of previous action rather than being explicitly designed by members. Even in the context of "participants" as the leadership medium, leadership is not solely the role of *members* of the collaboration. External stakeholders such as customers or local public figures often strongly direct the territory of a partnership or alliance. A strong lead is often also given by support staff who are not strictly members. For example, the information manager of a retail property development alliance commented about his role in moving the alliance members toward agreement about action:

I find that attrition helps . . . I am a stubborn old devil.

Managing Leadership Media

This perspective demonstrates the ease with which collaborations can move out of the control of their membership. Recognizing the at least partial inevitability of this and working around it is part of the practical response required. Diagramming techniques such as those in Figure 3 may be helpful in exploring the nature of the structure as a first step toward gaining an understanding of its leadership consequences.

For managers who wish to lead more actively, the implication appears to be that part of their activity must be concerned with the design of structures and processes that are effective for the particular purpose, and with monitoring their performance and evolution. We look further at active leadership in the final perspective.

Perspective 7: Leadership Activities Continually Meet with Dilemmas and Difficulties

Despite the strong contextual leadership derived from structures and processes, participants (whether or not they actually are members) do carry out *leadership activities* in order to move a collaboration forward in ways that they regard as beneficial. In carrying out these activities, they do affect the outcomes of collaborative initiatives. However, they are frequently thwarted by difficulties, so that the outcomes are not as they intend. For example, despite his war of attrition, the information manager quoted earlier was continuously thwarted in his attempts to create events in which key members of the partnering organizations would jointly consider their modes of thinking and working. Several dates set aside for group workshops were ultimately used for other kinds of meetings, as issues needing immediate attention emerged.

In practice, much of what is done by those who aim to take a lead in moving a collaboration forward may be said to be fundamentally *within the spirit of collaboration.* Activities of this sort are highly facilitative and are concerned with embracing, empowering, involving, and mobilizing members. However, the same people are also engaged in activities that, on the face of it, are much less collaborative. Many of them are adept at manipulating agendas and playing the politics. We have characterized these kinds of activities as being *toward collaborative thuggery* after the member of a city partnership who told us that a partnership that he was involved with had been successful:

> . . . because the convenor is a thug . . . if people are not pulling their weight he pushes them out.

He appeared to be arguing that this was a positive and effective mode of leadership.

Managing Leadership Activities

Does this, then, suggest a dilemma between the ideology of collaborative working and the pragmatism needed to get things done? Not necessarily. One way of thinking about this is to consider the nature of nurturing. Nurturing is often talked about in the context of the gentle care required for fragile plants. However, rather more decisive tactics have to be taken if the object is to nurture an overgrown garden back to health. Chopping down of excess growth and pulling up of weeds are likely to be key activities, in addition to the nurturing back to health of individual plants that have become overpowered by others. While it is not possible to produce hard evidence of this, those who lead more successfully seem to operate from both perspectives—the *spirit of collaboration* and *toward collaborative thuggery*—and to continually switch between them, often carrying out both types of leadership in the same act.

Realizing Collaborative Advantage

Our aim here has been to convey some of the complexity that underlies collaborative situations in a way that should seem real to those involved. Obviously the set of seven perspectives does not, in itself, provide any precise recipes for managerial action. It does, however, provide a dual basis for thoughtful action.

The first basis is through legitimizing the pain and addressing the isolation that people often feel when trapped in collaborative inertia:

> I have been working in a health education partnership . . . for about a year, and it is a relief and a reassurance to see that the "pain and grind" of partnership work exists in other partnerships, not just my situation.

Like this person, many managers are empowered simply by understanding that the problems they are experiencing are inevitable. This is partly because this awareness increases self-confidence, and partly because it immediately highlights the need to tackle the problem at a different level. Legitimizing a degree of manipulative and political activity through the notion of *collaborative thuggery* can also be helpful in this respect.

The second, and perhaps more significant, basis for action is through the conceptual handles that the perspectives provide. As presented here in summary, the combined picture gives a sense of the kinds of issues that have to be managed (a more detailed version of each perspective is available). Like the summary, the detailed perspectives do not provide a recipe for good practice, because to do so would be to oversimplify. Rather, they are intended to alert managers to challenges of collaborative situations that will need active attention and nurturing if problems of collaborative inertia are to be minimized. Each perspective provides a particular view on this, and can be used in isolation to stimulate thinking about that in particular. However, the issues raised by each perspective overlap with those raised by others, so the combination of perspectives always needs to be in the background, even if the focus at a particular time is a specific one. Many of the challenges are inherent, and there are often tensions between directly opposed possible ways of tackling them. This approach to practical support regards the action to be taken as a matter for managerial judgment. This includes making informed judgments about the resource that needs to be available to support the nurturing activities.

Don't Work Collaboratively Unless You Have to

One definite conclusion can, however, be drawn: Making collaboration work effectively is highly resource-consuming and often painful. The strongest piece of advice to managers (and policy makers) that derives from the discussed perspectives, therefore, is "don't do it unless you have to." Put rather more formally, the argument is that unless potential for real collaborative advantage is clear, it is generally best, *if there is a choice,* to avoid collaboration. It is worth noting, however, that collaborative advantage sometimes comes in nonobvious forms and may be concerned with the process of collaborating— for example, from the development of a relationship with a partner—rather than the actual output.

Selected Bibliography

This article draws on the *theory of collaborative advantage,* which we have developed gradually from extensive research with practitioners of collaboration over the last 15 years. The notions of collaborative advantage and collaborative inertia are central to this theory. *Collaborative advantage* was first used in this way in the early 1990s. See for example, C. Huxham and D. Macdonald, "Introducing Collaborative Advantage," *Management Decision* 30, no. 3 (1992), pp. 50–56. Rosabeth Moss Kanter used the term differently in her 1994 article "Collaborative Advantage: The Art of Alliances," *Harvard Business Review* 72, no. 4, pp. 96–108. *Collaborative inertia* was introduced in C. Huxham, "Advantage or Inertia: Making Collaboration Work," in R. Paton, G. Clark, G. Jones, and P. Quintas (eds.), *The New Management Reader* (London: Routledge, 1996), pp. 238–54.

Theory relating to the aims framework of perspective one can be found in C. Eden and C. Huxham, "The Negotiation of Purpose in Multi-Organizational Collaborative Groups," *Journal of Management Studies* 38, no. 3 (2001), pp. 351–69. A detailed discussion on the points of power in perspective two can be found in C. Huxham and N. Beech, "Points of Power in Interorganizational Forms: Learning from a Learning Network," *Best 10%, Proceedings of the Academy of Management Conference,* 2002.

The development of the trust-building loop and its implication for the management of trust in perspective three is explored in S. Vangen and C. Huxham, "Nurturing Collaborative Relations: Building Trust in Interorganizational Collaboration," *Journal of Applied Behavioral Science* 39, no. 1 (2003), pp. 5–31. A detailed exposition of perspectives four and five can be found in C. Huxham and S. Vangen, "Ambiguity, Complexity, and Dynamics in the Membership of Collaboration," *Human Relations* 53, no. 6 (2000), pp. 771–806. For a detailed discussion on the conceptualization and enactment of leadership in perspectives six and seven see C. Huxham and S. Vangen, "Leadership in the Shaping and Implementation of Collaboration Agendas: How Things Happen in a (Not Quite) Joined Up World," *Academy of Management Journal* (Special Forum on Managing in the New Millennium) 43, no. 6 (2000), pp. 1159–75; and S. Vangen and C. Huxham, "Enacting Leadership for Collaborative Advantage: Dilemmas of Ideology and Pragmatism in the Activities of Partnership Managers," *British Journal of Management* 14 (2003), pp. 61–74.

Reading 6.2

Taking Steps toward "Getting to Yes" at Blue Cross and Blue Shield of Florida

Bridget Booth
Matt McCredie

Never before has there been a more opportune time for Blue Cross and Blue Shield of Florida, Inc., (BCBSF) to benefit from the concepts of principled negotiation outlined in the book *Getting to Yes.*

BCBSF is the industry leader in Florida, providing health benefit plans and health-related services. The company and its subsidiaries serve more than 6 million people. However, maintaining a market leadership position is difficult in light of the many challenges facing today's health care marketplace.

Factors such as rising health care costs, increased competition, consumerism, and shifting demographics have caused the company to search for new and different ways of doing business as customers' health care needs expand. Inherent in these new and different business models is the need for more collaborative business practices, such as those outlined in *Getting to Yes.*

Different Times Call for Different Approaches

Today's health care marketplace is becoming increasingly consumer driven. Consumers expect the same level of service and convenience from health organizations that they receive from other companies, such as online retailers, banks, and investment firms. The Institute of the Future predicts that by the end of 2010, the health market will be an innovative economy demanding nontraditional offerings such as wellness, food, cosmetics, fashion, health information, and even biosecurity.[1] Developing alliances with other organizations is one way the company is positioning itself for the health industry of the future. BCBSF's Alliance Group, a small department formed in 2001, enables business areas to develop strategic relationships with other entities.

Capitalizing on business opportunities through alliances enables BCBSF and other companies to pursue the risks and rewards of mutually compatible goals that would be difficult to achieve alone. Alliances include outsourcing partnerships, joint operating agreements, and joint ventures. These alliances provide the companies with access to new markets, capabilities, knowledge, and capital, along with the ability to share development and acquisition costs. Alliances also enable each party to bring products to market quickly in a cost-effective manner, which is critical in today's health care industry.

BCBSF's Alliance Group is experiencing positive outcomes by applying concepts outlined in *Getting to Yes* and is helping to move the organization more toward the management concepts of principled negotiation. Historically, however, businesses have not formally practiced or rewarded employees for these types of behaviors. For example,

Source: "Taking Steps toward 'Getting to Yes at Blue Cross and Blue Shield of Florida," by Bridget Booth and Matt McCredie, from *Academy of Management Executive* 18, no. 3, 2004, pp. 109–112. Used with permission.

contract negotiations between companies often focus on each individual organization championing its own positions without considering the other's interests. Rewards are often linked to how well an organization's position is defended or "won" without giving thought to what bigger solutions could emerge by focusing on mutual gains.

To expand beyond this type of traditional mind-set, BCBSF is seeking out ways to indoctrinate the concepts of principled negotiation throughout the entire organization. Principled negotiation, according to *Getting to Yes,* involves looking at issues based on their merits rather than defending steadfast positions. Its goal is to meet the underlying concerns of the parties. Shifting behavior away from a contest of wills toward this type of collaborative mind-set can be challenging. To help make the transition, BCBSF is emphasizing three major steps: top-level executive support; a disciplined, programmed approach to alliance management; and reinforcement of desired behaviors and related outcomes.

BCBSF is further embracing the concepts of principled negotiation by working with Vantage Partners, a consulting firm that partners with leading companies to institutionalize the capability to negotiate, build, and manage critical relationships effectively. Initially, BCBSF was seeking external perspectives for establishing superior alliance management capabilities. As part of that process, the company was introduced to mutual-gains behavior as a necessary component of developing successful alliances and other collaborative relationships. Vantage, founded by *Getting to Yes* coauthor Roger Fisher, helps its clients incorporate concepts from the book into their daily management practices. BCBSF has been working with Vantage Partners for approximately two years and has experienced increased trust and alignment with business associates as a result of implementing *Getting to Yes* concepts.

Putting the Concepts into Practice

On a daily basis, BCBSF is learning firsthand about the benefits of applying principled negotiation concepts in its alliances, as well as the pitfalls of what happens when the concepts are not applied consistently.

The company's movement toward applying *Getting to Yes* concepts is illustrated by the formation and management of a strategic alliance with a key competitor. Availity, LLC, a joint venture between subsidiaries of BCBSF and Humana, Inc., was conceived out of a desire to lower health costs, improve efficiencies, and provide more timely service to physicians and hospitals. Humana is one of the nation's leading publicly traded health benefits companies, with approximately 7 million medical members in 19 states and Puerto Rico. The company offers coordinated health insurance coverage and related services to employer groups, government-sponsored plans, and individuals. Both Humana and BCBSF were trying to reach the same goal of improving the manner in which hospitals and physicians conducted business with their organizations.

The resulting joint venture, Availity, is an Internet-based solution that streamlines administrative workflow and improves communication between physicians, hospitals, payers, and pharmacies. Through a secure website, physicians can submit requests for payments, check the status of payments for services, verify patients' coverage and eligibility, and receive authorizations for referrals and other medical services online. This streamlined process replaces time-consuming manual interactions such as phone calls and paperwork.

Currently, there are more than 9,000 physician offices, 208 hospitals, and more than 27,000 physicians in Florida using the Availity platform to process routine transactions.

The challenges of managing a joint venture with a key competitor could be daunting, if not impossible, without a shift in behavior by both parties to think of the other as a partner. Adding to the complexity are the organizations' differing corporate cultures, due in part to their structures: Humana is a for-profit publicly traded company, while BCBSF is a private, not-for-profit policyholder-owned mutual company. In addition, Humana serves a national market, while BCBSF primarily serves Florida. The change in mind-set to be collaborative versus competitive in the development of this solution was critical to the formation and ongoing success of the joint venture.

Separating the People from the Problem

Although BCBSF had not yet institutionalized *Getting to Yes* concepts during the early formation of Availity, the company became more deliberate in following the concepts after the alliance was operational and the organization became more aware of the benefits of principled negotiation. Looking back, despite a lack of formal training in *Getting to Yes* concepts, the company unconsciously implemented some of the concepts during the formation of Availity, which helped greatly in building the alliance.

As outlined in the book, separating the people from the problem requires emphasizing relationships by dealing directly with perceptions. BCBSF looked for ways to demonstrate its desire to collaborate by coming to the table with a sincere intent to build a relationship and determine common interests. Although it was not formally stated that the concepts of principled negotiation would be followed, the negotiators realized that forming a successful joint venture would require a collaborative approach. Both parties approached initial discussions in an open manner by listening rather than trying to debate or persuade. The two parties invested substantial amounts of time at the executive level to build the relationship. As the book says, prevention works best—and building this type of personal relationship "cushioned the people on each side against the knocks of negotiation." A strong relationship at the senior level continues to benefit the alliance today through subsequent governance activities.

Once Availity was established and operational, BCBSF began to interact with Availity as a business associate. This new relationship benefited from additional collaborative negotiation skills.

A significant challenge in implementing the concept of separating the people from the problem was the complex nature of the multiple relationships inherent in the Availity alliance. On the surface, it seemed as though only one relationship existed: the two initial owners. A closer look revealed several different relationships between BCBSF and Availity, ranging from BCBSF having an ownership interest in Availity, to BCBSF being the largest customer of Availity, to BCBSF being a vendor for Availity for technical development. Similarly, Humana has multiple relationships with Availity.

Many of the people involved in the formation had multiple accountabilities reflecting different aspects of the relationship. These multiple relationships and their corresponding accountabilities made it difficult to understand a person's perspective on a given issue. By mapping out the different relationships and corresponding accountabilities, ambiguity was reduced and problem solving improved. The exercise helped the parties understand the various perspectives and clarified accountabilities. Mapping out accountabilities in alliances is an approach that BCBSF is adopting, which is starting to result in more favorable outcomes in learning to separate people from problems. In addition, when individuals have several roles, the organization is learning the value of having those individuals clearly communicate which role they are representing.

Focus on Interests, Not Positions

During initial discussions, Humana and BCBSF laid the groundwork to understand each other and see the situation from the other's perspective. General discussions about how each party viewed the industry, the future of health care, opportunities for collaboration, and anticipated future challenges helped both parties to identify and understand the other's interests regarding electronic connectivity. At later stages—for example, during the testing phase—this exercise served as a strong foundation in helping the parties to separate people from problems because there was an understanding of the other's viewpoints.

One challenge in focusing on interests rather than positions had to do with the two organizations having different approaches to testing the various capabilities of Availity. One party was accustomed to using a prescribed methodology for testing the various capabilities. The other, being a new organization, had processes that were still under development. The "positions" had to do with which organization's testing procedures to follow, but the underlying interests for both parties were identical: for Availity to be up and running error-free.

After holding a number of brainstorming sessions, it became evident that the parties could combine components of their methodologies to create a joint solution. By focusing on interests rather than positions, the parties realized that testing did not have to follow a certain methodology; it just had to result in error-free operations. By shifting the focus to interests rather than the positions, a new solution involving leveraging existing resources in a more effective manner was designed. A joint testing approach was agreed upon to meet mutual interests, and the parties were able to learn from each other in creating the solution.

Inventing Options for Mutual Gain

Getting to Yes says, "Skill at inventing options can be one of your most useful assets." This was especially evident in the formation of Availity. Before Availity was conceived, Humana and BCBSF came together and identified their interests regarding electronic connectivity. Both parties wanted to improve relationships with hospitals and physicians, reduce health care industry costs for consumers, and improve workflow for hospitals, physicians, and payers. The solution resulted in the joint venture that became Availity, which mutually benefited both organizations.

To assure that options for mutual gain were being sought throughout the development of Availity, relationship manager responsibilities were assigned to individuals to keep the best interests of the alliance in the forefront. Each party had someone who functioned in this capacity, which helped with the overall success of the alliance. Relationship manager roles are now included in many of BCBSF's alliances to serve as objective arbitrators between the parties and to look for options for mutual gain.

Additional Lessons Learned

BCBSF has learned a number of lessons about how to develop collaborative and productive alliance relationships.

In general, the company's experience has been that applying the concepts from *Getting to Yes* came more naturally at the executive/strategic level and required much more deliberation at subsequent levels. When alliance parties moved away from the conceptual level and into daily operations, implementing *Getting to Yes* concepts became more challenging. There are several reasons for this, including the experience levels of those involved, challenges with establishing strategic alignment throughout all levels, and varying reward systems at different levels of the organization. Among the steps that BCBSF is taking to address these challenges are establishing alliance specialists at the middle management level, and providing training regarding principled negotiation concepts at all levels of the organization.

Many of the lessons learned involve setting clear expectations in the beginning of the alliance formation. One is the importance of being deliberate in establishing ground rules for interacting with others early in the relationship before negotiation begins. Agreed-upon methods for communicating, making decisions, and handling conflicts, although somewhat awkward to create, are critical in relationship building and can help the parties to separate people from problems, especially when conflicts arise and emotions are high.

Along the same lines, a documented business plan that defines the market opportunity, product or service, sales and promotion approach, as well as validates financial forecasts, can prove beneficial. The business plan is not only an effective tool for guiding the alliance; it also clarifies the interests and expectations of the parties.

In addition to a business plan, the alliance parties have found benefits in clearly defined strategies with supporting organizational goals. In addition, the company is establishing metrics that measure not only the business results of alliances but the quality and strength of the relationships as well.

Establishing early on what each party will contribute in terms of capital, resources, and revenue is also a lesson that the company has learned in forming successful alliances. Without this foundation, the parties may have differing viewpoints of what the other is contributing, which often lead to misunderstanding and can prevent the alliance from progressing smoothly.

Perhaps the biggest reward for implementing the concepts from *Getting to Yes* is being able to see firsthand the benefits—meeting business goals, spending less time defending positions, creating a less stressful business environment, and meeting the underlying interests of both parties. The concepts have helped the company discover new ways of doing business—opening a new world of possibilities never imagined before.

Endnote

1. *The Emerging Health Economy: A Special Report,* SR-787 B 2003. Menlo Park, CA: Institute for the Future.

Reading 6.3

Taking the Stress Out of Stressful Conversations
Holly Weeks

We all get caught in conversations fraught with emotion. Usually, these interactions end badly—but they don't have to, thanks to a handful of techniques you can apply unilaterally.

We live by talking. That's just the kind of animal we are. We chatter and tattle and gossip and jest. But sometimes—more often than we'd like—we have stressful conversations, those sensitive exchanges that can hurt or haunt us in ways no other kind of talking does. Stressful conversations are unavoidable in life, and in business they can run the gamut from firing a subordinate to, curiously enough, receiving praise. But whatever the context, stressful conversations differ from other conversations because of the emotional loads they carry. These conversations call up embarrassment, confusion, anxiety, anger, pain, or fear—if not in us, then in our counterparts. Indeed, stressful conversations cause such anxiety that most people simply avoid them. This strategy is not necessarily wrong. One of the first rules of engagement, after all, is to pick your battles. Yet sometimes it can be extremely costly to dodge issues, appease difficult people, and smooth over antagonisms because the fact is that avoidance usually makes a problem or relationship worse.

Since stressful conversations are so common—and so painful—why don't we work harder to improve them? The reason is precisely because our feelings are so enmeshed. When we are not emotionally entangled in an issue, we know that conflict is normal, that it can be resolved—or at least managed. But when feelings get stirred up, most of us are thrown off balance. Like a quarterback who chokes in a tight play, we lose all hope of ever making it to the goal line.

For the past 20 years, I have been teaching classes and conducting workshops at some of the top corporations and universities in the United States on how to communicate during stressful conversations. With classrooms as my laboratory, I have learned that most people feel incapable of talking through sensitive issues. It's as though all our skills go out the window and we can't think usefully about what's happening or what we could do to get good results.

Stressful conversations, though, need not be this way. I have seen that managers can improve difficult conversations unilaterally if they approach them with greater self-awareness, rehearse them in advance, and apply just three proven communication techniques. Don't misunderstand me: There will never be a cookie-cutter approach to stressful conversations. There are too many variables and too much tension, and the interactions between people in difficult situations are always unique. Yet nearly every stressful conversation can be seen as an amalgam of a limited number of basic conversations, each with its own distinct set of problems. In the following pages, we'll explore how you can anticipate and handle those problems. But first, let's look at the three basic stressful conversations that we bump up against most often in the workplace.

Source: "Taking the Stress Out of Stressful Conversations," by Holly Weeks, from *Harvard Business Review,* July–August 2001, pp. 113–119. Harvard Business School Publishing. Used with permission.

"I Have Bad News for You"

Delivering unpleasant news is usually difficult for both parties. The speaker is often tense, and the listener is apprehensive about where the conversation is headed. Consider David, the director of a nonprofit institution. He was in the uncomfortable position of needing to talk with an ambitious researcher, Jeremy, who had a much higher opinion of his job performance than others in the organization did. The complication for David was that, in the past, Jeremy had received artificially high evaluations. There were several reasons for this. One had to do with the organization's culture: The nonprofit was not a confrontational kind of place. Additionally, Jeremy had tremendous confidence in both his own abilities and the quality of his academic background. Together with his defensive response to even the mildest criticism, this confidence led others—including David—to let slide discussions of weaknesses that were interfering with Jeremy's ability to deliver high-quality work. Jeremy had a cutting sense of humor, for instance, which had offended people inside and outside his unit. No one had ever said anything to him directly, but as time passed, more and more people were reluctant to work with him. Given that Jeremy had received almost no concrete criticism over the years, his biting style was now entrenched and the staff was restive.

In conversations like this, the main challenge is to get off to the right start. If the exchange starts off reasonably well, the rest of it has a good chance of going well. But if the opening goes badly, it threatens to bleed forward into the rest of the conversation. In an effort to be gentle, many people start these conversations on a light note. And that was just what David did, opening with, "How about those Red Sox?"

Naturally Jeremy got the wrong idea about where David was heading; he remained his usual cocky, superior self. Sensing this, David felt he had to take off the velvet gloves. The conversation quickly became brutally honest, and David did almost all the talking. When the monologue was over, Jeremy stared icily at the floor. He got up in stiff silence and left. David was relieved. From his point of view, the interaction had been painful but swift. There was not too much blood on the floor, he observed wryly. But two days later, Jeremy handed in his resignation, taking a lot of institutional memory—and talent—with him.

"What's Going On Here?"

Often we have stressful conversations thrust upon us. Indeed, some of the worst conversations—especially for people who are conflict averse—are the altogether unexpected ones that break out like crackling summer storms. Suddenly the conversation becomes intensely charged emotionally, and electricity flies in all directions. What's worse, nothing makes sense. We seem to have been drawn into a black cloud of twisted logic and altered sensibilities.

Consider the case of Elizabeth and Rafael. They were team leaders working together on a project for a major consulting firm. It seemed that everything that could have gone wrong on the project had, and the work was badly bogged down. The two consultants were meeting to revise their schedule, given the delays, and to divide up the discouraging tasks for the week ahead. As they talked, Elizabeth wrote and erased on the white board. When she had finished, she looked at Rafael and said matter-of-factly, "Is that it, then?"

Rafael clenched his teeth in frustration. "If you say so," he sniped.

Elizabeth recoiled. She instantly replayed the exchange in her mind but couldn't figure out what had provoked Rafael. His reaction seemed completely disconnected from her comment. The most common reaction of someone in Elizabeth's place is to guiltily defend herself by denying Rafael's unspoken accusation. But Elizabeth was uneasy with confrontation, so she tried appeasement. "Rafael," she stammered, "I'm sorry. Is something wrong?"

"Who put you in charge?" he retorted. "Who told you to assign work to me?"

Clearly, Rafael and Elizabeth have just happened into a difficult conversation. Some transgression has occurred, but Elizabeth doesn't know exactly what it is. She feels blindsided—her attempt to expedite the task at hand has clearly been misconstrued. Rafael feels he's been put in a position of inferiority by what he sees as Elizabeth's controlling behavior. Inexplicably, there seem to be more than two people taking part in this conversation, and the invisible parties are creating lots of static. What childhood experience, we may wonder, is causing Elizabeth to assume that Rafael's tension is automatically her fault? And who is influencing Rafael's perception that Elizabeth is taking over? Could it be his father? His wife? It's impossible to tell. At the same time, it's hard for us to escape the feeling that Rafael is overreacting when he challenges Elizabeth about her alleged need to take control.

Elizabeth felt Rafael's resentment like a wave and she apologized again. "Sorry. How do you want the work divided?" Deferring to Rafael in this way smoothed the strained atmosphere for the time being. But it set a precedent for unequal status that neither Elizabeth nor the company believed was correct. Worse, though Rafael and Elizabeth remained on the same team after their painful exchange, Elizabeth chafed under the status change and three months later transferred out of the project.

"You Are Attacking Me!"

Now let's turn our attention to aggressively stressful conversations, those in which people use all kinds of psychological and rhetorical mechanisms to throw their counterparts off balance, to undermine their positions, even to expose and belittle them. These "thwarting tactics" take many forms—profanity, manipulation, shouting—and not everyone is triggered or stumped by the same ones. The red zone is not the thwarting tactic alone but the pairing of the thwarting tactic with individual vulnerability.

Consider Nick and Karen, two senior managers working at the same level in an IT firm. Karen was leading a presentation to a client, and the information was weak and disorganized. She and the team had not been able to answer even basic questions. The client had been patient, then quiet, then clearly exasperated. When the presentation really started to fall apart, the client put the team on the spot with questions that made them look increasingly inadequate.

On this particular day, Nick was not part of the presenting team; he was simply observing. He was as surprised as the client at Karen's poor performance. After the client left, he asked Karen what happened. She lashed out at him defensively: "You're not my boss, so don't start patronizing me. You always undercut me no matter what I do." Karen continued to shout at Nick, her antagonism palpable. Each time he spoke, she interrupted him with accusations and threats: "I can't wait to see how you like it when people leave you flailing in the wind." Nick tried to remain reasonable, but Karen didn't wind down. "Karen," he said, "pull yourself together. You are twisting every word I say."

Here Nick's problem is not that Karen is using a panoply of thwarting tactics, but that all her tactics—accusation, distortion, and digression—are aggressive. This raises the stakes considerably. Most of us are vulnerable to aggressive tactics because we don't know whether, or how far, the aggression will escalate. Nick wanted to avoid Karen's aggression, but his insistence on rationality in the face of emotionalism was not working. His cool approach was trumped by Karen's aggressive one. As a result, Nick found himself trapped in the snare of Karen's choosing. In particular, her threats that she would pay him back with the client rattled him. He couldn't tell whether she was just huffing or meant it. He finally turned to the managing director, who grew frustrated, and later angry, at Nick and Karen for their inability to resolve their problems. In the end, their lack of skill in handling their difficult conversations cost them dearly. Both were passed over for promotion after the company pinned the loss of the client directly on their persistent failure to communicate.

Preparing for a Stressful Conversation

So how can we prepare for these three basic stressful conversations before they occur? A good start is to become aware of your own weaknesses to people and situations. David, Elizabeth, and Nick were unable to control their counterparts, but their stressful conversations would have gone much better if they had been more usefully aware of their vulnerabilities. It is important for those who are vulnerable to hostility, for example, to know how they react to it. Do they withdraw or escalate—do they clam up or retaliate? While one reaction is not better than the other, knowing how you react in a stressful situation will teach you a lot about your vulnerabilities, and it can help you master stressful situations.

Recall Nick's problem. If he had been more self-aware, he would have known that he acts stubbornly rational in the face of aggressive outbursts such as Karen's. Nick's choice of a disengaged demeanor gave Karen control over the conversation, but he didn't have to allow Karen—or anyone else—to exploit his vulnerability. In moments of calm self-scrutiny, when he's not entangled in a live stressful conversation, Nick can take time to reflect on his inability to tolerate irrational aggressive outbursts. This self-awareness would free him to prepare himself—not for Karen's unexpected accusations but for his own predictable vulnerability to any sudden assault like hers.

Though it might sound like it, building awareness is not about endless self-analysis. Much of it simply involves making our tacit knowledge about ourselves more explicit. We all know from past experience, for instance, what kinds of conversations and people we handle badly. When you find yourself in a difficult conversation, ask yourself whether this is one of those situations and whether it involves one of those people. For instance, do you bare your teeth when faced with an overbearing competitor? Do you shut down when you feel excluded? Once you know what your danger zones are, you can anticipate your vulnerability and improve your response.

Explicit self-awareness will often help save you from engaging in a conversation in a way that panders to your feelings rather than one that serves your needs. Think back to David, the boss of the nonprofit institution, and Jeremy, his cocky subordinate. Given Jeremy's history, David's conversational game plan—easing in, then when that didn't work, the painful-but-quick bombshell—was doomed. A better approach would have been for David to split the conversation into two parts. In a first meeting, he could have raised the central issues of Jeremy's biting humor and disappointing performance. A second meeting could have been set up for the discussion itself. Handling the situation incrementally would have allowed time for both David and Jeremy to prepare for a two-way conversation instead of one of them delivering a monologue. After all, this wasn't an emergency; David didn't have to exhaust this topic immediately. Indeed, if David had been more self-aware, he might have recognized that the approach he chose was dictated less by Jeremy's character than by his own distaste for conflict.

An excellent way to anticipate specific problems that you may encounter in a stressful conversation is to rehearse with a neutral friend. Pick someone who doesn't have the same communication problems as you. Ideally, the friend should be a good listener, honest but nonjudgmental. Start with content. Just tell your friend what you want to say to your counterpart without worrying about tone or phrasing. Be vicious, be timid, be sarcastically witty, jump around in your argument, but get it out. Now go over it again and think about what you would say if the situation weren't emotionally loaded. Your friend can help you because he or she is not in a flush of emotion over the situation. Write down what you come up with together because if you don't, you'll forget it later.

Now fine-tune the phrasing. When you imagine talking to the counterpart, your phrasing tends to be highly charged—and you can think of only one way to say anything. But when your friend says, "Tell me how you want to say this," an interesting thing happens: Your phrasing is often much better, much more temperate, usable. Remember, you can say what you want to say, you just can't say it *like that*. Also, work on your body language with your friend. You'll both soon be laughing because of the expressions that sneak out unawares—eyebrows skittering up and down, legs wrapped around each other like licorice twists, nervous snickers that will certainly be misinterpreted. (For more on preparing for stressful conversations, see the sidebar "The DNA of Conversation Management.")

Managing the Conversation

While it is important to build awareness and to practice before a stressful conversation, these steps are not enough. Let's look at what you can do as the conversation unfolds. Consider Elizabeth, the team leader whose colleague claimed she was usurping control. She couldn't think well on her feet in confrontational situations, and she knew it, so she needed a few hip-pocket phrases—phrases she could recall on the spot so that she wouldn't have to be silent or invent something on the spur of the moment. Though such a solution sounds simple, most of us don't have a tool kit of conversational tactics ready at hand. Rectifying this gap is an essential part of learning how to handle stressful conversations better. We need to learn communication skills in the same way that we learn CPR: well in advance, knowing that when we need to use them, the situation will be critical and tense. Here are three proven conversational gambits. The particular wording may not suit your style, and that's fine. The important thing is to understand how the techniques work, and then choose phrasing that is comfortable for you.

The DNA of Conversation Management

The techniques I have identified for handling stressful conversations all have tucked within them three deceptively simple ingredients that are needed to make stressful conversations succeed. These are clarity, neutrality, and temperance, and they are the building blocks of all good communication. Mastering them will multiply your chances of responding well to even the most strained conversation. Let's take a look at each of the components in turn.

Clarity means letting words do the work for us. Avoid euphemisms or talking in circles—tell people clearly what you mean: "Emily, from your family's point of view, the Somerset Valley Nursing Home would be the best placement for your father. His benefits don't cover it." Unfortunately, delivering clear content when the news is bad is particularly hard to do. Under strained circumstances, we all tend to shy away from clarity because we equate it with brutality. Instead, we often say things like "Well, Dan, we're still not sure yet what's going to happen with this job, but in the future we'll keep our eyes open." This is a roundabout—and terribly misleading—way to inform someone that he didn't get the promotion he was seeking. Yet there's nothing inherently brutal about honesty. It is not the content but the delivery of the news that makes it brutal or humane. Ask a surgeon; ask a priest; ask a cop. If a message is given skillfully—even though the news is bad—the content may still be tolerable. When a senior executive, for example, directly tells a subordinate that "the promotion has gone to someone else," the news is likely to be highly unpleasant, and the appropriate reaction is sadness, anger, and anxiety. But if the content is clear, the listener can better begin to process the information. Indeed, bringing clarity to the content eases the burden for the counterpart rather than increases it.

Tone is the nonverbal part of delivery in stressful conversations. It is intonation, facial expressions, conscious and unconscious body language. Although it's hard to have a neutral tone when overcome by strong feelings, *neutrality* is the desired norm in crisis communications, including stressful conversations. Consider the classic neutrality of NASA. Regardless of how dire the message, NASA communicates its content in uninflected tones: "Houston, we have a problem." It takes practice to acquire such neutrality. But a neutral tone is the best place to start when a conversation turns stressful.

Temperate phrasing is the final element in this triumvirate of skills. English is a huge language, and there are lots of different ways to say what you need to say. Some of these phrases are temperate, while others baldly provoke your counterpart to dismiss your words—and your content. In the United States, for example, some of the most intemperate phrasing revolves around threats of litigation: "If you don't get a check to me by April 23, I'll be forced to call my lawyer." Phrases like this turn up the heat in all conversations, particularly in strained ones. But remember, we're not in stressful conversations to score points or to create enemies. The goal is to advance the conversation, to hear and be heard accurately, and to have a functional exchange between two people. So next time you want to snap at someone—"Stop interrupting me!"—try this: "Can you hold on a minute? I want to finish before I lose my train of thought." Temperate phrasing will help you take the strain out of a stressful conversation.

Honor Thy Partner

When David gave negative feedback to Jeremy, it would have been refreshing if he had begun with an admission of regret and some responsibility for his contribution to their shared problem. "Jeremy," he might have said, "the quality of your work has been undercut—in part by the reluctance of your colleagues to risk the edge of your humor by talking problems through with you. I share responsibility for this because I have been reluctant to speak openly about these difficulties with you, whom I like and respect and with whom I have worked a long time." Acknowledging responsibility as a technique—particularly as an opening—can be effective because it immediately focuses attention, but without provocation, on the difficult things the speaker needs to say and the listener needs to hear.

Is this always a good technique in a difficult conversation? No, because there is never any one good technique. But in this case, it effectively sets the tone for David's discussion with Jeremy. It honors the problems, it honors Jeremy, it honors their relationship, and it honors David's responsibility. Any technique that communicates honor in a stressful conversation—particularly a conversation that will take the counterpart by surprise—is to be highly valued. Indeed, the ability to act with dignity can make or break a stressful conversation. More important, while Jeremy has left the company, he can still do harm by spreading gossip and using his insider's knowledge against the organization. The more intolerable the conversation with David has been, the more Jeremy is likely to make the organization pay.

Disarm by Restating Your Intentions

Part of the difficulty in Rafael and Elizabeth's "What's Going On Here?" conversation is that Rafael's misinterpretation of Elizabeth's words and actions seems to be influenced by instant replays of other stressful conversations that he has had in the past. Elizabeth doesn't want to psychoanalyze Rafael; indeed, exploring Rafael's internal landscape would exacerbate this painful situation. So what can Elizabeth do to defuse the situation unilaterally?

Elizabeth needs a technique that doesn't require her to understand the underlying reasons for Rafael's strong reaction but helps her handle the situation effectively. "I can see how you took what I said the way you did, Rafael. That wasn't what I meant. Let's go over this list again" I call this the clarification technique, and it's a highly disarming one. Using it, Elizabeth can unilaterally change the confrontation into a point of agreement. Instead of arguing with Rafael about his perceptions, she grants him his perceptions—after all, they're his. Instead of arguing about her intentions, she keeps the responsibility for aligning her words with her intentions on her side. And she goes back into the conversation right where they left off. (For a fuller discussion of the disconnect between what we mean and what we say, see the sidebar "The Gap between Communication and Intent.")

This technique will work for Elizabeth regardless of Rafael's motive. If Rafael innocently misunderstood what she was saying, she isn't fighting him. She accepts his take on what she said and did and corrects it. If his motive is hostile, Elizabeth doesn't concur just to appease him. She accepts and retries. No one loses face. No one scores points off the other. No one gets drawn off on a tangent.

The Gap between Communication and Intent

One of the most common occurrences in stressful conversations is that we all start relying far too much on our intentions. As the mercury in the emotional thermometer rises, we presume that other people automatically understand what we mean. We assume, for instance, that people know we mean well. Indeed, research shows that in stressful conversations, most speakers assume that the listener believes that they have good intentions, regardless of what they say. Intentions can never be that powerful in communications—and certainly not in stressful conversations.

To see what I mean, just think of the last time someone told you not to take something the wrong way. This may well have been uttered quite sincerely by the speaker; nevertheless, most people automatically react by stiffening inwardly, anticipating something at least mildly offensive or antagonistic. And that is exactly the reaction that phrase is always going to get. Because the simplest rule about stressful conversations is that people don't register intention despite words; we register intention through words. In stressful conversations in particular, the emphasis is on what is actually said, not on what we intend or feel. This doesn't mean that participants in stressful conversations don't have feelings or intentions that are valid and valuable. They do. But when we talk about people in stressful communication, we're talking about communication between people—and not about intentions.

Of course, in difficult conversations we may all wish that we didn't have to be so explicit. We may want the other person to realize what we mean even if we don't spell it out. But that leads to the wrong division of labor—with the listener interpreting rather than the speaker communicating. In all conversations, but especially in stressful ones, we are all responsible for getting across to one another precisely what we want to say. In the end, it's far more dignified for an executive to come right out and tell an employee, "Corey, I've arranged a desk for you—and six weeks of outplacement service—because you won't be with us after the end of July." Forcing someone to guess your intentions only prolongs the agony of the inevitable.

Fight Tactics, Not People

Rafael may have baffled Elizabeth, but Karen was acting with outright malice toward Nick when she flew off the handle after a disastrous meeting with the client. Nick certainly can't prevent her from using the thwarting tactics with which she has been so successful in the past. But he can separate Karen's character from her behavior. For instance, it's much more useful for him to think of Karen's reactions as thwarting tactics rather than as personal characteristics. If he thinks of Karen as a distorting, hostile, threatening person, where does that lead? What can anyone ever do about another person's character? But if Nick sees Karen's behavior as a series of tactics that she is using with him because they have worked for her in the past, he can think about using countering techniques to neutralize them.

The best way to neutralize a tactic is to name it. It's much harder to use a tactic once it is openly identified. If Nick, for instance, had said, "Karen, we've worked together pretty well for a long time. I don't know how to talk about what went wrong in the meeting when your take on what happened, and what's going on now, is so different from mine," he would have changed the game completely. He neither would have attacked Karen nor remained the pawn of her tactics. But he would have made Karen's tactics in the conversation the dominant problem.

Openly identifying a tactic, particularly an aggressive one, is disarming for another reason. Often we think of an aggressive counterpart as persistently, even endlessly, contentious, but that isn't true. People have definite levels of aggression that they're comfortable with—and they are reluctant to raise the bar. When Nick doesn't acknowledge Karen's tactics, she can use them unwittingly, or allegedly so. But if Nick speaks of them, it would require more aggression on Karen's part to continue using the same tactics. If she is at or near her aggression threshold, she won't continue because that would make her uncomfortable. Nick may not be able to stop Karen, but she may stop herself.

People think stressful conversations are inevitable. And they are. But that doesn't mean they have to have bad resolutions. Consider a client of mine, Jacqueline, the only woman on the board of an engineering company. She was sensitive to slighting remarks about women in business, and she found one board member deliberately insensitive. He repeatedly ribbed her about being a feminist and, on this occasion, he was telling a sexist joke.

This wasn't the first time that something like this had happened, and Jacqueline felt the usual internal cacophony of reactions. But because she was aware that this was a stressful situation for her, Jacqueline was prepared. First, she let the joke hang in the air for a minute and then went back to the issue they had been discussing. When Richard didn't let it go but escalated with a new poke—"Come on, Jackie, it was a *joke*"—Jacqueline stood her ground. "Richard," she said, "this kind of humor is frivolous to you, but it makes me feel pushed aside." Jacqueline didn't need to say more. If Richard had continued to escalate, he would have lost face. In fact, he backed down: "Well, I wouldn't want my wife to hear about my bad behavior a second time," he snickered. Jacqueline was silent. She had made her point; there was no need to embarrass him.

Stressful conversations are never easy, but we can all fare better if, like Jacqueline, we prepare for them by developing greater awareness of our vulnerabilities and better techniques for handling ourselves. The advice and tools described in this article can be helpful in unilaterally reducing the strain in stressful conversations. All you have to do is try them. If one technique doesn't work, try an other. Find phrasing that feels natural. But keep practicing—you'll find what works best for you.

Renegotiating Existing Agreements: How to Deal with "Life Struggling against Form"

Jeswald W. Salacuse

Renegotiation of existing agreements is constant in all areas of life. In this article, the author examines the nature and causes of renegotiation and offers guidance to persons involved in the renegotiation process. He identifies three distinct types of renegotiations—postdeal, intradeal, and extradeal renegotiation. Each of the three types poses particular problems and opportunities, and each requires different techniques to deal with those problems and opportunities.

Despite lengthy discussions, skilled drafting, and strict enforcement mechanisms, parties to solemnly signed and sealed agreements often find themselves returning to the bargaining table later on to "renegotiate" them. Thus a key challenge in negotiating any agreement is not just "getting to yes" but also staying there.

The renegotiation of existing agreements is a constant in all areas of life. Economic recessions or significant changes in prices invariably lead to restructurings and workouts of thousands of business arrangements made in better times. Companies facing financial crises sometimes try to find a solution to their problems by renegotiating their labor contracts. In the international arena, the world has witnessed the renegotiation of mineral and petroleum agreements of the 1960s and 1970s, often in the face of threatened host country nationalizations and expropriations; the loan reschedulings of the 1980s following the debt crisis in developing countries; and the restructuring of project and financial agreements as a result of the Asian financial crisis of the late 1990s. In 2001 the American government launched a major foreign policy initiative by asking Russia to renegotiate the Anti-Ballistic Missile Treaty so the United States could develop a missile defense system. Later this same year, the terrorist attacks in New York and Washington on September 11 inaugurated a new era of insecurity that has prompted the review and renegotiation of existing agreements in many domains.

Through renegotiation, business executives, lawyers, and government officials continually seem to be seeking either to alleviate a bargain that has become onerous or to hold onto a good deal that the other side wants to change. The examples are so numerous that renegotiating existing agreements seems as basic to human relations as is negotiating new agreements. Seventy years ago, Karl Llewellyn, a noted American legal scholar, captured the tension between negotiated agreements and subsequent reality in the conclusion of his thoughtful inquiry into the role of contract in the social order: "One turns from the contemplation of the work of contract as from the experience of Greek tragedy. Life struggling against form . . ." (Llewellyn 1931: 751). Renegotiation

Source: "Renegotiating Existing Agreements: How to Deal with 'Life Struggling against Form,'" by Jeswald W. Salacuse, from the *Negotiation Journal* 17, no. 4, October 2001, pp. 311–331. Blackwell Publishers, Ltd. Used with permission.

is one of the most important theaters in which parties to existing agreements play out the continuing struggle of life against form.

The purpose of this article is to examine the phenomenon of renegotiation, to explore its nature and causes, and to offer advice on how best to conduct the renegotiation process.

The Three Types of Renegotiation

Discussions of renegotiation apply the term to three fundamentally different situations, each of which presents different problems that require different solutions. The three situations are postdeal renegotiations, intradeal renegotiations, and extradeal renegotiations.

Postdeal renegotiation takes place at the expiration of a contract when the two sides, though legally free to go their own way, nonetheless try to renew their formal relationship. For example, consider the case of a power company that has built an electrical generating station and entered into a 20-year contract to supply electricity to a state public utility. At the end of 20 years, when local law considers their legal relationship at an end, the power company and the public utility begin discussions on a second long-term electricity supply contract, thereby renegotiating their original relationship. While this second negotiation process—a postdeal renegotiation—may at first glance seem to resemble the negotiation of their original contract, it also has some notable differences that influence renegotiation strategies, tactics, and outcomes.

Intradeal renegotiation occurs when the agreement itself provides that, at specified times or as the result of specified events occuring during the term of the contract, the parties may renegotiate or review certain of its provisions. For example, the just-mentioned electricity supply contract might include a provision calling for the renegotiation of the agreement's pricing terms in the event of dramatic changes in fuel costs, which could occur over a 20-year period. Here renegotiation is anticipated as a legitimate activity in which both parties, while still bound to each other in a valid contract, are to engage in good faith. It is an intradeal renegotiation because it takes places within the legal framework established for the original transaction.

The most difficult, stressful, and emotional renegotiations are those undertaken in apparent violation of the contract or at least in the absence of a specific clause authorizing a renegotiation. These negotiations take place extradeal, for they occur outside the framework of the existing agreement. The negotiations to reschedule loans following the Third World debt crisis of the early 1980s, the effort by the American government to renegotiate the ABM Treaty with the Russians, and attempts by companies to secure changes in existing union contracts all fit within the category of extradeal renegotiations. In each case, one of the participants is seeking relief from a legally binding obligation without any basis for renegotiation in the agreement itself.

Renegotiation has thus become a constant and ever-present fact of contemporary life, whether it is postdeal, intradeal, or extradeal. Renegotiation can be distinguished from initial negotiations by three factors that significantly affect the renegotiation process itself. They are *increased mutual knowledge, increased transactional understanding,* and *increased mutual linkage.* First, as a result of working together during their first agreement, the parties know much more about each other than when they negotiated that first agreement. Second, many of the questions that they had about their contemplated transaction during the initial negotiation have now been answered. And third, as a result of their investments in the transaction during the first agreement, it may now be more costly to abandon renegotiations than it was to have walked away from the initial negotiations.

In each type of renegotiation, different relationships and process dynamics are taking place among the parties. These dynamics lead to possible strategies and tactics that are worthy of consideration by thoughtful negotiators. Let's examine the processes at work in the three kinds of renegotiation.

Postdeal Renegotiations

Although a postdeal renegotiation takes place when the original transaction has reached or is approaching its end, several factors distinguish it from a negotiation in first instance—factors that may also significantly affect the renegotiation process. First, by virtue of law, custom, or express or implied contractual commitments, the parties may have a legal obligation to negotiate in good faith with one another despite the fact that their original contract has terminated; consequently, their ability to refuse to engage in postdeal renegotiations may be limited. The existence and precise nature of such a duty will depend on the law governing the contract.

Anglo-American law traditionally has recognized a broad, unrestrained freedom of negotiation that permits a party to begin or end negotiation at any time for any reason (Farnsworth 1987: 220–21). The rationale for this rule is that a limitation on the freedom to negotiate might discourage persons from undertaking transactions in the first place. By contrast, the law in certain other countries is less liberal, holding that once the parties have commenced negotiations, they may have an obligation to negotiate in good faith (Litvinoff 1997: 1659–62).

But even in common-law countries, the parties may have an obligation to renegotiate an agreement in good faith at its end because of an express provision in the original contract; the prevailing practices and customs of the business concerned; or the conduct of the parties toward one another during the life of their agreement. In contrast, parties seeking to negotiate a transaction in first instance have no such obligation and can abandon negotiations at any time.

The precise content of the obligation to renegotiate in good faith an existing negotiated agreement varies from country to country. It may include a duty not to negotiate with a third person until postdeal negotiations with a party in the original transaction have failed. Or it may also require a party not to terminate renegotiations without reasonable cause and without having persevered for a reasonable length of time (Farnsworth 1987: 269–85). Failure by either side to fulfill its obligations to renegotiate in good faith may result in liability in damages.

Even if the applicable law imposes no legal obligation to renegotiate in good faith, the original contract, as well as current economic factors, may constrain the postdeal renegotiation process in ways not present in the original negotiations. For example, the 20-year electricity supply contract mentioned earlier might provide that, if the power company and the public utility fail to negotiate a second 20-year supply contract, the public utility company will be obligated to purchase the project company's electrical generating station according to a pricing formula specified in the original agreement.

Beyond the legal and contractual constraints, the parties' increased mutual knowledge, increased transactional understanding, and increased mutual linkage will significantly influence the course of negotiations. For example, in renegotiating the electricity supply agreement, the power company's approach will be more cautious and reluctant if the history of the first contact was plagued by late and contested payments than if the public utility had always paid on time and in full. Similarly, if over the first 20 years the price of power under the contract had proven to be much higher than competing forms of energy, the public utility would seek changes in the pricing formula during the renegotiation. Finally, the fact that the power company organized itself and trained its employees to provide electricity over the long term to a single specific purchaser will probably mean that, all other things being equal, the power company would prefer to enter into a new contract with the utility rather than to make an agreement with another purchaser, a course of action entailing significant new risks and costs. Then too, the public utility, having come to rely on the power company for a major portion of its electrical supply, may wish to avoid the costs of finding another supplier or creating its own electrical generating capacity.

In any negotiation, a party's actions at the negotiating table are influenced by its evaluation of available alternatives to the deal it is trying to negotiate. Rational negotiators will not ordinarily agree to a transaction that is inferior to their best alternative to a negotiated agreement, or BATNA (Fisher, Ury, and Patton 1991: 99–102). In a postdeal renegotiation, each party's evaluation of its BATNA will be heavily influenced by knowledge of the other side obtained during the first agreement, its understanding of the transaction gained during that time, and the extent of the investment that it has made in the relationship.

In general, the success of postdeal renegotiations will depend on the nature of the relationship that developed between the parties during the original contract. If that relationship was strong and productive, the atmosphere at the renegotiation bargaining table will be that of two partners trying to solve a common problem. However, if the relationship was weak and troubled during the term of the initial agreement, the prevailing mood will be that of two cautious adversaries who know each other only too well.

These factors give rise to three general principles that negotiators should consider as they structure and conduct the process of postdeal renegotiations.

1.   *Provide for postdeal renegotiations in the original contract.* In transactions in which the desirability or likelihood of postdeal renegotiations is high, the parties should specify in their original agreement the process and rules that they will follow in conducting a postdeal renegotiation. For example, among other similar provisions, the contract should specify such matters as how soon before the end of the contract term renegotiations are to begin; how long the renegotiations are to continue before either party may legally abandon them; where the renegotiations are to take place; and the nature of the information that each side is to provide the other. Recognizing that postdeal renegotiations may become problematic, the contract might also authorize the use of mediators or other third-party helpers in the process.

2. *Individually and jointly review the history of the relationship during the original contract.* As part of its preparation, each party to a postdeal renegotiation should review, carefully and thoroughly, the experience of working with the other side during the first contract. An understanding of the problems encountered during that period will enable each side to shape proposals to remedy them during a contemplated second agreement. To make that review an opportunity for creative problem solving rather than mutual acrimony over past mistakes, the parties should structure a joint review of past experience, perhaps with the help of a neutral facilitator, at the beginning of the postdeal renegotiation process. For example, as a first step in the renegotiation process, the power company and the public utility might give a review team consisting of executives from each side the task of preparing a mutually acceptable history of their relationship. Inevitably, during the course of postdeal renegotiations, each side will refer to past events. The renegotiation process will proceed more smoothly and efficiently if, at the beginning of the process, the parties have a common understanding of their history together than if they engage in a continuing debate throughout the renegotiation about the existence and significance of past events.

3. *Understand thoroughly the alternatives to a renegotiated deal.* Negotiators should not only evaluate their own alternatives to the deal that they are trying to make, but they should also try to estimate their counterparts' alternatives. In a postdeal renegotiation, these two tasks are often complicated by the fact that the parties may have conducted their activities in such a way during the first contract that few realistic alternatives to a second contract seem possible. For example, the power company that owns a generating facility may feel that it has few other options than to enter into a second contract with the state public utility. Or the public utility company, in time of energy shortage, may see no realistic alternatives to making a second electricity power purchase agreement with the project company. Rather than accept the inevitability of a second contract, each side, long before the termination of the first contract, should carefully examine all options and seek to develop possible new alternatives before entering into postdeal renegotiations with the other side. For example, the state public utility, perhaps several years in advance of the end of the first contract, should contact other potential project companies to determine their interest in developing electrical generation plants.

Intradeal Renegotiations

Contractual stability is a goal sought by all sides in any negotiation. Parties to a contract obviously need the assurance that the terms of their agreement will be respected in the future. At the same time, most parties know that unforeseen events may arise during a contract term that drastically change the balance of benefits originally contemplated by their agreement. Consequently, a fundamental challenge in contracting practice is to achieve contractual stability but, at the same time, allow the parties to deal with changing circumstances in the future. The traditional approach to resolving this dilemma is for the parties during their original negotiation to attempt to anticipate all possible contingencies and to provide solutions for them in their agreement. This approach rejects the idea of intradeal renegotiation.

Another solution to the problem of balancing the imperatives of stability and change is for the contract itself to authorize the parties to renegotiate key elements of their relationship, should specified events or circumstances occur. In view of the impossibility of predicting all possible future contingencies, the inclusion in the agreement of some type of intradeal renegotiation clause would appear to be a useful device to give needed flexibility to long-term agreements. In fact, however, Western organizations rarely use them.

The traditional reluctance to use renegotiation clauses stems from a variety of factors, both legal and practical. First is the concern among lawyers that renegotiation clauses are merely "agreements to agree" and therefore may be unenforceable (Carter 1999: 188). On the other hand, although English common law has tended to dismiss agreements to negotiate as unenforceable, the contemporary approach in most American courts is to enforce agreements to negotiate in good faith. According to one recent case from a U.S. federal district court, "the critical inquiry in evaluating the enforceability of an express or implied agreement to negotiate in good faith is whether the standard against which the parties' good-faith negotiations are to be measured is sufficiently certain to comport with the applicable body of contract law" (*Howtek, Inc. v. Relisys et al.* [1999]). It would seem that a specific renegotiation clause in an existing contract with definite terms as to how the parties are to conduct the renegotiation process would easily meet this standard of enforceability. The required certainty would be further satisfied by specifying the precise events that give rise to the obligation to renegotiate and by specifically providing for the timing, locale, and conditions of the renegotiation process, among others.

Practical considerations have also led Western executives to view renegotiation clauses with suspicion on grounds that they increase uncertainty and risk in transactions and offend Western concepts of the "sanctity" of contract. Their presence in a contract also creates a risk that one of the parties will use a renegotiation clause as a lever to force changes in provisions that, strictly speaking, are not open to revision. The challenge of drafting these provisions and the heightened risks to contractual stability by renegotiation clauses that have yet to be tested in the courts are additional factors that have deterred their use in long-term contracts.

Despite these potential pitfalls, the inclusion of a renegotiation clause may actually contribute to transactional stability in certain situations. First, in cases in which significant changes in circumstances may result in severe unexpected financial hardship, a renegotiation clause may permit the parties to avoid default, with the attendant risk of litigation and extradeal renegotiations. During the original negotiations, it may be wiser for the parties to recognize the risk of changed circumstances and create within the contract a process to deal with them rather than to try to predict all eventualities and then be subject to the uncertain decisions of courts when those predictions prove to be flawed.

A second situation in which a renegotiation clause may be helpful occurs in cases in which the parties, by virtue of their differing cultures, understand and perceive the basis of their transaction in fundamentally different ways. For example, Western notions of business transactions as being founded upon law and contract often clash with Asian conceptions of business arrangements as based on personal relationships (Salacuse 1998: 225–27). In some Asian nations, executives often consider the essence of a business deal to be the relationship between the parties, rather than the written contract, which in their view can only describe that relationship imperfectly and incompletely. They may also assume that any long-term business relationship includes an implicit, fundamental principle: In times of change, parties in a business relationship should decide together how to cope with that change and adjust their relationship accordingly.

However, the Western party may view the long-term business transaction as set in the concrete of a lengthy and detailed contract without the possibility of modification. This sharply contrasts with the Asian side viewing the transaction as floating on the parties' fluid personal relationships, which always have within them an implicit commitment to renegotiate the terms of the transaction in the event of unforeseen happenings.

In long-term transactions, such as joint venture projects between Asian and Western companies whose success depends on close and continuing cooperation, it may be wise to recognize this difference of view at the outset of negotiations and attempt to find some middle ground. A renegotiation clause may represent such middle ground between total contractual rigidity on the one hand and complete relational flexibility on the other. It recognizes the possibility of redoing the deal, but controls the renegotiation process. An intradeal renegotiation clause, then, may give stability to an arrangement whose long-term nature creates a high risk of instability.

The use of renegotiation clauses in long-term agreements seems to be on the increase in recent years (Carter 1999: 189). A variety of intradeal renegotiation clauses exist to cope with the challenge of balancing contractual stability with adaptation to change. The following are some of the principal types.

1. *The implicit minor renegotiation clause.*   Despite some lawyers' claims to the contrary, contracts in long-term arrangements, no matter how detailed, are not a kind of comprehensive instruction booklet that the parties follow blindly. At best, such agreements are *frameworks* within which the participants constantly adjust their relationship. Karl Llewellyn (1931: 736–37) underscored this point many years ago when he wrote,

> . . . the major importance of a legal contract is to provide a framework for well-nigh every type of group organization and for well-nigh every type of passing or permanent relation between individuals and groups, up to and including states—a framework highly adjustable, a framework which almost never accurately indicates real working relations, but which affords a rough indication around which such relations vary, an occasional guide in cases of doubt, and a norm of final appeal when the relations cease in fact to work.

Executives responsible for implementing long-term transactions have consistently confirmed Llewellyn's observation in similar terms: "Once the contract is signed, we put it in the drawer. After that, what matters most is the relationship between us and our partner, and we are negotiating that relationship all the time." What this view means in practice is that certain matters in the agreement, usually but not always of a minor nature, are subject to renegotiation by the parties as part of their ongoing relationship, despite the fact that their contract contains no specific renegotiation clause (Kolo and Walde 2000: 45).

One can therefore argue that an "implicit minor renegotiation clause" is part of any transaction agreement. For example, if a long-term supply agreement provides that the supplier make deliveries in a country on June 30 of each year, but the government of the country later declares a national holiday on that date, making it difficult for the public utility to accept delivery, the parties would renegotiate a more appropriate time for delivery.

2. *Review clauses.* Long-term contracts, particularly in the oil and mineral industries, sometimes commit the parties to meet at specific times to review the operation of their agreement. For example, one mining agreement provided that the parties were to meet together every seven years "with a view to considering in good faith whether this agreement is continuing to operate fairly . . . and with a view further to discussing in good faith any problems arising from the practical operation of this agreement" (Peter 1995: 79). Although the words *negotiation* or *renegotiation* appear nowhere in this clause, one reasonable interpretation of the provision is that it carries an implicit obligation for the parties to resolve problems through good faith negotiation.

3. *Automatic adjustment clauses.* Transaction agreements often contain certain terms, such as those concerning prices or interest rates, subject to automatic change by reference to specified indexes, such as a cost-of-living index or the London Interbank Offered Rate (LIBOR). For example, the electricity supply contract might link the price to be paid for the electricity by the public utility to variations in fuel costs or the local cost-of-living index. While the aim of such a provision is to provide for flexibility without the risks inherent in renegotiation, negotiation may still be necessary to apply the index in unanticipated situations or in the event that the index itself disappears or becomes inappropriate (Kolo and Walde 2000: 44).

4. *Open-term provisions.* Because of the difficulties and risks inherent in trying to negotiate arrangements to take place far in the future, some transaction agreements specifically provide that certain matters will be negotiated at a later time, perhaps years after the contract has been signed and the transaction implemented. For example, a foreign investor seeking approval for a factory from a host government might agree to negotiate appropriate senior management training schemes after it has constructed the facility and begun to hire local managers. This type of provision might be called an *open-term* clause because the matter in question has been left open for negotiation at a later time (Farnsworth 1987: 250).

In a strict sense, of course, the subsequent negotiation of an open term is not really a renegotiation of anything, since the parties have not yet agreed on any elements of that provision. In a broader sense, however, the negotiation of an open term at a later time will have the effect of modifying the overall relationship among the parties. Moreover, it is not inconceivable that one or more of the parties could use the opportunity of negotiating the open term as an occasion to seek concessions or changes in other terms through the common negotiating device of linking issues. For example, the foreign investor might offer the host government a particularly attractive management training program if the government would agree to certain desired regulatory changes.

5. *Formal renegotiation clauses*.   In an effort to balance the imperatives of contractual stability with flexibility, long-term agreements sometimes contain formal wording that obligates the parties to renegotiate specified terms affected by changes in circumstances or unforeseen developments, such as those concerning construction costs, governmental regulations, or commodity prices. For example, an oil exploration contract between the government of Qatar and a foreign oil company provided that the two sides would negotiate future arrangements for the use of natural gas not associated with oil discoveries if commercial quantities of such "nonassociated" gas were later found in the contract area (Carver and Hossain 1990: 311). In addition, renegotiation clauses in investment contracts often accompany stabilization clauses by which a host country promises that any changes in laws or regulations will not adversely affect the foreign investment project. The effect of the two clauses is to obligate the host government and the project company to enter into negotiations to restore the financial equilibrium that such new laws and regulations may have destroyed.

An intradeal renegotiation clause obligates the parties only to negotiate, not to agree. If the two sides have negotiated in good faith but fail to agree, that failure cannot justify liability on the part of one of the parties. In order to bring finality to the process of intradeal renegotiation, long-term agreements sometimes include a *contract adaptation clause,* which stipulates that when certain specified events occur, the parties will first seek to negotiate a solution and, failing that, refer their problem to a third party for either a recommendation or a binding decision, depending on the desire of the parties to the contract. Certain institutions, such as the International Chamber of Commerce, have developed rules and facilities to help carry out the contract adaptation process.

Extradeal Renegotiation

In an extradeal renegotiation, one party is insisting on renegotiating terms of a valid contract that contains no express provision authorizing renegotiation. Unlike negotiations for the original transaction, which are generally fueled by both sides' hopes for future benefits, extradeal negotiations usually begin with both parties' shattered expectations. One side has failed to achieve the benefits expected from the transaction, and the other is being asked to give up something for which it bargained hard and which it hoped to enjoy for a long time. And whereas both parties to the negotiation of a proposed new venture participate willingly, if not eagerly, one party always participates reluctantly, if not downright unwillingly, in an extradeal renegotiation.

Beyond mere disappointed expectations, extradeal renegotiations, by their very nature, can create bad feeling and mistrust. One side believes it is being asked to give up something to which it has a legal and moral right. It views the other side as having gone back on its word, as having acted in bad faith by reneging on the deal. Indeed, the reluctant party may even feel that it is being coerced into participating in extradeal renegotiations since a refusal to do so would result in losing the investment it has already made in the transaction.

In most cases, it is very difficult for the parties to see extradeal renegotiations as anything more than a process in which one side wins and the other side loses. While the negotiation of any transaction initially is usually about the degree to which each side will share in expected benefits, an extradeal renegotiation is often about allocating a loss. At the same time, because the parties are bound together in a legal and economic relationhip, it is usually much more difficult for one or both of them to walk away from a troubled transaction than it is for two unconnected parties to a proposed agreement in the first instance.

In most countries, the law does not oblige a party to enter into renegotiations, no matter how much conditions have changed or how heavy the costs incurred by the other side since the contract was originally made (Carter 1999: 185).[1] In general, a party being asked to renegotiate an existing agreement has a legal right to refuse to renegotiate and to insist on performance in accordance with the letter of the contract. On the other hand, requests—or in some cases, demands—for renegotiation of an existing agreement are often accompanied by express or implied threats, including governmental intervention, expropriation, a slowdown in performance, or the complete repudiation or cancellation of the contract itself.

Parties facing a demand for renegotiation usually have an available legal remedy to enforce their existing contract and will often threaten to go to court to assert it. However, a willingness to pursue a legal remedy to its conclusion, rather than renegotiate, will usually depend on the party's evaluation of that remedy in relation to the results it expects from renegotiation. To the extent that the net benefits (i.e., benefits minus costs) from renegotiation exceed the expected net benefits from litigation, a rational party will ordinarily engage in the requested renegotiation. But if either before or during the renegotiation, a party decides that the net benefits to be derived from litigation will exceed the net benefits to be gained in renegotiation, that party will normally pursue its legal remedies.

On its side, the party asking for renegotiation will be making its own cost–benefit analysis of the relative merits of contract repudiation and its probable fate in litigation. As long as this party believes that the net benefits of repudiating the contract are less than the net benefits of respecting it, the contractual relationship will continue. But when (for whatever reason) it judges the respective net benefits to be the opposite, the result will be a demand for renegotiation with the threat of eventual repudiation in the background. Figure 1 seeks to capture this dynamic.

A party's reluctance to agree to an extradeal renegotiation may be due to the impact of renegotiation not only on the contract in question but on other contracts and relationships as well. Renegotiation of a transaction with one particular party may set an undesirable precedent for other renegotiations with other parties. For example, concessions

FIGURE 1 | Assessing the Effects of Changing Circumstances

Events	increase / decrease		Agreement benefits	
Net benefits of no contract	<	Net benefits of contract	=	Acceptance
Net benefits of no contact	>	Net benefits of contract	=	Rejection

by a union to one employer may lead another employer to seek equal treatment by demanding extradeal renegotiations of its own labor agreements.

Although the causes of extradeal renegotiations in individual cases are numerous, they generally fall into one of two basic categories: (1) the parties' imperfect contract with respect to their underlying transaction; and (2) changed circumstances after they have signed their agreement.

1. *The parties' imperfect contract.*   The goal of any written contract is to express the full meaning of the parties' agreement concerning their proposed transaction. Despite lawyers' belief in their abilities to capture that agreement in lengthy and detailed contracts, in practice a written contract, particularly in long-term arrangements, can achieve that goal only imperfectly, largely for three reasons. First, the parties to long-term agreements are inherently incapable of predicting all of the events and conditions that may affect their transactions in the future because that would require perfect foresight. Second, the transaction costs of making contracts limit the resources that the parties are able to devote to the contracting process and thus further restrict the ability of the parties to make a contract that perfectly reflects their understanding (Talley 1999: 1206; Tracht 1999: 623–24). Third, even if the parties had the requisite foresight and resources to draft a perfect contract, they have no assurance that a court will interpret their contract exactly as they intended.

Adding even more complexity to the problem of accurately negotiating and articulating the parties' intent in a long-term international transaction are the parties' differing cultures, business practices, ideologies, political systems, and laws—factors that often impede a true common understanding and inhibit the development of a working relationship (Salacuse 1991).

2. *Changed circumstances.*   Changes in circumstances since the time of the original contract are a second major cause for postdeal renegotiations. A sudden fall in commodity prices, the outbreak of civil war, a terrorist attack, the development of a new technology, or the imposition of currency controls are examples of changes in circumstance that often force the parties back to the negotiating table. As Raymond Vernon argued over three decades ago with respect to foreign investment projects, a bargain once struck will inevitably become obsolete for one of the parties, and issues once agreed upon will be reopened at a later time. Long-term agreements, in Vernon's words, are "obsolescing bargains" (Vernon 1971: 46).

Generally speaking, changes in circumstances can either increase or decrease the costs and benefits of the agreement to the parties. As Figure 1 shows, when a change in circumstances means that the cost of respecting a contract for one of the parties is greater than the cost of abandoning it, the result is usually rejection of the deal or a demand for its renegotiation. The notions of *costs* and *benefits* are not limited to purely economic calculations. Political and social costs and benefits must also be accounted for. For example, in one case involving an investment project to build a luxury resort near the Giza Pyramids in Egypt, the Egyptian government originally signed the agreement because it believed the economic benefits of the project to exceed its potential costs. But when public and international opposition became strong and persistent, the government canceled the project because it judged the political costs to outweigh the economic benefits to be derived from its construction.

Since the risk of extradeal renegotiation is always present in any agreement, negotiators should ask themselves two basic questions:

- How can the likelihood of extradeal renegotiations be reduced?
- When renegotiations actually occur, how should the parties conduct them to make the process as productive and fair as possible?

In answering these questions, negotiators need to distinguish actions they should take before and after the transaction has broken down and one party is demanding renegotiation or threatening to reject the deal entirely. Some renegotiation principles to follow before deal breakdown include the following.

1. *Recognize that a signed contract does not necessarily create a relationship*. For a long-term transaction to be stable and productive for both sides, it must be founded on a relationship, a complex set of interactions characterized by cooperation and trust. A relationship also implies a connection between the parties. It is the existence of a solid relationship between the parties to a transaction that allows them to face unforeseen circumstances and hardships in a productive and creative manner.

A contract, no matter how detailed and lengthy, does not create a business relationship. Just as a map is not a country, but only an imperfect description thereof, a contract is not a business relationship, but only an imperfect sketch of what the relationship should be. A contract may be a necessary condition for certain kinds of relationships, but it is usually not a sufficient condition.

While negotiators must be concerned about the adequacy of contractual provisions, they should also seek to determine that a solid foundation for a relationship is in place. Accordingly, a negotiator should also ask a variety of noncontractual questions during the negotiating process: How well do the parties know one another? What mechanisms are in place to foster communications between the two sides after the contract is signed? To what extent are there genuine links and connections between the parties to the agreement? Is the deal balanced and advantageous for both sides?

Regardless of culture, in most countries whenever one party fails to respect its contractual obligations to another party, the existence of a valuable relationship between the parties is more likely to facilitate a negotiated resolution of their dispute than if no such relationship exists. The reason for this phenomenon is that the aggrieved party views the relationship with the offending party as more valuable than the individual claim arising out of the failure to honor the contractual provision. Thus in a workout, a bank is often willing to renegotiate a loan with a delinquent debtor company or country when the bank considers that the prospect of future business with the debtor is likely. Bondholders of the same debtor, on the other hand, will generally be more resistant to renegotiation than banks since bondholders generally do not have the same opportunity for a profitable business relationship in the future.

2. *Building a relationship takes time, so don't rush initial negotiations.*   Negotiators who are concerned to lay the foundation for a relationship as well as to conclude a contract know that sufficient time is required to achieve this goal. While speed of negotiation may appeal to Americans as "efficient" and a recognition of the fact that "time is money," for other cultures a quick negotiation of a complicated transaction may imply overreaching by one of the parties, insufficient consideration of the public interest, or even corruption.

A negotiation done in haste invites renegotiation later on. For example, in one case that attracted significant media attention in the mid-1990s, the fact that Enron, a major American energy company, negotiated a memorandum of understanding with the Maharashtra state government in India to build a $2 billion power plant after just three days of discussions during Enron's first visit to the Indian state made the subsequent power purchase agreement vulnerable to challenges from many quarters. Ultimately, the two sides were only able to resolve their conflict through a lengthy extradeal renegotiation that changed important terms in the 20-year contract by which Enron's project was to sell electricity to the Maharashtra State public utility (Salacuse 2001: 1342–57).

3. *Provide for intradeal renegotiations in appropriate transactions.*   If the risk of change and uncertainty is constant in long-term agreements, how should deal makers cope with it? The traditional method is to write detailed contracts that seek to foresee all possible eventualities. Most modern contracts deny the possibility of change. They therefore rarely provide for adjustments to meet changing circumstances. This assumption of contractual stability has proven false time and time again.

As suggested earlier, rather than viewing a long-term transaction as frozen in the detailed provisions of a lengthy contract, it may be more realistic to think of a long-term agreement as a *continuing negotiation* between the parties as they seek to adjust their relationship to the rapidly changing environment in which they must work together. Accordingly, the parties should consider providing in their contract that, at specified times or on the happening of specified events, they will renegotiate or at least review certain of the contract's provisions.

In this approach, the parties deal with the problem of renegotiation before, rather than after, they sign their contract. Both sides recognize at the outset that the risk of changed circumstances is high in any long-term relationship and that at sometime in the future either side may seek to renegotiate or adjust the contract accordingly. Rather than dismiss the possibility of renegotiation and then be forced to review the entire contract at a later time in an atmosphere of hostility between the partners, it may be better to recognize the possibility of renegotiation at the outset and set down a clear framework to conduct the process.

4. *Consider a role for mediation or conciliation in the deal.*   A third party can often help the two sides with their negotiations and renegotiations. Third parties, whether called mediators, conciliators, or advisers, can assist in building and preserving business relations and in resolving disputes without resorting to litigation. Consequently, negotiators should consider the possibility of building into their transactions a role for some form of mediation. For example, the contract might provide that before either party can resort to litigation to settle a dispute, they must use the services of a mediator or conciliator for a specific period of time in an attempt to negotiate a settlement of their conflict.

* * * *

When one side has demanded renegotiation of the basic contract governing their relationship, how should one or both of the parties proceed? Following are some renegotiation principles after a deal has broken down.

1. *Resist the temptation to make belligerent or moralistic responses to a demand for renegotiation, but seek to understand the basis of the demand.* A party facing a demand for extradeal renegotiations often counters it with hostile, belligerent, or moralistic objections. Such responses are hardly ever effective in persuading the other side to end its insistence on renegotiation since that party has already determined that its own vital interests require repudiation or renegotiation of the agreement. Normally, it is only by dealing with those interests that the two sides in a renegotiation can resolve the conflict. Moreover, the party asking for renegotiation almost always asserts equally moralistic arguments to justify its own demands: The contract is exploitative, the negotiators were corrupt, one side used duress, the other side was ignorant of all the underlying factors, or the basic circumstances of the deal have changed in a fundamental way.

While respect for agreements is indeed a norm in virtually all societies (and may even rise to the level of a universal principle of law), most cultures also provide relief, in varying degrees, from the binding force of a contract in a variety of circumstances. "A deal is a deal" (*pacta sunt servanda*) is certainly an expression of a fundamental rule of human relations, but so is the statement "things have changed" (*rebus sic stantibus*). While a request for extradeal renegotiations may provoke bad feelings in one party, an outright refusal to renegotiate may also create ill will on the other side, which will see it as an attempt to impose an unjust bargain.

One may also argue that in many transactions (particularly between parties from different cultures) there are, in effect, two agreements: the legal contract, which sets out enforceable rights and duties, and the parties' "foundation relationship," which reflects their fundamental understanding in all its dimensions, legal and nonlegal. An important implied aspect of this relationship is an understanding, given the impossibility of predicting all future contingencies, that if problems develop in the future the two sides will engage in negotiations to adjust their relationship in a mutually beneficial way.

2. *Evaluate the benefits of a legal proceeding against the benefits of a future relationship.* The extent of a party's willingness to renegotiate an agreement will usually be in direct proportion to the value it attaches to its potential future relationship with the other side. If a party judges that relationship to be worth more than its claim for breach of contract, it will ordinarily be willing to engage in extradeal renegotiation. On the other hand, if the party concludes that its claim is worth more than the benefits from a continuing relationship, it will usually insist on its contractual rights to the point of using litigation to protect them.

For example, one of the factors that encouraged Enron to renegotiate with the Maharashtra government after the cancellation of its electricity supply contract was the prospect of undertaking numerous energy projects throughout India in the years ahead.

Enron clearly judged those potential relationships to be worth more than winning an arbitration award in a case that would certainly be a long protracted struggle. Looking forward, Enron therefore constantly remained open to renegotiation throughout its conflict with the state of Maharashtra.

Often an aggrieved party facing a demand for renegotiation cannot accurately evaluate the worth of its claim or the value of a renegotiated contract without first engaging in some kind of discussions with the other side. Moreover, satisfaction of its claim through litigation against the other side is almost always subject to long delays, a further inducement to enter into renegotiations. Indeed, one of the functions of the delays inherent in pursuing legal remedies is to give the parties an opportunity to negotiate an efficient solution to their conflict (Tracht 1999: 622).

3.   *Look for ways to create value in the renegotiation.* A party facing a demand for renegotiation has a tendency to see the process as the worst kind of win–lose activity in which any advantage gained by the other side is an automatic loss to itself. As a result, an unwilling participant in an extradeal renegotiation tends to be intransigent, to quibble over the smallest issues, to voice recriminations, and generally to fight a rearguard action throughout the process. By pursuing this approach, the parties may fail to capture the maximum gains possible from their encounter.

Joint problem-solving negotiation and integrative bargaining are as applicable to an extradeal renegotiation as they are to the negotiation of the deal in the first instance. The challenge for both sides in a renegotiation is to create an atmosphere in which problem solving can readily take place. Even if a party feels forced into an extradeal renegotiation, it should approach the process as an opportunity to secure gains from the process. Thus in the renegotiations between Enron and the Maharashtra State government over their electricity supply contract, while Maharashtra State gained a reduced power tariff, Enron secured the right to increase the capacity of its power plant.

4.   *The parties should fully understand the alternatives to succeeding in the renegotiation—especially their costs.* The alternative to a successful extradeal renegotiation in most cases is litigation in which the party seeking renegotiation will be the defendant and the party refusing it is the plaintiff. Litigation has risks and costs for both sides, and it is important that both sides understand them thoroughly as they approach the renegotiation process so they can accurately evaluate the worth of any proposal put forward.

Often the party demanding renegotiation has a tendency to undervalue the risks and costs of litigation while the party facing that demand tends to overvalue its benefits. It is therefore important for each side as part of its negotiating strategy to be sure that the other has a realistic evaluation of its BATNA.

Sometimes an aggrieved party may try to focus the other's attention on those costs by commencing a lawsuit while the renegotiation discussions are in progress. In the Enron case, at the time the Maharashtra government canceled the electricity supply agreement, it probably assumed that its action would entail relatively little cost. It also seemed to have assumed that other investors would be willing to take Enron's place or that it would be able to find indigenous solutions to the state's power shortage. Once those assumptions proved false and once Enron had begun an arbitration case in London with a claim of $300 million, the state of Maharashtra became considerably more open to renegotiation than it was at the time it canceled the contract.

5. *Involve, either directly or indirectly, all necessary parties in the renegotiation.* A successful renegotiation may not only require the participation of the parties who signed the original agreement, but it may also necessitate the involvement of other parties who did not sign it but who gained an interest in the transaction afterward. Such secondary parties may include labor unions, creditors, suppliers, governmental departments, and in the case of diplomatic negotiations, other states.

For example, in the renegotiation of a loan between a bank and a troubled real estate developer with a partially completed office building, no new agreement can be reached without the participation, directly or indirectly, of the unpaid construction contractor whose lien on the property can block refinancing of the project. It is therefore important in organizing any renegotiation to determine all the parties, both primary and secondary, that should participate and then to decide whether they should be involved in the face-to-face renegotiations between the primary parties or dealt with in separate discussions.

6. *Design the right forum and process for the renegotiation.* Both sides should think hard about the appropriate process for launching and conducting extradeal renegotiations. Renegotiations often emerge out of crisis characterized by severe conflict, threats, and high emotion. An appropriate process for the renegotiation may help to mollify the parties and reduce the negative consequences of the crisis on their subsequent discussions. An inappropriate process, on the other hand, may serve to heighten those negative consequences and impede the renegotiations.

The government of the state of Maharashtra, for example, after receiving the recommendation of a cabinet subcommittee, canceled the contract with Enron and also declared publicly that it would not renegotiate the agreement. In that context, if renegotiations were ever to take place, the parties would need to create a process that would preserve the government's dignity and prestige. Ultimately, the government chose to appoint a "review panel" consisting of energy experts to reexamine the project. The panel met with Enron representatives, as well as project critics, and then submitted a proposal to the government, containing the terms of a renegotiated electricity supply agreement to which Enron had agreed. The use of a panel of experts to conduct what amounted to a renegotiation, rather than face-to-face discussions between the government and Enron, served to protect governmental dignity. Moreover, the panel's status as a group of independent experts, rather than politicians, tended to give its recommendations a legitimacy needed to persuade the public that the renegotiated agreement protected Indian interests.

In some cases, the way in which the parties frame the renegotiation may influence its success. For example, rather than use the label *renegotiation,* a term that conjures up negative implications of fundamental changes in the sanctity of contract, the parties may refer to the process as a *review, restructuring, rescheduling, modification,* or an effort to clarify ambiguities in the existing agreement, rather than to change basic principles.[2] This approach, at least formally, respects the sanctity of contract and thereby may avoid some of the friction and hostility engendered by demanding outright extradeal renegotiations.

Yet another way of framing a renegotiation is a time-sensitive waiver, an approach that respects the agreement yet enables the burdened party to obtain temporary relief from certain contractual obligations.

7.   *Involve the right mediator in the renegotiation process.* In the stress and hostility often engendered by an extradeal renegotiation, a mediator or other neutral third person may be able to aid the parties to overcome the obstacles between them so as to reach a satisfactory renegotiated agreement. A mediator may make a positive contribution by helping design and manage the renegotiation process so that the parties will have the maximum opportunities to create value through their interaction; by assisting with the communications between the two sides in a way that will facilitate positive results from their interactions; and by suggesting substantive solutions to the problems that the parties encounter during the course of their extradeal renegotiation. To be effective, the mediator must have the blend of skills, experience, and confidence of the parties appropriate to the renegotiation in question. The wrong mediator, on the other hand, can make a difficult renegotiation impossible.

Concluding Thoughts

Many persons view a contract renegotiation in negative terms. For them, it is an aberration, a disreputable practice that evokes images of broken promises, disappointed expectations, and bargains made but not kept. From the viewpoint of anyone facing demands for an unwanted renegotiation, such a reaction is normal and understandable. But from the vantage of society, renegotiation plays a constructive role in human relations at all levels.

If Karl Llewellyn is correct—that the work of agreements in society is a struggle of life against form—the function of renegotiation in the social order is to mediate that struggle, to allow life and form to adjust to one another over the long term at least cost.

Endnotes

1.   Indeed, English common law at one time viewed renegotiated contracts under certain conditions as invalid since they lacked the legal requirement of consideration in those cases in which, as a result of renegotiation, a party was promising to do no more than it was already obligated to do under its original contract (Waddams 1999: 204).

2.   In the economic slowdown of 2001, increasing numbers of borrowers in the United States have been unable to make regular mortgage payments on their homes. Instead of foreclosing on delinquent borrowers judged to have the potential to make payments at some point in the future, some banks have established *loan modification programs,* by which they renegotiate the terms of the loan to prevent default (for example, by adding the unpaid interest to the principal of the loan). The banks frame these loans as *modified,* not *renegotiated,* mortgage agreements. See "Pinched homeowners are finding shelter in modified loans," *Wall Street Journal,* October 30, 2001, p. A1.

References

Carter, J.W. 1999. The renegotiation of contracts. *Journal of Contract Law* 13, pp. 185–98.

Carver, J., and H. Hossain. 1990. An arbitration case: The dispute that never was. *ICSID Review* 5, pp. 311–25.

Farnsworth, E. A. 1987. Precontractual liability and preliminary agreements: Fair dealing and failed negotiation. *Columbia Law Review* 87, pp. 217–94.

Fisher, R., W. Ury, and B. Patton. 1991. *Getting to YES: Negotiating agreement without giving in.* 2nd ed. New York: Penguin.

Howtek, Inc. v. Relisys et al. 1999. 958 F. Supp. 46 (D.N.H.)

Litvinoff, S. 1997. Good faith. *Tulane Law Review* 87, pp. 1645–74.

Llewellyn, K.N. 1931. What price contract? An essay in perspective. *Yale Law Journal* 40, pp. 704–51.

Kolo, A., and T. Walde. 2000. Renegotiation and contract adaptation in international investment projects. *Journal of World Investment* 1, pp. 5–28.

Peter, W. 1995. *Arbitration and renegotiation in international investment agreements.* 2nd ed. The Hague and Boston: Kluwer Law International.

Salacuse, J. W. 1991. *Making global deals: Negotiating in the international marketplace.* Boston: Houghton Mifflin.

———. 1998. Ten ways that culture affects negotiation. *Negotiation Journal* 13, pp. 199–205.

———. 2001. Renegotiation international project agreement. *Fordham International Law Journal* 24, pp. 1319–70.

Talley, E. L. 1999. Renegotiation, mechanism design, and the liquidated damages rule. *Stanford Law Review* 46, pp. 1195–1242.

Tracht, M. E. 1999. Renegotiation and secured credit: Explaining the equity of redemption. *Vanderbilt Law Review* 52, pp. 599–643.

Vernon, R. 1971. *Sovereignty at bay: The international spread of U. S. enterprises.* New York: Basic Books.

Waddams, S. M. 1999. Commentary on "The renegotiation of contracts." *Journal of Contract Law* 13, pp. 199–205.

Reading 6.5

Negotiating with Disordered People
Elizabeth L. Jeglic
Alexander A. Jeglic

Editors' Note: It's all but routine for a negotiator leaving a meeting to mutter under her breath concerning the perceived mental health issues of someone on the other side. Unfortunately the research now demonstrates that such suspicions may not always be unreasonable. Mental health issues, it turns out, do not prevent people from assuming and holding high status in many kinds of organizations, so you may be negotiating with borderline mentally ill people with some regularity. Furthermore, we know that high-stress situations like death of a family member, divorce, or job changes, which often lead to negotiations, can trigger mental illness. Here, a psychologist and a lawyer analyze the most common types of mental illness and tell you what to expect from each of the types you are most likely to encounter in negotiations.

One assumption that is commonly made when negotiating is that the other negotiator is rational and thus capable of making logical decisions. However, approximately one in five Americans ages 18 and older suffer from a diagnosable mental disorder during the course of any given year.[1] This means that an estimated 44.3 million people in the United States have a diagnosable mental illness that could significantly impair their ability to engage in rational negotiations.[2]

The presence of a mental disorder can cause the person to distort information and facts, process information incorrectly, or be detached from reality. Certain mental disorders can also cause the person to be callous, manipulative or delusional.[3] In addition, we must take into account that individuals with a mental disorder may have limited insight into their disorder, and it is possible that they may be unaware of how the disorder may be impacting their functioning.

To further complicate matters, it may not be immediately obvious that someone has a mental disorder. Unlike a medical disorder, a mental disorder does not have readily identifiable physical symptoms. Therefore, significant negotiations may have already taken place before a red flag is raised and those involved in the negotiations realize that something is amiss. Mental disorders such as major depression, bipolar disorder, anxiety spectrum disorders, psychopathy, and psychotic disorders can all impact an individual's ability to engage in rational negotiations. The goal of this essay is to outline some of the effects that mental illness can have on negotiations.

Major Depression

Major depression is one of the most common mental disorders, affecting an estimated 9.5 percent of Americans ages 18 and over in a given year.[4] Based upon the 1998 census

Source: "Negotiating with Disordered People," by Elizabeth L. Jeglic and Alexander A. Jeglic, from *The Negotiator's Fieldbook,* with Andrea Kupfer Schneider and Christopher Honeyman (Eds.), 2006, pp. 335–341. American Bar Association. Used with permission.

residential population estimate, this translates into about 18.8 million people in the United States who are suffering from major depression annually.[5] It is the leading cause of disability in the world,[6] and is characterized by feelings of depression, hopelessness, and a loss of interest and pleasure in daily activities that last for at least two weeks and that interfere with a person's ability to function on a daily basis. Furthermore, depression can cause eating disturbances (eating too much or too little), sleeping disturbances (sleeping too much or too little), a loss of energy, psychomotor agitation or retardation, feelings of guilt or worthlessness problems concentrating or making decisions, and suicidal thoughts or actions.[7]

According to the cognitive theory of depression, a key feature of the disorder is the depressed individuals' negative view of themselves, their future, and the world.[8] These views are maintained by negative mental biases, which cause the depressed person to interpret innocuous information in a negative way. For example, depressed individuals are more likely to draw strong negative conclusions without supporting evidence.[9] This type of thinking bias could have a large impact on negotiations as depressed individuals may interpret and distort the information that is presented to them, thus potentially negatively affecting the outcome of the negotiations.

Additionally, depressed people are more likely than non-depressed people to provide irrational explanations. A study by Cook and Peterson compared explanations for negative life events in a sample of depressed and non-depressed individuals.[10] They found that the depressed people offered significantly fewer "rational" or evidence-based explanations for their decisions. This has a direct impact on the process of negotiation as negotiators presuppose that their counterparts are rational and will partake in dialogue based upon logic. However, if negotiators suffer from major depression their ability to think logically may be impaired, thus affecting their ability to adequately represent their cause, or their client's.

Finally, depression is also characterized by concentration difficulties. This can be manifested through difficulty in collecting one's thoughts, trouble focusing on written materials, and difficulty following conversations.[11] In a negotiation, it is vital to be able to think on your feet and respond immediately to situations as they arise. If the negotiator is experiencing depressive symptoms that have impaired his or her concentration, then the individuals' ability to adequately fulfill the ordinary expectations of their negotiating counterpart is put into question.

Bipolar Disorder

Similar to major depression, bipolar disorder (also known as manic depression) is a mood disorder. More than 2 million Americans (approximately 1 percent of the population) carry this diagnosis.[12] The key diagnostic symptom of bipolar disorder is the dramatic changes in moods: from feelings of being high, elated, or irritable to feelings of sadness, despair, and hopelessness, with periods of normal moods in between. These periods of highs and lows are referred to as manic and depressive episodes. Along with the changes in mood, individuals with this disorder may also experience significant changes in energy and behavior. These fluctuations in mood are much more severe than just the regular "highs" and "lows" that we all experience. Individuals with bipolar disorder who do not receive treatment have serious impairments in all aspects of their functioning.[13]

The symptoms of an episode of mania include a decreased need for sleep, pressured speech, excessive talking, racing thoughts or flight of ideas, distractibility, increased libido, reckless behavior without regard for consequences, grandiosity (i.e., false conviction of personal wealth, power, inventiveness, and genius, or temporary assumption of a grandiose identity), and severe thought disturbances, which unless treated could result in psychosis.[14]

In contrast, the depressive phase of bipolar disorder is the same as a major depression. During this phase, a person may feel hopeless and lose all interest in other people or usual activities, experience weight fluctuation and feel tired all the time, sleep more than usual or have insomnia, complain of unexplained aches or pains, and have trouble concentrating. A person in the depressive phase is a suicide risk. Individuals with bipolar disorder who are experiencing a depressive episode will have similar thinking impairments to those exhibited by people with major depression including negative biases and irrationality.[15]

Neuropsychological investigations have yielded evidence suggesting that individuals with bipolar disorder may also experience enduring cognitive dysfunction. This dysfunction may best be described as an impairment in the attentional or executive control of action. This includes deficits in skills such as conflict resolution and switching from one task to another. Furthermore, it is suggested that these deficits worsen with the progression and severity of the bipolarity.[16]

Individually, each of these symptoms could impact a person's ability to negotiate rationally. However, when these symptoms are combined during the course of a manic or depressive episode, the consequences can be severe. The impairments experienced by a person with bipolar disorder, especially one who is not participating in treatment, could serve to undermine the negotiation process as their attentional and cognitive processing may be impaired while their thinking may be bordering on psychosis.

Anxiety

In any given year, over 40 million Americans experience an anxiety-related impairment.[17] There are several specific disorders that fall under the broader category of anxiety including panic disorder, social phobia, post traumatic stress disorder (PTSD). generalized anxiety disorder (GAD), and obsessive compulsive disorder (OCD).[18] The lifetime prevalence for a diagnosable anxiety disorder ranges from 1 to 14 percent with OCD being the least common and GAD and PTSD being the most common. It should be considered that, although many individuals do not meet the threshold for a diagnosable anxiety, most individuals have experienced some debility from anxiety at some point in their lives.[19]

A recent study found that people diagnosed with an anxiety disorder show neuropsychological impairments compared with people without an anxiety.[20] Overall, the results showed that participants with anxiety disorders were significantly impaired in episodic memory (memory for episodes in your own life) and executive functioning (higher level information processing). When the investigators studied the relation between the type of anxiety and impairment, they found that patients with panic disorder and OCD had impairments in both episodic memory and executive functioning. In contrast, the impairment for patients with social phobia was limited only to their episodic memory. These findings suggest that anxiety disorders have an impact on brain functioning. At present, we do not know if these changes are limited to the course of the anxiety disorder, or if they persist once the disorder has remitted.

Cognitive biases have also been found in patients with anxiety disorders. Patients with anxiety disorders tend to focus more attention on information related to their fears.[21] Therefore, if a fear/anxiety producing stimulus is present, their ability to focus elsewhere can be limited. Research suggests that this bias for stimuli that elicit anxiety is produced without the intervention of conscious strategies such as focusing attention on the fear producing stimulus.[22]

Psychopathy

Psychopathy (also referred to as sociopathy or antisocial personality disorder) is a personality disorder that is characterized by enduring patterns of perceiving, relating to, and thinking about oneself and the environment in ways that are inconsistent with acceptable social behaviors.[23] Robert Hare, a world-renowned expert in the evaluation of psychopathy, defines psychopathy as a socially devastating disorder characterized by a constellation of affective, interpersonal, and behavioral features. These include egocentricity, impulsivity, irresponsibility, shallow emotions, lack of empathy, guilt or remorse, pathological lying, manipulativeness, and the persistent violation of social norms and expectations.[24] It is estimated that between 15 and 20 percent of the offenders in state and federal prisons are psychopaths.[25] Recently, researchers have focused their attention on the concept of "successful" psychopaths.[26] Lynam and his colleagues define "successful psychopaths to be individuals who have patterns of psychopathic behavior, but who do not have the characteristic arrest and incarceration histories that are found among psychopaths in the prison population."[27] It is estimated that approximately 1 percent of the general population would meet the diagnostic criteria for psychopathy.

Babiak conducted a series of case studies where he profiled "industrial" or "corporate" psychopaths.[28] These are individuals who meet diagnostic criteria for psychopathy and are found to be working within organizations; often in positions of leadership. As part of his research, Babiak studied a half-dozen unnamed companies. One company was a fast-growing, high-tech firm, while the rest of the companies he profiled were large, multinational organizations that were undergoing dramatic organizational changes. These changes included severe downsizing, restructuring, mergers and acquisitions, and joint ventures. Babiak found that periods of organization instability and change created a favorable environment for the "corporate psychopath," with many actually thriving under such circumstances. The chaotic environment provided the psychopaths with stimulation while affording them ample opportunity to engage in manipulation. The consequences include a disproportionate number of negotiations and disputes, colored by the personalities of these executives.

It has been suggested by Emmons that psychopaths are frequently driven by the need for power, control, dominance, and prestige. Emmons cites these as characteristics that are valued by corporations, and search committees frequently recruit leaders possessing these traits. These are also qualities that are often cited and singled out for promotion within organizations. Therefore, it has been speculated, by Emmons and others, that many of our top business and political leaders, and perhaps even our negotiating counterparts, may, in fact, be psychopaths.[29]

One reason that these "corporate psychopaths" may go undetected is that they have the ability to present themselves as normal and extremely charming while causing great distress to their co-workers and organizations.[30] Psychopaths have been described as cunning, manipulative, untrustworthy, unethical, parasitic, and utterly remorseless: "There's nothing they won't do, and no one they won't exploit, to get what they want."[31]

In terms of negotiation, psychopaths fall into a completely different category from individuals with other mental disorders. While those with disorders such as depression and anxiety may exhibit impaired functioning, illogical thought processes, and limited rationality, they do not intend their colleagues and counterparts any harm. Psychopaths, on the other hand, are more than willing to wreak havoc in an effort to attain their goals. Psychopaths may appear both logical and rational during the course of a negotiation. But in violation of reasonable expectations of a certain amount of trust and goodwill in a typical negotiation, a psychopath may use whatever means are necessary to achieve what he desires.

Another personality disorder that is commonly associated with psychopathy is narcissism. While diagnostically distinct from psychopathy, narcissism and psychopathy have many overlapping traits. In both cases, these individuals exploit others to meet their own needs and exhibit little or no empathy. However, it is speculated that the key distinction between the two disorders is that psychopaths engage in this type of behavior with malevolent intent, while narcissists do it to compensate for low self esteem.[32]

Narcissism has been defined as a pattern of traits and behaviors that signify infatuation and obsession with one's self to the exclusion of all others and the egotistic and ruthless pursuit of one's gratification, dominance, and ambition. Furthermore, narcissistic individuals require constant admiration and adulation, always need to be right, and hold the belief that ordinary people cannot understand them. Since narcissistic individuals are very self involved, this could easily hinder the negotiation as they will be unlikely to view matters from a perspective outside of their own. There is some evidence suggesting that narcissists may become aggressive and violent if their ideas and status are challenged.[33] In the world of negotiations, having one's ideas challenged can be expected, if not guaranteed. Therefore, negotiations with a narcissist may quickly break down.

Psychotic Disorders

Psychotic disorders are characterized by trouble with reality testing—discriminating what is real from what is imagined. Common psychotic symptoms are hallucinations (hearing, seeing, or otherwise sensing the presence of things not actually there) and delusions (false, strongly held beliefs not influenced by logical reasoning or explained by a person's usual cultural concepts). Psychotic disorders include schizophrenia, schizoaffective disorder, and delusional disorder. It is estimated that 1 percent of the population is afflicted with a psychotic disorder.[34]

Psychotic disorders modify a person's ability to think clearly, make good judgments, respond emotionally, communicate effectively, and behave appropriately—all hallmark characteristics of a skilled negotiator. When the psychotic symptoms are severe, people with psychotic disorders often are unable to meet the ordinary demands of daily life.

Unlike many of the other mental disorders whose clinical presentation (or public face) may be more subtle, individuals with schizophrenia and schizoaffective disorder are readily identifiable by their disordered thinking and disorganized behavior. However, it is possible to enter into a negotiation with someone who is suffering from delusional disorder and for the disorder to go undetected. This disorder is characterized by the presence of non-bizarre delusions. These typically are beliefs of something occurring in a person's life which is not out of the realm of possibility (e.g., a spouse is unfaithful, or a friend is a government agent). Unlike the other psychotic disorders, people who have delusional disorder generally don't experience a marked impairment in functioning and their behavior is not noticeably bizarre.[35] It is only if the delusion pertains to the negotiation that the individual's thinking and behavior will be impacted.

Conclusions

It is commonly believed that individuals in positions of authority are psychologically healthier than those who did not achieve such career success. While this may be true, many individuals do not reveal a mental illness, as they fear the stigma and potential fallout. They may struggle to maintain a sheen of normality rather than seek help. Additionally, when one considers the prevalence of mental disorders in our society, there is a reasonable probability that an opposing negotiator or even a colleague may have a diagnosable mental illness. Given the number of impairments that are associated with mental disorders, it is perhaps most logical to enter into a negotiation prepared to face a counterpart that is not rational—with the hope that the evidence will suggest otherwise as the negotiation progresses, but with some forewarning of the likely symptoms if, in fact, you are negotiating with a disordered person.[36]

Endnotes

1. David A. Reiger, et al., "The De Facto U.S. Mental and Addictive Disorders Service System. Epidemiologic Catchment Area Prospective 1-Year Prevalence Rates of Disorders and Services," *Archives of General Psychiatry* 50 (1993), pp. 85–94.

2. William E. Narrow, "One-Year Prevalence of Mental Disorders, Excluding Substance Use Disorders, in the U.S.: NIMH ECA Prospective Data" (unpublished paper on file with author, July 1,1998); Population estimates based on "U.S. Census Estimated Residential Population Age 18 and Over" (July 1,1998).

3. American Psychiatric Association, *Diagnostic and Statistic Manual of Mental Disorders, 4th ed. (Arlington, VA: American Psychiatric Association, 1994). (Hereinafter DSM–IV.)*

4. Reiger, et al., "The De Facto U.S. Mental and Addictive Disorders Service System. Epidemiologic Catchment Area Prospective 1-Year Prevalence Rates of Disorders and Services," pp. 85–94.

5. William Narrow, "Table: One-Year Prevalence of Depressive Disorders Among Adults 18 and Over in the U.S.: NIMH ECA Prospective Data" (personal communication on file with author, 1998); Population estimates based on "U.S. Census Estimated Residential Population Age 18 and Over" (July 1,1998).

6. World Health Organization, *The World Health Report 2001—Mental Health: New Understanding, New Hope* (Geneva, Switzerland: World Health Organization, 2001), available at *http://www.who.int/whr/2001/en/index.html.*

7. *DSM-IV.*

8. Aaron T. Beck, "Thinking and Depression: Idiosyncratic Content and Cognitive Distortions," *Archives of General Psychiatry* 9 (1963), pp. 324–333; Aaron T. Beck, "Cognitive Models of Depression," *Journal of Cognitive Psychotherapy: An International Quarterly* 1 (1987), pp. 5–37.

9. David A. Haaga, et al., "Empirical Status of Cognitive Theory of Depression," *Psychological Bulletin* 110 (1991), pp. 215–36.

10. Michele L. Cook and Christopher Peterson, "Depressive Irrationality," *Cognitive Therapy and Research* 10 (1986), pp. 293–298.

11. Ibid, pp. 293–298.

12. Reiger, et al., pp. 85–94.

13. *DSM-IV.*

14. Ibid.

15. Ibid.

16. I. Nicol Ferrier and Jill M. Thompson, "Cognitive Impairment in Bipolar Affective Disorder: Implications for the Bipolar Diathesis," *British Journal of Psychiatry* 180 (2002), p. 293.

17. William E. Narrow, et al., "NIMH Epidemiology Note: Prevalence of Anxiety Disorders, One-Year Prevalence Best Estimates Calculated from ECA and NCS Data" (unpublished note, on file with author, 1998); Population estimates based on "U.S. Census Estimated Residential Population Age 18 and Over" (July 1,1998).

18. *DSM-IV.*

19. William E. Narrow, et al., "NIMH Epidemiology Note: Prevalence of Anxiety Disorders, One-Year Prevalence Best Estimates Calculated from ECA and NCS Data."

20. Eija Airaksinen, et al., "Neuropsychological Functions in Anxiety Disorders in Population-Based Samples: Evidence of Episodic Memory Dysfunction," *Journal of Psychiatric Research* 39 (2005), p. 207.

21. Andrew Matthews and Colin MacLeod, "Selective Processing of Threat Cues in Anxiety State," *Behaviour Research and Therapy* 23 (1985), p. 563.

22. Colic MacLeod and Elizabeth Rutherford, "Anxiety And the Selective Processing of Emotional Information: Mediating Roles of Awareness, Trait and State Variables, and Personal Relevance of Stimulus Materials," *Behaviour Research and Therapy* 30 (1992), p. 479.

23. *DSM-IV.*

24. *See generally,* Robert D. Hare, *Without Conscience: The Disturbing World of the Psychopaths Among Us* (New York: Guilford Press, 1999).

25. Robert D. Hare, "A Research Scale for the Assessment of Psychopathy in Criminal Populations," *Personality and Individual Differences* 1(1980), p. 111.

26. Paul Babiak, "When Psychopaths Go to Work: A Case Study of Industrial Psychopaths," *Applied Psychology: An International Review* 44 (1995), pp. 171–188.

27. Donald R. Lyman, et al., "Self-Reported Psychopathy: A Validation Study," *Journal of Personality Assessment* 73 (1999), p. 110.

28. Babiak, "When Psychopaths Go to Work: A Case Study of Industrial Psychopaths."

29. Robert A. Emmons, "Narcissism: Theory and Measurement," *Journal of Personality and Social Psychology* 52 (1987), p. 11.

30. Ibid.

31. Hare, *Without Conscience: The Disturbing World of the Psychopaths Among Us.*

32. *DSM-IV.*

33. Roy F. Baumeister, et al., "Relation of Threatened Egotism to Violence and Aggression: The Dark Side of High Self-Esteem," *Psychological Review* 103 (1996), pp. 5–33.

34. *DSM-IV.*

35. Ibid.

36. Actual strategies for dealing with disordered individuals are beyond the scope of this chapter. For further discussion see Jeffery P. Kahn and Alan M. Lanlieb, eds., *Mental Health and Productivity in the Workplace: A Handbook for Organizations and Clinicians* (San Francisco: Jossey-Bass, 2003).

When and How to Use Third-Party Help

Roy J. Lewicki
Alexander Hiam
Karen W. Olander

It may be that in spite of your best efforts to move the negotiations back on track, the two sides are still stuck, unable to go anywhere. In that case, you should consider asking a third party to step in. A third party is someone who is not directly involved in your negotiation or dispute, but who can be helpful in resolving it. This impartial party may be a friend, in the case of a simple negotiation, or it may be a neutral person whom both parties know and invite to assist, or it might even be someone with professional credentials whose job it is to intervene in such cases.

A third party is likely to use a number of conflict resolution techniques, engaging you and the other party in activities designed to reduce tension, improve communication, change the options, adjust the number of players or issues, or help find common ground. With outside help, the disputing parties may be able to move back on track and bring the negotiation to conclusion and closure.

When to Ask a Third Party to Intervene

In general, it is best to try everything you can to remedy the situation before you move to third-party intervention. However, when conflict escalates in negotiation, the parties often become suspicious of each other's motives, intentions, and behavior. One of the parties may try to use the tactics in a "partisan" way, with a bias toward achieving a specific outcome. Moreover, even when that party implements the practices in good faith, the other party doesn't see the efforts as genuine. Instead, he or she sees it as a ruse, a ploy, a tactic, or a way for the other to gain advantage. If the parties just cannot find a way to become "unstuck," then both parties should agree on the need for a third party. Although third parties can be very helpful, negotiators often resist using them because they feel they are decreasing the likelihood of achieving their preferred outcome.

Sometimes a third-party intervention will be imposed by an outside group that has the power or authority to do so and is anxious to resolve the matter. In an intrafamily dispute, when two children are fighting, a parent may intervene. In other cases, an intervention may be imposed by a constituency or higher-level authority, or it may result from a rule or legal procedure. For example, a number of warranties and contracts now specify that if there is a question as to liability or fault, the dispute will automatically go to an arbitrator or mediator.

Source: "When and How to Use Third-Party Help," by Roy J. Lewicki, Alexander Hiam, and Karen W. Olander, from *Think Before You Speak,* 1996, pp. 177–197. John Wiley & Sons, Inc. Publishers. Used with permission.

When two negotiating parties invite the third party to intervene, then the intervention is usually friendly and progresses smoothly. If the intervention is imposed by an outside authority, then the relationship between the disputing parties and the third party may not necessarily be friendly, and the negotiating environment may become even more hostile.

Reasons to Use a Third Party

You may want to consider using third-party help if[1]

- The emotional level between the parties is high, with lots of anger and frustration.
- Communication between the parties is poor or has completely broken down, or the parties appear to be talking "past" each other.
- Stereotypic views of each other's position and motives are preventing resolution.
- Behavior is negative (e.g., there is intense anger or name-calling).
- The parties have serious disagreements about what information is necessary, available, or required.
- The parties disagree on the number, order, or combination of issues.
- Differences in interests appear to be irreconcilable.
- Values differ greatly, and the parties disagree about what is fundamentally right.
- There are no established procedures for resolving the conflict, or the procedures have not been followed.
- Negotiations have completely broken down and there is an impasse.

There can be several objectives in bringing in a third party to achieve a resolution. First, the parties want to resolve the dispute; they care about the *outcome* dimension. A second reason is to smooth, repair, or improve the *relationship* between the parties—to reduce the level of conflict and the resultant damages. Finally, third parties are often used simply to stop the dispute—to get the parties to separate and not fight any more, or to make sure that they have as little future interaction as possible (e.g., when the United Nations intervenes in conflicts around the world, its first objective is often to stop warring groups from fighting). Depending on which type of objective is most important—resolving the dispute, repairing the relationship, or separating the parties—different types of third parties with different skills may be needed. The type of third party selected will focus on some or all of these objectives, and it is important to know which ones are most important and in what order they should be pursued.

Each type of third party has advantages and disadvantages, depending on the situation. Which type you choose will depend not only on the situation, but also on what services are available, who specifically is available, and, if applicable, what may be required by rules and regulations that govern the conflict and its resolution (e.g., laws, contracts, documents, precedents). After we discuss the types of interventions, we will look at how to select the appropriate one for your circumstances.

The term *ADR* is used in the literature and elsewhere in reference to third-party resolution of disputes. ADR stands for Alternative Dispute Resolution. ADR procedures are alternatives to taking the conflict into the court system, hiring an attorney, and pursuing litigation. Since the early 1980s, there has been a major social movement to take *civil* disputes (where there is no criminal violation of law) out of the courts and, instead, refer them to third parties. There are a number of reasons for this: The parties have more control over what happens, the process is often quicker and less costly, and it keeps the court system from becoming hopelessly overburdened, particularly when key issues of law are not in question.

There are many people who perform ADR services, including the more formal labor arbitrators, divorce mediators, community mediators, and process consultants. Dispute resolution is also performed informally by ombudspersons, fact finders and referees, ministers, social workers, teachers, managers, or even friends of the disputing parties. There are also quasi-substitutes for formal court proceedings, such as summary jury trials and minitrials, judicial reference, court-annexed arbitration, settlement conferences, tribunals, and judicial committees.

In this reading we will define and discuss the formal and informal processes of arbitration, mediation, and process consultation. We will discuss what these people do and how they work to resolve disputes. These methods are separate from the arena of actual litigation, which will not be discussed here, but which will be used as a point of comparison. For example, all the preceding processes are generally of shorter duration and less costly than a court trial.

Advantages and Disadvantages of Using a Third Party

Some of the advantages of employing a third party to assist in resolving a dispute are

- The parties gain time to cool off as they break their conflict and describe the problem to the third party.

- Communication can be improved because the third party slows the communication down, helps people be clear, and works to improve listening.

- Parties often have to determine which issues are really important because the third party may ask for some prioritizing.

- The emotional climate can be improved as the parties discharge anger and hostility and return to a level of civility and trust.

- The parties can take steps to mend the relationship, particularly if this work is facilitated by the third party.

- The time frame for resolving the dispute can be established or reestablished.

- The escalating costs of remaining in conflict can be controlled, particularly if continuing the dispute is costing people money or opportunity (paying fees for attorneys becomes very costly).

- By watching and participating in the process, parties can learn how the third party provides assistance and in the future may be able to resolve their disputes without this help.

- Actual resolutions to the dispute and closure may be achieved.

FIGURE 1 | Different Types of Third-Party Involvement in Disputes

| | | **Level of Third-Party Control over Outcome** | |
		High	Low
Level of Third-Party Control over Process	High	"Inquisition"	Mediation Process consultation
	Low	Arbitration	Negotiation

Disadvantages of ADR include

- The parties potentially lose face when the third party is called in, since there may be an image that the parties are somehow incompetent or incapable of resolving their own fight (this is true when those who are judging the negotiators are others who can publicly criticize them or move to have them replaced).

- There is also a loss of control of the process or the outcome or both, depending on which type of third party is called in to help. Relative to what they think they could have achieved had they "held out longer" or "fought harder," parties may be forced to accept less than 100 percent of their preferred target.

In general, when you bring a third party into the negotiations, the two contending parties will have to give up control over one or both aspects of the negotiation: the *process* and the *outcome*. The process is how the negotiation is conducted; the outcome is the result of the negotiation. As we discuss each type of third-party intervention, we will point out what the parties gain or lose in terms of process and outcome. Figure 1 depicts types of third-party involvement.

In negotiation without a third party, the opposing parties maintain control over both process and outcome. If they move to mediation, they give up control of the process but maintain control of the outcome. If they move to arbitration, they give up control of the outcome but retain control of the process. The fourth area in the diagram reflects a situation where the parties have control of neither process nor outcome—and no negotiation occurs. We now consider the major types of third-party behavior individually.

Arbitration

Arbitration is the most common form of third-party dispute resolution.[2] When an arbitrator is called into a situation, the negotiators retain control of the process, but the arbitrator takes control of shaping and determining the outcome. Each party presents its position to the arbitrator, who then makes a ruling on either a single issue or on a package of issues.[3] This depends on the rules of the arbitration process, if any, and the request of the parties, if applicable. The arbitrator's ruling (decision) may be voluntary or binding, according to laws or a previous commitment of the parties.

The arbitrator can arrive at a recommended outcome in several ways. Usually the arbitrator selects one side's position or the other's ("rules" in favor of one party or the other's preferred settlement). But sometimes third parties may also offer an entirely different resolution. The arbitrator may suggest a "split" between the two parties' positions, in essence creating a compromise between their positions. In formal proceedings that are governed by law and contract agreements, such as labor and management negotiations, there is usually a very clear and strict set of policies about how arbitration rulings are to be made.

Arbitration is used in business conflicts, disputes between business and union workers, labor relations, contracts (usually in the public sector), and grievances. In the case of grievances, the arbitrator is bound to decide how the grievance should be resolved, whether consistent with the labor–management contract or current labor law.

Advantages of Arbitration

The major advantages of arbitration are:

1. A clear solution is made available to the parties (though it may not be one or both parties' choice).

2. The solution may be mandated on them (they can't choose whether to follow it or not).

3. Arbitrators are usually selected because they are wise, fair, and impartial, and therefore the solution comes from a respected and credible source.

4. The costs of prolonging the dispute are avoided. It is interesting to note that arbitrators' decisions tend to be consistent with judgments received from courts.[4] In a sense, they are "judges without robes," and their decisions are usually governed by public law or contract law.

Disadvantages of Arbitration

There are some disadvantages to arbitration.[5]

1. The parties relinquish control over shaping the outcome; thus the proposed solution may not be one that they prefer or are even willing to live with.

2. The parties may not like the outcome, and it may impose additional costs, sacrifices, or burdens on them.

3. If the arbitration is voluntary (they have a choice whether to follow the recommended solution or not), they may lose face if they decide not to follow the arbitrator's recommendation.

4. There is a *decision-acceptance effect*—there is less commitment to an arbitrated resolution, for at least two reasons: They did not participate in the process of shaping the outcome, and the recommended settlement may be inferior to what they preferred. If parties are less committed to an outcome, they will be less likely to implement it. (As we will see when we discuss mediation, there is better

commitment to a resolution and its implementation because the parties are fully involved in making the decision.) For example, when divorce proceedings go to arbitration—particularly regarding alimony or child custody issues—the party who "loses" is often uncommitted to the settlement and refuses to follow the mandate, and the parties wind up back in court.

5. Research on arbitration has often shown that it has a *chilling effect.*[6] During negotiation, the parties may behave differently if they expect that the dispute will have to go to arbitration. During the negotiation, they may hold back on compromises so they do not lose anything in arbitration, particularly when they anticipate that the arbitrator will "split the difference." In essence, you might get a better settlement if you refuse to make any concessions, because if the arbitrator splits the difference, you can do better than if you made concessions and then the arbitrator split the difference. So negotiators may take a hard-line position. To avoid this, parties who expect to go to arbitration often use a method called *final-offer arbitration.* In this procedure, the arbitrator asks the parties to make their "best final offer," and then the arbitrator rules for one side or the other with no split. This in effect forces the parties to make the best deal they can during a negotiation, which reduces the distance between them as they approach arbitration. The more extreme the final offer, the less likely the arbitrator may be to rule in favor of it.

6. In the *narcotic effect,*[7] parties with a history of recurring arbitration tend to lose interest in trying to negotiate, become passive, and grow very dependent on the third party for helping them move toward resolution. Their attitude is, "We're not going to be able to agree, and a settlement is going to be imposed anyway, so why should I work hard to try to negotiate?" Thus parties become "addicted" to arbitration and take less responsibility for themselves and resolving their own conflict. Further, a party with a strong-willed constituency may be uncompromising and unyielding during negotiation, and then blame the arbitrator for any compromises that have to be made in arbitration.

7. In the *half-life effect,*[8] the results of more and more arbitration are less and less satisfaction with the outcomes. Because the parties have become passive in the process and have less control over the outcomes as well, arbitration frequently becomes ritualistic and simply loses its effectiveness. Eventually the parties refuse to participate, take their case elsewhere, or remove themselves completely.

8. In the *biasing effect,* the arbitrators may be perceived not to be neutral and impartial, but to be biased. This is most likely to occur when an arbitrator makes a whole sequence of decisions that favors one side over the other. Interestingly, parties in strong conflict often try to bias the third party, and then reject the third party for being biased. (Witness the harassment that referees and umpires receive in most sporting events!) This shows how insidious and problematic destructive conflict can become. If an arbitrator is seen as biased, the parties will move toward selecting another arbitrator who will be neutral, or preferably, will favor their position.

Mediation

Formal mediation is based on established rules and procedures.[9] The objective of the mediator is to help the parties negotiate more effectively. The mediator does not solve the problem or impose a solution. He or she helps the disputing parties to develop the solution themselves and then to agree to it.[10] Thus the mediator takes control of the process, but not the outcome.

A major concern for the mediator is to assist the parties in areas of communication. The intent is to improve the parties' skills so they will be able to negotiate more effectively. The assumption in mediation is twofold. First, the parties can and will come up with a better solution than one that is invented by a third party; and second, the relationship is an important one, and the parties want to develop their ability to problem-solve about their conflict.

How Mediation Works[11]

There are a number of variations on the mediation process, but in general it tends to follow a reasonably common process. First, the mediator needs to be selected. The mediator can be a member of a professional mediation center or service, or can be acting informally as a mediator while in some other capacity (minister, manager, social worker, teacher, counselor, etc.).

The mediator begins by taking an active role. Usually, the mediator invites both sides to attend a meeting. The mediator sets ground rules by which the mediation will occur:

- The parties agree to follow a procedure set forth by the mediator.
- The parties agree to listen to each other and follow some rules of civility and respect toward each other.
- The role of the mediator is not to solve the parties' dispute, but to work with the parties to achieve a "negotiated" outcome.

As actual mediation starts, the mediator then takes on a more passive role. He or she meets with each party to listen to them and learn about the dispute. In most cases, the mediator does this with the other party in the room, so that each can hear how the other sees the dispute. However, if the parties cannot be candid in front of the other, or conflict is likely to erupt, the mediator may hold these meetings with each party separately. Through active listening and questions, the mediator tries to identify and understand the issues. The mediator looks for underlying interests, priorities, and concerns, and finds areas for potential collaboration or compromise.

In the next stage, the parties agree on the agenda—the key issues to be discussed, and the order for discussion. The mediator will help them prioritize and package their proposals and counterproposals as needed.

The mediator brings the parties together and encourages exploration of possible solutions, trade-offs, or concessions. These are designed to help communication flow more freely, reduce tension, and so forth. The mediator may invent proposals or suggest possible solutions, but will not impose any of these on the parties.

The final stage is agreement, which may be made public with an announcement of the settlement. There may be a written agreement, and it may or may not be signed. Many mediators push for some form of written agreement, to help the parties be clear about who is going to do what, and to enhance their commitment.

A long time may be involved in the mediation process, depending on the nature and degree of difficulty between the two parties. However, mediation is still less costly than going to court. The length of the stages may vary. For example, in divorce mediation, the preference is usually for both parties to begin meeting together as soon as possible, rather than having long individual meetings with the mediator. The objective is to move the parties toward communicating and working out their problems, but it will depend on the degree of cooperation of the parties and the skills of the mediator.

How Mediators Help

In addition to facilitating the negotiation process, mediators can help the parties save face when they need to make concessions. They can assist in resolving internal disagreements and help parties deal with their constituencies (e.g., by explaining the agreement to the constituency, or helping the negotiator save face with the constituency by portraying the negotiator as tough, fair, and effective). They may offer the parties incentives for agreement or concession, or offer negative incentives for noncooperation.

Mediators maintain control if the parties are unable to do so, largely by controlling the process (e.g., making sure the conflict between the parties does not escalate again, or that one side does not take undue advantage of the other). Mediators push when needed, and move into the background when the negotiators seem to be able to move forward themselves.

When Mediation Can Be Helpful

Mediation may be used in labor relations, or as a precursor to arbitration in grievance and contractual negotiations. It has also been used successfully in settling malpractice suits, tort cases, small claims, consumer complaints, liability claims, divorce,[12] civil and community disputes,[13] business disputes,[14] business and government cases involving the environment,[15] and international disputes.[16] It is increasingly being used in communities to resolve disputes between landlords and tenants or merchants and customers, and on college campuses to resolve conflicts in residence halls or between students of different genders, ethnic groups, and nationalities.

Most of these types of disputes are self-explanatory. What is interesting is to see the variety of ways that mediation can be taught and used. For example, children are being taught, as early as elementary school age, the art of mediation, and then taught how to use it to resolve conflicts in the classroom, on the playground, and in the home. While the techniques taught to children are probably not as sophisticated as they would be in a major international negotiation, the principles are exactly the same, and the dispute resolution skills children learn at an early age can carry over into their adult lives.

Factors Necessary for Success in Mediation

First, mediators *need to be seen by the disputants* as neutral, impartial, and unbiased. This is critical, because if mediators are seen by one or both disputants as "biased" toward one side or having a preferred outcome, then their actions will not be trusted. It is not enough for mediators themselves to believe they are neutral or can act in an unbiased manner—the acid test is that the *parties must see them as unbiased.*

Second, mediators may need to be expert in the field where the dispute occurs, although mediation requires less expertise than arbitration. An arbitrator has to know the key laws or contract issues in the area, and usually has to make a decision that is consistent with previous rulings. In contrast, as long as a mediator is neutral and smart enough to understand the key issues and arguments of both sides, he or she can be effective. Sometimes, in fact, naive mediators have so few biases about the dispute in question that they may discover helpful approaches that experts in this area have become blind to. Expertise is especially important to industrial conflicts, where industry-specific knowledge may be important. In divorce mediation, a knowledge of marital law is helpful. (For an agreement to be legally binding, a lawyer probably has to write the document, but parties can achieve fundamental agreements in principle with almost any kind of a mediator.) It is also useful for the mediator to have experience in mediating similar disputes.

Although it is not required by law, certification of mediation training enhances the mediator's credibility. The Federal Mediation and Conciliation Service of the U.S. Department of Labor is one group that certifies mediators. There are also local mediation services and dispute settlement centers that "certify" mediators by having them participate in a mandatory training program, as well as an apprenticeship with an experienced mediator. Mediation centers can assist disputing parties in finding a mediator.

Successful mediation depends to a large degree on timing. Mediation cannot be used as a technique for dispute resolution if the parties do not agree that they need help, or are so angry and upset at each other that they cannot even civilly sit in the same room together. Mediation also depends on the willingness of the parties to make some concessions and find a compromise solution. If they are so committed to their point of view that no compromise is even possible—a problem we see in attempting to mediate value-based disputes around issues like abortion and environmental management—then mediation is doomed to fail. If the parties are not both willing to accept mediation, then it is unlikely that other techniques will work until the parties soften their views.

Success

Mediation tends to be successful in 60 to 80 percent of cases, according to statistics. Success of using mediation as an ADR technique is most likely when[17]

- The conflict is moderate but not high.
- The conflict is not excessively emotional and polarized.
- There is a high motivation by both parties to settle.
- The parties are committed to follow the process of mediation.
- Resources are not severely limited.
- The issues do not involve a basic conflict of values.
- The power is relatively equal between the parties.
- Mediation is seen as advantageous relative to going to arbitration (or no agreement).

- The bargainers have experience and understand the process of give and take, and the costs of no agreement.[18]

In successful mediation, negotiators tend to be committed to the agreement that is generated.[19] Thus the implementation rate is high.

Disadvantages

Mediation is not effective or is more difficult to use when

- The bargainers are inexperienced and assume that if they simply take a hard line, the other party will eventually give in.
- There are many issues, and the parties cannot agree on priorities.
- The parties are strongly committed to their positions (and are held to them by an uncompromising constituency).
- There is very strong emotion, passion, and intensity to the conflict.
- A party has an internal conflict and isn't sure what to do.
- The parties differ on major social values.
- The parties differ greatly on their expectations for what is a fair and reasonable settlement.
- The parties' resistance points do not overlap—the most one party will give is still much less than the minimum the other will accept.

Mediation can be more time-consuming than arbitration. The parties have to take a lot of time explaining the dispute to the third party, and then participating in the process of searching for a resolution. Also, because mediation is not binding, there is no impetus for the parties to commit to the settlement or even to settle at all. Thus there is always the potential for the dispute to reappear and continue—perhaps even for a long time. And it is always possible that the dispute will escalate.

Combining Mediation and Arbitration

Some who monitor third-party interventions have suggested that even better than mediation, in some cases, may be requiring a sequence of dispute resolution events, such as mediation followed by arbitration. This sequence seems to minimize the liabilities of each type of ADR (arbitration and mediation) and to obtain better compromises.[20] If the parties expect that they will have to progress to arbitration, they may be more willing to modify their positions in mediation to improve their chances of ruling in favor of their side. On the other hand, the expectation of arbitration may make the parties "lazy" in mediation, particularly if they think the arbitrator will ultimately rule in their favor.

Assisting the Mediator

Mediators succeed when both parties are agreeable to the mediation. Further, there are ways you can help the process.

You can help a mediator to help you negotiate by being cooperative and giving clear information. Tell the mediator what is important to you and why you want it. If you do not understand something, speak up. Express your concerns if necessary. Remember that the mediator is there to assist in the negotiation process, not to remake it. Finally, be willing to make concessions or problem solve. The objective of mediation is to move the dispute from a competitive solution to a compromise or collaborative solution, and this requires the work of all parties. Ultimately, the success of the negotiation is your responsibility. You and the other party need to find, select, and implement a workable outcome. The mediator will assist you in this endeavor, but will not do the work for you.

Process Consultation

Another way of getting help with a stalled negotiation is to use a process consultant. Process consultants serve as counselors who focus on the *process* of negotiation, as their title would suggest. They assist parties in improving communication, reducing the emotionality of the proceedings, and increasing the parties' dispute resolution skills. Their objective is to enable parties to solve their own disputes in the future. Process consultants are thus useful if the relationship between the opposing parties is a long-term one.

A process consultant is somewhat like a mediator in that he or she helps with the steps in the process. But this person differs from the mediator in that there is no discussion of the specific issues or any attempt to solve them. Thus process consultants are often more like counselors who help the parties to get along better so that they can engage in better negotiation and problem solving.

The Process

Process consultants (PCs) first interview the parties individually. Then they design a schedule of structured meetings for the parties. At these meetings, the PCs have the disputing parties discuss their past conflicts and perceptions of each other. The PCs remain neutral, guiding the parties as needed. They keep people on track, keep the emotional level from escalating, and move the parties toward problem-solving behavior. Their objective is to change the conflict management climate, improve communication, promote constructive dialogue, and create the capacity for people to act as "their own third party."

PCs have expertise in the areas of conflict and emotions. They provide emotional support to their clients. They confront and diagnose problems while remaining neutral and unbiased. They must also be authoritative to keep the process moving. They control and manage the agenda of how the parties engage each other, but not what actually happens.

Process consultation is used in marital therapy, family therapy, organizational development, and team building. It is also used in labor–management disputes and international conflict where there are ethical, political, and cultural difficulties to contend with.

Process consultation is less likely to work in the following circumstances:

- There are severe, polarized disputes over large issues.
- The relationship is short-term and the parties have no stake in improving it.
- The issues are fixed (competitive rather than collaborative negotiation).
- The party's constituency is not supportive of improving the relationship.
- One or both parties are intent on revenge or retribution.

Other, Less Formal Methods of Dispute Resolution

"Ombuds" and Others

Ombudspersons, fact finders, and referees are employed by various organizations to deal with matters before they turn into disputes. In many cases, their job is to hear and investigate conflicts between employees, or between an individual employee and "the system" (the rules, practices, and policies of the organization). At NCR,[21] as at other companies, ombuds are trained in problem solving, dispute avoidance, negotiation, and dispute resolution.

Their mission is to limit and resolve problems quickly and informally. They usually are not part of the chain of command in an organization and may report directly to the CEO rather than to a specific department. They often have links with the legal and human resources departments, so they can discuss trends in compliance or legal issues. But it is essential for ombuds to be impartial, and hence they are often unattached to the organizational hierarchy.

When an employee takes a problem to an ombud or the equivalent, the ombud engages in confidential fact-finding, then informs both sides of their rights and the opportunities for resolving the conflict. The ombud may use a combination of counseling, conciliation, negotiation, and mediation. If the complaint involves corporate policy, salary, promotion, tenure, discharge, liability, discriminatory treatment, or the like, the ombud may recommend a settlement, but usually management is involved in the final decision.

The main reason for using an ombudsperson is to make sure the process is fair and that the individual employees, with very little power, have a way to get a fair investigation and hearing about their concerns. If you are negotiating within a system or organization, an ombud can make sure you know the channels that are available to you, your rights, and what kind of outside help you may need. Ombuds can often act as "change agents," pushing an organization to change its rules and policies to deal with unfair treatment practices.

Advantages and Disadvantages of Ombuds

Using an ombud or other type of counselor can be to your advantage if the power between the two disputing parties is out of balance. This is particularly true when a lower-level employee tries to challenge his or her employer and doesn't want to get fired simply for asking questions or raising concerns about "fairness" and "rights." As with other third-party practices, however, the final outcome may not be what you hoped for.

Some organizations specify a formal process for expressing and hearing problems and disputes in this system. They may require a staged approach, where the first step is an ombud, the next is mediation, and the final step is arbitration.

Managers as Third Parties

Finally, we turn to managers, supervisors, and others whose jobs do not consist primarily of mediating disputes, but who nevertheless often must intervene to get work done or deal with unproductive conflicts in the workplace. It is estimated that managers spend 20 percent of their time in conflict management.[22] Their methods tend to be informal since most work environments do not have established rules or guidelines for how to mediate a dispute. Few managers have any formal training in settling disputes, and many are uncomfortable with conflict. But they need to know that some conflict is all right[23] and to seek assistance themselves if they often find themselves refereeing employee disputes.

Styles

Managers tend to solve disputes along the lines we discussed for other types of interventions—high or low process control, high or low outcome control.[24] The style used will depend on the manager's tolerance for conflict, the time frame, and, to some degree, the personalities of the parties involved.

High Control of Both Process and Outcome   If a manager wants to maintain control of both the process and the outcome (which is the most typical scenario), the manager's style will be inquisitorial or autocratic. The manager behaves more like a judge in a European court, or like the infamous judge on the TV show *The People's Court*. The manager runs his or her own investigation, and then makes a decision. The manager will listen to both parties' stories, structure the process as he or she pleases, asking questions to learn more information, and then will decide on the solution. This method tends to be the most common among managers. It is frequently used when the issues are minor, quick decisions are needed, or management needs to implement an unpopular action.[25]

High Outcome Control, Low Process Control   A manager who wants to retain high control of the outcome, but low control of the process, will use passive listening and then will make a decision. This is most like the arbitration style described earlier. This is somewhat like the "high–high" method, except that the manager listens to both sides; he or she makes little effort to gather more information, ask questions, or structure the process other than to render a decision after hearing the arguments.

High Process Control, Low Outcome Control   This approach is most like mediation. More managers are learning to use this approach, although not as much as would be hoped. In many disputes, the manager considers the outcome more important than the process and wants to have some control over it, so this method is used less than it might be.

Low Process and Outcome Control   If the manager does not care about controlling either process or outcome, he or she will either ignore the dispute and let the parties deal with it by themselves, or tell the disputing employees, "You solve the problem yourselves, or I will impose a solution that probably neither of you will like." This may sound like a parent acting as intervener between two arguing children.

Factors Affecting the Choice of Method

The choice of dispute resolution method will often be based on the time frame. Because outcome control methods are believed to be quicker by the third party (hence often ignoring a lot of the "disadvantages" of arbitration and outcome control), high outcome control methods are used when efficiency and saving time are high priorities. Other factors that affect the choice of resolution method are

- The objectivity (neutrality) of the manager.
- The relationship of the parties (long-term or short-term).
- The effect of how this confrontation is resolved on future negotiations.
- The expected ability of the parties to resolve conflicts for themselves in the future.
- The extent of training of the manager in conflict resolution techniques.

Keys for Managers Helping Employees with Conflict

- Select a neutral site for the meeting.
- Be empathetic; listen as well as you can, and practice listening skills.
- Be assertive, particularly about setting guidelines for how the parties should deal with each other in a more productive manner.
- Ask for cooperation and be cooperative yourself.
- Ask what the parties want you to do to help solve the problem.
- When there is a resolution, if appropriate, get it in writing.
- Help the parties plan for implementation. And do not forget to follow-up.

ADR's Usefulness

Since 95 percent of all civil cases are settled out of court, there is room in the area of dispute resolution for ADR.[26] Alternative methods of dispute resolution can save time and money, reduce the number of cases on court dockets, and provide timely solutions to problems. In fact, about half of state court systems now require that certain civil complaints be referred to arbitration prior to trial. Thirty-three jurisdictions require that family disputes regarding custody and visitation be brought into mediation.[27]

At the federal level, the U.S. district courts increasingly order civil cases into mandatory arbitration or refer parties to moderated settlement conferences, minitrials, and summary jury trials. The U.S. Court of Appeals for the District of Columbia and the U.S. Court of Claims are also experimenting with mediation programs.

As an example of costs, a commercial suit with a $200,000 claim will cost parties almost that much in legal fees, discovery costs, and actual trial costs. Mediation for this situation would cost about $2,500, usually shared between the two parties. So it makes sense to use third-party intervention before taking a case to court. And, as stated previously, mediation has a good track record—70 to 80 percent of all cases are successfully mediated.

Many employers now include in contracts, employment agreements, and other related documents an ADR clause that defines the dispute resolution process. It may specify[28]

- The rules or laws that apply to the process.
- The ADR methods to use and in what order to apply them.

- The location for the ADR procedure.
- The official language of the ADR process.
- Whether the outcome will be binding.
- How the costs will be allocated among the parties.

In fact, at NCR, ADR is specified as the first, preferred method for dispute settlement.

However, ADR is not always the perfect solution. As an example, in the case of a rate-setting dispute with the Public Utilities Commission of Ohio (PUCO),[29] ADR appeared not to work well for this regulated utility, and was not a viable solution. There were several reasons. First, the intervention was not voluntary, so there was lower commitment to the process. Time constraints for public utilities prohibited the long periods of consideration that tend to be required in mediated situations. Resources were strained because the utility had to prepare for court at the same time as pursuing ADR in case ADR failed. Statutory requirements added further constraints and costs. Utilities in dispute need to have mediators who are fully aware of industry-specific details (especially in the area of regulation) in order to be effective, and this was not true in this case.

How Some Organizations Solve Disputes

Many organizations follow a "line authority" approach to solving problems: First you go to a supervisor, then to a division supervisor, then to a panel of supervisors, and finally to top management. If one of the parties is a union, the fourth step is binding arbitration. But there are other, more effective, more proactive ways to solve problems.

One such plan is PGR—peer group resolution[30]—which is used by the Northern States Power Company. The purpose of the process is to investigate, review, and resolve disputes; employee peer groups serve on the panel and execute the process. The PGR steps are very specific.

Step 1.   The employee with a complaint completes a PGR form and submits a copy of it to the human resources department within 10 days of the incident. The employee gives the original form to the immediate supervisor, who completes a meeting with the employee within three working days. The supervisor writes a response to the problem on the form, and returns it to the employee within two working days. The employee then has two days to decide whether the response satisfies the complaint, or whether to progress to step 2.

Step 2.   The employee's second-level supervisor schedules and completes a meeting with the employee within three working days of receiving the form. This person writes a response on the form, and returns it to the employee within two working days of meeting with the employee. The employee has two working days after receiving the written response to complete the appropriate section of the form, either indicating satisfaction with the response and sending it to human resources, or going to step 3.

Step 3.   In this step, the employee can select from one of two options listed on the PGR form: Meet either with a third-level supervisor or with a peer group panel.

The supervisor meeting process is similar to that in step 2. If the employee selects the peer group panel, the human resources department coordinates the random selection of panel members and schedules a panel review. The peer group panel consists of five employees, randomly chosen from two panelist pools. If the employee is nonsupervisory, then five panelists are selected from the nonsupervisory pool and four panelists from the supervisory pool. If the employee is supervisory, five panelists come from the supervisory pool, and four from the nonsupervisory pool. In either case the employee chooses two names from each pool to discard, resulting in a total of five panelists.

Within 10 working days of the employee choosing the final option, the panel meets with the employee and reviews the documentation and facts. The panel reaches a decision by majority vote to grant, modify, or deny the remedy requested by the employee. The panelists sign the form, adding explanations as appropriate. Human resources distributes copies of the decision to the employee and supervisors. The decision reached in this manner is binding and cannot be appealed. All materials are kept confidential.

The program is successful in part because all who volunteer to be panelists receive a full day of training for this role. They practice reviewing sample cases using the role-play process.

The results of peer group resolution at the Northern States Power Company have been rewarding. Many disputes have been resolved before they get to step 3. Accountability of management has improved. Communication and problem-solving skills have improved. Concerns can be voiced and dealt with before they become major problems or disputes. The process allows all parties to deal with conflict in an organized manner. Productivity and morale are higher because employees feel they can be heard. They also learn, as panelists, to better appreciate what goes into management decisions and participate in a process of resolving disputes.

The company requires everyone to complete an evaluation form to assess the process, and this has provided positive feedback. In addition, each party with a grievance must be interviewed three months after settlement to ensure that there is no retaliation.

Finding Third-Party Help

There are many organizations for mediators, arbitrators, and other third-party professionals. Among them are the Federal Mediation and Conciliation Service and the American Arbitration Association. There are private organizations that provide professional services, such as Endispute. There are also local mediation services in many communities, as well as consumer protection services available through district attorneys' offices. In most communities, you can simply look up "Mediation Services" in your classified telephone directory, and find a list of individuals and organizations providing services.

If you are interviewing a potential candidate for third-party help, you may want to find out about availability, interests, and potential conflicts. Select someone who has a knowledge of the subject area that is the center of your dispute. Do not use a person who is likely to be partisan.[31]

Endnotes

1. C. Moore, *The Mediation Process: Practical Strategies for Resolving Conflict* (San Francisco: Jossey-Bass, 1986).

2. See F. Elkouri and E. Elkouri, *How Arbitration Works,* 4th ed. (Washington, DC: BNA, 1985); P. Prasow and E. Peters, *Arbitration and Collective Bargaining: Conflict Resolution in Labor Relations,* 2nd ed. (New York: McGraw-Hill, 1983); and R. N. Corley, R. L. Black, and O. L. Reed, *The Legal Environment of Business,* 4th ed. (New York: McGraw-Hill, 1977).

3. C. Feigenbaum, "Final-Offer Arbitration: Better Theory Than Practice," *Industrial Relations* 14 (1975), pp. 311–317.

4. D. Golann, "Consumer Financial Services Litigation: Major Judgments and ADR Responses," *The Business Lawyer* 48 (May 1993), pp. 1141–49.

5. T. A. Kochan, *Collective Bargaining and Industrial Relations* (Homewood, IL: Irwin, 1980).

6. G. Long and P. Feuille, "Final Offer Arbitration: Sudden Death in Eugene," *Industrial and Labor Relations Review* 27 (1974), pp. 186–203; F. A. Starke and W. W. Notz, "Pre- and Postintervention Effects of Conventional versus Final-Offer Arbitration," *Academy of Management Journal* 24 (1981), pp. 832–50.

7. V. H. Vroom, "A New Look at Managerial Decision Making," *Organizational Dynamics* 1 (Spring 1973), pp. 66–80.

8. J. C. Anderson and T. Kochan, "Impasse Procedures in the Canadian Federal Service," *Industrial and Labor Relations Review* 30 (1977), pp. 283–301.

9. T. A. Kochan and T. Jick, "The Public Sector Mediation Process: A Theory and Empirical Examination," *Journal of Conflict Resolution* 22 (1978), pp. 209–40; T. A. Kochan, *Collective Bargaining and Industrial Relations* (Homewood, IL: Irwin, 1980).

10. P. J. D. Carnevale and D. G. Pruitt, "Negotiation and Mediation," in M. Rosenberg and L. Porter (eds.), *Annual Review of Psychology* 43 (Palo Alto, CA: Annual Reviews, 1992), pp. 531–582; J. A. Wall and A. Lynn, "Mediation: A Current Review," *Journal of Conflict Resolution* 37 (1993), pp. 160–94; R. J. Lewicki, S. Weiss, and D. Lewin, "Models of Conflict, Negotiation and Third Party Intervention: A Review and Synthesis," *Journal of Organizational Behavior* 13 (1992), pp. 209–52.

11. Carnevale and Pruitt, "Negotiation and Mediation."

12. See W. A. Donohue, *Communication, Marital Dispute and Divorce Mediation* (Hillsdale, NJ: Erlbaum, 1991); K. Kressel, N. Jaffe, M. Tuchman, C. Watson, and M. Deutsch, "Mediated Negotiations in Divorce and Labor Disputes: A Comparison," *Conciliation Courts Review* 15 (1977), pp. 9–12; O. J. Coogler, *Structural Mediation in Divorce Settlement: A Handbook for Marital Mediators* (Lexington, MA: Lexington Books, 1978).

13. K. Duffy, J. Grosch, and P. Olczak, *Community Mediation: A Handbook for Practitioners and Researchers* (New York: Guilford, 1991); P. Lovenheim, *Mediate, Don't Litigate: How to Resolve Disputes Quickly, Privately, and Inexpensively without Going to Court* (New York: McGraw-Hill, 1989); L. Singer, *Settling Disputes: Conflict Resolution in Business, Families, and the Legal System* (CO: Boulder, Westview Press, 1990).

14.   R. Coulson, *Business Mediation: What You Need to Know* (New York: American Arbitration Association, 1987).

15.   W. Drayton, "Getting Smarter about Regulation," *Harvard Business Review* 59 (July–August 1981), pp. 38–52; R. B. Reich, "Regulation by Confrontation or Negotiation," *Harvard Business Review* 59 (May–June 1981), pp. 82–93; L. Susskind and J. Cruikshank, *Breaking the Impasse: Consensual Approaches to Resolving Public Disputes* (New York: Basic Books, 1987).

16.   R. Fisher, *International Mediation: A Working Guide* (New York: International Peace Academy, 1978).

17.   Carnevale and Pruitt, "Negotiation and Mediation"; K. Kressel and D. Pruitt (eds.), *Mediation Research* (San Francisco: Jossey-Bass, 1989).

18.   T. A. Kochan and T. Jick, "The Public Sector Mediation Process: A Theory and Empirical Examination," *Journal of Conflict Resolution* 22 (1978), pp. 209–40.

19.   C. Moore, The *Mediation Process: Practical Strategies for Resolving Conflict* (San Francisco: Jossey-Bass, 1986).

20.   Starke and Notz, "Pre- and Postintervention Effects"; D. W. Grigsby, *The Effects of Intermediate Mediation Step on Bargaining Behavior under Various Forms of Compulsory Arbitration,* paper presented to the Annual Meeting of the American Institute for Decision Sciences, Boston, MA, November 1981; D. W. Grigsby and W. J. Bigoness, "Effects of Mediation and Alternative Forms of Arbitration on Bargaining Behavior: A Laboratory Study," *Journal of Applied Psychology* 67 (1982), pp. 549–54.

21.   T. B. Carver and A. A. Vondra, "Alternative Dispute Resolution: Why It Doesn't Work and Why It Does," *Harvard Business Review,* May–June 1994, p. 124.

22.   M. A. Rahim, J. E. Garrett, and G. F. Buntzman, "Ethics of Managing Interpersonal Conflict in Organizations," *Journal of Business Ethics* 14 (1992), pp. 423–32.

23.   Rahim, Garrett, and Buntzman, "Ethics of Managing Interpersonal Conflict."

24.   B. H. Sheppard, "Managers as Inquisitors: Some Lessons from the Law," in M. Bazerman and R. J. Lewicki (eds.), *Negotiating in Organizations* (Beverly Hills, CA: Sage, 1983), pp. 193–213.

25.   Rahim, Garrett, and Buntzman, "Ethics of Managing Interpersonal Conflict."

26.   G. M. Flores, "Handling Employee Issues through Alternative Dispute Resolution," *Bankers Magazine,* July/August 1993, pp. 47–50.

27.   From American Bar Association material—Section of Dispute Resolution (1800 M Street, Washington, DC).

28.   M. S. Lans, "Try an ADR and You'll Save Yourself a Court Date," *Marketing and the Law,* June 21, 1993, p. 14.

29.   D. C. Bergmann, "ADR: Resolution or Complication?" *Public Utilities Fortnightly,* January 15, 1993, pp. 20–22.

30.   D. B. Hoffman and N. L. Kluver, "How Peer Group Resolution Works at Northern States Power Co.," *Employment Relations Today,* Spring 1992, pp. 25–30.

31.   J. Greenwald, "Resolving Disagreements: Alternative Market Finds ADR Works to Its Advantage," *Business Insurance,* June 7, 1993, p. 45.

Investigative Negotiation

Deepak Malhotra
Max H. Bazerman

The best way to get what you're after in a negotiation—sometimes the only way—is to approach the situation the way a detective approaches a crime scene.

Chris, a *Fortune* 500 Executive, is known in his firm as a gifted negotiator who can break impossible deadlocks. Consider his performance in the following deal.

A few years ago, Chris's company entered into negotiations with a small European firm to buy an ingredient for a new health care product. (Some details have been changed to protect the companies involved.) The two sides settled on a price of $18 a pound for a million pounds of the substance annually. However, a disagreement developed over the terms. The European supplier refused to sell the ingredient exclusively to the U.S. firm, and the U.S. firm was unwilling to invest in a product that was based on an ingredient its competitors could easily acquire. With considerable hesitation, the U.S negotiators sweetened the deal, offering guaranteed minimum orders and a higher price. To their shock, the supplier still balked at providing exclusivity—even though it had no chance of selling anything close to a million pounds a year to anyone else. The negotiation seemed to be at a dead end, with the U.S. negotiators out of ideas for pushing through a deal. Even worse, the relationship had deteriorated so much that neither side trusted the other to continue bargaining in good faith.

At that point the stymied U.S. team brought in Chris to help improve relations. He did more than that. After listening to the facts, he asked the Europeans a simple question: Why? *Why* wouldn't they provide exclusivity to his corporation, which would buy as much of the ingredient as they could produce? The response surprised the Americans. Exclusivity would require the supplier's owner to violate an agreement with his cousin, who bought 250 pounds of the ingredient each year to make a locally sold product. Armed with this new knowledge, Chris proposed a solution that allowed the two firms to quickly wrap up a deal. The European firm would provide exclusivity with the exception of a few hundred pounds annually for the supplier's cousin.

In retrospect, that solution seems obvious. But as we've seen in real-world negotiations, as well as in classroom simulations with seasoned deal makers, this type of problem solving is exceedingly rare. That's because most negotiators wrongly assume that they understand the other side's motivations and, therefore, don't explore them further. The U.S. team members initially failed because they thought they knew why the supplier was being difficult: Clearly, they assumed, the Europeans were holding out for a higher price or didn't want to lose out on future deals with other customers.

Source: "Investigative Negotiation," by Deepak Malhotra and Max H. Bazerman, from *Harvard Business Review*, September 2007, pp. 73–78. Harvard Business School Publishing. Used with permission.

Would you have made the same mistake? We have presented this case to hundreds of experienced executives in negotiation courses at Harvard Business School. When we asked them to strategize on behalf of Chris's team about how to break the impasse, roughly 90 percent of their answers sounded like these: "Consent to a larger minimum purchase agreement." "Ask for a shorter exclusivity period." "Buy out the supplier." "Increase your offer price." "Threaten to walk away." All those suggestions share the same flaw: They are solutions to a problem that has not been diagnosed. Moreover, even if one of them had been effective in securing exclusivity, it would have been more costly than Chris's solution.

Chris succeeded because he challenged assumptions and gathered critical information regarding the other party's perspective—the first step in what we call "investigative negotiation." This approach, introduced in our new book, *Negotiation Genius*, entails both a mind-set and a methodology. It encourages negotiators to enter talks the same way a detective enters a crime scene: by learning as much as possible about the situation and the people involved.

Though the solution to every negotiation may not be as straightforward as Chris's, his approach can help in even the most complex deals. In this article, we delineate five principles underlying investigative negotiation and show how they apply in myriad situations.

Principle 1: Don't Just Discuss *What* Your Counterparts Want—Find Out *Why* They Want It

This principle works in fairly straightforward negotiations, like Chris's, and can be applied fruitfully to complex multiparty negotiations as well. Consider the dilemma facing Richard Holbrooke in late 2000, when he was the U.S. ambassador to the United Nations. At the time, the United States was more than $1 billion in arrears to the UN but was unwilling to pay it unless the UN agreed to a variety of reforms. As a result, U.S. representatives were being sidelined in UN committee meetings, and the country faced losing its vote in the General Assembly. Meanwhile, U.S. senators were calling for a withdrawal from the organization.

Why the turmoil? For decades the United States had paid 25 percent of the regular UN budget. Believing that was too large a share, Congress decided to hold the $1 billion hostage until the UN agreed to, among other changes, reduce the U.S. assessment from 25 percent to 22 percent of the budget. The other UN member states saw this as a nefarious tactic.

Ambassador Holbrooke faced a tough challenge. According to UN regulations, a change in the allocation of dues needed the approval of all 189 members. What's more, a hard deadline was fast approaching. The Helms-Biden bill, which had appropriated close to $1 billion to cover much of what the United States owed, stipulated that if a deal was not struck by January 1, 2001, the money would disappear from the federal budget.

Holbrooke's team had hoped that Japan and some European countries would absorb most of the U.S. reductions. Unfortunately, the Japanese (who were already the second-highest contributors) rejected that idea outright. The Europeans also balked. How could Holbrooke break the impasse?

With the clock ticking, he and his team decided to concentrate less on persuading member states of the need for change and more on better understanding their perspectives. Whenever a member resisted an increase, Holbrooke, instead of arguing, would push further to discover precisely why it could not (or would not) pay more. Soon, one entirely unanticipated reason became salient: Many countries that might otherwise agree to increase their contributions did not have room to do so in their 2001 budgets, because they had already been finalized. The January 1 deadline was marking the deal unworkable.

This new understanding of the problem gave rise to a possible solution. Holbrooke's proposal was to immediately reduce U.S. assessments from 25 percent to 22 percent to meet Congress's deadline but delay the increase in contributions from other nations until 2002. (The 2001 shortfall was covered by CNN founder and philanthropist Ted Turner, who agreed to make a onetime personal contribution of $34 million to the UN.) The key to resolving the conflict, however, was discovering that the dispute entailed not one issue but two: the timing of assessments as well as their size. Once the negotiators broadened their focus to include the issue of the timing, they could strike a deal that allowed each side to get what it wanted on the issue it cared about most.

Principle 2: Seek to Understand and Mitigate the Other Side's Constraints

Outside forces can limit our ability to negotiate effectively. We may be constrained by advice from lawyers, by corporate policies that prohibit making concessions, by fear of setting a dangerous precedent, by obligations to other parties, by time pressure, and so on. Similarly, the other side has constraints that can lead it to act in ways that don't seem rational—and that can destroy value for both sides but unfortunately, the constraints of the other side are often hidden from (or ignored by) us.

Smart negotiators attempt to discover the other party's constraints—and to help overcome them—rather than dismiss the other side as unreasonable or the deal as unworkable. Above all, investigative negotiators never view the other side's constraints as simply *"their* problem."

The experience of a company we'll call HomeStuff demonstrates why. At HomeStuff, a producer of household appliances, the CEO was negotiating the purchase of mechanical parts from a supplier we'll call Kogs. The two key issues were price and delivery date. HomeStuff wanted to pay a low price and get immediate delivery; Kogs sought a high price and more time to deliver the goods.

Eventually, the parties agreed on a price of $17 million and delivery within three months. "Meeting that deadline will be difficult for me," said the supplier, "but I'll manage." The CEO of HomeStuff was tempted to let the discussion end there—the deal was already done and meeting the deadline was now the supplier's problem—but she decided to explore matters further. Aware that a delivery after three months would cost her company close to $1 million, she offered to accept a delay if Kogs would drop the price by that amount. "I appreciate the offer," the supplier responded, "but I can't accommodate such a large price cut."

Curious, the CEO pressed on. "I'm surprised that a three-month delivery would be so costly to you," she said to the supplier. "Tell me more about your production process so that I can understand why you can't cheaply manufacture the parts in that time frame." "Ah! But that's not the problem," the supplier explained. "We can easily manufacture the products in three months. But we have no way of cheaply shipping the order so it would arrive on time."

When the HomeStuff CEO heard this, she was thrilled. Because her firm often had to transport products quickly, it had arranged favorable terms with a shipping company. Using that service, HomeStuff could have the parts delivered in *less than* three months for a small fraction of what the supplier would have paid.

The CEO made the following offer, which the supplier immediately accepted: HomeStuff would arrange for its own shipper to deliver the parts in two and a half months, the supplier would pay the shipping costs, and the price would drop from $17 million to $16.5 million.

As this story illustrates, the other side's problem can quickly become your own. This is true not only when the other party is quietly accepting its constraints but also when it's being disagreeable. Often, when the other side refuses to meet demands, its intransigence is interpreted as a sure sign it's acting in self-interest, but in fact its hands may be tied. Through investigation, negotiators may find that they can help mitigate the other side's constraints to their own advantage.

Principle 3: Interpret Demands as Opportunities

The CEO of a successful construction company was negotiating a deal to build a number of midsize office buildings. After months of talks — but just before the contract was signed—the developer approached the CEO with an entirely new and potentially costly demand: a clause that would require the builder to pay large penalties if the project fell more than one month behind schedule. The CEO, understandably, was irritated by this last-minute attempt to squeeze more concessions from him.

The builder weighed his options. He could accept the new clause and seal the deal, he could reject it and hope the deal would survive, or he could try to negotiate lower penalties. As he thought more deeply, he began to focus less on possible responses and more on what the demand revealed. At the very least, it showed that the developer had a strong interest in timely project completion. But might it also suggest that the developer valued *early* completion? With that in mind, the CEO approached the developer with a new proposal: He would pay even higher penalties than the developer wanted if the project was delayed. If the project was completed earlier than scheduled, however, the developer would give the construction company a bonus. Both sides agreed to that clause and were happier with the new terms. The builder was confident that his company would finish ahead of schedule and receive the bonus, and the developer minimized his downside risk.

Typically, When the other side makes seemingly unreasonable demands, negotiators adopt a defensive mind-set: "How can I avoid having to accept this?" In contrast, investigative negotiators confront difficult demands the same way they confront any statement from the other party: "What can I learn from the other side's insistence on this issue? What does this demand tell me about this party's needs and interests? How can I use this information to create and capture value?" The construction company CEO's breakthrough came from his ability to shift his efforts away from fighting the other side's demand and toward investigating the opportunities hidden beneath it.

Principle 4: Create Common Ground with Adversaries

Negotiation professors often engage their students in a complex simulation called "The Commodity Purchase," written by Leonard Greenhalgh of Dartmouth's Tuck School of Business. In it, one student plays the role of the seller of 100,000 pheasant eggs, and five other students play potential egg buyers. The buyers have different motives (for example, some want chemicals in the eggs to manufacture health products) and need a variety of quantities, encouraging the formation of coalitions among them. The alliance that will create the most value, however, involves two competing pharmaceutical firms that, by cooperating, have the potential to outbid the other three buyers. The problem is that one of the firms needs at least 80,000 eggs, the other needs at least 70,000, and it is not obvious how both can get what they want, given that there are only 100,000 eggs. In fact, only about 5 percent of MBA students and executives that participate in this simulation manage to discover the solution.

To find it, the company reps must first realize that the needs of their respective pharmaceutical firms are complementary, not competitive. Specifically, one firm needs the whites of the eggs, and the other needs the yolks. Once they know this, the two firms can split the cost of the eggs and each take what they need from the acquired product. However, few come to this conclusion, because to develop it, the parties must adopt an investigative negotiation approach, overcome their reluctance to seek common ground with someone who is considered the enemy, and attempt to understand their competitor's perspective. The naive assumption that other firms in the same industry are strictly competitors typically prevents negotiators from taking an investigative approach.

As professors Adam Brandenburger of New York University and Barry Nalebuff of Yale University demonstrate in their book *Co-opetition*, it is often possible to simultaneously cooperate and compete with others. Investigative negotiators understand this. Those who view their relationship with the other side as one-dimensional—"He is my competitor"—forgo opportunities for value creation, whereas those who appreciate the complexity of relationships and explore areas of mutual interest are able to find common ground.

Principle 5: Continue to Investigate even after the Deal Appears to Be Lost

How many times have you tried to close a deal only to have your final offer rejected? If you are like most people, once someone has said no to your best offer, you presume there is nothing left to do. Often, this is the case. Sometimes, however, you are wrong—and you lose the deal not because there was no viable agreement but because you did not negotiate effectively.

A few years ago the chief executive of a specialty-gift-item manufacturer learned that a *Fortune* 500 company she had courted for months had decided to purchase from her competitor. Though she had no further plans for winning the deal, the CEO placed one final call to the prospect's vice president, asking why her offer was rejected and explaining that an answer could help her improve future offerings.

To the CEO's surprise, the VP explained that the competitor, despite charging more, had beaten her offer by including product features that his company valued. Under the false assumption that the prospect cared mostly about price, the CEO had made a final offer that reduced the prospect's cost as much as possible. The CEO thanked the VP for his explanation and added that she had misunderstood his position earlier. "Knowing what I know now," she told him, "I'm confident that I could have beaten their offer. Would you consider a revised offer?" The answer was yes. One week later the CEO won over the prospect—and signed the deal.

After being rejected, an investigative negotiator should immediately ask, "What would it have taken for us to reach agreement?" Though it may appear costly to continue negotiating when a "no deal" response appears certain, if you're confused about the *reason* your deal fell through in the first place, it could be even more costly to abandon the discussion.

Even if you find that you cannot win the deal, you may still acquire important information that will help in future negotiations. By staying at the table, you can learn about this customer's future needs, the interests and concerns of similar customers, or the strategies of other players in the industry. Keep in mind that it is often easier to get candid information from the other side when you are not in selling mode and there is little reason to distrust your motives. Next time you've lost the deal and been asked to leave the room, see if you can stick around and investigate further. You may be surprised by what you find out.

As these five principles demonstrate, successful investigative negotiation requires challenging some time honored negotiation approaches. Chief among these is the reflex to "sell" your position.

Imagine that you're observing a salesperson at work. What is he doing? Most people picture a smooth talker with a briefcase making a pitch—arguing his case and trying to persuade a potential target to buy what he has to offer. Now imagine that you're observing a negotiator at work. What is he doing? If, once again, you picture a smooth talker with a briefcase making a pitch, you are missing a crucial distinction between selling and negotiating.

Selling involves telling people about the virtues of your products or services, focusing on the strengths of your case, and trying to induce agreement or compliance. While effective negotiating requires some of those activities, as the previous cases demonstrate, it also requires a strong focus on the other side's interests, priorities, and constraints. Investigative negotiators—like truly effective salespeople—keep this focus top of mind. They also understand that constructing a value-maximizing deal often hinges not on their ability to persuade but on their ability to listen.

In the end, negotiation is an information game. Those who know how to obtain information perform better than those who stick with what they know. In the situations described here, the decision to challenge assumptions, probe below the surface, and avoid taking no for an answer helped negotiators improve their options and strike better deals. More generally, the investigative negotiation approach can help you transform competitive negotiations into ones with potential for building trust and cooperation, creating value, and engendering mutual satisfaction.

Getting Information from Distrustful Negotiators

Negotiation Entails Risk

If you share private information with the people on the other side, they might use it to their advantage. Guess what? The other side feels the same way. When other parties seem to be hiding information and evading your questions, you are likely to see them as deceptive or conniving rather than simply nervous and afraid. Try giving them the benefit of the doubt, recognizing that most people are reluctant to open up in negotiations because they don't know whether you can be trusted. The following three tactics can help you elicit information when trust is in short supply.

Share Information and Encourage Reciprocity

If you are up against a reticent negotiator, be the first to share information, making it clear that you expect reciprocity. For example, you might say; "I know that there are many things we need to discuss. If you prefer I can get the ball rolling by describing some of my key interests, concerns and constraints. Then you can do the same. Does that sound like a reasonable way to proceed?" Such an approach helps reduce the other side's anxiety, because the other party knows that both sides will be vulnerable.

Keep in mind two things. First, you want to explicitly state the ground rules up front: I will start, and then you will follow suit. Make sure that the other side commits to reciprocating. Second, if the parties don't have full confidence in each other, share information incrementally taking turns with the other side. That minimizes your own risks. If the other party fails to be forthcoming, you can hold back.

Negotiate Multiple Issues Simultaneously

In most complex negotiations, issues are discussed one at a time. You might start by discussing what's presumed to be the most important (for example, price). When you have reached some agreement on price, you turn your attention to another concern (such as contract length), and then another (such as exclusivity). However, when there is only one issue on the table at any given moment, both sides behave as if it is the most important issue to them. When you move to the second concern, that concern appears to be the most critical. And so you continue to clash on each issue and never learn what the other party truly values or needs most.

Often, it's better to negotiate multiple issues simultaneously. That is identify all the issues up front and put everything on the table at the same time. Then, go back and forth between the issues as you make offers and counteroffers. Doing so allows you to get information regarding the other side's true interest and priorities.

To determine what is really most important to the other side, look at the following signs:

- Which issue does the other party want to return to constantly?

- Which issue makes him or her the most emotional, tense, or stressed?

- Which issues are most likely to lead your counterpart to try to control the conversation, rather then listen?

- What is the other side most obstinate about when you ask for a concession or compromise?

Make Multiple Offers at the Same Time

Not only is it useful to negotiate multiple issues simultaneously, but it is also useful to make multiple *offers* at once. The next time you are preparing to make an offer to the other side, stop. Instead, make two offers at the same time that are equally valuable to you but differ on the details of one pair of issues.

Consider the case of a business owner who was negotiating with an ex-employee. The ex-employee was threatening to sue for having been fired without cause. The business owner preferred to settle out of court and soon discovered that the ex-employee was offering to settle for $15,000 in cash plus six months of temporary employer-paid health insurance. The business owner felt this amount was unjustified but was willing to negotiate. He started by asking whether the ex-employee cared more about the cash or about the health coverage. The ex-employee refused to offer this information. The business owner, having first calculated that the cost of providing the insurance would be approximately $2,500 for three months, decided to propose two options.

Offer X: $7,500 plus three months of health insurance.

Offer Y: $5,000 plus six months of health insurance.

The ex-employee was unwilling to accept either of the offers outright but voiced a preference for something closer to Y than X. This revealed that health insurance was more valuable to him than the cash. Offering him two options had prompted him to divulge his relative preferences. The final arrangement, then, could be made more attractive to the ex-employee and less costly to the business owner if further concessions were more heavily weighted toward insurance than toward cash.

Making multiple offers simultaneously is a great tactic for other reasons as well. It allows you to discover the interests of reticent negotiators, and it also makes you appear flexible and empathetic. It signals to the people on the other side that you are willing to be accommodating and interested in understanding their needs.

Summary

Reading 7.1

Best Practices in Negotiation

Roy J. Lewicki
Bruce Barry
David M. Saunders

Negotiation is an integral part of daily life, and the opportunities to negotiate surround us. While some people may look like born negotiators, negotiation is fundamentally a skill involving analysis and communication that everyone can learn. The purpose of this book is to provide students of negotiation with an overview of the field of negotiation, perspective on the breadth and depth of the subprocesses of negotiation, and an appreciation for the art and science of negotiation. In this final chapter we reflect on negotiation at a broad level by providing 10 "best practices" for negotiators who wish to continue to improve their negotiation skills (see Table 1).

1. Be Prepared

We cannot overemphasize the importance of preparation, and we strongly encourage all negotiators to prepare properly for their negotiations. Preparation does not have to be a time-consuming or arduous activity, but it should be right at the top of the best practices list of every negotiator. Negotiators who are better prepared have numerous advantages, including the ability to analyze the other party's offers more effectively and efficiently, to understand the nuances of the concession-making process, and to achieve their negotiation goals. Preparation should occur *before* the negotiation begins so that the time spent negotiating is more productive. Good preparation means understanding one's own goals and interests as well as possible and being able to articulate them to the other party skillfully. It also includes being ready to understand the other party's communication in order to find an agreement that meets the needs of both parties. Few negotiations are going to conclude successfully without both parties achieving at least some of their goals, and solid work up front to identify your needs and to understand the needs of the other party is a critical step to increasing the odds of success.

Source: "Best Practices in Negotiation," by Roy J. Lewicki, Bruce Barry, and David M. Saunders, from *Negotiation: Sixth Edition,* 2009. McGraw-Hill/Irwin, a business unit of The McGraw-Hill Companies. Used with permission.

TABLE 1 | Ten Best Practices for Negotiators

1. Be prepared.
2. Diagnose the fundamental structure of the negotiation.
3. Work the BATNA.
4. Be willing to walk.
5. Master paradox.
6. Remember the intangibles.
7. Actively manage coalitions.
8. Savor and protect your reputation.
9. Remember that rationality and fairness are relative.
10. Continue to learn from the experience.

Good preparation also means setting aspirations for negotiation that are high but achievable. Negotiators who set their sights too low are virtually guaranteed to reach an agreement that is suboptimal, while those who set them too high are more likely to stalemate and end the negotiation in frustration. Negotiators also need to plan their opening statements and positions carefully so they are especially well prepared at the start of negotiations. It is important to avoid preplanning the complete negotiation sequence, however, because while negotiations do follow broad stages, they also ebb and flow at irregular rates. Overplanning the tactics for each negotiation stage in advance of the negotiation is not a good use of preparation time. It is far better that negotiators prepare by understanding their own strengths and weaknesses, their needs and interests, the situation, and the other party as well as possible so that they can adjust promptly and effectively as the negotiation proceeds.

Finally, it is important to recognize and prepare for the effects of the broader context of the negotiation, such as the nature of existing relationships, the presence of audiences, opportunities for forming coalitions, and negotiation within or between teams, as well as for the effects of cross-cultural differences. Negotiators need to consider how these broad contextual factors will influence the negotiation.

2. Diagnose the Fundamental Structure of the Negotiation

Negotiators should make a conscious decision about whether they are facing a fundamentally distributive negotiation, an integrative negotiation, or a blend of the two, and choose their strategies and tactics accordingly. Using strategies and tactics that are mismatched will lead to suboptimal negotiation outcomes. For instance, using overly distributive tactics in a fundamentally integrative situation will almost certainly result in reaching agreements that leave integrative potential untapped because negotiators tend not to share readily the information needed to succeed in integrative negotiations in response to distributive tactics. In these situations, money and opportunity are often left on the table.

Similarly, using integrative tactics in a distributive situation may not lead to optimal outcomes either. For instance, one of the authors of this book was recently shopping for a new car, and the salesman spent a great deal of time and effort asking questions about the author's family and assuring him that he was working hard to get the highest possible value for his trade-in. Unfortunately, requests for clarification about the list price of the car and information about manufacturer incentives described in a recent newspaper advertisement were met with silence or by changing the topic of conversation. This was a purely distributive situation for the author, who was not fooled by the salesman's attempt to bargain "integratively." The author bought a car from a different dealer who was able to provide the requested information in a straightforward manner—and whose price was $1,500 lower than the first dealer for the same car!

Negotiators also need to remember that many negotiations will consist of a blend of integrative and distributive elements and that there will be distributive and integrative phases to these negotiations. It is especially important to be careful when transitioning between these phases within the broader negotiation because missteps in these transitions can confuse the other party and lead to impasse.

Finally, there are also times when accommodation, avoidance, and compromise may be appropriate strategies. Strong negotiators will identify these situations and adopt appropriate strategies and tactics.

3. Identify and Work the BATNA

One of the most important sources of power in a negotiation is the alternatives available to a negotiator if an agreement is not reached. One alternative, the best alternative to a negotiated agreement (BATNA), is especially important because this is the option that likely will be chosen should an agreement not be reached. Negotiators need to be vigilant about their BATNA. They need to know what their BATNA is relative to a possible agreement and consciously work to improve the BATNA so as to improve the deal. Negotiators without a strong BATNA may find it difficult to achieve a good agreement because the other party may try to push them aggressively, and hence they may be forced to accept a settlement that is later seen as unsatisfying.

For instance, purchasers who need to buy items from sole suppliers are acutely aware of how the lack of a positive BATNA makes it difficult to achieve positive negotiation outcomes. Even in this situation, however, negotiators can work to improve their BATNA in the long term. For instance, organizations in a sole supplier relationship have often vertically integrated their production and started to build comparable components inside the company, or they have redesigned their products so they are less vulnerable to the sole supplier. These are clearly long-term options and are not available in the current negotiation. However, it may be possible to refer to these plans when negotiating with a sole supplier in order to remind them that you will not be dependent forever.

Negotiators also need to be aware of the other negotiator's BATNA and to identify how it compares to what you are offering. Negotiators have more power in a negotiation when their potential terms of agreement are significantly better than what the other negotiator can obtain with his or her BATNA. On the other hand, when the difference between your terms and the other negotiator's BATNA is small, then negotiators have less room to maneuver. There are three things negotiators should do with respect to the other negotiator's BATNA: (1) Monitor it carefully in order to understand and retain your competitive advantage over the other negotiator's alternatives; (2) remind the other negotiator of the advantages your offer has relative to her BATNA; and (3) in a subtle way, suggest that the other negotiator's BATNA may not be as strong as he or she thinks it is (this can be done in a positive way by stressing your strengths or in a negative way by highlighting competitors' weaknesses).

4. Be Willing to Walk Away

The goal of most negotiations is achieving a valued outcome, not reaching an agreement per se. Strong negotiators remember this and are willing to walk away from a negotiation when no agreement is better than a poor agreement or when the process is so offensive that the deal isn't worth the work. While this advice sounds easy enough to take in principle, in practice, negotiators can become so focused on reaching an agreement that they lose sight of the real goal, which is to reach a good outcome (and not necessarily an agreement). Negotiators can ensure that they don't take their eye off the goal by making regular comparisons with the targets they set during the planning stage and by comparing their progress during their negotiation against their walkaway and BATNA. While negotiators are often optimistic about goal achievement at the outset, they may need to reevaluate these goals during the negotiation. It is important to continue to compare progress in the current negotiation with the target, walkaway, and BATNA and to be willing to walk away from the current negotiation if their walkaway or BATNA becomes the truly better choice.

Even in the absence of a good BATNA, negotiators should have a clear walkaway point in mind where they will halt negotiations. Sometimes it is helpful if the walkaway is written down or communicated to others so that negotiators can be reminded during difficult negotiations. When in team negotiations, it is important to have a team member monitor the walkaway point and be responsible for stopping the negotiation if it appears that a final settlement is close to this point.

5. Master the Key Paradoxes of Negotiation

Excellent negotiators understand that negotiation embodies a set of paradoxes—seemingly contradictory elements that actually occur together. We will discuss five common paradoxes that negotiators face. The challenge for negotiators in handling these paradoxes is to strive for *balance* in these situations. There is a natural tension between choosing between one or the other alternative in the paradox, but the best way to manage a paradox is to achieve a balance between the opposing forces. Strong negotiators know how to manage this tension.

Claiming Value versus Creating Value

All negotiations have a value *claiming* stage, where parties decide who gets how much of what, but many negotiations also have a value *creation* stage, where parties work together to expand the resources under negotiation. The skills and strategies appropriate to each stage are quite different; in general terms, distributive skills are called for in the value claiming stage and integrative skills are useful in value creation. Typically the value creation stage will precede the value claiming stage, and a challenge for negotiators is to balance the emphasis on the two stages and the transition from creating to claiming value. There is no signpost to mark this transition, however, and negotiators need to manage it tactfully to avoid undermining the open brainstorming and option-inventing relationship that has developed during value creation. One approach to manage this transition is to publicly label it. For instance, negotiators could say something like "It looks like we have a good foundation of ideas and alternatives to work from. How can we move on to decide what is a fair distribution of the expected outcomes?" In addition, research shows that most negotiators are overly biased toward thinking that a negotiation is more about claiming value rather than creating value, so managing this paradox will likely require an overemphasis on discussing the creating value dynamics.

Sticking by Your Principles versus Being Resilient to the Flow

The pace and flow of negotiations can move from an intense haggle over financial issues to an intense debate over deeply held principles about what is right or fair or just. These transitions often create a second paradox for negotiators. On the one hand, effective negotiation requires flexible thinking and an understanding that an assessment of a situation may need to be adjusted as new information comes to light; achieving any deal will probably require both parties to make concessions. On the other hand, core principles are not something to back away from easily in the service of doing a deal. Effective negotiators are thoughtful about the distinction between issues of principle, where firmness is essential, and other issues where compromise and accommodation are the best route to a mutually acceptable outcome. A complex negotiation may well involve both kinds of issues in the same encounter. And it is not enough for the negotiator to know in her own mind that an unwavering commitment on issue X is grounded in some deep personal value or principle; good negotiators know that it is critical to convey that principle to the other party so that he or she will not misread firmness based on principle as hostility or intransigence.

Sticking with the Strategy versus Opportunistic Pursuit of New Options

New information will frequently come to light during a negotiation, and negotiators need to manage the paradox between sticking with their prepared strategy and pursuing a new opportunity that arises during the process. This is a challenging paradox for negotiators to manage because new "opportunities" may in fact be Trojan horses harboring unpleasant surprises. On the other hand, circumstances do change, and legitimate "one-time," seize-the-moment deals do occur. The challenge for negotiators is to distinguish phantom opportunities from real ones; developing the capacity to recognize the distinction is another hallmark of the experienced negotiator.

Strong preparation is critical to being able to manage the "strategy versus opportunism" paradox. Negotiators who have prepared well for the negotiation and who understand the circumstances are well positioned to make this judgment. We also suggest that negotiators pay close attention to their intuition. If a deal doesn't feel right, if it "seems too good to be true," then it probably *is* too good to be true and is not a viable opportunity. If negotiators feel uneasy about the direction the negotiation is taking, then it is best to take a break and consult with others about the circumstances. Often explaining the "opportunity" to a colleague, friend, or constituent will help to distinguish real opportunities from Trojan horses.

We are not suggesting that negotiators become overly cautious, however. There frequently are genuinely good opportunities that occur during a negotiation, legitimately caused by changes in business strategy, market opportunities, excess inventory, or a short-term cash flow challenge. Negotiators who have prepared well will be able to take full advantage of real opportunities when they arise and reduce the risk presented by Trojan horses.

Honest and Open versus Closed and Opaque

Negotiators face the *dilemma of honesty:* How open and honest should I be with the other party? Negotiators who are completely open and tell the other party everything expose themselves to the risk that the other party will take advantage of them. In fact, research suggests that too much knowledge about the other party's needs can actually lead to suboptimal negotiation outcomes. On the other hand, being completely closed will not only have a negative effect on your reputation, but it is also an ineffective negotiation strategy because you don't disclose enough information to create the groundwork for agreement. The challenge of this paradox is deciding how much information to reveal and how much to conceal, both for pragmatic and ethical reasons.

Strong negotiators have considered this paradox and understand their comfort zone, which will likely vary depending on the other party. We suggest that negotiators should remember that negotiation is an ongoing process. As the negotiators make positive progress, they should be building trust and feeling more comfortable about revealing more information to the other party. That said, there is some information that should probably not be revealed (e.g., the bottom line in a distributive negotiation) regardless of how well the negotiation is progressing.

Trust versus Distrust

As a mirror image of the dilemma of honesty, negotiators also face the *dilemma of trust:* how much to trust what the other party tells them. Negotiators who believe everything the other party tells them make themselves vulnerable to being taken advantage of by the other party. On the other hand, negotiators who do not believe anything the other party tells them will have a very difficult time reaching an agreement. As with the dilemma of honesty, we suggest that negotiators remember that negotiation is a process that evolves over time. First, as we noted, trust can be built by being honest and sharing information with the other side, which hopefully will lead to reciprocal trust and credible disclosure by the other side. Moreover, there will be individual differences in trust. Some negotiators will start off by being more trusting, but become less trusting if information comes to light showing that the other party is not trustworthy. Other negotiators will be more comfortable having the other party "earn their trust" and will be more skeptical early in negotiations. There is no right or wrong approach to managing this dilemma. Strong negotiators are aware of this dilemma, however, and constantly monitor how they are managing this challenge.

6. Remember the Intangibles

It is important that negotiators remember the intangible factors while negotiating and remain aware of their potential effects. Intangibles frequently affect negotiation in a negative way, and they often operate out of the negotiator's awareness. Intangibles include winning, avoiding loss, looking tough or strong to others, not looking weak, being fair, and so on. For instance, if the other party is vying with his archrival at the next desk for a promotion, he may be especially difficult when negotiating with you in front of his boss in order to "look tough." It is unlikely that the other negotiator will tell you this is what he is doing, and in fact he may not even be aware of it himself. The best way to identify the existence of intangible factors is to try to "see what is not there." In other words, if your careful preparation and analysis of the situation reveals no tangible explanation for the other negotiator's behavior—adamant advocacy of a certain point, refusal to yield another one, or behavior that just doesn't "make sense"—then it is time to start looking for the intangibles driving his behavior.

For example, several years ago one of the authors of this book was helping a friend buy a new car, and the price offered from the dealer was $2,000 less than any other dealer in town. The only catch was that the car had to be sold that day. On the surface this looked like a trick (see the previous discussion of strategy versus opportunism), but there was no obvious tangible factor that explained this special price. The friend had never purchased from the dealer before, the car was new and fully covered by a good warranty, and the friend had visited several dealers and knew this price was substantially lower than at other dealers. As we continued to discuss the potential deal, the salesman became more and more agitated. Sweat was literally falling from his brow. The friend decided to purchase the car, and as soon as he signed the salesman was simultaneously relieved and excited. He asked for a moment to telephone his wife to share with her some good news. It turned out that the salesman had just won a complicated incentive package offered by the dealer, and the prize was a two-week all expenses paid Caribbean vacation for his family of four. The incentive package required that a total of 10 vehicles be sold in a month, and that one of each category of vehicles at the dealership be sold. The salesman specialized in selling trucks, and the friend was buying a sports car, so you can imagine the pressure the salesman felt when he had given a huge discount to secure the deal and the friend was hesitating.

The intangible factor of trying to win the vacation package explained the salesman's behavior in this example. The buyer learned of this only when the salesman could no longer contain his excitement and shared the good news with his family. Often negotiators do not learn what intangible factors are influencing the other negotiator unless the other chooses to disclose them. Negotiators can "see" their existence, however, by looking for changes in the other negotiator's behavior from one negotiation to another, as well as by gathering information about the other party before negotiation begins. For instance, if you find out that the other party has a new boss that she doesn't like and she is subsequently more difficult to deal with in the negotiation, the intangible of the new boss may be to blame.

There are at least two more ways to discover intangibles that might be affecting the other. One way to surface the other party's intangibles is to ask questions. These questions should try to get the other party to reveal why he or she is sticking so strongly to a given point. It is important to remember that strong emotions and/or values are the root of many intangibles, so surfacing intangibles may result in the discussion of various fears and anxieties. The question-asking process should also be gentle and informal; if the questioning is aggressive, it may only make the other defensive, adding another intangible to the mix and stifling effective negotiations! A second way is to take an observer or listener with you to the negotiation. Listeners may be able to read the other's emotional tone or nonverbal behavior, focus on roadblock issues, or try to take the other's perspective and put themselves in the other's shoes (role reversal). A caucus with this listener may then help refocus the discussion so as to surface the intangibles and develop a new line of questions or offers.

Negotiators also need to remember that intangible factors influence their own behavior (and that it is not uncommon for us to not recognize what is making us angry, defensive, or zealously committed to some idea). Are you being particularly difficult with the other party because he "does not respect you"? Are you "trying to teach a subordinate a lesson"? Or do you want to "win" this negotiation to "look better" than another manager? Without passing judgment on the legitimacy of these goals, we strongly urge negotiators to be aware of the effect of intangible factors on their own aspirations and behavior. Often talking to another person—a sympathetic listener—can help the negotiator figure these out. Strong negotiators are aware of how both tangible and intangible factors influence negotiation, and they weigh both factors when evaluating a negotiation outcome.

7. Actively Manage Coalitions

Coalitions can have very significant effects on the negotiation process and outcome. Negotiators should recognize three types of coalitions and their potential effects: (1) coalitions against you, (2) coalitions that support you, and (3) loose, undefined coalitions that may materialize either for or against you. Strong negotiators assess the presence and strength of coalitions and work to capture the strength of the coalition for their benefit. If this is not possible, negotiators need to work to prevent the other party from capturing a loose coalition for their purposes. When negotiators are part of a coalition, communicating with the coalition is critical to ensuring that the power of the coalition is aligned with their goals. Similarly, negotiators who are agents or representatives of a coalition must take special care to manage this process.

Successfully concluding negotiations when a coalition is aligned against a negotiator is an extremely challenging task. It is important to recognize when coalitions are aligned against you and to work consciously to counter their influence. Frequently this will involve a "divide and conquer" strategy, where negotiators try to increase dissent within the coalition by searching for ways to breed instability within the coalition.

Coalitions occur in many formal negotiations, such as environmental assessments and reaching policy decisions in an industry association. Coalitions may also have a strong influence in less formal settings, such as work teams and families, where different subgroups of people may not have the same interests. Managing coalitions is especially important when negotiators need to rely on other people to implement an agreement. It may be possible for negotiators to forge an agreement when the majority of people influenced are not in favor, but implementing the outcomes of that agreement will be very challenging. Strong negotiators need to monitor and manage coalitions proactively, and while this may take considerable time throughout the negotiation process, it will likely lead to large payoffs at the implementation stage.

8. Savor and Protect Your Reputation

Reputations are like eggs—fragile, important to build, easy to break, and very hard to rebuild once broken. Reputations travel fast, and people often know more about you than you think that they do. Starting negotiations with a positive reputation is essential, and negotiators should be vigilant in protecting their reputations. Negotiators who have a reputation for breaking their word and not negotiating honestly will have a much more difficult time negotiating in the future than those who have a reputation for being honest and fair. Consider the following contrasting reputations: "tough but fair" versus "tough and underhanded." Negotiators prepare differently for others with these contrasting reputations. Negotiating with a tough but fair negotiator means preparing for potentially difficult negotiations while being aware that the other party will push hard for her perspective but will also be rational and fair in her behavior. Negotiating with a tough but underhanded other party means that negotiators will need to verify what the other says, be vigilant for dirty tricks, and be more guarded about sharing information.

How are you perceived as a negotiator? What is your reputation with others at this point? What reputation would you like to have? Think about the negotiators you respect the most and their reputation. What is it about their behavior that you admire? Also think about the negotiators that have a bad reputation. What would it take for them to change your image of them?

Rather than leaving reputation to chance, negotiators can work to shape and enhance their reputation by acting in a consistent and fair manner. Consistency provides the other party with a clear set of predictable expectations about how you will behave, which leads to a stable reputation. Fairness sends the message that you are principled and reasonable. Strong negotiators also periodically seek feedback from others about the way they are perceived and use that information to strengthen their credibility and trustworthiness in the marketplace.

9. Remember That Rationality and Fairness Are Relative

Research on negotiator perception and cognition is quite clear: People tend to view the world in a self-serving manner and define the "rational" thing to do or a "fair" outcome or process in a way that benefits themselves. First, negotiators need to be aware of this tendency in both themselves and the other party. Negotiators can do three things to manage these perceptions proactively. First, they can question their own perceptions of fairness and ground them in clear principles. Second, they can find external benchmarks and examples that suggest fair outcomes. Finally, negotiators can illuminate definitions of fairness held by the other party and engage in a dialogue to reach consensus on which standards of fairness apply in a given situation.

Moreover, negotiators are often in the position to collectively define what is right or fair as a part of the negotiation process. In most situations, neither side holds the keys to what is absolutely right, rational, or fair. Reasonable people can disagree, and often the most important outcome that negotiators can achieve is a common, agreed-upon perspective, definition of the facts, agreement on the right way to see a problem, or standard for determining what is a fair outcome or process. Be prepared to negotiate these principles as strongly as you prepare for a discussion of the issues.

10. Continue to Learn from the Experience

Negotiation epitomizes lifelong learning. The best negotiators continue to learn from experience—they know there are so many different variables and nuances when negotiating that no two negotiations are identical. These differences mean that for negotiators to remain sharp, they need to continue to practice the art and science of negotiation regularly. In addition, the best negotiators take a moment to analyze each negotiation after it has concluded, to review what happened and what they learned. We recommend a three-step process:

- Plan a personal reflection time after each negotiation.
- Periodically "take a lesson" from a trainer or coach.
- Keep a personal diary on strengths and weaknesses and develop a plan to work on weaknesses.

This analysis does not have to be extensive or time-consuming. It should happen after every important negotiation, however, and it should focus on *what* and *why* questions: What happened during this negotiation, why did it occur, and what can I learn? Negotiators who take the time to pause and reflect on their negotiations will find that they continue to refine their skills and that they remain sharp and focused for their future negotiations.

Moreover, even the best athletes—in almost any sport—have one or more coaches on their staff, and stop to "take a lesson." Negotiators have access to seminars to enhance their skills, books to read, and coaches who can help refine their skills. This book should be seen as one step along the way to sharpening and refining your negotiation skills, and we encourage you to continue to learn about the art and science of negotiation. We wish you the best of luck in all of your future negotiations!

Getting Past Yes: Negotiating as if Implementation Mattered

Danny Ertel

The Idea in Brief

Why do so many deals that looked great on paper end up in tatters? Negotiators on both sides probably focused too much on closing the deals and squeezing the best terms out of one another—and not enough on implementation. Bargainers with this **deal-maker mind-set** never ask how—or whether—their agreement will work *in practice*. Once implementation begins, surprises and disappointments crop up—often torpedoing the deal.

How to avoid this scenario? Bargain using an **implementation mind-set.** Define negotiation not as closing the deal but as setting the stage for a successful long-term relationship. Brainstorm and discuss problems you might encounter 12 months down the road. Help the other party think through the agreement's practical implications, so your counterparts won't promise something they can't deliver. Ensure that both sides' stakeholders support the deal. And communicate a consistent message about the deal's terms and spirit to both parties' implementation teams.

Deals negotiated from an implementation mind-set don't "sizzle" like those struck by bargainers practicing brinksmanship. But as companies like HP Services and Procter & Gamble have discovered, a deal's real value comes not from a signature on a document but from the real work performed long after the ink has dried.

The Idea in Practice

To adopt an implementation mind-set, apply these practices *before* inking a deal:

Start with the End in Mind

Imagine that it's a year into implementation of your deal. Ask:

- **Is the deal working?** What metrics are you using to measure its success?

- **What has gone wrong so far?** What have you done to put things back on course? What signals suggest trouble ahead?

- **What capabilities are needed to accomplish the deal's objectives?** What skills do your implementation teams need? Who has tried to block implementation, and how have you responded?

(continued)

Source: " 'Getting Past Yes': Negotiating as if Implementation Mattered," by Danny Ertel, from *Harvard Business Review*, November 1, 2004, pp. 1–10. Harvard Business School Publishing. Used with permission.

By answering these questions now, you avoid being blindsided by surprises during implementation.

Help the Other Party Prepare

Coming to the table prepared to negotiate a workable deal isn't enough—your *counterpart* must also prepare. Before negotiations begin, encourage the other party to consult with their internal stakeholders throughout the bargaining process. Explain who you think the key players are, who should be involved early on, and what key questions about implementation you're asking yourself.

Treat Alignment as a Shared Responsibility

Jointly address how you'll build broad support for the deal's implementation. Identify both parties' stakeholders—those who will make decisions, affect the deal's success through action or inaction, hold critical budgets, or possess crucial information. Map how and when different stakeholders' input will be solicited. Ask who needs to know what in order to support the deal and carry out their part of its implementation.

Send One Message

Ensure that each team responsible for implementing the deal understands what the agreement is meant to accomplish. Communicate *one* message to them about the terms of the deal, the spirit in which it was negotiated, and the trade-offs that were made to craft the final contract.

- **Example**

   During IBM Global Services' "joint handoff meetings," the company's negotiators *and* their counterparts brief implementation teams on what's in the contract, what's different or nonstandard, and what the deal's ultimate intent is.

Manage Negotiation Like a Business Process

Establish a disciplined process for negotiation preparation in your company. Provide training in collaborative negotiation tools and techniques for negotiators *and* implementers. Use post-negotiation reviews to capture learning. And reward individuals for the delivered success of the deals they negotiated—not for how those deals look on paper.

In July 1998, AT&T and BT announced a new 50/50 joint venture that promised to bring global interconnectivity to multinational customers. Concert, as the venture was called, was launched with great fanfare and even greater expectations: The $10 billion start-up would pool assets, talent, and relationships and was expected to log $1 billion in profits from day one. Just three years later, Concert was out of business. It had laid off

2,300 employees, announced $7 billion in charges, and returned its infrastructure assets to the parent companies. To be sure, the weak market played a role in Concert's demise, but the way the deal was put together certainly hammered a few nails into the coffin.

For example, AT&T's deal makers scored what they probably considered a valuable win when they negotiated a way for AT&T Solutions to retain key multinational customers for itself. As a result, AT&T and BT ended up in direct competition for business—exactly what the Concert venture was supposed to help prevent. For its part, BT seemingly outnegotiated AT&T by refusing to contribute to AT&T's purchase of the IBM Global Network. That move saved BT money, but it muddied Concert's strategy, leaving the start-up to contend with overlapping products. In 2000, Concert announced a complex new arrangement that was supposed to clarify its strategy, but many questions about account ownership, revenue recognition, and competing offerings went unanswered. Ultimately, the two parent companies pulled the plug on the venture.[1]

Concert is hardly the only alliance that began with a signed contract and a champagne toast but ended in bitter disappointment. Examples abound of deals that look terrific on paper but never materialize into effective, value-creating endeavors. And it's not just alliances that can go bad during implementation. Misfortune can befall a whole range of agreements that involve two or more parties—mergers, acquisitions, outsourcing contracts, even internal projects that require the cooperation of more than one department. Although the problem often masquerades as one of execution, its roots are anchored in the deal's inception, when negotiators act as if their main objective were to sign the deal. To be successful, negotiators must recognize that signing a contract is just the beginning of the process of creating value.

During the past 20 years, I've analyzed or assisted in hundreds of complex negotiations, both through my research at the Harvard Negotiation Project and through my consulting practice. And I've seen countless deals that were signed with optimism fall apart during implementation, despite the care and creativity with which their terms were crafted. The crux of the problem is that the very person everyone thinks is central to the deal—the negotiator—is often the one who undermines the partnership's ability to succeed. The real challenge lies not in hammering out little victories on the way to signing on the dotted line but in designing a deal that works in practice.

The Danger of Deal Makers

It's easy to see where the deal maker mind-set comes from. The media glorifies big-name deal makers like Donald Trump, Michael Ovitz, and Bruce Wasserstein. Books like *You Can Negotiate Anything, Trump: The Art of the Deal*, and even my own partners' *Getting to Yes* all position the end of the negotiation as the destination. And most companies evaluate and compensate negotiators based on the size of the deals they're signing.

But what kind of behavior does this approach create? People who view the contract as the conclusion and see themselves as solely responsible for getting there behave very differently from those who see the agreement as just the beginning and believe their role is to ensure that the parties involved actually realize the value they are trying to create. These two camps have conflicting opinions about the use of surprise and the sharing of information. They also differ in how much attention they pay to whether the parties' commitments are realistic, whether their stakeholders are sufficiently aligned, and whether those who must implement the deal can establish a suitable working relationship with one another. (For a comparison of how different mind-sets affect negotiation behaviors, see the figure 1 "Deal-Minded Negotiators versus Implementation-Minded Negotiators.")

This isn't to say deal makers are sleazy, dishonest, or unethical. Being a deal maker means being a good closer. The deal maker mind-set is the ideal approach in certain circumstances. For example, when negotiating the sale of an asset in which title will simply be transferred and the parties will have little or no need to work together, getting the signatures on the page really does define success.

But frequently a signed contract represents a commitment to work together to create value. When that's the case, the manner in which the parties "get to yes" matters a great deal. Unfortunately, many organizations structure their negotiation teams and manage the flow of information in ways that actually hurt a deal's chances of being implemented well.

An organization that embraces the deal maker approach, for instance, tends to structure its business development teams in a way that drives an ever growing stream of new deals. These dedicated teams, responsible for keeping negotiations on track and getting deals done, build tactical expertise, acquire knowledge of useful contract terms, and go on to sign more deals. But they also become detached from implementation and are likely to focus more on the agreement than on its business impact. Just think about the language deal-making teams use ("closing" a deal, putting a deal "to bed") and how their performance is measured and rewarded (in terms of the number and size of deals closed and the time required to close them). These teams want to sign a piece of paper and book the expected value; they couldn't care less about launching a relationship.

The much talked about Business Affairs engine at AOL under David Colburn is one extreme example. The group became so focused on doing deals—the larger and more lopsided the better—that it lost sight of the need to have its business partners actually remain in business or to have its deals produce more than paper value. In 2002, following internal investigations and probes by the SEC and the Department of Justice, AOL Time Warner concluded it needed to restate financial results to account for the real value (or lack thereof) created by some of those deals.[2]

The deal maker mentality also fosters the take-no-prisoners attitude common in procurement organizations. The aim: Squeeze your counterpart for the best possible deal you can get. Instead of focusing on deal volume, as business development engines do, these groups concentrate on how many concessions they can get. The desire to win outweighs the costs of signing a deal that cannot work in practice because the supplier will never be able to make enough money.

Think about how companies handle negotiations with outsourcing providers. Few organizations contract out enough of their work to have as much expertise as the providers themselves in negotiating deal structures, terms and conditions, metrics, pricing, and the like, so they frequently engage a third-party adviser to help level the playing field as they select an outsourcer and hammer out a contract. Some advisers actually trumpet their role in commoditizing the providers' solutions so they can create "apples to apples" comparison charts, engender competitive bidding, and drive down prices. To maximize competitive

Deal–Minded Negotiators   *versus*   Implementation-Minded Negotiators

Negotiation Tactics

Deal–Minded Negotiators		Surprise	Implementation-Minded Negotiators	
Assumption	**Behaviors**		**Assumption**	**Behaviors**
"Surprising them helps me. They may commit to something they might not have otherwise, and we'll get a better deal."	Introduce new actors or information at strategic points in negotiation. Raise new issues at the end.	= **Surprise** =	"Surprising them puts us at risk. They may commit to something they cannot deliver or will regret."	Propose agendas in advance so both parties can prepare. Suggest questions to be discussed and provide relevant data. Raise issues early.
Assumption	**Behaviors**		**Assumption**	**Behaviors**
"It's not my role to equip them with relevant information or to correct their misperceptions."	Withhold information. Fail to correct mistaken impressions.	= **Information Sharing** =	"I don't want them entering this deal feeling duped, I want their goodwill during implementation, not their grudging compliance."	Create a joint fact-gathering group. Commission third-party research and analysis. Question everyone's assumptions openly.
Assumption	**Behaviors**		**Assumption**	**Behaviors**
"My job is to get the deal closed. It's worth putting a little pressure on them now and coping with their unhappiness later."	Create artificial deadlines. Threaten escalation. Make "this day only" offers.	= **Closing techniques** =	"My job is to create value by crafting a workable agreement. Investing a little extra time in making sure both sides are aligned is worth the effort."	Define interests that need to be considered for the deal to be successful. Define joint communication strategy.
Assumption	**Behaviors**		**Assumption**	**Behaviors**
"As long as they commit, that's all that matters. Afterward, it's their problem if they don't deliver."	Focus on documenting commitments rather than on testing the practicality of those.commitments. Rely on penalty clauses for protection.	= **Realistic commitments** =	"If they fail to deliver, we don't get the value we expect."	Ask tough questions about both parties' ability to deliver. Make implementability a shared concern. Establish early warning systems and contingency plans.
Assumption	**Behaviors**		**Assumption**	**Behaviors**
"The fewer people involved in making this decision, the better and faster this will go."	Limit participation in discussions to decision makers. Keep outsiders in the dark until it is too late for them to derail things.	= **Decision making and stakeholders** =	"If we both fail to involve key stakeholders sufficiently and early enough, whatever time we save now will be lost during implementation."	Repeatedly ask about stakeholders. Whose approval is needed? Whose cooperation is required? Who might interfere with implementation?

tension, they exert tight control, blocking virtually all communications between would-be customers and service providers. That means the outsourcers have almost no opportunity to design solutions tailored to the customer's unique business drivers.

The results are fairly predictable. The deal structure that both customer and provider teams are left to implement is the one that was easiest to compare with other bids, not the one that would have created the most value. Worse yet, when the negotiators on each side exit the process, the people responsible for making the deal work are virtual strangers and lack a nuanced understanding of why issues were handled the way they were. Furthermore, neither side has earned the trust of its partner during negotiations. The hard feelings created by the hired guns can linger for years.

The fact is, organizations that depend on negotiations for growth can't afford to abdicate management responsibility for the process. It would be foolhardy to leave negotiations entirely up to the individual wits and skills of those sitting at the table on any given day. That's why some corporations have taken steps to make negotiation an organizational competence. They have made the process more structured by, for instance, applying Six Sigma discipline or a community of practice principles to improve outcomes and learn from past experiences.

Sarbanes-Oxley and an emphasis on greater management accountability will only reinforce this trend. As more companies (and their auditors) recognize the need to move to a controls-based approach for their deal-making processes—be they in sales, sourcing, or business development—they will need to implement metrics, tools, and process disciplines that preserve creativity and let managers truly manage negotiators. How they do so, and how they define the role of the negotiator, will determine whether deals end up creating or destroying value.

Negotiating for Implementation

Making the leap to an implementation mindset requires five shifts.

1. Start with the End in Mind

For the involved parties to reap the benefits outlined in the agreement, goodwill and collaboration are needed during implementation. That's why negotiation teams should carry out a simple "benefit of hindsight" exercise as part of their preparation.

Imagine that it is 12 months into the deal, and ask yourself:

Is the deal working? What metrics are we using? If quantitative metrics are too hard to define, what other indications of success can we use?

What has gone wrong so far? What have we done to put things back on course? What were some early warning signals that the deal may not meet its objectives?

What capabilities are necessary to accomplish our objectives? What processes and tools must be in place? What skills must the implementation teams have? What attitudes or assumptions are required of those who must implement the deal? Who has tried to block implementation, and how have we responded?

If negotiators are required to answer those kinds of questions before the deal is finalized, they cannot help but behave differently. For example, if the negotiators of the Concert joint venture had followed that line of questioning before closing the deal, they might have asked themselves, "What good is winning the right to keep customers out of the deal if doing so leads to competition between the alliance's parents? And if we have to take that risk, can we put in mechanisms now to help mitigate it?" Raising those tough questions probably wouldn't have made a negotiator popular, but it might have led to different terms in the deal and certainly to different processes and metrics in the implementation plan.

Most organizations with experience in negotiating complex deals know that some terms have a tendency to come back and bite them during implementation. For example, in 50/50 ventures, the partner with greater leverage often secures the right to break ties if the new venture's steering committee should ever come to an impasse on an issue. In practice, though, that means executives from the dominant party who go into negotiations to resolve such impasses don't really have to engage with the other side. At the end of the day, they know they can simply impose their decision. But when that happens, the relationship is frequently broken beyond repair.

Tom Finn, vice president of strategic planning and alliances at Procter & Gamble Pharmaceuticals, has made it his mission to incorporate tough lessons like that into the negotiation process itself. Although Finn's alliance management responsibilities technically don't start until after a deal has been negotiated by the P&G Pharmaceuticals business development organization, Finn jumps into the negotiation process to ensure negotiators do not bargain for terms that will cause trouble down the road. "It's not just a matter of a win-win philosophy," he says. "It's about incorporating our alliance managers' hard-won experience with terms that cause implementation problems and not letting those terms into our deals."

Finn and his team avoid things like step-down royalties and unequal profit splits with 50/50 expense sharing, to name just a few. "It's important that the partners be provided [with] incentives to do the right thing," Finn says. "When those incentives shift, you tend to end up [with] difficulties." Step-down royalties, for instance, are a common structure in the industry. They're predicated on the assumption that a brand is made or lost in the first three years, so that thereafter, payments to the originator should go down. But P&G Pharmaceuticals believes it is important to provide incentives to the partner to continue to work hard over time. As for concerns about overpaying for the licensed compound in the latter years of the contract, Finn asserts that "leaving some money on the table is OK if you realize that the most expensive deal is one that fails."

2. Help Them Prepare, Too

If implementation is the name of the game, then coming to the table well prepared is necessary—but not sufficient. Your counterpart must also be prepared to negotiate a workable deal. Some negotiators believe they can gain advantage by surprising the other side. But surprise confers advantage only because the counterpart has failed to think through all the implications of a proposal and might mistakenly commit to something it wouldn't have if it had been better prepared. While that kind of an advantage might pay off in a simple buy-sell transaction, it fails miserably—for both sides—in any situation that requires a long-term working relationship.

That's why it's in your best interest to engage with your counterpart before negotiations start. Encourage the other party to do its homework and consult with its internal stakeholders before and throughout the negotiation process. Let the team know who you think the key players are, who should be involved early on, how you hope to build implementation planning into the negotiation process, and what key questions you are asking yourself.

Take the example of Equitas, a major reinsurer in the London market. When preparing for commutations negotiations—whereby two reinsurers settle their mutual book of business—the company sends its counterpart a thorough kickoff package, which is used as the agenda for the negotiation launch meeting. This "commutations action pack" describes how the reinsurer's own commutations department is organized, what its preferred approach to a commutations negotiation is, and what stages it follows. It also includes a suggested approach to policy reconciliation and due diligence and explains what data the reinsurer has available—even acknowledging its imperfections and gaps. The package describes critical issues for the reinsurer and provides sample agreements and memorandums for various stages of the process.

The kickoff meeting thus offers a structured environment in which the parties can educate each other on their decision-making processes and their expectations for the deal. The language of the commutations action pack and the collaborative spirit of the kickoff meeting are designed to help the parties get to know each other and settle on a way of working together before they start making the difficult trade-offs that will be required of them. By establishing an agreed-upon process for how and when to communicate with brokers about the deal, the two sides are better able to manage the tension between the need to include stakeholders who are critical to implementation and the need to maintain confidentiality before the deal is signed.

Aventis Pharma is another example of how measured disclosure of background and other information can pave the way to smoother negotiations and stronger implementation. Like many of its peers, the British pharmaceutical giant wants potential biotech partners to see it as a partner of choice and value a relationship with the company for more than the size of the royalty check involved. To that end, Aventis has developed and piloted a "negotiation launch" process, which it describes as a meeting during which parties about to enter into formal negotiations plan together for those negotiations. Such collaboration allows both sides to identify potential issues and set up an agreed upon process and time line. The company asserts that while "formally launching negotiations with a counterpart may seem unorthodox to some," the entire negotiation process runs more efficiently and effectively when partners "take the time to discuss how they will negotiate before beginning."

3. Treat Alignment as a Shared Responsibility

If their interests are not aligned, and they cannot deliver fully, that's not just their problem—it's your problem, too.

Unfortunately, deal makers often rely on secrecy to achieve their goals (after all, a stakeholder who doesn't know about a deal can't object). But leaving internal stakeholders in the dark about a potential deal can have negative consequences. Individuals and departments that will be directly affected don't have a chance to weigh in with suggestions to mitigate risks or improve the outcome. And people with relevant information about the deal don't share it, because they have no idea it's needed. Instead, the typical reaction managers have when confronted late in the game with news of a deal that will affect their department is "Not with my FTEs, you don't."

Turning a blind eye to likely alignment problems on the other side of the table is one of the leading reasons alliances break down and one of the major sources of conflict in outsourcing deals. Many companies, for instance, have outsourced some of their human resource or finance and accounting processes. Service providers, for their part, often move labor-intensive processes to Web-based self-service systems to gain process efficiencies. If users find the new self-service system frustrating or intimidating, though, they make repeated (and expensive) calls to service centers or fax in handwritten forms. As a result, processing costs jump from pennies per transaction to tens of dollars per transaction.

But during the initial negotiation, buyers routinely fail to disclose just how undisciplined their processes are and how resistant to change their cultures might be. After all, they think, those problems will be the provider's headache once the deal is signed. Meanwhile, to make requested price concessions, providers often drop line items from their proposals intended to educate employees and support the new process. In exchange for such concessions, with a wink and a nod, negotiators assure the provider that the buyers will dedicate internal resources to change-management and communication efforts. No one asks whether business unit managers support the deal or whether function leaders are prepared to make the transition from managing the actual work to managing the relationship with an external provider. Everyone simply agrees, the deal is signed, and the frustration begins.

As managers and employees work around the new self-service system, the provider's costs increase, the service levels fall (because the provider was not staffed for the high level of calls and faxes), and customer satisfaction plummets. Finger-pointing ensues, which must then be addressed through expensive additions to the contract, costly modifications to processes and technology, and additional burdens on a communication and change effort already laden with baggage from the initial failure.

Building alignment is among negotiators' least favorite activities. The deal makers often feel as if they are wasting precious time "negotiating internally" instead of working their magic on the other side. But without acceptance of the deal by those who are essential to its implementation (or who can place obstacles in the way), proceeding with the deal is even more wasteful. Alignment is a classic "pay me now or pay me later" problem. To understand whether the deal will work in practice, the negotiation process must encompass not only subject matter experts or those with bargaining authority but also those who will actually have to take critical actions or refrain from pursuing conflicting avenues later.

Because significant deals often require both parties to preserve some degree of confidentiality, the matter of involving the right stakeholders at the right time is more effectively addressed jointly than unilaterally. With an understanding of who the different stakeholders are—including those who have necessary information, those who hold critical budgets, those who manage important third-party relationships, and so on—a joint communications subteam can then map how, when, and with whom different inputs will be solicited and different categories of information might be shared. For example, some stakeholders may need to know that the negotiations are taking place but not the identity of the counterpart. Others may need only to be aware that the organization is seeking to form a partnership so they can prepare for the potential effects of an eventual deal. And while some must remain in the dark, suitable proxies should be identified to ensure that their perspectives (and the roles they will play during implementation) are considered at the table.

4. Send One Message

Complex deals require the participation of many people during implementation, so once the agreement is in place, it's essential that the team that created it get everyone up to speed on the terms of the deal, on the mind-set under which it was negotiated, and on the trade-offs that were made in crafting the final contract. When each implementation team is given the contract in a vacuum and then is left to interpret it separately, each develops a different picture of what the deal is meant to accomplish, of the negotiators' intentions, and of what wasn't actually written in the document but each had imagined would be true in practice.

"If your objective is to have a deal you can implement, then you want the actual people who will be there, after the negotiators move on, up front and listening to the dialogue and the give-and-take during the negotiation so they understand how you got to the agreed solution," says Steve Fenn, vice president for retail industry and former VP for global business development at IBM Global Services. "But we can't always have the delivery executive at the table, and our customer doesn't always know who from their side is going to be around to lead the relationship." To address this challenge, Fenn uses joint hand-off meetings, at which he and his counterpart brief both sides of the delivery equation. "We tell them what's in the contract, what is different or nonstandard, what the schedules cover. But more important, we clarify the intent of the deal: Here's what we had difficulty with, and here's what we ended up with and why. We don't try to reinterpret the language of the contract but [we do try] to discuss openly the spirit of the contract." These meetings are usually attended by the individual who developed the statement of work, the person who priced the deal, the contracts and negotiation lead, and occasionally legal counsel. This team briefs the project executive in charge of the implementation effort and the executive's direct reports. Participation on the customer side varies, because the early days in an outsourcing relationship are often hectic and full of turnover. But Fenn works with the project executive and the sales team to identify the key customer representatives who should be invited to the hand-off briefing.

Negotiators who know they have to brief the implementation team with their counterparts after the deal is signed will approach the entire negotiation differently. They'll start asking the sort of tough questions at the negotiating table that they imagine they'll have to field during the postdeal briefings. And as they think about how they will explain the deal to the delivery team, they will begin to marshal defensible precedents, norms, industry practices, and objective criteria. Such standards of legitimacy strengthen the relationship because they emphasize persuasion rather than coercion. Ultimately, this practice makes a deal more viable because attention shifts from the individual negotiators and their personalities toward the merits of the arrangement.

5. Manage Negotiation Like a Business Process

Negotiating as if implementation mattered isn't a simple task. You must worry about the costs and challenges of execution rather than just getting the other side to say yes. You must carry out all the internal consultations necessary to build alignment. And you must make sure your counterparts are as prepared as you are. Each of these actions can feel like a big time sink. Deal makers don't want to spend time negotiating with their own people to build alignment or risk having their counterparts pull out once they know all the details. If a company wants its negotiators to sign deals that create real value, though, it has to weed out that deal maker mentality from its ranks. Fortunately, it can be done with simple processes and controls. (For an example of how HP Services structures its negotiation process, see the sidebar "Negotiating Credibility.")

More and more outsourcing and procurement firms are adopting a disciplined negotiation preparation process. Some even require a manager to review the output of that process before authorizing the negotiator to proceed with the deal. KLA-Tencor, a semiconductor production equipment maker, uses the electronic tools available through its supplier-management Web site for this purpose, for example. Its managers can capture valuable information about negotiators' practices, including the issues they are coming up against, the options they are proposing, the standards of legitimacy they are relying on, and the walkaway alternatives they are considering. Coupled with simple postnegotiation reviews, this information can yield powerful organizational insights.

Preparing for successful implementation is hard work, and it has a lot less sizzle than the brinksmanship characteristic of the negotiation process itself. To overcome the natural tendency to ignore feasibility questions, it's important for management to send a clear message about the value of postdeal implementation. It must reward individuals, at least in part, based on the delivered success of the deals they negotiate, not on how those deals look on paper. This practice is fairly standard among outsourcing service providers; it's one that should be adopted more broadly.

Negotiating Credibility

HP Services is growing in a highly competitive market, and its success is partly due to its approach to negotiating large outsourcing transactions. In a maturing market, where top tier providers can demonstrate comparable capabilities and where price variations inevitably diminish after companies bid against one another time and time again, a provider's ability to manage a relationship and build trust are key differentiators. The negotiation and the set of interactions leading up to it give the customer a first taste of what it will be like to solve problems with the provider during the life of the contract "Decisions made by clients regarding selection have as much to do with the company they want to do business with as with price, capability, and

(continued)

reliability," acknowledges Steve Huhn, HP Services' vice president of strategic outsourcing. "Negotiating these kinds of deals requires being honest, open, and credible. Integrity is critical to our credibility."

Huhn's team of negotiators uses a well-structured process designed to make sure
that the philosophy of integrity is pervasive throughout the negotiation and not just a
function of who happens to be at the table on any given day. It begins with the formation of a negotiation team. Because transition in complex outsourcing transactions
represents a period of high vulnerability, it is important to involve implementation
staff early on; that way, any commitments made can be validated by those who will
be responsible for keeping them. A typical negotiation team consists of a business
leader, or pursuit lead, who is usually responsible for developing the business and
structuring the transaction; a contract specialist, who brings experience with outsourcing contract terms and conditions; and the proposed client manager, who will
be responsible for delivery.

Negotiation leads work with a high degree of autonomy. Huhn believes that a
negotiator without authority is little more than a messenger, and messengers are unlikely to earn trust or build working relationships with counterparts. At HP, negotiators earn that autonomy by preparing extensively with templates and by reviewing
key deal parameters with management. A negotiator's mandate does not just cover
price: It also encompasses margins, cash flow, and ROI at different times in the life
of the contract; the treatment of transferred employees; the ways various kinds of
risk will be allocated; and how the relationship will be governed. All these interests
must be addressed—both in preparation and at the negotiation table.

HP's outsourcing negotiators are subject to informal reviews with full-time deal
coaches as well as formal milestone reviews. The reviews, which are designed to get
key stakeholders committed to implementation, happen before the formal proposal is
delivered and before the deal is signed.

The pursuit team leaders aren't finished once the agreement is signed. In fact,
they retain responsibility during the transition phase and are considered "liable" for
the deal's performance during the next 18 to 24 months. That means negotiators can't
simply jump to the next alluring deal. On the contrary, they have a vested interest in
making sure the closed deal actually meets its targets.

Improving the implementability of deals is not just about layering controls or capturing data. After all, a manager's strength has much to do with the skills she chooses to
build and reward and the example she sets with her own questions and actions. In the
health care arena, where payer-provider contentions are legion, forward-thinking payers
and innovative providers are among those trying to change the dynamics of deals and
develop agreements that work better. Blue Cross and Blue Shield of Florida, for example, has been working to institutionalize an approach to payer-provider negotiations that
strengthens the working relationship and supports implementation. Training in collaborative negotiation tools and techniques has been rolled down from the senior executives
to the negotiators to the support and analysis teams. Even more important, those who

manage relationships with providers and are responsible for implementing the agreements are given the same training and tools. In other words, the entire process of putting the deal together, making it work, and feeding the lessons learned through implementation back into the negotiation process has been tightly integrated.

. . .

Most competitive runners will tell you that if you train to get to the finish line, you will lose the race. To win, you have to envision your goal as just beyond the finish line so you will blow right past it at full speed. The same is true for a negotiator. If signing the document is your ultimate goal, you will fall short of a winning deal.

The product of a negotiation isn't a document; it's the value produced once the parties have done what they agreed to do. Negotiators who understand that prepare differently than deal makers do. They don't ask, "What might they be willing to accept?" but rather, "How do we create value together?" They also negotiate differently, recognizing that value comes not from a signature but from real work performed long after the ink has dried.

Endnotes

1. For more perspectives on Concert's demise, see Margie Semilof's 2001 article "Concert Plays Its Last Note" on *InformationWeek.com;* Brian Washburn's 2000 article "Disconcerted" on *CallCenterMagazine.com;* and Charles Hodson's 2001 article "Concert: What Went Wrong?" on CNN.com.

2. See Alec Klein, "Lord of the Flies," *Washington Post*, June 15, 2003, and Gary Rivlin, "AOL's Rough Riders," *Industry Standard*, October 30, 2000, for more information on the AOL Business Affairs department's practices.

Reading 7.3

Seven Strategies for Negotiating Success
Max Messmer

Executive Summary

- **Enter negotiations with a salary range in mind**, but also understand which benefits and other elements of compensation you must have and which you are willing to give up.

- **Focus on the employer's needs** and why you are uniquely qualified to meet them. Do your research and ask your networking contacts to determine a fair wage and list of benefits.

- **Consider the leverage you might be entitled to** because of your special qualifications or the pressing needs of your employer or the marketplace.

- **If at all possible, make the employer come up with a number first.** If you absolutely must name a price yourself, remember that the employer is psychologically committed to hiring you at this point and give a range instead of a flat figure.

- **Consider the intangibles** as well as the money.

- **Be sure you understand any bonus or incentive payments;** ask for specifics on how bonuses are determined.

Receiving a job offer may seem like the pinnacle of your employment search—and, in many ways, it is. Before you start celebrating, however, you need to achieve the peace of mind that comes with knowing the offer meets your needs. This usually involves a negotiation process.

Discussing salary and benefits is not always an easy conversation, even for accounting professionals who are accustomed to discussing numbers. You must strike the right balance between being appreciative of an offer and making sure it fairly represents your worth in the marketplace and helps you realize the primary goals of your job search. This article will offer seven tips to ensure the best possible outcome for job applicants, plus some food for thought for the partners and human-resources professionals sitting across the negotiating table from them.

1. Know Your Priorities

Before you can negotiate with confidence, you need a firm grasp of what is most important to you. If you have researched the position, then you will have an idea of competitive salaries for the role. You should enter negotiations with a range in mind.

Source: "Seven Strategies for Negotiating Success," by Max Messmer, from *Journal of Accountancy* 202, no. 2, August 2006, pp. 34–37. Used with permission.

FIGURE 1 | What Benefits Do Employees Value Most?

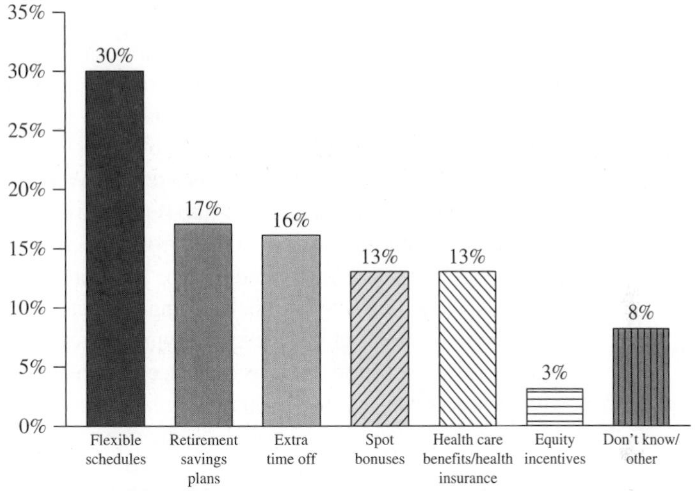

Source: Robert Half International survey of 1,400 chief financial officers.

Aside from salary though, many other elements of the total package can be negotiated to make the offer more attractive. These include bonuses (signing, annual, performance-based), profit-sharing and equity incentives, paid time off, tuition reimbursement, relocation assistance, job title, support of continuing education, flexible scheduling options, how the firm handles personal and family emergencies, and severance provisions.

Decide which elements are most important to you. It can help to sort them into essential and nonessential categories and rank them in priority order. As long as you are not making unreasonable requests, avoid worrying too much about whether the hiring manager will be receptive to your proposals. You will not know unless you ask, and employers often are willing to approve various smaller requests in exchange for reaching a compromise on a more significant issue, such as salary.

Interviewing Insights

- Arrive on time or a few minutes early.
- Project energy and enthusiasm. Smile and shake hands firmly.
- Wait to be offered a chair.
- At the beginning of the interview, ask the hiring manager to describe the job. Then tailor your responses accordingly.
- Sit upright, look the interviewer in the eye, and respond succinctly and articulately.

2. Address the Employer's Needs, Not Just Your Own, as a Basis for Determining Compensation

In negotiations, keep the focus on the employer's needs and how you are uniquely qualified to address them. This may require you to demonstrate that the market value for someone with your experience and the ability to truly satisfy the demands of the position is higher than what the company is offering.

Research financial publications, career-related Web sites, information from professional associations and resources such as the Bureau of Labor Statistics' *Occupational Outlook Handbook* and the annual *Salary Guide* from Robert Half International to establish pay ranges for a variety of accounting and finance positions in different geographic locations. These sources, combined with your networking contacts, can help you determine which incentives or benefits others at your level are typically receiving. You also may find specific examples that will be useful, such as evidence of recent accounting hires at a competing firm who have received signing bonuses or guaranteed salary increases over a certain period. The more facts you have on your side, the more reasonable your requests will seem.

3. Know How Much Leverage You Have

In addition to your research, there are other ways to gauge how much bargaining power you have. For example, if you are a CPA with compliance experience who constantly receives calls from recruiters trying to entice you to consider other opportunities, you are in a strong position to negotiate the terms you want. You should, of course, be completely truthful about this and all other information you provide.

Consider, too, any pressures the prospective employer may be under. If you are interviewing for an assistant controller position at the midpoint of the fourth quarter, you can probably assume your interviewer is eager to hire someone. Even if you have significant leverage, though, be careful not to come across as unreasonable or overly confident. Remember that you are supposed to be negotiating, not making demands. Assuming an inflexible stance likely will backfire and knock you out of the running.

4. Persuade the Interviewer to Name the First Figure, if Possible

Negotiation experts generally agree that being asked to name a specific dollar figure—whether it is what you currently are making or what you are seeking to make—is always tricky. Although you want to avoid playing games with a prospective employer, you also don't want to disqualify yourself or sell yourself short by naming a figure that seems too high or too low.

The best way around this situation is to try to get the interviewer to name the initial figure, such as the budgeted salary range for the position. If you must cite a number first, you might give a range that reflects your current and targeted salary or say something like, "I would expect a position with these responsibilities to be worth approximately $75,000 to $85,000." This approach gives the hiring manager something to react to and builds in room for negotiating. One exception to this guiding principle applies when you're working with recruiters: They generally need to know your salary level to gauge whether it's in line with a potential opportunity.

Keep in mind that at this stage of the negotiation process, the prospective employer already is psychologically committed to hiring you. It is now just a matter of settling on terms, and both parties usually are willing to make adjustments to strike a deal.

Case Study—Give a Little, Take a Little

Sue Blair wanted to leave the pressures of her divisional controller position at a large public company. Hoping to find a role that would allow her to perform a broader range of financial tasks and to become more involved in making day-to-day business decisions, she applied for a position as chief financial officer at a small private manufacturing company.

The hiring manager and Sue talked extensively about the nature of the job and Sue's abilities and experience. By the time they came around to discussing salary, it was clear that the manager wanted to hire Sue, and Sue wanted the job.

When Sue revealed her current total compensation, it was higher than the predecessor's salary. In addition, by changing jobs, Sue would have to give up a 401(k) plan with an employer match.

The manufacturing firm offered her additional salary to offset the loss of retirement benefits and to make the offer more financially appealing than Sue's current position. Upon accepting the offer, Sue also was encouraged to use her new role to explore the possibility of setting up a retirement plan for the company.

Case Study—More Than Just Money

For one accounting professional, the opportunity to make a lifestyle change outweighed a higher salary. Kevin Clark had become burned out on his job as a consultant at a large public accounting firm. Ever since the birth of his first child, the 12-hour days and frequent travel that accompanied the position had become especially burdensome. Hoping to scale back his work hours and travel requirements, Kevin pursued a corporate accounting position at a bank holding company.

The hiring manager pressed Kevin to reveal what he was currently making. Saying that he did not think his current job made for a good comparison with the one for which he was interviewing, he asked instead about the salary range for the position. The hiring manager eventually gave him a range, and Kevin negotiated a salary at the top end.

As negotiations were concluding, Kevin tipped his hand about his current salary. The hiring manager was surprised to discover that he was taking a pay cut to accept the position. Asked why, he reminded her of certain aspects of the position that she had used as selling points: the 40 to 45 hour week, competitive benefits, lack of travel and a generous number of paid days off. To Kevin, what he gave up in salary was insignificant compared to what he gained in terms of lifestyle.

5. Consider More Than Just Money

The decision about whether to accept an offer rarely boils down to just a dollar figure. Other advantages, such as a dynamic corporate culture, professional advancement and development opportunities, the option to occasionally telecommute, or a perk such as an early office closure on Fridays during the summer, may ultimately be more important than an extra $5,000 in salary. Also inquire about work/life benefits offered by the organization. Employers recognize that professionals are striving to gain greater control over their time and better balance their personal and professional priorities. As a result, flexible scheduling options are growing in popularity. In fact, a survey of chief financial officers commissioned by our company found that flexible schedules are the benefit workers value most.

6. Understand the Variable Pay Components

Before accepting an offer, make sure you have a solid grasp of the value of any bonus or incentive-pay aspects of your employment package. This is especially important if you are counting on variable pay making up a sizable portion of your compensation.

Ask about the company's history of awarding annual bonuses or long-term performance incentives and for specific guidelines about what you can expect in the future. For instance, inquire whether bonuses are awarded solely at the discretion of management or are triggered by the firm's ability to hit certain targets.

Write a Résumé That Resonates

- Don't just list the requirements of each job. Instead, describe what you achieved. Use action verbs, like "managed" or "developed." Note how your efforts improved the bottom line.
- Use a professional-looking typeface, white or ivory paper and black ink. Proofread carefully.
- List any professional designations or certifications you have obtained or are working toward, such as CPA or CITP, as well as any involvement with professional, trade, and civic associations.

7. Remain Professional

Although you owe it to yourself to push for the best possible employment package, there is no reason for the negotiations to become contentious. After all, the prospective employer thinks well enough of you to offer you a job. Be willing to meet an accommodating hiring manager halfway if at all possible. Keep in mind that establishing a good relationship is critical not only to receiving the best deal but also to laying the groundwork for a positive start with your new company.

When it comes to negotiating salary, there is no substitute for being prepared. By coming to the bargaining table with a clear sense of your goals for salary and other elements of the employment package, you should be able to reach a deal that is satisfactory for both you and your prospective employer.

Final Considerations Before Saying Yes

Compensation is an important factor in the decision of whether to accept a position—but it's not the only factor. See if you agree with the statements below as you evaluate offers.

- The salary and benefits package is competitive and commensurate with my experience level and the responsibilities of the position.

- This opportunity will allow me to grow professionally and bring me closer to my ultimate career objectives.

- The incentives offered are motivational yet attainable.

- I am likely to find the challenges of the position stimulating.

- The hours required, and the travel and commuting requirements, are acceptable and in line with my goals for work/life balance.

- The company culture is a match with my values and personality.

- The work environment seems positive and professional.

- My prospective colleagues appear to be people with whom I would enjoy working.

Reading 7.4

Six Habits of Merely Effective Negotiators

James K. Sebenius

Global deal makers did a staggering $3.3 trillion worth of M&A transactions in 1999—and that's only a fraction of the capital that passed through negotiators' hands that year. Behind the deal-driven headlines, executives endlessly negotiate with customers and suppliers, with large shareholders and creditors, with prospective joint venture and alliance partners, with people inside their companies and across national borders. Indeed, wherever parties with different interests and perceptions depend on each other for results, negotiation matters. Little wonder that Bob Davis, vice chairman of Terra Lycos, has said that companies "have to make deal making a core competency."

Luckily, whether from schoolbooks or the school of hard knocks, most executives know the basics of negotiation; some are spectacularly adept. Yet high stakes and intense pressure can result in costly mistakes. Bad habits creep in, and experience can further ingrain those habits. Indeed, when I reflect on the thousands of negotiations I have participated in and studied over the years, I'm struck by how frequently even experienced negotiators leave money on the table, deadlock, damage relationships, or allow conflict to spiral.

There are as many specific reasons for bad outcomes in negotiations as there are individuals and deals. Yet broad classes of errors recur. In this article, I'll explore those mistakes, comparing good negotiating practice with bad. But first, let's take a closer look at the right negotiation problem that your approach must solve.

Solving the Right Negotiation Problem

In any negotiation, each side ultimately must choose between two options: accepting a deal or taking its best no-deal option—that is, the course of action it would take if the deal were not possible. As a negotiator, you seek to advance the full set of your interests by persuading the other side to say yes—and mean it—to a proposal that meets your interests better than your best no-deal option does. And why should the other side say yes? Because the deal meets its own interests better than its best no-deal option. So, while protecting your own choice, your negotiation problem is to understand and shape your counterpart's perceived decision—deal versus no deal—so that the other side chooses *in its own interest* what you want. As Italian diplomat Daniele Vare said long ago about diplomacy, negotiation is "the art of letting them have your way."

This approach may seem on the surface like a recipe for manipulation. But in fact, understanding your counterpart's interests and shaping the decision so the other side agrees for its own reasons is the key to jointly creating and claiming sustainable value

Source: "Six Habits of Merely Effective Negotiators," by James K. Sebenius, from *Harvard Business Review,* April 1, 2001, pp. 87–95. Harvard Business School Publishing. Used with permission.

from a negotiation. Yet even experienced negotiators make six common mistakes that keep them from solving the right problem.

Mistake 1: Neglecting the Other Side's Problem

You can't negotiate effectively unless you understand your own interests and your own no-deal options. So far, so good—but there's much more to it than that. Since the other side will say yes for its reasons, not yours, agreement requires understanding and addressing your counterpart's problem as a means to solving your own.

At a minimum, you need to understand the problem from the other side's perspective. Consider a technology company, whose board of directors pressed hard to develop a hot new product shortly after it went public. The company had developed a technology for detecting leaks in underground gas tanks that was both cheaper and about 100 times more accurate than existing technologies—at a time when the Environmental Protection Agency was persuading Congress to mandate that these tanks be continuously tested. Not surprisingly, the directors thought their timing was perfect and pushed employees to commercialize and market the technology in time to meet the demand. To their dismay, the company's first sale turned out to be its only one. Quite a mystery, since the technology worked, the product was less expensive, and the regulations did come through. Imagine the sales engineers confidently negotiating with a customer for a new order: "This technology costs less and is more accurate than the competition's." Think for a moment, though, about how intended buyers might mull over their interests, especially given that EPA regulations permitted leaks of up to 1,500 gallons while the new technology could pick up an 8-ounce leak. Potential buyer: "What a technological tour de force! This handy new device will almost certainly get me into needless, expensive regulatory trouble. And create public relations problems too. I think I'll pass, but my competition should definitely have it." From the technology company's perspective, "faster, better, cheaper" added up to a sure deal; to the other side, it looked like a headache. No deal.

Social psychologists have documented the difficulty most people have understanding the other side's perspective. From the trenches, successful negotiators concur that overcoming this self-centered tendency is critical. As Millennium Pharmaceuticals' Steve Holtzman put it after a string of deals vaulted his company from a start-up in 1993 to a major player with a $10.6 billion market cap today, "We spend a lot of time thinking about how the poor guy or woman on the other side of the table is going to have to go sell this deal to his or her boss. We spend a lot of time trying to understand how they are modeling it." And Wayne Huizenga, veteran of more than a thousand deals building Waste Management, AutoNation, and Blockbuster, distilled his extensive experience into basic advice that is often heard but even more often forgotten. "In all my years of doing deals, a few rules and lessons have emerged. Most important, always try to put yourself in the other person's shoes. It's vital to try to understand in depth what the other side really wants out of the deal."

Tough negotiators sometimes see the other side's concerns but dismiss them: "That's their problem and their issue. Let them handle it. We'll look after our own problems." This attitude can undercut your ability to profitably influence how your counterpart sees its problem. Early in his deal-making career at Cisco Systems, Mike Volpi had trouble completing proposed deals, his "outward confidence" was often mistaken for arrogance. Many acquisitions later, a colleague observed that "the most important part of [Volpi's] development is that he learned power doesn't come from telling people you are powerful. He went from being a guy driving the deal from his side of the table to the guy who understood the deal from the other side."

An associate of Rupert Murdoch remarked that, as a buyer, Murdoch "understands the seller—and, whatever the guy's trying to do, he crafts his offer that way." If you want to change someone's mind, you should first learn where that person's mind is. Then, together, you can try to build what my colleague Bill Ury calls a "golden bridge," spanning the gulf between where your counterpart is now and your desired end point. This is much more effective than trying to shove the other side from its position to yours. As an eighteenth-century pope once noted about Cardinal de Polignac's remarkable diplomatic skills, "This young man always seems to be of my opinion [at the start of a negotiation], and at the end of the conversation I find that I am of his." In short, the first mistake is to focus on your own problem, exclusively. Solve the other side's as the means to solving your own.

Mistake 2: Letting Price Bulldoze Other Interests

Negotiators who pay attention exclusively to price turn potentially cooperative deals into adversarial ones. These "reverse Midas" negotiators, as I like to call them, use hard-bargaining tactics that often leave potential joint gains unrealized. That's because, while price is an important factor in most deals, it's rarely the only one. As Felix Rohatyn, former managing partner of the investment bank Lazard Frères observed, "Most deals are 50 percent emotion and 50 percent economics."

There's a large body of research to support Rohatyn's view. Consider, for example, a simplified negotiation, extensively studied in academic labs, involving real money. One party is given, say, $100 to divide with another party as she likes; the second party can agree or disagree to the arrangement. If he agrees, the $100 is divided in line with the first side's proposal; if not, neither party gets anything. A pure price logic would suggest proposing something like $99 for me, $1 for you. Although this is an extreme allocation, it still represents a position in which your counterpart gets something rather than nothing. Pure price negotiators confidently predict the other side will agree to the split; after all, they've been offered free money—it's like finding a dollar on the street and putting it in your pocket. Who wouldn't pick it up?

In reality, however, most players turn down proposals that don't let them share in at least 35 percent to 40 percent of the bounty—even when much larger stakes are involved and the amount they forfeit is significant. While these rejections are "irrational" on a pure price basis and virtually incomprehensible to reverse Midas types, studies show that when a split feels too unequal to people, they reject the spoils as unfair, are offended by the process, and perhaps try to teach the "greedy" person a lesson.

An important real-world message is embedded in these lab results: people care about much more than the absolute level of their own economic outcome; competing interests include relative results, perceived fairness, self-image, reputation, and so on. Successful negotiators, acknowledging that economics aren't everything, focus on four important nonprice factors.

The Relationship   Less experienced negotiators often undervalue the importance of developing working relationships with the other parties, putting the relationships at risk by overly tough tactics or simple neglect. This is especially true in cross-border deals. In much of Latin America, Southern Europe, and Southeast Asia, for example, relationships—rather than transactions—can be the predominant negotiating interest when working out longer term deals. Results-oriented North Americans, Northern Europeans, and Australians often come to grief by underestimating the strength of this interest and insisting prematurely that the negotiators "get down to business."

The Social Contract   Similarly, negotiators tend to focus on the economic contract— equity splits, cost sharing, governance, and so on—at the expense of the social contract, or the "spirit of a deal." Going well beyond a good working relationship, the social contract governs people's expectations about the nature, extent, and duration of the venture, about process, and about the way unforeseen events will be handled. Especially in new ventures and strategic alliances, where goodwill and strong shared expectations are extremely important, negotiating a positive social contract is an important way to reinforce economic contracts. Scurrying to check founding documents when conflicts occur, which they inevitably do, can signal a badly negotiated social contract.

The Process   Negotiators often forget that the deal-making process can be as important as its content. The story is told of the young Tip O'Neill, who later became Speaker of the House, meeting an elderly constituent on the streets of his North Cambridge, Massachusetts, district. Surprised to learn that she was not planning to vote for him, O'Neill probed, "Haven't you known me and my family all my life?" "Yes." "Haven't I cut your grass in summer and shoveled your walk in winter?" "Yes." "Don't you agree with all my policies and positions?" "Yes." "Then why aren't you going to vote for me?" "Because you didn't ask me to." Considerable academic research confirms what O'Neill learned from this conversation: process counts. What's more, sustainable results are more often reached when all parties perceive the process as personal, respectful, straightforward, and fair.[1]

The Interests of the Full Set of Players   Less experienced negotiators sometimes become mesmerized by the aggregate economics of a deal and forget about the interests of players who are in a position to torpedo it. When the boards of pharmaceutical giants Glaxo and SmithKline Beecham publicly announced their merger in 1998, investors were thrilled, rapidly *increasing* the combined company's market capitalization by a stunning $20 billion. Yet despite prior agreement on who would occupy which top executive positions in the newly combined company, internal disagreement about management control and position resurfaced and sank the announced deal, and the $20 billion evaporated. (Overwhelming strategic logic ultimately drove the companies back together, but only after nearly two years had passed.) This episode confirms two related lessons. First, while favorable overall economics are generally necessary, they are often not sufficient. Second, keep all potentially influential internal players on your radar screen; don't lose sight of their interests or their capacity to affect the deal. What is "rational" for the whole may not be so for the parts.

It can be devilishly difficult to cure the reverse Midas touch. If you treat a potentially cooperative negotiation like a pure price deal, it will likely become one. Imagine a negotiator who expects a hardball, price-driven process. She initiates the bid by taking a tough preemptive position; the other side is likely to reciprocate. "Aha!" says the negotiator, her suspicions confirmed. "I *knew* this was just going to be a tough price deal."

A negotiator can often influence whether price will dominate or be kept in perspective. Consider negotiations between two companies trying to establish an equity joint venture. Among other issues, they are trying to place a value on each side's contribution to determine ownership shares. A negotiator might drive this process down two very different paths. A price-focused approach quickly isolates the valuation issue and then bangs out a resolution. Alternatively, the two sides could first flesh out a more specific shared vision for the joint venture (together envisioning the "pot of gold" they could create), probe to understand the most critical concerns of each side—including price—and craft trade-offs among the full set of issues to meet these interests. In the latter approach, price becomes a component or even an implication of a larger, longer-term package, rather than the primary focus.

Some negotiations are indeed pure price deals and only about aggregate economics, but there is often much more to work with. Wise negotiators put the vital issue of price in perspective and don't straitjacket their view of the richer interests at stake. They work with the subjective as well as the objective, with the process and the relationship, with the "social contract" or spirit of a deal as well as its letter, and with the interests of the parts as well as the whole.

Mistake 3: Letting Positions Drive Out Interests

Three elements are at play in a negotiation. *Issues* are on the table for explicit agreement. *Positions* are one party's stands on the issues. *Interests* are underlying concerns that would be affected by the resolution. Of course, positions on issues reflect underlying interests, but they need not be identical. Suppose you're considering a job offer. The base salary will probably be an issue. Perhaps your position on that issue is that you need to earn $100,000. The interests underlying that position include your need for a good income but may also include status, security, new opportunities, and needs that can be met in ways other than salary. Yet even very experienced deal makers may see the essence of negotiation as a dance of positions. If incompatible positions finally converge, a deal is struck; if not, the negotiation ends in an impasse. By contrast, interest-driven bargainers see the process primarily as a reconciliation of underlying interests: you have one set of interests, I have another, and through joint problem solving we should be better able to meet both sets of interests and thus create new value.

Consider a dispute over a dam project: Environmentalists and farmers opposed a U.S. power company's plans to build a dam. The two sides had irreconcilable positions: "absolutely yes" and "no way." Yet these incompatible positions masked compatible interests. The farmers were worried about reduced water flow below the dam, the environmentalists were focused on the downstream habitat of the endangered whooping crane, and the power company needed new capacity and a greener image. After a costly legal stalemate, the three groups devised an interest-driven agreement that all of them considered preferable to continued court warfare. The agreement included a smaller dam built on a fast track, water flow guarantees, downstream habitat protection, and a trust fund to enhance whooping crane habitats elsewhere.

Despite the clear advantages of reconciling deeper interests, people have a built-in bias toward focusing on their own positions instead. This hardwired assumption that our interests are incompatible implies a zero-sum pie in which my gain is your loss. Research in psychology supports the mythical fixed-pie view as the norm. In a survey of 5,000 subjects in 32 negotiating studies, mostly carried out with monetary stakes, participants failed to realize compatible issues fully half of the time.[2] In real-world terms, this means that enormous value is unknowingly left uncreated as both sides walk away from money on the table.

Reverse Midas negotiators, for example, almost automatically fixate on price and bargaining positions to claim value. After the usual preliminaries, countless negotiations get serious when one side asks, "So, what's your position?" or says, "Here's my position." This positional approach often drives the process toward a ritual value-claiming dance. Great negotiators understand that the dance of bargaining positions is only the surface game; the real action takes place when they've probed behind positions for the full set of interests at stake. Reconciling interests to create value requires patience and a willingness to research the other side, ask many questions, and listen. It would be silly to write off either price or bargaining position; both are extremely important. And there is, of course, a limit to joint value creation. The trick is to recognize and productively manage the tension between cooperative actions needed to create value and competitive ones needed to claim it. The pie must be both expanded and divided.

Mistake 4: Searching Too Hard for Common Ground

Conventional wisdom says we negotiate to overcome the differences that divide us. So, typically, we're advised to find win–win agreements by searching for common ground. Common ground is generally a good thing. Yet many of the most frequently overlooked sources of value in negotiation arise from differences among the parties.

Recall the battle over the dam. The solution—a smaller dam, water flow guarantees, habitat conservation—resulted not from common interests but because farmers, environmentalists, and the utility had different priorities. Similarly, when Egypt and Israel were negotiating over the Sinai, their positions on where to draw the boundary were incompatible. When negotiators went beyond the opposing positions, however, they uncovered a vital difference of underlying interest and priority: the Israelis cared more about security, while the Egyptians cared more about sovereignty. The solution was a demilitarized zone under the Egyptian flag. Differences of interest or priority can open the door to unbundling different elements and giving each party what it values the most—at the least cost to the other.

Solving Teddy Roosevelt's Negotiation Problem

Theodore Roosevelt, nearing the end of a hard-fought presidential election campaign in 1912, scheduled a final whistle-stop journey. At each stop, Roosevelt planned to clinch the crowd's votes by distributing an elegant pamphlet with a stern presidential portrait on the cover and a stirring speech, "Confession of Faith," inside. Some 3 million copies had been printed when a campaign worker noticed a small line under the photograph on each brochure that read, "Moffett Studios, Chicago." Since Moffett held the copyright, the unauthorized use of the photo could cost the campaign one dollar per reproduction. With no time to reprint the brochure, what was the campaign to do?

Not using the pamphlets at all would damage Roosevelt's election prospects. Yet, if they went ahead, a scandal could easily erupt very close to the election, and the campaign could be liable for an unaffordable sum. Campaign workers quickly realized they would have to negotiate with Moffett. But research by their Chicago operatives turned up bad news: although early in his career as a photographer, Moffett had been taken with the potential of this new artistic medium, he had received little recognition. Now Moffett was financially hard up and bitterly approaching retirement with a single-minded focus on money.

Dispirited, the campaign workers approached campaign manager George Perkins, a former partner of J. P. Morgan. Perkins lost no time summoning his stenographer to dispatch the following cable to Moffett Studios: "We are planning to distribute millions of pamphlets with Roosevelt's picture on the cover. It will be great publicity for the studio whose photograph we use. How much will you pay us to use yours? Respond immediately." Shortly, Moffett replied, "We've never done this before, but under the circumstances we'd be pleased to offer you $250." Reportedly, Perkins accepted— without dickering for more.

Perkins's misleading approach raises ethical yellow flags and is anything but a model negotiation on how to enhance working relationships. Yet this case raises a very interesting question: why did the campaign workers find the prospect of this negotiation so difficult? Their inability to see what Perkins immediately perceived flowed from their anxious obsession with their own side's problem: their blunders so far, the high risk of losing the election, a potential $3 million exposure, an urgent deadline, and no cash to meet Moffett's likely demands for something the campaign vitally needed. Had they avoided mistake 1 by pausing for a moment and thinking about how Moffett saw his problem, they would have realized that Moffett didn't even know he had a problem. Perkins's tactical genius was to recognize the essence of the negotiator's central task: shape how your counterpart sees its problem such that it chooses what you want.

The campaign workers were paralyzed in the face of what they saw as sharply conflicting monetary interests and their pathetic BATNA. From their perspective, Moffett's only choice was how to exploit their desperation at the prospect of losing the presidency. By contrast, dodging mistake 5, Perkins immediately grasped the importance of favorably shaping Moffett's BATNA perceptions, both of the campaign's (awful) no-deal options and Moffett's (powerful) one. Perkins looked beyond price, positions, and common ground (mistakes 2, 3, and 4) and used Moffett's different interests to frame the photographer's choice as "the value of publicity and recognition." Had he assumed this would be a standard, hardball price deal by offering a small amount to start, not only would this assumption have been dead wrong but, worse, it would have been self-fulfilling.

Risky and ethically problematic? Yes . . . but Perkins saw his options as certain disaster versus some chance of avoiding it. And was Moffett really entitled to a $3 million windfall, avoidable had the campaign caught its oversight a week beforehand? Hard to say, but this historical footnote, which I've greatly embellished, illuminates the intersection of negotiating mistakes, tactics, and ethics.

Even when an issue seems purely economic, finding differences can break open deadlocked deals. Consider a small technology company and its investors, stuck in a tough negotiation with a large strategic acquirer adamant about paying much less than the asking price. On investigation, it turned out that the acquirer was actually willing to pay the higher price but was concerned about raising price expectations in a fast-moving sector in which it planned to make more acquisitions. The solution was for the two sides to agree on a modest, well-publicized initial cash purchase price; the deal included complex-sounding contingencies that virtually guaranteed a much higher price later.

Differences in forecasts can also fuel joint gains. Suppose an entrepreneur who is genuinely optimistic about the prospects of her fast-growing company faces a potential buyer who likes the company but is much more skeptical about the company's future cash flow. They have negotiated in good faith, but, at the end of the day, the two sides sharply disagree on the likely future of the company and so cannot find an acceptable sale price. Instead of seeing these different forecasts as a barrier, a savvy negotiator could use them to bridge the value gap by proposing a deal in which the buyer pays a fixed amount now and a contingent amount later on the basis of the company's future performance. Properly structured with adequate incentives and monitoring mechanisms, such a contingent payment, or "earn-out," can appear quite valuable to the optimistic seller—who expects to get her higher valuation—but not very costly to the less optimistic buyer. And willingness to accept such a contingent deal may signal that the seller's confidence in the business is genuine. Both may find the deal much more attractive than walking away.

A host of other differences make up the raw material for joint gains. A less risk-averse party can "insure" a more risk-averse one. An impatient party can get most of the early money, while his more patient counterpart can get considerably more over a longer period of time. Differences in cost or revenue structure, tax status, or regulatory arrangements between two parties can be converted into gains for both. Indeed, conducting a disciplined "differences inventory" is at least as important a task as is identifying areas of common ground. After all, if we were all clones of one another, with the same interests, beliefs, attitudes toward risk and time, assets, and so on, there would be little to negotiate. While common ground helps, differences drive deals. But negotiators who don't actively search for differences rarely find them.

Mistake 5: Neglecting BATNAs

BATNAs—the acronym for "best alternative to a negotiated agreement" coined years ago by Roger Fisher, Bill Ury, and Bruce Patton in their book *Getting to Yes*—reflect the course of action a party would take if the proposed deal were not possible. A BATNA may involve walking away, prolonging a stalemate, approaching another potential buyer, making something in-house rather than procuring it externally, going to court rather than settling, forming a different alliance, or going on strike. BATNAs set the threshold—in terms of the full set of interests—that any acceptable agreement must exceed. Both parties doing better than their BATNAs is a necessary condition for an agreement. Thus, BATNAs define a zone of possible agreement and determine its location.

A strong BATNA is an important negotiation tool. Many people associate the ability to inflict or withstand damage with bargaining power, but your willingness to walk away to an apparently good BATNA is often more important. The better your BATNA appears both to you and to the other party, the more credible your threat to walk away becomes, and the more it can serve as leverage to improve the deal. Roger Fisher has dramatized this point by asking which you would prefer to have in your back pocket during a compensation negotiation with your boss: a gun or a terrific job offer from a desirable employer who is also a serious competitor of your company?

Not only should you assess your own BATNA, you should also think carefully about the other side's. Doing so can alert you to surprising possibilities. In one instance, a British company hoped to sell a poorly performing division for a bit more than its depreciated asset value of $7 million to one of two potential buyers. Realizing that these buyers were fierce rivals in other markets, the seller speculated that each party might be willing to pay an inflated price to keep the other from getting the division. So they made sure that each suitor knew the other was looking and skillfully cultivated the interest of both companies. The division sold for $45 million.

Negotiators must also be careful not to inadvertently damage their BATNAs. I saw that happen at a Canadian chemical manufacturing company that had decided to sell a large but nonstrategic division to raise urgently needed cash. The CEO charged his second-in-command with negotiating the sale of the division at the highest possible price.

The target buyer was an Australian company, whose chief executive was an old school friend of the Canadian CEO. The Australian chief executive let it be known that his company was interested in the deal but that his senior management was consumed, at the moment, with other priorities. If the Australian company could have a nine-month negotiating exclusive to "confirm their seriousness about the sale," the Australian chief executive would dedicate the top personnel to make the deal happen. A chief-to-chief agreement to that effect was struck. Pity the second-in-command, charged with urgently maximizing cash from this sale, as he jetted off to Sydney with no meaningful alternative for nine endless months to whatever price the Australians offered.

Negotiators often become preoccupied with tactics, trying to improve the potential deal while neglecting their own BATNA and that of the other side. Yet the real negotiation problem is "deal versus BATNA," not one or the other in isolation. Your potential deal and your BATNA should work together as the two blades of the scissors do to cut a piece of paper.

Mistake 6: Failing to Correct for Skewed Vision

You may be crystal clear on the right negotiation problem—but you can't solve it correctly without a firm understanding of both sides' interests, BATNAs, valuations, likely actions, and so on. Yet, just as a pilot's sense of the horizon at night or in a storm can be wildly inaccurate, the psychology of perception systematically leads negotiators to major errors.[3]

Self-Serving Role Bias   People tend to unconsciously interpret information pertaining to their own side in a strongly self-serving way. The following experiment shows the process at work. Harvard researchers gave a large group of executives financial and industry information about one company negotiating to acquire another. The executive subjects were randomly assigned to the negotiating roles of buyer or seller; the information provided to each side was identical. After plenty of time for analysis, all subjects were asked for their private assessment of the target company's fair value—as distinct from how they might portray that value in the bargaining process. Those assigned the role of seller gave median valuations more than twice those given by the executives assigned to the buyer's role. These valuation gulfs had no basis in fact; they were driven entirely by random role assignments.

Even comparatively modest role biases can blow up potential deals. Suppose a plaintiff believes he has a 70 percent chance of winning a million-dollar judgment, while the defense thinks the plaintiff has only a 50 percent chance of winning. This means that, in settlement talks, the plaintiff's expected BATNA for a court battle (to get $700,000 minus legal fees) will exceed the defendant's assessment of his exposure (to pay $500,000 plus fees). Without significant risk aversion, the divergent assessments would block any out-of-court settlement. This cognitive role bias helps explain why Microsoft took such a confrontational approach in its struggle with the U.S. Department of Justice. The company certainly appeared overoptimistic about its chances in court. Similarly, Arthur Andersen likely exhibited overconfidence in its arbitration prospects over the terms of separation from Andersen Consulting (now Accenture). Getting too committed to your point of view—"believing your own line"—is an extremely common mistake.

Partisan Perceptions   While we systematically err in processing information critical to our own side, we are even worse at assessing the other side—especially in an adversarial situation. Extensive research has documented an unconscious mechanism that enhances one's own side, "portraying it as more talented, honest, and morally upright," while simultaneously vilifying the opposition. This often leads to exaggerated perceptions of the other side's position and overestimates of the actual substantive conflict. To an outsider, those caught up in disintegrating partnerships or marriages often appear to hold exaggerated views of each other. Such partisan perceptions can become even more virulent among people on each side of a divide, such as Israelis and Palestinians, Bosnian Muslims and the Serbs, or Catholics and Protestants in Northern Ireland.

Partisan perceptions can easily become self-fulfilling prophecies. Experiments testing the effects of teachers' expectations of students, psychiatrists' diagnoses of mental patients, and platoon leaders' expectations of their trainees confirm the notion that partisan perceptions often shape behavior. At the negotiating table, clinging firmly to the idea that one's counterpart is stubborn or extreme, for example, is likely to trigger just that behavior, sharply reducing the possibility of reaching a constructive agreement.

As disagreement and conflict intensify, sophisticated negotiators should expect biased perceptions, both on their own side and the other side. Less seasoned players tend to be shocked and outraged by perceived extremism and are wholly unaware that their own views are likely colored by their roles. How to counteract these powerful biases? Just knowing that they exist helps. Seeking the views of outside, uninvolved parties is useful, too. And having people on your side prepare the strongest possible case for the other side can serve as the basis for preparatory role-playing that can generate valuable insights. A few years ago, helping a client get ready for a tough deal, I suggested that the client create a detailed "brief" for each side and have the team's best people negotiate for the other side in a reverse role-play. The brief for my client's side was lengthy, eloquent, and persuasive. Tellingly, the brief describing the other side's situation was only two pages long and consisted mainly of reasons for conceding quickly to my client's superior arguments. Not only were my client's executives fixated on their own problem (mistake 1), their perceptions of each side were also hopelessly biased (mistake 6). To prepare effectively, they needed to undertake significant competitive research and reality-test their views with uninvolved outsiders.

From Merely Effective to Superior Negotiation

So you have navigated the shoals of merely effective deal making to face what is truly the right problem. You have focused on the full set of interests of all parties, rather than fixating on price and positions. You have looked beyond common ground to unearth value-creating differences. You have assessed and shaped BATNAs. You have taken steps to avoid role biases and partisan perceptions. In short, you have grasped your own problem clearly and have sought to understand and influence the other side's such that what it chooses is what you want.

Plenty of errors still lie in wait: cultural gaffes, an irritating style, inadvertent signals of disrespect or untrustworthiness, miscommunication, bad timing, revealing too much or too little, a poorly designed agenda, sequencing mistakes, negotiating with the wrong person on the other side, personalizing issues, and so on. Even if you manage to avoid these mistakes as well, you may still run into difficulties by approaching the negotiation far too narrowly, taking too many of the elements of the "problem" as fixed.

The very best negotiators take a broader approach to setting up and solving the right problem. With a keen sense of the potential value to be created as their guiding beacon, these negotiators are game-changing entrepreneurs. They envision the most promising architecture and take action to bring it into being. These virtuoso negotiators not only play the game as given at the table, they are masters at setting it up and changing it away from the table to maximize the chances for better results.

To advance the full set of their interests, they understand and shape the other side's choice—deal versus no deal—such that the other chooses what they want. As François de Callières, an eighteenth-century commentator, once put it, negotiation masters possess "the supreme art of making every man offer him as a gift that which it was his chief design to secure."

Endnotes

1. W. Chan Kim and Renée Mauborgne, "Fair Process: Managing in the Knowledge Economy," *HBR,* July–August 1997.

2. This and other studies illustrating this point can be found in Leigh Thompson's *The Mind and Heart of the Negotiator* (Prentice Hall, 1998).

3. See Robert J. Robinson, "Errors in Social Judgment: Implications for Negotiation and Conflict Resolution, Part I: Biased Assimilation of Information." Harvard Business School, 1997; and Robert J. Robinson, "Errors in Social Judgment: Implications for Negotiation and Conflict Resolution, Part II: Partisan Perceptions," Harvard Business School, 1997.

Exercise 1

The Subjective Value Inventory (SVI)

Introduction

This exercise is designed to help you explore the psychological outcomes of a negotiation, including satisfaction, trust, rapport, and self-impressions. It involves completing a questionnaire following a simulated or actual negotiation. Your instructor will tell you which negotiation to use as the basis for filling it out.

Instructions for Completing the SVI

For each question, please circle a number from 1 to 7 that most accurately reflects your opinion. You will notice that some of the questions are similar to one another; this is primarily to ensure the validity and reliability of the questionnaire. Please answer each question independently, without reference to any of the other questions.

Important: If you encounter a particular question that is not applicable to your negotiation, simply circle "NA." Even if you did not reach agreement, please try to answer as many questions as possible.

1. How satisfied are you with your own outcome—that is, the extent to which the terms of your agreement (or lack of agreement) benefit you?

1	2	3	4	5	6	7	NA
Not at all satisfied			Moderately satisfied			Perfectly satisfied	

2. How satisfied are you with the balance between your own outcome and your counterpart(s)'s outcome(s)?

1	2	3	4	5	6	7	NA
Not at all satisfied			Moderately satisfied			Perfectly satisfied	

3. Did you feel like you forfeited or "lost" in this negotiation?

1	2	3	4	5	6	7	NA
Not at all			A moderate amount			A great deal	

4. Do you think the terms of your agreement are consistent with principles of legitimacy or objective criteria (e.g., common standards of fairness, precedent, industry practice, legality)?

1	2	3	4	5	6	7	NA
Not at all			Moderately			A great deal	

Source: Developed by Jared R. Curhan, Hillary A. Elfenbein, and Heng Xu. Copyright © 2005 by Curhan, Elfenbein, & Xu. Used with permission.

5. Did you "lose face" (i.e., damage your sense of pride) in the negotiation?

1	2	3	4	5	6	7	NA
Not at all			Moderately			A great deal	

6. Did you feel as though you behaved appropriately in this negotiation?

1	2	3	4	5	6	7	NA
Not at all			Moderately			A great deal	

7. Did this negotiation make you feel more or less competent as a negotiator?

1	2	3	4	5	6	7	NA
It made me feel *less* competent.			It did not make me feel more or less competent.			It made me feel *more* competent.	

8. Did you behave according to your own principles and values?

1	2	3	4	5	6	7	NA
Not at all			Moderately			A great deal	

9. Do you feel your counterpart(s) listened to your concerns?

1	2	3	4	5	6	7	NA
Not at all			Moderately			A great deal	

10. Would you characterize the negotiation process as fair?

1	2	3	4	5	6	7	NA
Not at all			Moderately			A great deal	

11. How satisfied are you with the ease (or difficulty) of reaching an agreement?

1	2	3	4	5	6	7	NA
Not at all satisfied			Moderately satisfied			Perfectly satisfied	

12. Did your counterpart(s) consider your wishes, opinions, or needs?

1	2	3	4	5	6	7	NA
Not at all			Moderately			Very much	

13. How satisfied are you with your relationship with your counterpart(s) as a result of this negotiation?

1	2	3	4	5	6	7	NA
Not at all satisfied			Moderately satisfied			Perfectly satisfied	

14. What kind of overall impression did your counterpart(s) make on you?

1	2	3	4	5	6	7	NA
Extremely *negative*			Neither negative nor positive			Extremely *positive*	

15. Did the negotiation make you trust your counterpart(s)?

1	2	3	4	5	6	7	NA
Not at all			Moderately			A great deal	

16. Did the negotiation build a good foundation for a future relationship with your counterpart(s)?

1	2	3	4	5	6	7	NA
Not at all			Moderately			A great deal	

Pemberton's Dilemma

Introduction

This exercise creates a situation in which you and the other person(s) will be making separate decisions about how to manage your firm. In this situation, the outcomes (profits and losses) are determined not only by what you do, but also by a number of other factors such as the goals and motives that you and the other party have and the communication that takes place between you and them.

Read the background information for Pemberton's Dilemma that follows. In this exercise, you will represent your store in discussions with the other store about the hours that each store should open on Sundays. You and the other store will be making decisions simultaneously, and your profits will be directly affected by these decisions.

Background Information

Pemberton is a quaint little town located in the heartland of our great country. Although it is only a 30-minute drive to a major metropolitan center, most of the townsfolk prefer to do their shopping at one of the two general stores located in Pemberton. At these stores, one can buy a variety of goods, ranging from groceries to hardware equipment. Both establishments boast a soda fountain, which is quite popular among both the younger and older generations as well.

Like most small towns, Pemberton is proud of the fact that it has been able to preserve its many traditions, some of which date back to the 1890s. One of these grand traditions, which became official in 1923 when the Town Hall passed a resolution to this effect, is the cessation of all commercial activity on Sunday. Times have changed, however, and "Sunday shoppers" are becoming more and more prevalent. In fact, every Sunday there is a mass exodus to the nearby metropolitan center, where Sunday shopping has been permitted for years.

You are a member of the management team from one of the two general stores in Pemberton. Both the Country Market and the Corner Store have been consistently losing potential profit as Sunday shopping becomes more popular. Your management team, as well as the team from the competing general store, has recently contemplated opening the store on Sunday, in spite of the municipal resolution that prohibits this.

The ramifications of such decisions are important, since the profitability of such an action will depend on the decision made by the competing store. For instance, if neither store decides to open on Sunday, it will be business as usual, and both stores will make a profit of $20,000 in a given week.

Source: Written in collaboration with Gregory Leck.

If only one store decides to open on Sunday, that particular store would enjoy the patronage of all those Sunday shoppers and would manage to make a $40,000 profit for the week. Unfortunately, the store that decided to remain closed on that Sunday would actually incur a loss of $40,000 that week. This would be due to various reasons, most notably the preference of customers to continue to do their shopping throughout the week at the store that remained open on Sunday.

If both stores decided to stay open on Sunday, adverse consequences would be faced by both establishments. Although Town Hall may be able to turn a blind eye to one store violating the municipal resolution, two stores would be looked upon as a conspiracy against the traditionalists of Pemberton. Artemus Hampton, Pemberton's mayor and a direct descendant of one of the town's founders, would no doubt pressure Town Hall into levying the highest possible fine allowable by law. In this case, the penalty would be so excessive that both stores would incur losses of $20,000 each for the week. While your lawyers have suggested that the municipal resolutions prohibiting Sunday shopping in Pemberton might be overturned in a court case, this too would be a costly option. In either case, if both stores open on Sunday, they will each incur losses of $20,000 for the week.

Keeping this information in mind, your team is to decide each week, for the next 12 weeks, whether your store is to remain open on the Sunday of that week. The decision made for the first week must be made without prior consultation with the management team of the competing store. Subsequent decisions may be made after consulting with your competitors. Both teams shall reveal their decisions simultaneously. *Remember, the goal is to maximize profits over the next 12-week period.*

Familiarize yourself with the following profit chart. There will be 12 one-minute rounds where the stores will either open or close. Each round represents one Sunday, and every *fourth* Sunday is part of a long weekend. A three-minute planning session separates each Sunday. *There may not be any communication between the stores during the planning sessions.*

The exercise begins when representatives from the stores (one from each) meet and indicate with a card if their store will open or close on the first Sunday. Each team will record the outcome of each Sunday on their profit chart. The time periods between each Sunday are fixed and may not be altered. Each team will complete a total of 12 moves. Profits and losses are calculated after each Sunday and are cumulative for the 12 weeks (see the accompanying sample profit chart).

		Country Market			
		Close Sunday		**Open Sunday**	
Corner Store	**Close Sunday**	Corner:	+$20,000	Corner:	−$40,000
		Country:	+$20,000	Country:	+$40,000
	Open Sunday	Corner:	+$40,000	Corner:	−$20,000
		Country:	−$40,000	Country:	−$20,000

Profit Chart				
			Profit	
	Corner Store's Choice	**Country Market's Choice**	**Corner Store**	**Country Market**
First 15-minute planning period				
1.				
2.				
3.				
4. **Double** profit/loss, *this round only*				
Five-minute negotiation period				
5.				
6.				
7.				
8. **Triple** profit/loss, *this round only*				
Five-minute negotiation period				
9.				
10.				
11.				
12. **Quadruple** profit/loss, *this round only*				

Exercise 3

The Commons Dilemma

Introduction

This is a simulation about the dynamics of competition and cooperation in a situation where there are multiple actors. The entire class will participate, with each individual student making a series of decisions over the course of several class periods. At each decision point, your outcomes will be determined by what everyone else does as well as by your own actions. At the end of the simulation, when all decisions have been made, you will receive an overall score that can be converted into a grade for the exercise. Although the instructor will not discuss or debrief this exercise until after the final decision has been made, you and your fellow students are free to discuss it as you wish.

Source: This version of the Commons Dilemma was developed by Michael Morris; it is based on a presentation made by Gary Throop at the 1990 Organizational Behavior Teaching Conference. Used with permission.

The Used Car

Introduction

The scenario for this role-play involves a single issue: the price of a used car that is for sale. While there is a great deal of other information that may be used to construct supporting arguments or to build in demands and requests in addition to the price, the sale price will ultimately be the indicator used to determine how well you do in comparison to other role-play groups.

Background Information

You are about to negotiate the purchase/sale of an automobile. The seller advertised the car in the local newspaper. (*Note:* Both role-players should interpret "local" as the town in which the role-playing is occurring.) Before advertising it, the seller took the car to the local Volkswagen dealer, who has provided the following information:

> 2006 Volkswagen Jetta 2.5 sedan, five-cylinder, automatic transmission, power steering, air conditioning, front-wheel drive, dual air bags, cruise control.
>
> Black with gray interior, power door locks, power windows, and AM/FM/CD stereo.
>
> Mileage: 51,000 miles; radial tires expected to last another 30,000 miles.
>
> Fuel economy: 22 mpg city, 30 mpg highway; uses regular (87 octane) gasoline.
>
> No rust; dent on passenger door barely noticeable.
>
> Mechanically perfect except exhaust system, which may or may not last another 10,000 miles (costs $600 to replace).
>
> Blue book (2005) values: retail, $13,200; trade-in, $9,250; private party, $10,250.
>
> Car has been locally owned and driven (one owner).

Source: Revised version of an original role-play that was developed by Professor Leonard Greenhalgh, Dartmouth College. Used with permission.

Statement of Agreement for Purchase of the Automobile

Price: _____

Manner of payment: _____

Special terms and conditions: _____

_____

_____

_____

_____

We agree to the terms above:

_____   _____

           Seller   Buyer

* *

Who made the first offer? _____

Initial Settlement Proposals

Seller: _____

_____

Buyer: _____

_____

_____

Exercise 5

Knight Engines/Excalibur Engine Parts

Introduction

The process of negotiation combines economic transactions with verbal persuasion. A great deal of what transpires during a negotiation is the verbal persuasion—people arguing for and supporting their own preferred position, and resisting similar arguments from the other party. At the same time, underlying this layer of persuasive messages is a set of economic transactions—bids and counterbids—that are at the economic core of the negotiation process.

The purpose of this exercise is to provide some experience with combining the economic transactions and the persuasive messages to support preferred economic outcomes. You will be assigned the role of Knight Engines or Excalibur Engine Parts for this exercise. Your objective is to negotiate a deal that is most advantageous to you and your company.

Source: Written in collaboration with Gregory Leck.

Exercise 6

GTechnica—AccelMedia

Introduction

The scenario for this simulation is a negotiation between a supplier of electronic components and a computer hardware maker over the price of a processor needed for the manufacture of a computer graphics accelerator adapter. The role-play information you will be given by your instructor provides details about the context of the negotiation that may help you to understand the situation, develop a bargaining strategy, and form arguments or demands to implement that strategy. Ultimately, however, how well you do in this negotiation in relation to other negotiating groups is determined by the final sale price for the part, if you are able to reach an agreement.

When you read your role information and are preparing to negotiate, keep these guidelines in mind:

- Use any plan or strategy that will help you achieve your objectives.

- If you are negotiating in a team, you may call a caucus at any time to evaluate your strategy or the opponent's strategy.

- Reach an agreement by the end of the specified time period, or conclude that you are not able to agree and that buyer and seller will explore other alternatives.

- Complete the negotiation outcome form as directed by your instructor. Be sure to write down any additional terms or conditions that were agreed to.

Source: This exercise was developed by Bruce Barry.

Toyonda

Introduction

The options available to us in a negotiation encounter are often related to the amount of power and leverage that we think we have going in to the situation. This exercise revolves around the kind of situation that many will experience at one time or another: an individual negotiating with a representative of a large corporation over dissatisfaction with a consumer experience.

You will be assigned either to the role of a consumer who owns an automobile with a faulty transmission, or to the role of a regional manager for the company that manufactured the car. As you prepare for and conduct the negotiation, think about the sources of power each party has in this situation, and how that affects the process and outcome of the encounter.

Source: This exercise was developed by Roger C. Mayer and Edward C. Tomlinson. Used with permssion.

Exercise 8

Planning for Negotiations

Introduction

This exercise asks you to focus on either an upcoming role-play negotiation or a real negotiation that will occur within your life within the next several weeks or months. In this exercise, your objective is to develop a plan for that negotiation.

Here you will find 10 question areas that can be used as a planning guide for this negotiation. These questions reflect the important elements to consider when you prepare to negotiate. Not all of these questions will be relevant to every negotiation, so you may not have a specific answer for every question. The purpose of the planning process is to make sure you consider all of the major factors that may impact the upcoming negotiation, and assemble information, arguments, or analysis so that you can be more effective in achieving your goals in that negotiation. The detailed questions are presented next, and a blank abbreviated planning guide is available after the questions for you to complete about your own upcoming negotiation. The readings in this book may offer additional help in considering how to plan most effectively.

If you are using this planning guide as part of a class exercise, your instructor may give you additional instructions on how to use the guide.

Planning Questions

Here are the major dimensions you should address in planning for a negotiation:

1. Understanding the issues—that is, what is to be negotiated.

2. Assembling the issues and defining the bargaining mix:

   - Which issues are most important and which issues are less important?

   - Which issues are linked to other issues, and which are separate or unconnected?

3. Defining the interests: What are the other's primary underlying interests?

4. Defining limits:

   - What is our walkaway point on each issue—that is, what is a minimally acceptable settlement for each issue or the issues as a package?

   - If this negotiation fails, what is our best alternative to a negotiated agreement (BATNA)?

5. Defining targets and openings:

   - What will be our preferred settlement in each issue?

   - What will be our opening request for each issue?

   - Where are we willing to trade off issues against each other in the bargaining mix?

6. Constituencies: To whom is the other accountable for the solution—that is, to whom does he or she report or have to explain or defend the outcome? Does this party also have to be involved in issue definition and goal setting?

Source: Developed by Roy J. Lewicki and John W. Minton.

7. Opposite negotiators: Who is the other party (or parties) in the negotiation?

    - What information do we have about them?
    - What issues will they have?
    - What priorities are they likely to have for their issues?
    - What are their interests?
    - What has been my past relationship with them? What future relationship do I need to have, or would I like to have with them?
    - What is their reputation and style, and how should I take this into consideration?

8. Selecting a strategy:

    - What overall negotiation and strategy do I want to select? How important are the outcome and the relationship with the other?
    - What strategy do I expect the other will be selecting?

9. Planning the issue presentation and defense:

    - What research do I need to do on the issues so that I can argue for them convincingly and compellingly?
    - Do I have (or can I prepare) graphs, charts, and figures that will clearly communicate my preferences?
    - In what order and sequence should I present the information?
    - What arguments can I anticipate from the other party, and how am I going to counteract their arguments?
    - What tactics will I use to present my arguments or defend against the other's arguments?
    - What tactics will I use to try to move us toward agreement?
    - What roles will different people play in the negotiation?

10. Protocol:

    - Where will we negotiate? Do we wish to influence the choice of location?
    - When will we negotiate? Do we wish to influence the time and length of negotiation?
    - Who will be at the actual negotiation meeting? Do we want to bring other parties to serve a particular purpose (e.g., an expert or an observer)?
    - Do we have an agenda? How can we help to either create the agenda or participate in its development?
    - What will we do if the negotiation fails?
    - Who will write down and confirm the agreement? Do we need to have the contract reviewed by a professional (e.g., attorney, accountant, agent)?

One member of each group should record the results of the group's work and be able to report the plan back to the group (you may wish to use large paper, overhead transparencies, or a written handout).

Planning Guide

This planning guide may be completed for any important upcoming negotiation:

1. What are the issues to be negotiated? _____
   _____
   _____

2. What are the priorities among the issues in the bargaining mix? _____
   _____
   _____

3. What are the primary underlying interests? _____
   _____
   _____

4. What are my limits on each issue—walkaway points and BATNAs?_____
   _____
   _____

5. What are my target points and opening requests on these issues? _____
   _____
   _____

6. Who are the important constituencies to whom I am accountable? _____
   _____
   _____

7. What do I know about the other negotiator's interests, negotiating style, and personal reputation? _____
   _____
   _____

8. What overall strategy do I want to pursue?_____
   _____
   _____

9. What do I need to assemble—research, documents, charts and graphs, and so on—to make the most effective presentation on what I want to achieve? What tactics will I use to present my arguments or defend against the other negotiator's arguments? _____
   _____
   _____

10. What protocol is important for this negotiation: where we negotiate, when we negotiate, who is present for the negotiation, agenda to be followed, note taking? Also, what is our backup plan if this negotiation fails? _____
    _____
    _____

The Pakistani Prunes

Introduction

In many work settings it is not possible for people to work independently as they pursue their work goals. Often we find ourselves in situations where we must obtain the cooperation of other people, even though the other people's ultimate objectives may be different from our own. Getting things done in organizations requires us to work together in cooperation, even though our ultimate objective may be only to satisfy our own needs. Your task in this exercise is to learn how to work together more productively with others.

Source: Adapted by Roy J. Lewicki and John W. Minton.

Universal Computer Company

Introduction

In this exercise you will play the role of a plant manager who has to negotiate some arrangements with another plant manager. You will be in a potentially competitive situation where cooperation is clearly desirable. Your task is to find some way to cooperate, when to do so might seem to put you at a disadvantage.

Read the background information section and the role information that the instructor has provided. Do not discuss your role with other class members. Plan how you will handle the forthcoming meeting with the other plant manager. Record your initial proposal on the Initial Settlement Proposal form. Do not show this to the other party you are negotiating with until after the negotiations are completed.

Background Information

The Universal Computer Company is one of the nation's major producers of computers. Plants in the company tend to specialize in producing a single line of products or, at the most, a limited range of products. The company has considerable vertical integration. Parts made at one plant are assembled into components at another, which in turn are assembled into final products at still another plant. Each plant operates on a profit center basis.

The Crawley plant produces computer chips, modules, cable harnesses, and terminal boards, which are shipped to other company plants. In addition to numerous computer chips, the Crawley plant makes more than 40 different modules for the Phillips plant. The two plants are about five miles apart.

The Quality Problem

Production at the Phillips plant has been plagued by poor quality. Upon examination it has been found that a considerable portion of this problem can be traced to the quality of the modules received from the Crawley plant.

The Crawley plant maintains a final inspection operation. There has been considerable dispute between the two plants as to whether the Crawley plant is to maintain a 95 percent overall acceptance level for all modules shipped to the Phillips plant, or to maintain that standard for *each* of the 42 modules shipped. The Phillips plant manager has insisted that the standard has to be maintained for each of the 42 individual modules produced. The Crawley plant manager maintains that the requirements mean that the 95 percent level has to be maintained overall for the sum of modules produced. Experience at the Phillips plant shows that while some module types were consistently well above the 95 percent acceptance level, 12 types of modules had erratic quality and would often fall far below the 95 percent level. As a result, while individual types of modules might fall below standard, the quality level

---

Initial Settlement Proposal

_____ Plant

How do you propose that the following expenses and repairs should be handled?

Expense of repairing all faulty modules: _____

_____

Expense of repairing faulty modules other than the 12 types that fall below the 95 percent level:

_____

_____

Expense of repairing the faulty modules of the 12 types that fall below the 95 percent level:

_____

_____

How to handle the repair of the faulty modules of the 12 types that fall below the 95 percent level:

_____

_____

How to handle the repair of the modules other than the 12 types that fall below the 95 percent level:

_____

_____

---

for all modules was at or above the 95 percent level. This raised serious problems at the Phillips plant, since the quality of its products is controlled by the quality of the poorest module.

The Interplant Dispute

The management of the Phillips plant felt that the quality problem of the modules received from the Crawley plant was causing them great difficulty. It caused problems with the customers, who complained about the improper operation of the products that contained the Crawley modules. As a result, the Phillips plant operation had earlier added secondary final inspection of its completed products. More recently it had added an incoming inspection of 12 poor-quality modules received from the Crawley plant. There were times when the number of modules rejected was large enough to slow or even temporarily stop production. At those times, to maintain production schedules, the Phillips plant had to work overtime. In addition, the Phillips plant had the expense of correcting all the faulty units received from the Crawley plant.

Ideally, the management of the Phillips plant would like to receive all modules free of defects. While this was recognized as impossible, they felt that the Crawley plant should at least accept the expense of repairs, extra inspections, and overtime required by the poor quality of the parts.

Since installing incoming inspection procedures on the 12 modules, the Phillips plant had been rejecting about $15,000 of modules a week. For the most part, these had been put into storage pending settlement of the dispute as to which plant should handle

---

Final Settlement Agreement

How, exactly, did you agree that the following expenses and repairs would be handled?

Expense of repairing all faulty modules: _____

_____

Expense of repairing faulty modules other than the 12 types that fall below the 95 percent level:

_____

_____

Expense of repairing the faulty modules of the 12 types that fall below the 95 percent level:

_____

_____

How to handle the repair of the faulty modules of the 12 types that fall below the 95 percent level:

_____

_____

How to handle the repair of the modules other than the 12 types that fall below the 95 percent level:

_____

_____

_____   _____
Representative, Phillips Plant   Representative, Crawley Plant

---

repairing them. Occasionally, when the supply of good modules had been depleted, repairs were made on some of the rejected units to keep production going. The Phillips plant had continued to make repairs on the remaining 30 types or modules as the need for repairs was discovered in assembly or final inspection.

From its perspective, the Crawley plant management felt that it was living up to its obligation by maintaining a 95 percent or better quality level on all its modules shipped to the Phillips plant. Further, they pointed out that using sampling methods on inspection meant that some below-standard units were bound to get through and that the expense of dealing with these was a normal business expense that the Phillips plant would have to accept as would any other plant. They pointed out that when buying parts from outside suppliers it was common practice in the company to absorb the expenses from handling the normal level of faulty parts.

The Phillips plant management argued that the Crawley plant management was ignoring its responsibility to the company by forcing the cost of repairs onto their plant, where only repairs could be made—rather than having the costs borne by the Crawley plant, where corrections of faulty processes could be made.

Exercise 11

Twin Lakes Mining Company

Introduction

In this role-play you will have the opportunity to negotiate a serious problem—a conflict between a mining company and the government of a small city regarding an environmental cleanup. While the issues in this scenario have been simplified somewhat for the purpose of this role-play, such conflicts between industry and governmental groups are typical throughout the country. Try to introduce as much realism into this situation as you can, based on your own personal experiences.

Background Information

The Twin Lakes Mining Company is located in Tamarack, Minnesota, in the northern part of the state. It was established there in 1961. The city of Tamarack has a year-round population of approximately 18,000. Although there is a growing revenue that accrues to the city as a result of heavy summer tourism (summer homes, fishing, etc.) and several cottage industries, Tamarack is basically a one-industry city. Twenty-five hundred people, 60 percent of whom live within city limits, work for the Twin Lakes Mining Company; 33 percent of the city's real estate tax base of about $5 million consists of Twin Lakes Mining Company property and operations. Both in terms of direct tax revenue and indirect contribution to the economic stability of the local population, Tamarack is strongly dependent on the continued success of the Twin Lakes Mining Company.

The Twin Lakes Mining Company is an open-pit, iron ore mine. Open-pit mining consists of stripping the topsoil from the ore deposit with the use of power shovels. Train rails are then laid, and most of the ore is loaded into railroad cars for transportation to a central collecting point for rail or water shipment. As mining operations progress, rails are relaid or roads constructed to haul ore by truck. The ore is transported to a "benefication plant" located on the outskirts of Tamarack. Benefication of ore involves crushing, washing, concentration, blending, and agglomerating the ore. In the early days of ore production, such treatment was unnecessary; however, benefication is necessary today for several reasons. First, transportation costs of rejected material (gangue) are minimized. The crude ore may lose as much as one-third of its weight in grading, and, in addition, impurities are removed at a much lower cost than if removed during smelting. Second, ores of various physical and chemical properties can be purified and blended during this process. Finally, fine ore materials, which previously may have been rejected as a result of smelting problems, can now be briquetted and pelletized to increase their value. After the ore proceeds through this process of cleaning and agglomerating into larger lumps or pellets, it is shipped by railroad car to steel mills throughout the Midwest. Rejected materials are returned to "consumed" parts of the mine, and the land is restored.

Twin Lakes' benefication plant is located approximately five miles outside of Tamarack. As a result of the expansion of the residential areas of the city, summer home development, and various Twin Lakes operations, the plant has become a major problem for local citizens. For years, the Tamarack City Council has been pressing the company to clean up the most problematic operations.

While most of these discussions have been amicable, Twin Lakes has done little or nothing to remedy the major concerns. Now, as a result of more stringent environmental laws and regulations, Twin Lakes has come under pressure from both the state of Minnesota and the federal government for environmental cleanup. Both the state and the federal Environmental Protection Agency have informed Twin Lakes that the company is in major violation of water and air pollution quality standards, and that immediate action must be taken. Twin Lakes' estimates indicate that total compliance with the cleanup regulations will cost the company over $36 million. Because Twin Lakes is now mining relatively low-grade ore and because foreign competition in the steel market has significantly eroded the demand for ore, environmental compliance may seriously influence the profitability of the company. Many local citizens, as individuals and through the local chapter of the United Mineworkers Union, are putting significant pressure on the City Council to help the Twin Lakes Company in its environmental cleanup operations.

The imposition of the environmental controls on Twin Lakes, and the resulting pressure from all segments of the community, have led to renewed discussions between company officials and the City Council. As a result of these discussions, the following environmental issues have emerged:

1. *Water quality:* The Twin Lakes plant requires large amounts of water to wash the crushed ore. In addition, much of the highest-quality ore is reduced to an almost powderlike texture after washing and is being lost in the washing operation. As a result, the company has built a series of settlement recovery ponds alongside Beaver Brook near the plant. Water that has been used for washing ore is allowed to stand in these ponds; they are periodically drained and the ore recovered. Nevertheless, granules of iron ore and other impurities continue to wash downstream from the plant. The environmental agents have insisted that the effluent from the plant and the ponds be cleaned up. Estimates for the cost of a filtration plant are $20 million. Twin Lakes claims that it cannot afford to build the plant with its own revenue. Since Tamarack has periodically talked about Beaver Brook as a secondary water source for the city (and residential development makes this a more pressing concern in two to three years), the Twin Lakes officials hope that they might interest Tamarack in a joint venture.

2. *Air quality:* The entire process of mining, transporting, and crushing ore generates large amounts of dust. This has significantly increased the levels of particulates in the air. In addition, during the dry summer months, the operation of many large trucks along dirt roads intensifies the problem considerably. Twin Lakes believes that it can control a great deal of the dust generated immediately around the plant at a cost of approximately $8 million. The most significant debate with the city has been over a series of roads around the city outskirts. Approximately half of the roads are city owned; the rest have been specially constructed for the transportation of ore and material. Estimates for paving all the roads are $4.8 million, with a yearly maintenance cost of $600,000; periodic oil spraying of the roads, to

keep down the dust, would run approximately $800,000 annually, but an agreement to do this as a short-term measure may not satisfy the environmental agencies.

3.   *Taxation of company land:* The land for the mine itself is outside city limits. However, the plant lies within city boundaries, and current taxes on the city land are $800,000 annually. The company has always felt that this taxation rate is excessive. In addition, several of the railroad spurs used to move ore into the plant, and out to the major railway line, cross city land. The city has continued to charge a flat rate of $400,000 annually for right-of-way use. It has occasionally offered the land for sale to the company at rates varying from $2.2 million to $2.4 million. Again, the company has felt that this rate is excessive.

Both the company and the city believe that if some resolution could be obtained on these three major issues, the remaining problems could be easily resolved, and Twin Lakes would agree to keep the mine open.

City of Tamarack

Introduction

In this role-play, you will have the opportunity to negotiate a serious problem—a conflict between a mining company and the government of a small city regarding an environmental cleanup. Conflicts among community, government, and industry groups are very common, particularly around environmental management issues. The issues in this simulation may be similar to environmental cleanup, development, or management problems ongoing in your own community.

Background Information

The largest regional office of the Twin Lakes Mining Company is located in Tamarack, Minnesota, in the northern part of the state. It was established there in 1941. The city of Tamarack has a population of approximately 18,000. Although there is a growing revenue that accrues to the city as a result of heavy summer tourism (summer homes, fishing, etc.) and several cottage industries, Tamarack is basically a one-industry city. Two thousand five hundred people, 60 percent of whom live within city limits, work for the Twin Lakes Mining Company; 33 percent of the city's real estate tax base consists of Twin Lakes property and operations. Both in terms of direct tax revenue and indirect contribution to the economic stability of the local population, Tamarack is strongly dependent on the continued success of the Twin Lakes Mining Company.

The primary activity of the Twin Lakes Mining Company consists of mining iron ore from open-pit mines. Open-pit mining consists of stripping the topsoil from the ore deposit with the use of a power shovel. Train rails are then laid, and most of the ore is loaded into railroad cars for transportation to a central collecting point for rail or water shipment. As mining operations progress, rails are relaid or roads constructed to haul ore by truck. The ore is transported to a plant located on the outskirts of Tamarack, where it is crushed, washed, concentrated, blended, and agglomerated into larger lumps or pellets. After the ore proceeds through this process of cleaning and agglomerating, it is shipped by railroad car to steel mills throughout the Midwest. Rejected materials are returned to parts of the mine where the mining process has been completed. Mines that are no longer in use are called *consumed* mines.

Twin Lakes' plant is located approximately five miles outside Tamarack. As a result of the expansion of the residential areas of the city, summer home development, and various Twin Lakes operations, the plant has become an environmental problem for local citizens. The primary problem is that the mining operations pollute the air with dust. For years, the Tamarack City Council has been pressing the company to clean up the most problematic operations. Although several discussions between the city and the company have occurred, Twin Lakes has done little to remedy the major concerns. Now, as a

Source: This exercise was written by Jeff Polzer. Used with permission.

result of more stringent environmental laws and regulations, Twin Lakes has come under pressure from the state of Minnesota and the federal government for environmental cleanup. Both the state and the federal Environmental Protection Agency have informed Twin Lakes that it is in major violation of air pollution quality standards and that immediate action must be taken. Because Twin Lakes is now mining relatively low-grade ore and because foreign competition in the steel market has significantly eroded the demand for ore, the high cost of environmental compliance might force the company to shut down its Tamarack operations. Many local citizens, as individuals and through the local chapter of the United Mineworkers Union, are putting significant pressure on the City Council to help the Twin Lakes Company in its environmental cleanup operations.

The imposition of the environmental controls on Twin Lakes, and the resulting pressure from all segments of the community, have led to renewed discussions between company and city officials about the future of Twin Lakes in the Tamarack area. As a result of these discussions, the following major issues, including environmental issues and others, have emerged:

Air quality—paving dirt roads: The entire process of mining, transporting, and crushing ore generates large amounts of dust. This has significantly increased the levels of particulates in the air. During the dry summer months, the operation of many large trucks along dirt roads intensifies the problem considerably.

Twin Lakes believes that it can control a great deal of the dust generated immediately around the plant and is planning to incur this expense without help from Tamarack. The most significant debate with the city has been over a series of roads around the outskirts of the city. They need to be paved to reduce the dust in the air to acceptable levels. Many of the roads are city-owned, and some have been specially constructed by the company for the transportation of ore and material. Almost all of the roads, including those constructed by the company, are used frequently by tourists. All of the roads have to be paved for Twin Lakes to comply with the environmental regulations and stay in business.

Air quality—road maintenance: The roads in question currently require a minimal amount of maintenance. They will require a much higher degree of maintenance if they are paved, however, especially because the harsh winters tend to break up paved roads. To keep the roads in an acceptable condition, the city and company will have to agree on who will maintain them.

Site of next mine: Twin Lakes has been testing several locations in the Tamarack area to determine the extent of iron ore deposits. Several of the locations have enough ore to be profitable, and Twin Lakes would like to open a new mine. Although the actual mining may not begin immediately, the decision concerning the location of a new site has to be made now to allow time for both the company to plan for a new mine and the city to plan its expansion around any new mining site.

Restoration of consumed mines: The consumed mines that are no longer used by the company are outside city limits. Some of these mines lie alongside main roads leading into the city from the most popular resort areas on local lakes. The city considers the consumed mines unsightly and is afraid that tourists may be repelled by the mines. The company has restored the land to the extent required by law, but the city would like to see further restoration.

Tax rate on company land: The land for the mine currently in operation is outside city limits. However, the plant lies within city boundaries, and Twin Lakes pays a substantial amount of money in taxes. The company has always felt that the Tamarack taxation rate is excessive.

Both the company and the city believe that if some resolution could be obtained on these major issues, the remaining problems could be easily resolved, and Twin Lakes would agree to keep its operations in the Tamarack area in business. Toward this end, a formal negotiation has been arranged between the City of Tamarack and the Twin Lakes Mining Company.

Exercise 13

Island Cruise

Introduction

In this exercise you will participate in a negotiation about a cruise ship and its rights to visit a tropical island. You will role-play this negotiation as either the director of the cruise ship or the mayor of the island. The issues to be discussed during the negotiation include the number of visits per year that the ship can make, the length of individual visits, and the volume of passengers allowed to disembark from the ship on each day when it visits. This simulation provides a rich context for a business negotiation in which economic, cultural, and ecological factors all come into play.

Background Information

The *Island Queen* is a privately owned and operated luxury cruise ship. Cruise ship passenger demand has steadily fallen over the past few years due to the poor economy, fear of worldwide terrorism, and recurring cases of the Norwalk virus on cruise ships. Norwalk-like viruses, which have afflicted hundreds of passengers on several cruise ships, cause diarrhea, stomach pain, and vomiting. The *Island Queen's* operations department has decided that adding a new exotic destination to the standard 16-day itinerary will help stimulate passenger demand. While many islands in the region are possible candidates, Tropical Island is its first choice due to the island's reputation as an exotic and pristine locale.

Tropical Island

Tropical Island is part of a chain of lush Pacific islands in one of the most remote spots on earth. At 10 miles wide by 38 miles long, the island is not large. However, it is home to an extensive array of rare and endangered plant and animal species, many found only on Tropical Island. The traditional rural and native culture of the island has remained relatively unchanged over time, earning it the nickname "The Last Unspoiled Island."

The island is a wonderful combination of rain forests, desert lands, waterfalls, and black- and white-sand beaches. Weather on the island is pleasant year round, with maximum daytime temperatures ranging from 88 degrees Fahrenheit in the summer (May to October) to 80 degrees in the winter (November to April). Nighttime temperatures rarely fall below 60 degrees. As a result, the island's tourism, though considered minimal, remains almost constant year-round, at about 70,000 visitors per year.

Approximately 60 percent of the island's 7,000 residents have true Pacific Island ancestry. This makes Tropical Island the only one in the region where true natives are

Source: This exercise was written by Jeff Peddie in collaboration with Lisa Barron. Copyright © 2003 by Jeff Peddie. Used with permission.

the majority. These natives continue to practice the region's old traditions while trying to minimize the influence of the rampant commercialism found on other islands. The two closest islands are more than 25 miles away and are far more commercialized than Tropical Island.

Compared to the other islands in the region, Tropical Island is a quiet and pristine world of breathtaking beauty, where one can easily escape to peaceful solitude or participate in a myriad of outdoor activities. In addition, prices on the island are generally lower than on surrounding islands. As a result, many visitors are actually repeat customers, reimmersing themselves in the idyllic lifestyle they know they will find on the island.

Typical island activities include surfing, kayaking, fishing, and hiking. Snorkeling and scuba diving are especially spectacular due to the abundance of giant sea turtles. The island is also home to the longest barrier reef in the region, which stretches 28 miles. Guided hiking tours of the island's extensive rain forests allow visitors to learn about the flora and fauna unique to the region. For the less sure-footed, guided mule rides down the highest oceanfront cliffs in the world offer dramatic views of the unspoiled coastline.

With only one movie theater, one public restroom, and no stoplights, the island takes pride in its lack of development. A weekly Saturday morning farmer's market offers a vibrant taste of the rich local heritage. In addition, the island's macadamia nut farm, coffee plantation, and kite factory provide abundant opportunities to explore the island's unique character. Dining options cover the full spectrum from inexpensive eateries to extravagant gourmet feasts, complete with traditional native entertainment.

In addition to tourism, major industries on the island include fishing, farming, and retail sales. With the collapse of the sugar and pineapple industries in the 1990s, the island has moved to replace these once dominant industries with more diversified aquaculture and agriculture.

Tropical Island is governed by an autonomous council. Residents elect a mayor, who serves a three-year term with a two-term limit, and an eight-member island council with two-year terms. The island council, with current mayor Gil Egan as its representative, is responsible for making all decisions regarding the island community. Decisions are made by majority vote of the council. The mayor performs the function of "tie-breaker" when necessary.

There are five public and two private schools on the island serving 2,000 students from kindergarten through twelfth grade. Residents seeking a college-level education typically move off the island for the duration of their studies. These students rarely return to live permanently on the island. This has been a major concern of the islanders, who wish to reduce the loss of native residents. Therefore, construction of a local community college is under consideration.

Current means for tourists to access the island include small aircraft and small sea vessels. There are also two inter-island flights per day between Tropical Island and the surrounding islands, with each flight carrying about 50 passengers. On any given day, about 200 tourists arrive or depart Tropical Island, with a total of 500 tourists on the island at any given time. Electric cart rentals are available at the airport for transportation around the island.

Marine ecological studies performed on Tropical Island by the United Nations' International Maritime Organization Agency indicate that for each day a cruise ship operates in Tropical Island's sensitive coastal waters, at least two weeks of undisturbed marine environment must be maintained afterward to avoid permanent ecological damage. Each additional day of operation requires two additional weeks of recovery. The ecosystem, however, is not able to sustain more than five consecutive days of abuse. These figures assume no intentional damage to the ecosystem, such as removal of coral or wildlife as a result of cruise ship–related tourism.

During the time that a cruise ship is anchored near the island, and for four days following its departure, local residents are advised not to fish or swim within a two-mile radius of where the cruise ship had been anchored because of potential health hazards. The island's only natural harbor is the best location for anchoring cruise ships. Unfortunately, this two-mile-wide bay is also the island's most productive fishing spot.

The *Island Queen*

At 971 feet in length and weighing 91,000 tons, the $400 million *Island Queen* is the largest cruise ship ever to service the Tropical Island region. It accommodates 2,200 passengers and 1,100 crew members. Operation of the *Island Queen* is handled through Island Queen, Inc., a private corporation. Captain Stuart (Stu) Bing is the director of cruise ship operations for the *Island Queen.* While he has sole responsibility for negotiating all contracts governing the vessel's operation, he ultimately answers to the CEO and the board of directors of Island Queen, Inc., regarding all corporate matters.

With 10 distinctive restaurants and 14 separate lounges and bars, the *Island Queen* has a venue for the most discriminating guest. Passengers who desire the excitement of gambling will enjoy the lavish Grand Casino with its glass elevators, floating staircases, stained glass domes, and ocean view windows. The magnificent Riviera Deck, adorned with sparkling pools, bars, hamburger grill, ice cream bar, gymnasium, and spa, is the perfect spot for outdoor activities and food. The *Island Queen* sets a new standard for luxury cruise ships with its unique alternative 24-hour dining in the panoramic Horizon Court, two theaters, computerized golf, and a library featuring "listening chairs" for music and audio books. Industry standard venues and amenities such as buffet meals, theaters, and gyms are included in the price of the cruise. Dining in the more exclusive restaurants and some personal services such as massages and beauty treatments are an additional expense billed separately to the passenger.

The standard *Island Queen* cruise is 16 days and 15 nights. The itinerary consists of five days sailing to the island region, six days visiting various tropical islands, and five days returning to its home port. An island visit generally involves passengers disembarking at 8 a.m. and returning to the ship by 8 p.m. On more popular islands, the ship will remain in port for two days. At these ports, passengers may elect to spend the night on the island, but they must return to the ship by 8 p.m. the following evening when the ship sets sail for the next port.

Island Queen, Inc., has provided luxury cruises to the island region for over 20 years, but Tropical Island has never allowed cruise ships to visit. For economic reasons, Tropical Island is now considering offering exclusive visitation rights to a cruise line company. Though other cruise line companies are vying for the right to add Tropical Island to their itinerary, the *Island Queen* is the most luxurious prospect. An agreement with the *Island Queen* is expected to provide greater income per tourist for the island than an agreement with any of the other cruise lines because of the *Island Queen*'s wealthier clientele.

During one-day port visits, about half of the ship's passengers typically disembark. As the length of stay increases, fewer passengers disembark per day. Those who remain on the ship are an important revenue source as they continue to patronize onboard facilities including the casino, shops, and restaurants. Island disembarkation agreements are negotiated in increments of 100 passengers. Thus an agreement for 500 passengers per day would include any number of visitors up to 500. There are currently no island visits longer than two days because this would not leave enough time to visit all the other popular ports. However, a visit longer than two days is certainly possible given sufficient demand.

Because there is no suitable deepwater dock on Tropical Island, cruise ships will have to anchor in the ecologically sensitive coastal waters surrounding the island. A smaller vessel must then make multiple trips ferrying passengers back and forth between the ship and the island. The island's harbor area is considered the best location for anchoring cruise ships due to its proximity to the main island community.

Tropical Island and *Island Queen* Concerns

Large cruise ships, like the *Island Queen,* can severely impact the local marine ecology during their stay. According to one environmental group, typical cruise ships "produce massive volumes of waste, including sewage, nonsewage wastewater or gray water, ballast water, oily bilge water, air pollution, solid waste, and hazardous waste, each of which may harm sensitive marine ecosystems like the island's through the addition of harmful pathogens and chemicals, or the introduction of alien species."[1] There are, however, international environmental standards under which cruise lines must operate. These standards, set forth in international conventions, create strict guidelines for all commercial vessels, including passenger vessels, to prevent ship-generated pollution for oil, garbage, and waste.[2]

Still, the island community has strong reservations about allowing cruise-based tourism because of the industry's dismal record of environmental compliance and poor enforcement of laws regarding ship pollution.

There is also concern that a sudden increase in tourism will adversely affect the social makeup of the quiet rural island. Environmentalists point to small islands and towns in Alaska and the Caribbean whose local lifestyle, culture, and economy become crowded out by foreign visitors. The island council's community plan defines its primary economic focus as agricultural industries. Tourism is to be limited to a level that will not adversely affect the community's traditional, social, economic, and environmental characteristics. An agreement between the *Island Queen* and Tropical Island must take into account the impact it will have on the traditional lifestyle and customary rights of the native inhabitants.

The main reason cruise ship companies have been hesitant to add Tropical Island to their itinerary has been the lack of island infrastructure to support the needs of a typical cruise ship visit. Too many cruise tourists descending upon the island all at once may overwhelm existing island facilities, resulting in an unpleasant experience for everyone. The fact that there is only one public restroom on the island is enough to dissuade even the most optimistic tour operator. Limiting the number of tourists disembarking will help preserve the island's natural character and benefit the cruise ship since remaining passengers will spend their money on board the ship.

Conclusion

Traditional island culture and mores, as well as island law, forbid council members, and Mayor Gil Egan as their representative, from accepting any form of financial incentives, such as bribes, from the cruise lines to gain commercial access to Tropical Island. A respectful and mutually beneficial relationship between Tropical Island and the *Island Queen* is desirable.

Any agreement between Tropical Island and the *Island Queen* should take into account the current economic environment, existing resources and infrastructure, expected tourism income for both parties, and any damage to local ecology and native culture resulting from added cruise line tourism. International maritime law requires that any agreement between the parties remain in force for six years following its adoption, so it is important to consider anticipated trends with any agreement since renegotiating in the near term will be very difficult, if not impossible.

Endnotes

1. "Moloka'i Citizens Sue for Environmental Review of Cruise Ship Visits," *Earthjustice*, December 3, 2002.

2. "Technical and Regulatory", Cruise Lines International Association, *http://www.Crusing.org/industry/environment/cfm.*

Salary Negotiations

Introduction

In this simulation, you will play the role of either a manager or subordinate in a negotiation over the subordinate's salary. Both in securing employment as well as promotions, we are frequently in a position to negotiate with our superiors over salary. Moreover, once we achieve managerial rank, we do the same with subordinates. This is one of the most common and, at the same time, most personal forms of negotiation. For many people, it is also the most difficult. Since salary can be a means of satisfying many needs—economic, recognition, status, or competitive success measure—it naturally leads to complex negotiations.

Source: Developed from examples used by John Tarrant, *How to Negotiate a Raise* (New York: Van Nostrand Reinhold, 1976).

Job Offer Negotiation: Joe Tech and Robust Routers

Introduction

The scenario for this simulation is a negotiation over a job offer that has been extended by a technology company to an MBA student nearing graduation. The background information introduces the principals involved, recaps their prior relationship, and presents a detailed summary of the terms of the offer that the firm has extended to the student. For the negotiation simulation, you will be assigned to assume the role of either the student or a representative of the hiring company. The role-play information that your instructor will then provide gives details about the specific interests and objectives of the party to which you are assigned.

In many ways, negotiations about job offers are just like any other negotiation: Parties try to pursue their own interests while keeping an eye on relationship concerns and seeking areas of common ground that might allow them to bridge compatible interests. In other ways, however, job offer negotiations may be perceived as distinctive because of the stakes involved: For the job seeker, they involve the negotiation of one's personal circumstances, often with an opponent who is someone you will have to "live with" on a day-to-day basis for what could be a long time to come. As you read your role information and prepare for the encounter, think about how the pursuit of your goals—whether you are in the role of the hiring firm or the job-seeking student—may or should be affected by the unique context involved when one is negotiating about employment.

Background Information

Joe Tech, an MBA student in the final semester before graduation, has an offer (see Offer Letter, below) for permanent employment from Robust Routers (RR), and the deadline for accepting the offer is next week. Joe spent the summer before his final year in the MBA program working for RR in Mountain View, California. His boss during the summer internship was Leigh Bultema, the product manager for RR's flagship product—a new terabit router. Leigh is the person at RR with whom Joe will speak to negotiate the terms of the offer.

Economic and Industry Conditions

At the time of the job offer, the U.S. economy has leveled off following a prolonged upswing. Economic growth is significantly lower than it was just a couple of years ago. The mixed news for MBA students, however, is that although the unemployment rate is

Source: This simulation was developed by Jorge Ferrer, Andy Lauman, Fred Smith, and Tobey Sommer. It is adapted and used here with permission.

elevated, and the job market for new MBA graduates has remained reasonably strong. In recent years, "traditional" MBA employers such as banks and consulting firms have felt pressure to compete with aggressive technology companies recruiting top MBA prospects with potentially lucrative stock options. More recently, the stock market entered a period of high turbulence, dampening the outlook for smaller technology firms. Even the most promising and profitable tech companies have seen their share prices come under pressure. Companies like RR, which make Internet "backbone" equipment, operate with extraordinary profit margins, and yet even their shares have fallen.

Just last week, however, there was a rebound in tech share prices, in part due to the resolution of a strike at Horizon Communications. Horizon settled its labor dispute and reaffirmed its commitment to capital spending, which Wall Street analysts had predicted would slow over the next two years. That potential slowdown would have eroded the stock valuations of network infrastructure manufacturers in general, and market leader RR in particular. Now Horizon has reaffirmed its capital expenditure plans and announced a multiyear purchase of RR's high-end terabit routers.

Company Background

Robust Routers (RR) was started by several enterprising graduate business students who had helped their university tie its computer lab machines together into a local area network. Anticipating a market for networking devices, the two borrowed money from friends and family, maxed out their credit cards, and started a company. Two years later they sold their first network router.

Originally targeting universities, RR by the late 1990s had expanded its marketing to include large and medium-sized corporations. As an early player with a proven track record, RR had a head start when the market for network routers took off in the early 1990s. RR's sales lept from $1 million in 1993 to $30 million in 2000. The company went public in 2001. Since then, RR has acquired several niche players in the market and currently has a market capitalization of $120 billion, a significant accomplishment for a company its age.

The computer hardware networking industry consists of companies designing, developing, and manufacturing products that provide connectivity solutions for multiuse computing environments, local area networks, and wide area networks. Network hardware products include PC cards, routers, hubs, remote access servers, switches, and adapters. At the time of Joe Tech's job offer, RR controls more than two-thirds of the global market and offers the industry's broadest range of products used to form information networks and power the Internet.

RR sells in approximately 75 countries through a direct sales force, distributors, value-added resellers, and system integrators. RR continues to purchase companies at a frenzied pace—it has made close to 10 acquisitions per year during the last two years. RR serves customers in three target markets: (1) enterprises—large organizations with complex networking needs, including corporations, government agencies, utilities, and educational institutions; (2) service providers—firms providing information services, including telecommunications carriers, Internet service providers, cable companies, and wireless communication providers; and (3) small/medium businesses—firms with a need for data networks of their own, as well as connection to the Internet and/or to business partners.

Joe Tech's Internship Experience at RR

Joe worked at RR during the summer between his first and second years of graduate school. He was fortunate to have secured an internship at the leading router company because they don't normally recruit from his school. He contacted an alumnus who worked for Horizon (one of RR's largest customers), who put him in touch with a friend at RR. Joe and Leigh Bultema hit it off from the initial exchange of e-mails, and after a fast-track series of telephone interviews, Joe had his internship set up for the summer.

Leigh Bultema began working at RR eight years ago, when the company took the market and really began to pull away from its competition. She was in the right place at the right time. RR had proprietary technology that promised to revolutionize the telecom industry, and Leigh had drive, ambition, and brains. Leigh rose through the ranks at RR quickly, working in positions in sales, marketing, manufacturing, and business development activities. A proven performer, Leigh has been assigned to pivotal and vital roles within RR during her tenure. RR has identified product management of the new terabit router as a priority function, and the CEO personally placed Leigh in this crucial role.

When he landed the summer internship, Joe expressed an interest in working in business development. However, because he did not enter RR through traditional recruiting channels from a top five MBA program, the business development internships were already filled. There were 50 MBA interns working at RR over the summer. They were spread out among marketing, strategic alliances, technical development, business development, treasury, and corporate marketing. Joe worked on product management for Leigh during the summer. The internship exposed Joe to senior management and different groups within the company, including the business development group for which Joe hoped to work after completing his MBA. Business development maintained all key business relationships at RR and was considered one of the preeminent functions within the firm. Joe received accolades from very senior executives on his internal product presentations of the terabit router.

The internship ended on a high note for the company and for Joe Tech. RR received an order from Horizon for its terabit router, and Joe received an offer letter from RR. The offer came from Leigh Bultema's product management group, not the business development group Joe was targeting. However, job assignments at RR changed frequently. At the end of the summer, Leigh assured Joe that if his interest truly lay with business development, all he had to do was perform well within product management and he could write his own ticket internally. Leigh herself had performed well in her initial job assignment within RR, and subsequently found herself courted by executives from several different internal groups who wanted her on their teams.

Although the permanent job offer was tendered back in August at the conclusion of the internship, RR told Joe that the offer would remain available until March 1. The specific terms of the offer are shown in the offer letter. Now it is February 20, and Joe has arranged to speak with Leigh to discuss the offer before making a decision.

Offer Letter

Robust Routers, Inc.
One Robust Center
555 Silicon Way
Mountain View, CA 94201

August 25, 2009

Joe Tech
401 Owen Way
Nashville, TN 37220

Dear Joe,

On behalf of Robust Routers, Inc., I am delighted to confirm our offer to you of the position of Associate Product Manager. Your appointment will be effective June 1, 2010. The specifics of this offer are as follows:

Position: Associate Product Manager, Terabit Router Group

Salary: Starting salary will be $88,000 annually, paid monthly.

Signing bonus: You will receive a signing bonus of $15,000, paid as a lump sum within 30 days after you accept the offer in writing.

Options: You will receive 1,000 stock options at a strike price equal to the share price of RR on the date of employment. Additionally, you will be eligible to receive a minimum grant of 500 incentive options after your first year of employment, and on each subsequent employment anniversary, provided your performance fully meets expectations and that you are an active employee on the subsequent grant date. The strike price for these options is set by company management and ratified by the board of directors annually. Options vest over a three-year period (33.3% per year).

Benefits: Robust Routers provides a comprehensive benefit plan to its employees. You will be entitled to the benefits detailed in the applicable plan document in effect at the time you join the company. Current benefits include health insurance, basic life insurance, dependent life insurance, long-term disability coverage, and immediate participation in Robust Router's matched savings plan for retirement. The Human Resources Department will send details on these benefits, along with specifics regarding paid sick leave, vacation leave, and holiday leave, under separate cover.

Relocation: You will receive a lump sum cash payment of $5,000 to help defray expenses associated with moving to Silicon Valley. Upon acceptance of our offer, you will receive a relocation handbook, which will provide detailed instructions regarding relocation benefits and information on the local area provided by several real estate firms.

Robust Routers is offering you a position with the understanding that you are not a party to a written agreement containing either a noncompete or nonsolicitation clause. Our corporation conducts routine employment checks on prospective employees. Your employment is contingent upon the successful completion and satisfactory results of these checks.

This offer remains in force until March 1, 2010. If you choose to accept the offer, please sign and return a copy of this offer letter on or before that date. Should you have any questions, the appropriate point of contact is the hiring manager, Leigh Bultema.

We are impressed with your background and experience, and we look forward to having you join the Robust Router team in June.

Sincerely,

Keith Hernandez
Managing Director
Product Management Group

cc: Leigh Bultema
     Human Resources

The Employee Exit Interview

Introduction

This exercise involves a negotiation between the managing director of a small, privately held consulting firm and an employee who wishes to leave the firm for personal reasons. There are two main issues under discussion: (1) back pay for sick days, and (2) stock that the employee wishes to sell back to the firm under its stock buyback plan.

Source: This exercise was written by G. Richard Shell and is used with permission.

Live8

Introduction

The Live8 exercise involves a negotiation between parties who have never met in person, and are negotiating an important transaction using e-mail. It provides a context for thinking about how negotiation skills, cultural differences, and ideology all play out in an online environment. As you negotiate this exercise, think about how negotiating face-to-face with someone differs from negotiating through indirect channels, such as by telephone or over e-mail. Does that make it easier or harder to reach a satisfactory outcome in negotiation? When is it better to negotiate in person and when is it better to use e-mail? This exercise is designed to stimulate thought and discussion around the role of communication channels through which negotiation occurs.

Source: This exercise was developed by Noam Ebner, who teaches in the Werner Institute's Masters Program on Negotiation & Dispute Resolution at Creighton University. Used with permission. Although this exercise alludes to the "LIVE8" concerts that actually occurred in July 2005, the circumstances presented within the exercise are fictitious.

Exercise 18

Ridgecrest School Dispute

Introduction

In this simulation, you will play a member of either a school board or teachers' association bargaining team. You and the other members of your team, and the members of the other team, are negotiators representing constituencies. You will deal with a complex mix of bargaining issues; these issues have different preference functions for each side. Finally, you will be subject to a variety of pressures during the negotiation.

Background Information

(Reprint of a recent, widely read article in *The Ridgecrest Gazette*)

The next round of negotiations between the board of education and the teachers' association is scheduled for the evening of August 24; the final round is scheduled for August 31, the evening before the opening day of the school year (September 1) in Ridgecrest, New Jersey. The contract between the Ridgecrest Teachers' Association (which represents the teachers in Ridgecrest) and Ridgecrest School District expired on June 30. Since then, the board of education and representatives of the teachers' association have met on several occasions in an attempt to finalize a contract, but these attempts have not been successful.

If either party were to declare an impasse after the final round of negotiations, then the state would provide a mediator; if the parties still could not agree, then they would enter "fact finding" (essentially, non-binding arbitration) and a written report would be made public; and if an agreement still could not be reached, then the state would appoint a "super conciliator" (essentially, another mediator). Prior to June 30 and during the summer months, there was increasing talk among the membership of the teachers' association of the desirability of calling a strike if the contract was not finalized by opening day. While it is true that a school board can often get a court order preventing teachers from striking, it is also true that emotions in Ridgecrest are running high, and teacher strikes have been known to happen despite court orders. However, the leadership of the teachers' association has agreed, for the benefit of the community, to maintain normal operations throughout the system (without a contract) *on a day-to-day basis*. This is in response to parent pressures to maintain normal operations. Parents have been placing pressure on both teachers and the board to keep the schools operating.

For the past two consecutive years, voters have defeated referendums for increased taxes to cover unavoidable budgetary increases. Due to decreases in enrollments and in income from state and federal aid, as well as increased costs, maintenance of the school

Source: This exercise was written by Daniel Z. Levin and is an adaptation of the "Newtown School Dispute," by Frank Masters, from *Negotiation: Readings, Exercises, and Cases,* 3rd ed., with R. Lewicki, D. Saunders, and J. Minton, eds. 1998. New York: Irwin. Special thanks to Nareatha L. Studdard and Dan Coulthard for research and other assistance.

budget at par with the previous year would produce a 4.08 percent budgetary shortfall, which the board feels would begin to exhaust budgetary categories beginning in the coming April. Therefore, the board feels that programs and personnel must be cut while, at the same time, productivity (workload) of teachers must be increased if the system is to function effectively within its budgetary constraints to the end (June 30) of the current fiscal year. The district is mandated by New Jersey state law to provide 180 instructional days during the school year.

The board of education is caught between the teachers' association and community pressure groups. Board members, who are elected but not paid, believe that they must satisfy these pressure groups, while at the same time keeping the teachers on the job with a contract that is acceptable to the bargaining unit's membership. The board is concerned that if it fails to respond appropriately to community pressures for cost reductions, it may be removed. The board's primary objective, therefore, is to cut costs while retaining as many programs as possible. It hopes to do so through cutbacks in teaching personnel and benefits. The board also wishes to eliminate certain existing agreements in order to increase productivity. In this connection, the board wants to negotiate a three-year contract that will "stabilize" the situation by creating orderly and predictable budgetary needs that will be less likely to be seen as excessive by various community groups. In contrast, the teachers' association wants to obtain a one-year contract to maintain flexibility.

The teachers' association also feels caught between community pressure groups, who want to avert a strike, and the board's apparent unwillingness to fight for increased budget allocations to run the system. The teachers feel the board has not faced up to the community's unwillingness to accept increased taxation to pay for education, and that the board is simply responding to community unwillingness by passing the burden along to teachers.

Normally, New Jersey state law leaves issues such as reductions in staff entirely at the school board's discretion (i.e., they cannot be negotiated). Governor Fictitious, however, has just signed a new law (passed over the strong objections of the state's school boards association) that allows the teachers' union in one school district in the state, as an experiment, to negotiate over all six issues involved in this negotiation. Moreover, any signed agreement that results from these negotiations will be legally enforceable. The Ridgecrest Teachers' Association applied for and was granted permission for Ridgecrest to be that one school district. As part of the new experimental law that now applies to Ridgecrest, the Ridgecrest Board of Education has until the opening day of school to finalize its budget. In addition, under the new law, any involuntary reductions in teaching staff—if agreed to by the union—must still comply with prior state law on tenure and seniority. That is, untenured teachers must be laid off first but can be laid off in any order. Among tenured teachers (essentially, anyone with three years and one day of experience), however, all teachers in a lower step must be laid off before anyone in a higher step can be laid off.

Ridgecrest is an average-sized, relatively settled, and stable upper-middle-income community, with a strong interest in quality education, but is disinclined to increase its already burdensome tax rate. Like the state as a whole, Ridgecrest has a high cost of living. The Ridgecrest School District consists of 8 schools: 6 elementary schools (K-8) and 2 senior high schools. The student population is 6,200, with 4,135 elementary and 2,065 high school students. The bargaining unit consists of 315 elementary teachers in all categories and 144 high-school teachers in all categories.

Both sides wish to conclude an agreement to avert state involvement (or a strike). However, the teachers' association bargaining team is adamantly committed to improving the lot of its membership, and the board is just as committed to keeping its costs as low as possible. Nevertheless, each side feels it has some room to move on certain issues.

The following three official tables accompanied *The Ridgecrest Gazette* article and are available in print to all parties.

TABLE 1 | Ridgecrest School District Teachers' Salary Schedule

Step	Amount	Last Year's Number of Teachers	Cost	Current Year's Number of Teachers	Cost
1	$38,000	26	$988,000	0	$0
2	$39,000	20	$780,000	25	$975,000
3	$40,000	30	$1,200,000	19	$760,000
4	$41,000	22	$902,000	26	$1,066,000
5	$42,000	31	$1,302,000	22	$924,000
6	$44,600	38	$1,694,800	31	$1,382,600
7	$47,000	30	$1,410,000	38	$1,786,000
8	$50,100	22	$1,102,200	29	$1,452,900
9	$53,400	29	$1,548,600	22	$1,174,800
10	$55,400	30	$1,662,000	27	$1,495,800
11	$57,300	16	$916,800	30	$1,719,000
12	$59,000	15	$885,000	15	$885,000
13	$60,700	13	$789,100	15	$910,500
14	$62,100	10	$621,000	11	$683,100
15	$63,500	9	$571,500	10	$635,000
16	$65,600	10	$656,000	7	$459,200
17	$67,700	8	$541,600	10	$677,000
18	$70,100	9	$630,900	6	$420,600
19	$73,700	7	$515,900	6	$442,200
20	$77,500	107	$8,292,500	110	$8,525,000
Totals		482	$27,009,900	459	$26,373,700

TABLE 2 | Ridgecrest School District Teachers' Ages

Age Range	Current Year's Number of Teachers	Retirement Eligibility[a]
22–46	371	Not eligible.
47–54	28	Most are likely eligible for early retirement, but pension would be cut by 3% for each year under the age of 55.
55–70	60	Probably all are eligible for early or regular retirement. No penalties if eligible.
Total	459	—

[a] Plan is administered by the state. New Jersey law forbids providing an explicit cash incentive to public school teachers solely in exchange for their taking early or regular retirement.

TABLE 3 | Ridgecrest School District Budget

	Last Year Jul 1–Jun 30 Actual Audit	Current Year Jul 1–Jun 30 Projected	Notes
Revenue			
Local property tax	$68,022,021	$68,595,244	a
State aid	$9,060,136	$8,835,494	
Federal grants	$1,687,329	$1,468,536	
TOTAL REVENUE	$78,769,486	$78,899,274	
Expenditures			
Salaries of teachers	$27,009,900	$26,373,700	b
Salaries of aides	$2,085,731	$2,153,076	
Textbooks and supplies	$1,365,124	$1,941,977	c, d
Purchased services	$102,601	$112,189	
Total: Instruction	$30,563,356	$30,580,942	
Salaries of other professional staff	$983,484	$1,023,724	
Purchased training services	$193,729	$200,056	
Total: Improvement of Instructional Svcs.	$1,177,213	$1,223,780	e
Salaries for extracurricular activities	$272,301	$282,786	
Materials and supplies	$20,719	$28,066	d
Total: Extracurricular Activities	$293,020	$310,852	
Salaries for athletics	$427,513	$447,484	
Materials and supplies	$167,652	$175,198	
Total: Athletics	$595,165	$622,682	

(continued)

TABLE 3 | Ridgecrest School District Budget

	Last Year Jul 1–Jun 30 Actual Audit	Current Year Jul 1–Jun 30 Projected	Notes
Salaries of student support professionals	$3,761,263	$3,889,045	f
Salaries of clerical/secretaries	$350,369	$377,784	
Purchased services (specialists)	$813,700	$838,446	
Materials and supplies	$148,194	$214,053	d
Total: Student Support Services	$5,073,526	$5,319,328	
Salaries of school nurses	$727,172	$807,341	
Purchased professional & technical services	$67,607	$68,197	
Materials and supplies	$17,916	$18,730	
Total: Health Services	$812,695	$894,268	
Salaries of librarians/educational media staff	$713,818	$773,014	g
Materials and supplies	$119,468	$157,605	d
Total: Educ'l Media Services/School Library	$833,286	$930,619	
Salaries for general administration	$1,883,023	$1,983,967	
Salaries of clerical/secretaries	$83,277	$86,608	
Legal services	$179,221	$184,494	
Communications/telephone	$270,405	$279,028	
Materials and supplies	$308,608	$402,004	d
Miscellaneous expenditures	$563,984	$575,213	
Total: General Administration	$3,288,518	$3,511,314	
Salaries of principals/assistant principals	$2,057,932	$2,146,188	
Salaries of other professional staff	$19,992	$21,588	
Salaries of clerical/secretaries	$1,285,810	$1,325,063	
Purchased services	$0	$200,000	h
Materials and supplies	$108,526	$142,210	d
Total: School Administration	$3,472,260	$3,835,049	
Salaries for plant operations/maintenance	$3,632,806	$3,742,402	
Cleaning/repair/maintenance services	$243,807	$500,894	i
Purchased services, professional & technical	$481,113	$506,550	
Insurance	$438,853	$489,786	
Materials and supplies	$149,535	$155,118	
Energy (heat and electricity)	$1,713,856	$1,998,402	j
Total: Plant Operation/Maintenance	$6,659,970	$7,393,152	
Salaries for pupil transport coordination	$74,961	$78,634	
Purchased services	$3,262,524	$3,554,649	k
Materials and supplies	$100,766	$102,781	
Total: Student Transportation	$3,438,251	$3,736,064	

(*continued*)

TABLE 3 | Ridgecrest School District Budget

	Last Year Jul 1–Jun 30 Actual Audit	Current Year Jul 1–Jun 30 Projected	Notes
Social Security and Medicare contributions	$996,530	$1,038,174	l
Workmen's compensation	$277,778	$299,340	
Health benefits	$10,117,070	$10,914,664	m
Other employee benefits	$295,140	$323,564	
Total: Employee Benefits	$11,686,518	$12,575,742	
Equipment	$207,456	$193,813	
Facilities acquisition and construction services	$1,171,939	$1,093,206	
Total: Capital Outlay	$1,379,395	$1,287,019	
Out-of-district tuition	$3,674,983	$3,898,099	n
State and federal projects	$2,157,254	$2,100,133	o
Funds for charter schools	$861,133	$897,258	p
Total: Externally Designated Funds	$6,693,370	$6,895,490	
Total: Debt Service	$2,802,943	$3,138,988	
TOTAL EXPENDITURES	$78,769,486	$82,255,289	

Notes on Table 3:

a   Local property tax rate for schools is $1.65 per $100 of assessed real property. Assessment is at full value. No significant change in assessed values expected.

b   Twenty-three teachers from last year did not return to the system for this current year (i.e., they left the system nearly two months ago, on June 30) due to either retirement or other reasons. Teachers' salaries are paid over the course of 10 months (September 1 to June 30).

c   New textbooks are needed to comply with extensive state-mandated curriculum changes.

d   Even after switching to a low-cost supplier, costs of materials and supplies will be up dramatically over last year's cost based largely on the rising cost of paper.

e   Includes mainly curriculum development.

f   Student support professionals include guidance counselors, psychologists, substance abuse coordinators, social workers, and speech therapists.

g   Educational media staff include a school's audiovisual technicians and educational computing staff. These positions tend not to require state certification, whereas librarians do.

h   Includes $200,000 in current year for cost of consultant to redesign the teacher evaluation system.

i   Includes $250,000 for overdue, deferred maintenance.

j   Cost of utilities is expected to increase dramatically due to rate increases set by regulators.

k   Transportation costs are up due to increases in operating and maintenance costs.

l   The state—not Ridgecrest—pays the employer's contribution for Social Security (6.2% of salary, up to the maximum dollar amount required) and Medicare (1.45%) for all teachers, former teachers still employed by Ridgecrest, and many employees whose position require state certification. The state also pays the employer's retirement contributions for these employees, as well as for custodians. Ridgecrest pays the employer contribution for Social Security and Medicare on salaries of employees whose positions do not require state certification, such as aides, secretaries, custodians, some administrators, etc. In addition, Ridgecrest pays the employer's retirement contributions ("other employee benefits") for these employees, with the exception of custodians (whose employer's retirement contributions are paid for by the state).

m Applies to all 783 current employees, all of whom are full time (459 teachers, 92 aides, 55 student support professionals, 41 secretaries, 12 nurses, 9 librarians/media staff, 15 general administrators, 18 principals or assistant principals, 81 custodians, and 1 pupil transportation coordinator).

n Tuition is for special education students whose needs cannot be addressed in-district. The amount is set by the other districts' costs.

o State and federal projects are targeted projects paid entirely by federal grants or state aid earmarked solely for those projects.

p The amount of funds transferred to the charter schools can only be changed by the state legislature.

Total number of pupils: 6,200 (current year); 6,510 (last year)

Total number of teachers: 459 (current year); 482 (last year)

Per pupil expenditure: $13,267 (current year); $12,100 (last year)

Exercise 19

Bestbooks/Paige Turner

Introduction

This situation involves a negotiation between two representatives: one for an author, Paige Turner, and the other for a publishing company, Bestbooks. This is clearly a competitive situation, but some cooperation is also required. Your challenge is to get the best contract possible for your side.

Read the private material that your instructor has provided, and prepare your strategy for the negotiations. Each dyad of representatives will conduct its meeting trying to reach a new contract between Paige Turner and Bestbooks. When an agreement is reached, write down the settlement on the final settlement agreement form. Agreement must be reached on all eight issues in order for a final agreement to be struck.

Final Agreement Settlement Form	
Issue	**Settlement Point**
Royalties	
Signing bonus	
Print runs	
Weeks of promotion	
Number of books	
Advance	
Countries distributed	
Book clubs	

Source: Written in collaboration with Gregory Leck.

Strategic Moves and Turns

Introduction

This exercise involves two short vignettes about negotiation situations within organizations. In each situation, the protagonist has a challenging negotiation that involves getting the other person to negotiate seriously. In the first one, a health care agency director is negotiating with her CEO for a promotion. In the second one, a pharmaceutical company executive is negotiating with an executive from a partner company about a joint venture in South America. Both situations involve challenges associated with overcoming resistance and getting one's proposals heard.

Vignette #1: Cynthia's Challenge[1]

Cynthia is a program director in a large home health care agency. She has worked there for five years and received salary increases as she has been promoted. With the resignation of the vice president, Cynthia is now one of the most senior people in the agency in terms of responsibility, but not in terms of salary. At the same time she has been taking on added responsibilities because of turnover and finds herself working more than 80 hours a week and picking up the slack from the vice president's departure. She knows that others with less responsibility are paid more than she is, and that eats at her. She also wants the vice president position. She's been essentially doing the job in an "acting" role and wants it to be official. She's always been on good terms with George, the CEO, helping him out when he needed it. Recently she oversaw an audit of the agency where she worked around the clock, making sure it was successful, and it was. Deciding the time was right, she planned to see George about a promotion to the vice president position with an increase in pay the job merited.

Cynthia had a negotiation with George about salary a year ago. Although she ultimately got a raise, the negotiations were difficult and she felt she deserved more. George praised her, telling her how much he valued her contributions to the organization. But when she raised the salary issue, he became angry and accused her of being inconsiderate and irresponsible in bringing the issue up. Cynthia did not want this situation to be repeated.

Vignette #2: Marjorie's Mandate[2]

As the newly appointed vice president of global joint ventures for ABCO, a large pharmaceutical company, Marjorie is responsible for monitoring and managing the firm's portfolio of joint venture projects. Always a vocal supporter of ABCO's emerging markets division, she was excited when Jim Drake, the CEO, gave her the opportunity to head this new function in the business. She knew that Jim, a risk-averse fellow, was skeptical about how profitable some of the joint ventures in South America and Asia would turn out to be. Marjorie's mandate was to analyze the existing joint ventures worldwide. Based on this analysis, the firm would invest in the profitable ventures, but "clean house," meaning disband the unprofitable ones. Jim, however, was prone to sending mixed messages. Over her 10 years at ABCO, Marjorie had learned that even with clear evidence that a project was a losing proposition, he hated to kill it.

Marjorie's recent challenge was a struggling marketing initiative in Chile that ABCO had undertaken with one of its South American partners—Sorso, Inc. Despite the losses mounting on the venture's books, Sorso was requesting an additional infusion of capital. Although other joint venture initiatives with Sorso continued to be reasonably successful in other countries in South America, this three-year-old project had problems from the beginning. Based on her current numbers and financial modeling, she saw further deterioration ahead. Additional funding, Marjorie decided, was not warranted until the political and economic climate in the region improved.

Dick Cortez headed ABCO's operations in South America. Although Marjorie had complete faith in Dick's abilities, she was concerned that he was not on top of this problem. The picture was not altogether clear, however, since Dick reported to Greg— the vice president of the International division and Marjorie's peer—and not to her. Further, Dick had generally had free reign in how he managed operations in his area.

Marjorie began to push Dick hard on cutting back in Chile. "Dick believed the currency crunch was a temporary setback," she said. "Although he agreed that revenues had been slow to materialize, he pointed out that we had invested significant sums in building distribution channels in the region. These would be put at risk were we to scale back." Marjorie thought that Dick was too heavily involved with Sorso on other ventures to be able to see the benefits of shutting this losing proposition down. Moreover, Dick handled only South America. "He didn't want his budget sliced. I, on the other hand, had overall responsibility for these distribution arrangements, and I, not Dick, would be held accountable for poor performance."

CEO Jim Drake, impatient with Dick's foot-dragging, told Marjorie to get a handle on the Chilean joint venture. Although Dick thought that he should control what happened in his area, Marjorie decided she needed to intervene directly in the negotiations with Sorso in order to dismantle the project. Under pressure from Jim, she felt she had to move quickly and planned to travel to South America within the next few months to negotiate the venture's dissolution. Since the other South American joint ventures with Sorso would be continued, she hoped that Dick wouldn't see this decision as a harbinger of things to come, but rather as the phasing out of one unsuccessful experiment within a larger operation.

At her first meeting with Sorso, Marjorie learned that Dick had already been negotiating with them without telling her. Their understanding was that Dick was ABCO's chief negotiator with Sorso based on the excellent working relationship they had established. Marjorie proposed several options for ending the Chilean joint venture, but they responded that Dick had assured them the venture would continue. After the meeting, Marjorie confronted Dick about these private and unauthorized negotiations. He was nonchalant and told her not to get so excited. He was simply trying to maintain the good working relations that he had spent so long setting up with Sorso. He assured her that he would take care of it and that she shouldn't worry. This arrangement was not agreeable to Marjorie.

Endnotes

1. This vignette was developed by Deborah M. Kolb, Deloitte Ellen Gabriel Professor for Women and Leadership, Simmons School of Management, 2002. Used with permission.

2. This vignette was written by Fleur Weigert under the direction of Deborah M. Kolb, 2000. Used with permission.

Elmwood Hospital Dispute

Introduction

In this exercise you will be dealing with a very complex negotiation situation. In contrast to earlier exercises, where there may have been a single opponent and one or two clearly defined issues, this simulation creates a negotiation between larger groups with less clearly defined issues—and perhaps stronger emotions. The key roles played by mediators are also introduced in this simulation.

Background Information

The situation described here is a composite, with some data drawn from a number of similar disputes, and other information constructed specifically for this training exercise. The scenario is not to be interpreted as an account of any actual dispute. This simulation is one of several developed and tested by the Institute for Mediation and Conflict Resolution in New York, and adapted with permission by the Community Conflict Resolution Program.

Elmwood is a medium-sized, 450-bed private hospital in a southwestern city of approximately 600,000. It is well equipped for inpatient care and has an open-heart surgery team that is a matter of special pride to the board of trustees and the hospital's director. None of the trustees live in the hospital's immediate neighborhood, though some of their parents once did. Most of them are professionals or business-people, and one of their main functions as trustees is to help in fund-raising for the hospital.

Until 10 years ago, Elmwood was in the middle of a white, middle-class community. Now, however, it is on the eastern edge of an expanding low-income neighborhood, which has moved across the nearby expressway and is continuing to grow eastward. A good part of the low-income community is served by West Point Hospital, back on the western side of the expressway. People on the east, however, are turning to Elmwood. There are very few private physicians left in the Elmwood area, and the hospital, through its outpatient clinic, is the main source of medical care for the newer residents.

These newer residents, who now make up approximately 65 percent of the service area, are a mix of relatively recent newcomers to the city, some from other parts of the United States and others from various foreign countries. Most are in low-paying service jobs. Many are on public assistance. Infant mortality is three times as high as in the rest of the city. Malnutrition is a problem, as are tuberculosis, lead poisoning, and other diseases associated with a slum environment. Most of these new residents cannot afford to be admitted to the hospital when sick and rely instead on outpatient treatment in what is now an overburdened facility at Elmwood.

Source: Adapted from an activity developed for the Institute for Mediation and Conflict Resolution.

Like most hospitals, Elmwood is in a financial squeeze. In addition, it has become increasingly difficult to attract new interns and residents and harder to retain present professionals. Although the hospital director is somewhat sympathetic to the medical care problems of the community, he sees his first priority as building the hospital's institutional strength by such measures as increasing intern- and resident-oriented research opportunities and adding facilities that would induce the staff to stay on rather than go elsewhere. He has apparently given some thought to sponsoring a neighborhood health center, but it has been put off by location problems. He has also heard about some heated conflicts over control of services at other hospitals in the state that took state and federal health grants. Right now, the director apparently intends to put these matters on the back burner until he gets the other things going.

Residents of the low-income community have organized a Concerned Community Coalition (CCC). The community has been asking the hospital to increase its almost nonexistent efforts in preventive medical care, improve and expand outpatient facilities, establish a satellite health center with day care facilities, and train a roving paraprofessional health team to administer diagnostic tests throughout the community. Elmwood is their neighborhood hospital, and to them, this is what a neighborhood hospital should be doing for the residents.

Two weeks ago, the CCC sent a letter to the director asking that the hospital initiate these efforts and requesting that he meet with them to discuss how the community and the hospital could work together. Although the community is deeply concerned about its medical problems and resents the fact that a city institution has not acted before this of its own volition, the letter was not unfriendly.

To date, the letter has not been answered.

Three days ago, the director and the chairman of the board announced the acquisition of a site about 15 blocks from the hospital on which it said it would build a heart research facility, a six-story nurses' residence, and a staff parking lot, with shuttle bus service to the hospital grounds.

On learning of the plans, the leaders and members of the CCC were incensed. They decided to sit in at the director's office until the hospital met their needs.

The day before yesterday, about 50 CCC supporters took over the director's office, vowing not to leave until the hospital agreed to meet the following demands:

1. Replacement of the board of trustees with a community-controlled board.

2. A 100 percent increase in outpatient facilities.

3. Establishment of a neighborhood health center and a day care facility on the newly acquired site.

4. Establishment of a preventive diagnostic mobile health team, consisting of neighborhood residents chosen by the CCC.

5. Replacement of the director by one chosen by the community.

While the hospital director indicated that he would be glad to meet with the group's leader to discuss the matters raised in its letter, he also stated quite forcefully that he considered the new demands arrogant and destructive and that, in any event, he would not meet under duress (i.e., as long as the sit-in continued).

The CCC said it would not leave until a meeting took place and the demands were accepted.

The sit-in began two days ago. This morning the hospital's lawyers moved to get an injunction against the sit-in. The CCC, aided by a legal services attorney, resisted.

The judge reserved decision, stating that to grant an injunction might only make the situation worse. He noted that both the hospital and the CCC would have to learn to live together for their own joint best interest. He therefore instructed the parties to meet to try to work out the problems between them, and has appointed a mediator to assist them. The mediator is a staff member of the city's Human Rights Commission, a unit of the municipal government.

At the judge's suggestion, the sides have agreed to meet with the mediator in the hospital library. The meeting has been scheduled for later today.

Exercise 22

The Power Game

Introduction

The concept of *power* is a complex, elusive, and almost paradoxical one. It is complex because there is a wide variety of definitions of what constitutes power, and how it is effectively accumulated and used. It is elusive because there seems to be very little consensus about the definitions, or the best way to describe power and talk about it in action. Finally, power is paradoxical because it doesn't always work the way it is expected to; sometimes those who seem to have the most power really have the least, while those who may appear to have the least power are most in control.

This simulation offers an opportunity to experience power in a wide variety of forms and styles. During the activity, you may become aware of your own power and the power of others. Your objective will be to determine who has power, how power is being used, and how to use your own power to achieve your goals. This type of analysis is essential to effective negotiations when power relationships have not been well defined.

Source: Adapted from an exercise developed by Lee Bolman and Terrence Deal, Harvard Graduate School of Education, and published in *Exchange: The Organizational Behavior Teaching Journal.* Used with permission.

Exercise 23

Coalition Bargaining

Introduction

The word *coalition* may be loosely defined as a group of individuals or subgroups who assemble to *collectively* exert influence on another group or individual. In an environment where there are many individuals, there are often many different points of view (different interests). Each individual views things differently, and each individual would like to have the "system" represent his or her views. In a dictatorship, the system usually represents the views of the dictator; but in a democratic environment, the views that are represented are usually those of a subgroup who have agreed to work together and collectively support one another's views in exchange for having a stronger impact on the system than each individual could have alone.

Many of us are familiar with the work of coalitions. The patterns of influence in national politics, governments, and communities provide us with some excellent examples. Whether it be the coalitions that are formed along traditional party ties (Democrats or Republicans) or along the concerns of special interest groups (Common Cause, the Sierra Club, the AFL–CIO, the National Rifle Association, the National Organization for Women, or hundreds of others), each group is attempting to influence the direction of the larger system by effectively pooling its resources, working together as a team, and persuading those who have control of the current system.

Coalitions are a common phenomenon in organizations as well. We have seen a significant emergence of coalitions in the business sector. In earlier times, these may have been no more than cooperative agreements and licensing between companies, or efforts to work together to influence political and economic policy. But the demands for increased business competitiveness have spawned a significant number of mergers, partnerships, and strategic alliances between companies, as they attempt to compete in the international marketplace or move into new markets, product lines, and spin-off businesses. Organizations are a complex web of cross-pressures among various subgroups, each one striving to have its own priorities adopted as the primary goals of the total organization. Those who are initiating and leading these efforts must have excellent strategic skills to assess the "power dynamics" that each party brings to this game and sophisticated negotiating skills to forge and manage the relationships between the parties.

The purpose of this exercise is to help you understand the different sources and expressions of power, or *leverage,* that individuals and groups can use in multiparty decision making. In this exercise, you will see people use power and influence in a variety of different ways. See if you can determine what kind of power is being used,

Source: Adapted from Roy J. Lewicki and Joseph Litterer, *Negotiation: Readings, Exercises, and Cases,* 1st ed. (Homewood, IL: Richard D. Irwin, 1985); and from Donald D. Bowen, Roy J. Lewicki, D. T. Hall, and F. Hall, *Experiences in Management and Organizational Behavior,* 2nd and 4th eds. (New York: John Wiley, 1996). Reprinted by permission of John Wiley & Sons, Inc.

and how effective that power is at gaining the other's compliance or cooperation. In addition, this exercise will help you explore the dynamics of trust and cooperation in a strongly competitive situation.

Rules of the Game

Objective

The objective is to form a coalition with another team in order to divide the stake. The coalition must also decide on a way of dividing the stake so as to satisfy both parties.

The Stake

Each team has unequal resources. In spite of the fact that you each contributed $X, you will receive a different stake, depending on the coalition you form. The following table should be filled in with information provided by the group leader (the individual pay-offs are determined by the number of participants in the activity and the total money collected):

If an AB coalition forms, it will receive a stake of $_____.

If an AC coalition forms, it will receive a stake of $_____.

If a BC coalition forms, it will receive a stake of $_____.

The Strategy

Each team will meet separately to develop a strategy before the negotiations. You should also select a negotiator.

Rules for Negotiation

1. All members on a team may be present for negotiations; however, only the negotiator may speak.
2. Notes may be passed to negotiators if desired.
3. A team may change its negotiator between conversations.
4. At the termination of the game, the stake will be allocated only if a coalition has been formed.
5. Only one formal coalition is permitted.
6. A coalition will be recognized by the group leader only if (*a*) no two teams are permitted to receive the same amount of money, and (*b*) neither team in the coalition is allowed to receive zero.
7. If no coalition is reached, no funds are allocated.
8. Negotiations will be conducted in the following fixed order, and for the following fixed periods of time:

Order of Negotiation	Time for First Round of Negotiation	Time for Second and Third Rounds of Negotiation
Teams A and B	5 minutes	4 minutes
Teams A and C	5 minutes	4 minutes
Teams B and C	5 minutes	4 minutes

9.   The team *not* in negotiations—that is, while the other two teams are negotiating—must leave the negotiation room. Other members of the companies who are *not* in the negotiating teams may not speak with any of the negotiators.

10.   There cannot be any conversation between team members and observers at any time.

Valid Coalitions

1.   A coalition will be recognized by the group leader only if (*a*) no teams are permitted to receive the same amount of money, and (*b*) neither team in the coalition is allowed to receive zero.

2.   After negotiations, all three teams are given the opportunity to submit a written statement in the following form: "Team X has a coalition with Team Y, whereby Team X gets $X.xx and Y gets $Y.yy." When written statements meeting these requirements from any two teams agree, a valid coalition has been formed.

End of the Game

The group leader will ask each team to meet separately and to submit a ballot stating the coalition that they believe was formed. A blank ballot may be distributed by the referee, or should be written on a blank sheet of paper, in the following format:

Team (*your team*) has a coalition with Team _____, whereby Team _____ receives _____ (dollars or points) and Team _____ receives _____ (dollars or points).

Put your own team letter (A, B, or C) on the ballot.

Each team brings its written statement to the negotiating room. The group leader will announce whether a valid coalition has been formed (two ballots agree); the money is then distributed as specified on the ballots. If a coalition has not been formed, or if the coalition that has formed does not use up all of the initial stake, a problem will arise as to what to do with the funds.

Exercise 24

The Connecticut Valley School

Introduction

In this situation you must allocate a limited capital budget among seven competing projects. Three parties are involved in the negotiation: the headmaster, the faculty budget committee, and the board of trustees. While the issues in this exercise appear straightforward, the parties do not necessarily perceive the budget process in the same manner.

Read the background information for the Connecticut Valley School; then read the role information that the instructor has provided for you. Participants who have been assigned to the same team (faculty budget committee, board of trustees, headmaster) will meet separately to decide how to manage the upcoming meeting.

The different parties will meet together to negotiate an agreement about the capital projects that will be funded. The chairperson of the board of trustees will chair this meeting. Participants will leave this meeting with an agreement about the priority of the capital spending projects. If no agreement is reached, each team should have a record of their final rankings and where they are willing to make further concessions.

Background Information

The Connecticut Valley School (CVS) is a private boarding school in Massachusetts. Headmaster John Loring has just submitted his annual recommendations for capital spending to the board of trustees. Capital spending will be funded from two sources: new debt and the accumulated interest on the school's endowment. Since the school is approaching its debt capacity and trustees are committed not to draw on the principal of the endowment, the school can afford to spend only $900,000 to $1,000,000 on capital improvements over the next year. The seven major projects under consideration are described briefly here:

1. *Swimming pool*

   Cost: $640,000   Expected life: 15 years

   Currently the school rents a local facility for $60,000 per year. In addition, the school pays $10,000 per year to bus students to the facility. If the school owned a pool, it could rent out pool time to local organizations for $30,000 per year. The headmaster feels that more students would use the pool if it were located on campus.

2. *Buses*

   Cost: $270,000 (3 buses)   Expected life: 6 years
   Salvage value: Nil

Source: Written by Peter Nye, University of Washington at Bothell. Used with permission.

CVS owns two campuses several miles apart. A private bus company transports students between campuses at a cost of $180,000 per year. If the school owns and operates its buses, it will incur $80,000 in operating expenses each year.

3. *New roof for hockey rink*

Cost: $60,000

A new roof is essential to prevent further damage to the rink and to the arena's infrastructure. The project could be delayed one year; but due to the additional damage that would result, total repair costs would jump to $120,000.

4. *Wood chip heating system*

Cost: $800,000   Expected life: 15 years

Cold New England winters and the high cost of fuel oil have been draining the school's operating funds. This new heating system could save the school between $140,000 and $160,000 per year over the next 15 years.

5. *Renovation of fine arts building*

Cost: $300,000

The faculty and trustees agree that an improved fine arts program is critical to the school's liberal arts mission. The renovated fine arts building would include a photography lab, a pottery shop, and art studios, as well as a small gallery. The building would not generate any incremental revenues or cost savings. However, a wealthy benefactor (after whom the building would be named) has offered to contribute $150,000 to subsidize the project. In addition, the facility would provide some marketing benefits, as a strong arts program attracts quality students.

6. *Renovations to women's locker room*

Cost: $40,000

The women's locker room has not been renovated since it was built 33 years ago for visiting men's teams. Many of the women have complained that the facility is dirty, depressing, and overcrowded. Some women refuse to use the facility. The headmaster insists that these complaints are unfounded. The renovations would generate no incremental revenues or cost savings.

7. *Upgrading the computer lab*

Cost: $120,000

Over the past eight years computer equipment has been purchased on a piecemeal basis with surplus operating funds. To support curricular goals, the school needs state-of-the-art computers and more workstations. The director of computing has proposed that the equipment be upgraded over three years. The first stage of this plan would require spending $120,000 on personal computers in the coming year. An additional $160,000 would be spent over the following two years.

The school uses a 12 percent annual discount rate to evaluate all cost-saving investment projects.

Since not all of these projects can be undertaken, they must be prioritized. In his report to the trustees, Headmaster Loring ranked the seven projects as follows:

1. Swimming pool $640,000
2. Hockey rink roof $60,000
3. Buses $270,000
4. Heating system $800,000
5. Fine arts building $300,000
6. Women's locker room $40,000
7. Computer lab $120,000

He recommended that this year's capital funds be spent on the construction of a swimming pool, repairs to the roof of the hockey rink, and the purchase of three buses. These projects would require a total expenditure of $970,000. Loring's rankings were based on his subjective evaluation of cost–benefit trade-offs.

While the trustees must make the final decision, they have solicited advice from the faculty. The faculty is in touch with the day-to-day operations of the school and with the needs of the students. In addition, many faculty members feel that they were closed out of the decision process last year and that the ultimate allocation of funds was inconsistent with the school's objectives. In an attempt to improve the decision process, the trustees appointed a faculty budget committee to advise them on capital spending priorities. A meeting of the trustees, the budget committee, and the headmaster has been scheduled. The purpose of this meeting is to prioritize capital spending projects. It is expected to be a lively and productive session.

Exercise 25

Bakery–Florist–Grocery

Introduction

This is a negotiation involving three parties. Representatives of three retail businesses—a bakery, a florist, and a grocery—will be meeting to negotiate details regarding a proposed joint market that would house all three of them. The tentative plan is to open a large market together in which each of the three shops will be located in a separate space, but in which there will also be shared market space. The idea is to make this joint space look attractive by furnishing it with benches, fountains, and plants, and by installing facilities such as an automatic bank teller machine (ATM). The goal is to make it possible for customers to shop in a pleasant and convenient way in a roofed-in shopping area, which (they hope) should eventually lead to increased sales.

The owner of each shop has appointed someone as a representative to participate in this negotiation. Your instructor will assign you to one of the three shop roles and provide detailed instructions for that role. In the negotiation, there will be three issues to be jointly decided: store design, temperature, and distribution of rental costs.

Source: This simulation was developed by Bianca Beersma, who adapted the "Towers Market" case (see L. R. Weingart, R. J. Bennett, and J. M. Brett, "The Impact of Consideration of Issues and Motivational Orientation on Group Negotiation Process and Outcome," *Journal of Applied Psychology* 78 [1993], pp. 504–17) in order to fit a three-person negotiation context. Used with permission.

The New House Negotiation

Introduction

Many negotiations involve only two parties—a buyer and a seller. However, there are many other negotiations in which the parties are represented by agents. An agent is a person who is hired to negotiate on behalf of the buyer or seller and usually collects some fee or commission based on these services.

The purpose of this negotiation is to gain experience by negotiating through agents. The negotiation simulates the sale and purchase of a piece of real estate, a transaction which is normally conducted through agents. Some of you will play the role of agents; others will play the role of buyers and sellers. This experience should provide a simple but rich context in which to observe the ways that negotiation can very quickly become highly complex.

The House

The property in question is a three-bedroom, two-bath, one-story house. It was listed in the local real estate multiple listings service two weeks ago at $250,000. The house has the following features:

- 2,100 square feet.
- Six years old (one owner prior to current owner).
- Two-car garage.
- Contemporary styling (back wall of house is basically all glass, with sliding draperies).
- Half-acre lot (no flooding problems).
- Brick exterior.
- Built-in range, dishwasher, garbage disposal, and microwave.
- Electric cooling and gas heat.
- Fireplace and ceiling fan in the family room.
- No fence.
- Assumable FHA loan.

Source: This simulation was developed by Conrad Jackson, College of Administrative Science, the University of Alabama at Huntsville. Adapted and used with permission.

EXHIBIT 1

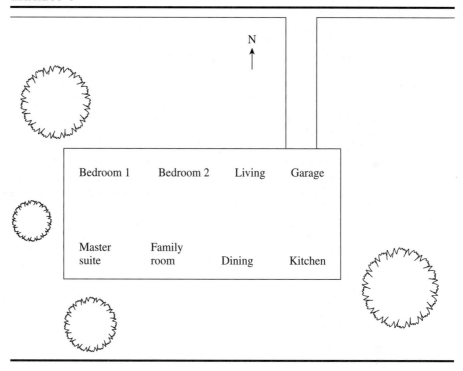

The Buena Vista Condo

Introduction

This exercise is a simulated negotiation regarding the sale of a condominium between a real estate agent representing the sellers and a buyer interested in the property. There are several issues of interest to the two negotiating parties and these will become apparent when you read the role-play information provided to you by your instructor. Your performance in this negotiation will depend on your ability to bargain and come up with creative solutions. Although you are encouraged to think creatively, it is inappropriate to add information that you do not know to be factual. For instance, if you are the buyer, you can not make-believe that your wealthy uncle passed away and left you a fortune that you can use to buy the condo.

Please complete the exercise in the time frame specified by your instructor. After the negotiation, record the outcome of the negotiation (terms of a deal or the absence of a deal, as appropriate).

Source: This exercise was developed by Sreedhari D. Desai. Used with permission.

Eurotechnologies, Inc.

Introduction

This role-play brings three additional new features to your negotiating experience. First, the context of this negotiation is *inside* an organization. In this scenario, you will be asked to represent one of two groups: a management team or a group of scientists who are protesting against a major management decision. Second, this simulation is considerably less structured than others, in that there is a great deal more flexibility and opportunity for creative solutions. Finally, the negotiation occurs in an international context, which may provide a new experience for many of you. We hope you find this simulation an interesting negotiating opportunity.

Eurotechnologies, Inc., General Information

Eurotechnologies, Inc. (ETI), is a Munich-area firm that employs about 900 people. It is a high-technology division of Mentor, whose corporate offices are in Paris. ETI's primary product is an elaborate bioelectronic detection system developed and manufactured under contract with a consortium of European governments. This system is used for detecting various types of life forms through radarlike procedures. Because of the highly classified nature of the manufacturing process and the need for manufacturing to occur in a relatively pollution-free environment, ETI has chosen to separate its manufacturing facilities from its main offices.

The manufacturing facilities are located in a remote area near Wasserburg, Germany, approximately 64 kilometers from downtown Munich. ETI has purchased several hundred acres of land that provide the adequate security and air quality for manufacturing and full-scale test operations. While it is a picturesque area far away from the congestion of the Munich area, it is not without its faults. Access to the plant requires travel over 16 kilometers of a poor locally maintained road; manufacturing employees constantly complain of worn brakes, tire wear, and strain on their cars. The road is often rain-slicked, muddy, and treacherous in the winter. Most of the 630 workers (480 hourly, 140 staff, and 10 R&D personnel who run the test facility) employed in this plant commute from a 45 to 60 kilometer radius over this road into the plant; traffic congestion, particularly around the times of shift changes, makes travel and access a highly undesirable aspect of working for this plant.

The manufacturing facility itself is not air-conditioned and hence frequently hot in the summer and stuffy in the winter. The closest town, Wasserburg, is 16 kilometers away. The Wasserburg plant has a cafeteria, but the food is cooked elsewhere and reheated at the plant. The menu is limited and expensive.

Source: This role-play is developed by Robert Reinheimer, adapted from a scenario developed by Robert Reinheimer and Roy Lewicki. Used with permission. The case and role-play have been prepared for class discussion rather than to illustrate effective or ineffective handling of an administrative situation.

There are two groups of support personnel at Wasserburg. One group (approximately 110 employees) is directly connected with the manufacturing operations as supervisors, shipping and receiving, plant operation and maintenance, stock and inventory, clerical, and so on. The remainder (30 employees) are professional engineers responsible for providing technical support and quality maintenance for manufacturing. Facilities for this support staff are somewhat better than for hourly employees; office space and lighting are adequate and the building is air-conditioned. There is no separate cafeteria, and no place to entertain visitors; staff alternate between bringing their lunch, occasionally purchasing the cafeteria food and taking it back to their offices to eat, or carpooling for the 20-minute drive down to Wasserburg. Dissatisfaction and low morale among the professional staff are rampant.

The Downtown Location

The executive staff offices, the government liaison offices, and the research and development laboratory are located in suburban Munich, just north of the city center. Also, there are test facilities on a one-tenth scale for ongoing research and development programs. All administrative services are conducted from here: employment, payroll, security, data processing and system analysis, and research engineering and design. The buildings are spacious, clean, and air-conditioned and boast two cafeterias: one for hourly workers and one for research personnel and executive officers. Employees can also go out for lunch, and many good restaurants are nearby. Working hours are more flexible, and the environment is more relaxed with less visible pressure. While the normal starting time is 8:00 a.m., professional staff drift in as late as 9:30 and often leave early in the afternoon; working at home is frequent. On the other hand, when deadlines or schedules have to be met, it is not unusual to find them working 60 hours a week. The work environment is more informal and displays casualness similar to a university setting.

As the majority of the Munich-based employees are professional people, they consider themselves a cut above the manufacturing and technical service employees at Wasserburg. While they will acknowledge the value of the revenue generated by Wasserburg, they are convinced that it is really the Munich area group that carries the company. Without their high-level technical advances, ETI would not have the outside reputation it has for premium-quality products. Inside ETI, however, the rivalries between various engineering and scientific personnel led to the creation of "domains" or "kingdoms." The primary split is between Wasserburg and Munich, and over the years it has fostered extensive duplication of efforts. Each group (testing, maintenance, etc.) has been able to procure tools and equipment for itself that normally would be shared if the two locations were closer. The Munich technical divisions have even subcontracted certain testing and development operations to suppliers who are competitors of ETI, due to their basic lack of respect for in-house capabilities at Wasserburg and the red tape and expense of having to work through their own planning and scheduling staffs.

Additionally, the Munich R&D group has taken consulting contracts from other firms and has consistently failed to involve any Wasserburg personnel in those projects.

The Contract Bidding History

In recent years, ETI has put out numerous competitive bids for civilian and military contracts, but few projects have been forthcoming. Analysis of failures revealed that rejections have been due to excessive cost estimates rather than weak technical capabilities. ETI is considered to be one of the top 10 quality-based manufacturing firms of its kind on the continent. However, its overhead costs are prohibitive. The cost of operating two sites, duplication of effort, overstaffing, and a blurring of goals for corporate growth and expansion have caused the overhead rate to be 30 to 40 percent higher than that of competitors. For example, the United Kingdom had recently issued a request for bids on the development of a new bioelectronic system, similar to ETI's current product. The development contract alone was worth 12.25 million euros; and production of these units would be worth 73.35 million euros. ETI was positive it would get the contract. However, when the government evaluated the bids from five different companies, ETI came in first in the technical aspect of the bidding and fifth in the cost aspect; the company did not get the contract.

The Alternatives

Top management's reaction to this setback was to propose a 20 percent cost reduction plan. Many high-salaried technical and engineering personnel were destined to be laid off. The housecleaning was overdue; some deadwood and duplication of effort was eliminated. But after six months, it became a hard, cold fact that further reductions in overhead costs would be necessary in order to continue to be competitive.

ETI owned the Munich-area facility, and top management believed the most obvious way to achieve this reduction was to close it, move all of the Munich-area employees to the Wasserburg facility, and lease out the vacated buildings. The leases would be excellent tax shelters and an additional source of revenue. This consolidation was expected to reduce much of the duplication of effort, as well as provide better coordination on existing and future projects.

In thinking through how the proposed move might be accomplished, top management considered features designed to make it as palatable as possible. First, they proposed to spread the relocations over one full year. Each employee could either accept the move or reject it and accept termination from the company. ETI management would go as far as possible with those employees who rejected the relocation. They would offer a liberal time-off policy to those involved so the employee could seek other employment, provide a special bonus of one month's salary for relocation expenses, notify other companies in the Munich area of the names and résumés of terminating employees, and set up employment interviews with these companies. They also would notify all placement agencies in the area and pay all placement agency fees.

It was clear to management that even with the generous plan they had outlined, the move would be hugely painful for the organization and would represent some very real costs in terms of overall effectiveness. Yet they saw no alternative but to proceed with studying the proposed consolidation.

When the details of the proposal leaked, the plan was met with a massive reaction of hostility and despair. Almost all the Munich-area professional employees felt that a transfer to Wasserburg would mean a sharp decline in status with their peers in similar industries. Most had their homes close to Munich, and the drive to Wasserburg would increase their commuting time and cause wear and tear on their automobiles. The company thus knew that a certain percentage of employees would terminate because of the relocation. It estimated that a "safe level" of termination was 22 percent; if it reached 35 percent in any occupational group, it could be considered a critical problem. Management informally surveyed employees and found that among the administrative staff, the termination rate was likely to be near 25 percent.

The strongest reaction came from the company's research and development staff. They had grown used to having their laboratory and test facilities in the Munich area and drew heavily on informal relationships with faculty at the area's most prestigious universities for ideas and information. Their view was that being forced to move to Wasserburg, in addition to being undesirable, would cripple their ability to function effectively because of their loss of contact with other professionals. Of the 11 members of the research and development staff, only two expressed a willingness to consider the move to Wasserburg. The others claimed they would avail themselves of the many other employment opportunities their specialties commanded. They formally expressed their resistance in a letter to the company president (Exhibit 1).

The letter was written by a committee of R&D personnel formed to represent the group's interests regarding the proposed move. In the letter, they outlined their concerns and volunteered to take 20 percent salary cuts to contribute to the reduction of overhead costs. This reduction would total approximately 183,375 euros.

The committee members consisted of the following six employees:

- Axle Pederson, age 52. Oldest member of the group, but only one year at ETI. Previously worked with several environmental engineering firms in the Munich area. Moved to ETI because of the quality of the other people in the research group and because of interest in the projects that were being considered.

- Thomas Hoffmann, age 49. Most senior member of the ETI group (24 years), and a likely candidate to be the next vice president of research and development. Lived near Munich all his life, and currently lives a block away from Pieter Jensen, the president.

- Manfred Berkowitz, age 42. Fifteen years with ETI, and the most professionally aggressive of the group. Most active in research with high professional visibility.

- Volker Schmidt, age 47. Twenty-two years with ETI. Also very professionally active, second to Berkowitz. Schmidt has spent a number of years developing professional contacts in the Munich area and has been the most articulate in defending the richness of the professional stimulation to be derived from the area.

- Pieter van der Velden, age 36. Five years with ETI. Worked for two years at Wasserburg before being assigned to the Munich group. A definite up and comer in this group.

- Michael Blank, age 32. Four years with ETI. Strong research orientation, a close collaborator with Berkowitz on several professional papers. Berkowitz also served as a mentor to Blank while Blank was completing his PhD at Heidelberg University.

EXHIBIT 1

Mr. Pieter Jensen, President
Eurotechnologies, Inc.
300 Reinstrasse
Munich, Germany

Dear Mr. Jensen:

Our committee, representing your research and development personnel, wishes to express its serious concern about the recent events which have affected our company. We believe that ETI's survival depends on our retaining our technical excellence. We are dismayed that you and your management team seem to be contemplating actions that could cripple that capability.

We have all been shocked by our recent loss of contracts. However, it is critical for you to note that we have never been faulted for our technical expertise. It is our cost structure that prevents us from winning these bids. But an action which addresses the cost problem, while destroying our ability to compete technically, simply trades one problem for a more disastrous one. Closing the Munich facility and consolidating operations at Wasserburg creates just such a trade, and that is unacceptable.

Although no formal announcement of management's response to the current situation has been provided, it is clear that consolidation is in the wind. We believe that forcing R&D to move to the Wasserburg location will ruin the professional network that is our (and the company's) treasured asset. Some alternative must be found and, if it is not, the members of our department will seek individual solutions to their personal problems.

It is time that management emerges from behind closed doors and asks vital members of the company team to become involved in this decision. If management intends to launch this consolidation effort, we believe it will have disastrous results and that it is unlikely that research and development personnel will remain with the company.

Our interest is in the company's survival. If it were necessary, the members of the committee would be willing to agree to a 20 percent salary reduction in return for being able to remain in the Munich-area network. We request an opportunity to speak with management about this vital decision which massively affects all of us.

Sincerely,
(signed by all members of the committee)

After reading the statement sent by the committee, the president of Eurotechnologies, Pieter Jensen, conferred with the vice president for research and development (and the immediate superior of the scientists) and the vice president for human resources. The three discussed the statement that they had received and agreed that the situation was serious. It was clear that the Wasserburg move created unforeseen, legitimate problems for the vital R&D personnel and that management had erred in not seeking wider input in considering their cost reduction alternatives.

The management team debated the alternatives. They understood the frustrations of the research and development staff but were faced with having to cut almost 6,500,000 euros from annual costs in order for ETI to remain competitive. Consolidation still seemed the obvious answer, but the problems were mounting with this employee disclosure.

EXHIBIT 2

(addressed to all committee members)
Research and Development
Eurotechnologies, Inc.
300 Reinstrasse
Munich, Germany

Dear (names):

I have given my most serious consideration to the points you raised in your recent letter. We share your interest in doing what is best for ETI and welcome your interest in contributing to that goal.

It is clear that our technical expertise is one of our greatest assets and that your work in research and development is a vital contributor to that expertise. We have no wish to reduce our technical competitiveness. Nevertheless, our failure to produce cost-competitive contract bids is a problem that requires a painful solution, and we have only 18 months to produce an effective response.

We acknowledge that we have begun to examine the consolidation of our operations at the Wasserburg facility. Such a consolidation would reduce duplication of facilities, equipment, and personnel. These reductions would contribute significantly to an overall cost saving. Page two of this letter is an exhibit of the ongoing cost savings we believe would result from such a move.

At the same time, we believe that this action would be unwise if it truly has the crippling effect on your effectiveness that you forecast. Our dilemma, as the management team for ETI, is to address the need for major, fast cost reduction while providing for the continuation of our technical excellence. We also believe that any proposal must be fair to the many employees who are a part of the Eurotechnologies family.

In response to your letter, I have ordered that further evaluation of the Wasserburg alternative be halted for the time being. I ask that your committee send some of its members to a meeting with myself and other members of the management team to discuss the situation as it has evolved. We share an interest in ETI's survival if we can develop a plan that is mutually acceptable in achieving that goal. I look forward to meeting with you.

Sincerely,
(signed, Pieter Jensen)

Jensen wrote a letter to the committee acknowledging their concerns and inviting the members of that group to come to a meeting with the president, the VP of research and development, the VP of human resources, and other senior company officials. Jensen was careful to make no commitments or promises in the letter; he simply invited them to come to a meeting (Exhibit 2).

ETI Expense Statement (in thousands of euros)				
			Totals	
Overhead	**Wasserburg**	**Munich**	**Current**	**Consolidated**
Manufacturing	18,035			18,035
Administrative	2,662	5,406		2,906
R&D	483	4,343		4,531
Total	21,180	9,749	30,929	25,472
R&D Expenses				
Utilities	82	204		173
Computer lease		1,019		1,019
Supplies	212	449		492
Consulting		749		663
Total	294	2,421	2,715	2,347
Salaries and Benefits				
Professional	1,630	2,282		3,912
Benefits	245	342		587
Hourly	8,137	305		8,325
Benefits	813	31		824
Relocation				750*
Total	10,825	2,960	13,785	14,398
				13,648[†]
Facilities				
Debt service	815	2,630		815
Insurance/ maintenance/taxes	408	1,070		408
Total	1,223	3,700	4,923	1,223
Grand total: Current versus consolidated			52,352	42,656[†]

*One-time expense

[†]Ongoing total

Exercise 29

Third-Party Conflict Resolution

Introduction

In addition to being involved in their own conflicts, managers are often called upon to intervene and to settle conflicts between other people. The two activities in this section are designed to explore how third parties may enter conflicts for the purpose of resolving them, and to practice one very effective approach to intervention. In the first activity, you will read about a manager who has a problem deciding how to intervene in a dispute, and you will discuss this case in class. Part 2 of this exercise contains a mediation guide.

Part 1: The Seatcor Manufacturing Company

You are senior vice president of operations and chief operating officer of Seatcor, a major producer of office furniture. Joe Gibbons, your subordinate, is vice president and general manager of your largest desk assembly plant. Joe has been with Seatcor for 38 years and is two years away from retirement. He worked his way up through the ranks to his present position and has successfully operated his division for five years with a marginally competent staff. You are a long-standing personal friend of Joe's and respect him a great deal. However, you have always had an uneasy feeling that Joe has surrounded himself with minimally competent people by his own choice. In some ways, you think he feels threatened by talented assistants.

Last week you were having lunch with Charles Stewart, assistant vice president and Joe's second in command. Upon your questioning, it became clear that he and Joe were engaged in a debilitating feud. Charles was hired last year, largely at your insistence. You had been concerned for some time about who was going to replace Joe when he retired, especially given the lack of really capable managerial talent on Joe's staff. Thus you prodded Joe to hire your preferred candidate—Charles Stewart. Charles is relatively young, 39, extremely tenacious and bright, and a well-trained business school graduate. From all reports he is doing a good job in his new position.

Your concern centers on a topic that arose at the end of your lunch. Charles indicated that Joe Gibbons is in the process of completing a five-year plan for his plant. This plan is to serve as the basis for several major plant reinvestment and reorganization decisions that would be proposed to senior management. According to Charles, Joe Gibbons has not included Charles in the planning process at all. You had to leave lunch quickly and were unable to get much more information from Charles. However, he did admit that he was extremely disturbed by this exclusion and that his distress was influencing his work and probably his relationship with Joe.

Source: Developed by Roy J. Lewicki. "The Mediation Guide" developed by Larry Ray, American Bar Association, and Robert Helm, Oklahoma State University. "The Seatcor Manufacturing Company" and "The Summer Interns" developed by Blair Sheppard, Duke Corporate Education. Used with permission.

You consider this a very serious problem. Charles will probably have to live with the results of any major decisions about the plant. More important, Joe's support is essential if Charles is to properly grow into his present and/or future job. Joe, on the other hand, runs a good ship and you do not want to upset him or undermine his authority. Moreover, you know Joe has good judgment; thus he may have a good reason for what he is doing.

How would you proceed to handle this issue?

Part 2: The Mediation Guide

This section presents a series of steps for effectively conducting a mediation. You may use this checklist and the flowchart depicted in Exhibit 1.

Step 1: Stabilize the Setting

Parties often bring some strong feelings of anger and frustration into mediation. These feelings can prevent them from talking productively about their dispute. You, as mediator, will try to gain their trust for you and for the mediation process. Stabilize the setting by being polite; show that you are in control and that you are neutral. This step helps the parties feel comfortable, so they can speak freely about their complaints, and safe, so they can air their feelings.

1. _____ Greet the parties.

2. _____ Indicate where each of them is to sit.

3. _____ Identify yourself and each party, by name.

4. _____ Offer water, paper and pencil, and patience.

5. _____ State the purpose of mediation.

6. _____ Confirm your neutrality.

7. _____ Get their commitment to proceed.

8. _____ Get their commitment that only one party at a time will speak.

9. _____ Get their commitment to speak directly to you.

10. _____ Use calming techniques as needed.

Step 2: Help the Parties Communicate

Once the setting is stable and the parties seem to trust you and the mediation process, you can begin to carefully build trust between them. Both must make statements about what has happened. Each will use these statements to air negative feelings. They may express anger, make accusations, and show frustration in other ways. But with your help, this mutual ventilation lets them hear each other's side of the story, perhaps for the first time. It can help calm their emotions, and can build a basis for trust between them.

1. _____ Explain the rationale for who speaks first.

2. _____ Reassure them that both will speak without interruption, for as long as necessary.

3. _____ Ask the first speaker to tell what has happened.

 a. _____ Take notes.

 b. _____ Respond actively; restate and echo what is said.

 c. _____ Calm the parties as needed.

 d. _____ Clarify, with open or closed questions, or with restatements.

 e. _____ Focus the narration on the issues in the dispute.

 f. _____ Summarize, eliminating all disparaging references.

 g. _____ Check to see that you understand the story.

 h. _____ Thank this party for speaking, the other for listening quietly.

4. _____ Ask the second speaker to tell what has happened.

 a. _____ Take notes.

 b. _____ Respond actively; restate and echo what is said.

 c. _____ Calm the parties as needed.

 d. _____ Clarify, with open or closed questions, or with restatements.

 e. _____ Focus the narration on the issues in the dispute.

 f. _____ Summarize, eliminating all disparaging references.

 g. _____ Check to see that you understand the story.

 h. _____ Thank this party for speaking, the other for listening quietly.

5. _____ Ask each party, in turn, to help clarify the major issues to be resolved.

6. _____ Inquire into basic issues, probing to see if something instead may be at the root of the complaints.

7. _____ Define the problem by restating and summarizing.

8. _____ Conduct private meetings, if needed (explain what will happen during and after the private meetings).

9. _____ Summarize areas of agreement and disagreement.

10. _____ Help the parties set priorities on the issues and demands.

Step 3: Help the Parties Negotiate

Cooperativeness is needed for negotiations that lead to agreement. Cooperation requires a stable setting, to control disruptions, and exchanges of information, to develop mutual trust. With these conditions, the parties may be willing to cooperate, but still feel driven to compete. You can press for cooperative initiatives by patiently helping them to explore alternative solutions, and by directing attention to their progress.

1. _____ Ask each party to list alternative possibilities for a settlement.

2. _____ Restate and summarize each alternative.

3. _____ Check with each party on the workability of each alternative.

4. _____ Restate whether the alternative is workable.

5. _____ In an impasse, suggest the general form of other alternatives.

6. _____ Note the amount of progress already made, to show that success is likely.

7. _____ If the impasse continues, suggest a break or a second mediation session.

8. _____ Encourage them to select the alternative that appears to be workable.

9. _____ Increase their understanding by rephrasing the alternative.

10. _____ Help them plan a course of action to implement the alternative.

Step 4: Clarify Their Agreement

Mediation should change each party's attitude toward the other. When both have shown their commitment through a joint declaration of agreement, each will support the agreement more strongly. For a settlement that lasts, each component of the parties' attitudes toward each other—their thinking, feeling, and acting—will have changed. Not only will they now *act* differently toward each other, but they are likely to *feel* differently, more positively, about each other and to *think* of their relationship in new ways.

1. _____ Summarize the agreement terms.

2. _____ Recheck with each party on his or her understanding of the agreement.

3. _____ Ask whether other issues need to be discussed.

4. _____ Help them specify the terms of their agreement.

5. _____ State each person's role in the agreement.

6. _____ Recheck with each party on when he or she is to do certain things, where, and how.

7. _____ Explain the process of follow-up.

8. _____ Establish a time for follow-up with each party.

9. _____ Emphasize that the agreement is theirs, not yours.

10. _____ Congratulate the parties on their reasonableness and on the workability of their resolution.

EXHIBIT 1 | Steps in a Mediation Process

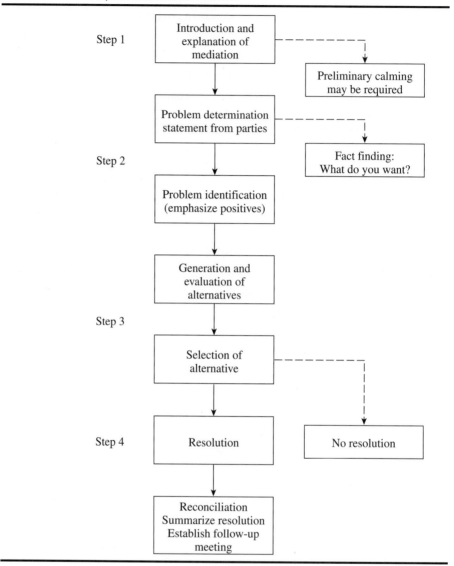

AuraCall Inc.

Introduction

We often think of an agreement as the finished product of a negotiation encounter. In many situations, however, the implementation of the deal—how the parties put the settlement they have negotiated into practice—is just as important as the deal itself. Sometimes the implementation of a deal creates problems of its own, leading the parties back into conflict or into a new set of conflicts that need to be resolved.

This exercise involves just this sort of situation: Two parties are now having some serious problems with a business relationship defined by a negotiation that they successfully completed in the recent past (or so they thought). It turns out that the implementation of the arrangement has led to some unanticipated problems, and now the parties sharply disagree about the causes and sources of the difficulties they are experiencing.

Before the parties can resolve their substantive differences, which are serious, they need to consider options for the process of dispute resolution in this situation and agree on the *method* for resolving the dispute. Accordingly, your task as a representative for one of the parties in this exercise will *not* be to negotiate a substantive agreement that solves the underlying problems in the business relationship. Instead, your goal in a meeting with the other party is to advocate and negotiate for a suitable dispute resolution *process* that will best serve your interests in this relationship.

Source: This exercise was developed by Noam Ebner, who teaches in the Werner Institute's Masters Program on Negotiation & Dispute Resolution at Creighton University. Used with permission.

Exercise 31

500 English Sentences

Introduction

This exercise involves a cross-cultural negotiation where there are several tangible and intangible factors at stake. You will play the role of either a Japanese teacher who is head of the English Department that is responsible for the publication of an English textbook, or an American assistant English teacher who has been asked to work on the book.

Source: This exercise was written by Laura Turek. Copyright 2006. Used with permission.

Sick Leave

Introduction

This exercise involves a cross-cultural negotiation where there are several tangible and intangible factors at stake. You will play the role of either a Japanese manager responsible for the supervision of several foreign assistant English teachers, or an American assistant English teacher.

Source: This exercise was written by Laura Turek. Copyright 2006. Used with permission.

Alpha–Beta

Introduction

In this situation you will negotiate a possible robot manufacturing and marketing agreement with another company. You will be a member of a team that represents either an electrical company in the nation of Alpha or a manufacturer of electrical machinery in the nation of Beta.

Background Information

Alpha

Alpha Inc. is a large, broadly diversified electrical company based in the nation of Alpha. The company is one of the leading makers of numerical control equipment and plans to become a leader in equipping the "factory of the future." It has recently spent hundreds of millions of dollars putting together a collection of factory automation capabilities ranging from robotics to computer-aided design and manufacturing. Alpha Inc. has been acquiring companies, investing heavily in new plants, and spending considerable sums on product development. Innovative robots, some equipped with vision, are being developed, but they have been a bit slow in making their way out of the company's R&D labs. To meet its objective of quickly becoming a major worldwide, full-service supplier of automation systems, Alpha Inc. has found it necessary to tie up, in various ways, with foreign firms that are further up the robotics learning curve.

Robotics in the Nation of Alpha

There are 30 robot manufacturers in Alpha, and big computer and auto firms have recently been entering the business. During 1980, use and production of robots in Alpha was only about 33 percent of what it was in the nation of Beta. One survey reported 4,370 robots in use in Alpha in 1980, mainly in the auto and foundry-type industries, and 1,269 produced. Robot sales in 1980 were estimated at $92 million, with a significant share accounted for by imports. The industrial automation market as a whole is growing at well over 20 percent a year, and the robotics portion of it is expected to become a $2 billion-a-year domestic market by 1990.

Beta

Beta Inc. is the leading manufacturer of integrated electrical machinery in the nation of Beta. Run by scientists since its founding, the company is Beta's most research-oriented corporation: It employs over 9,000 researchers, and its R&D spending equals 5.9 percent

Source: This exercise was first developed by Thomas N. Gladwin in 1984, and is copyrighted 1990–91 by Thomas N. Gladwin, Stephen E. Weiss, and Allen J. Zerkin. Used with permission.

of corporate sales. Beta Inc. started producing robots only in 1979 but plans within a few years to become the world's largest robot producer. To do so, it must double its manufacturing capacity and strongly push exports (to date, nearly all of its output has been sold at home). The company's deep commitment to robotics is reflected in the recent formation of a 500-person technical task force to develop a universal assembly robot with both visual and tactile sensors. Beta Inc. expects to be using the new robots for some 60 percent of its in-house assembly operations within three years.

Robotics in the Nation of Beta

Beta Inc. is only 1 of 150 companies making or selling robots in Beta, a nation with "robot fever" and a government that has declared automation a national goal. An estimated 12,000 to 14,000 programmable robots are already on the job in the nation, representing 59 percent of those in use worldwide. In 1980, Betan firms churned out nearly $400 million worth of robots (approximately 3,200 units, or 50 percent of world production). The nation exported only 2.5 percent of its production and imported fewer than 5 percent of its robots. Industry analysts see robot production in Beta rising to $2 billion in 1985 and to $5 billion in 1990.

Over the past five months, Alpha Inc. and Beta Inc. have held preliminary negotiations over a possible robot manufacturing and marketing tie-up. The two companies have reached the following tentative agreement:

1. The tie-up over seven years will proceed in two phases: (*a*) in years 1 through 4, Beta will supply Alpha with fully assembled Beta Inc. robots for sale under Alpha's brand name; (*b*) in years 5 through 7, Alpha will begin producing these robots themselves in Alpha, using Beta technology and key components.

2. The tie-up will focus on the robots that Beta Inc. currently has on the market.

3. The agreement will be nonexclusive; that is, Beta Inc. will be allowed to enter the Alphan market directly at any time and allowed to tie up with other Alphan firms.

The two companies' negotiation teams are now scheduled to meet for discussion of remaining issues. They include the following:

1. The number of different models involved.

2. The quantity of Beta Inc. units to be imported and/or produced under license by Alpha during each year.

3. The unit price to be paid to Beta.

4. Access to Alpha's vision technology.

5. The royalty rate to be paid to Beta.

Exercise 34

Galactica SUV

Introduction

Even relatively simple negotiation encounters can turn into complex situations when negotiators interact across a national or cultural divide. This exercise, which on the surface is a negotiation encounter over the purchase of a "vehicle," introduces a variety of cultural issues that often can and do occur in a real world intercultural or international negotiation. The encounter will test your ability to contend with cultural ambiguity, to learn from mistakes, and to overcome them, all while trying to negotiate the best deal you can in the transaction at hand.

Source: This exercise was developed by Craig B. Barkacs and Linda L. Barkacs. Used with permission.

Bacchus Winery

Introduction

This exercise is a three-party negotiation between representatives of three cultural groups: an American, a Japanese, and a Serbian. The American firm (Bacchus) produces a variety of wines; the Japanese firm (Tokyo Saki) produces saki and rice wines; the Serbian firm (Serbian Steins & Stems) produces fine decanters, wineglasses, and accessories. The three firms will discuss the terms of a possible merger/joint venture between them.

Source: Adapted by Roy J. Lewicki from an exercise developed by Judi McLean Parks, Washington University. Used with permission.

Exercise 36

Collecting Nos

Introduction

In all work settings, there comes a time when we need something from someone else. It might be an approval, it might be resources, or it might be some form of assistance. Whatever it might be, it is virtually impossible for us to get our work done without the cooperation of others. And the best way to get what you want from others is to ask them for it. Yet many people would rather do it themselves than ask someone else. One reason people are hesitant to ask for things is because they do not want to get a "no."

A similar problem exists in negotiations. On the one hand, inexperienced negotiators often are afraid to ask for what they want or need because they are afraid to get a no. On the other hand, those who are asked will frequently *not* say no, in spite of their strong dislike of the request or having to fulfill it. Therefore, many negotiations are incomplete because the requester did not ask for enough, or the respondent actually gave more than he or she wanted to. Several negotiation experts have argued that negotiation only *begins* when the other party says no; if you do not get a no, you probably have not asked for enough!

The purpose of this exercise is to give you experience in making requests and dealing with others' objections. Your task in this exercise is to collect nos.

Part A

Continue to make requests until you have collected 10 nos. Keep a verbatim written record of *each* request you make, the response you receive to each request, and what meaning or interpretation you gave to the response (what thoughts or feelings you had in reaction to the response). Create the following table:

Request I Made	Response I Received	My Reaction to the Response
1.		
2.		
3.		
etc.		

Source: Developed by Professor Jeffrey Ford of the Fisher College of Business, The Ohio State University, for this volume. Used with permission.

Part B

Pick one of the requests for which you received a no, and make that same request of the same person a second time. If you receive another no, wait until later and make the same request yet a third time. Write down what the person says each time.

Part C

Pick at least one of the requests for which you received a no, and ask the person who said no, "What would have to happen for you to say yes to my request?" Write down what the person says. Your instructor will help you process these reactions in class.

Exercise 37

A Team in Trouble

Introduction

In this exercise you will read about a situation involving conflict that often arises when students are formed into teams for academic work. Student members of the team described in the case have different personalities, interests, skills, and goals. The team has been working together for almost a month. During that time they have had some successes, but also some very difficult encounters. Alliances are forming, and at least one member feels not just marginalized, but angry and frustrated.

Your instructor will provide you with a short case handout containing details about the situation this team is experiencing. After reading the case, your role will be to act as a coach for the team, helping them find a way to become more effective. As you read about the team, think about these questions:

- What is the underlying cause of the team's internal conflict?
- What should your role be as a third party helping this team?
- What steps would you take next to manage the conflict?
- What are the basic options, and for each option what are the risks and potential benefits?
- Who you would talk to, what you would say to them or ask of them, and in what order?

Source: This exercise was developed by Ray Friedman. Used with permission.

Capital Mortgage Insurance Corporation (A)

Frank Randall hung up the telephone, leaned across his desk, and fixed a cold stare at Jim Dolan.

> OK, Jim. They've agreed to a meeting. We've got three days to resolve this thing. The question is, what approach should we take? How do we get them to accept our offer?

Randall, president of Capital Mortgage Insurance Corporation (CMI), had called Dolan, his senior vice president and treasurer, into his office to help him plan their strategy for completing the acquisition of Corporate Transfer Services (CTS). The two men had begun informal discussions with the principal stockholders of the small employee relocation services company some four months earlier. Now, in late May 1979, they were developing the terms of a formal purchase offer and plotting their strategy for the final negotiations.

The acquisition, if consummated, would be the first in CMI's history. Furthermore, it represented a significant departure from the company's present business. Randall and Dolan knew that the acquisition could have major implications, both for themselves and for the company they had revitalized over the past several years.

Jim Dolan ignored Frank Randall's intense look and gazed out the eighth-floor window overlooking Philadelphia's Independence Square.

> That's not an easy question, Frank. We know they're still looking for a lot more money than we're thinking about. But beyond that, the four partners have their own differences, and we need to think through just what they're expecting. So I guess we'd better talk this one through pretty carefully.

Company and Industry Background

CMI was a wholly owned subsidiary of Northwest Equipment Corporation, a major freight transporter and lessor of railcars, commercial aircraft, and other industrial equipment. Northwest had acquired CMI in 1978, two years after CMI's original parent company, an investment management corporation, had gone into Chapter 11 bankruptcy proceedings. CMI had been created to sell mortgage guaranty insurance policies to residential mortgage lenders throughout the United States. Mortgage insurance provides banks, savings and loans, mortgage bankers, and other mortgage lenders with protection against financial losses when homeowners default on their mortgage loans.

Lending institutions normally protect their property loan investments by offering loans of only 70 percent to 80 percent of the appraised value of the property; the

Source: Capital Mortgage Insurance Corporation (A), Harvard Business School Case 9-480-057.
Copyright ©1980 by the President and Fellows of Harvard College.

This case was prepared by James P. Ware as a basis for class discussion rather than to illustrate either effective or ineffective handling of an administrative situation. Reprinted by permission of the Harvard Business School. This case written in 1979. For a variety of reasons, it is not possible to update the financial information or the fact pattern in the case. We contiue to use it in this book because of the teaching value of the case, in spite of its age.

remaining 20 to 30 percent constitutes the homeowner's down payment. However, mortgage loan insurance makes it possible for lenders to offer so-called high-ratio loans of up to 95 percent of a home's appraised value. High-ratio loans are permitted only when the lender insures the loan; although the policy protects the lender, the premiums are paid by the borrower, as an addition to monthly principal and interest charges.

The principal attraction of mortgage insurance is that it makes purchasing a home possible for many more individuals. It is much easier to produce a 5 percent down payment than to save up the 20 to 30 percent traditionally required.

CMI had a mixed record of success within the private mortgage insurance industry. Frank Randall, the company's first and only president, had gotten the organization off to an aggressive beginning, attaining a 14.8 percent market share by 1972. By 1979, however, that share had fallen to just over 10 percent even though revenues had grown from $18 million in 1972 to over $30 million in 1979. Randall attributed the loss of market share primarily to the difficulties created by the bankruptcy of CMI's original parent. Thus he had been quite relieved when Northwest Equipment acquired CMI in January 1978. Northwest provided CMI with a level of management and financial support it had never before enjoyed. Furthermore, Northwest's corporate management had made it clear to Frank Randall that he was expected to build CMI into a much larger, diversified financial services company.

Northwest's growth expectations were highly consistent with Frank Randall's own ambitions. The stability created by the acquisition, in combination with the increasing solidity of CMI's reputation with mortgage lenders, made it possible for Randall to turn his attention more and more toward external acquisitions of his own. During 1978 Randall, with Jim Dolan's help, had investigated several acquisition opportunities in related insurance industries, with the hope of broadening CMI's financial base. After several unsuccessful investigations, the two men had come to believe that their knowledge and competence was focused less on insurance per se than it was on residential real estate and related financial transactions. These experiences had led to a recognition that, in Frank Randall's words, "we are a residential real estate financial services company."

The Residential Real Estate Industry

Frank Randall and Jim Dolan knew from personal experience that real estate brokers, who play an obvious and important role in property transactions, usually have close ties with local banks and savings and loans. When mortgage funds are plentiful, brokers often steer prospective home buyers to particular lending institutions. When funds are scarce, the lenders would then favor prospective borrowers referred by their favorite brokers. Randall believed that these informal relationships meant that realtors could have a significant impact on the mortgage loan decision and thus on a mortgage insurance decision as well.

For this reason, CMI had for many years directed a small portion of its marketing effort toward real estate brokers. CMI's activities had consisted of offering educational programs for realtors, property developers, and potential home buyers. The company derived no direct revenues from these programs, but offered them in the interest of stimulating home sales and, more particularly, of informing both realtors and home buyers of how mortgage insurance makes it possible to purchase a home with a relatively low down payment.

Because he felt that real estate brokers could be powerful allies in encouraging lenders to use mortgage insurance, Randall had been tracking developments in the real estate industry for many years. Historically a highly fragmented collection of local, independent entrepreneurs, the industry in 1979 appeared to be on the verge of a major restructuring and consolidation. For the past several years many of the smaller brokers had been joining national franchise organizations in an effort to gain a brand image and to acquire improved management and sales skills.

More significantly, in 1979, several large national corporations were beginning to acquire prominent real estate agencies in major urban areas. The most aggressive of these appeared to be Merrill Lynch and Company, the well-known Wall Street securities trading firm. Merrill Lynch's interest in real estate brokers stemmed from several sources; perhaps most important were the rapidly rising prices on property and homes. Realtors' commissions averaged slightly over 6 percent of the sales price; *Fortune* magazine estimated that real estate brokers had been involved in home sales totaling approximately $190 billion in 1978, netting commissions in excess of $11 billion (in comparison, stockbrokers' commissions on all securities transactions in 1978 were estimated at $3.7 billion).[1] With property values growing 10 to 20 percent per year, commissions would only get larger; where 6 percent of a $30,000 home netted only $1,800, 6 percent of a $90,000 sale resulted in a commission well in excess of $5,000—for basically the same work.

There were also clear signs that the volume of real estate transactions would continue to increase. Although voluntary intercity moves appeared to be declining slightly, corporate transfers of employees were still rising. One of Merrill Lynch's earliest moves toward the real estate market had been to acquire an employee relocation company several years earlier. Working on a contract basis with corporate clients, Merrill Lynch Relocation Management (MLRM) collaborated with independent real estate brokers to arrange home sales and purchases for transferred employees. Like other relocation companies, MLRM would purchase the home at a fair market value and then handle all the legal and financial details of reselling the home on the open market. MLRM also provided relocation counseling and home search assistance for transferred employees; its income was derived primarily from service fees paid by corporate clients (and augmented somewhat by referral fees from real estate brokers, who paid MLRM a portion of the commissions they earned on home sales generated by the transferred employees).

Later, in September 1978, Merrill Lynch had formally announced its intention to acquire at least 40 real estate brokerage firms within three to four years. Merrill Lynch's interest in the industry stemmed not only from the profit opportunities it saw but also from a corporate desire to become a "financial services supermarket," providing individual customers with a wide range of investment and brokerage services. In 1978 Merrill Lynch had acquired United First Mortgage Corporation (UFM), a mortgage banker. And in early 1979 Merrill Lynch was in the midst of acquiring

AMIC Corporation, a small mortgage insurance company in direct competition with CMI. As *Fortune* reported,

> In combination, these diverse activities hold some striking possibilities. Merrill Lynch already packages and markets mortgages through its registered representatives. . . . If all goes according to plan, the company could later this year be vertically integrated in a unique way. Assuming the AMIC acquisition goes through, Merrill Lynch will be able to guarantee mortgages. It could then originate mortgages through its realty brokerages, process and service them through UFM, insure them with AMIC, package them as pass-through or unit trusts, and market them through its army of registered representatives.[2]

It was this vision of an integrated financial services organization that also excited Frank Randall. As he and Jim Dolan reviewed their position in early 1979, they were confident that they were in a unique position to build CMI into a much bigger and more diversified company. The mortgage insurance business gave them a solid financial base, with regional offices throughout the country. Northwest Equipment stood ready to provide the capital they would need for significant growth. They already had relationships with important lending institutions across the United States, and their marketing efforts had given them a solid reputation with important real estate brokers as well.

Thus Randall, in particular, felt that at least he had most of the ingredients to begin building that diversified "residential real estate financial services company" he had been dreaming about for so long. Furthermore, Randall's reading of the banking, thrift, and real estate industries suggested that the time was ripe. In his view, the uncertainties in the financial and housing industries created rich opportunities for taking aggressive action, and the vision of Merrill Lynch "bulling" its way into the business was scaring realtors just enough for CMI to present a comforting and familiar alternative.

The Metropolitan Realty Network

Frank Randall spent most of the fall of 1978 actively searching for acquisition opportunities. As part of his effort, he contacted David Osgood, who was the executive director of the Metropolitan Realty Network, a national association of independent real estate brokers. The association, commonly known as MetroNet, had been formed primarily as a communication vehicle so its members could refer home buyers moving from one city to another to a qualified broker in the new location.

Randall discovered that Osgood was somewhat concerned about MetroNet's long-term health and viability. Though MetroNet included over 13,000 real estate agencies, it was losing some members to national franchise chains, and Osgood was feeling increasing pressures to strengthen the association by providing more services to member firms. Yet the entrepreneurial independence of MetroNet's members made Osgood's task particularly difficult. He had found it almost impossible to get them to agree on what they wanted him to do.

One service that the MetroNet brokers *were* agreed on developing was the employee relocation business. Corporate contracts to handle transferred employees were especially attractive to the brokers because the contracts virtually guaranteed repeat business in the local area, and they also led to intercity referrals that almost always resulted in a home sale.

MetroNet brokers were also resentful of how Merrill Lynch Relocation Management and other relocation services companies were getting a larger and larger share of "their" referral fees. Osgood told Randall that he had already set up a committee of MetroNet brokers to look into how the association could develop a corporate relocation and third-party equity capability of its own.[3] Osgood mentioned that their only effort to date was an independent firm in Chicago named Corporate Transfer Services, Inc. (CTS), that had been started by Elliott Burr, a prominent Chicago broker and a MetroNet director. CTS had been formed with the intention of working with MetroNet brokers, but so far it had remained relatively small and had not met MetroNet's expectations.

As Randall explained to Osgood what kinds of activities CMI engaged in to help lenders and increase the volume of home sales, Osgood suddenly exclaimed, "That's exactly what *we're* trying to do!" The two men ended their initial meeting convinced that some kind of working relationship between CMI and MetroNet could have major benefits for both organizations. Osgood invited Randall to attend the next meeting of MetroNet's Third-Party Equity Committee, scheduled for March 1. "Let's explore what we can do for each other," said Osgood. "You're on," concluded Randall.

The Third-Party Equity Business

Randall's discussion with David Osgood had opened his eyes to the third-party equity business, and he and Jim Dolan spent most of their time in preparation for the March 1 committee meeting steeped in industry studies and pro forma income statements.

They quickly discovered that the employee relocation services industry was highly competitive, though its future looked bright. Corporate transfers of key employees appeared to be an ingrained practice that showed no signs of letting up in the foreseeable future. Merrill Lynch Relocation Management was one of the two largest firms in the industry; most of the prominent relocation companies were well-funded subsidiaries of large, well-known corporations. Exhibit 1 contains Jim Dolan's tabulation of the seven major relocation firms, along with his estimates of each company's 1978 volume of home purchases.

Dolan also developed a pro forma income and expense statement for a hypothetical firm handling 2,000 home purchases annually (see Exhibit 2). His calculations showed a potential 13.1 percent return on equity (ROE). Dolan then discovered that some companies achieved a much higher ROE by using a home purchase trust, a legal arrangement that made it possible to obtain enough bank financing to leverage a company's equity base by as much as 10 to 1.

Randall and Dolan were increasingly certain that they wanted to get CMI into the employee relocation services business. They saw it as a natural tie-in with CMI's mortgage insurance operations—one that could exploit the same set of relationships that CMI already had with banks, realtors, savings and loans, and other companies involved in the development, construction, sale, and financing of residential real estate. The two men felt that real estate brokers had a critically important role in the process. Brokers were not only involved in the actual property transactions, but in addition they almost always had local contacts with corporations that could lead to the signing of employee relocation contracts. Equally important, from Randall's and Dolan's perspective, was their belief that a close relationship between CMI and the MetroNet brokers would also lead to significant sales of CMI's mortgage insurance policies.

EXHIBIT 1 | Major Employee Relocation Services Companies

Relocation Company	Parent Organization	Estimated 1978 Home Purchases	Estimated Value of Home Purchases*	Estimated Gross Fee Income†
Merrill Lynch Relocation	Merrill Lynch	13,000	$975,000,000	$26,800,000
Homequity	Peterson, Howell, & Heather	12,000	900,000,000	24,750,000
Equitable Relocation	Equitable Life Insurance	5,000	375,000,000	10,300,000
Employee Transfer	Chicago Title and Trust	5,000	375,000,000	10,300,000
Relocation Realty Corporation	Control Data Corporation	3,000	225,000,000	6,200,000
Executrans	Sears/Coldwell Banker	3,000	225,000,000	6,200,000
Transamerica Relocation	Transamerica, Inc.	3,000	225,000,000	6,200,000

*Assumes average home values of $75,000.

†Assumes fee averaging 2.75 percent of value of homes purchased.

EXHIBIT 2 | Hypothetical Employee Relocation Company Pro Forma Income Statement

Key assumptions

1. Annual purchase volume of 2,000 homes.
2. Assume average holding period of 120 days. Inventory turns over three times annually, for an average of 667 units in inventory at any point in time.
3. Average home value of $75,000.
4. Existing mortgages on homes average 50 percent of property value. Additional required capital will be 40 percent equity, 60 percent long-term debt.
5. Fee income from corporate clients will average 2.75 percent of value of properties purchased (based on historical industry data).
6. Operating expenses (marketing, sales, office administration) will average 1 percent of value of properties purchased (all costs associated with purchases, including debt service, are billed back to corporate clients).

Calculations

Total value of purchases	
(2,000 units at $75,000)	$150,000,000
Average inventory value	50,000,000
Capital required	
Existing mortgages	25,000,000
New long-term debt	15,000,000
Equity	10,000,000
Fee income at 2.75%	4,125,000
Operating expenses at 1%	1,500,000
Net income	$2,625,000
Tax at 50%	(1,312,500)
Profit after tax	$1,312,500
Return on equity	13.1%

The March 1 meeting with MetroNet's Third-Party Equity Committee turned into an exploration of how CMI and MetroNet might help each other by stimulating both home sales and high-ratio mortgage loans. After several hours of discussion, Frank Randall proposed specifically that CMI build an operating company to handle the corporate relocation business jointly with the MetroNet brokers. As a quid pro quo, Randall suggested that the brokers could market CMI mortgage insurance to both potential home buyers and lending institutions.

The committee's response to this idea was initially skeptical. Finally, however, they agreed to consider a more formal proposal at a later date. MetroNet's board of directors was scheduled to meet on April 10; the Third-Party Equity Committee could review the proposal on April 9 and, if they approved, present it to the full board on the 10th.

As the committee meeting broke up, Randall and Dolan began talking with Elliott Burr and Thomas Winder, two of the four owners of Corporate Transfer Services, Inc. (CTS). Though Burr had been the principal founder of CTS, his primary business was a large real estate brokerage firm in north suburban Chicago that he operated in partnership with William Lehman, who was also a CTS stockholder.

The four men sat back down at the meeting table, and Randall mentioned that his primary interest was to learn more about how an employee relocation business operated. Burr offered to send him copies of contracts with corporate clients, sample financial statements, and so on. At one point during their discussion Burr mentioned the possibility of an acquisition. Randall asked, somewhat rhetorically, "How do you put a value on a company like this?" Burr responded almost immediately, "Funny you should ask. We've talked to an attorney and have put together this proposal." Burr reached into his briefcase and pulled out a two-page document. He then proceeded to describe a complex set of terms involving the sale of an 80 percent interest in CTS, subject to guarantees concerning capitalization, lines of credit, data processing support, future distribution of profits and dividends, and more.

Randall backed off immediately, explaining that he needed to learn more about the nature of the business before he would seriously consider an acquisition. As Jim Dolan later recalled,

> I think they were expecting an offer right then and there. But it was very hard to understand what they really wanted; it was nothing we could actually work from. Besides that, the numbers they were thinking about were ridiculously high—over $5 million. We put the letter away and told them we didn't want to get specific until after the April 10 meeting. And that's the way we left it.

Preparation for the April 10 Meeting

During the next six weeks Randall and Dolan continued their investigations of the employee relocation industry and studied CTS much more closely.

One of their major questions was how much additional mortgage insurance the MetroNet brokers might be able to generate. Frank Randall had CMI's marketing staff conduct a telephone survey of about 25 key MetroNet brokers. The survey suggested that most brokers were aware of mortgage insurance, although few of them were actively pushing it. All of those questioned expressed an interest in using CMI's marketing programs, and were eager to learn more about CMI insurance.

By early May a fairly clear picture of CTS was emerging. The company had been founded in 1975; it had barely achieved a break-even profit level. Annual home purchases and sales had reached a level of almost 500 properties, and CTS had worked with about 65 MetroNet brokers and 35 corporate clients. Tom Winder was the general manager; he supervised a staff of about 25 customer representatives and clerical support staff. Conversations with David Osgood and several MetroNet brokers who had worked with CTS suggested that the company had made promises to MetroNet about developing a nationwide, well-financed, fully competitive organization. To date, however, those promises were largely unfulfilled. Osgood believed that CTS's shortage of equity and, therefore, borrowing capacity, had severely limited its growth potential.

Jim Dolan obtained a copy of CTS's December 1978 balance sheet that, in his mind, confirmed Osgood's feelings (see Exhibit 3). The company had a net worth of only $420,000. Three of the four stockholders (Elliott Burr, William Lehman, and Michael Kupchak) had invested an additional $2 million in the company—$1.3 million in short-term notes and $700,000 in bank loans that they had personally guaranteed. While CTS owned homes valued at $13.4 million, it also had additional bank loans and

EXHIBIT 3 | CTS Balance Sheet

CORPORATE TRANSFER SERVICES, INC.
Unaudited Balance Sheet
December 1978

Assets	($ 000)
Cash	$ 190
Homes owned	13,366
Accounts and acquisition fees receivable	665
Other (mainly escrow deposits)	143
	$14,364

Liabilities	
Client prepayments	$ 1,602
Notes payable to banks	4,161
Assumed mortgages payable	5,670
Loan from stockholders	700
Advance from MetroNet	300
Other liabilities	211
	$12,644

Capital	
Subordinated debenture due stockholder (April 1981)	1,300
Common stock	450
Deficit	(30)
	$14,364

assumed mortgages totaling $9.8 million. Furthermore, the company had a highly uncertain earnings stream; Frank Randall believed the current business could tail off to almost nothing within six months.

During late March both Randall and Dolan had a number of telephone conversations with Burr and Winder. Their discussions were wide ranging and quite open; the CTS partners struck Randall as being unusually candid. They seemed more than willing to share everything they knew about the business and their own company. On one occasion, Burr asked how much of CTS Randall wanted to buy and how Randall would feel about the present owners retaining a minority interest. Burr's question led Randall and Dolan to conclude that in fact they wanted full ownership. They planned to build up the company's equity base considerably and wanted to gain all the benefits of a larger, more profitable operation for CMI.

In early April, Randall developed the formal proposal that he intended to present to MetroNet's board of directors (see Exhibit 4). The proposal committed CMI to enter negotiations to acquire CTS and to use CTS as a base for building a third-party equity company with a capitalization sufficient to support an annual home purchase capability of at least 2,000 units. In return, the proposal asked MetroNet to begin a program of actively supporting the use of CMI's insurance on high-ratio loans.

EXHIBIT 4 | Letter of Intent

Board of Directors
The Metropolitan Realty Network
New York, NY

April 9, 1979

Gentlemen:

It is our intention to enter negotiations with the principals of Corporate Transfer Services, Inc., for the acquisition of the equity ownership of this Company by Capital Mortgage Insurance Corporation.

In the event Capital Mortgage Insurance Corporation is successful in the acquisition of Corporate Transfer Services, Inc., it is our intention to capitalize this Company to the extent required for the development of a complete bank line of credit. The initial capital and bank line of credit would provide the MetroNet association members an annual equity procurement of 1,500 to 2,000 units. In addition, we would be prepared to expand beyond this initial capacity if the MetroNet Association volume and profitability of business dictate.

We are prepared to develop an organizational structure and support system that can provide a competitive and professional marketing and administrative approach to the corporate transfer market.

Our intentions to enter negotiations with Corporate Transfer Services, Inc., are subject to the following:

1. The endorsement of this action by you, the board of directors of MetroNet, for Capital Mortgage Insurance Corporation to acquire this organization.

2. The assurance of the MetroNet Association for the continuation of their support and use of CTS. Upon completion of the acquisition, the MetroNet Association would agree to sign a Letter of Agreement with the new owners of Corporate Transfer Services.

3. The assurance of the MetroNet Association to cooperate in the development of a close working relationship with CMI for the influence and control they may provide when seeking high-ratio conventional mortgage loans using mortgage insurance.

Capital Mortgage Insurance will need the support of expanded business by the MetroNet Association, due to the heavy capital commitment we will be required to make to CTS to make this acquisition feasible. In this regard, CMI is prepared to offer the MetroNet nationwide members a range of marketing programs and mortgage financing packages that will help earn and deserve the mortgage insurance business and expand the listings, sales, and profitability of the MetroNet members.

Upon receiving the endorsement and support outlined in this letter from the board of directors of MetroNet, we will proceed immediately with the negotiations with Corporate Transfer Services, Inc. It would be our intention to have the acquisition completed and the company fully operational by the time of the MetroNet national convention in San Francisco in July 1979.

Sincerely,

Franklin T. Randall
President and Chief Executive Officer

Randall and Dolan met again with the Third-Party Equity Committee in New York on April 9 to preview the CMI proposal. The committee reacted favorably, and the next day MetroNet's board of directors unanimously accepted the proposal after discussing it for less than 15 minutes.

Formal Negotiations with Corporate Transfer Services

On the afternoon of April 10, following the MetroNet board meeting, Randall and Dolan met again with Elliott Burr and Tom Winder. Now that CMI was formally committed to acquisition negotiations, Burr and Winder were eager to get specific and talk numbers. However, Randall and Dolan remained very cautious. When Burr expressed an interest in discussing a price, Randall replied, "We don't know what you're worth. But we'll entertain any reasonable argument you want to make for why we should pay more than your net worth." The meeting ended with a general agreement to firm things up by April 25. Later, reflecting on this session, Jim Dolan commented,

> Our letter of agreement committed us to having an operating company by July 12, so the clock was running on us. However, we know that after the April 10 board meeting they would be hard pressed not to be bought, and besides they were obviously pretty eager. But at that point in time we had not even met the other two stockholders; we suspected the high numbers were coming from them.

Further Assessment of CTS

Even though the April 10 meeting had ended with an agreement to move ahead by April 25, it quickly became evident that a complete assessment of CTS and preparation of a formal offer would take more than two weeks. Other operating responsibilities prevented both Randall and Dolan from devoting as much time as they had intended to the acquisition, and the analysis process itself required more time than they had expected.

During the first week of May, Jim Dolan made a "reconnaissance" trip to Chicago. His stated purpose was to examine CTS's books and talk with the company's local bankers. He also scrutinized the office facilities, met and talked with several office employees, observed Tom Winder interacting with customers and subordinates, and generally assessed the company's operations. Dolan spent most of his time with Winder, but he also had an opportunity to have dinner with William Lehman, another of CTS's stockholders. Dolan returned to Philadelphia with a generally favorable set of impressions about the company's operations and a much more concrete understanding of its financial situation. He reported to Randall, "They're running a responsible organization in a basically sensible manner." At the same time, however, Dolan also reported that CTS was under increasing pressure from its bankers to improve its financial performance.

Dolan's trip also provided him with a much richer understanding of the four men who owned CTS: Elliott Burr, William Lehman (Burr's real estate partner), Michael Kupchak (a private investor), and Tom Winder. Of these four, only Winder was actively involved in the day-to-day management of the company, although Elliott Burr stayed in very close touch with Winder and was significantly more involved than either Lehman or Kupchak. From their meetings and telephone conversations, Randall and Dolan pieced together the following pictures of the four men:

- *Elliott Burr,* in his middle 50s, had been the driving force behind Corporate Transfer Services. He was a classic real estate salesman—a warm, straightforward, friendly man who enthusiastically believed in what he was doing. An eternal optimist, he had been an early advocate of MetroNet's getting into the employee relocation business. Burr knew the relocation business extremely well; he personally called on many of the large Chicago corporations to sell CTS's services.

  Burr appeared to be very well off financially. Burr and Lehman Real Estate was one of the largest realty firms on Chicago's North Shore, and Burr was held in high regard by local bankers. One banker had told Dolan, "Burr's word is his bond."

- *William Lehman,* Burr's real estate partner, was in his mid-60s. He appeared to be much more of a financial adviser and investor than an operating manager. Lehman personally owned the shopping center where Burr and Lehman Real Estate was located, as well as the office building where CTS was leasing space.

  Dolan characterized Lehman as an "elder statesman—a true gentleman." Dolan recalled that when he had had dinner with Lehman during his visit to Chicago, Lehman had kept the conversation on a personal level, repeatedly expressing concern about Dolan's plane reservations, hotel accommodations, and so on. He had hardly mentioned CTS during the entire dinner.

- *Michael Kupchak* was the third principal stockholder. Kupchak, about 50, had been a mortgage banker in Chicago for a number of years. Recently, however, he had left the bank to manage his own investments on a full-time basis.

  Dolan met Kupchak briefly during his Chicago visit, and characterized him as a "bulldog"—an aggressive, ambitious man much more interested in financial transactions than in the nature of the business. He had apparently thought Dolan was coming to Chicago to make a firm offer and had been irritated that one had not been forthcoming. Frank Randall had not yet met Kupchak face-to-face, although they had talked once by telephone.

- *Thomas Winder,* 44, had spent most of his career in real estate–related businesses. At one time he had worked for a construction company, and then he had joined the mortgage bank where Michael Kupchak worked.

  Kupchak had actually brought Winder into CTS as its general manager, and the three original partners had offered him 25 percent ownership in the company as part of his compensation package.

  Winder was not only CTS's general manager, but its lead salesperson as well. He called on prospective corporate clients all over the country, and he worked closely with MetroNet. That activity primarily involved appearing at association-sponsored seminars to inform member brokers about CTS and its services.

It was obvious to Jim Dolan that CTS had become an important source of real estate sales commissions for the Burr and Lehman partnership. Most of CTS's clients were in the Chicago area, and a large portion of the real estate transactions generated by CTS were being handled by Burr and Lehman Real Estate.

Dolan also inferred that the three senior partners—Burr, Lehman, and Kupchak—were close friends socially as well as professionally. The men clearly respected each other and valued each other's opinions. On one occasion Burr had told Dolan, "It's because of Bill Lehman that I have what I have today. I can always trust his word." Tom Winder was also woven into the relationship, but he was apparently not as closely involved as the other three. Randall and Dolan both sensed that Elliott Burr was the unofficial spokesman of the group. "I have the impression he can speak for all of them," commented Dolan.

In late April, Randall obtained a copy of a consultant's report on the employee relocation industry that had been commissioned by MetroNet's Third-Party Equity Committee. The report estimated that there were more than 500,000 homeowner/employees transferred annually, generating over 1 million home purchases and sales. However, fewer than 55,000 of these transfers were currently being handled by relocation services companies. Dolan's own analysis had projected a 10 to 15 percent annual growth rate in the use of relocation companies, leading to industry volume estimates of 60,000 in 1979, 67,000 in 1980, and 75,000 by 1981. The consultant's report stressed that success in the relocation business depended on a company's ability to provide services to its corporate clients at lower cost than the clients could do it themselves. In addition, profitability depended on a company's ability to turn over its inventory of homes quickly and at reasonable prices. Dolan's own financial projections showed a potential return on equity of over 30 percent by 1983, assuming only an 8 percent share of the market. And that return did not include any incremental profits resulting from new sales of CMI mortgage insurance policies generated by MetroNet brokers. Randall in particular was confident that the close ties between CMI and MetroNet would result in at least 5,000 new mortgage insurance policies annually—a volume that could add over $400,000 in after-tax profits to CMI's basic business.

On May 10, Randall and Dolan attended a Northwest Equipment Corporation financial review meeting in Minneapolis. Prior to their trip west Randall had prepared a detailed analysis of the CTS acquisition and the employee relocation industry. The analysis, in the form of a proposal, served as documentation for a formal request to Northwest for a capital expenditure of $9 million. Randall had decided that he was willing to pay up to $600,000 more than the $420,000 book value of CTS's net worth; the remaining $8 million would constitute the initial equity base required to build CTS into a viable company. The financial review meeting evolved into a lengthy critique of the acquisition proposal. Northwest's corporate staff was initially quite skeptical of the financial projections, but Randall and Dolan argued that the risks were relatively low (the homes could always be sold) and the potential payoffs, both economic and strategic, were enormous. Finally, after an extended debate, the request was approved.

Formal Negotiations with CTS

When Randall and Dolan returned from Minneapolis, they felt it was finally time to proceed in earnest with the acquisition negotiations. Randall sensed that at present CTS was limping along to no one's satisfaction—including Elliott Burr's. The company was sucking up much more of Burr's time and energy than he wanted to give it, and its inability to fulfill MetroNet's expectations was beginning to be an embarrassment for Burr personally.

In spite of these problems, Randall remained interested in completing the acquisition. Buying CTS would get CMI into the relocation business quickly, would provide them with immediate licensing and other legal documentation in 38 states, and would get them an experienced operations manager in Tom Winder. More important, Randall knew that Elliott Burr was an important and respected MetroNet broker, and buying CTS would provide an effective, influential entry into the MetroNet "old boy" network. Though he couldn't put a number on the value of that network, Randall believed it was almost more important than the acquisition of CTS itself. Randall was convinced that the connection with the MetroNet brokers would enable him to run CTS at far lower cost than the established relocation companies, and he also expected to realize a significant increase in CMI's mortgage insurance business.

May 21, 1979

Now, as Randall and Dolan sat in Randall's office on May 21, they discussed the draft of a formal purchase offer that Dolan had prepared that morning (see Exhibit 5 for relevant excerpts). The two men had decided to make an initial offer of $400,000 more than the $420,000 book value of CTS's net worth, subject to a formal audit and adjustments depending on the final sales prices of all homes owned by CTS as of the formal purchase date. This opening bid was $200,000 below Randall's ceiling price of $600,000 for the firm's goodwill. The offer was for 100 percent of the ownership of the company. The $2 million in outstanding notes would pass through to the new company owned by Randall and Dolan. The offer also included a statement of intent to retain Tom Winder as CTS's general manager and to move the company to CMI's home office in Philadelphia.

As Randall and Dolan reviewed their plans, it was clear that they were more concerned about how to conduct the face-to-face negotiations than with the formal terms themselves. In the telephone call he had just completed, Randall had told Elliott Burr only that they wanted to meet the other stockholders and review their current thinking. At one point during the conversation Jim Dolan commented,

> I really wonder how they'll react to this offer. We've been putting them off for so long now that I'm not sure how they feel about us anymore. And our offer is so much less than they're looking for.

Randall replied,

> I know that—but I have my ceiling. It seems to me the real question now is what kind of bargaining stance we should take, and how to carry it out. What do you think they are expecting?

Discussion Questions

1. Prepare, and be ready to discuss, a negotiation strategy for Randall and Dolan.
2. What should CMI be expecting from CTS?

EXHIBIT 5 | Draft of Purchase Letter

The Board of Directors and Stockholders
Corporate Transfer Services, Inc.
Chicago, IL

May 24, 1979

Gentlemen:

Capital Mortgage Insurance Corporation (the "Purchaser") hereby agrees to purchase from you (the "Stockholders"), and you, the Stockholders, hereby jointly and severally agree to sell to us, the Purchaser, 100 percent of the issued and outstanding shares of capital stock of Corporate Transfer Services (the "Company") on the following terms and conditions.

Purchase Price. Subject to any adjustment under the following paragraph, the Purchase Price of the Stock shall be the sum of $400,000.00 (four hundred thousand dollars even) and an amount equal to the Company's net worth as reflected in its audited financial statements on the closing date (the "Closing Date Net Worth").

Adjustment of Purchase Price. The Purchase Price shall be reduced or increased, as the case may be, dollar-for-dollar by the amount, if any, by which the net amount realized on the sale of homes owned as of the Closing Date is exceeded by, or exceeds, the value attributed to such homes in the Closing Date Net Worth.

Continuation of Employment. Immediately upon consummation of the transaction, the Purchaser will enter into discussion with Mr. Thomas Winder with the intent that he continue employment in a management capacity at a mutually agreeable rate of pay. Mr. Winder will relocate to Philadelphia, Pennsylvania, and will be responsible for the sale of all homes owned by the Company at the Closing Date.

Covenant-Not-to-Compete. At the closing, each Stockholder will execute and deliver a covenant-not-to-compete agreeing that he will not engage in any capacity in the business conducted by the Company for a period of two years. If the foregoing correctly states our agreement as to this transaction, please sign below.

Very truly yours,

CAPITAL MORTGAGE INSURANCE
CORPORATION

The foregoing is agreed to and accepted.   By _____
                                                    President

---

Endnotes

1. "Why Merrill Lynch Wants to Sell Your House," *Fortune,* January 29, 1979.

2. Ibid., p. 89.

3. The term *third-party equity capability* derived from the fact that a relocation services company actually purchased an employee's home, freeing up the owner's equity and making it available for investment in a new home. Within the industry, the terms *third-party equity company* and *employee relocation services company* were generally used interchangeably.

Case 2

Pacific Oil Company (A)

For the discussion of Pacific Oil Company, please prepare the following:

1. As background information, read the appendix to this case: "Petrochemical Supply Contracts: A Technical Note" (p. 601).

2. Read the Pacific Oil Company case.

3. Prepare the following questions for class discussion:

   a. Describe the problem that Pacific Oil Company faced as it reopened negotiations with Reliant Chemical Company in early 1985.

   b. Evaluate the styles and effectiveness of Messrs. Fontaine, Gaudin, Hauptmann, and Zinnser as negotiators in this case.

   c. What should Frank Kelsey recommend to Jean Fontaine at the end of the case? Why?

The Pacific Oil Company

"Look, you asked for my advice, and I gave it to you," Frank Kelsey said. "If I were you, I wouldn't make any more concessions! I really don't think you ought to agree to their last demand! But you're the one who has to live with the contract, not me!"

Static on the transatlantic telephone connection obscured Jean Fontaine's reply. Kelsey asked him to repeat what he had said.

"OK, OK, calm down, Jean. I can see your point of view. I appreciate the pressures you're under. But I sure don't like the looks of it from this end. Keep in touch—I'll talk to you early next week. In the meantime, I will see what others at the office think about this turn of events."

Frank Kelsey hung up the phone. He sat pensively, staring out at the rain pounding on the window. "Poor Fontaine," he muttered to himself. "He's so anxious to please the customer, he'd feel compelled to give them the whole pie without getting his fair share of the dessert!"

Kelsey cleaned and lit his pipe as he mentally reviewed the history of the negotiations. "My word," he thought to himself, "we are getting completely taken in with this Reliant deal! And I can't make Fontaine see it!"

Background

Pacific Oil Company was founded in 1902 as the Sweetwater Oil Company of Oklahoma City, Oklahoma. The founder of Sweetwater Oil, E.M. Hutchinson, pioneered a major oil strike in north central Oklahoma that touched off the Oklahoma "black gold" rush

Source: Case prepared by Roy J. Lewicki.

Although this case is over 20 years old, the editors of this volume believe that it presents valuable lessons about the negotiation process.

of the early 1900s. Through growth and acquisition in the 1920s and 1930s, Hutchinson expanded the company rapidly and renamed it Pacific Oil in 1932. After a period of consolidation in the 1940s and 1950s, Pacific expanded again. It developed extensive oil holdings in North Africa and the Middle East, as well as significant coal beds in the western United States. Much of Pacific's oil production is sold under its own name as gasoline through service stations in the United States and Europe, but it is also distributed through several chains of independent gasoline stations. In addition, Pacific is also one of the largest and best-known worldwide producers of industrial petrochemicals.

One of Pacific's major industrial chemical lines is the production of vinyl chloride monomer (VCM). The basic components of VCM are ethylene and chlorine. Ethylene is a colorless, flammable, gaseous hydrocarbon with a disagreeable odor; it is generally obtained from natural or coal gas, or by "cracking" petroleum into smaller molecular components. As a further step in the petroleum cracking process, ethylene is combined with chlorine to produce VCM, also a colorless gas.

VCM is the primary component of a family of plastics known as the vinyl chlorides. VCM is subjected to the process of polymerization, in which smaller molecules of vinyl chloride are chemically bonded together to form larger molecular chains and networks. As the bonding occurs, polyvinyl chloride (PVC) is produced; coloring pigments may be added, as well as "plasticizer" compounds that determine the relative flexibility or hardness of the finished material. Through various forms of calendering (pressing between heavy rollers), extruding, and injection molding, the plasticized polyvinyl chloride is converted to an enormous array of consumer and industrial applications: flooring, wire insulation, electrical transformers, home furnishings, piping, toys, bottles and containers, rainwear, light roofing, and a variety of protective coatings. (See Exhibit 1 for a breakdown of common PVC-based products.) In 1979, Pacific Oil established the first major contract with the Reliant Corporation for the purchase of vinyl chloride monomer. The Reliant Corporation was a major industrial manufacturer of wood and petrochemical products for the construction industry. Reliant was expanding its manufacturing operations in the production of plastic pipe and pipe fittings, particularly in Europe. The use of plastic as a substitute for iron or copper pipe was gaining rapid acceptance in the construction trades, and the European markets were significantly more progressive in adopting the plastic pipe. Reliant already had developed a small polyvinyl chloride production facility at Abbeville, France, and Pacific constructed a pipeline from its petrochemical plant at Antwerp to Abbeville.

The 1979 contract between Pacific Oil and Reliant was a fairly standard one for the industry and due to expire in December of 1982. The contract was negotiated by Reliant's purchasing managers in Europe, headquartered in Brussels, and the senior marketing managers of Pacific Oil's European offices, located in Paris. Each of these individuals reported to the vice presidents in charge of their companies' European offices, who in turn reported back to their respective corporate headquarters in the States. (See Exhibits 2 and 3 for partial organization charts.)

EXHIBIT 1 | Polyvinyl Chloride Major Markets, 1982 (units represented in MM pounds)

Market	MM Pounds	Percentage of Market Share
Apparel		
Baby pants	22	0.6
Footwear	128	3.2
Miscellaneous	60	1.5
	210	5.3
Building and construction		
Extruded foam moldings	46	1.2
Flooring	428	10.8
Lighting	10	0.3
Panels and siding	64	1.6
Pipe and conduit	720	18.5
Pipe fittings	78	2.0
Rainwater systems	28	0.7
Swimming pool liners	40	1.0
Weather stripping	36	0.9
Miscellaneous	50	1.2
	1,500	38.2
Electrical		
Wire and cable	390	9.9
Home furnishings		
Appliances	32	0.8
Miscellaneous	286	9.8
	318	10.6
Housewares	94	2.4
Packaging		
Blow molded bottles	64	1.6
Closure liners and gaskets	16	0.4
Coatings	16	0.4
Film	124	3.2
Miscellaneous	80	2.0
	300	7.6
Recreation		
Records	136	3.4
Sporting goods	46	1.2
Miscellaneous	68	1.7
	250	6.3
Transportation		
Auto mats	36	0.9
Auto tops	32	0.8
Miscellaneous	164	4.2
	232	5.9

(*continued*)

EXHIBIT 1 | (concluded)

Market	MM Pounds	Percentage of Market Share
Miscellaneous		
Agriculture (including pipe)	106	2.6
Credit cards	24	0.4
Garden hose	40	1.0
Laminates	44	1.1
Medical tubing	42	1.1
Novelties	12	0.3
Stationery supplies	32	0.8
Miscellaneous	12	0.3
	312	7.6
Export	146	3.7
Miscellaneous	98	2.5
	244	6.2
Total	3,850	100.0

The 1982 Contract Renewal

In February 1982, negotiations began to extend the four-year contract beyond the December 31, 1982, expiration date. Jean Fontaine, Pacific Oil's marketing vice president for Europe, discussed the Reliant account with his VCM marketing manager, Paul Gaudin. Fontaine had been promoted to the European vice presidency approximately 16 months earlier after having served as Pacific's ethylene marketing manager. Fontaine had been with Pacific Oil for 11 years and had a reputation as a strong up-and-comer in Pacific's European operations. Gaudin had been appointed as VCM marketing manager eight months earlier; this was his first job with Pacific Oil, although he had five years of previous experience in European computer sales with a large American computer manufacturing company. Fontaine and Gaudin had worked well in their short time together, establishing a strong professional and personal relationship. Fontaine and Gaudin agreed that the Reliant account had been an extremely profitable and beneficial one for Pacific and believed that Reliant had, overall, been satisfied with the quality and service under the agreement as well. They clearly wanted to work hard to obtain a favorable renegotiation of the existing agreement. Fontaine and Gaudin also reviewed the latest projections of worldwide VCM supply, which they had just received from corporate headquarters (see Exhibit 4). The data confirmed what they already knew—that there was a worldwide shortage of VCM and that demand was continuing to rise. Pacific envisioned that the current demand–supply situation would remain this way for a number of years. As a result, Pacific believed that it could justify a high favorable formula price for VCM.

Fontaine and Gaudin decided that they would approach Reliant with an offer to renegotiate the current agreement. Their basic strategy would be to ask Reliant for their five-year demand projections on VCM and polyvinyl chloride products. Once these projections were received, Fontaine and Gaudin would frame the basic formula price that

EXHIBIT 2 | Partial Organization Chart—Pacific Oil Company

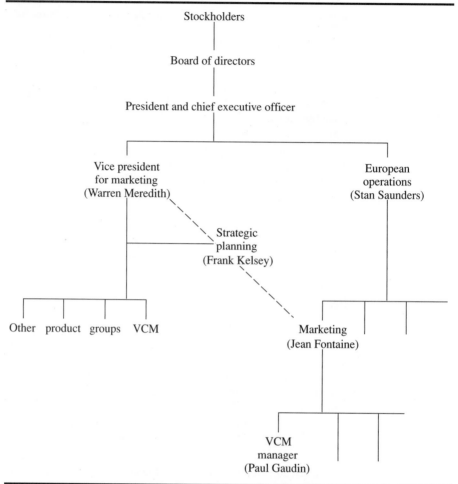

they would offer. (It would be expected that there would be no significant changes or variations in other elements of the contract, such as delivery and contract language.) In their negotiations, their strategy would be as follows:

1. To dwell on the successful long-term relationship that had already been built between Reliant and Pacific Oil, and to emphasize the value of that relationship for the success of both companies.

2. To emphasize all of the projections that predicted the worldwide shortage of VCM and the desirability for Reliant to ensure that they would have a guaranteed supplier.

3. To point out all of the ways that Pacific had gone out of its way in the past to ensure delivery and service.

EXHIBIT 3 | Partial Organization Chart—Reliant Chemical Company

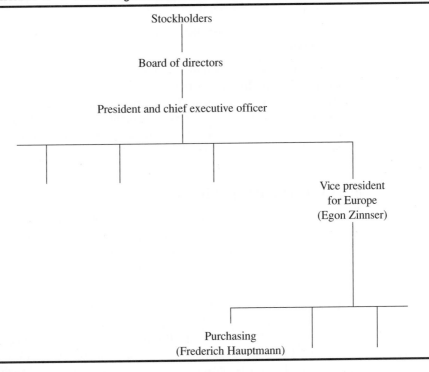

Stockholders

Board of directors

President and chief executive officer

Vice president
for Europe
(Egon Zinnser)

Purchasing
(Frederich Hauptmann)

EXHIBIT 4 | Memorandum, January 17, 1982

TO: All VCM Marketing Managers
FROM: F. Kelsey, Strategic Planning Division
RE: Worldwide VCM Supply–Demand Projections
DATE: January 17, 1982
CONFIDENTIAL—FOR YOUR EYES ONLY

Here are the data from 1980 and 1981, and the five-year projections that I promised you at our last meeting. As you can see, the market is tight, and is projected to get tighter. I hope you will find this useful in your marketing efforts—let me know if I can supply more detailed information.

Year	Total Projected Demand (in MM pounds)	Supply Plant Capacities	Operating Rates to Meet Demand (percent)
1980	4,040	5,390	75%
1981	4,336	5,390	80
1982	5,100	6,600	77
1983	5,350	6,600	81
1984	5,550	6,600	83
1985	5,650	7,300	75
1986	5,750	7,300	78

4. To use both the past and future quality of the relationship to justify what might appear to be a high formula price.

5. To point out the ways that Pacific's competitors could not offer the same kind of service.

Over the next six months, Gaudin and Fontaine, independently and together, made a number of trips to Brussels to visit Reliant executives. In addition, several members of Pacific's senior management visited Brussels and paid courtesy calls on Reliant management. The net result was a very favorable contract for Pacific Oil, signed by both parties on October 24, 1982. The basic contract, to extend from January 1983 to December 1987, is represented as Exhibit 5.

A Changed Perspective

In December of 1984, Fontaine and Gaudin sat down to their traditional end-of-year review of all existing chemical contracts. As a matter of course, the Reliant VCM contract came under review. Although everything had been proceeding very smoothly, the prospects for the near and long-term future were obviously less clear, for the following reasons:

1. Both men reviewed the data that they had been receiving from corporate headquarters, as well as published projections of the supply situation for various chemicals over the next 10 years. It was clear that the basic supply–demand situation on VCM was changing (see Exhibit 6). While the market was currently tight—the favorable supply situation that had existed for Pacific when the Reliant contract was first negotiated—the supply of VCM was expected to expand rapidly over the next few years. Several of Pacific's competitors had announced plans for the construction of VCM manufacturing facilities that were expected to come on line in 20–30 months.

2. Fontaine and Gaudin knew that Reliant was probably aware of this situation as well. As a result, they would probably anticipate the change in the supply–demand situation as an opportunity to pursue a more favorable price, with the possible threat that they would be willing to change suppliers if the terms were not favorable enough. (Although rebuilding a pipeline is no simple matter, it clearly could be done, and had been, when the terms were sufficiently favorable to justify it.)

3. Fontaine was aware that in a situation where the market turned from one of high demand to excess supply, it was necessary to make extra efforts to maintain and re-sign all major current customers. A few large customers (100 million pounds a year and over) dominated the marketplace, and a single customer defection in an oversupplied market could cause major headaches for everyone. It would simply be impossible to find another customer with demands of that magnitude; a number of smaller customers would have to be found, while Pacific would also have to compete with spot market prices that would cut profits to the bone.

EXHIBIT 5 | Agreement of Sale

This Agreement, entered into this *24th* day of *October 1982,* between *Pacific Oil Company,* hereinafter called Seller, and *Reliant Chemical Company of Europe,* hereinafter called Buyer. WITNESSETH:

Seller agrees to sell and deliver and Buyer agrees to purchase and receive commodity (hereinafter called "product") under the terms and conditions set forth below.

1. Product: Vinyl Chloride Monomer

2. Quality: ASTM requirements for polymer-grade product

3. Quantity: 1983: 150 million pounds

    1984: 160 million pounds

    1985: 170 million pounds

    1986: 185 million pounds

    1987: 200 million pounds

4. Period: Contract shall extend from January 1, 1983, until December 31, 1987, and every year thereafter, unless terminated with 180 days' prior notification at the end of each calendar year, but not before December 31, 1987.

5. Price: See Contract formula price.

6. Payment Terms:

    a. Net 30 days.

    b. All payments shall be made in United States dollars without discount or deduction, unless otherwise noted, by wire transfer at Seller's option, to a bank account designated by Seller. Invoices not paid on due date will be subject to a delinquency finance charge of 1 percent per month.

    c. If at any time the financial responsibility of Buyer shall become impaired or unsatisfactory to Seller, cash payment on delivery or satisfactory security may be required. A failure to pay any amount may, at the option of the Seller, terminate this contract as to further deliveries. No forbearance, course of dealing, or prior payment shall affect this right of Seller.

7. Price Change:

    The price specified in this Agreement may be changed by Seller on the first day of any calendar *half-year* by written notice sent to the Buyer not less than thirty (30) days prior to the effective date of change. Buyer gives Seller written notice of objection to such change at least ten (10) days prior to the effective date of change. Buyer's failure to serve Seller with written notice of objection thereto prior to the effective date thereof shall be considered acceptance of such change. If Buyer gives such notice of objection and Buyer and Seller fail to agree on such change prior to the effective date thereof, this Agreement and the obligations of Seller and Buyer hereunder shall terminate with respect to the unshipped portion of the Product governed by it. Seller has the option immediately to cancel this contract upon written notice to Buyer, to continue to sell hereunder at the same price and terms which were in effect at the time Seller gave notice of change, or to suspend performance under this contract while pricing is being resolved. If Seller desires to revise the price, freight allowance, or terms of payment pursuant to this agreement, but is restricted to any extent against doing so by reason of any law, governmental decree, order, or regulation, or if the price, freight allowance, or terms of payment then in effect under this contract are nullified or reduced by reason of any law, governmental decree, order, or regulation, Seller shall have the right to cancel this contract upon fifteen (15) days' written notice to purchaser.

8. Measurements:

    Seller's determinations, unless proven to be erroneous, shall be accepted as conclusive evidence of the quantity of Product delivered hereunder. Credit will not be allowed for shortages of

(*continued*)

EXHIBIT 5 | (continued)

1/2 of 1 percent or less of the quantity, and overages of 1/2 of 1 percent or less of the quantity will be waived. The total amount of shortages or overages will be credited or billed when quantities are greater and such differences are substantiated. Measurements of weight and volume shall be according to procedures and criteria standard for such determinations.

9. Shipments and Delivery:

Buyer shall give Seller annual or quarterly forecasts of its expected requirements as Seller may from time to time request. Buyer shall give Seller reasonably advanced notice for each shipment which shall include date of delivery and shipping instructions. Buyer shall agree to take deliveries in approximately equal monthly quantities, except as may be otherwise provided herein. In the event that Buyer fails to take the quantity specified or the pro rata quantity in any month, Seller may, at its option, in addition to other rights and remedies, cancel such shipments or parts thereof.

10. Purchase Requirements:

   a. If during any consecutive three-month period, Buyer for any reason (but not for reasons of force majeure as set forth in Section 12) takes less than 90 percent of the average monthly quantity specified, or the prorated minimum monthly quantity then applicable to such period under Section 12, Seller may elect to charge Buyer a penalty charge for failure to take the average monthly quantity or prorated minimum monthly quantity.

   b. If, during any consecutive three-month period, Buyer, for any reason (but not, however, for reasons of force majeure as set forth in Section 12) takes Product in quantities less than that equal to at least one-half of the average monthly quantity specified or the prorated minimum monthly quantity originally applicable to such period under Section 12, Seller may elect to terminate this agreement.

   c. It is the Seller's intent not to unreasonably exercise its right under (a) or (b) in the event of adverse economic and business conditions in general.

   d. Notice of election by Seller under (a) or (b) shall be given within 30 days after the end of the applicable three-month period, and the effective date of termination shall be 30 days after the date of said notice.

11. Detention Policy:

Seller may, from time to time, specify free unloading time allowances for its transportation equipment. Buyer shall be liable to the Transportation Company for all demurrage charges made by the Transportation Company, for railcars, trucks, tanks, or barges held by Buyer beyond the free unloading time.

12. Force Majeure:

Neither party shall be liable to the other for failure or delay in performance hereunder to the extent that such failure or delay is due to war, fire, flood, strike, lockout, or other labor trouble, accident, breakdown of equipment or machinery, riot, act, request, or suggestion of governmental authority, act of God, or other contingencies beyond the control of the affected party which interfere with the production or transportation of the material covered by this Agreement or with the supply of any raw material (whether or not the source of supply was in existence or contemplated at the time of this Agreement) or energy source used in connection therewith, or interfere with Buyer's consumption of such material, provided that in no event shall Buyer be relieved of the obligation to pay in full for material delivered hereunder. Without limitation on the foregoing, neither party shall be required to remove any cause listed above or replace the affected source of supply or facility if it shall involve additional expense or departure from its normal practices. If any of the events specified in this paragraph shall have occurred, Seller shall have the right to allocate in a fair and reasonable manner among its customers and Seller's own requirements any supplies of material Seller has available for delivery at the time or for the duration of the event.

(continued)

EXHIBIT 5 | (concluded)

13. Materials and Energy Supply:

If, for reasons beyond reasonable commercial control, Seller's supply of product to be delivered hereunder shall be limited due to continued availability of necessary raw materials and energy supplies, Seller shall have the right (without liability) to allocate to the Buyer a portion of such product on such basis as Seller deems equitable. Such allocation shall normally be that percentage of Seller's total internal and external commitments which are committed to Buyer as related to the total quantity available from Seller's manufacturing facilities.

14. Disclaimer:

Seller makes no warranty, express or implied, concerning the product furnished hereunder other than it shall be of the quality and specifications stated herein. Any implied warranty of FITNESS is expressly excluded and to the extent that it is contrary to the foregoing sentence; any implied warranty of MERCHANTABILITY is expressly excluded. Any recommendation made by Seller makes no warranty of results to be obtained. Buyer assumes all responsibility and liability for loss or damage resulting from the handling or use of said product. In no event shall Seller be liable for any special, indirect, or consequential damages, irrespective of whether caused or allegedly caused by negligence.

15. Taxes:

Any tax, excise fee, or other charge or increase thereof upon the production, storage, withdrawal, sale, or transportation of the product sold hereunder, or entering into the cost of such product, imposed by any proper authority becoming effective after the date hereof, shall be added to the price herein provided and shall be paid by the Buyer.

16. Assignment and Resale:

This contract is not transferable or assignable by Buyer without the written consent of Seller. The product described hereunder, in the form and manner provided by the Seller, may not be assigned or resold without prior written consent of the Seller.

17. Acceptance:

Acceptance hereof must be without qualification, and Seller will not be bound by any different terms and conditions contained in any other communication.

18. Waiver of Breach:

No waiver by Seller or Buyer of any breach of any of the terms and conditions contained in this Agreement shall be construed as a waiver or any subsequent breach of the same or any other term or condition.

19. Termination:

If any provision of this agreement is or becomes violate of any law, or any rule, order, or regulation issued thereunder, Seller shall have the right, upon notice to Buyer, to terminate the Agreement in its entirety.

20. Governing Law:

The construction of this Agreement and the rights and obligations of the parties hereunder shall be governed by the laws of the State of New York.

21. Special Provisions:

BUYER: SELLER:
                                          PACIFIC OIL COMPANY

(firm)
By: By:
Title: Senior Purchasing Manager   Title: Marketing Vice President
Date: Date:

EXHIBIT 6 | Memorandum, December 9, 1984

TO: All VCM Marketing Managers
FROM: F. Kelsey, Strategic Planning Division
RE: Worldwide VCM–Supply–Demand Projections
DATE: December 9, 1984
CONFIDENTIAL—FOR YOUR EYES ONLY

This will confirm and summarize data that we discussed at the national marketing meeting last month in Atlanta. At that time, I indicated to you that the market projections we made several years ago have changed drastically. In early 1983, a number of our competitors announced their intentions to enter the VCM business over the next five years. Several facilities are now under construction, and are expected to come on line in late 1986 and early 1987. As a result, we expect a fairly significant shift in the supply–demand relationship over the next few years.

I hope you will give this appropriate consideration in your long-range planning effort. Please contact me if I can be helpful.

Year	Total Projected Demand (in MM pounds)	Supply Plant Capacities	Operating Rates to Meet Demand (percent)
1982	5,127 (actual)	6,600	78%
1983	5,321 (actual)	6,600	81
1984	5,572 (rev. 11/84)	6,600	84
1985	5,700	7,300	78
1986	5,900	8,450	70
1987	6,200	9,250	64
1988	6,500	9,650	67
1989	7,000	11,000	63

4. In a national product development meeting back in the States several weeks prior, Fontaine had learned of plans by Pacific to expand and diversify its own product line into VCM derivatives. There was serious talk of Pacific's manufacturing its own PVC for distribution under the Pacific name, as well as the manufacture and distribution of various PVC products. Should Pacific decide to enter these businesses, not only would they require a significant amount of the VCM now being sold on the external market, but Pacific would probably decide that, as a matter of principle, it would not want to be in the position of supplying a product competitor with the raw materials to manufacture the product line, unless the formula price was extremely favorable.

As they reviewed these factors, Gaudin and Fontaine realized that they needed to take action. They pondered the alternatives.

A New Contract Is Proposed

As a result of their evaluation of the situation in December 1984, Fontaine and Gaudin decided to proceed on two fronts. First, they would approach Reliant with the intent of reopening negotiation on the current VCM contract. They would propose to renegotiate the current agreement, with an interest toward extending the contract five years from the point of agreement on contract terms. Second, they would contact those people at corporate headquarters in New York who were evaluating Pacific's alternatives for new product development, and inform them of the nature of the situation. The sooner a determination could be made on the product development strategies, the sooner the Pacific office would know how to proceed on the Reliant contract.

Gaudin contacted Frederich Hauptmann, the senior purchasing manager for Reliant Chemicals in Europe. Hauptmann had assumed the position as purchasing manager approximately four weeks earlier, after having served in a purchasing capacity for a large German steel company. Gaudin arranged a meeting for early January in Hauptmann's office. After getting acquainted over lunch, Gaudin briefed Hauptmann on the history of Reliant's contractual relationships with Pacific Oil. Gaudin made clear that Pacific had been very pleased with the relationship that had been maintained. He said that Pacific was concerned about the future and about maintaining the relationship with Reliant for a long time to come. Hauptmann stated that he understood that the relationship had been a very productive one, too, and also hoped that the two companies could continue to work together in the future. Buoyed by Hauptmann's apparent enthusiasm and relative pleasure with the current agreement, Gaudin said that he and Jean Fontaine, his boss, had recently been reviewing all contracts. Even though the existing Pacific–Reliant VCM agreement had three years to run, Pacific felt that it was never too soon to begin thinking about the long-term future. In order to ensure that Reliant would be assured of a continued supply of VCM, under the favorable terms and working relationship that was already well established, Pacific hoped that Reliant might be willing to begin talks now for contract extension past December 31, 1987. Hauptmann said that he would be willing to consider it but needed to consult other people in the Brussels office, as well as senior executives at corporate headquarters in Chicago. Hauptmann promised to contact Gaudin when he had the answer.

By mid-February, Hauptmann cabled Gaudin that Reliant was indeed willing to begin renegotiation of the current agreement, with interest in extending it for the future. He suggested that Gaudin and Fontaine come to Brussels for a preliminary meeting in early March. Hauptmann also planned to invite Egon Zinnser, the regional vice president of Reliant's European operations and Hauptmann's immediate superior.

March 10

Light snow drifted onto the runway of the Brussels airport as the plane landed. Fontaine and Gaudin had talked about the Reliant contract, and the upcoming negotiations, for most of the trip. They had decided that while they did not expect the negotiations to be a complete pushover, they expected no significant problems or stumbling points in the deliberations. They thought Reliant negotiators would routinely question some of the coefficients that were used to compute the formula price as well as to renegotiate some of the minimum quantity commitments. They felt that the other elements of the contract would be routinely discussed but that no dramatic changes should be expected.

After a pleasant lunch with Hauptmann and Zinnser, the four men sat down to review the current VCM contract. They reviewed and restated much of what Gaudin and Hauptmann had done at their January meeting. Fontaine stated that Pacific Oil was looking toward the future and hoping that it could maintain Reliant as a customer. Zinnser responded that Reliant had indeed been pleased by the contract as well but that it was also concerned about the future. They felt that Pacific's basic formula price on VCM, while fair, might not remain competitive in the long-run future. Zinnser said that he had already had discussions with two other major chemical firms that were planning new VCM manufacturing facilities and that one or both of these firms were due to come on line in the next 24 to 30 months. Zinnser wanted to make sure that Pacific could remain competitive with other firms in the marketplace. Fontaine responded that it was Pacific's full intention to remain completely competitive, whether it be in market price or in the formula price.

Zinnser said he was pleased by this reply and took this as an indication that Pacific would be willing to evaluate and perhaps adjust some of the factors that were now being used to determine the VCM formula price. He then presented a rather elaborate proposal for adjusting the respective coefficients of these factors. The net result of these adjustments would be to reduce the effective price of VCM by approximately 2 cents per pound. It did not take long for Fontaine and Gaudin to calculate that this would be a net reduction of approximately $4 million per year. Fontaine stated that they would have to take the proposal back to Paris for intensive study and analysis. The men shook hands, and Fontaine and Gaudin headed back to the airport.

Throughout the spring, Gaudin and Hauptmann exchanged several letters and telephone calls. They met once at the Paris airport when Hauptmann stopped over on a trip to the States and once in Zurich when both men discovered that they were going to be there on business the same day. By May 15, they had agreed on a revision of the formula price that would adjust the price downward by almost one cent per pound. Gaudin, believed that the price had finally been established, reported back to Fontaine that significant progress was being made. Gaudin expected that the remaining issues could be closed up in a few weeks and a new contract signed.

May 27

Hauptmann contacted Gaudin to tell him that Reliant was now willing to talk about the remaining issues in the contract. The two men met in early June. Gaudin opened the discussion by saying that now that the formula price had been agreed upon, he hoped that Reliant would be willing to agree to extend the contract five years from the point of signing. Hauptmann replied that Reliant had serious reservations about committing the company to a five-year contract extension. He cited the rapid fluctuations in the demand, pricing structure, and competition of Reliant's various product lines, particularly in the construction industry, as well as what appeared to be a changing perspective in the overall supply of VCM. Quite frankly, Hauptmann said, Reliant didn't want to be caught in a long-term commitment to Pacific if the market price of VCM was likely to drop in the foreseeable future. As a result, Reliant wanted to make a commitment for only a two-year contract renewal.

Gaudin tried to give Hauptmann a number of assurances about the continued integrity of the market. He also said that if changing market prices were a concern for Reliant, Pacific Oil would be happy to attempt to make adjustments in other parts of the contract to ensure protection against dramatic changes in either the market price or the demand for Reliant's product lines. But Hauptmann was adamant. Gaudin said he would have to talk to Fontaine and others in Paris before he could agree to only a two-year contract.

The two men talked several times on the telephone over the next two months and met once in Paris to discuss contract length. On August 17, in a quick 45-minute meeting in Orly Airport, Gaudin and Hauptmann agreed to a three-year contract renewal. They also agreed to meet in early September to discuss remaining contract issues.

September 10

Hauptmann met Gaudin and Fontaine in Pacific's Paris office. Hauptmann stressed that he and Zinnser were very pleased by the formula price and three-year contract duration that had been agreed to thus far. Fontaine echoed a similar satisfaction on behalf of Pacific and stated that they expected a long and productive relationship with Reliant. Fontaine stressed, however, that Pacific felt it was most important to them to complete the contract negotiations as quickly as possible, in order to adequately plan for product and market development in the future. Hauptmann agreed, saying that this was in Reliant's best interest as well. He felt that there were only a few minor issues that remained to be discussed before the contract could be signed.

Fontaine inquired as to what those issues were. Hauptmann said that the most important one to Reliant was the minimum quantity requirements, stipulating the minimum amount that Reliant had to purchase each year. Gaudin said that based on the projections for the growth of the PVC and fabricated PVC products over the next few years, and patterns established by past contracts, it was Pacific's assumption that Reliant would want to increase their quantity commitments by a minimum of 10 percent each year. Based on minimums stipulated in the current contract, Gaudin expected that Reliant would want to purchase at least 220 million pounds in year 1, 240 million pounds in year 2, and 265 million pounds in year 3. Hauptmann responded that Reliant's projections were very different. The same kind of uncertainty that had led to Reliant's concern about the term of the contract also contributed to a caution about significantly overextending themselves on a minimum quantity commitment. In fact, Reliant's own predictions were that they were likely to take less than the minimum in the current year (*underlifting,* in the parlance of the industry) and that, if they did so, they would incur almost a $1 million debt to Pacific. Conservative projections for the following year (1987) projected a similar deficit, but Reliant hoped that business would pick up and that the minimum quantities would be lifted. As a result, Hauptmann and Zinnser felt that it would be in Reliant's best interest to freeze minimum quantity requirements for the next two years—at 200 million pounds—and increase the minimum to 210 million pounds for the third year. Of course, Reliant *expected* that, most likely, they would be continuing to purchase much more than the specified minimums. But given the uncertainty of the future, Reliant did not want to get caught if the economy and the market truly turned sour.

Fontaine and Gaudin were astonished at the conservative projections Hauptmann was making. They tried in numerous ways to convince Hauptmann that his minimums were ridiculously low and that the PVC products were bound to prosper far more than Hauptmann seemed willing to admit. But Hauptmann was adamant and left Paris saying he needed to consult Zinnser and others in Brussels and the States before he could revise his minimum quantity estimates upward. Due to the pressure of other activities and vacation schedules, Gaudin and Hauptmann did not talk again until late October. Finally, on November 19, the two men agreed to a minimum quantity purchase schedule of 205 million pounds in the first year of the contract, 210 million pounds in the second year, and 220 million pounds in the third year. Moreover, Pacific agreed to waive any previous underlifting charges that might be incurred under the current contract when the new contract was signed.

October 24

Jean Fontaine returned to Paris from meetings in New York and a major market development meeting held by senior Pacific executives at Hilton Head. After a number of delays due to conflicting market research and changes in senior management, as well as the general uncertainty in the petroleum and chemical markets, Pacific had decided not to develop its own product lines for either PVC or fabricated products. The decision was largely based on the conclusion—more gut feel than hard fact—that entry into these new markets was unwise at a time when much greater problems faced Pacific and the petrochemicals industry in general. Fontaine had argued strenuously that the VCM market was rapidly going soft, and that failure to create its own product lines would leave Pacific Oil in an extremely poor position to market one of its basic products. Fontaine was told that his position was appreciated but that he and other chemical marketing people would simply have to develop new markets and customers for the product. Privately, Fontaine churned on the fact that it had taken senior executives almost a year to make the decision, while valuable time was being lost in developing the markets; but he wisely decided to bite his tongue and vent his frustration on 36 holes of golf. On the return flight to Paris, he read about Pacific's decision in the October 23 issue of *The Wall Street Journal* and ordered a double martini to soothe his nerves.

December 14

Fontaine and Gaudin went to Brussels to meet with Hauptmann and Zinnser. The Pacific executives stressed that it was of the utmost importance for Pacific Oil to try to wrap up the contract as quickly as possible—almost a year had passed in deliberations, and although Pacific was not trying to place the "blame" on anyone, it was most concerned that the negotiations be settled as soon as possible.

Zinnser emphasized that he, too, was concerned about completing the negotiations quickly. Both he and Hauptmann were extremely pleased by the agreements that had been reached so far and felt that there was no question that a final contract signing was imminent. The major issues of price, minimum quantities, and contract duration had been solved. In their minds, what remained were only a few minor technical items in contract language. Some minor discussion of each of these should wrap things up in a few weeks.

Fontaine asked what the issues were. Zinnser began by stating that Reliant had become concerned by the way that the delivery pipeline was being metered. As currently set up, the pipeline fed from Pacific's production facility in Antwerp, Belgium, to Reliant's refinery. Pacific had built the line and was in charge of maintaining it. Meters had been installed at the exit flange of the pipeline, and Reliant was paying the metered amount to Pacific. Zinnser said that some spot-checking by Reliant at the manufacturing facility seemed to indicate that they may not be receiving all they were being billed for. They were not questioning the integrity of the meters or the meter readers, but felt that since the pipe was a number of years old, it may have developed leaks. Zinnser felt that it was inappropriate for Reliant to absorb the cost of VCM that was not reaching its facility. They therefore proposed that Pacific install meters directly outside of the entry flange of Reliant's manufacturing facility and that Reliant only be required to pay the meter directly outside the plant.

Fontaine was astonished. In the first place, he said, this was the first time he had heard any complaint about the pipeline or the need to recalibrate the meters. Second, if the pipeline was leaking, Pacific would want to repair it, but it would be impossible to do so until spring. Finally, while the meters themselves were not prohibitively expensive, moving them would mean some interruption of service and definitely be costly to Pacific. Fontaine said he wanted to check with the maintenance personnel at Antwerp to find out whether they could corroborate such leaks.

Fontaine was unable to contact the operating manager at Antwerp or anyone else who could confirm that leaks may have been detected. Routine inspection of the pipeline had been subcontracted to a firm that had sophisticated equipment for monitoring such things, and executives of the firm could not be reached for several days. Fontaine tried to raise other contract issues with Zinnser, but Zinnser said that this was his most important concern, and this issue needed to be resolved before the others could be finalized. Fontaine agreed to find out more about the situation and to bring the information to the next meeting. With the Christmas and New Year holidays approaching, the four men could not schedule another meeting until January 9.

January Meetings

The January 9 meeting was postponed until January 20, due to the death of Hauptmann's mother. The meeting was rescheduled for a time when Hauptmann needed to be in Geneva, and Gaudin agreed to meet him there.

Gaudin stated that the investigation of the pipeline had discovered no evidence of significant discharge. There were traces of *minor* leaks in the line, but they did not appear to be serious, and it was currently impossible to determine what percentage of the product may be escaping. The most generous estimate given to Gaudin had been 0.1 percent of the daily consumption. Hauptmann stated that their own spot monitoring showed it was considerably more and that Reliant would feel infinitely more comfortable if the new metering system could be installed.

Gaudin had obtained estimates for the cost of remetering before he left Paris. It was estimated that the new meters could be installed for approximately $20,000.

Tracing and fixing the leaks (if they existed) could not be done until April or May and might run as much as $50,000 if leaks turned out to be located at some extremely difficult access points. After four hours of debating with Hauptmann in a small conference room off the lobby of the Geneva Hilton, Gaudin agreed that Pacific would remeter the pipeline.

Hauptmann said that as far as he was concerned, all of his issues had been settled; however, he thought Zinnser might have one or two other issues to raise. Hauptmann said that he would report back to Zinnser and contact Gaudin as soon as possible if another meeting was necessary. Gaudin, believing that Pacific was finally beginning to see the light at the end of the tunnel, left for Paris.

January 23

Hauptmann called Gaudin and said that he and Zinnser had thoroughly reviewed the contract and that there were a few small issues of contract language which Zinnser wanted to clarify. He said that he would prefer not to discuss them over the telephone and suggested that since he was going to be in Paris on February 3, they meet at the Pacific offices. Gaudin agreed.

Fontaine and Gaudin met Hauptmann on February 3. Hauptmann informed them that he felt Reliant had been an outstanding customer for Pacific in the past and that it probably was one of Pacific's biggest customers for VCM. Fontaine and Gaudin agreed, affirming the important role that Reliant was playing in Pacific's VCM market. Hauptmann said that he and Zinnser had been reviewing the contract and were concerned that the changing nature of the VCM market might significantly affect Reliant's overall position in the marketplace as a purchaser. More specifically, Reliant was concerned that the decline in market and price for VCM in the future might endanger its own position in the market, since Pacific might sign contracts with other purchasers for lower formula prices than were currently being awarded to Reliant. Since Reliant was such an outstanding customer of Pacific—and Fontaine and Gaudin had agreed to that— it seemed to Reliant that Pacific Oil had an obligation to write two additional clauses into the contract that would protect Reliant in the event of further slippage in the VCM market. The first was a "favored nations" clause, stipulating that if Pacific negotiated with another purchaser a more favorable price for VCM than Reliant was receiving now, Pacific would guarantee that Reliant would receive that price as well. The second was a "meet competition" clause, guaranteeing that Pacific would willingly meet any lower price on VCM offered by a competitor, in order to maintain the Reliant relationship. Hauptmann argued that the "favored nations" clause was protection for Reliant, since it stipulated that Pacific valued the relationship enough to offer the best possible terms to Reliant. The "meet competition" clause, he argued, was clearly advantageous for Pacific since it ensured that Reliant would have no incentive to shift suppliers as the market changed.

Fontaine and Gaudin debated the terms at length with Hauptmann, stressing the potential costliness of these agreements for Pacific. Hauptmann responded by referring to the costliness that the absence of the terms could have for Reliant and suggesting that perhaps the Pacific people were truly *not* as interested in a successful long-term relationship as they had been advocating. Fontaine said that he needed to get clearance from senior management in New York before he could agree to these terms and that he would get back to Hauptmann within a few days when the information was available.

Frank Kelsey's View

Frank Kelsey was strategic planning manager, a staff role in the New York offices of the Pacific Oil Company. Kelsey had performed a number of roles for the company in his 12 years of work experience. Using the chemistry background he had achieved in college, Kelsey worked for six years in the research and development department of Pacific's Chemical Division before deciding to enter the management ranks. He transferred to the marketing area, spent three years in chemical marketing, and then assumed responsibilities in marketing planning and development. He moved to the strategic planning department four years ago.

In late 1985, Kelsey was working in a staff capacity as an adviser to the executive product vice president of Pacific Oil Company. Pacific had developed a matrix organization. Reporting relationships were determined by business areas and by regional operating divisions within Pacific Oil. Warren Meredith, the executive vice president, had responsibility for monitoring the worldwide sale and distribution of VCM. Jean Fontaine reported to Meredith on all issues regarding the overall sale and marketing of VCM and reported to the president of Pacific Oil in Europe, Stan Saunders, on major issues regarding the management of the regional chemicals business in Europe. In general, Fontaine's primary working relationship was with Meredith; Saunders became involved in day-to-day decisions only as an arbiter of disputes or interpreter of major policy decisions.

As the negotiations with Reliant evolved, Meredith became distressed by the apparent turn that they were taking. He called in Frank Kelsey to review the situation. Kelsey knew that the VCM marketing effort for Pacific was going to face significant problems. Moreover, his dominant experience with Pacific in recent years had been in the purchasing and marketing operations, and he knew how difficult it would be for the company to maintain a strong negotiation in VCM contracts.

Meredith asked Kelsey to meet with Fontaine and Gaudin in Paris and review the current status of negotiations on the Reliant contract. While Kelsey could act only in an advisory capacity—Fontaine and Gaudin were free to accept or reject any advice that was offered, since they were the ones who had to live with the contract—Meredith told Kelsey to offer whatever services the men would accept.

Kelsey flew to Paris shortly after New Year's Day 1986. He met with Fontaine and Gaudin, and they reviewed in detail what had happened in the Reliant contract negotiations over the past year. Kelsey listened, asked a lot of questions, and didn't say much. He felt that offering advice to the men was premature and perhaps even unwise; Fontaine and Gaudin seemed very anxious about the negotiations and felt that the new contract would be sealed within a month. Moreover, they seemed to resent Kelsey's visit and clearly didn't want to share more than the minimum amount of information. Kelsey returned to New York and briefed Meredith on the state of affairs.

When Fontaine called Meredith for clearance to give Reliant both "favored nations" and "meet competition" clauses in the new contract, Meredith immediately called Kelsey. The two of them went back through the history of events in the negotiation and realized the major advantages that Reliant had gained by its negotiation tactics.

Meredith called Fontaine back and advised against granting the clauses in the contract. Fontaine said that Hauptmann was adamant and that he was afraid the entire negotiation was going to collapse over a minor point in the contract language. Meredith said he still thought it was a bad idea to make the concession. Fontaine said he thought he needed to consult Saunders, the European president of Pacific Oil, just to make sure.

Two days later, Saunders called Meredith and said that he had complete faith in Fontaine and Fontaine's ability to determine what was necessary to make a contract work. If Fontaine felt that "favored nations" and "meet competition" clauses were necessary, he trusted Fontaine's judgment that the clauses could not cause significant adverse harm to Pacific Oil over the next few years. As a result, he had given Fontaine the go-ahead to agree to these clauses in the new contract.

March 11

It was a dark and stormy night, March 11, 1986. Frank Kelsey was about to go to bed when the telephone rang. It was Jean Fontaine. Kelsey had not heard from Fontaine since their meeting in Paris. Meredith had told Kelsey about the discussion with Saunders, and he had assumed that Fontaine had gone ahead and conceded on the two contract clauses that had been discussed. He thought the contract was about to be wrapped up, but he hadn't heard for sure.

The violent rainstorm outside disrupted the telephone transmission, and Kelsey had trouble hearing Fontaine. Fontaine said that he had appreciated Kelsey's visit in January. Fontaine was calling to ask Kelsey's advice. They had just come from a meeting with Hauptmann. Hauptmann and Zinnser had reported that recent news from Reliant's corporate headquarters in Chicago projected significant downturns in the sale of a number of Reliant's PVC products in the European market. While Reliant thought it could ride out the downturn, they were very concerned about their future obligations under the Pacific contract. Since Reliant and Pacific had already settled on minimum quantity amounts, Reliant wanted the contractual right to resell the product if it could not use the minimum amount.

Kelsey tried to control his emotions as he thought about this negative turn of events in the Reliant negotiations. He strongly advised against agreeing to the clause, saying that it could put Pacific in an extremely poor position. Fontaine debated the point, saying he really thought Reliant might default on the whole contract if they didn't get resale rights. "I can't see where agreeing to the right to resale is a big thing, Frank, particularly given the size of this contract and its value to me and Pacific."

> KELSEY: Look, you asked for my advice, and I gave it to you. If I were you, I wouldn't make any more concessions. Agreeing to a resale clause could create a whole lot of unforeseen problems. At this point I think it's also the principle of the thing!

FONTAINE: Who cares about principles at a time like this! It's my neck that's on the line if this Reliant contract goes under! I'll have over 200 million pounds of VCM a year to eat in an oversupplied market! It's my neck that's on the line, not yours! How in the world can you talk to me about "principle" at this point?

KELSEY: Calm down, Jean! I can see your point of view! I appreciate the pressures on you, but I really don't like the looks of it from this end. Keep in touch—let me ask others down at the office what they think, and I'll call you next week.

Kelsey hung up the telephone, and stared out of the windows at the rain. He could certainly empathize with Fontaine's position—the man's neck was on the block. As he mentally reviewed the two-year history of the Reliant negotiations, Kelsey wondered how they had gotten to this point and whether anyone could have done things differently. He also wondered what to do about the resale clause, which appeared to be the final sticking point in the deliberations. Would acquiescing to a resale clause for Reliant be a problem to Pacific Oil? Kelsey knew he had to take action soon.

APPENDIX *Petrochemical Supply Contracts: A Technical Note*

Supply contracts between chemical manufacturing/refining companies and purchasing companies are fairly standard in the industry trade. They are negotiated between supplier and purchaser in order to protect both parties against major fluctuations in supply and demand. Any purchaser wishing to obtain a limited amount of a particular product could always approach any one of a number of chemical manufacturing firms and obtain the product at *market price*. The market price is controlled by the competitive supply and demand for the particular product on any given day. But purchasers want to be assured of a long-term supply and do not want to be subject to the vagaries of price fluctuation; similarly, manufacturers want to be assured of product outlets in order to adequately plan manufacturing schedules. Long-term contracts protect both parties against these fluctuations.

A supply contract is usually a relatively standard document, often condensed to one page. The major *negotiable* elements of the contract, on the *front side* of the document, include the price, quantity, product quality, contract duration, delivery point, and credit terms (see Exhibit 1A for a sample blank contract). The remainder (*back side*) of the contract is filled with traditionally fixed legal terminology that governs the conditions under which the contract will be maintained. While the items are seldom changed, they may be altered or waived as part of the negotiated agreement.

The primary component of a long-term contract is the price. In the early years of the petrochemical industry, the raw product was metered by the supplier (either in liquid or gaseous form) and sold to the purchaser. As the industry became more competitive, as prices rose rapidly, and as the products developed from petrochemical supplies (called *feedstocks*) became more sophisticated, pricing became a significantly more complex

EXHIBIT 1A | Agreement of Sale

This Agreement, entered into this _____ day of _____, _____, between *Pacific Oil Company,* hereinafter called Seller, and _____, hereinafter called Buyer.

WITNESSETH:

Seller agrees to sell and deliver and Buyer agrees to purchase and receive commodity (hereinafter called "product") under the terms and conditions set forth below.

1. Product:

2. Quality:

3. Quantity:

4. Period:

5. Price:

6. Payment Terms:

   a. Net _____.

   b. All payments shall be made in United States dollars without discount or deduction, unless otherwise noted, by wire transfer at Seller's option, to a bank account designated by Seller. Invoices not paid on due date will be subject to a delinquency finance charge of 1% per month.

   c. If at any time the financial responsibility of Buyer shall become impaired or unsatisfactory to Seller, cash payment on delivery or satisfactory security may be required. A failure to pay any amount may, at the option of the Seller, terminate this contract as to further deliveries. No forbearance, course of dealing, or prior payment shall affect this right of Seller.

7. Price Change:

   The price specified in this Agreement may be changed by Seller on the first day of any calendar _____ by written notice sent to the Buyer not less than thirty (30) days prior to the effective date of change. Buyer gives Seller written notice of objection to such change at least ten (10) days prior to the effective date of change. Buyer's failure to serve Seller with written notice of objection thereto prior to the effective date thereof shall be considered acceptance of such change. If Buyer gives such notice of objection and Buyer and Seller fail to agree on such change prior to the effective date thereof, this Agreement and the obligations of Seller and Buyer hereunder shall terminate with respect to the unshipped portion of the Product governed by it. Seller has the option immediately to cancel this contract upon written notice to Buyer, to continue to sell hereunder at the same price and terms which were in effect at the time Seller gave notice of change, or to suspend performance under this contract while pricing is being resolved. If Seller desires to revise the price, freight allowance, or terms of payment pursuant to this agreement, but is restricted to any extent against doing so by reason of any law, governmental decree, order, or regulation, or if the price, freight allowance, or terms of payment then in effect under this contract are nullified or reduced by reason of any law, governmental decree, order, or regulation, Seller shall have the right to cancel this contract upon fifteen (15) days' written notice to purchaser.

8. Measurements:

   Seller's determinations, unless proven to be erroneous, shall be accepted as conclusive evidence of the quantity of Product delivered hereunder. Credit will not be allowed for shortages of 1/2 of 1% or less of the quantity and overages of 1/2 of 1% or less of the quantity will be waived. The total amount of shortages or overages will be credited or billed when quantities are greater and such differences are substantiated. Measurements of weight and volume shall be according to procedures and criteria standard for such determinations.

(continued)

EXHIBIT 1A | *(continued)*

9. Shipments and Delivery:

Buyer shall give Seller annual or quarterly forecasts of its expected requirements as Seller may from time to time request. Buyer shall give Seller reasonably advanced notice for each shipment, which shall include date of delivery and shipping instructions. Buyer shall agree to take deliveries in approximately equal monthly quantities, except as may be otherwise provided herein. In the event that Buyer fails to take the quantity specified or the pro rata quantity in any month, Seller may, at its option, in addition to other rights and remedies, cancel such shipments or parts thereof.

10. Purchase Requirements:

a. If during any consecutive three-month period, Buyer for any reason (but not for reasons of force majeure as set forth in Section 12) takes less than 90 percent of the average monthly quantity specified, or the prorated minimum monthly quantity then applicable to such period under Section 12, Seller may elect to charge Buyer a penalty charge for failure to take the average monthly quantity or prorated minimum monthly quantity.

b. If, during any consecutive three-month period, Buyer, for any reason (but not, however, for reasons of force majeure as set forth in Section 12) takes Product in quantities less than that equal to at least one-half of the average monthly quantity specified, or the prorated minimum monthly quantity originally applicable to such period under Section 12, Seller may elect to terminate this agreement.

c. It is the Seller's intent not to unreasonably exercise its rights under (*a*) or (*b*) in the event of adverse economic and business conditions in general.

d. Notice of election by Seller under (*a*) or (*b*) shall be given within 30 days after the end of the applicable three-month period, and the effective date of termination shall be 30 days after the date of said notice.

11. Detention Policy:

Seller may, from time to time, specify free unloading time allowances for its transportation equipment. Buyer shall be liable to the Transportation Company for all demurrage charges made by the Transportation Company, for railcars, trucks, tanks, or barges held by Buyer beyond the free unloading time.

12. Force Majeure:

Neither party shall be liable to the other for failure or delay in performance hereunder to the extent that such failure or delay is due to war, fire, flood, strike, lockout, or other labor trouble, accident, breakdown of equipment or machinery, riot, act, request, or suggestion of governmental authority, act of God, or other contingencies beyond the control of the affected party which interfere with the production or transportation of the material covered by this Agreement or with the supply of any raw material (whether or not the source of supply was in existence or contemplated at the time of this Agreement) or energy source used in connection therewith, or interfere with Buyer's consumption of such material, provided that in no event shall Buyer be relieved of the obligation to pay in full for material delivered hereunder. Without limitation on the foregoing, neither party shall be required to remove any cause listed above or replace the affected source of supply or facility if it shall involve additional expense or departure from its normal practices. If any of the events specified in this paragraph shall have occurred, Seller shall have the right to allocate in a fair and reasonable manner among its customers and Seller's own requirements any supplies of material Seller has available for delivery at the time or for the duration of the event.

13. Materials and Energy Supply:

(continued)

EXHIBIT 1A | (*concluded*)

If, for any reasons beyond reasonable commercial control, Seller's supply of product to be delivered hereunder shall be limited due to continued availability of necessary raw materials and energy supplies, Seller shall have the right (without liability) to allocate to the Buyer a portion of such product on such basis as Seller deems equitable. Such allocation shall normally be that percentage of Seller's total internal and external commitments which are committed to Buyer as related to the total quantity from Seller's manufacturing facilities.

14. Disclaimer:

Seller makes no warranty, express or implied, concerning the product furnished hereunder other than it shall be of the quality and specification stated herein. Any implied warranty of FITNESS is expressly excluded and to the extent that it is contrary to the foregoing sentence; any implied warranty of MERCHANTABILITY is expressly excluded. Any recommendation made by Seller makes no warranty of results to be obtained. Buyer assumes all responsibility and liability for loss or damage resulting from the handling or use of said product. In no event shall Seller be liable for any special, indirect or consequential damages, irrespective of whether caused or allegedly caused by negligence.

15. Taxes:

Any tax, excise fee, or other charge or increase thereof upon the production, storage, withdrawal, sale, or transportation of the product sold hereunder, or entering into the cost of such product, imposed by any proper authority becoming effective after the date hereof, shall be added to the price herein provided and shall be paid by the Buyer.

16. Assignment and Resale:

This contract is not transferable or assignable by Buyer without the written consent of Seller. The product described hereunder, in the form and manner provided by the Seller, may not be assigned or resold without prior written consent of the Seller.

17. Acceptance:

Acceptance hereof must be without qualification, and Seller will not be bound by any different terms and conditions contained in any other communication.

18. Waiver of Breach:

No waiver by Seller or Buyer of any breach of any of the terms and conditions contained in this Agreement shall be construed as a waiver or any subsequent breach of the same or any other term or condition.

19. Termination:

If any provision of this agreement is or becomes violate of any law, or any rule, order, or regulation issued thereunder, Seller shall have the right, upon notice to Buyer, to terminate the Agreement in its entirety.

20. Governing Law:

The construction of this Agreement and the rights and obligations of the parties hereunder shall be governed by the laws of the State of _____.

21. Special Provisions:

BUYER: SELLER:

_____   _____
                (firm)   (firm)
By: _____   By: _____
Title: _____   Title: _____
Date: _____   Date: _____

process. Most contemporary contract prices are determined by an elaborate calculation called a *formula price,* composed of several elements:

1. *Feedstock characteristics:* Petrochemical feedstock supplies differ in the chemical composition and molecular structure of the crude oil. Differences in feedstocks will significantly affect the refining procedures and operating efficiency of the refinery that manufactures a product, as well as their relative usefulness to particular purchasers. While some chemical products may be drawn from a single feedstock, large-volume orders may necessitate the blending of several feedstocks with different structural characteristics.

2. *Fuel costs:* Fuel costs include the price and amount of energy that the manufacturing company must assume in cracking, refining, and producing a particular chemical stream.

3. *Labor costs:* Labor costs include the salaries of employees to operate the manufacturing facility for the purpose of producing a fixed unit amount of a particular product.

4. *Commodity costs:* Commodity costs include the value of the basic petrochemical base on the open marketplace. As the supply and demand for the basic commodity fluctuate on the open market, this factor is entered into the formula price.

A formula price may therefore be represented as a function of the following elements:

$$\text{Formula price} = \text{Feedstock cost} + \text{Energy cost} + \text{Labor cost} + \text{Commodity cost (per unit)}$$

If only one feedstock were used, the chemical composition of the feedstock would determine its basic cost and the energy, labor, and commodity costs of producing it. If several feedstocks were used, the formula price would be a composite of separate calculations for each particular feedstock, or a weighted average of the feedstock components, multiplied by the cost of production of each one.

Each of the elements in the formula price is also multiplied by a weighting factor (coefficient) that specifies how much each cost will contribute to the determination of the overall formula price. The supplier generally sets a *ceiling price,* guaranteeing that the formula price will not exceed this amount. Below the ceiling price, however, the supplier endeavors to maximize profits while clearly specifying the costs of production to the purchaser, while the purchaser attempts to obtain the most favorable formula price for himself. Since basic cost data and cost fluctuations are well known, negotiations typically focus on the magnitude of the coefficients that are applied to each element in the formula. Hence the actual formula computation may be represented as follows:

$$\text{Formula price} = (\text{Weighting coefficient} \times \text{Feedstock cost})$$
$$+ (\text{Weighting coefficient} \times \text{Energy cost})$$
$$+ (\text{Weighting coefficient} \times \text{Labor cost})$$
$$+ (\text{Weighting coefficient} \times \text{Commodity cost})$$

A fairly typical ratio of the weighting coefficients in this formula would be 70 percent (0.7) for feedstock cost, 20 percent (0.2) for energy costs, 5 percent (0.05) for labor costs, and 5 percent (0.05) for commodity costs. Multiple feedstocks supplied in a particular contract would be composed of a different set of costs and weighting elements for each feedstock in the supply.

The computation of a formula price, as opposed to the determination of a market price, has a number of advantages and disadvantages. Clearly, it enables the supplier to pass costs along to the purchaser, which minimizes the risk for both parties in the event of rapid changes in cost during the duration of the contract. The purchaser can project directly how cost changes will affect his supply costs; the supplier is protected by being able to pass cost increases along to the purchaser. However, when the market demand for the product is very high, the formula price constrains the seller in the ceiling price he can charge, hence curtailing potential profit for the product compared to its value on the open marketplace. Conversely, when market demand is very low, the contract may guarantee a large market to the supplier, but at a price for the product that could be unprofitable compared to production costs.

Quantity

Formula prices are typically computed with major attention given to quantity. Costs will fluctuate considerably based on the efficiency with which the production plant is operated, number of labor shifts required, and so on. Hence, in order to adequately forecast demand, attain particular economies of scale in the manufacturing process, and plan production schedules, suppliers must be able to determine the quantities that a particular customer will want to acquire. (Because of the volumes involved, no significant inventory is produced.) Quantities will be specified in common units of weight (pounds, tons, etc.) or volume (gallons, etc.).

Quantity specifications are typically treated as minimum purchase amounts. If a purchaser desires significantly more than the minimum amount (*overlifting*) in a given time period (e.g., a year), the amount would be sold contingent on availability and delivered at the formula price. Conceivably, *discount* prices or adjustments in the formula price could be negotiated for significant purchases over minimum quantity. Conversely, underpurchase of the minimum amount (*underlifting*) by a significant degree typically results in penalty costs to the purchaser. These are typically referred to as *liquidated damages* in the industry and may be negotiated at rates anywhere from a token fine of several thousand dollars to as much as 30 percent of the formula price for each unit underlifted. Faced with the possibility of underlifting (due to market or product demand changes that require less raw material in a given time period), purchasers typically handle underlifting in one of several ways:

1. Pay the underlifting charges (liquidated damages) to the supplier, either as stated or according to some renegotiated rate.

2. Not pay the liquidated damages, under the assumption that the supplier will not want to press legal charges against the purchaser at the expense of endangering the entire supply contract.

3. Resell the commodity to another purchaser who may be in need of supply, perhaps at a discounted price. Such action by the purchaser could cause major

instability in the market price and in supply contracts held at the original manufacturer or other manufacturers. For this reason, sellers typically preclude the right of the purchaser to resell the product as part of the standard contract language.

Quality

The quality of the product is related to the particular feedstock from which it is drawn, as well as the type and degree of refining that is employed by the supplier. Standard descriptions for gradations of quality are common parlance for each major chemical product.

Delivery

Most contracts specify the method of delivery, point of delivery, and way that the quantity amounts will be measured as the product is delivered. Gases are typically metered and delivered by direct pipeline from the manufacturer to the purchaser; liquids and liquefied gases may be sold by pipeline or shipped via tank truck, railroad tank car, tank barges, and tank ships.

Contract Duration

Most typical supply contracts extend for a period from one to five years; significantly longer or shorter ones would probably only be negotiated under extreme circumstances. Negotiations for contract renewal are typically begun several months prior to contract expiration.

Payment Terms

Payment terms are determined by the credit ratings and cash flow demands of both parties. Typical contracts specify payment within 30 days of delivery, although this time period may be shortened to payment on delivery or lengthened to a period of three months between delivery and payment.

Contract Language

As can be determined from Exhibit 1A, there are a number of elements in the contract that delineate the conditions under which the parties agree to bind themselves to the contract, or to deviate from it. Terminology and agreements are typically standard unless altered by negotiation prior to contract signing. These elements include the following:

1. *Measurements:* A mechanism for specifying how quantity amounts will be determined and how disputes over differences in delivered quantity will be resolved.

2. *Meet competition:* The seller agrees to meet competitive market prices for the product if they become substantially lower than the current negotiated formula price.

3. *Favored nations:* The supplier agrees that if he offers a better price on the product to any of the purchaser's competitors, he will offer the same price to this buyer.

4. *Purchase requirements:* The purchase requirements govern the conditions and terms under which liquidated damages may be invoked.

5. *Force majeure:* The force majeure clause exempts the parties from contract default in the event of major natural disasters, strikes, fires, explosions, or other events that could preclude the seller's ability to deliver the product or the buyer's ability to purchase.

6. *Disclaimers:* The disclaimers protect both buyer and seller against unreasonable claims about the product or its quality.

7. *Assignability:* The assignability clause limits the right of either party to assign the contract to another purchaser or supplier if they so desire.

8. *Notifications:* The notifications section specifies the lead time during which one or both parties must notify the other party of any change in the contract or its renewal.

9. *Other clauses:* Other clauses include conditions under which the product may be assured delivery, application of taxes, provisions for resale, definitions of contract breach and termination, the legal framework used to enforce the contract (in the event of cross-state or cross-national agreements), and methods of notification of one party to the other.

Contract Management and Maintenance

While a supply contract is a legally binding document that attempts to articulate the way two companies will work together, it more commonly stands as the cornerstone of a complex long-term social relationship between buyer and seller. This relationship requires constant monitoring, evaluation, and discussion by representatives of both organizations. Thus, while similar supply contracts may exist between a particular manufacturer and three different buyers, there may be major differences in the day-to-day interactions and quality of relationships between the manufacturer and each buyer. Experienced sales representatives have defined a good seller–buyer relationship as meeting the following criteria:

• *The purchaser can be counted on to live up to the terms and conditions of the contract as negotiated.* The purchaser accepts a fair formula price in price negotiations and does not attempt to push the supplier into an artificially low price. The purchaser lifts as much of the product per time period as he agreed to lift under the contract. The purchaser is trustworthy and follows a course of action based on sound business ethics.

• *The purchaser does not attempt to take advantage of fluctuations or aberrations in the spot market price to gain advantage.* He accepts the fact that a formula price has been negotiated and that both parties agree to live up to this price for the duration of the contract. He does not seek contract price changes as the market price may drop for some time period.

• *When there is a mutual problem between seller and purchaser, it can be openly discussed and resolved between the two parties.* Problems resulting from the continued inability of the supplier to provide the product, and/or the continued inability of the buyer to consume the product, can be openly addressed and resolved. Problems in the quality of the product, labor difficulties resulting in problems in manufacturing, loading, shipping, unloading, cleanliness of the shipping equipment, and so on can be promptly explored and resolved to mutual satisfaction. Finally, changes in the business projections of one or both parties can be shared, so that difficulties anticipated by the supplier in providing all of the product, or difficulties anticipated by the purchaser in consuming all of the product, can lead to amicable and satisfactory resolutions for both parties. Ability to resolve these problems requires mutual trust, honesty, open lines of communication, and an approach to problem solving that seeks the best solution for both sides.

Negotiating on Thin Ice: The 2004–2005 NHL Dispute (A)

Introduction

National Hockey League veteran player Trevor Linden was gearing up for another face-off. But this time, he was not wearing his skates and helmet; he was wearing a business suit. And, instead of walking onto the ice, clutching his hockey stick, he was walking into yet another union meeting, clutching his briefcase. The irony of the situation was not lost on Trevor: his toughest and most consequential of battles had not lasted three periods in a skating rink, but five months in negotiations with the National Hockey League. And now, as the "game" went into overtime, he was unsure which side would prevail.

At issue was the negotiation of a new collective bargaining agreement (CBA) between the players, represented by the National Hockey League Players' Association (NHLPA), and the team owners, represented by the National Hockey League (NHL). The CBA provided the basic framework for players' salary contracts, and was the keystone for agreements on a wide array of issues, including salary arbitration, free agency, and guaranteed contracts.

The CBA had been renegotiated many times before, but this time was different. The league, insistent on cutting costs and curtailing the growth of players' salaries, was resolute on two key issues: 1) the introduction of a salary cap, which would establish a limit on player salaries, and 2) the linkage of salary to revenues, such that league-wide salaries would not exceed a fixed percentage of league-wide revenues. Meanwhile, the players adamantly opposed both proposals. As a result, this negotiation had been longer, more acrimonious, and less productive than any in the past.

The previous CBA had expired on September 15, 2004. Since the two sides had failed to negotiate a new CBA by that date, NHL Commissioner Gary Bettman locked out the players.[a] This meant that no hockey would be played, no revenues would be collected, and no salaries would be paid. This was no idle threat, and it was not taken idly. With the lockout in effect, 150 NHL players promptly joined European hockey clubs,[1] sports arenas began finding other sources of revenue, and the Canadian Broadcasting Corporation (CBC) replaced "Hockey Night in Canada" with "Movie Night in Canada." Meanwhile, millions of hockey fans turned their attention to other professional sports. The start date for the 2004–2005 NHL season—October 13, 2004—came, and went.

Source: "Negotiating on Thin Ice: The 2004–2005 NHL Dispute (A)," by Deepak Malhotra and Maly Hout, Harvard Business School. Case 9-906-038, revised March 4, 2006. Boston, MA: Harvard Business School Publishing. http://www.hbsp.harvard.edu. © *2006 President and Fellows of Harvard College.* Used with permission.

Months of negotiations had produced only rejected offers. Now, in mid-February 2005, Union President Linden wondered what lay in store for the players he represented and for the sport he loved. The union had flexed its muscles in the past—and won—numerous times. Could they pull it off one more time? With almost half the season already lost, and the rest of the season on the verge of being cancelled, which side had the power to hold out longer, or to negotiate a more favorable CBA?

Background on the NHL

Professional hockey came onto the ice in the 1900s, and the National Hockey League was established in Montreal in November 1917.[2] The league, now headquartered in New York, was the official body representing the collective interests of the NHL team owners. The league's responsibilities included operational and administrative tasks such as setting game rules, scheduling seasons, selling national television rights and, of course, negotiating the CBA with the NHLPA.

The NHL Board of Governors oversaw the league, but most of the operations were carried out under the supervision of the Board-elected NHL commissioner. The NHL commissioner worked on behalf of the 30 NHL teams across Canada and the United States. (See Exhibit 1 for the structure of the NHL, and Exhibit 2 for a list of NHL teams.) Teams were typically owned privately or by large corporations, (e.g., Comcast owns the Flyers).

While each team had only six players (five skaters and one goal tender) on the ice at any time during the game, each team was required to have between 20 and 23 players on its roster (with up to 3 goal tenders) and up to 50 on its reserve list.[3] Each team played 82 regular season games from October to mid-April. The playoffs ran from mid-April to early June, and culminated with the Stanley Cup Finals which were "broadcast to more than 150 countries, from Albania to Zimbabwe, and watched in more than 300 million homes."[4]

EXHIBIT 1 | NHL Structure

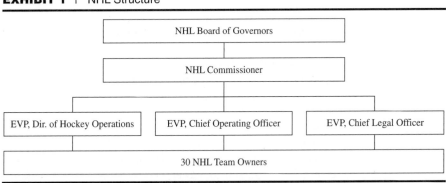

Source: Canadian Press, "Chronology of the Lockout," Globe and Mail, July 13, 2005, http://www.the globeandmail.com/servlet/story/RTGAM.20050713.wchrono13/BNStory/, accessed July 2005.

EXHIBIT 2 | NHL Teams (2002–2003 season)

EASTERN CONFERENCE

Atlantic Division	Northeast Division	Southeast Division
New Jersey Devils	Boston Bruins	Atlanta Thrashers
New York Islanders	Buffalo Sabres	Carolina Hurricanes
New York Rangers	Montreal Canadiens	Florida Panthers
Philadelphia Flyers	Ottawa Senators	Tampa Bay Lightning
Pittsburgh Penguins	Toronto Maple Leafs	Washington Capitals

WESTERN CONFERENCE

Central Division	Northwest Division	Pacific Division
Chicago Blackhawks	Calgary Flames	Mighty Ducks of Anaheim
Columbus Blue Jackets	Colorado Avalanche	Dallas Stars
Detroit Red Wings	Edmonton Oilers	Los Angeles Kings
Nashville Predators	Minnesota Wild	Phoenix Coyotes
St. Louis Blues	Vancouver Canucks	San Jose Sharks

Source: "Teams," NHL website, http://www.nhl.com/teams/index.html, accessed January 2006.

At the end of each hockey season, the league required all teams to report their financial performance by preparing a Unified Report of Operations (URO). The URO included all hockey-related revenues and expenses, and was designed to standardize financial reporting methods in order for the league to compile league-wide financial results. The league's reporting of its financial results has been a point of contention throughout the NHL's history.

During the early years of the NHL's existence, the players accused team owners of concealing actual revenues and underreporting the profitability of the game.[5] The players received only league-wide information, and perceived a difference between observable revenues (e.g., sum of ticket sales, concession and parking revenues) and the reported revenues of teams. Consequently, the players believed that the league reported financial data selectively, and that each team's idiosyncratic method of reporting revenues disguised actual performance. Meanwhile, team owners were unwilling to engage in any debate regarding the players' mistrust of their reporting, contending that teams were private enterprises, and thus not obligated to disclose any financial information.[6] According to team owners, players should simply be grateful for making two to three times more than the average person, staying at the best hotels, and being role-models to boys young and old.[7] The situation worsened until 1967, when the players banded together to create a players' union: the NHLPA.

Background on the NHLPA

From 1917 to 1967, players had no collective bargaining rights and few options when it came to playing professional hockey—the number of NHL teams was limited, growing from five to six during this entire period.[b,8] Consequently, team owners were able to negotiate highly favorable contracts. Money was not the only problem facing players. The game was also incredibly rough and it was not uncommon to see a player with blood running down his face, cracked teeth, a broken nose, or a bruised shoulder. This was not surprising: there were no rules requiring goalies to wear facemasks, nor for players to wear helmets.[c] In addition to risking physical injury, players endured significant verbal abuse from team owners, who did it partly to conjure up a sense of aggression for games and partly to cement players' feebleness in their relationship. Unsurprisingly, the relationship between players and team owners was marked with hostility and distrust in the early years.

The first significant step towards unionization came in 1957, when Detroit Red Wing's team captain and nine-time All Star, "Terrible" Ted Lindsay, brought in New York lawyer Milton Mound to establish a players' union. However, it would be another 10 years before the union was founded, as team owners did everything possible to prevent unionization.[9] Most effective was their punishment of players who led the charge in creating a union. For his unionization efforts, Lindsay was immediately demoted as Detroit's captain, transferred to Chicago (considered the NHL equivalent of Siberia at the time), and portrayed in the media by team owners as greedy.[10] Under intense pressure from team owners to disband, the initial group of union organizers dissolved. However, in 1967, under the leadership of Toronto Maple Leafs' Bob Pulford, a new, more sizable and unified group of players emerged and was successful in establishing the NHLPA. It was not long before the union was successful in negotiating higher salaries, increased benefits, and the adoption of a salary arbitration process.

Headquartered in Toronto, Ontario, Canada, the NHLPA was founded as the labor union representing NHL players' interests. The players had power over all NHLPA activities. The players annually elected representatives from their respective NHL teams to form an executive board. This board was overseen by an executive committee, which was comprised of the union president and five to six vice-presidents. (See Exhibit 3 for the structure of the NHLPA.) The executive board and executive committee were largely comprised of veteran players.

By the 2003–2004 season, the union's negotiating team was working on behalf of over 700 NHL players, who automatically became members of the union when they joined the NHL.[11] These players hailed from 23 different countries, but over half of

EXHIBIT 3 | NHLPA Structure

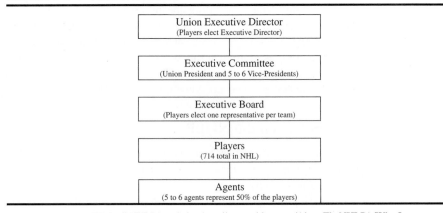

Source: "About the NHLPA," NHLPA website, http://www.nhlpa.com/AboutTheNHLPA/WhatIs.asp, accessed January 2006.

EXHIBIT 4 | NHL Player Breakdown by Nationality (2002–2003 season)

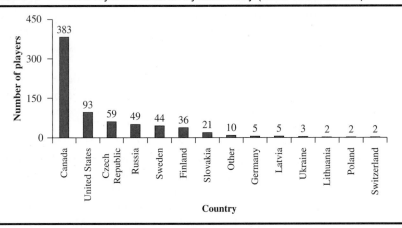

Source: "NHL Player Breakdown by Nationality," NHL website, www.nhl.com, accessed July 2005.

them came from Canada.[12] (See Exhibit 4 for NHL player breakdown by nationality.) As a result of the NHLPA's success, most of these players were well compensated for their work. According to the league's reporting, more than 400 of the current NHL players would make over $10 million during their careers.[d,13] Superstar players could earn as much as $50 to $70 million during their careers.[14]

Head-to-Head

The 2004–2005 CBA negotiations were conducted by the NHL commissioner (on behalf of the league) and the NHLPA's executive director (on behalf of the union). The current NHL commissioner, Gary Bettman, began his tenure on February 1, 1993.[15]

During his tenure, the league grew from 24 to 30 franchises, revenues grew from US $400 million to over US $1.6 billion, and licensing revenues grew by a staggering 700 percent.[16] Bettman also signed TV deals with major American broadcasters ABC and ESPN, played a major role in changing the rules of the game and, for the first-time, permitted NHL players to participate in the Olympic Winter Games.[17]

Although Bettman was successful in reaching out to broadcasters, he was less successful in establishing a positive rapport with the union. Some of his critics charged that Bettman was "not a hockey guy."[18] In some obvious ways he was not. He was a New York lawyer and a former senior executive in the National Basketball Association (NBA). As a result, Bettman was perceived by many as motivated by money and not by the love of hockey.[19]

The entire burden of negotiating with the union did not rest on Bettman's shoulders alone. NHL chief legal officer, Bill Daly, participated in the negotiation of all major issues. In an otherwise contentious negotiation, Daly stood out as one with the joint virtues of being well-respected both by the union and by the league. He was close to Bettman, and could "stroll into Bettman's office and the commissioner [would listen] to every word."[20]

On the other side of the table, representing the NHLPA, was executive director Bob Goodenow. Bob Goodenow was elected in 1992 when the previous executive director, Alan Eagelson, was accused of fraud and was forced to step down.[e] A 1979 graduate of Harvard University, Goodenow went on to study law at the University of Detroit, and subsequently became a corporate and commercial lawyer. His days as a hockey player on the Junior Wings and as captain of Harvard's hockey team underpinned his interest in hockey. Through hockey friends, he eventually transitioned into the world of professional hockey, first as an agent, then as deputy to Eagelson, and now as executive director of the NHLPA.

What Bettman did for the NHL, Goodenow did for the NHLPA: He grew the organization and he delivered results. During his tenure, NHLPA revenues increased 25-fold, and the NHLPA administration team grew from 2.5 employees to 50 employees.[21] He also helped players negotiate higher salaries; under his leadership, players' salaries had increased by 240 percent since 1995.[22] Goodenow was a hands-on leader, and spent much of his time communicating directly with players. He was always "available to take a player's phone call" and was well-respected by them.[23] His reputation was that of an energetic, militant advocate of players' interests. For players who remembered (or knew of) a past in which they had been pushed around and out-muscled, such leadership was welcomed.

Goodenow's top aide in the negotiations was NHLPA Senior Director Ted Saskin. Saskin was known to be less confrontational than Goodenow and was seen as an effective communicator of the union's interests.[24] Alongside Goodenow and Saskin stood union president, and sixteen-year NHL veteran, Trevor Linden. Linden was elected president in June 1998.[25] As president, he was the primary voice for the NHL players, was involved in planning union strategies, and was responsible for bringing player demands to union management (i.e., to Goodenow). (See Exhibit 5 for other NHL individuals at the negotiating table.)

In some ways, Bettman and Goodenow were entering the 2004–2005 negotiations as they had entered so many other negotiations. There were differences in perspective, differences in interests, differences in priorities, and differences of opinion. But what made this negotiation more difficult was not what made Bettman and Goodenow different, but what made them similar. Both of these men had come into their positions in the early 1990s. Both had performed incredibly well in their assigned roles. Both were seen

EXHIBIT 5 | Key Negotiators

NHL		NHLPA	
League Management		**Union Leadership**	
Gary Bettman	Commissioner	Bob Goodenow	Executive Director
Bill Daily	Chief Legal Officer	Trevor Linden	Union President
Bob Batterman	Labor Lawyer	Ted Saskin	Senior Director
David Zimmerman	VP, Gen. Counsel	John McCambridge	Labor Lawyer
		Executive Committee	Vice Presidents
		Mike Gartner	Ex-NHLPA President
Team Owners		**Player Agents**	
Lou Lamoriello	Devils President/GM	Don Baizley	
Wayne Gretzky	Coyotes Co-Owner	J.P. Barry and Pat Brisson	
Mario Lemieux	Penguins Owner/Player	Steve Bartlett	
Jeremy Jacobs	Bruins Owner	Larry Kelly	
Kevin Lowe	Oilers GM	Mike Gillis	
Harley Hotchkiss	Flames Co-Owner		
Ed snider	Flyers Owner		
Glen Sather	Rangers President/GM		

Source: CBC, "Faceoff 2002: Who's who: The Negotiators," from *CBC Sports Online* website, 2005, http://www.cbc.ca/sports/indepth/cba/who/bettman_gary.html, accessed July 2005.7

as capable, competent, and caring by their constituents. And both had the same problem: they were negotiating in the dark shadows of their shared past.

More Money, More Problems

1992 Strike[26]

Following his election to executive director, Goodenow had led the players on their first-ever strike in NHL history. The principal issue in this negotiation was the players demand for full control of the marketing rights to their images, (e.g., on trading cards, posters, and other merchandise). As the sport gained popularity, the value associated with marketing rights grew.

What could have become a long protracted battle over a significant sum of money was in fact settled quickly. The timing of the strike may have contributed: the strike occurred just before the start of the season's playoffs. It lasted only 10 days, from April 1 to 11, 1992.

When the smoke cleared, the players had been given full control over the marketing rights to their images. In return, they agreed to accept a shorter CBA contract length. Although the players had originally asked for a three-year contract, they settled on a two-year deal (for the 1991–1992 and 1992–1993 seasons). The collateral damage was minimal: the 30 games that were supposed to be played during the strike were rescheduled, and four games were added to the regular schedule to pay for increased league costs. The players were largely regarded as the victors in this negotiation.[27]

1994–1995 Season Lock Out[28]

The expiration of the 1991–1993 CBA again resulted in conflict. This time, the issue was the league's financial concerns. Although the two sides were unable to agree on a new CBA for the 1993–1994 season, both sides agreed to continue playing the game under the existing CBA terms by agreeing to a "no-strike, no-lockout" pledge. One year later, there was still no new CBA. This time, believing that the economic state of the league was getting progressively worse, Bettman insisted on signing a new CBA before the 1994–1995 season began. When the two sides were unable to agree on a new CBA before the season's start, the NHL locked out the players for the first time in NHL history.

The primary issue in the negotiation was how to help small market teams (those that brought in less revenue) become more competitive. Both the team owners and the players saw that doing so was necessary: more competition meant more rivalries, more exciting games, and more potential revenue for the league. Unfortunately, as the NHL grew, the revenue gap between small market teams and large market teams had widened, enabling large market teams to continually attract better players and thus consistently win more games. However, while both the league and the union agreed that this situation had to be fixed, they disagreed on how to make this happen.

The league's proposal had three key components:

1. A payroll tax system that would fine teams who exceeded the league's average payroll. The collected taxes would then be redistributed to cash-strapped clubs.

2. An unrestricted free-agency system that would limit players' mobility early in their careers but enhance it later. This issue, the league hoped, would reduce the bidding-up of players' salaries, because it would limit the amount of time during their career that players could accept competing salaries.[f]

3. A cap (i.e., limit) on rookie (i.e., new player) salaries and on rookie signing bonuses to curb the amount players initially made. This issue, it was hoped, would not only cut compensation to rookies, but also provide a drag on their future salaries.

Of the issues presented by the league, the union outright rejected the NHL's proposed payroll tax. The union argued that the tax would inhibit owners from paying fair (i.e., "market") rates, and would thus artificially deflate salaries. Instead, the union proposed alternative schemes, such as managing the franchises better and sharing revenues among them, or instituting a gate receipt tax of 5 percent that could be levied on the top 16 teams. The NHL rejected all union proposals: none, they argued, would be as effective as the payroll tax in lessening the revenue gap between small and large market teams.

While the two sides tried to find a way to work through these issues, Bettman embittered the union by tabling additional demands that scaled back existing player rights, (e.g., eliminating salary arbitration and per diems, stipulating that players had to pay their own medical insurance, life insurance, and travel expenses for training camp, etc.). All of these, argued Bettman, were necessary to reduce costs. The union saw it differently. They felt that Bettman was using these issues as threats to speed up the negotiation.

After four months of negotiation, Bettman agreed to remove the payroll tax from his proposal. In return, the union agreed to the rookie salary cap, the unrestricted free agency system, and some modifications to the salary arbitration process. By the time the new CBA was signed, the lockout had lasted 104 days, from Oct. 1 to Jan. 11, and had thus eliminated nearly half of the scheduled season.

The league believed that the concessions they had extracted would curb escalating salaries and thereby help small market teams to afford better hockey players and compete more effectively. According to media sources, there were collective high-fives among NHL management.[29] This interpretation—that team owners had "won" in the 1995 negotiation—would not last long.

1998–1999 Season Renegotiation Request

By the start of the 1998–1999 season, the league was claiming that its last CBA negotiation had been ineffective in curbing runaway player salaries. Indeed, the opposite seemed to have resulted. Extending the age of unrestricted free agents limited the number of players in the market at any time.[30] As a result, quality free agents became scarcer and could command top dollars.[31] Moreover, creative contracts (featuring signing and performance bonuses) countered the effects of delayed free agency and of restrictions on rookie pay.[32] For example, on top of a lowered salary base, a rookie could earn significant bonuses for scoring a certain number of goals or achieving a certain number of assists. As a result, team owners were able to compensate players lucratively while adhering to restrictions. Finally, and again to the disappointment of team owners, despite changes in the arbitration clause, players continued to win most salary arbitrations.[33] Looking back, Bill Daly conceded, "We felt that we had addressed escalating salaries in a number of ways that would work. But it quickly became apparent that it wasn't working."[34]

While the existing CBA was seen as problematic by the league, there was little that team owners could do about it: the CBA did not expire until 2004. On March 19, 1999, Bettman wrote to Goodenow to propose a voluntary renegotiation of the CBA in the near term.[35] Otherwise, warned Bettman, the players would have to prepare for major concessions in the 2004–2005 season (once the CBA had expired). However, the union rejected the league's request for a renegotiation. The consequences were clear: both sides knew now that the 2004–2005 season would entail a critical, high-stakes negotiation. And both started to prepare for battle.

Preparing for a Face-off

As the 1998–1999 season came to an end, both sides started to build their war chests in preparation for the impending negotiation. The NHLPA held onto union dues, which it typically repaid to players at the end of each year. Plus, the NHLPA did not cut any licensing checks to players, which it typically did every few years. Meanwhile, the league required each team to set aside $10 million apiece in an account to help fund operations during a potential lock out or strike.

As the 2004–2005 negotiation neared, the team owners also voted unanimously to modify the league's ratification rules for a new CBA. Previously, a simple majority was required to institute a lock out or to ratify a new CBA.[36] The new rules stated that any CBA which the commissioner (Bettman) did not support would require approval by three-quarters of the teams in order to be accepted.[37] The league also voted to give the commissioner authority, in advance, to call a lockout immediately after the CBA expired.

According to media reports, the league was also successful in securing a unified commitment to the 2004–2005 lock out from all 30 team owners.[38] To uphold this unity, the league benefited from a by-law that prohibited team owners from speaking out about the lock out.[39] The consequences of breaking rank would be severe, as Atlanta Thrashers owner Steve Belkin would soon discover; he was slapped with a US$250,000 fine in October, 2004, for mentioning to the *Boston Herald* that the NHL would consider using replacement players for the 2005–2006 season if a new collective bargaining agreement wasn't reached. According to media sources, "No information got out unless it was an official league statement. There were no renegades here. It all went through Bettman."[40]

Saskin summarized each side's bargaining position: "At the end of the day, you had two very powerful groups. On one side, billionaire owners, for whom this was typically not their primary business. On the other side, players who had made a lot of money as of late, but who cared more for the game itself."[41]

The Puck Drops

Underpinning the current dispute was the league's precarious and contentious financial situation. For the 2002–2003 season, the league had reported combined operating revenues of $1.996 billion and a combined operating loss of $273 million.[42] (See Exhibit 6 for the league's financial performance.) The league also pointed out that NHL player costs were 75 percent of revenues, a higher percentage of revenue than in other major league sports.[43] (See Exhibit 7 for a comparison of player costs across leagues.) Also, that season, only 11 teams reported operating profits, while 19 teams reported operating losses.[44] The NHLPA disputed the NHL's operating loss numbers and their percentage of revenues going to player costs. Media also expressed some skepticism since the league refused access to their financial books. However, the league charged that their economic troubles were grave.

To avoid continued operating losses, the league demanded "cost certainty" in this negotiation.[45] To achieve this, the league wanted two things above all else: 1) a salary cap, and 2) a linkage of salary to revenues. Bettman argued that these were the only viable solutions to the growing evidence that NHL revenues were not keeping up with increasing player salaries. While revenues had increased 160 percent since 1995, player salaries had increased by 240 percent over this same time period.[46] The league believed that player salaries were escalating because team owners, willing to pay big money for top players in the hopes of winning a championship, were engaged in unhealthy bidding wars. As a result, the average NHL salary was close to $2 million in 2002–2003, compared to only $733,000 in 1994–1995.[47] (See Exhibit 8 for the average player salary over time.) The league also released the results of a fan poll that

EXHIBIT 6 | NHL Financial Performance (in millions of U.S. dollars)

	1993–1994	2002–2003	2003–2004
Combined Revenues	$732	$1,996	$2,083
Less: Player Salaries	$414	$1,494	$1,511
Less: Other Operating Costs	$358	$ 775	$ 795
Operating Profit (Loss)	$ (40)	$ (273)	$ (224)

Source: Arthur Levitt Jr., "Independent Review of the Combined Financial Results of the National Hockey League 2002–2003 Season," Feb. 5, 2004, p. 21; "2003–04 League Revenues and Player Expenses," Andrew's Dallas Stars Page, http://www.andrewsstarspage.com/NHL-Business/03-04revenue-expense.htm, accessed January 2006; Bill Daly, "A Few Follow-up Questions on the NHL Lockout," e-mail message to Deepak Malhotra, February 8, 2006.

EXHIBIT 7 | Comparison of Player Salaries as a Percentage of Revenue (2002–2003 season)

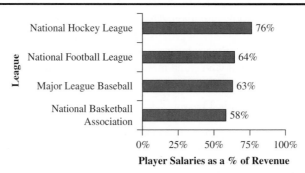

Source: CBC, "Faceoff 2002: What Each Side Wants," *CBC Sports Online* website, 2005, http://www.cbc.ca/sports/indepth/cba/issues/index.html, accessed July 2005.

EXHIBIT 8 | Average NHL Player Salary (in thousands of U.S. dollars)

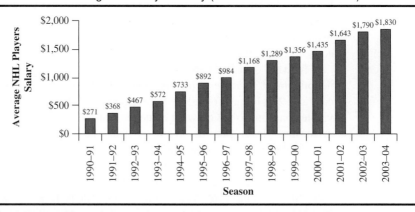

Source: "Average NHL Player Salary," Andrew's Dallas Stars Page, http://www.andrewsstarspage.com/NHL-Business/average-salary.htm, accessed January 2006.

EXHIBIT 9 | Percentage of Fans Who Agree With . . .

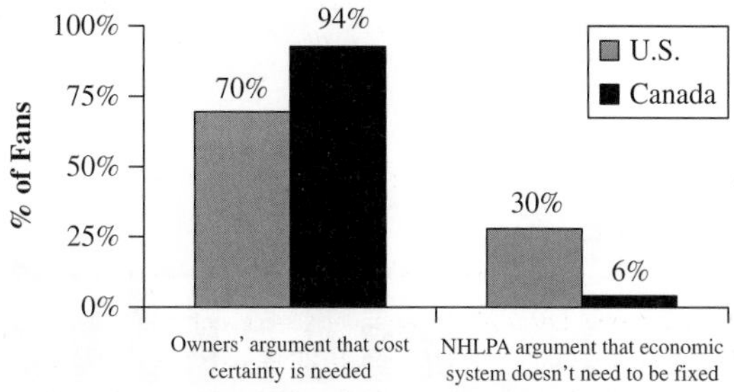

Source: "What Fans Say September 2004," *NHL CBA News* website, http://nhlcbanews.com/reaction/
fansurvey0904.html, accessed January 2006, accessed July 2005.

revealed fans' concerns regarding the financial health of the league, (see Exhibit 9 for
poll results.) The NHL's financial condition was precarious, Bettman argued, and
"what we need to achieve is a system that enables all of our clubs to be economically
stable and competitive."[48]

The union rejected the notion that players needed to help team owners avoid bidding up their salaries, arguing that "the free market should determine players' salaries
and that the owners should be their own salary controllers."[49] Goodenow also rejected
Bettman's argument that salaries needed to be tied explicitly to revenue: "They say they
want a relationship between revenues and player costs. We say it already exists."[50] The
union's reluctance to accept a system that tied player salaries to revenues was not only
a matter of principle; the union mistrusted the financial and accounting numbers
presented by the league. The union believed that teams had under-reported their revenues and over-reported their losses. Saskin called the teams' accounting "garbage in
and out."[51] How could players link their salaries to revenue numbers they did not trust?

Goodenow, though well aware that the league was willing to fight harder now than
in the past, remained resolute: "I've told the players to be prepared for a long lockout by
the owners. It may last a year, it may last two or three years, but we will never accept a
salary cap."[52]

2003 to September 15, 2004

On September 19, 2003, news of the NHL's losses of nearly $300 million for the
2002–2003 season hit *The Wall Street Journal*.[53] Within weeks of this report, the union
proposed a deal that included a 5 percent salary rollback.[54] The league countered with
its first salary cap demand: limiting team payrolls to $31 million per team.[55] This salary
cap was a significant decrease in the current average team payroll of $44 million. (See
Exhibit 10 for the average team payroll). No deal seemed possible.

The situation intensified as the tension between Bettman and Goodenow mounted
publicly. The media reported that the two sides seemed to disagree not only on the CBA,
but also on what constituted a meeting. While Bettman claimed all meetings before
October 1 were "informal conversations," Goodenow retorted that the two sides had

EXHIBIT 10 | Average NHL Team Payroll (in millions of U.S. dollars)

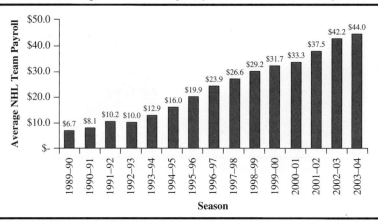

Source: "NHL Team Payrolls," Andrew's Dallas Stars Page, http://www.andrewsstarspage.com/NHL-Business/historical-payrolls.htm, accessed January 2006.

"12-plus meetings," which were "full-day meetings between the two parties, not casual phone conversations between Gary and I."[56] Hockey agent Ritch Winter proffered his point-of-view on the relationship between Bettman and Goodenow: "What [scared] me [was] that there [were] so few people involved in the process. It [was] Gary Bettman and Bob Goodenow and they [didn't] appear very cordial in their relationship."[57]

The situation worsened as the union publicly reported its mistrust of the losses reported by the league. In response, the league hired former chairman of the Securities and Exchange Commission, Arthur Levitt Jr., to perform an independent audit of its 2002–2003 URO. The league believed that Levitt's former leadership of an independent regulatory body would establish his impartiality and credibility. The "Levitt Report," dated February 5, 2004, confirmed the league's accounting and financial conclusions.[58] The players, however, were unimpressed: the league had notified them of the "Levitt Report" only one day before the report hit the newsstands. As Goodenow explained, ". . . The League did not advise the NHLPA of this initiative and there has been no discussion of it by the parties . . . Against this background, it is clear the Levitt report is simply another League public relations initiative. To suggest the report is in any way independent is misleading."[59] Because Levitt had been hired by the league, the union also questioned his objectivity and whether he had been provided access to all relevant data. The relationship between the parties remained contentious.

Five months passed with very little progress. At the end of July 2004, Bettman wrote a letter to Goodenow highlighting 19 additional aspects of the CBA that the league would like to modify, including salary guarantees, the rookie salary cap, salary arbitration, etc. The players again saw this tactic as a way to put pressure on the union, and again this tactic embittered the union.

A week before the CBA was to expire, the union made another proposal: a 5 percent rollback in salaries, a payroll tax system like the one the league had proposed during the 1994–1995 season, changes to rookie salary contracts, and revenue sharing.[60] The league immediately rejected this proposal because it did not contain a salary cap. On September 15, 2004, Bettman announced the lockout: the players would not get on the ice for the start of a new season.

September 16, 2004 to February 16, 2005

Shortly after the lockout announcement, the International Ice Hockey Federation (IIHF) reported that more than 150 NHL players had signed contracts to play with European teams. By mid-January, this number grew to 393.[61] Meanwhile, the league advised team owners to allow other interested parties to book their sports arenas for non-NHL events on a 45-day rolling basis, two weeks longer than the previous allowance of 30 days.[62]

Both the union and the league knew it was important to maintain order in their respective ranks, but dissension among union members began to surface early. On October 27, 2004, two weeks after what would have been the first official day of the NHL season, Calgary Flames defenseman Mike Commodore admitted that he would play under a salary cap: "I don't want to spend the next uh, however, long my career lasts, playing here in the American Hockey League (with the Lowell Lock Monsters) . . . So I think whatever it takes."[63] Saskin was quick to respond: "We know that the overwhelming majority of our members do not support the views that were expressed by Mike Commodore, but as I've said before we have over 700 members with no gag orders or fines for players speaking out."[64] The next day, Montreal Canadiens' winger Pierre Dagenais also admitted that he would play under a salary cap.[65]

The following week, the union held a four-hour meeting with team representatives and 74 players—including Dagenais.[66] According to the media, "the [union emerged] from the meeting as united as ever" and several players publicly supported the union's strategy.[67] Notably, Dagenais, wearing an NHLPA cap, responded to a reporter's question regarding whether he would still play under a cap by stating, "I don't have to answer that. All I want is to play hockey and these guys are working hard to fix the problem."[68]

On December 9, 2004, the union shocked the hockey world by offering a 24 percent salary rollback on all existing player contracts, a slightly better payroll tax, and other concessions on the rookie salary cap and salary arbitration issues.[69] Notably, the union was still unwilling to consider a salary cap. The league countered with an offer that included a salary cap, eliminated salary arbitration, and restructured the salary rollback to take more money away from higher-end players and none from lower-paid ones.[70] Even as the days progressed closer and closer to what would have been the halfway point of the season, little headway was made in the negotiation. On February 9, 2005, Bettman raised the stakes by threatening to cancel the entire season.

Bettman's announcement was followed by a flurry of activity aimed at salvaging the season. With little progress being made towards a new CBA, on February 11, 2005, the league released its "gag order on owners, GMs, and coaches of [the] 30 teams allowing them to talk about the lockout to the media and reach out to players if they want."[71] The league hoped that engaging other individuals in the negotiation would help to break the impasse.

Two days later, on February 13, 2005, at the request of the director of the U.S. Federal Mediation and Conciliation Service, the two sides met with U.S. federal mediators in Washington, D.C. NHL Chief Legal Officer Bill Daly and labor lawyer Bob Batterman represented the league while NHLPA Senior Director Ted Saskin and labor lawyer John McCambridge represented the players. Bettman and Goodenow were not present.

The day after, on Valentine's Day, February 14, 2005, Saskin and Daly met secretly and, for the first time, both sides drastically altered their negotiating positions. The league increased its proposed salary cap from $31 million to $40 million, and, to address the union's mistrust of league-reported revenues, relinquished its demand for linking salary to revenue. For its part, the union, for the first time, accepted the idea of instituting a salary cap, but rejected the $40 million offer; the union proposed a $52 million salary cap.[72]

The next day, the league offered a "take-it-or-leave-it" offer: a $42.5 million salary cap and a deadline to accept by 11 a.m. the following day.[73] Bettman, feeling strongly that the league had reached its limit, clarified: "This offer is not an invitation to begin negotiations—it's too late for that."[74] Goodenow called his bluff, and counter-offered with a $49 million salary cap. Bettman rejected the offer immediately, stating simply: "We cannot afford your proposal."[75]

The following day, February 16, 2005, Bettman cancelled the 2004–2005 season. Rumors circulated that backroom phone calls were made by players and owners, while emergency sessions were called with hockey superstars Wayne Gretzky and Mario Lemieux, all in an effort to "uncancel" the season. It was too late.

What to Do Now?

Linden reflected on where things stood. On the one hand, substantive progress had been made: the league had relinquished its demand for linking salaries to revenues, and the union had accepted—at least in principle—a salary cap. On the other hand, animosity and mistrust had been exacerbated, an entire season had been cancelled, billions in revenue had been lost, and the two sides were still millions apart on the most important issue in the negotiation.

Linden was reminded of frustrating times he had spent in the penalty box. At least in the penalty box, players knew that they would be back on the ice within minutes. In this negotiation, the players had no idea as to when they would return to the game. As he walked into the union's strategy meeting, he wondered what kind of power play could help the NHLPA score a new and fair CBA with the NHL.

Bibliography

Andrew's Dallas Stars Page website, http://www.andrewsstarspage.com/NHL-Business/index.htm, accessed January 2006.

Canadian Press. "Chronology of the Lockout." Globe and Mail. July 13, 2005. http://www.theglobeandmail.com/servlet/story/RTGAM.20050713.wchrono13/BNStory/, accessed July 2005.

CBC. "Faceoff 2004–05." *CBC Sports Online* Web site, 2005. http://www.cbc.ca/sports/indepth/cba/, accessed July and October 2005.

Daly, Bill, "A Few Follow-Up Questions on the NHL Lockout." E-mail message Deepak Malhotra, February 8, 2006.

Daly, Bill. NHL Chief Legal Officer. Phone interview by authors. February 1, 2006.

Davidson, John with John Steinbreder. *Hockey for Dummies.* Indianapolis, Indiana: Wiley Publishing, 2000.

Levitt Jr., Arthur. "Independent Review of the Combined Financial Results of the National Hockey League 2002–2003 Season." February 5, 2004.

Networth. Directed by Jerry Ciccoritti, Canadian Broadcasting Corporation/Morningstar Entertainment Inc., 1995.

NHL website, http://www.nhl.com, accessed July 2005.

NHL CBA News website, http://www.nhlcbanews.com/bythenumbers/index.html, accessed October 2005.

NHLPA website, http://www.nhlpa.com/, accessed January 2006.

NHLPA–NHL, 1997 CBA.

"Goodenow Comments on League Commissioned Report." NHLPA media release. Toronto, ON, February 12, 2004.

Saskin, Ted. NHLPA Senior Director. Phone Interview by authors. February 13, 2006.

Tavares, Dan and John Molinaro. CBC Online Sports Journalists. Phone Interview by authors. December 6, 2005.

Weatherdon, Jonathan. NHLPA Media Relations. Phone Interview by authors. February 13, 2006.

Weatherdon, Jonathan, "NHLPA." E-mail Message Maly Hout , February 13, 2006.

Endnotes

a. A lockout is initiated by owners; it forcibly suspends salary payments by halting operations. A strike, in contrast, is initiated by players; it forcibly halts operations through a collective refusal to work. In this case, it was the owners that had decided not to start the season until a new CBA was signed.

b. The "original six" teams included the Boston Bruins, Chicago Blackhawks, Detroit Red Wings, Montreal Canadiens, New York Rangers, and Toronto Maple Leafs.

c. Such rules were adopted only after players were unionized. Goalies were required to wear facemasks starting in 1973, and players entering the league were required to wear helmets starting in 1979.

d. The average hockey player's career lasted five to six years.

e. In January 1998, Eagelson pleaded guilty to defrauding hockey players and the NHL. As a result, he faced six counts of fraud, was fined $1 million CDN, and was sentenced to 18 months in jail for his conduct.

f. Unrestricted free agents can be offered (and can accept) an offer from any team. Under most conditions, new players cannot accept competing offers for a specified number of years (i.e., they must play for the team that initially hired them).

1. Canadian Press, "Chronology of the Lockout," *Globe and Mail,* July 13, 2005, http://www.theglobeandmail.com/servlet/story/RTGAM.20050713.wchrono13/BNStory/, accessed July 2005.

2. Ibid, p. 45.

3. NHLPA–NHL, 1997 CBA, p.5.

4. John Davidson with John Steinbreder, *Hockey for Dummies* (Indianapolis: Wiley Publishing, 2000), p. 47.

5. *Networth,* directed by Jerry Ciccoritti (Canadian Broadcasting Corporation/Morningstar Entertainment Inc., 1995).

6. Ibid.

7. Ibid.

8. "NHL Expansion & Relocation Since 1967," Andrew's Dallas Stars Page website, http://www.andrewsstarspage.com/NHL-Business/Expansion.htm, accessed January 2006.

9. Ibid.

10. Ibid.

11. "NHL Player Breakdown by Nationality as of the Start of the 2002–2003 NHL Season," NHL website, www.nhl.com, accessed July 2005.

12. Ibid.

13. CBA By the Numbers, "Career Gross Salary Earnings of $10M or More, Players Under Contract for 2003–2004," *NHL CBA News* website, http://www.nhlcbanews.com/careerearnings_numbers.html, accessed October 2005.

14. Ibid.

15. CBC, "Faceoff 2004–05: Who's who: Gary Bettman," *CBC Sports Online* website, 2005, http://www.cbc.ca/sports/indepth/cba/who/bettman_gary.html, accessed October 2005.

16. Ibid.

17. Ibid.

18. Ibid.

19. Ibid.

20. CBC, "Faceoff 2004–05: Who's who: NHL Executives," *CBC Sports Online* website, 2005, http://www.cbc.ca/sports/indepth/cba/who/nhl.html#daly, accessed October 2005.

21. CBC, "Faceoff 2004–05: Who's who: Bob Goodenow," *CBC Sports Online* website, 2005, http://www.cbc.ca/sports/indepth/cba/who/goodenow_bob.html, accessed October 2005.

22. Ibid.

23. Ibid.

24. CBC, "Faceoff 2004–05: Who's who: NHLPA Officials," *CBC Sports Online* website, 2005, http://www.cbc.ca/sports/indepth/cba/who/nhlpa.html#linden, accessed October 2005.

25. Ibid.

26. CBC, "Faceoff 2004–05: Flashback to 1992 & 1994," *CBC Sports Online* website, 2005, http://www.cbc.ca/sports/indepth/cba/features/flashback.html, accessed July 2005.

27. Dan Tavares and John Molinaro (CBC Online Sports Journalists) in a phone interview with the authors, December 6, 2005.

28. CBC, "Faceoff 2004–05: Flashback to 1992 & 1994," *CBC Sports Online* website, 2005.

29. Dan Tavares and John Molinaro (CBC Online Sports Journalists) in a phone interview with the authors, December 6, 2005.

30. Ibid.

31. Ibid.

32. Ibid.

33. Ibid.

34. Bill Daly (NHL Chief Legal Officer) in a phone interview with the authors, February 1, 2006.

35. Canadian Press, "Chronology of the Lockout," *Globe and Mail*, July 13, 2005.

36. Bill Daly (NHL Chief Legal Officer) in a phone interview with the authors, February 1, 2006.

37. Ibid.

38. Dan Tavares and John Molinaro, phone interview.

39. Bill Daly, phone interview.

40. Dan Tavares and John Molinaro, phone interview.

41. Ted Saskin (NHLPA Senior Director) in a Phone Interview with the authors, February 13, 2006.

42. Arthur Levitt Jr., "Independent Review of the Combined Financial Results of the National Hockey League 2002–2003 Season," February 5, 2004, p. 21.

43. CBC, "Faceoff 2004–05: What Each Side Wants," *CBC Sports Online* website, 2005, http://www.cbc.ca/sports/indepth/cba/issues/index.html, accessed July 2005.

44. Arthur Levitt Jr., "Independent Review of the Combined Financial Results of the National Hockey League 2002–2003 Season," p. 22.

45. CBC, "Faceoff 2004–05: What Each Side Wants: Salary Cap," *CBC Sports Online* website, 2005, http://www.cbc.ca/sports/indepth/cba/issues/index.html, accessed July 2005.

46. Ibid.

47. Ibid.

48. Ibid.

49. Ibid.

50. Ibid.

51. Ibid.

52. Ibid.

53. Ibid.

54. Ibid.

55. Ibid.

56. Ibid.

57. Report on Business Magazine, August 2001 Edition, as reported on the *CBC Sports Online* website, "Faceoff 2004: Who's who: Gary Bettman," 2005, http://www.cbc.ca/sports/indepth/cba/who/bettman_gary.html, accessed October 2005.

58. Canadian Press, "Chronology of the Lockout," *Globe and Mail,* July 13, 2005.

59. "Goodenow Comments on League Commissioned Report," NHLPA media release (Toronto, ON, February 12, 2004).

60. Ibid.

61. Jonathan Weatherdon, "NHLPA", e-mail message to Maly Hout, February 13, 2006.

62. Canadian Press, "Chronology of the Lockout," *Globe and Mail,* July 13, 2005.

63. Ibid.

64. Ibid.

65. Ibid.

66. Ibid.

67. Ibid.

68. Ibid.

69. Ibid.

70. Ibid.

71. Ibid.

72. Ibid.

73. Ibid.

74. Ibid.

75. Ibid.

Collective Bargaining at Magic Carpet Airlines: A Union Perspective (A)

History of Magic Carpet Air

Magic Carpet Air (MCA) began operations in 1961, serving 2 cities, and grew to serve 18 cities by 1987. River City Airlines (RCA) began in 1969 with service to 4 cities and grew to serve 12 cities by 1987. In January 1987, Magic Carpet Air purchased River City Airlines and merged the two operations. The joining of these two regional airlines created a small "national" airline (defined as a carrier with sales between $100 million and $1 billion) with sales of $140,265,000 in 1987. Even so, the firm competed primarily in only one region of the country, and managers constantly compared it to other large regional airlines.

In May 1988, Magic Carpet Air entered into a marketing agreement with a major national carrier and became a "feeder" airline for that carrier (e.g., American Eagle is a feeder airline for American Airlines, United Express is a feeder for United Airlines). That is, MCA delivered passengers from small airports to larger ones, where passengers could make connections using that airline. Subsequently, no more reservations were given to the public as Magic Carpet Air; passengers believed that they bought tickets for the major carrier. The company also repainted all aircraft to make the public believe Magic Carpet Air was part of the major carrier.

Prior to 1989, the flight attendants at neither company were unionized. However, both MCA and RCA flight attendants worried about what they perceived as the arbitrary way that MCA management resolved personnel issues such as merging seniority lists. Such fears led several workers to contact the League of Flight Attendants (LFA), a union whose membership consisted solely of flight attendants. Despite opposition to unionization from MCA, the LFA won a union certification election with 82 percent of the vote.

Previous Contract Negotiations

Negotiations for the first MCA–LFA contract began in November 1989, and negotiators from both sides cooperated effectively. The committee borrowed language from other airline contracts (e.g., Piedmont Airlines). The committee also incorporated the past practices and working conditions that were used at River City Airlines. These rules had

Source: This case was prepared by Peggy Briggs and William Ross of the University of Wisconsin–LaCrosse and is intended to be used as a basis for class discussion rather than to illustrate either effective or ineffective handling of the situation. The names of the firms, individuals, and locations; dates; conversation quotations; and financial information have all been disguised to preserve the firm's and union's desire for anonymity.

An earlier version of this case was presented and accepted by the refereed Midwest Society for Case Research and appeared in *Annual Advances in Case Research, 1991.* All rights reserved to the authors and the MSCR.

not been written down but had been mutually acceptable past practices. Negotiators signed the final contract in August 1990. The contract was effective until August 1994.

Negotiations for the second contract also went smoothly. In terms of contract provisions, the second contract was basically an extension of the first, with a modest pay increase and one additional paid holiday. The agreement was effective until August 31, 1997.

What follows is a synopsis of the 1997 contract negotiations from a union negotiator's perspective.

League of Flight Attendants (LFA) Negotiating Team

Whenever an LFA carrier began negotiations, the National Office of LFA sent a national bargaining representative (NBR) to the scene. Dixie Lee, the NBR assigned to the MCA negotiations, met with the flight attendants' Master Executive Council (MEC) to select a negotiating team. The negotiating team prepared for negotiations and conducted the actual bargaining sessions. Once at the table, Dixie spoke for the committee. Using an NBR as the spokesperson lessened the likelihood that a flight attendant who was emotionally involved with an issue might say something inappropriate while trying to negotiate. Dixie had 14 years' experience and had also assisted with the 1994 MCA contract negotiations. Although Dixie was the spokesperson, the negotiating team was formally chaired by Ruth Boaz, LFA MEC president at Magic Carpet Air. Other members of the team included local LFA union presidents Peggy Hardy, Marie Phillips, and Jody Rogers.

Determining the Union's Bargaining Objectives

The LFA negotiating committee members first identified their bargaining objectives. For the 1997 contract, the LFA negotiating committee devised an opening offer based on the average working conditions and wage rates for flight attendants offered by other, similarly sized carriers. They looked at wage, unemployment, and cost-of-living data from government sources such as the *Monthly Labor Review.* The committee members knew the financial history of MCA and kept their proposals within financial reach of the company. They also used other employee groups (e.g., pilots, mechanics) within MCA as a guide—many of the LFA proposals were items that these other unions already had in their contracts. The LFA negotiating committee hoped to bring wages and work rules in line with the company's financial performance and industry standards (see Table 1). Finally, they looked at past grievances and arbitration cases to determine if contract wording needed changes.

Committee members also considered the wishes of the rank-and-file members. To do this, the committee mailed a survey to the 115 LFA members asking questions regarding wages, working conditions, and issues of concern to flight attendants. They received a 75 percent response rate; results are shown in Table 2.

After tallying the responses, negotiating team members discovered that the flight attendants' major concern was wage determination. MCA currently paid flight attendants for the time they were in the aircraft with it moving under its own power—they

TABLE 1 | 1996–97 Regional Airline Industry Comparisons

Airline	Starting Wage/Hour	Days off per Month	Duty Rig* as Airline (percentage of time)
A	$17.00	11	60%
B	$15.00	12	62%
C	$15.00	12	none
D	$14.00	13	none
E	$14.00	10	none
F	$13.50	10	33%
Magic Carpet	$13.00	10	none

*Duty rig is a pay calculation that is a certain percentage of the period of time which a flight attendant is on duty with the company. Duty time normally begins 45 minutes prior to first scheduled trip departure time and ends 15 minutes after final arrival time at the end of the day.

TABLE 2 | Results of the Flight Attendant Survey

Questionnaires mailed: 115	
Questionnaires returned: 86	
Question: What was the flight attendant's top priority for the new contract?	
Direct wages	40%
Job security	31%
Working conditions	26%
Other	3%
Question: How did the flight attendant want to receive her/his direct wages?	
Duty rigs	47%
Hourly rate	34%
Holiday pay	15%
Other	4%
Question: How did the flight attendant want her/his job security?	
Seniority protection	60%
Protection from layoffs	28%
Protection of contract	12%

were not paid for the time spent sitting in airports waiting for flights. Union members wanted MCA to implement *duty rigs*. A duty rig paid the attendant a fixed percentage of the period of time he or she was on duty with the company.

For example, suppose an attendant worked a 15-hour day, but worked in moving aircraft for only six hours. Under the current system, MCA paid wages for six hours, plus one hour for preparation time (*duty time*) at the beginning of the day. However, if the duty rig pay rate was 67 percent, MCA would pay the attendant for 10 hours of work, plus 1 hour for duty time. Thus duty rigs would require the airline to pay a percentage of the wage for all time at work, whether flying or sitting.

Flight attendants also voiced concern over job security and working conditions. When they analyzed the job security issue, team members found that in the event of any merger or buyout of MCA, the flight attendants wanted their seniority with the carrier to be continued by any new company. Second, flight attendants sought protection from layoffs in the event of a merger or acquisition.

The survey also had a section for employee comments. The area that members most frequently relayed as a concern was their current sick leave program. Many flight attendants complained that they were not allowed to use their accrued sick time when they were sick. Others complained that they had to give management a five-day notice whenever they wanted to swap routes with other MCA attendants.

From this information, union negotiating committee members identified two broad objectives: increased wages via a duty rig provision, and increased job security. They also decided that their initial package would be very close to their final objectives. The committee members proposed a duty rig clause with the same standards as the pilots, although the dollar amount was less important than just obtaining the provision itself. They also devised a "successorship clause" allowing attendants to arbitrate their seniority rights in the event someone bought MCA. In order to obtain these clauses, the union also proposed two throwaway clauses: an expensive health care package and double-time wages for working holidays.

Strategies of the Union

During planning sessions, the negotiating committee identified four strategies for achieving its objectives through bargaining:

1. Keeping union members informed of negotiation progress.
2. Getting union members involved.
3. Convincing the company that the union's demands were serious.
4. Settling an issue only with the unanimous consent of the negotiating committee.

Informing Union Members

The first strategy attempted to keep the union members informed. The negotiating committee mailed a short letter after each bargaining session, explaining the issues discussed and the general content of any agreed-upon sections. Members were also sent *Negotiation Update* newsletters every two weeks, telling flight attendants of their progress. These newsletters did not reveal any initial proposals because committee members knew that union members would be disappointed if the union did not receive what was initially requested.

Involving Union Members

The second strategy sought to get the union members involved. The negotiating committee printed the slogan, "We make the difference and they make the money" on pens, buttons, and T-shirts. These were distributed to all members and to all passengers on selected flights. This program was loosely modeled after the United Airlines' 1996–97

Create Havoc Around Our System (CHAOS) program, where the union sought to enlist the aid of the public and employed creative tactics (e.g., intermittent strikes, informational picketing) to pressure management to resolve their contract dispute. The union also invited any member in good standing to attend any negotiation session.

Convincing the Company

The third strategy attempted to convince the company to take the LFA seriously. In a widely publicized move, negotiation team members did extensive research on both economic picketing and informational picketing, inquiring at all of their domicile cities as to what permits would be needed to picket. The union mailed their *Negotiation Update* newsletters to each manager's home address, informing managers of the LFA's preparations in the event of a future strike. Committee members hoped these actions would convince management that the LFA made serious proposals—and would strike if those proposals were not met.

Settling Issues

The fourth strategy was that the team would not proceed with an item without the entire team being in total agreement. All planning meetings and caucuses (meetings without the company team member present) during negotiations would involve every committee member.

Company Negotiating Team

The company negotiating team consisted of the following people:

- Bill Orleans, director of labor relations.
- Ross Irving, director of human resources.
- Kristine Lamb, director of in-flight services.
- Christian Andrew, executive vice president.
- Willie Sanders, senior vice president of operations.
- Tom Windham, chief executive officer (CEO) and president.

The company team was in a state of transition, and consequently seemed to suffer from much confusion. Bill Orleans had recently been demoted from director of human resources to director of labor relations—a move he resented. Ross Irving, the new director of human resources, hired from another firm, avoided the sessions; he seemed uncomfortable sitting next to his predecessor, particularly since Orleans had negotiated most of the union contracts at MCA. Finally, Lamb, who was used to giving orders to flight attendants, acted as if the negotiations reflected a lack of loyalty on the part of the workers and interference with her job on the part of management. Tom Windham was grooming Willie Sanders to take over upon Windham's retirement.

The Negotiating Process: Initial Positions

Airlines are governed under the Railway Labor Act of 1926, as amended. This act states that labor contracts never expire, but may be amended on their amendable dates. When the amendable date comes near, a letter is mailed by the party requesting changes in the contract to the counterparty in the contract. This letter allows contract talks to begin. Dixie mailed MCA such a letter on March 31, giving a full 60 days notice of the flight attendants' intent to open talks for amending their current contract before September 1.

Inasmuch as the company would not meet in a neutral city, LFA negotiators agreed to an MCA proposal to meet at a hotel located near corporate headquarters. MCA paid for the meeting room. The first negotiation session was scheduled for May 29, 1997.

Everyone on the LFA committee had the jitters. It was the first time in negotiations for Marie, Jody, and Peggy. Dixie gave them some last-minute instructions:

> I don't want y'all to speak or use any facial expressions at the table. Instead, I want all of y'all to silently take notes. Draw a vertical line down the middle of each note page. Write whatever the managers say on the left side of the page and write whatever I say on the right-hand side of the page. Is it OK with y'all if I do the negotiating? I've found things go best if only one person talks at the bargaining table.

As the LFA negotiators filed into the conference room, they saw it was empty. Each of the managers arrived late. Twenty minutes later, Orleans still had not come. As everyone waited, CEO Tom Windham arrived. Small talk began as Windham glanced over his notes and spoke:

> You know that as a feeder airline we do not have full control over our own destiny; the marketing agreement with the major carrier restricts our flexibility. Even so, I am willing to give your flight attendant group a modest increase. I am not looking for any concessions. Also, my philosophy is that all the groups (pilots, agents, office personnel) should be treated equally. However, your union does have a good agreement right now—say, why don't we just agree to continue the present contract for another six years? It could save a lot of time!

As everyone chuckled at Windham's joke, Orleans arrived. The union negotiators could tell by the expression on his face that he was surprised and embarrassed to see Tom Windham there. Windham stood up, wished everyone good luck, and left.

The Union's Initial Position

Dixie spent the first day describing problems with the current contract. At 4:15 p.m., the union presented the company with its neatly typed contract proposal. Dixie had written "change," "new," "clarification," and so on in the margin next to each paragraph that had been changed in any way from the 1994 contract.

> ORLEANS: This is a "wish book"! Do I look like Santa Claus?

> LEE: Stop fidgeting, Mr. Orleans. Let me explain why we are insisting on these changes.

Dixie read only about one-third of the provisions in the union's contract proposal. Two additional sessions were necessary to read through the entire proposal. The major changes are summarized in Table 3.

TABLE 3 | Changes in the Magic Carpet Air–League of Flight Attendants Contract

Contract Provision	1994–97 Contract	Union Proposal
Compensation		
Base wage	$13.00	$15.45
Wage after five years	$20.20	$25.55
Duty rig pay	None	1 hour pay per 2 hour duty (50%)
Daily guarantee	3.25 hours	4.5 hours
Holiday pay	None	8 holidays at double-time rate
Job security		
Successorship	None	Contract will still be binding
Protection of seniority rights in the event of a merger	None	Arbitrator combines MCA seniority list with that of the other airline
Working conditions		
Trip trading lead time	5 days	24 hours
Shoe allowance	None	$100/year
Winter coat	None	Total cost
Uniform maintenance	$16/month	$20/month

Management's Initial Position

On the fourth day, company representatives presented their initial offer to the union. Orleans handed each of the LFA committee members a book in a binder. As they leafed through the book, members were puzzled. They did not see any notations indicating changes from the current contract. Orleans talked quickly, summarizing the provisions in the contract; most of the proposed provisions included some type of union concessions, but he did not highlight these.

LEE: Is this a serious proposal? The union presented a realistic proposal using industry standards, and your opener (opening offer) is totally unreasonable.

ORLEANS: Don't get your panties in a wad. The party has just begun and there is lots of time to dance. Why, we didn't even list any wages in our proposal—we were hoping you would work for free, ha ha.

Orleans then gave a long, patronizing sermon regarding MCA's poor financial health and how the company could be bankrupt at any time. However, in the history of Magic Carpet Air, the company had never shown a loss on its financial statement.

A recess was called for lunch. As the union members caucused, Peggy looked depressed. Marie sat with fists clenched.

MARIE: I can't eat anything! I am furious at Mr. Orleans—he has some nerve!

JODY: The others were not much better. Did you hear their snide remarks about us when they went to lunch?

PEGGY: What are we going to do? They have asked for concessions on everything! And Mr. Windham promised us just the opposite.

DIXIE: Now girls, just relax. It is still the first week of negotiations. I suggest that we just work from our initial contract proposal and ignore theirs. It can't be taken seriously anyway, in my opinion.

MARIE: Well, you'll have to carry on without me tomorrow; I have to work. Management won't let me rearrange my schedule to negotiate. At least I won't have to watch Mr. Orleans chain smoke!

Talks resumed after lunch break. Dixie summarized each section of the LFA proposal. Orleans fidgeted and kept saying "No." Nothing was settled that day.

By noon the next day, it became obvious that not much was getting accomplished. Finally, the union moved to sections where it did not propose any changes and the managers tentatively agreed to keep those intact. It seemed like a mountain had been climbed just to get the company to agree to those "no changes." Negotiations were adjourned for the day.

LEE: When can we meet? Monday, at 8:30?

SANDERS: No good for me. I have important meetings that day.

LEE: How about Tuesday?

ANDREW: I can't make it. Every day next week is bad.

ORLEANS: The following week I will be out of town. Sorry!

LEE: OK, y'all tell us when y'all's schedules are free.

ORLEANS: We'll have to caucus. We'll get back to you.

Instead of caucusing and deciding when they could next meet, the managers simply went home, leaving the union negotiating team to wonder when—or if—bargaining would continue.

Round 2

On Wednesday, July 16, Ruth Boaz got a letter from management asking for a meeting two days later. Ruth quickly scheduled a planning session for Thursday night, where the LFA team members reviewed their objectives and the progress to date. Negotiations with MCA resumed Friday.

July 18: Grievances and Uniforms

Irving proposed using the same language for a revised grievance procedure as that printed in the pilot's contract. The union caucused. Ruth telephoned the pilot's union and, once she was satisfied that the pilots were happy with their grievance procedure, convinced the union negotiating team to agree.

The discussion moved to the section on uniforms. After some countering back and forth on various issues, a winter coat was added as an optional item; however, who would pay the cost was still an issue. The union wanted MCA to pay the total cost.

ORLEANS: Unacceptable. You'll have to buy your own coats. We already give $16 per month for uniform cleaning.

LEE: But a winter coat is expensive. Surely y'all recognize that a poor little ol' flight attendant couldn't be expected to shoulder the entire cost of a new coat. Mr. Orleans, have a heart.

ORLEANS: I do have a heart; fortunately, it is not attached to my wallet, ha ha. OK, we will allow $40 every five years to buy a coat.

LEE: According to my research, a new coat costs $120. And it costs $10 per month to clean.

ORLEANS: How often does someone dry-clean a coat she only wears three months of the year? She doesn't clean it 12 times! (*Pause.*) OK, if you drop this silly request for free shoes, then we'll raise the combined uniform and coat maintenance allowance to $16.50 per month.

LEE: But, Mr. Orleans, shoes are a part of our uniform, too. You expect us to all wear the same type of shoes, don't you? You pay for the other parts of our uniforms, so it is only reasonable that MCA should also pay for shoes. Our research shows that two pairs of standard shoes cost, on average, $100.

ORLEANS: However, you can wear the shoes when you are not on duty, too. You probably wouldn't do that with other parts of your uniforms. So we're not paying for shoes you can wear other places.

BOAZ: Mr. Orleans, I can assure you that we don't wear our uniform shoes when we go dancing on the weekends. (Everyone laughed.)

ORLEANS: If we pay $25 for shoes and $45 for a coat, then we will pay $17.50 per month for uniform maintenance.

LEE: Good, but not good enough.

> (*Both sides sat in silence for nearly four minutes. Mr. Orleans was obviously uncomfortable with this period of silence.*)

ORLEANS: Let's see . . . (*fumbling with a pen and paper*) we'll split the cost of the new coat, so that is $60 and we'll pay $25 for shoes. Good enough now?

LEE: Raise the combined uniform and coat maintenance to $18 per month and you have a deal.

LEE: (*As they were writing the agreed-upon section.*) Why don't we make it one new coat for the life of the three-year contract, instead of one new coat every five years? That makes it so much easier for everyone to keep track of.

Orleans rolled his eyes and nodded in acquiescence. The meeting then adjourned for the weekend. At last the union team felt that some progress was being made.

Bargaining Strategy in Major League Baseball

Introduction

During the winter of 2005–2006, Donald Fehr was faced with some monumental decisions. As the head of the Major League Baseball Players Association (MLBPA), he had been arduously preparing for the upcoming round of negotiations between his union and the owners of the 30 major league baseball clubs (collectively known as Major League Baseball, or MLB). Being the representative of the labor force in a multi-billion dollar business was no easy task, even for a seasoned negotiating veteran. The health—even the very survival—of his union had hung in the balance each time a new basic agreement (the uniform contract between the two sides) was negotiated, and Fehr couldn't help but remember past work stoppages, which hurt both sides tremendously. Fehr knew that hard bargaining with the ownership group might cause another strike or lockout, but with attendance levels at the highest they had ever been in the history of the sport, he needed to gauge his constituents' (and his opposition's) resolve to decide how to approach the process.

History

The Early Years

Tumultuous labor relations in professional baseball were almost as old as the sport itself. What started as a "gentlemen's game" in the mid-1800's quickly turned into business when the general public started taking interest in the sport. Throughout the second half of the 19th century, different leagues were formed by American industrialists whose intentions were to capitalize financially on the sport's growing popularity. Only two leagues stood the test of time, the National League, formed in 1875, and the American League, formed in 1901. In 1903 the two leagues merged to become Major League Baseball, which quickly became the most profitable sports business in America.

When players began to realize that their unique skills could be marketed to the highest bidder, nervous owners began to seek ways to ensure that their moneymakers would not jump ship. In the most controversial move in baseball's early history, the "reserve clause" was developed and implemented into player contracts. In a move that some considered a form of outright collusion, owners agreed amongst themselves that after each season, each club was able to "reserve" five players that could not be sought after by the other teams. In this regard, the five players on each team that were reserved had no right to switch teams if they found the conditions deplorable or found that they could make more money elsewhere. Eventually this clause would be written into all contracts, and players who chose to dishonor the clause were blacklisted from organized baseball.

Source: This case was prepared by Daniel T. Romportl and William H. Ross, Jr., both of the University of Wisconsin–La Crosse. Used with permission from the authors and the Society for Case Research.

Opposition to the reserve clause became a rallying point for the players, and several unions were formed over the next few decades in an attempt to give players bargaining leverage and a bigger voice. The Brotherhood of Professional Base Ball Players (1885), the Players Protective Association (1900), the Baseball Players' Fraternity (1912), the National Baseball Players' Association of the United States (1922), and the Association of Professional Ballplayers (1924) all had formed, in part, to oppose the reserve clause. However, those unions had trouble sustaining member interest and financial backing and eventually disbanded. During the time of these unions' formations, the anti-union sentiment was high among the general public due to several highly publicized instances of labor union violence. The unions' failures meant the owners maintained complete control over their players' salaries, benefits, and livelihoods.

Illegal Restraint of Trade?

By restricting the movement of labor from team to team, which in almost all cases would be over state lines, it seemed to many that the owners were illegally restraining trade, a violation of the *Sherman Antitrust Act.* Several legal challenges were mounted against organized baseball by rival start-up leagues who were angered when they were denied access to the player market. In 1922, the United States Supreme Court ruled that baseball was a sport, not a business, and since it was conducted in local ballparks for local fans, it was mainly involved in *intrastate* commerce. The *Federal Baseball Club v. National League* decision (aka the *Holmes* decision, named after Judge Oliver Wendell Holmes) would ultimately give baseball an "antitrust exemption." In 1953, the Supreme Court would reaffirm the ruling after a player (George Toolson of the New York Yankees) filed suit, claiming the reserve clause was illegal and was threatening his livelihood. Chief Justice Earl Warren reiterated that baseball "was not within the scope of federal antitrust laws,"[1] and that action taken against the exemption should be by the U.S. Congress, not the courts. The reserve clause would remain untouched and embedded in players' contracts until the mid-1970s.

The Major League Baseball Players Association

In 1946, a Mexican league was hiring several prominent U.S. players, creating competitive pressure on American player salaries. U.S. owners wanted to avoid a bidding war with the Mexican League. That same year, a labor lawyer convinced U.S. players to organize the American Baseball Guild. This union's existence concerned management enough to cause them to bargain over a uniform players' contract. The contract called for a minimum player salary ($5,000) and a guaranteed pension plan. Players contributed the bulk of the retirement funds, paying into the pension plan until their tenth season; owners contributed to it primarily from radio, television, and post-season ticket revenue. The union was short-lived, fading into obscurity by the end of that same year; however, the pension fund endured. By the early 1950s funds for the pension plan fell short, and the players felt it was in their best interest to organize once again.

In 1953, the Major League Baseball Players Association (MLBPA) was formed to serve as the players' main bargaining body and the owners implicitly voluntarily recognized the union by allowing it to operate the pension fund and by contributing to the fund. The union was led by player representatives and legal advisors until 1965 when it hired its first full-time executive, Marvin Miller, an economist with the Steelworkers Union. Miller brought with him experience in industrial relations and a hard-line bargaining approach. In response, the owners formed the Major League Player Relations Committee (PRC) to serve as their negotiating body. In 1968, the two sides hammered out the 1st Basic Agreement, a uniform contract that established (among other things) a formal grievance procedure for players and a significantly increased minimum salary level. Baseball historian Lee Lowenfish writes, "[the owners] conceded more rights in the 1st Basic Agreement than in all previous decades of the sport."[2]

The Early 1970s: Players Challenge the Reserve Clause

In 1972, the MLBPA and the PRC ran into trouble while negotiating the 3rd Basic Agreement. The major disagreement between the two sides stemmed from the amount the owners were willing to contribute to the players' pension fund. Players union head Marvin Miller claimed that there was a surplus of pension funding that could be used to offset increased cost-of-living expenses that the players had been incurring. The owners showed solidarity (which has been rare throughout the league's history) by refusing the MLBPA's demands. The union even went so far as to file an "unfair labor practice" claim with the National Labor Relations Board when the owners refused to share certain financial information with them (the information was eventually provided). On April 1, 1972, a day that the *Sporting News* would call "the darkest day in sports history,"[3] the players went on strike. The strike did not last long, as the two sides eventually reached a compromise on the contribution amount ($500,000). The half-million dollars that the players received in increased pension contributions was far less than the salary losses they incurred during the two-week long strike. The owners, who had talked the union down from their initial proposal of a $1 million increase in contributions, had lost $5.2 million in revenue.[4]

Shortly after the strike of 1972, the reserve clause was threatened once again. Outfielder Curt Flood of the St. Louis Cardinals challenged the legality of the reserve clause in court, and in *Flood v. Kuhn,* the Supreme Court once again upheld the *Holmes* decision. Flood was successful, however, in attracting Congress's and the media's attention to the reserve clause issue. In 1974, pitcher Catfish Hunter sought to become the league's first free agent when the owner of his team (the Oakland A's) dishonored a provision in his contract. Hunter's case went to a three-man arbitration panel, which had been created and outlined in the 3rd Basic Agreement. The panel voted 2 to 1 that Hunter had the right to "shop his services" to other clubs since his own club did not honor the legally binding contract. Hunter became baseball's first free agent.

A year later, two players (Dave McNally and Andy Messersmith) challenged the clause once again. The two teams that held the rights to McNally and Messersmith had renewed the players' contracts for the 1975 season, and for different reasons, both players refused to sign them. They played out the season anyway, without being under contract, and when the season concluded, the clubs employed the reserve clause once again. The players claimed that the reserve clause only provided that clubs could *renew* the contracts for one year, and that since they were not under contract during the 1975 season, the clubs were not within their rights to renew them for the 1976 season. The case went to arbitration, and by a 2 to 1 vote, the McNally and Messersmith won. The players had won the right to offer their services to the highest bidder (a process called "free agency"), and the reserve clause was dead. The new labor environment would become even more turbulent as free agency shook the economics of the game to its core.

1976 to 1989: Free Agency Becomes the Norm

In 1976, the MLBPA and the PRC were split on the new free agency issue. The owners wanted players to gain free agency eligibility after 10 years of professional service, while the union proposed a five-year requirement. During Spring Training, the owners instituted a lockout. Commissioner Bowie Kuhn, who was technically an "employee of the owners," ordered the owners to end the lockout, a move that lost him favor with many on the management side. The two sides eventually agreed on an eligibility minimum of six years of professional service, and compensation in the form of a draft pick for the team who was losing the player.

Prior to the start of the 1980 season, the two sides were again far apart when negotiating the 5th Basic Agreement. The major issue was the compensation that a team would receive after losing a free agent. The proposals that the PRC presented were seen by Marvin Miller as an attempt to "dismantle free agency in its infancy."[5] On April 1, the players again went on strike. They agreed to start the season on the scheduled opening day, but promised to resume the strike on May 23 (the week that attendance usually plateaued) if no agreement had been reached. On the morning of May 23, the two sides reached a deal which basically provided that the free-agent compensation issue be studied for a year, after which negotiations regarding the issue would reopen.

The committee that was selected to study the issue produced nothing substantial, and in 1981, the two sides were again having trouble finding common ground. The MLBPA's Marvin Miller and the PRC's president Ray Grebey had developed a bitter rivalry that the press could not get enough of. On May 29, the players went on strike once again. The strike lasted 50 days. The National Labor Relations Board, Congress's Federal Mediation and Conciliation Services, and the Department of Labor all attempted to help the parties end their strike. On July 31, the two sides reached a deal that would provide the team losing a free agent compensation. The team that lost the player would receive a player from the "signing" team. The union won a free agency system that was similar to their own bargaining position—but at a heavy price. Players lost a total of $30 million in wages, and the owners lost roughly $72 million in revenues.[6] Miller, Grebey, Kuhn, and other key figures in the negotiation process left their positions, and baseball witnessed labor peace and an attendance boom over the next four years.

In 1985, with Donald Fehr heading the MLBPA, the two sides were determined to avoid a work stoppage while negotiating the 6th Basic Agreement. The two main issues that divided the two sides were once again free agent compensation and pension contribution levels. Several issues were agreed upon early (e.g., a drug review board would investigate cases where a player was accused of using cocaine), but it was still not enough to avoid another work stoppage. On August 6, the players went on strike, but with the 1981 strike still fresh in their minds, the two sides reached an agreement within a day.

The risk of alienating the fans, who were spending more money than ever on baseball, proved to be the driving force behind the speedy resolution.

The Early 1990s: Salary Arbitration, Revenue Sharing, and "The Big Strike"

In 1990, the owners instituted another lockout while bargaining with the union over the 7th Basic Agreement. The disparity between large market teams (such as the New York Yankees and Los Angeles Dodgers) and small market teams (such as the Kansas City Royals and Milwaukee Brewers) was growing. With a larger fan base, large market teams were able to attract significantly richer television contracts from local networks. Because no salary cap existed, large market teams could sign better players due to their ability to offer high salaries. The owners saw this as a major problem, and proposed a "revenue sharing" program, in which large market teams would share a certain portion of their local revenue with small market teams. Their justification was that by increasing competitive balance, playoff races would be closer, attracting more people to the ballparks late in the season and producing higher television ratings. The union opposed a revenue sharing proposal because, if the large market teams had less money, they could not afford to offer top dollar contracts to free agents. Players employed by teams that received revenue sharing would not necessarily benefit either, because those teams were not obligated to spend the funds on player salaries. The owners tried to preempt a strike by locking the players out of spring training. After 32 days, an agreement was reached; the revenue sharing issue was put on hold.

In 1994, the owners realized that not only was competitive and financial disparity hurting their profits, but salary arbitration was driving up salary levels. Beginning with the 1985 contract, players with three years of major-league service who felt that they were underpaid could demand that their salaries be adjusted upward through a process called "final offer arbitration." The process worked as follows: The player's representative presented evidence that the player was underpaid, relative to peers with comparable records. The team owner's representative presented evidence that the player was equitably compensated, given other players in his peer group. Each side proposed a salary figure. The arbitrator then had to select either the player's proposal or the owner's proposal. Teams had been more inclined to pay players a little bit more than what they were worth instead of risking a loss in the final-offer arbitration process (where they stood to pay considerably more). The owners suggested an overhaul of the entire economic structure of the league: eliminating salary arbitration, phasing in a "salary cap" (where a team's total payroll was limited to a specified amount), lowering free agency eligibility, and splitting television revenue 50/50 with the players. Fehr and the MLBPA, on the other hand, rejected these proposals. On August 11, 1994, the players went on strike.

This time, the strike lasted 232 days, and the World Series was cancelled for the first time ever. The courts, the NLRB, Congress, the FMCS, and President Clinton all intervened at some point during the stoppage. The strike eventually ended when Judge Sonia Sotomayor of the United States District Court in Manhattan granted the NLRB's request for an injunction. The NLRB was claiming that the owners had implemented their proposals during the strike without the existence of a good-faith impasse. Baseball

resumed on April 26, 1995, with the old contract provisions being re-implemented. Historian Paul Staudohar calls the strike "one of the most eventful, but unproductive, ever."[7]
The owners estimated their total losses to be in upwards of $1 billion, and the players
saw their salaries drop considerably as cash-strapped clubs sought cheaper talent from
the minor leagues. Some fans turned to minor league teams for baseball entertainment;
others abandoned the game altogether. Meanwhile bargaining continued. The 8th Basic
Agreement wasn't agreed upon until late December, 1996. A revenue sharing program
was implemented, but the owners did not receive their highly sought salary cap.

Labor Relations Developments from 1998 to 2002: The Curt Flood Act and Contraction

In 1998, Congress passed the *Curt Flood Act*. The law called for an end to baseball's sto-
ried antitrust exemption, but only as it applied to labor relations. The premise of the bill was
to "reduce the chance of future strikes by allowing players to bring an antitrust suit against
the owners if labor negotiations stall."[8] All other aspects of the exemption still applied.

In July 2000, the owners tried to partially rectify the problem of competitive and
financial disparity by eliminating (or contracting) two teams from Major League Baseball. Their rationalization was that by having two of the poorly performing clubs gone,
the revenue sharing burden would be eased substantially. Congress unsuccessfully
attempted to stop the contraction, and the union responded by filing a grievance. Eventually, the owner of the Montreal Expos (one of the teams that was being considered for
contraction) sold his team to an ownership group made up of the other 29 owners for
$120 million. They moved the team to Washington, D.C., renamed it the Nationals, and
then found a buyer for the team.[9] The issue of contraction was put on hold.

In 2002, the two sides entered a bargaining process that was calmer and more
productive than in previous bargaining sessions. The owners wanted to implement a
"luxury tax" (a team exceeding a certain payroll threshold would pay money to MLB
and those funds would be redistributed among the other teams) and a competitive balance draft (the eight worst teams could select players from the eight best teams). Fehr
and the union opposed these provisions (the original proposal by the owners was a
50 percent tax on all salary spending over $84 million), and disagreements over a
proposed expansion of the drug testing policy also arose. The union set a strike date of
August 30, and the two sides struck a deal the night before the work stoppage was to
take place. A luxury tax with higher thresholds than originally proposed was implemented as a way to slow rising player salaries, and, perhaps just as importantly, the post-
season (which accounts for a large portion of baseball's revenue) was saved.

The Upcoming 10th Basic Agreement

The 2002 contract was set to expire in December 2006. The history of labor relations in
professional baseball—the lost revenue from strikes and lockouts, attempts to control
escalating players' salaries, and clauses found in prior contracts—all cast a long
shadow over the 2006 negotiations. Baseball Commissioner Allen H. (Bud) Selig issued
an order to all MLB employees that no one outside of his office was to discuss upcoming

labor negotiations. While the MLBPA's Fehr planned to travel to each of the teams to listen to player concerns in the early spring, as of December 2005 the following issues seemed prominent:

1. Steroids

In the fall of 2005, with negotiations over the 10th Basic Agreement still months away, the two sides were forced to bargain over a drug testing program. The endless media coverage over certain players' alleged steroid usage was harming Major League Baseball's image greatly, and Congress (most notably Senator John McCain, R-Arizona) had been threatening to act if the two sides could not develop a tougher policy.[10] The controversy began when a book by ex-slugger Jose Canseco claimed to reveal the extent to which major league ballplayers were using and abusing steroids. The steroid issue had been gaining momentum for several years prior, as home-run records were broken and balls were flying out of the park like never before. In what some say was an attempt to garner media attention and solidify anti-drug stances with the public, several Congressmen became involved, even subpoenaing several former players and executives to testify in front of the Government Reform Committee in March of 2005.[11] The MLBPA complained that the union should be contacted before either current or former players spoke out publicly on this issue.

Fehr and Commissioner Selig were far apart on the issue of punishment for steroid users, with Fehr's proposal being far more lenient than Selig's.[12] Fehr was calling for suspensions of 20 games for the first time a player was tested positive for steroids, 75 games for the second penalty (with some flexibility, based on circumstances), and a lifetime ban for the third penalty. Selig countered with an absolute ban of 50 games for the first penalty, 100 games for the second penalty, and a lifetime ban "for anybody dumb enough to be caught a third time."[13] Congress was threatening to act if the two sides could not voluntarily agree on a drug testing program for steroids.

Amphetamines also became a topic for discussion. Owners wanted to expand the drug testing program to include amphetamines, albeit with lighter penalties than for steroids. The union leadership generally opposed this expansion of the drug testing program, but again Fehr was sensitive to Congressional pressure.

2. Contraction

In 2002, "contraction"—a possible decrease in the number of MLB teams and/or relocation of poorly performing clubs—was a prominent topic. However, with the transformation of the Montreal Expos into the Washington, D.C. Nationals, it was unlikely that the topic would be a part of the 2006 negotiations; the owners had sent signals that contraction was no longer a pressing issue. However, it was possible that the topic could reemerge, if only as a "throw-away" issue. The 9th Basic Agreement stated that the owners had until July 2006 to notify the union of contraction/relocation plans.

3. The "Luxury Tax"

Financial disparity was a topic that the PRC would certainly not consider to be "throw-away" issues. Owners argued that because some teams could afford to pay high salaries, they could hire the best players and make it unlikely that most other teams could make the playoffs. To restore competitive parity, the owners wanted to continue, and even expand, the luxury tax that had been implemented in 2002. The players union remained philosophically opposed to any formula such as the luxury tax (which they considered to be a type of flexible salary cap) that might hurt player incomes. However, as Murray Chass of *The New York Times* wrote, ". . . the owners would be hard pressed to make proposals based on economic hardship. Industry revenues didn't reach $2 billion until 1997, and last year [2005] it soared to $4.7 billion."[14] The luxury tax which was laid out in the 9th Basic Agreement only affected a few teams (most of the penalties were paid by the New York Yankees), so both sides could have trouble proving or disproving its worth. It started in 2003 with a tax threshold of $117 million and rose to $136.5 million in 2006. Certain alterations to the complicated tax formula—the tax increased with each offense—could be proposed during bargaining, but it was doubtful that team owners would agree to a complete overhaul of the system so early in its existence.

4. Revenue Sharing

In addition to the luxury tax, MLB used revenue sharing (e.g., from television contract rights and ticket sales) to distribute income from the most profitable teams to the least profitable teams. In 2004 and 2005, Major League Baseball witnessed its highest attendance levels ever, with 73,022,969 and 74,915,268 fans passing through the turnstiles, respectively.[15] With luxury box and ticket prices rising, this attendance boom signaled an unprecedented rise in gate revenue. While this helped improve the profitability of the smaller-market teams, the union was concerned about how these funds were used. Minimum team salary levels needed to be addressed. After the Florida Marlins club received luxury tax and revenue sharing funds, it slashed its payroll to $15 million ($20 million less than the second lowest payroll). To the union leaders, such a move exposed holes in the revenue sharing program—in effect, funds were being transferred from some owners to other owners, but there was no guarantee that the players would see any of those funds.

5. Salary Levels

The average salary earned by a MLB player rose 7 percent—about double the inflation rate for 2005. The average MLB player certainly seemed well-paid, with a 2005 salary of $2.4 million. However, this figure was skewed by the very high salaries paid to star players, some of whom earned over $20 million annually. The minimum annual salary was $327,000. The union wanted to increase that minimum.

6. Salary Arbitration and Free Agency

How long one must play before becoming eligible for salary arbitration and/or free agency remained an issue. The union wanted to shorten the length of time so that high-performing players could increase their income to be comparable to their peers. The owners wanted to keep it where it was, or perhaps even lengthen the eligibility requirements. The appropriate compensation a signing team should pay to the team losing a free agent also remained a topic of potential discussion in contract negotiations.

7. Pension Contribution Levels

The union wanted owners to increase their contributions to the player's pension fund. Owners balked at this request, citing declining television revenues, which were used to fund pension contributions. The World Series television contract that Major League Baseball could sign with the FOX network might be the X-factor in the owners' approach to bargaining over economic matters. A large percentage of baseball's revenues came from national broadcasting contracts, which gave a network the right to broadcast playoff games, the All-Star Game, and a certain number of games throughout the regular season. The previous contract with FOX, which ran from 2000 through 2006, was worth $2.5 billion, but unfortunately coincided with the lowest television ratings in the sport's history. The World Series ratings in 2000, 2002, and 2005 were the three lowest-rated broadcasts since the Series began airing in 1968.[16] Because of this surprising trend, the new contract with FOX, which was to be signed in July of 2006, was rumored to be worth significantly less (estimated at $1.75 billion over seven years).[17] Since the owners used large portions of the television contract to fund the players' pension fund, the claim of financial hardship by the PRC could rear its ugly head during Basic Agreement negotiations.

8. Strike Risks

The potential alienation of baseball's fan base by undergoing another work stoppage might prove to exert more influence over bargaining matters than any other factor. Past work stoppages had cost both players and owners significant amounts of money. A strike could result in team owners attempting to bring in "scab" players (e.g., minor league players) or it could result in the decertification of the union by disgruntled players.

9. The Media and Public Perception

Finally, with any labor relations situation, the media play an important role in the approaches that the two sides take to bargaining. In prior negotiations, national media attention to labor contract negotiations was considerably more intense than in other industries. The ESPN television network only added to the scrutiny as it complemented traditional media outlets, such as *Sports Illustrated* magazine and the *USA Today, New York Times,* and *Washington Post* newspapers. The MLBPA was recently accused of shielding drug addicts and criminals because of its stance on steroid testing. Yet to give in to owner demands for a tough new drug testing policy would only lead to media criticism that "the strongest union in America" was ineffective and could be beaten by determined owners. Such criticism could cause some union leaders to encourage taking a hard-line approach to regain the confidence of their constituents.

The Big Decision: What Bargaining Strategy Should Fehr Adopt?

Donald Fehr realized that he could go one of two ways when the bargaining sessions were to begin during the 2006 season. On one hand, he could probably secure the "basic" increases in minimum salary and pension contributions without a lot of resistance from the PRC and its leader, Commissioner Bug Selig. Although the owners might claim that the decreased television revenue put them in a less desirable financial position, Fehr knew that he could retaliate by going to the media with the astronomical industry revenue figures that baseball was currently realizing. With gate revenues and industry profits at an all time high, a hard-line approach and the threat of a strike or antitrust lawsuit might allow the union to secure better wages and benefits than they had ever imagined. On the other hand, Fehr knew that the public image of the union had suffered because of past "strikes by millionaires" and because of the union's current resistance to a tougher steroid policy. As Fehr mulled his options and planned his bargaining strategy, he perhaps hoped that Jose Canseco wasn't planning on writing another book anytime soon.

Bibliography

Bumgardner, L. G. (2000). Baseball's Antitrust Exemption: While the Lawyers Warmed Up in the Bullpen, the Game Was Called Due to the Reign of Compromise. In P. D. Staudohar (Ed.), *Diamond Mines: Baseball & Labor* (pp. 83–95). Syracuse, NY: Syracuse University Press.

Dworkin, J. (1981). *Owners versus players: baseball and collective bargaining.* Boston: Auburn House Publishing Company.

Gelzheiser, R. (2006). *Labor and capital in 19th century baseball.* Jefferson, NC: McFarland and Company, Inc.

Korr, C. P. (2000). From Judge Cannon to Marvin Miller. In P. D. Staudohar (Ed.), *Diamond Mines: Baseball and Labor* (pp. 1–20). Syracuse, NY: Syracuse University Press.

Miller, M. (1991). *A whole different ballgame.* New York: Carol Publishing Group.

Powers, A. (2003). *The business of baseball.* Jefferson, NC: McFarland and Company, Inc., Publishers.

Endnotes

1. McKelvey, G. (2001). *For it's one, two, three, four strikes you're out at the owners' ball game.* Jefferson, NC: McFarland and Company, Inc.

2. Lowenfish, L. (1991). *The imperfect diamond: a history of baseball's labor wars* (2nd ed). New York: Da Capo Press, Inc.

3. McKelvey, *For it's one, two, three, four strikes you're out at the owners' ball game.*

4. Jennings, K. (1990). *Balls and strikes: the money game in professional baseball.* New York: Praeger Publishers.

5. McKelvey, *For it's one, two, three, four strikes you're out at the owners' ball game.*

6. Burk, R. (2001). *Much more than a game: players, owners, & American baseball since 1921.* Chapel Hill, NC: The University of North Carolina Press.

7. Staudohar, P. D. (2000). The baseball strike of 1994–95. In P. D. Staudohar (Ed.), *Diamond Mines: Baseball and Labor* (pp. 48–61). Syracuse, NY: Syracuse University Press.

8. Bumgardner, L. G. (2000). Baseball's antitrust exemption: While the lawyers warmed up in the bullpen, the game was called due to the reign of compromise. In P. D. Staudohar (Ed.), *Diamond Mines: Baseball & Labor* (pp. 83–95). Syracuse, NY: Syracuse University Press.

9. Boeck, S. (2004, September 30). Expos relocation timeline. *USA Today.* Retrieved April 24, 2006, from EbscoHost Database.

10. Brodley, H. (2004). McCain, baseball labor boss to discuss steroid testing. *USA Today,* December 7, 2004.

11. Lazarus, E. (2005). Congress' decision to subpoena former baseball players to testify. *CNN.com,* March 17, 2005. http://www.cnn.com/2005/LAW/03/17/lazarus.steroids/

12. Curry, J. (2005). Selig cool toward Fehr's new offer on steroid testing. *New York Times,* September 27, 2005.

13. Wilbon, M. (2005). Finally, baseball's steroid policy shows a little muscle. *Washington Post,* November 16, 2005, p. E1.

14. Chass, M. (2006). Labor talks: don't worry, there must be something to fight over. *New York Times,* April 2, 2006.

15. "Major League Baseball's record attendance reaches nearly 75 million." MLB press release, October 3, 2005. Online at http://www.mlb.com/news/press_releases/

16. World Series TV Ratings. Baseball Almanac Website: http://www.baseball-almanac.com/ws/wstv.shtml

17. Gough, P. (2006). Fox gets relief in MLB deal. *Hollywood Reporter,* July 12, 2006.

Midwestern::Contemporary Art
(A) Who Is in Charge?

The Midwestern::Contemporary Art (MCA) museum is one of the nation's largest facilities devoted to modern art, exhibiting some of the most compelling and thought-provoking works of art created since 1945. The MCA documents contemporary visual culture through painting, sculpture, photography, video, film, and performance arts. The museum is located in a new facility near the historic White Tower in the heart of the city of Great Lakes, and boasts a gift shop, bookstore, restaurant, 300-seat theater, terraced sculpture garden, and spectacular view of Lake Michigan. Under the leadership of several directors over four decades, the MCA was transformed from an insignificant art showroom in a converted bakery into what is known today as a major shrine to contemporary art. The MCA's continued success can be attributed to the vision of its leaders, succinctly captured in the museum's mission statement:

> The mission of MCA is to be an innovative center of contemporary art where the public can directly experience the work and ideas of living artists as well as understand the historical, social, and cultural context of the art of our time.
>
> The museum boldly interweaves exhibitions, performances, collections, and educational programs to form a challenging, refreshing, and exciting atmosphere for our visitors. In addition, we take pride in providing insights into the creative process for our public viewers.
>
> MCA aspires to attract a broad and diverse audience, create a sense of community, and act as a venue for contemplation and discussion about contemporary art and culture.

Peter and Catherine Smith

Peter and Catherine Smith met when they were teenagers. Friends of the couple said the two functioned as a unit. The couple was not well known among the downtown crowd of collectors until they became involved with contemporary art in the 1970s. Thereafter, the Smiths tended to shy away from the social limelight.

Both Smiths had careers in the legal sector—Peter graduated from an Ivy League school and became the assistant to the chairman of a national retailer headquartered in Great Lakes. He later served as a municipal judge. Catherine graduated from a Great Lakes law school and became the first female lawyer in the state attorney's office, handling cases in child and spousal abuse.

The couple began collecting art after Catherine experienced cerebral vascular spasms in the late 1960s and was forced to give up her legal career. In an assessment of her life, Catherine told her husband that she would be unable to fulfill three of her lifelong dreams: raising their daughters, breeding horses, and acquiring a collection of

Source: Research assistant Rudolph Ng and Professor Matthew Liao-Troth prepared this case as a basis for class discussion, not to illustrate effective or ineffective handling of an administrative situation. Jane Lee assisted with preliminary work on this case and made suggestions for the teaching notes.

art. Upon Catherine's unexpected recovery, the couple dedicated more time to their children, invested in a horse, and made their first art purchases.

A visit to New York's Museum of Modern Art in the early 1970s prompted the couple's interest in works created by contemporary artists. After much research and first-hand observations at galleries, the Smiths began to purchase works of art in the minimalist genre, along with examples of new realist paintings and conceptual art. Such works had not been acquired in depth by Great Lakes collectors, but by 1980 the Smiths' intense collecting activity was recognized by supporters of the MCA.

In June of 1981, Peter was invited to be a member of the MCA board of trustees. Catherine recalled later,

> Board President Heidi Goldman visited us, saying, "I have good news and bad news. You
> have been asked onto the board, and we need a check for $10,000." I admired that directness.

Peter Smith joined the board and began pushing his desire that the MCA would attract more artists and a broader audience base to appreciate contemporary art. He and his wife were prepared to donate more money to make the MCA a better museum with a facility larger than the three-story townhouse it then occupied. In 1989, Peter Smith was elected the board chairman. He then devoted more time to managing the MCA with the hope that his business acumen could make the MCA a more nationally prominent museum.

Keith Schmidt

Keith Schmidt was hired as the MCA's executive director at the start of 1989. Before that, Schmidt served as director of the Seaside Art Museum on the West Coast. Prior to that, he was director of the Southern Museum of Art. At both museums, Schmidt successfully instigated novel building programs, including plans for a new museum building in Seaside and the design and construction of a 70,000-square-foot, $12.1 million adaptive reuse project of historic National Register buildings for the Southern Museum of Art.

During his first month at the MCA, Schmidt showed that his reputation was well earned. One of the first things he did at the MCA was to set goals for the museum. He wanted the museum to be the best in the Midwest and among the top five across the nation in five years. To achieve such an ambitious objective, he realized the necessity of large donations and media attention. Henceforth his time was split among fund-raising, recruiting the best curators, and obtaining and showing the best artwork.

The Conflict between the Chairman and Director

During the two-year overlap of Smith's chairmanship and Schmidt's term as executive director, the two men often had intense debates at board meetings. These confrontations were rooted in a number of areas: what artifacts to show, which artist to invite to forums, and when to hold exhibitions. However, the most heated arguments occurred over the direction and speed of the MCA's expansion.

John Stuart, a former board member and chairman of the museum's budget committee, commented on the differences between Smith and Schmidt:

> I remember a specific meeting when Peter challenged Keith. We were coming out of a
> rough time—having funded some very expensive exhibitions—and were just about to break

even financially. Keith wanted to rent extra office space and hire more staff. Peter asked why we were moving so quickly, but he didn't give orders or intimidate anyone. Besides, any good board chairman had to ask, and it was his responsibility to make intelligent business decisions. During the first six months of 1990, Peter asked a lot of questions. He wanted to proceed in a conservative manner and be assured that there was a backup plan if we didn't continue the plans with the new building. Yet Keith proceeded, racing ahead like a wild bull and perhaps without authority to take such action. There was no question that Keith and Peter disagreed on a number of financial issues. However, each year, we always ended up with a balanced budget, and so I feel that Schmidt acted very responsibly in dealing with fiscal matters.

By October 1991, tension between the two had become very visible to others in the museum. Smith approached his friend and fellow board member, Jennifer Lee, for advice. At a loss for how to handle the aggressive style of Schmidt, Smith expressed his frustration:

> Jennifer, I don't know how other folks on the board feel, but I'm pretty darn sure about my duties and responsibility as a chairperson. You know, they didn't put me in this position without a charge. I'm here to oversee the museum's operation, and Keith's exceedingly ambitious agenda isn't financially sound. I feel that as the board chairman, I should have the final say on this serious matter.

On the other hand, Keith Schmidt also sought to build coalition support from board members. He approached Richard Lang, counsel to the board, and told him his problem with the chairman:

> Throughout my 12-year experience as an art museum director in three other places, I have never had so much interference from the board and chairpersons. I always thought that if the board hired me, then they must trust my ability as a leader and manager of their institution. Rarely had previous chairpersons or board members questioned or objected to my proposals since they had faith in my professional knowledge. After all, my recommendations and proposals have almost always resulted in prosperity and development of their institutions. However, sometimes at MCA, some members of the board, and especially Peter, seem to be downright intrusive and skeptical of my day-to-day management.

In November 1991, the board decided to vote on whether to go with Schmidt's advice to rapidly expand the MCA or to adhere to Smith's conservative policy. Although most members were somewhat skeptical about Schmidt's aggressive plan to develop the museum, most of them felt that they should take the risk. After the vote, Smith was reasonably upset since his opinion was not supported by the majority. Soon after, Peter and Catherine Smith disappeared from the Chicago art community, and repeated phone calls from the MCA were not returned. At this point, the board elected a new chairperson for the MCA.

Discussion Questions for Part (A)

1. Is Peter Smith micromanaging Keith Schmidt?
2. What type of conflict are they experiencing?

3. What can an organization do structurally to reduce conflict resulting from role ambiguity?

4. How should Peter Smith react when his advice is not followed by the board?

5. How are the roles of board chairman and an executive director different in an organization such as the MCA?

(B) The Decision

It is now the fall of 1997. Peggy Fischer, who earlier this year was elected chair of the Midwestern::Contemporary Art (MCA) board, pored over the messages that her secretary had left on her desk. Almost immediately, Fischer's attention turned to a message marked "urgent" on the very top of the stack. Bob Hatchs, the museum's treasurer, had left a memo stating that the MCA was currently facing a very critical financial situation because a $5 million pledge to the museum had not been honored. After reading Hatchs's memo, Fischer realized the gravity of the MCA's financial situation—without the $5 million promised by Peter Smith, the museum's ability to fulfill its mission and attract important exhibits to its state-of-the-art facility would be jeopardized. The new chairperson was determined to resolve the issue as soon as possible in order to preserve both her and the museum's reputation in the art world as well as the local community.

Peggy Fischer

As a modern art enthusiast, Peggy Fischer collected a wide variety of artifacts ranging from postmodernist paintings to surrealist sculptures. In 1980, her friends in the Chicago art community suggested that she join the MCA, and after several financial contributions to the museum she became a board member. In 1989, after Peter Smith became chairman of the MCA's board and Schmidt became the director, Fischer, like other members, often noticed that there were conflicts between two strong-willed men. Nevertheless, she chose to remain quiet as the heated debates between the two escalated. After Smith left the MCA board and Avery Truman replaced him, Fischer was chosen as the next chairperson because of her ability to establish excellent interpersonal relationships among board members.

Fischer knew that Peter Smith and his wife Catherine had been long-time supporters of the MCA until museum director Keith Schmidt was hired in 1989. After a series of explicit heated debates and covert power struggles between Peter Smith and Keith Schmidt, the Smiths disappeared from the Chicago art scene at the end of 1991 and missed all payments on their $5 million pledge toward the planned new building for the museum.

Like many nonprofit organizations, the MCA typically does not receive the full amount of pledges. Some donors are unable to fulfill pledges because of unexpected financial hardship. Others simply change their giving priorities between the time they sign the letter of intent to give and the point where payment becomes due. Normally a nonprofit would defer obligations based on such a pledge until it was realized, but at the time the Smiths' pledge failed to materialize, the MCA was in a fiscal bind: Construction funding depended on that pledge. In addition, in 1995 while construction was under way, a revision of accounting rules by the Financial Accounting Standards Board (FASB) had big implications for how the MCA could treat the pledge.

The New Building for the MCA

After receiving promises and pledges from a variety of board members and other donors, the MCA board went ahead with construction of a new building for the institution starting in 1993. Not only was the new MCA to be the first project designed in the United States by architect Mattias Lee Bollinger, but it would also be the first building made specifically for the MCA's use since the institution's founding in 1967. With almost seven times the square footage of the museum's previous facility, the new home of the MCA would provide space for installing both temporary exhibitions and works from the permanent collection. The building also would give the MCA a terraced outdoor sculpture garden, a museum store for books and design objects, a café and special events area, and a 15,000-volume art library. In addition, there was to be room for the Gibbons Education Center, which incorporates studio classrooms—or a space suitable for symposia and performances—and a 300-seat auditorium. The new MCA facility opened in mid-1996, about six months before Peggy Fischer became chair of the museum's board.

In 1995, while construction was in progress, revisions to FASB accounting rules forced many nonprofit organizations across the nation to record pledges as income at the time of the pledge. This impacted the MCA greatly because in the past, pledges were not recorded until the actual transfer of money from donor to museum occurred. The new rule forced the MCA to take greater action in enforcing pledges; they needed to keep their accounts receivables low for financial purposes, such as construction loans or bond issuance, while constructing the new facility. Because of this FASB rule revision, lawsuits to collect unpaid pledges became a hot topic among nonprofit organizations across the United States. Edward Able, head of the American Association of Museums representing 8,000 institutions, told reporters,

> We fought the changes made by the FASB to no avail, and the issue has been highly charged for nonprofit groups since that time. We have not polled our members to determine the amounts of the suits or their frequency, but people throughout the art community are hard pressed to cite any instances of museums suing over large pledges.

Today's Board Meeting

Now, in late 1997, the MCA finds itself in a financial crisis because of a high debt load resulting from construction and because of the Smiths' unfulfilled pledge, which by now was to have been fully paid. At a meeting today of the MCA board, Peggy Fischer sought advice from the board about how to proceed The board's chief counsel, board member Richard Lang, suggested that Fischer take legal action against Peter Smith. Lang explained his reasoning:

> From a legal standpoint, we have every reason to believe that the lawsuit will proceed in our interests. In 1990, Peter Smith made a written pledge on behalf of himself and his wife to give an endowment that would help build a new MCA facility. The pledge is legally

binding since we relied on his donations for our financial security and had reasonable expectation that he would indeed fulfill his pledge. We would not have proceeded with the construction of the new building without his pledge. In the court of law, we can make a plea of the reliance damages that we have suffered and, thus, seek remedies from the Smiths.[1]

Lang also cited a high-profile 1994 case involving the Philadelphia Museum of Art. Like the MCA situation, the Philadelphia Museum of Art received a $5 million pledge from one of its donors that was not honored. The donor in question passed away before the transfer of funds, and his estate refused to honor the pledge. Subsequently, the Philadelphia Museum sued the estate, and the two parties reached "an amicable settlement." He recalled another similar case in 1996 where the University of California–Irvine won a lawsuit against a donor who refused to pay up his $1 million pledge. Lang argued that even though the MCA may never receive the $5 million in its entirety, the lawsuit would send a strong message to its prospective donors that the museum takes pledges seriously and relies on them.

Andrew Whitehorse, another board member, agreed with Lang's suggestion. White-horse pointed out that it was unlikely for the MCA to gain other financial resources be-cause a stagnant economy and stock market would not benefit the endowment fund and the amount of donations. "How are we supposed to pay for the new building and the MCA's continuous exhibitions?" Whitehorse asked. He further expressed his concern that the board's long-standing prestige might be hurt if the financial crisis was not han-dled properly and swiftly.

On the other hand, Rich Steiner, a member on the board, objected to Lang's proposed legal strategy, and contended that the crisis would be best resolved through nonlegal avenues. Steiner argued that resorting to lawsuits will increase the MCA's fi-nancial burden due to enormous legal fees from prolonged legal proceedings or failed attempts to win court cases. Jennifer Lee, a longtime MCA board member, concurred:

> The lawsuit will not only irritate and anger the Smiths to the point that they will never voluntarily donate money to us again, but it will also cause other potential donors to view our actions as being insensible. Furthermore, we, the MCA—a nonprofit organization—should not behave like all other greedy businesses that resort to the court of law whenever there is a conflict. We can't be so shortsighted as to focus exclusively on the $5 million. Besides, how would other donors perceive our legal actions? Would they think twice in the future before placing their trust in us? What kind of image will we be sending out to the community?

Another MCA board member and friend of the Smiths, John Stuart, sided with Lee and Steiner by asserting that it would be callous to sue the couple at this time. He explained,

> Although it's Peter and Catherine's moral responsibility to honor their pledge, we should not sue them. This is strictly confidential, but I have recently learned that Peter has been diagnosed with terminal cancer and is undergoing a series of chemotherapy treatments. Pe-ter is now too weak to walk, and Catherine is physically and emotionally distressed to see her husband suffer. I strongly believe that it would be unwise and very insensitive to file a lawsuit against the Smiths. I am sure that they can be reasoned with; now is just not the time to approach them.

After the board meeting, Fischer reviewed the situation and became uncomfortable with several aspects of the legal route. Although she was concerned that the financial crisis may result in the museum's bankruptcy, Fischer feared the implications of a possible lawsuit against the Smiths. Fischer was unable to predict the consequences of taking the legal actions because, with the exception of Philadelphia Museum of Art, no lawsuit involving such a large amount of money had ever been filed by a nonprofit organization (the Philadelphia Museum signed a secrecy agreement barring both parties from discussing their settlement). Furthermore, even though Fischer was not a very close friend of the Smiths, she did work with them for a significant period of time, and was not particularly comfortable with the notion of filing a lawsuit against the couple during such an unfortunate time. Nonetheless, the financial pressure posed by the construction of the new facility was magnifying, and without income, the new facility might be unable to remain open.

As this intense day drew to a close, Fischer glanced at her calendar and noticed that the next board meeting was in five days. She knew that she had to make a decision by the next meeting, but Fischer suspected that decision making was only the first step in handling the situation.

Discussion Questions for Part (B)

1. What alternative approaches could Peggy Fischer use to collect the unfulfilled pledge?

2. Should Fischer involve the board in further discussions leading to a decision about whether or not to file a lawsuit? Or should she formulate a recommendation on her own for the board's next meeting?

3. Do you think the museum should sue the Smiths? Why or why not?

Endnote

1. *Reliance damages* are contract damages placing the injured party in as good a position as he would have been in had the contract terms been met.

500 English Sentences

Scott sat looking out the window, watching a group of boys playing baseball in the school yard. Poor kids, he thought, they are the real losers in all of this. He looked down at a copy of *500 English Sentences* and the endorsement letter on his desk. He glanced at the clock and realized that he had to have an answer for Mr. Honda within the hour. He was feeling very frustrated and stressed from the events of the past 10 days. He decided that he would go to the karate school after work, something that always made him feel better. He sighed as he thought about what he had to do next.

Scott

Scott was 26 years old and had been living in Japan for 18 months. He was born in Auburn, Massachusetts, and had spent most of his life in the United States. Scott's father was a successful entrepreneur who believed that hard work and good old-fashioned principles were the ingredients to success. He always taught his children to stand up for what they believed in and to never sacrifice their values in order to get ahead. Scott's mother was a housewife who took care of the family home and the children. She loved to travel and encouraged Scott's father to take the family abroad every year so that their children would have a better understanding of the world around them.

Scott was a very disciplined student. He was an English major and had been on the dean's honor role for every semester throughout his four years at college. During his senior year, Scott worked as a teaching assistant, grading papers and tutoring students.

Scott started studying karate when he was a junior in high school. He enjoyed the physical workout and the disciplinary aspect of the sport and continued to train throughout his undergraduate years. By the time he was ready to graduate, Scott had earned a third-degree black belt.

> It was through karate that I first became interested in Japan. I thought it would be enlightening to experience Japanese culture and learn more about their ways of thinking. My goal was to one day go over to Japan and train in a Japanese karate dojo (school) and learn from a real karate sensei. My biggest problem was to figure out how to go about doing this. I knew that I didn't have the luxury of just moving to Japan to study karate, and since I didn't speak the language I figured that my chances of working for a company in Japan were about nil.

In the fall of his senior year, Scott saw a poster for the Japan Exchange and Teaching (JET) Program at school that advertised teaching jobs in Japan. He had heard of other students going over to Japan to teach English but had never given any serious thought to a career in teaching, even if only for a short time. To work as an assistant

English teacher on the JET Program, applicants had to have a bachelor's degree and an interest in Japan. Knowledge of Japanese language or a degree in education were not listed as requirements. This was what Scott had been hoping for: an opportunity to go over to Japan to continue his karate under a Japanese instructor as well as a chance to put his English degree to good use. He wrote the address in his notebook and sent for an application that very night.

The Japan Exchange and Teaching (JET) Program
Before the JET Program

The origins of the JET Program can be traced back to 1982. In that year, the Japanese Ministry of Education (Monbusho) initiated a project known as the Monbusho English Fellows (MEF) Program, which hired Americans to work at the local boards of education in order to assist Japanese English teaching consultants who acted as advisers to the Japanese teachers of English in the public schools. The task of the MEFs was to oversee the junior and senior high school English teachers and to assist them with their training. In 1983, the British English Teachers Scheme (BETS) was inaugurated by the Ministry of Education. However, from the outset the British teachers were stationed at schools, and the goals of the program did not only concern English instruction but also sought to increase mutual understanding and improve friendly relations between the peoples of Japan and Britain. While there were some differences between the two programs, both shared a common goal: inviting native English speakers to Japan to assist in improving foreign language instruction.

The Birth of the JET Program

The realization that Japan must open itself more fully to contact with international societies resulted in an awareness of the importance of promoting internationalization and international exchange at the local level. This brought about not only expanded English instruction, but also a rapid increase in exchange programs. Taking these new circumstances into account, the Japanese Ministry of Home Affairs in 1985 released a paper titled "Plans for International Exchange Projects" as part of its priority policy of local governments for the following year. In the paper, the Ministry of Home Affairs proposed a definite course for the internationalization of local governments, which ideally would lead to smoothly functioning cultural exchanges. All of these ideas were finally implemented in a concrete project: the Japan Exchange and Teaching (JET) Program.

The Ministry of Home Affairs abolished the two projects currently in effect (MEF and BETS) and created a new one that was entrusted simultaneously to three ministries: the Ministry of Foreign Affairs, the Ministry of Education, and the Ministry of Home Affairs. However, the concept of appointing local authorities to implement the program and act as host institutions was preserved. While discussions were held with each of the local authorities to work out the details and ensure the smooth implementation of such a massive program, the formation of a cooperative organization for all local governments was expedited.

The Creation of CLAIR

CLAIR, originally the Conference of Local Authorities for International Relations, was established in October 1986 by the *Todofuken* (the 47 prefectures of Japan) and the *Seireishiteitoshi* (the [then] 10 designated cities) as a cooperative organization responsible for implementing the JET Program in conjunction with the three Japanese ministries just named.

CLAIR's Role in the JET Program

To ensure smooth implementation of the JET Program, the three ministries, the local authorities, and CLAIR were all given specific functions. The functions that the conference attempted to fulfill for implementing the JET Program were as follows:

1. Advice and liaison during recruitment and selection.
2. Placement of participants.
3. Participant orientation, conferences.
4. Guidance for local authority host institutions.
5. Participant welfare and counseling.
6. Travel arrangements for participants coming to Japan.
7. Liaison with related groups and institutions.
8. Publications and reference materials.
9. Publicity for the program.

The larger goal behind these functions of the conference was the promotion of international exchange at the local level. Independent of this development, the Council of Local Authorities for International Relations (a publicly endowed foundation) was inaugurated in July 1987. The council's main duty was to study and survey participating nations' local authorities overseas with the ultimate objective being to support local government programs for the promotion of internationalization. By fostering international exchange at the regional level, the council came to assume the same duties as the Conference of Local Authorities for International Relations. It was suggested that both organizations merge since they held information relevant to each other's work and shared the goals of improving work efficiency and performing their tasks more effectively. Moreover, the annual growth of the JET Program led to an increased number of interrelated duties and tasks. Thus it was necessary to strengthen the structure of the Conference of Local Authorities for International Relations.

It was decided that the operations and financial assets of the conference would be assumed by the council, and in August 1989 they were amalgamated, under the acronym of CLAIR, to form a joint organization of local public bodies in Japan to support and promote internationalization at the regional level.

Scott's Acceptance

Scott reviewed the JET information he had received. There were two different positions available: (1) the coordinator for international relations (CIR) and (2) the assistant language teacher (ALT). The first position, although it sounded interesting, was out of the question since knowledge of Japanese was a requirement. Scott applied for the second position because as an English major he felt that he was qualified to assist in the teaching of English. Scott was chosen for an interview and was successful in obtaining an offer to teach English in Japan.

> The JET Program and CLAIR were very good at trying to prepare the participants for their stay in Japan. I attended several workshops and orientations concerning my job in Japan as well as seminars on what to expect living in such a different culture from my own. I remember thinking some of the potential situations they were preparing us for seemed a bit unrealistic and that I would probably never encounter them, but I found out soon enough that Japan and the United States are culturally a world apart, and I was glad to have received the predeparture training. Without it, I would have thought that I had arrived in Wonderland with no idea on how to behave at the tea party.

Scott's Situation in Japan

Scott was sent to a small village on the northern island of Hokkaido, where he taught English at Naka High School. At first, Scott had some difficulties adjusting to living in such a remote place. The people were friendly, yet since they were not accustomed to seeing many foreigners, Scott always felt that he was on display, or that his every move was under scrutiny.

> It was strange being the only non-Japanese person living in the town. I was there to do my job, and study karate, but somehow ended up as the town celebrity. Everyone in town knew everything about me. They all knew where I lived, when I entertained guests. I felt like my every move was monitored. It got so bad that I even had to hang my wash inside my house because people started to tell me that they liked my colorful boxer shorts.
>
> People not only watched what I did, but how I did it. Everyone wanted to know how the American talked, walked, and ate. People asked me daily if I could eat with chopsticks. I made a conscious effort very quickly to blend in as much as I could. It was either that or get angry, and I don't think people were being malicious, they were just overly curious.

The biggest problem that Scott encountered from the start was feelings of incompetence and frustration. The only people in the whole village with whom he could speak without much difficulty were the Japanese English teachers at the high school. If he ran into problems at the bank or supermarket, he was forced to rely on a mixture of basic Japanese and English accompanied by an elaborate display of sign language which more often than not ended in frustration. To overcome the communication problems, Scott began studying Japanese every night at home. He also found a Japanese language teacher at the high school who agreed to tutor him.

> Until I moved to Japan, I never realized how frustrating life can be when you cannot even do the simplest tasks for yourself like read your electric bill or use an automated teller machine. I felt pretty helpless a lot of the time, and no one seemed to understand what I was going through. Whenever I had a problem involving a language or cultural misunderstanding, I would go see Mr. Honda, the head of English, not only because his

English was the best of all of the teachers, but also because he had lived abroad in England and Australia, and I figured that he would be able to understand what I was going through.

Mr. Honda

Mr. Honda was the head of English at Naka High School. He was 46 years old and had been teaching English at various schools in the prefecture for more than 22 years. In his youth, Mr. Honda had studied English at Oxford and had spent two summers in Australia on homestays. His command of spoken English and his vocabulary were quite remarkable. Mr. Honda acted as a mentor to Scott. He considered Scott as his *kohai* (junior) and believed that as a good Japanese manager, it was his duty to guide the young foreigner throughout his stay in Japan. Mr. Honda showed this same kind of paternalistic concern for all of the junior English teachers and counseled them on everything from lesson planning to when they should think about marrying. None of the younger teachers in the English department made any decision without the approval of Mr. Honda. Scott thought that this was a waste of talent and initiative. He knew a couple of young teachers who were very dynamic and had some creative teaching ideas, yet were forced to use the dated teaching methods of Mr. Honda because he was their superior.

Although he never expressed it openly, Mr. Honda did not really like dealing with these young ALTs. He found it insulting to work with such young foreigners, who more often than not had no formal training as English teachers yet were hired to tell him how to do his job better. He did not share in the opinion that these foreign assistants were experts in English teaching just because they could speak the language fluently. Mr. Honda, as well as the other teachers on the staff, had trouble adjusting to the ALTs since they were hired on a yearly contract basis, which was renewable only to a maximum of three years. This left the school barely enough time to get to know an ALT before he or she left and another took over. Mr. Honda also didn't like the fact that these young assistant teachers were earning nearly the same salary as he each month, despite his 22 years of experience.

In spite of his feelings for ALTs in general, Mr. Honda liked Scott. He not only felt that Scott was qualified to be doing the job but also thought that Scott was adapting very well to the Japanese style of management.

Scott works very hard. He shows great enthusiasm for teaching English at our school. He is very pleasant to work with and is making a big effort to learn the Japanese language and ways. It is a pleasure to have such a good teacher on our staff.

Acceptance in the Group

Scott joined the local karate school and began training every night after work.

I felt very much at ease at the karate dojo. Despite the fact that I had no idea what my karate teacher and the other men were saying to me, we seemed to get along very well because we were all there for a common goal: to study karate. I think the other members accepted me into their group because I showed them that I was serious about the sport and had a determination to learn. At first, I saw the other members only at the karate school, but after a few months, they started inviting me to dinners and other social gatherings. Sometimes we even went out drinking after practice. It was good to feel like I was a part of something. I was tired of being treated like the "funny *gaijin*" all the time.

For the first few months, Scott felt isolated at work. Excluding the English teachers, many of his coworkers did not talk to him at all, which made him feel unwelcome at the school. It wasn't until he asked a young English teacher about the situation that she told Scott how several of the teachers were afraid to speak to him because they felt that their English skills were too weak. Scott told the young teacher that it was he who should be embarrassed for not speaking Japanese. After that, Scott made an effort to speak in Japanese, even though his mistakes often made him feel ridiculous and self-conscious. The other teachers slowly began to warm up to Scott and started to converse more with him at school.

Scott went out of his way to get involved at school. He not only taught his courses but also became involved with many of the clubs after school. He ran the English-speaking club and helped coach the karate club. He was also willing to come in on weekends when there was a special event going on at the school.

> I got involved with extracurricular activities at school, not necessarily for altruistic reasons, but I guess because aside from karate, there was really not much for me to do in such a remote place where I could barely speak the language. I guess the other teachers thought that I was different from some of the other foreigners who had worked at Naka High because I was putting in extra time and work. Whatever the reason, they began to treat me like one of the group.

The Move

Scott had been in Japan almost a year and made the decision to renew for another. He asked to be transferred to Satsuki, the capital city of the prefecture, because his girlfriend back in the United States was thinking of coming over to Japan and there would be no work for her in such a small town as the one he was in. The teachers at Naka High were sad to see Scott leave and gave him a huge farewell party at which everyone made speeches saying how they would miss him.

> It was kind of sad to leave Naka High. Once I got to know them, the teachers at Naka were quite a down-to-earth group who treated me like I was one of the family. The problem was that life in such a small town no longer offered what I needed. My girlfriend wanted to come over to Japan and I knew that she could get a job in Satsuki. My karate sensei also told me that if I wanted to test for my fourth-degree black belt, I would get better training at one of the bigger karate dojos in the city, and this was the reason that I came to Japan in the first place.

The city was quite a change for Scott. Since many foreigners lived there—English teachers, university students, and businesspeople—he did not receive the same attention as he had in the village. Compared to the small town, it was like living back in the

United States. Nishi High, the school where Scott was assigned, was not at all like Naka High. Instead, it was a large academic high school where there was a particular emphasis placed on preparing for the rigorous university entrance exam. Only students who scored in the very top percentile were admitted to the best universities in the country, and Nishi prided itself on the number of students who were accepted to Tokyo University, the best in the country.

Scott was not the only foreigner working at this school. John, a 22-year-old from Australia, had just been hired to replace a Canadian woman who had spent two years teaching at the school. John had just graduated with a degree in chemistry, but he had studied Japanese for about seven years before moving to Japan.

One surprise Scott encountered was that Mr. Honda had also been transferred to Nishi High to head their English department. Mr. Honda spoke very highly of Scott to the teachers at Nishi and, as a result, Scott was put in charge of the advanced English class, which was cramming for the university entrance exams.

The English department used a textbook titled *500 English Sentences,* which had been written approximately 10 years before by members of Nishi's staff. The book had become a standard and was used by virtually every high school in the prefecture. The teachers who wrote it were all subsequently promoted to work as advisers at the Satsuki Board of Education. Scott had tried the book in his classes, but thought that it was an inferior text riddled with grammatical inconsistencies, spelling mistakes, and archaic usages of the English language. Although this book was part of the curriculum, Scott refused to use it and instead taught from the other texts. Scott assumed this was not a problem since none of the other teachers ever mentioned the fact that he did not use the text in his classes.

In the Limelight

After three months of working at Nishi, Scott found out that there was going to be a prefecturewide English teachers' convention held at the school. Scott was surprised when the English staff asked him to conduct a demonstration class for one of the seminars. He was told that, in total, about 200 teachers were expected to attend.

Despite initial misgivings and stage fright, Scott's demonstration class was a huge success, and Nishi High received outstanding commendations from all the teachers who attended and from the board of education. The English teachers at Nishi praised Scott for bringing honor to their school. Scott was glad that everything had gone well, but he did not think that he deserved the only credit.

> For various reasons, I was awarded much of the credit for the outstanding commendations, though I felt most of the work had been done by the regular English staff. Anyway, at this point I had built an excellent relationship with the school's staff, and found that this made the whole working situation function much easier, made getting things done possible, and kept me "part of the loop" in decisions in the English department.

Scott began to receive more and more responsibilities at work. The English staff would consult with him on problems big or small concerning the teaching of English. Although Scott and John both arrived at Nishi High at the same time, Scott was considered *sempai* (the senior). Scott attributed this to a combination of his age and the fact that he had already worked one year at another school in Japan.

> It was a bit unnerving that I was given more authority than John, I had been in Japan one year longer than he had and was a few years older, but he was able to speak their language fluently and was a capable teacher. The Japanese English teachers treated me as though I were John's superior and often put me in an awkward position by making John answer to me.

The Dilemma

One afternoon while Scott was sitting at his desk in the staff room, he was approached by several of the Japanese English teachers, including Mr. Honda. Mr. Honda began by inquiring after Scott's health and complimenting him on his students' recent test scores. After several minutes of small talk, Mr. Honda cleared his throat and got to the point. He laid a copy of *500 English Sentences* on Scott's desk and smiled at him. Scott thought that Mr. Honda and the other teachers had finally come to ask him to use the text in his class. "Yes, it's a textbook, and a humdinger at that," said Scott. Scott's comment was met with confusion, nervous laughs, and several coughs. "No," replied Mr. Honda, "We were hoping that you would be so kind as to help us in repairing any errors there might be in this text for republication by the prefecture." Mr. Honda continued saying that Nishi High had been assigned the duty of editing the text and resubmitting it to the publisher for printing. He said that Scott's help would be greatly appreciated since he had been an English major at university and the Japanese teachers already knew that he was a more capable teacher. Mr. Honda also said that they desired Scott's help because he was a native English speaker and he would have an excellent grasp of both current and colloquial usage of the language, something which none of the Japanese English teachers had.

Scott agreed to help them with the project and asked Mr. Honda how soon he wanted the manuscript returned. Again Mr. Honda cleared his throat and said, "Very soon."

"How soon is very soon?" asked Scott. Mr. Honda replied that the manuscript had to be into the publisher within 10 days. Ten days seemed unreasonably short to Scott, so he asked Mr. Honda how long he had known about the project. Mr. Honda replied that the school had been asked to do the project more than six months ago. Not wanting to ask why the English teachers took so long to begin working on the manuscript, Scott took the project and promised to have it back within a few days. Mr. Honda smiled and thanked Scott. Scott went home that night and started working on the project.

> I was glad to have the opportunity to do something productive and lasting. I had hated this text since I had first seen it and had secretly ridiculed the foolish foreigner whose name and recommendation graced its inner cover. I exalted in the opportunity to finally dismember the text and replace the reams of errors with actual functional English.

Scott worked on the manuscript every night for four nights, putting in an average of eight hours of work each night. He returned the text to Mr. Honda on the fifth day, full of red ink: corrections, sample replacement sentences, and explanations as to why the changes were necessary. To Scott's surprise, Mr. Honda did not thank him for the work. Instead, he looked very uncomfortable and smiled nervously as he flipped through the marked pages of the manuscript.

Two days later, Mr. Honda returned to Scott's desk. He praised Scott for his work and reminded him of their mutual indebtedness. He talked about the weather, asked Scott how his karate training was progressing, and inquired about Scott's girlfriend's health. Eventually, Mr. Honda turned the discussion to the manuscript. Apologetically, he said, most of the corrections could not be used. Scott was confused and asked why. Mr. Honda revealed that he had given the corrected manuscript to John to look at and that John had disagreed with some of the corrections. Scott became concerned and asked to see the manuscript to see the contended corrections. Upon reviewing the manuscript, Scott noted three places where John had marked disagreement. John had also noted that the differences with these three sentences were probably due to usage in Australia compared with the United States and that since he was not an English major, like Scott, Scott was probably correct. Mr. Honda agreed that Scott's corrections were valid and went back to his desk.

Mr. Honda returned an hour later to say that despite their earlier conversation all of the corrections could not be used because it was so late in the process and that it would be very troublesome for the publisher to make so many changes.

> By now I was getting frustrated. I told Mr. Honda that he should have thought of this six months ago when he first learned about the project and then asked him which was more important to him, the publisher or the students?

That night, one of the junior members of the Japanese English staff offered Scott a ride home. They discussed various topics, including how much Scott liked living in Japan. The young teacher then told Scott a story involving a junior member of the staff who tried to be helpful by correcting a memo that his boss had written. Since the memo had already been circulated once, the subsequent recirculation with the corrections resulted in a great loss of face for the boss. This resulted in strained relations, even though no offense was intended. By the time the teacher finished his anecdote, they had already arrived at Scott's house. He thanked the teacher for the ride, then got out of the car.

The next day, Scott did not discuss the topic of the manuscript and the situation seemed to have resolved itself. He assumed that Mr. Honda would go ahead and not use his changes, but he was unsure of what he could do about it.

After a few days of silence between Scott and the English teachers, Mr. Honda and the same group of English teachers came over to Scott's desk. This time they looked extremely nervous and spoke in very polite *keigo* (extremely respectful Japanese) that Scott could barely follow. Upon reaching some sort of consensus among themselves, they presented Scott with a single sheet of paper. On it was the verbatim endorsement of the previous issue of *500 English Sentences* with a blank line and Scott's name typed under the blank. "Would you be so kind as to sign this?" asked Mr. Honda. Scott was shocked. He thought the issue was closed when he had made a fuss about the corrections.

> I looked at the group and plainly and directly said that there was no way that I would sign such a statement since I felt that the text was substandard and that my integrity as a teacher would be compromised by signing the statement.

Scott suggested that Mr. Honda ask John to sign the endorsement, but Mr. Honda replied that due to his seniority, English degree, and good association with Nishi High, the board of education had personally asked for Scott's signature. Mr. Honda then added that he needed to send it in to the publisher by 5:00 p.m. that same day.

What to Do

Mr. Honda went back to his own desk, and Scott sat thinking about what he should do. All he could think about was having his name endorsing a text that he considered to be substandard. He didn't see how he could knowingly sign his name to a project that he knew was flawed.

Sick Leave

Kelly tried to control her anger as she thought about her supervisor. She couldn't understand why he was being so unreasonable. Maybe to him it was only a couple days of paid leave and not worth fighting over, but to her it meant the difference between being able to go on vacation during Golden Week or having to stay home.[1] She looked at her contract and the phone number of CLAIR on her desk. She wasn't the only person in the office affected by this. She sat and thought about how she should proceed.

Kelly

Kelly was 22 years old and had been working for the past six months at the Soto Board of Education office in Japan. This was her first job after graduating from college with a degree in management, and she was really excited to finally be in the real world.

Kelly was born in Calgary and had spent most of her life in Alberta, Canada. Kelly's father was a successful lawyer in Calgary, and her mother was a high school English teacher. Kelly had an older sister, Laurel, 27, who had just passed the bar exam and was working for a corporate law firm in Edmonton.

Kelly had studied Japanese in high school and in university and spoke and wrote the language quite well. When she was 15 years old, Kelly spent four months in Japan on a school exchange. She had enjoyed the time she spent there and always planned to return one day. Upon graduating from high school, Kelly went to the University of Alberta, in Edmonton, to study management.

During her final year at the university, Kelly heard some of her friends talking about the Japan Exchange and Teaching (JET) Program. She was told that it was quite easy to get accepted—all an applicant needed was a university degree and an interest in Japan—and that it would be a great way to make money and see another part of the world. Kelly would have her degree by the end of the year and thought that having lived in Japan and knowing the language showed enough interest to have her application considered. Kelly thought that a year or two in Japan after her management degree would improve her Japanese and give her more of a competitive advantage when she returned to Canada to begin her career. She also thought that it would be a great way to make money and have some fun before she came home to start a real job. She asked her friend how she could apply to the program and returned home that night to work on her résumé.

Source: This case was written by Laura Turek. Copyright ©2006 by Laura Turek. Used with permission. This case was prepared as a basis for classroom discussion, not to illustrate either the effective or ineffective management of an administrative situation.

The Japan Exchange and Teaching (JET) Program

Before the JET Program

The origins of the JET Program can be traced back to 1982. In that year, the Japanese Ministry of Education (Monbusho) initiated a project known as the Monbusho English Fellows (MEF) Program, which hired Americans to work at the local boards of education in order to assist Japanese English teaching consultants who acted as advisors to the Japanese teachers of English in the public schools. The task of the MEFs was to oversee the junior and senior high school English teachers and to assist them with their training. In 1983, the British English Teachers Scheme (BETS) was inaugurated by the Ministry of Education. However, from the outset the British teachers were stationed at schools, and the goals of the program did not only concern English instruction but also sought to increase mutual understanding and improve friendly relations between the peoples of Japan and Britain. While there were some differences between the two programs, both shared a common goal: inviting native English speakers to Japan to assist in improving foreign language instruction.

The Birth of the JET Program

The realization that Japan must open itself more fully to contact with international societies resulted in an awareness of the importance of promoting internationalization and international exchange at the local level. This brought about not only expanded English instruction, but also a rapid increase in exchange programs. Taking these new circumstances into account, the Japanese Ministry of Home Affairs in 1985 released a paper titled "Plans for International Exchange Projects" as part of its priority policy of local governments for the following year. In the paper, the Ministry of Home Affairs proposed a definite course for the internationalization of local governments, which ideally would lead to smoothly functioning cultural exchanges. All of these ideas were finally implemented in a concrete project: the Japan Exchange and Teaching (JET) Program.

The Ministry of Home Affairs abolished the two projects currently in effect (MEF and BETS) and created a new one that was entrusted simultaneously to three ministries: the Ministry of Foreign Affairs, the Ministry of Education, and the Ministry of Home Affairs. However, the concept of appointing local authorities to implement the program and act as host institutions was preserved. While discussions were held with each of the local authorities to work out the details and ensure the smooth implementation of such a massive program, the formation of a cooperative organization for all local government was expedited.

The Creation of CLAIR

CLAIR, originally the Conference of Local Authorities for International Relations, was established in October 1986 by the *Todofuken* (the 47 prefectures of Japan) and the *Seireishiteitoshi* (the [then] 10 designated cities) as a cooperative organization responsible for implementing the JET Program in conjunction with the three Japanese ministries just named.

CLAIR's Role in the JET Program

To ensure smooth implementation of the JET Program, the three ministries, the local authorities, and CLAIR were all given specific functions. The functions that the conference attempted to fulfill for implementing the JET Program were as follows:

1. Advice and liaison during recruitment and selection.
2. Placement of participants.
3. Participant orientation, conferences.
4. Guidance for local authority host institutions.
5. Participant welfare and counseling.
6. Travel arrangements for participants coming to Japan.
7. Liaison with related groups and institutions.
8. Publications and reference materials.
9. Publicity for the program.

The larger goal behind these functions of the conference was the promotion of international exchange at the local level. Independent of this development, the Council of Local Authorities for International Relations (a public endowed foundation) was inaugurated in July 1987. The council's main duty was to study and survey participating nations' local authorities overseas with the ultimate objective being to support local government programs for the promotion of internationalization. By fostering international exchange at the regional level, the council came to assume the same duties as the Conference of Local Authorities for International Relations. It was suggested that both organizations merge since they held information relevant to each other's work and shared the goals of improving work efficiency and performing their tasks more effectively. Moreover, the annual growth of the JET Program led to an increased number of interrelated duties and tasks. Thus it was necessary to strengthen the structure of the Conference of Local Authorities for International Relations.

It was decided that the operations and financial assets of the conference would be assumed by the council, and in August 1989 they were amalgamated, under the acronym of CLAIR, to form a joint organization of local public bodies in Japan to support and promote internationalization at the regional level.

Counseling System of the JET Program (Figure 1)

1. *Role of the host institution:* Basic problems that JET participants faced during their stay in Japan were addressed by the host institution. If a JET had a complaint or a problem at work or in his or her private life, the JET could alert his or her supervisor, who took up the matter and attempted to solve it.

2. *Role of CLAIR:* Problems or difficulties that JET Program participants faced were as a rule dealt with by host institutions. However, if the issues were difficult to solve at this level, or if they concerned grievances between the JET participant and the host institution, CLAIR employed a number of non-Japanese program coordinators who would intervene and respond directly to participants' needs.

FIGURE 1 | Counseling System

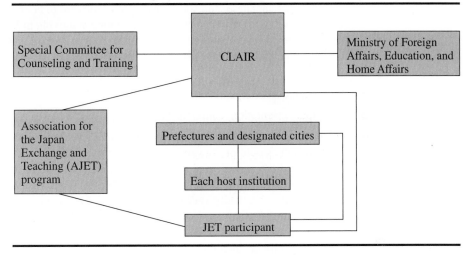

CLAIR would then step in on behalf of the JET participant and work to solve the problems with the host institution.

3. *The Special Committee for Counseling and Training:* The Special Committee for Counseling and Training consisted of the staff members of the three ministries (Foreign Affairs, Home Affairs, and Education), embassies of the participating countries, and host institutions. It took charge of orientation, conferences, public welfare, and counseling. If necessary, it answered the questions and concerns of the JET participants.

AJET

The Association for the Japan Exchange and Teaching (AJET) Program was an independent, self-supporting organization created by JET Program participants, whose elected officers were all volunteers. Membership in AJET was also voluntary. AJET provided members with information about working and living in Japan and provided a support network for members at the local, regional, and national levels. Many Japanese and JETs considered AJET to be the union of the JET Program participants.

The First Job

Kelly looked over the information she received from the JET Program. There were two different positions available: (1) the coordinator for international relations (CIR) and (2) the assistant language teacher (ALT). The first position sounded quite interesting to Kelly since applicants were required to have a functional knowledge of Japanese. ALTs, on the other hand, were not required to know any Japanese before arriving in Japan. She realized that her odds of getting accepted were greater if she applied to the second position since almost 600 ALTs were selected across Canada, compared with only 25 CIRs. Kelly was chosen for a CIR interview but in the end was offered a position as an ALT.

At first she was a little disappointed, but then she reminded herself that her original goal was to perfect her Japanese, and she started to look forward to her trip to Japan.

Kelly received a lot of information about working and living in Japan from CLAIR. CLAIR also offered several predeparture training sessions and orientations about life in Japan and its potential problems, but she decided not to attend because after four months in Japan she already knew what to expect.

The Placement

Kelly was sent to Soto, a medium-sized city on the island of Shikoku. Kelly found the area a far cry from Osaka, where she had stayed the previous time she was in Japan. Soto was, in Kelly's opinion, "a small provincial town, stuck in the middle of nowhere." She had enjoyed the activity and nightlife of Osaka and, except for sports, her only entertainment options in Soto were one movie theater, several pachinko parlors,[2] and scores of karaoke bars. Kelly very quickly developed the habit of going away on the weekends to tour different parts of the island. She would also use her holidays to take advantage of visiting parts of Japan that she might never again get a chance to see. After a few months, Kelly decided that Soto was at least a good place to improve her Japanese since not many people spoke English very well, and only a few other foreigners lived there.

Kelly worked at the board of education office three days a week and visited schools the other two days to help with their English programs. There were three other JET participants who worked in the same office: Mark, 27, another Canadian; Andrea, 26, an American; and Suzanne, 25, from Great Britain. Like Kelly, Suzanne had been in Japan for only the past six months, while Mark and Andrea had been working there for a year and a half. Kelly was on good terms with the other JETs in the office, although she was closest with Suzanne since they had both arrived in Japan at the same time and had met at their orientation in Tokyo.

Although Kelly had lived in Japan before, this was the first time she had worked in a Japanese office. She had learned about Japanese work habits in a cross-cultural management class at the university, yet she was still surprised at how committed the Japanese were to their jobs. The workday began each morning at 8:30 with a staff meeting and officially ended each night at 5:00 p.m., yet no one left the office before 7:00 or 8:00 p.m., The Japanese also came in on Saturdays, which Kelly thought was absurd since it left the employees with only one day a week to relax or spend time with their families.

Kelly and the other JETs in the office had a standard North American contract given to them by CLAIR which stipulated hours, number of vacation days, amount of sick leave, and so on (Figure 2). The contract stated that the JET participants only worked from Monday to Friday until 5:00 p.m. and did not mention working on Saturdays. Neither Kelly nor the other foreigners ever put in extra hours at the office, nor were they ever asked to do so.

Kelly's supervisor was Mr. Higashi. At first Kelly thought that he was very kind and helpful because he had picked her and Suzanne up from the airport and had arranged their housing before they arrived in Japan. Mr. Higashi even took the two women shopping to help them buy necessary items like bedding and dishes so they did not have to be without, even for one night.

FIGURE 2 | Contract of English Teaching Engagement

Article 11: Paid Leave

Section 1

During the period of employment and with the approval of his/her supervisor, the JET participant may use 20 paid holidays individually or consecutively.

Section 2

When the JET participant wishes to make use of one of the above-mentioned paid holidays,
he/she shall inform his/her supervisor three days in advance. Should the JET participant wish
to use more than three paid holidays in succession, he/she is required to inform his/her supervisor one month in advance.

Article 12: Special Holidays

Section 1

The JET participant shall be entitled to special holidays under the following circumstances:

1. Sick leave—the period of serious illness or injury resulting in an acknowledged inability
   to work.
2. Bereavement—the period of 14 consecutive days, including Sundays and national holidays, immediately after the loss of father, mother, or spouse.
3. Natural disaster—the period the board of education deems necessary in the event of destruction of or serious damage to the JET participant's place of residence.
4. Transportation system failure—the period until the said problem has been resolved.

Section 2

Under the conditions of Article 12, Section 1 (1), above, the JET participant may take not
more than 20 days of consecutive sick leave. Moreover, if the interval between two such periods of sick leave is less than one week, those two periods shall be regarded as continuous.

Section 3

The special holidays noted above in Article 12, Section 1, are paid holidays.

Article 17: Procedure for Taking (Sick) Leave

Section 1

When the JET participant wishes to make use of the special holidays/leave specified in Article 12, Section 1, he/she must apply and receive consent from his/her supervisor before taking the requested holidays. If circumstances prevent the JET participant from making
necessary application beforehand, he/she should do so as soon as conditions permit it.

Section 2

In the event of the JET participant taking three or more consecutive days of sick leave,
he/she must submit a doctor's certificate. The board of education may require the JET participant to obtain the said medical certificate from a medical practitioner specified by the board.

Mr. Higashi

Mr. Higashi was born and had lived all of his life in Soto. He was 44 years old and had
been teaching high school English in and around Soto for more than 20 years. Two years
ago, Mr. Higashi was promoted to work as an adviser to all English teachers at the Soto
Board of Education. This was a career-making move, and one that placed him on the
track to becoming a school principal.

This new position at the board of education made Mr. Higashi the direct supervisor
over the foreign JET participants in the office, as well as making him responsible for

their actions. He had worked with them before when he was still teaching in the schools, but since they only came once a week to his school, he had never had the chance to get to know any of them really well.

Mr. Higashi found it very difficult to work with JETs. Since they were hired on a one-year contract basis, renewable only to a maximum of three, he had already seen several come and go. He also considered it inconvenient that Japanese was not a requirement for the JET participants because, since he was the only person in the office who could speak English, he found that he wasted a lot of his time working as an interpreter and helping the foreigners do simple everyday tasks like reading electric bills and opening a bank account. Despite this, he did his best to treat the foreign assistants as he would any other *kohai,* or subordinate, by nurturing their careers and acting as a father to them, since he knew what was best for them. Mr. Higashi was aware that his next promotion was due not only to his own performance but also to how well he interacted with his subordinates, so he worked hard to be a good mentor.

Mr. Higashi took an instant liking to Kelly because she spoke Japanese well and had already lived in Japan. Although she was the youngest of the four ALTs, he hoped that she would guide the others and assumed that she would not be the source of any problems for him.

The ALTs' Opinion of Mr. Higashi

At first, Mr. Higashi seemed fine. All of the ALTs sat in two rows with their desks facing each other, as they used to do in grade school, with Mr. Higashi's desk facing Kelly's. The foreigners all agreed that Mr. Higashi acted more like a father than a boss. He continually asked Kelly and Suzanne how they were enjoying Japanese life and kept encouraging them to immerse themselves in Japanese culture. He left brochures on Kelly's desk for courses in flower arranging and tea ceremony and even one on Japanese cooking. At first Kelly found this rather amusing, but she soon tired of it and started to get fed up with this constant pressure to "sign up" for Japanese culture. What she resented the most was that Mr. Higashi kept insisting she try activities that were traditionally considered a woman's domain. Not that she had anything against flowers, but if she had been a man, she knew that Mr. Higashi would not have hassled her this much to fit in. She knew that Japanese society was a male-dominated one. On her first day at the office, Kelly had looked around and noticed that there were no Japanese women who had been promoted to such a senior level within the board of education. The only women who worked there were young and single "office ladies" or secretaries. Although they were all very sweet young women, Kelly was not about to become one of them and "retire" if and when she found a husband.

Kelly had been very active in sports back in Canada and bought herself a mountain bike when she arrived in Japan so that she could go for rides in the country. At Suzanne's encouragement, Kelly joined a local Kendo club. She had seen this Japanese style of fencing before back in Calgary, and had always been attracted to the fast movements and interesting uniforms. Kelly hoped that Mr. Higashi would be satisfied that she was finally getting involved in something traditionally Japanese and leave her alone.

On top of his chauvinistic attitudes, Kelly didn't think much of Mr. Higashi as a supervisor. If Kelly or any of the other foreigners had a problem or question concerning living in Japan, he would either ignore them or give them information that they later found out was incorrect. Andrea told Kelly that she stopped going to Mr. Higashi when she had problems and instead consulted the office lady, since she was always able to help her. Andrea had even joked that the office lady should be their supervisor because she was by far more effective than Mr. Higashi.

As far as Suzanne was concerned, Mr. Higashi was utterly exasperating. He was forever arranging projects and conferences for the ALTs to participate in, then changing his mind and canceling at the last minute without bothering to tell them. He would also volunteer the ALTs to work on special assignments over the holiday periods and then get angry when they told him that they had previous plans and were unable to go. Suzanne recalled that one week before the Christmas vacation, Mr. Higashi announced that he had arranged for her to visit a junior high school. Suzanne informed him that while she would love to go, it was impossible since she had already booked the time off and had arranged a holiday to Seoul, Korea. Mr. Higashi got angry and told her that he and the board of education would lose face if she didn't attend. Suzanne told Mr. Higashi that losing face would not have been an issue if he had told her about the visit in advance so she could have prepared for it. As a result, Suzanne lost all respect for Mr. Higashi as a manager and continually challenged his authority. Whenever a problem arose, she was quick to remind him that things were very different and much better in Great Britain.

Mark also had difficulties with Mr. Higashi. Mark was not much of a group player and resented Mr. Higashi's constantly telling him what to do. He preferred to withdraw and work on his own. He didn't like Mr. Higashi's paternalistic attitude. He just wanted to be treated like a normal, capable employee and be given free rein to do his work. As a show of his independence, Mark refused to join in on any of the "drinking meetings" after work.

The Japanese Opinion of the ALTs

The other Japanese employees in the office found it difficult to work with the ALTs because, as far as they were concerned, the ALTs were never there long enough to become part of the group. It seemed like just after they got to know one ALT, he or she left and was replaced by another. Another problem was that since the foreigners usually did not speak Japanese, communication with them was extremely frustrating.

The biggest problem that the employees at the board of education office had with the ALTs was that they were so young and inexperienced. All of the men in the office had worked a minimum of 20 years to reach this stage in their careers, only to find themselves working side by side with foreigners who had recently graduated from college. To make matters worse, these young foreigners were also hired to advise them how to do their jobs better. The employees were also aware that the ALTs earned practically the same salary as their supervisor each month.

The Japanese employees did not consider the ALTs to be very committed workers. They never stayed past 5:00 p.m. on weekdays, and never came to work on the weekends even though the rest of the office did. It seemed as though the ALTs were rarely at the office. The ALTs also made it very clear that they had a contract that allowed them vacation days, and they made sure that they used every single day. The Japanese employees, on the other hand, rarely ever made use of their vacation time and knew that if they took holidays as frequently as the foreigners, they could return to find that their desk had been cleared.

The Incident

Kelly woke up one Monday morning with a high fever and a sore throat. She phoned Mr. Higashi to let him know that she wouldn't be coming in that day and possibly not the next. Mr. Higashi asked if she needed anything and told her to relax and take care of herself. Before he hung up, Mr. Higashi told her that when she came back to the office, to make sure to bring in a doctor's note. Kelly was annoyed. The last thing she wanted to do was to get out of bed and go to the clinic for a simple case of the flu. As she was getting dressed she thought she was being treated like a schoolgirl by being forced to bring in a note.

Two days later, Kelly returned to the office with the note from a physician in her hand. Andrea informed her that Mark and Suzanne had also been sick and that she had been by herself in the office. She also said that Mr. Higashi was suspicious that the three of them had been sick at the same time and had commented that he knew that foreigners sometimes pretended to be sick in order to create longer weekends. Kelly was glad that she had gone to the doctor and got a note so she could prove that she was really sick. Kelly said good morning to Mr. Higashi and gave him her note. He took it from her without so much as looking at it and threw it onto a huge pile of incoming mail on his desk. He asked her if she was feeling better and then went back to his work.

At midmorning, the accountant came over to Kelly's desk and asked her to sign some papers. Kelly reached for her pen and started to sign automatically until she noticed that she was signing for two days of paid leave and not sick leave. She pointed out the error to the accountant, who told her that there had not been a mistake. Kelly told the accountant to come back later and went over to speak with Mr. Higashi. To her surprise, Mr. Higashi said that there had been no mistake and that this was standard procedure in Japan. He said that typical Japanese employees normally did not make use of their vacation time due to their great loyalty to the company. If an employee became sick, he often used his paid vacation first out of respect for his employers.

Kelly responded that this was fine for Japanese employees, but since she was not Japanese, she preferred to do things the Canadian way. Mr. Higashi replied that since she was in Japan, maybe she should start doing things the Japanese way. Kelly turned away and looked at Andrea, not believing what had just happened.

The next day, both Mark and Suzanne returned to the office only to find themselves in the same predicament as Kelly. Suzanne called Mr. Higashi a lunatic and Mark chose to stop speaking to him altogether. Kelly was furious that they were being forced to waste two of their vacation days when they were guaranteed sick leave. She threw the JET contract on Mr. Higashi's desk and pointed out the section that stipulated the number of sick days they were entitled to and demanded that he honor their contract as written.

Mr. Higashi looked extremely agitated and said that he had to go to a very important meeting and would discuss the situation later. The accountant reappeared with the papers for the three ALTs to sign, but they all refused. Suzanne started to complain about Mr. Higashi's incompetence, while Mark complained about the Japanese style of management. Suzanne said that it was a shame that none of them had bothered to join AJET, for wasn't this the kind of problem that unions were supposed to handle? Kelly stared at the contract on her desk and said that they could take it to a higher level and involve CLAIR. Andrea said that things could get ugly and people could lose face if it went that far. Kelly took her agenda out of her desk and started looking for CLAIR's phone number.

Discussion Questions

1. What should Kelly and the other ALTs do now?

2. Why did conflict occur? How could it have been prevented?

Endnotes

1. Golden Week is the period from April 29 to May 5, in which there are four Japanese national holidays. Many Japanese employees and their families take advantage of this period to go on vacation.

2. *Pachinko* is a Japanese-style game of chance that resembles a cross between pinball and a slot machine. It is a very popular pastime among certain groups and, like any form of gambling, can be quite lucrative.

The Personal Bargaining Inventory

Introduction

One way for negotiators to learn more about themselves, and about others in a negotiating context, is to clarify their own personal beliefs and values about the negotiation process and their style as negotiators. The questionnaire in this section can help you clarify perceptions of yourself on several dimensions related to negotiation—winning and losing, cooperation and competition, power and deception—and your beliefs about how a person "ought" to negotiate. Your instructor is likely to ask you to share your responses with others after you complete the questionnaire.

Advance Preparation

Complete the Personal Bargaining Inventory Questionnaire in this exercise. Bring the inventory to class.

Personal Bargaining Inventory Questionnaire

The questions in this inventory are designed to measure your responses to your perceptions of human behavior in situations of bargaining and negotiation. Statements in the first group ask you about *your own behavior* in bargaining; statements in the second group ask you to judge *people's behavior in general*.

Part I: Rating Your Own Behavior

For each statement, please indicate how much the statement is *characteristic of you* on the following scale:

1 Strongly uncharacteristic
2 Moderately uncharacteristic
3 Mildly uncharacteristic
4 Neutral, no opinion
5 Mildly characteristic
6 Moderately characteristic
7 Strongly characteristic

Rate each statement on the seven-point scale by writing in one number closest to your personal judgment of yourself:

Rating	Statement
_____	1. I am sincere and trustworthy at all times. I will not lie, for whatever ends.
_____	2. I would refuse to bug the room of my opponent.
_____	3. I don't particularly care what people think of me. Getting what I want is more important than making friends.
_____	4. I am uncomfortable in situations where the rules are ambiguous and there are few precedents.

Source: Adapted from an exercise developed by Bert Brown and Norman Berkowitz.

Personal Bargaining Inventory Questionnaire (*continued*)

Rating	Statement
_____	5. I prefer to deal with others on a one-to-one basis rather than as a group.
_____	6. I can lie effectively. I can maintain a poker face when I am not telling the truth.
_____	7. I pride myself on being highly principled. I am willing to stand by those principles no matter what the cost.
_____	8. I am a patient person. As long as an agreement is finally reached, I do not mind slow-moving arguments.
_____	9. I am a good judge of character. When I am being deceived, I can spot it quickly.
_____	10. My sense of humor is one of my biggest assets.
_____	11. I have above-average empathy for the views and feelings of others.
_____	12. I can look at emotional issues in a dispassionate way. I can argue strenuously for my point of view, but I put the dispute aside when the argument is over.
_____	13. I tend to hold grudges.
_____	14. Criticism doesn't usually bother me. Any time you take a stand, people are bound to disagree, and it's all right for them to let you know they don't like your stand.
_____	15. I like power. I want it for myself, to do with what I want. In situations where I must share power I strive to increase my power base, and lessen that of my co–power holder.
_____	16. I like to share power. It is better for two or more to have power than it is for power to be in just one person's hands. The balance of shared power is important to effective functioning of any organization because it forces participation in decision making.
_____	17. I enjoy trying to persuade others to my point of view.
_____	18. I am not effective at persuading others to my point of view when my heart isn't really in what I am trying to represent.
_____	19. I love a good old, knockdown, drag-out verbal fight. Conflict is healthy, and open conflict where everybody's opinion is aired is the best way to resolve differences of opinion.
_____	20. I hate conflict and will do anything to avoid it—including giving up power over a situation.
_____	21. In any competitive situation, I like to win. Not just win, but win by the biggest margin possible.
_____	22. In any competitive situation, I like to win. I don't want to clobber my opponent, just come out a little ahead.
_____	23. The only way I could engage conscientiously in bargaining would be by dealing honestly and openly with my opponents.

Part II: Rating People's Behavior in General

For each statement, please indicate how much you agree with the statement on the following scale:

1 Strongly disagree

2 Moderately disagree

3 Mildly disagree

4 Neutral, no opinion

5 Mildly agree

6 Moderately agree

7 Strongly agree

Think about what you believe makes people effective negotiators. Rate each statement on the seven-point scale by writing in one number closest to your judgment of what makes an excellent negotiator:

Rating	Statement

_____ 24. If you are too honest and trustworthy, most people will take advantage of you.

_____ 25. Fear is a stronger persuader than trust.

_____ 26. When one is easily predictable, one is easily manipulated.

_____ 27. The appearance of openness in your opponent should be suspect.

_____ 28. Make an early minor concession; the other side may reciprocate on something you want later on.

_____ 29. Personality and the ability to judge people and persuade them to your point of view (or to an acceptable compromise) are more important than knowledge and information about the issues at hand.

_____ 30. Silence is golden—it's the best reply to a totally unacceptable offer.

_____ 31. Be the aggressor. You must take the initiative if you are going to accomplish your objectives.

_____ 32. One should avoid frequent use of a third party.

_____ 33. Honesty and openness are necessary to reach equitable agreement.

_____ 34. It is important to understand one's values prior to bargaining.

_____ 35. Be calm. Maintaining your cool at all times gives you an unquestionable advantage. Never lose your temper.

_____ 36. Keep a poker face; never act pleased as terms are agreed upon.

_____ 37. A good negotiator must be able to see the issues from the opponent's point of view.

_____ 38. An unanswered threat will be read by your opponent as weakness.

_____ 39. In bargaining, winning is the most important consideration.

_____ 40. The best outcome in bargaining is one that is fair to all parties.

_____ 41. Most results in bargaining can be achieved through cooperation.

_____ 42. Principles are all well and good, but sometimes you have to compromise your principles to achieve your goals.

_____ 43. You should never try to exploit your adversary's personal weakness.

_____ 44. A member of a bargaining team is morally responsible for the strategies and tactics employed by that team.

_____ 45. Good ends justify the means. If you know you're right and your goal is worthy, you needn't be concerned too much about *how* your goal is achieved.

_____ 46. Honesty means openness, candor, telling all, and not withholding pertinent information, not exaggerating emotion. One should always be honest during bargaining.

_____ 47. Imposing personal discomfort on an opponent is not too high a price to pay for success in negotiation.

_____ 48. Regardless of personal considerations, team members should accept any role assigned to them by the bargaining team.

_____ 49. There is no need to deal completely openly with your adversaries. In bargaining as in life, what they don't know won't hurt them.

_____ 50. There is nothing wrong with lying to an opponent in a bargaining situation as long as you don't get caught.

The SINS II Scale

Introduction

The purpose of the SINS* II scale is to inquire about your general disposition toward ethical issues in negotiation. It will help you determine your views on a range of ethical and unethical negotiation tactics. The instructor will explain how to score and interpret this questionnaire.

Advance Preparation

Complete the SINS II scale as specified by your instructor.

Incidents in Negotiation Questionnaire

This questionnaire is part of research study on how negotiators decide when certain strategies and tactics are ethical and appropriate in negotiations.

In completing this questionnaire, *please try to be as candid as you can about what you think is appropriate and acceptable to do.* You are being asked about tactics that are controversial; however, your responses on this questionnaire are completely anonymous, and no one will ever know your individual responses.

You will be asked to consider a list of tactics that negotiators sometimes use. You should consider these tactics in the context of a *situation in which you will be negotiating for something that is very important to you and your business.* For each tactic, you will be asked to indicate how appropriate the tactic would be to use in this situation. Then assign a rating to each tactic, evaluating how appropriate it would be to use this tactic in the context specified above, based on the following scale:

1	2	3	4	5	6	7
Not at all appropriate			Somewhat appropriate			Very appropriate

(If you have any need to explain your rating on a tactic, please do so in the margin or at the end of the questionnaire.)

Rating

---

1. Promise that good things will happen to your opponent if he/she gives you what you want, even if you know that you can't (or won't) deliver these things when the other's cooperation is obtained. ____

2. Get the other party to think that you like him/her personally despite the fact that you don't really. ____

3. Intentionally misrepresent information to your opponent in order to strengthen your negotiating arguments or position. ____

4. Strategically express anger toward the other party in a situation where you are not really angry. ____

*SINS stands for *Self-Reported Inappropriate Negotiation Strategies.*
Source: Questionnaire developed by Robert Robinson, Roy J. Lewicki, and Eileen Donahue, 1998. Modified by Roy J. Lewicki, 2001, using items developed by Bruce Barry. Used with permission of the developers.

Incidents in Negotiation Questionnaire (*continued*)

	Rating
5. Attempt to get your opponent fired from his/her position so that a new person will take his/her place.	____
6. Intentionally misrepresent the nature of negotiations to your constituency in order to protect delicate discussions that have occurred.	____
7. Express sympathy with the other party's plight although in truth you don't care about their problems.	____
8. Gain information about an opponent's negotiating position by paying your friends, associates, and contacts to get this information for you.	____
9. Feign a melancholy mood in order to get the other party to think you are having a bad day.	____
10. Make an opening demand that is far greater than what you really hope to settle for.	____
11. Pretend to be disgusted at an opponent's comments.	
12. Convey a false impression that you are in absolutely no hurry to come to a negotiated agreement, thereby trying to put time pressure on your opponent to concede quickly.	____
13. Give the other party the false impression that you are very disappointed with how things are going.	____
14. In return for concessions from your opponent now, offer to make future concessions which you know you will not follow through on.	____
15. Threaten to make your opponent look weak or foolish in front of a boss or others to whom he/she is accountable, even if you know that you won't actually carry out the threat.	____
16. Deny the validity of information which your opponent has that weakens your negotiating position, even though that information is true and valid.	____
17. Give the other party the (false) impression that you care about his/her personal welfare.	____
18. Intentionally misrepresent the progress of negotiations to your constituency in order to make your own position appear stronger.	____
19. Talk directly to the people whom your opponent reports to, or is accountable to, and tell them things that will undermine their confidence in your opponent as a negotiator.	____
20. Stimulate fear on your part so that the other party will think you are tense about negotiating.	____
21. Gain information about an opponent's negotiating position by cultivating his/her friendship through expensive gifts, entertaining, or "personal favors."	____
22. Pretend to be furious at your opponent.	____
23. Make an opening demand so high/low that it seriously undermines your opponent's confidence in his/her ability to negotiate a satisfactory settlement.	____
24. Guarantee that your constituency will uphold the settlement reached, although you know that they will likely violate the agreement later.	____
25. Gain information about an opponent's negotiating position by trying to recruit or hire one of the opponent's teammates (on the condition that the teammate brings confidential information with him/her).	____

Six Channels of Persuasion Survey

Introduction

A very important element of negotiation is persuasion—getting others to see, understand, and accept your point of view. Some people rely on a very limited set of persuasive strategies, while others use different styles in different situations. Understanding your own preferred approaches to persuasion is a first step in learning how to adapt styles to meet different persuasive challenges, in negotiation encounters as well as in other social and professional settings.

This instrument is a tool for assessing two things:

1. the persuasive strategies with which you are personally most comfortable, and

2. the strategies that you feel are necessary to get ahead.

Regarding the second—strategies needed to succeed—the survey will asks you to describe what you think is necessary "in your organization." If you are not currently employed, then respond in terms of the *last organization* where you worked. If you haven't worked full-time in a "real job," then base your responses on the strategies you believe are necessary in a *typical* corporation or workplace.

Procedure

1. Complete the Six Channels Survey.

2. Your instructor will provide instructions for scoring the survey, as well as information about the questionnaire and what it measures.

Directions

Without giving the matter too much thought (and without revising your answers for any reason!), please select the statement in each pair below that *most accurately* describes what you do to exercise influence. Pick *one statement* in each pair of statements and record the letter associated with that statement in the "I select ___" space.

There are two columns for recording your choices:

- Column 1 is for the statement that describes *what you feel you must do in your organization to be effective most of the time.*

- Column 2 is for the statement that describes *what you would feel more comfortable doing* and would prefer to do if you had complete freedom to act as you would like.

Source: The Art of Woo: Using Strategic Persuasion to Sell Your Ideas, by G. Richard Shell and Mario Moussa. New York: Penguin, 2007. Used with permission.

For both columns, select the statement you think is *more accurate*—even if you think neither statement is very accurate or both are very accurate. If you do not currently work for an organization, you can skip Column 1 and record your choices only in Column 2.

Please note that you can select the same statement for both columns if what you generally do at work to influence others is also what you prefer doing.

Warning: Do not pick the statement you "ought" to agree with—just pick the one your gut tells you is more accurate most of the time. In addition, some statements repeat, but you should not worry about answering consistently. Just keep going. All answers are equally "correct."

Survey		
	Column 1 What I must do to be effective within my organization	Column 2 What I would be more comfortable doing if I could choose
1. A. I sometimes assert my control. B. I let the data do the talking.	I select ___.	I select ___.
2. C. I present the big picture. D. I reach out to be friends with the people I need to influence.	I select ___.	I select ___.
3. B. I use detailed information to support my points. D. I establish good relationships with others.	I select ___.	I select ___.
4. A. I use the authority I have to help me accomplish my goals. E. I negotiate so everyone wins.	I select ___.	I select ___.
5. B. I show people the logic of my proposal. E. I engage in a little give-and-take to get things done.	I select ___.	I select ___.
6. C. I try to inspire others. F. I assemble coalitions when necessary.	I select ___.	I select ___.
7. E. I negotiate to obtain others' support. C. I emphasize the broader goals of the organization.	I select ___.	I select ___.
8. A. I rely on whatever authority I have. D. I do favors to create good relationships.	I select ___.	I select ___.
9. B. I construct a tight case to argue for my ideas. F. I gather support by approaching key people.	I select ___.	I select ___.
10. D. I get to know people personally. F. I work hard to make sure "people who matter" support my idea.	I select ___.	I select ___.

11. A. I use the authority of my position.

    B. I present the data, point to the precedents, and argue the pros and cons.

    I select ___.   I select ___.

12. D. I socialize with people I want to influence.

    C. I show where my idea fits into the overall scheme.

    I select ___.   I select ___.

13. E. I find ways to negotiate so everyone wins.

    F. I establish a wide network of organizational contacts.

    I select ___.   I select ___.

14. B. I make my case with data and evidence.

    F. I focus on people and groups who can sway opinion.

    I select ___.   I select ___.

15. B. I use reasoned argument.

    D. I reach out to understand how other people feel.

    I select ___.   I select ___.

16. A. I use my position to get things done.

    F. I work behind the scenes to get support.

    I select ___.   I select ___.

17. D. I rely on relationships to accomplish my goals.

    E. I sometimes ask for a bit more than I expect to get.

    I select ___.   I select ___.

18. A. I get things done efficiently by using my authority.

    C. I inspire others to feel as I do about the proposal.

    I select ___.   I select ___.

19. B. I present objective information to convince others.

    C. I remind people of what the organization stands for.

    I select ___.   I select ___.

20. D. I win friends and influence people.

    F. I target key decision makers.

    I select ___.   I select ___.

21. A. I use whatever formal authority I have.

    E. I seek the middle ground when there are disagreements.

    I select ___.   I select ___.

22. B. I base my arguments on objective information.

    E. I negotiate so everybody wins.

    I select ___.   I select ___.

23. E. I provide incentives to gain support.

    F. I build momentum by winning over key individuals and groups.

    I select ___.   I select ___.

24. A. I assert the authority that goes with my position.

    C. I get people excited about the future.

    I select ___.   I select ___.

25. B. I use data and logic to make my case.

    C. I emphasize our common purpose.

    I select ___.   I select ___.

26. C. I frame my ideas in terms of our
    organization's goals.

    F. I take time to consult key individuals.

    I select ___.   I select ___.

27. A. I rely on my formal position to get things done.

    D. I make sure that others know I care
    about their needs.

    I select ___.   I select ___.

28. E. I give concessions and expect others
    to do the same.

    C. I remind people that what we do matters.

    I select ___.   I select ___.

29. A. I assert my authority.

    F. I anticipate the politics and work around them.

    I select ___.   I select ___.

30. D. I establish rapport and pay attention to feelings.

    E. I make deals that work for both sides.

    I select ___.   I select ___.

The Trust Scale

Introduction

The purpose of the Trust Scale is to inquire about your general level of trust and distrust in another person before or after a negotiation. Your instructor will explain how to score and interpret this questionnaire.

Advance Preparation

Complete the Trust Scale as specified by your instructor.

Procedure

1. Complete the Trust Scale.

2. Your instructor will hand out a scoring key for the Trust Scale. Follow the key to score your questionnaire. A description of the questionnaire and what it measures will be provided by the instructor.

3. Be prepared to share your answers to the questions with others in a small group or class discussion.

Trust Scale				

Identify a specific other person for whom you have some level of trust. Then rate that other person on the following five-point scale:

1	2	3	4	5
Strongly disagree		Undecided		Strongly agree

Rating

1. This person's behavior meets my expectations. _____
2. This person fears the consequences if he or she doesn't comply with our agreements. _____
3. This person will protect and defend me, even at his or her own expense. _____
4. I try to protect myself and my interests from this person. _____
5. This person does as he or she promises. _____
6. I can easily monitor what this person does to make sure he or she complies. _____
7. This person and I have the same basic values. _____
8. This person enjoys making my life miserable. _____
9. I communicate regularly with this person, and he or she keeps me informed about what he or she is doing. _____

Source: Questionnaire developed by Roy J. Lewicki. Please request permission if used for nonpedagogical purposes.

Trust Scale (*continued*)

	Rating
10. If this person doesn't do as he or she promises, I can "get even."	————
11. This person cares for me so much that he or she often does what is best for me even without asking me.	————
12. I see this person more as a competitor and an opponent.	————
13. I can check up on this person if I need to.	————
14. This person knows that I have lots of ways of retaliating if he or she doesn't follow through.	————
15. We identify with each other.	————
16. I don't expect this person to make any sacrifices for me.	————
17. I have interacted with this person a lot.	————
18. This person knows what I will do if he or she violates a commitment.	————
19. This person and I have the same fundamental views of the world.	————
20. When I am with this person, the atmosphere is always tense.	————
21. This person is honest with me.	————
22. This person is aware that I will know if he or she breaks his or her word.	————
23. This person will go out of his or her way to protect my interests if they are challenged or threatened.	————
24. This person's value system is fundamentally different from my own.	————
25. I think I can accurately predict what this person will do.	————
26. This person knows that it is in his or her own best interest to do what he or she promises.	————
27. This person and I really stand for the same basic things.	————
28. Whatever happens, you can expect this person to take care of only himself or herself.	————
29. In my experience, this person is very reliable.	————
30. This person cares for me a great deal.	————
31. If this person thought he or she could get away with it, he or she would take advantage of others.	————
32. Everything I know about this person makes me cautious and suspicious.	————

Discussion

In recent years, a great deal of research has been conducted on the nature of trust and the role it plays in critical social relationships. Trust is essential to productive social relationships with others, and it can play a critical role in negotiations, particularly integrative negotiations. High trust contributes to better negotiations, and more cooperative, productive negotiations are likely to enhance trust. Conversely, low trust may contribute to less productive negotiations, and less productive negotiations are likely to decrease trust.

There are many definitions of trust, reflecting different views about trust as either a core characteristic of one's personality or a set of perceptions, expectations, and judgments that are shaped by what we know about the other party and the situation in which our relationship with them takes place. In discussing trust here, we will define *trust* as "an individual's belief in, and willingness to act on the basis of, the words, actions, and decisions of another."

Recent research suggests that there are two different types of trust—calculus-based and identification-based trust. *Calculus-based trust* is based on consistency of behavior—that people will do what they say they are going to do. Behavioral consistency is sustained by offering either the promise of rewards for people to do what they say they are going to do, or the threat of punishment (e.g., loss of relationship) that will occur if consistency is not maintained—that is, people do *not* do what they say they will do. This type of trust is based on an ongoing, economic calculation of the value of the outcomes to be received by creating and sustaining the relationship relative to the costs of maintaining or severing it. Not only are these rewards and punishments given directly to the other, but we also can reward or punish the other by enhancing or destroying the other's reputation with friends, associates, and business partners if they honor or violate the trust.

Identification-based trust is based on complete empathy with or identification with the other party's desires and intentions. At this level, trust exists because each party effectively understands, appreciates, agrees with, empathizes with, and takes on the other's values because of the emotional connection between them—and thus can act for the other. Identification-based trust thus permits one to act as an "agent" for the other and substitute for the other in interpersonal transactions. The other can be confident that his or her interests will be fully protected, and that no surveillance or monitoring of the actor is necessary. A true affirmation of the strength of identification-based trust between parties can be found when one party acts for the other in a manner even more zealous than the other might demonstrate; the parties not only know and identify with each other, but understand what they must do to sustain the other's trust. One learns what "really matters" to the other and comes to place the same importance on those behaviors as the other does. When we watch very closely knit groups working together under pressure, such as jazz quartets, basketball teams, or very skilled work groups, we get to see identification-based trust in action.

In addition, research is beginning to confirm that distrust is fundamentally different from trust, rather than being more or less of the same thing. Although trust can be defined as "confident positive expectations regarding another's conduct," distrust can indeed be "confident negative expectations" regarding another's conduct. Moreover, research is confirming that there are two forms of distrust: calculus-based distrust and identification-based distrust.

Calculus-based distrust consists of confident negative expectations of another's conduct. Like calculus-based trust, it is also grounded in consistency of behavior—but consistency in that the other consistently *fails* to do as he or she says. This type of distrust is based on an ongoing, economically based calculation or what we stand to lose by maintaining the relationship with the other, relative to the costs of severing it or finding an alternative way to meet our needs. Distrust of the other can be enhanced or reduced based on the other's reputation with friends, associates, and business partners if they violate or honor the trust.

Similarly, *identification-based distrust* consists of confident negative expectations of another's conduct grounded in perceived incompatibility of closely held values, dissimilar or competing goals, or a negative emotional attachment. Identification-based distrust is based on a complete lack of empathy or lack of identification with the other party's desires and intentions. Such distrust is grounded in a visceral dissimilarity with and dislike for the other—we do not agree with or empathize with the other, and we hold very dissimilar values. We expect that we have little in common with the other and that in fact the other may be a committed adversary who is out to do us in.

There are many implications for understanding relationships as complex combinations of these two types of trust and distrust:

- First, and most important, a relationship with another party can have elements of both trust and distrust. Relationships with other people are complex; we come to know them in a variety of different situations and contexts, some of which create trust and some of which create distrust. While many of these relationships will be dominated by trust or distrust, some will contain elements of both; we characterize these relationships as ones laden with *ambivalence.*

- Trust and distrust build as we come to know another party and have direct and indirect experiences with them (i.e., we learn about them from both our own and other people's experience). As we gain more information about another, we draw a more complex and detailed picture of the other.

- Remarkably, most relationships do not start at zero trust. Research has tended to show that most people begin a relationship assuming that the other is reasonably trustworthy. Thus most relationships start with a moderately positive level of trust.

- A number of other factors will influence how much we trust or distrust another party. These include our own personality (individuals differ in the amount of trust they have for another party), our general motivation and disposition toward the other party (e.g., cooperative or competitive), the other's reputation and our judgments of his or her trustworthiness, and the context in which the trust judgments are occurring.

- When trust has been violated, rebuilding trust may not be the same as controlling or managing distrust. Rebuilding trust may require actions such as acknowledgment of responsibility for violating the trust, making an apology, or claiming responsibility for one's actions. However, managing distrust may require actions that bind or constrain any future harmful consequences from violating trust again. Being clear about expectations for the other's conduct, setting deadlines, explicitly specifying consequences for failing to comply, detailing procedures for monitoring and verifying the other's actions, and cultivating alternative ways to have one's needs met are all ways to manage distrust, but engaging in these actions does not necessarily rebuild trust.

Discussion Questions

1. Think about the person you rated in this questionnaire. How close and personal (or distant and impersonal) is your relationship with that person?

2. Experiment with the questionnaire by rating several different people. For example, rate

   - The person whom you trust the most.

   - A person whom you trust in a professional capacity (e.g., a doctor, counselor, adviser).

- A boss or colleague at work.
- A person whom you are very close to.
- A person whom you actively distrust.
- A person who has violated your trust.

How do your ratings differ for each? What does this say about the role of trust and distrust in your relationship with that person?

3. How do you build trust in order to make negotiation more effective? What kinds of things can you do to strengthen trust? What should you avoid if you do not want to damage existing trust?

4. What do you do to manage your relationship with someone you distrust? How are these actions different from trust building or trust rebuilding?

5. Think about the person who has violated your trust. What happened in this situation? Why do you no longer trust that person? What would it take to repair the relationship with that person?

Communication Competence Scale

Generally speaking, *communication competence* can be defined as the ability to enact both appropriate and effective messages in any communication setting. Appropriate communication conforms to the expectations and rules of a situation, while effective communication allows parties in an interaction to achieve their goals. Communication competence, then, is a broad construct that refers to the ability to accurately assess situations and other people and respond to them in ways that allow you to get what you want while still complying with social rules and expectations.

The scale here is a diagnostic tool to help you determine your current level of communication competence. Answer the questions as honestly as you can, thinking about what you actually do in most situations you encounter. Once you have completed the instrument, your instructor will help you interpret your score.

Directions

The following are statements about the communication process. Answer each as it relates to what you generally think about concerning social situations. Please indicate the degree to which each statement applies to you by placing the appropriate number (according to the scale below) in the space provided:

5 Always true of me

4 Often true of me

3 Sometimes true of me

2 Rarely true of me

1 Never true of me

Rating	Statement
_____	1. Before a conversation, I think about what people might be talking about.
_____	2. When I first enter a new situation, I watch who is talking to whom.
_____	3. During a conversation, I am aware of when a topic is going nowhere.
_____	4. After a conversation, I think about what the other person thought of me.
_____	5. Generally, I think about how others might interpret what I say.
_____	6. After a conversation, I think about my performance.
_____	7. During a conversation, I am aware of when it is time to change the topic.
_____	8. When I first enter a new situation, I try to size up the event.
_____	9. Before a conversation, I mentally practice what I am going to say.

Source: Adapted by Roy J. Lewicki. "Toward the Development and Validation of a Measure of Cognitive Communication Competence," by R. L. Duran and B. H. Spitzberg, from *Communication Quarterly* 43, 1995, pp. 259–75. Used with permission.

(*continued*)

Rating	Statement
_____	10. After a conversation, I think about what I said.
_____	11. Generally, I think about the consequences of what I say.
_____	12. Before a conversation, I think about what I am going to say.
_____	13. Generally, I study people.
_____	14. After a conversation, I think about what I could have said.
_____	15. When I first enter a new situation, I think about what I am going to talk about.
_____	16. Generally, I think about how what I say may affect others.
_____	17. During a conversation, I pay attention to how others are reacting to what I am saying.
_____	18. Generally, I am aware of people's interests.
_____	19. During a conversation, I think about what topic to discuss next.
_____	20. After a conversation, I think about what I have said to improve for the next conversation.
_____	21. Generally, I think about the effects of my communication.
_____	22. During a conversation, I know if I have said something rude or inappropriate.

The Cultural Intelligence Scale

Introduction

Cultural Intelligence (CQ) refers to an individual's ability to function well in situations characterized by cultural diversity. CQ has the potential to enhance personal and organizational effectiveness in a variety of settings. This questionnaire is designed to assess a person's cultural intelligence.

Procedure

1. Complete the Cultural Intelligence Scale.
2. Your instructor will provide instructions for scoring the scale, as well as a description of the questionnaire and what it measures.

Directions

Read each statement and select the response that best describes your capabilities. Select the answer that *best* describes you *as you really are.*

For each item below, enter a number from 1 to 7 based on the following scale:

1	2	3	4	5	6	7
Strongly disagree						Strongly agree

_____ 1. I am conscious of the cultural knowledge I use when interacting with people with different cultural backgrounds.

_____ 2. I adjust my cultural knowledge as I interact with people from a culture that is unfamiliar to me.

_____ 3. I am conscious of the cultural knowledge I apply to cross-cultural interactions.

_____ 4. I check the accuracy of my cultural knowledge as I interact with people from different cultures.

_____ 5. I know the legal and economic systems of other cultures.

_____ 6. I know the rules (e.g., vocabulary, grammar) of other languages.

_____ 7. I know the cultural values and religious beliefs of other cultures.

_____ 8. I know the marriage systems of other cultures.

_____ 9. I know the arts and crafts of other cultures.

_____ 10. I know the rules for expressing non-verbal behaviors in other cultures.

_____ 11. I enjoy interacting with people from different cultures.

_____ 12. I am confident that I can socialize with locals in a culture that is unfamiliar to me.

_____ 13. I am sure I can deal with the stresses of adjusting to a culture that is new to me.

_____ 14. I enjoy living in cultures that are unfamiliar to me.

_____ 15. I am confident that I can get accustomed to the shopping conditions in a different culture.

Source: © The Cultural Intelligence Center. Used with permission.

_____ 16. I change my verbal behavior (e.g., accent, tone) when a cross-cultural interaction requires it.

_____ 17. I use pause and silence differently to suit different cross-cultural situations.

_____ 18. I vary the rate of my speaking when a cross-cultural situation requires it.

_____ 19. I change my non-verbal behavior when a cross-cultural situation requires it.

_____ 20. I alter my facial expressions when a cross-cultural interaction requires it.

Appendix 1

Negotiating on Thin Ice:
The 2004–2005 NHL Dispute (B)

Introduction

It has been a bizarre, dysfunctional process from the get go. While it's hard to predict what will happen down the road, I'm sure that the Harvard Law School, business schools, and journalism schools will take what's happened over the past year between the NHL and NHLPA, and I guarantee that there will be case studies and books written about this very bizarre process.[1]

—Bob McKenzie, TSN Hockey Analyst

When news of the season's cancellation hit the stands, fans and sports analysts were quick to berate both sides. Jack Todd of *The Montreal Gazette* summarized, "For a difference that amounted to slightly more than the amount Jose Theodore [Montreal Canadiens goal tender] would have earned this year, they sunk the Stanley Cup playoffs. For the take from a single exhibition game, they became the first major pro league to scuttle an entire season."[2] Steve Bisheff of *The Orange Country Register* wrote, "That wasn't just the season, it was the entire future of professional hockey getting checked hard into the boards and left sprawled out on the deserted ice Wednesday."[3]

The season was now cancelled, but negotiations needed to continue. Initially, neither side seemed willing to soften. On March 1, 2005, the league hinted at hiring replacement players. After an NHL Board of Governor's meeting, Edmonton Oilers Chair Cal Nichols asserted, "I think that we can move forward and plan to play a season however it happens this coming year."[4] To further weaken the union's solidarity, the league then filed a charge with the United States National Labor Relations Board aimed at revoking a union policy that required members to repay any work stoppage benefits they had received if they became replacement players. In retaliation, and to thwart the potential use of replacement players, the NHLPA applied for union certification in two additional Canadian provinces, Quebec and British Columbia.

Tension finally began to subside when, in early April, the union brought to the table a proposal that might help to break the impasse. The union had already indicated, back in February, its willingness to accept a salary cap. Now, the union announced, it was also willing to link league-wide salaries to league revenues, provided that the two sides could agree to a number of other arrangements. First, and most critically, the two sides would have to agree upon a shared definition of what constituted hockey related revenues, and to institute a system that would require teams to report all sources of revenue that contributed to hockey.[5] The union insisted that each team owner be required to report revenue line items not only for their team, but also for any related entities owned by the team owner (e.g., some team owners own other teams that play in the same arena, or own the arena itself). Second, the union demanded a series of "systemic" improvements. In particular, if a salary cap was to be imposed, players needed to have greater mobility between teams in order for them to receive competing offers. This request would necessitate modifications to the current regulations regarding unrestricted free agency. Finally, the union insisted that, if players were going to be "majority partners" in the business (because salaries would be tied to revenue), they should have a greater voice in the way the game is played.[6] The league was willing to make these trades.

The threat of replacement players and of counter-moves by the NHLPA dissipated as the two side's proposals inched closer together and a deal seemed imminent. This was partially motivated by the eagerness of both sides to establish a new CBA by July; failure to do so would hurt the sale of season tickets for the 2005–2006 hockey season. As a result, the number of meetings increased substantially in May and June: the two sides met 31 times over these two months. Then, on July 13, 2005, a tentative deal was reached.

Among other things, the new CBA included an immediate salary rollback of 24 percent, a salary cap (per team) of $39 million, a salary minimum (per team) of $21 million, and the linkage of league-wide salaries to league-wide revenues. In other words, league-wide salaries (and hence, the team salary cap) would increase (or decrease) with future changes in league revenues. For the upcoming 2005–2006 season, revenues were expected to be $1.7 billion, and player salaries were capped at 54 percent of expected revenues. If the revenues for 2005–2006 season surpassed expectations, this percentage (and the team salary cap) would be raised the following year, according to the following scale:

Player Salaries as a Percentage of Revenues	Revenues
54%	<$2.2 billion
55%	$2.2–$2.4 billion
56%	$2.4–$2.7 billion
57%	>$2.7 billion

While the salary cap was aimed at equalizing salaries across teams, the new agreement also included terms that narrowed the salary gap between players. The new CBA restricted the maximum salary for a player to 20 percent of his team's salary cap, and increased the minimum salary for a player to $450,000 (previously, it was $185,000). The minimum player salary would be increased in the coming years according to the following scale:

Minimum Player Salary	Season
$450,000	2005–06 and 2006–07
$475,000	2007–08 and 2008–09
$500,000	2009–10 and 2010–11
$525,000	2011–12

In response to the union's other demands, the age of unrestricted free agency would be lowered from 31 to 27 years by 2008, and players would be given equal representation on a "Competition Committee" and a "Marketing Committee," allowing them to have the level of influence on the game that they had long sought. Moreover, players would continue to benefit from guaranteed contracts, and were granted permission to participate in the 2006 Winter Olympics. On the issue of salary arbitration, team owners would be granted the right to request salary arbitration (in the past only players could do so).

Finally, in order to alleviate any remaining concerns regarding the inequity of the six-year agreement, the players would have the right to re-open negotiations on this CBA in four years if desired.

The following week, on July 21, 87 percent of the NHLPA's members approved the CBA. The following day, the 30 NHL teams voted unanimously in favor of the deal. The agreement marked the end of 300 days of negotiations. The game would resume, and there would be a 2005–2006 season.

Endnotes

1. CBC, "Faceoff 2002: What They're Saying", *CBC Sports Online* website, 2005, http://www.cbc.ca/sports/indepth/cba/features/quotes.html, accessed July 2005.
2. Ibid.
3. Ibid.
4. Canadian Press, "Chronology of the Lockout," Globe and Mail, July 13, 2005 , http://www.globeandmail.com.
5. Ted Saskin (NHLPA Senior Director), in a phone interview with the authors, February 13, 2006.
6. Ibid.

Title Index

Name Index

Names printed in **bold face** are of authors with selections in this volume, along with the appropriate page references.